Llewellyn's Golden Dawn Series

SELF-INITIATION
into the Golden Dawn Tradition

A Complete Curriculum of Study
for Both the Solitary Magician
and the Working Magical Group

Chic Cicero
Sandra Tabatha Cicero

Llewellyn Publications
Saint Paul, Minnesota

FIRST EDITION
Fourth Printing, 2005

Cover painting of "The Mountain of Initiation"
        by Sandra Tabatha Cicero
Diagrams, artwork, and color paintings
        copyright © Sandra Tabatha Cicero

Library of Congress Cataloging-in-Publication Data

Cicero, Chic, 1936-
    Self-initiation into the Golden Dawn tradition : a complete
curriculum of study / Chic Cicero, Sandra Tabatha Cicero. — 1st ed.
        p. cm. — (Llewellyn's Golden Dawn series)
    Includes bibliographical references.
    ISBN 1-56718-136-8 (pbk.) : $39.95
    1. Hermetic Order of the Golden Dawn. I. Cicero, Sandra Tabatha,
1959-   . II. Title. III. Series.
BF1623.R7C484   1995
135' .4—dc20   95-1118
                                                          CIP

Permissions:

Cross and Triangle artwork copyright © Sandra Tabatha Cicero
The Godforms of the Visible Stations copyright © Adam P. Forrest
The quotation from Manly P. Hall's *Secret Teachings of All Ages* is reproduced by
        permission of the Philosophical Research Society, Inc.

Llewellyn Publications
A Division of Llewellyn Worldwide, Ltd.
P.O. Box 64383, St. Paul, MN 55164-0383

Printed in the United States of America

ABOUT LLEWELLYN'S GOLDEN DAWN SERIES

Just as, 100 years ago, the original Order of the Golden Dawn *initiated* a powerful rebirth of interest in the Western Esoteric Tradition that has lasted through this day, so do we expect this series of books to add new impetus to the Great Work itself among an ever broadening base of sincere students.

> *I further promise and swear that with the Divine Permission, I will from this day forward, apply myself to the Great Work—which is: to purify and exalt my Spiritual Nature so that with the Divine Aid I may at length attain to be more than human, and thus gradually raise and unite myself to my Higher and Divine Genius, and that in this event I will not abuse the great power entrusted to me.*

With this oath, the *Adeptus Minor* of the Inner Order committed him/herself to undertake, consciously and deliberately, that which was ordained as the birthright of all Humanity: TO BECOME MORE THAN HUMAN!

It is this that is the ultimate message of esotericism: that evolution continues, and the purpose of each life is to grow into the Image set for us by our Creator: to attain and reveal our own Divinity.

These books and tapes will themselves make more easily accessible the Spiritual Technology that is inherent in the Golden Dawn System. It is a system that allows for individual as well as group endeavor; a system that works within or without an organized lodge; a system that is based on universal principles that will be shown to be global in their impact today.

And practical. The works in this series will be practical in their applications and requirements for application. You need neither to travel to the mountain top nor obtain any tool other than your own consciousness. No garment need you other than that of your own imagination. No authority need you other than that of your own True Will.

Set forth, then, into the New Dawn—a New Start on the greatest adventure there is: to become One with the Divine Genius.

Also by Chic Cicero and Sandra Tabatha Cicero

The Golden Dawn Magical System Kit
  including:
  New Golden Dawn Ritual Tarot (deck)
  The New Golden Dawn Ritual Tarot (book)
Secrets of a Golden Dawn Temple
The Golden Dawn Journal, Book I: Divination
The Golden Dawn Journal, Book II: Qabalah: Theory and Magic
The Golden Dawn Journal, Book III: The Art of Hermes
The Magical Pantheons: A Golden Dawn Journal
Experiencing the Kabbalah
A Garden of Pomegranates by Israel Regardie (Third Editon, edited and annotated by the Ciceros)
The Middle Pillar by Israel Regardie (Third Editon, edited and annotated by the Ciceros)
The Tree of Life by Israel Regardie (Third Editon, edited and annotated by the Ciceros)
The Essential Golden Dawn

TABLE OF CONTENTS

The Hermetic Order of the Golden Dawn

The teachings of the Golden Dawn have regained popularity in recent times. Because of this, many fine groups calling themselves the Golden Dawn in various forms are now offering excellent Order teachings to aspiring students. We would like to take this opportunity to announce that there is only one *Hermetic Order of the Golden Dawn* operating in the United States and Canada that has a Vault which was consecrated by Israel Regardie and into which Regardie performed initiations for the purpose of establishing a Second Order with valid initiatory succession from the original Mother temple in London. This Order does not charge money for initiations or teachings, nor does it advertise or solicit for membership.

This book is recommended by the G.H. Chiefs of our Order. However readers of this book are not considered official members of the *Hermetic Order of the Golden Dawn*. The book was written primarily to give solitary students and unaffiliated groups of magicians the ability to tap into the Golden Dawn's current of magic without having to become a member of any organization.

Students who have any questions considering the material presented in this book, or who wish to inquire further about the Golden Dawn, may address their questions to the authors in care of the publisher.

DEDICATION

This book is dedicated to
our teacher and friend

Grady McMurtry

aka Hymenaeus Alpha,
former Caliph of the O.T.O.;

Israel Regardie

our teacher and friend
who put his trust in us
to preserve the traditions
of the Golden Dawn;
and

Adam P. Forrest

our teacher and brother
in the Great Work
who had enormous faith
and patience with us.

ACKNOWLEDGMENTS

We would like to acknowledge the following individuals for helping us complete this book: Mitch and Gail Henson, Adam and Isidora Forrest, John Plymale, Harvey Newstrom, Lisa Roggow, and a special thanks to Maria Babwahsingh.

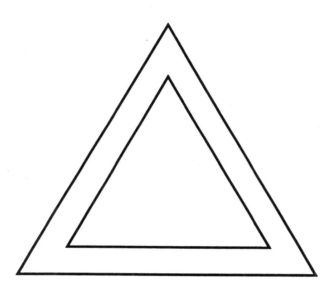

Introduction

nitiation means "to begin" or embark upon something new. It is the beginning of a new phase or outlook on life; the passage into a distinctly new type of existence. The characteristics of this event are marked by an expansion of the mind to include an awareness of higher levels of consciousness. Initiation represents spiritual growth; the commencement of a new life committed to an entirely new set of principles from those of mundane society. Initiation is the precursor of immortality. Humankind has the potential for immortality, but only obtains it when men and women align themselves with that immortal spiritual essence that underlies all aspects of the manifest universe; that same spiritual essence which is too often ignored by the great majority of humanity. Obtaining that rare and splendid essence is the supreme objective of that part of the Western Esoteric Tradition known as *magic*. The goal of all magical processes is the purification of the natural human being—that is, the extraction of the pure gold of spiritual *Selfhood* from the husk of the outer personality.

Magic is a spiritual science. It is a specialized system of discipline which has a spiritual rather than material goal. This is a personal science that is based upon the fundamental knowledge of the true human being which lies beneath the illusion of the outer, secular human. Ceremonial magic incorporates a process of memorization and ritual which results in the direct stimulation of the *Will* and the exaltation of the *Imagination*. The final objective of all this is the purification of the lower personality and the realization of an elevated state of consciousness, wherein the magician's ego enters into a union with his/her own Higher Self and ultimately with the Divine. Every action, idea and utterance in any ceremony is designed to bring about this final conclusion. Each and every detail of the ritual itself, including banishings, circumambulations, evocations and invocations, serves to remind the operator of this single goal. *"For the assault on the Holy City, every sense and every faculty is deliberately mobilized, and the whole individual soul of the operator must enter into the act."*[1] Every impression, by means of a Hermetic and Qabalistic system of associated ideas, is made the beginning of a sequence of related thoughts which culminate in the ultimate aim of the ceremony. When emblem after emblem has infiltrated the mind of the magician, and the ritual act has stimulated his/her emotions to a fever pitch, then the absolute moment of

---

[1] Israel Regardie, *The Tree of Life*, pg. 107.

spiritual ecstasy is attained. A clear and open channel is created between the mind and the soul, concluding in an increased concentration of magical abilities and the exaltation of the true and divine nature of the magician.

To accomplish these lofty goals in the tradition of the Golden Dawn, memorization of certain materials known collectively as "Knowledge Lectures" is very important. The Hermetic Art is a true science and would-be magicians must commit the rudimentary knowledge of the system to memory, just as if s/he were a student entering a school of medicine or engineering. Physicians and engineers require years of training to achieve their career goals. This training naturally includes much memorization of materials that are important to the specific trade. Training and study are no less imperative for the magician who seeks to journey between the astral realms and explore the inner workings of the human mind. Magic is real. It is not something that should be toyed with by "dabblers" who know next to nothing about the subject, but assume that it would be fun to "make something happen." Surgeons who practice medicine without a license often end up in jail. Superficial occultists who occasionally manage to open psychic doors without knowing what to do next sometimes end up in mental hospitals.

This is what makes the Golden Dawn's curriculum of study so important to any student of the Western Magical Tradition. Memorization of a large amount of information is required. This material is fundamental to building a solid foundation of knowledge that will steadily become second-nature to the magician, enabling him/her to perceive more clearly the astral influences that permeate the physical world—influences which the average person cannot perceive. The conscious commitment to learn the symbolic (magical) alphabet of the unconscious mind results in the cultivation of psychic reflexes which aid the magician and make all ceremonial work flow more smoothly. But more importantly than this, the memorization of magical data changes the very structure of the psyche, which is gradually infiltrated by holy symbols that speak on a subconscious level to the Divine Being in each of us. The mind of the magician is steadily purified by this process as an increasing percentage of mundane thoughts are supplanted or transformed by spiritual thoughts.

Initiation is the preliminary step in the realm of magic. A true initiation is the inner and hidden essence which pushes the student to seek the Path of Knowledge with a tenacity that cannot be denied. This initial step is the enfolding of the Divine Light; the gentle nurturing of the spark of consciousness within the Inner Self. Attaining this point of growth requires peace of mind, awareness of one's subconscious impulses, persistent hard work and a certain degree of self-sacrifice. When the secret recesses of the Inner Self have been reached, communication with the universal Power is then possible. And by the single act of one student tapping into this Divine Power, the whole of humanity is enriched.

The word "mystery" plays an important role in the drama of initiation. It is derived from the Greek word *mysteria*, meaning "that which is reserved for initiates only." Several magical groups and secret societies have a tradition of tracing their ancestral roots back to the mystery cults and religions that flourished in the ancient world. Many people were drawn to these mystery religions because of the sense of spiritual vitality and rapture they provided through elaborate induction ceremonies. To be an *initiate* means that one is accepted into an inner circle whose teachings and rituals are meaningful only to other members of the group who share this common experience. It confers a sense of status and belonging, and of having been uplifted through the disclosure of divinely inspired wisdom. The candidate seeking admittance must first prove him/her self worthy of inclusion into the group or magical tradition. The ritual of initiation is meant to purify and prepare the candidate to receive the secrets and teachings of that tradition or current. A new initiate does not receive the total volume of knowledge immediately, but in gradual stages. This process of spiritual evolution begins at the bottom of a hierarchical ladder, each step of which is accompanied by an additional initiation ceremony and further study.

Initiation is also a wonderfully fulfilling experience. A candidate entering the temple for the first time is in a heightened state of awareness; adrenaline is pumping through the body, the senses are amplified—the whole being of the candidate is poised and ready to receive an influx of energy. All of this is brought about by the conscious decision to be initiated. We have seen some candidates moved to tears or fainting with joy from the energy of an initiation ceremony. This is the power of the decision to begin a spiritual Path.[2]

"Long hast thou dwelt in Darkness, Quit the Night and Seek the Day." This one sentence from the Neophyte Ritual of the Golden Dawn encompasses the primary goal and aspiration of the student of the Mysteries; to exchange the mundane for the Divine. That goal is based upon a journey of self-discovery and spiritual attainment. It is not just the awareness of the Divine, but also the bringing forth of divinity into daily life. The very name of the Order—*The Golden Dawn*—alludes to the shining brilliance of the Eternal and Divine Light, breaking through the confines of Darkness to herald the birth of a new day in the evolution of humankind. The aim of all the rituals and practical magical work of the Golden Dawn is to create a spiritual bond between the magician and the Immortal Self.

The purposes for which the G∴D∴ was formed were twofold; first, through study, teaching, and organization, to serve as guardian of the Western Esoteric Tradition, and second, to initiate, educate, and nurture those individuals called to carry on the *Great Work* (that is, to become more than human, and to achieve union with the Divine). For those individuals who are called to the Western Esoteric Mysteries, the Golden Dawn system presents itself as a vital, consistent, and secure method for spiritual enhancement.

The fundamental practices and techniques of the Golden Dawn's system of psychic development are threefold; the first is initiation (astral and physical), the second is assimilation of Qabalistic and Hermetic knowledge (the basic alphabet of the magical language), and the third is personal ritual work. All three are

---

[2] For one of my initiation ceremonies, I had undertaken a three-day fast and frequent meditations beforehand. During the ritual, the smell of the incense, the symbols, the sounds, the speeches of the officers, and every single aspect of the ceremony was so powerful and overwhelming to me that at a moment of supreme realization and influx of energy, my knees began to fail me and I had to be supported by one of the officers as the ritual continued. It was without a doubt one of the turning points in my life.—STC

prerequisites for advancement into the Golden Dawn Tradition. Initiation by itself is pointless without the repeated practice of ritual techniques and individual ceremonial work. Likewise, performance of advanced Golden Dawn rituals, such as the consecration of Elemental weapons without the knowledge of certain fundamentals such as the Hebrew Alphabet, is similar to constructing a building without first pouring a foundation—the project is likely to collapse. All three aspects of the G∴D∴ system must be undertaken equally in order for the system to work the way that it was intended to work.

There is no need for us to present a history of the Hermetic Order of the Golden Dawn here, since that subject has already been covered at length by various authors. *The Magicians of the Golden Dawn* by Ellic Howe, *The Golden Dawn: Twilight of the Magicians* by R. A. Gilbert, *Sword of Wisdom* by Ithell Colquhoun, and *Ritual Magic in England* by Francis King should all be consulted for the light that they shed on the history of the G∴D∴ and its various offshoots. The history of the modern incarnation of the Hermetic Order of the Golden Dawn has been succinctly covered in the Epilogue of our book *Secrets of a Golden Dawn Temple*. This book will concentrate instead upon the techniques that are essential for the solitary student to be able to initiate him/her self into the Golden Dawn's current of magic from Neophyte through the Portal grade, providing a complete curriculum of study for the Outer Order grades.

Self-initiation into the G∴D∴ current of magic has been a subject of much speculation and discussion. However very little practical information has been presented upon the subject. Israel Regardie was a vocal champion of the idea that a student could initiate him/her self through the grades of the Golden Dawn. He put forth the opinion that by repeated performance of such rituals as the Opening by Watchtower and the Middle Pillar Exercise, the aspiring magician could effectively be considered an initiate of the G∴D∴ current. (Note: These rituals are provided in Chapter Six of this book.) However, he also stated that this hinged upon the student's own persistence, hard work and determination. The responsibility for spiritual progress is placed squarely on the shoulders of the student. There is only one person to blame if indolence keeps spiritual growth from occurring.

The need for *Self-initiation* is born out of the fact that it is not always possible for prospective students to live in an area that is close to an officially recognized initiatory temple. Especially here in the U.S., students have often had to spend a lot of money on transportation to an official temple in order to receive an initiation. Since there is a total of no less than seven initiation ceremonies required to become an Adeptus Minor, it is easy to see how expensive the process of traveling to a temple can become. This has led to various magical groups offering correspondence courses and astral initiation by proxy. However, these too are often highly expensive undertakings which do not address the solitary student's basic need to monitor his/her own psychic growth in a meaningful and spiritually fulfilling manner. (Some groups even bestow instant Adepthood with virtually no Outer Order training whatsoever; for a fee, almost anyone can get a certificate proclaiming one to be an Adeptus Minor [or even an Adeptus Exemptus!]. The spiritual value of grades obtained in such a manner is, of course, highly questionable.)

It was Israel Regardie's wish that students of the Golden Dawn tradition quietly and patiently continue the Order work and goals as instituted by Mathers and Westcott, without a lot of hoopla or fanfare. Regardie was a man of strong convictions who was adamantly opposed to several of the factors which historically tear magical groups of all traditions apart and shift the focus of such groups away from spiritual concerns—including schisms, egotistic pontificating or self-aggrandizement on the part of group leaders, the idea of soliciting money in return for grade initiations, and pointless bickering between this group and that group. And for all that Israel Regardie has done to singlehandedly keep the G∴D∴ tradition alive and available to all, some people now claim that Regardie had no lineage to the Golden Dawn, in the same manner that some Wiccans have tried to denounce Gerald Gardner after all he had done for Wicca. There are even some individuals, who after supposedly self-initiating themselves into high degrees, now claim that self-initiation is not possible for others—that the prospective student must go to them for a *proper* initiation. Not all magical groups or fraternities manage to maintain their high spiritual ideals under the onslaught of such integrity-killers as ego or profit-making.

Another problem with correspondence courses is that although they offer genuinely good material, it is often presented in a manner that is unrelated to the original Order teachings. Some groups add Thelema, Eastern esoteric practices, Odinism, or other elements which are totally unconnected to the established teachings of the Golden Dawn. This often results in a hybrid curriculum which no longer resembles that of the Golden Dawn, either in content or in essence.

Although most of the Golden Dawn's curriculum from Neophyte through the sub-grade of Zelator Adeptus Minor has already been published, there is no reason for Neophytes to be instructed to perform Inner Order rituals such as the Banishing Ritual of the Hexagram and the Rose Cross Ritual.[3] This problem originated from the fragmentary presentation of the Outer Order grade work given in Israel Regardie's *The Golden Dawn*. The Knowledge Lectures presented by Regardie are in reality little more than a student's lecture notes, which were originally supplemented by oral Order teachings. To "flesh out" the Outer Order curriculum as presented in *The Golden Dawn*, many magical correspondence groups have taken what was traditionally the Inner Order curriculum (study work and rituals) and transferred it to the grades of the First Order. The end result is Neophytes and Zelators being asked by their instructors to perform unnecessary busywork, complex Second Order studies,[4] and advanced work such as the construction of the Elemental weapons,[5] or the painting of several Trees of Life in the various Qabalistic color

---

[3] The Hexagram Ritual and the Rose Cross Ritual were traditionally taught in the Second Order, the R.R. et A.C., not in the First Order of the Golden Dawn.

[4] Such as Enochian. While I was in the Practicus grade, I once informed Regardie that I was taking up the study of the Enochian Alphabet. Regardie told me in no uncertain terms to "cease and desist." He was adamant in his belief that Outer Order students should leave Enochian alone.—STC

[5] The construction of these tools (Earth Pentacle, Air Dagger, Water Cup and Fire Wand) is part of the gradework of a Neophyte Adeptus Minor. That is why they are referred to as the tools of a Z.A.M.—(Zelator Adeptus Minor). They are never used in the Outer Order. A student who makes these tools during the Elemental grades will often express the desire to remake them in the Adept grade, due to

scales—work which is traditionally undertaken by the Adeptus Minor as part of his/her gradework.[6] By overloading the Outer Order student with Inner Order work, a curious thing often happens—the student is overwhelmed and eventually drops out. Moreover, there is certainly ample Order material to be found which is suitable for the Neophyte and Elemental grades, without having to loot the Inner Order curriculum and deprive the Adeptus Minor of his/her proper gradework.[7]

It is not that we condemn such practices or that we wish to brow-beat students into refraining from work that is "beyond their grade" (a phrase which often reeks of egotism and suggests that the teacher might be trying to conceal his/her own lack of knowledge). The point we are trying to make is that by adopting Second Order study work into the First Order curriculum, the student is no longer following the traditional teachings of the Golden Dawn in the manner in which they were intended to work. The First Order of the Golden Dawn was and is a solid foundation where the student gathers the tools, building materials and information necessary to: (1) receive an influx of Divine Light, (2) establish an alignment upon the Tree of Life and correspondingly imprint the Tree within the psyche, (3) stabilize the unbalanced portions of the psyche through Elemental equilibration, and (4) create the groundwork and solid substructure necessary for further magical work in the Adept grades. Teachings taken from the higher grades and given to Outer Order members often obscure the original goal of the Golden Dawn—that is to carefully and steadily build a firm bedrock of knowledge that will ground the student and insure that s/he will grow to be a psychically balanced and knowledgeable Adept who is then fully capable of safely performing advanced Elemental, Planetary, Zodiacal and Sephirotic workings. Many Neophytes and Zelators are simply not ready to take on Adept-level work in which the Golden Dawn system's built-in psychic safeguards are disregarded or abandoned.

We are not implying that the curriculum of the Golden Dawn has remained stagnant and unchanged for one hundred years, extolling the weary cry of "Tradition! Tradition!" Nothing could be further from the truth. The teachings of the Golden Dawn have evolved, are evolving, and will continue to evolve as modern Adepts add to the Golden Dawn's pool of knowledge. *The Golden Dawn Companion* by R. A. Gilbert provides good examples of how something as essential as the Neophyte obligation has changed over the years to better serve the needs of

---

added insights gained through initiatory experience. However, some of our temples still suggest that students construct these tools in the Elemental grades. Our advice to students who wish to make these implements in the Outer grades is this: paint all names and sigils on the implement except for the magical motto, which can be added after completion of the Portal grade—when the initiate traditionally changes his/her motto. It would be problematic to have a Second Order Implement with an Outer Order motto inscribed on it.

6 This is part of the grade work for the *Hodos Chamelionis*, an Adeptus Minor who is on the Path of the Chameleon—or the Path of Mixed Colors.

7 Our position on this matter is as follows: We never dissuade any responsible student from taking on study work or performing rituals that are beyond their grade, particularly if the student is already magically advanced and balanced—however, we do not encourage it either. We simply do not promote Second Order work in the First Order *as* Outer Order gradework. (Our one exception is the Middle Pillar exercise which Regardie advocated as a highly important exercise for maintaining psychic balance.)—CC & STC.

initiates. The teachings of the modern day *Hermetic Order of the Golden Dawn*, established by Israel Regardie, have also evolved and adapted to meet the needs of today's students; and new information on Egyptian magic, Coptic magic and more, continues to be discovered by archeologists and magicians—information that was simply not available in MacGregor Mathers' day.

One such modern change in Golden Dawn instruction is the teaching of Geomancy in the Earth grade of Zelator, rather than in the Water grade of Practicus where it was taught a century ago.[8] Another change is the re-introduction of basic Astrology into the Outer Order. The formal teaching of Astrology was at one time dropped from the Order, since it was then felt that the student could find ample information on the subject from sources outside the Golden Dawn. Although such reasoning is quite true, we have nonetheless seen fit to add this basic information back into the Outer Order curriculum, because it becomes all too easy for students to skip over information that they are not presented with up front.

Oftentimes students come into our Order with previous knowledge of advanced ritual work from the back of Regardie's *The Golden Dawn*. Inevitably they advance through the grades and discover that through the discipline of the traditional Outer Order curriculum, they experience completely new insights concerning the Golden Dawn that they never imagined beforehand.

This brings us to the idea of "legitimacy." Does a student who is working alone need to be a member of a legitimate initiatory temple of the Hermetic Order of the Golden Dawn? The answer is no. Whether or not one is a member of an officially recognized temple has no bearing on his/her spiritual and magical growth. With the Golden Dawn's curriculum and most of its important papers already published, the tools for advancement into the G∴D∴ current are already at the aspirant's fingertips. It is possible today for the student to become his/her own initiator. Any individual or group that claims sole ownership of the Hermetic Tradition or claims to be the official "Grand High Muckety-Muck of the World" is doing occult students a great disservice by blowing off a good deal of hot air. The same is true for anyone who claims to know magical "secrets" that can only be bought for a high price. The student needs to use discretion and put some measure of trust in his/her own latent spiritual abilities. Questions of the legitimacy or heredity of a magical group can in fact get in the way of spiritual progress if a student becomes more interested in buying or otherwise obtaining a magical merit badge from a recognized group, rather than securing union with one's Holy Guardian Angel. Empty gestures and hollow proclamations of high degrees and titles mean little or nothing to one's own Higher Self. The intent and determination to achieve union with the Divine is the only important consideration in advancing to the path of an initiate. And to do this, one need not be a member of any recognized magical group.

What is a *magical tradition* or *current*? This is a concept which may hold different meanings for different people. Here we will refer to the *current* of the Golden Dawn as a specific stream of energy that has empowered the Western

---

[8] The practice of Geomancy or "Earth Divination" is more appropriate to the grade of Zelator.

Magical Tradition since ancient times. This magical current has surfaced at various times and places in history as different magical groups with similar ideas, teachings, techniques and goals. As we have already stated, anyone can tap into this current by studying and applying oneself to the magical work of the current. An *egregore* is a specialized aspect of a current. The word *egregore* comes from a Greek word meaning "watcher." Whereas the current can be likened to a large river, the egregore is like a small adjoining stream. The current is the raw power—somewhat of a blind force—compared to the egregore, which is a more interactive and personal force. When we speak of a *group egregore,* we are talking about the distinctive energy of a specific group of magicians who are working together. The single current can sustain several different group egregores.

As indicated earlier, there are two forms of initiation: astral and physical. The first type occurs on the subtle planes of the astral and is not always perceived by the initiate until after the fact, although s/he can also sometimes be aware of it as it is occurring. This type of initiation is conferred upon a person directly by spiritual archetypes within the psyche. A physical initiation is just what it sounds like—an actual ceremony carried out by officers in a physical temple. Some might think that the astral initiation is the only kind that matters—the physical one being only an outward reflection of an inner process. This is simply not the case. A physical initiation reaffirms the candidate's spiritual intent and Will by the act of submitting him/her self to the process of the initiation ceremony. It is a physical proclamation to the manifest universe of one's desire to follow the path of an initiate of the Mysteries. Depending upon the candidate, it is sometimes unlikely that an astral initiation would ever occur without the physical initiation and the skill of the participating initiator. What is clear, however, is that one form of initiation, astral or physical, almost always precedes or occurs simultaneously with the other form. Both are important.

Any discussion of initiation into the G∴D∴ tradition must include a description of the various grades or levels of initiation. The grades of the Golden Dawn correspond to the Sephiroth on the Qabalistic Tree of Life. These grades are further divided into three separate groups known as the First, Second and Third Orders. The list of the grades (from lowest to highest) is as follows:

Grade	Corresponding Sephirah	Element
Neophyte $0^0=0^\Box$	——	——
Zelator $1^0=10^\Box$	Malkuth	Earth
Theoricus $2^0=9^\Box$	Yesod	Air
Practicus $3^0=8^\Box$	Hod	Water
Philosophus $4^0=7^\Box$	Netzach	Fire
Adeptus Minor $5^0=6^\Box$	Tiphareth	——
Adeptus Major $6^0=5^\Box$	Geburah	——
Adeptus Exemptus $7^0=4^\Box$	Chesed	——
Magister Templi $8^0=3^\Box$	Binah	——
Magus $9^0=2^\Box$	Chokmah	——
Ipsissimus $10^0=1^\Box$	Kether	——

The First Order consists of the grades from Neophyte through Philosophus. The grade of Neophyte is a probationary period which is not assigned a Sephirah on the Tree of Life. The grades from Zelator through Philosophus are known as the Elemental grades and are each attributed to one of the four Elements (Fire, Water, Air, Earth). Advancement through the grades of the First or Outer Order is designed to convey to the student an understanding of the four Elemental principles of nature. But, more importantly, the student must learn to realize and balance these four Elements as indispensable ingredients of his/her own psychological and spiritual make-up. We once read a criticism of the Golden Dawn by an author who claimed that the G∴D∴ taught its members to try to control the Elements in the outer world rather than controlling the Elements within. He couldn't have been more wrong. Equilibrating the Elemental components within is the primary goal of the Outer grades. The key objective of the First Order could be summed up in the phrase "learn to balance."

The Portal grade is another probationary period between the First and Second Orders. During this initiation, the candidate is introduced to the fifth and final Element of Spirit, thus completing the component parts of his/her Elemental constitution. The Portal is the final initiation ceremony that we will present in this book. Although Israel Regardie suggested that the Outer Order ceremonies could be converted over into self-initiation rituals, he was convinced that to do so with the Adeptus Minor Ceremony was impossible. (See *The Complete Golden Dawn System of Magic*, page 10.) Initiation into the Second Order grades (starting with Adeptus Minor) still requires an authentic initiator and a physical Vault of the Adepti. However we agree with Regardie in his belief that continued and persistent repetition of the Opening by Watchtower Ceremony over a long period of time can result in the acceptance of the performer as an Adept in the astral realms.

The various grades of the Order also correspond (in a general way) to the various stages of an initiate's life. The Outer Order grades fittingly correspond to the aspirant in his/her twenties. The minimum ideal age for Adeptus Minor would be around twenty-five to thirty, because a distinctive change of consciousness occurs when full adulthood is entered. It is difficult to conceive of a twenty-year-old Adept, unless the person is absolutely extraordinary, because at that age the student has simply not lived long enough to have gained the practical experiences of life. The grade of Adeptus Major would be most appropriate for someone from the age of forty to fifty, mature enough to have acquired some of life's scars—an experienced leader, warrior, and magician. Adeptus Exemptus is the highest grade of the Order and is to be ideally conferred upon someone who exemplifies the old and wise master magician—a person who has perfected his/her magical workings in this lifetime.[9] Keep in mind that these ages are given as suggested archetypal ages. They are not necessarily the actual ages of initiates in those specific grades.

---

[9] In the Golden Dawn, the Adeptus Minor grade was divided into the sub-grades of Neophyte Adeptus Minor, Zelator Adeptus Minor, Theoricus Adeptus Minor, Practicus Adeptus Minor, and Philosophus Adeptus Minor. The curriculum for these grades was extensive and required a minimum of six years to complete. (To say nothing of the time required in the grade of 6°=5□!) The Stella Matutina simplified the curriculum so that the studies for the higher grades of Adeptus Major and Adeptus

The Third Order consists of the grades from Magister Templi to Ipsissimus. These grades are not attained by living initiates; therefore we need not discuss them here.

The effectiveness of an initiation ceremony depends almost entirely upon the initiator. This is no less true of the self-initiator. In a fully operating temple of the Golden Dawn, an initiating Hierophant is required to have attained the grade of Zelator Adeptus Minor. To have reached that point, s/he will have undergone an extensive period of training in the grade of Neophyte Adeptus Minor and will have passed a series of examinations, written, oral, and practical. The power to confer a successful initiation comes from either having had it awakened internally by another proficient initiator or, in the case of self-initiation, by undertaking a great deal of magical and meditative work.

The goal of initiation is to bring about the illumination of the human soul by the Inner and Divine Light. A true "initiate" is an individual whose Higher Self (or Higher Genius) has merged with the Lower Personality and actually incarnated into the physical body. The Personality is left in charge of the day-to-day routines of living and working, but the Higher Genius is free to look out at the world through the eyes of the initiate. Through this experience, the individual is given a permanent extension of consciousness which is impossible to mistake. Many times a student of the mysteries is drawn to a particular mystical current without knowing it. A series of "coincidences" and synchronicities will often direct (or sometimes shove) a person toward that current through books or through meeting other people who also have a connection with the current. During this time, the student's psychic faculties are still relatively undeveloped, yet the inner spark has been ignited. However, a full initiation, or dawning of the Inner Light, is evident when the entire aura is illuminated.

The Higher Self, also called the *Augoides* or Body of Light, comes into manifestation in the material body when true initiation occurs. But a great deal of preparation is necessary prior to this. Before it is possible for the Higher Genius to manifest in the consciousness, the Lower Personality must be tuned to the same wavelength as that of the Inner Self. The Genius carries out its existence in the higher spiritual realms in the same manner that the Lower Personality carries out its functions in the secular world. The desire of the Higher Self is to maintain equilibrium with the Light Divine, while the ambition of the Lower Self is to maintain an alignment with the mundane world. In order for a spiritual initiation

---

Exemptus were actually based upon the work previously undertaken in the sub-grades of Adeptus Minor. By re-designing the curriculum, the magicians of the Stella Matutina were able to claim ever higher grades with ever less justification.

Although Regardie preferred the later format, we feel that the original curriculum is the better one. It is less subject to ego exploitation and better aligned to the archetypal energies which correspond to those grades. (It is amusing to consider that since Regardie's death a few years previous to the writing of this book, a plethora of individuals claiming the lofty degree of $7^\circ=4^\square$ (and even $8^\circ=3^\square$ have suddenly appeared in this country. If these individuals have not merely given themselves honorary degrees then surely, they have discovered H.G. Wells' Time Machine!)

to take place, the Lower Personality must be reoriented and realigned with the aspirations of the Higher Self. This requires a total shift in outlook and a single-minded devotion for the Divine Union. It also requires self-sacrifice on the part of the Lower Personality—the part of the psyche which is ruled by the principles of "me first" and "I want." To the average secular person, sacrificing the needs of the Lower Personality seems foolish, but the submission of the Lower to the Higher Divine Self truly results in the attainment of something which is far more satisfying and durable than momentary wants and desires.

The act of initiation is of prime importance to spiritual growth and personal evolution. As the Personality is gradually taught through magical studies, and moved into an alignment with the Higher Self through purification and ritual work, the Divine Light begins to permeate the aura (the sphere of sensation) of the individual. The seed that an initiation plants within the soul of the magician is a perpetual one that will remain intact throughout many different incarnations, growing stronger as the person rediscovers his/her psychic abilities with each new life cycle. None of this mystical knowledge is ever lost when an initiate undergoes physical death; it is recovered at the appropriate time in the next incarnation, and the process of mystical growth continues from the point where it left off. Spiritual evolution can take many life cycles to fully complete. The ultimate goal of an initiate undergoing this progression lifetime after lifetime is total and perfect union with the Divine Self, which frees him/her from the karmic wheel and the need to incarnate further into a physical body. At this pinnacle of spiritual attainment, the initiate has the choice of remaining in the glory of the Godhead or returning to physical form in order to teach and help other initiates who are "less evolved."

Spiritual growth is an essential step in human evolution. In the not-so-distant past, animal species that failed to evolve in order to meet the challenges of a changing environment died out. Humanity, too, needs to evolve in order to confront the difficult challenges of a world which is experiencing great ecological threats, a skyrocketing population explosion, and rampant violence committed against human beings in the name of race, religion, and resources. As the primary cause of all these problems, it is humanity's obligation to evolve spiritually and wisely, in order to correct them. If we as a species fail to evolve in this fashion, then we truly run the risk of extinction.

Failure to achieve an initiation on whatever level in any given spiritual path or current is usually due to the unwillingness of the individual to sacrifice the petty needs and wants of the Lower Personality for that which is Higher. The Personality and its attendant mental archetypes are quite comfortable in the mundane world and will often put up a fight when threatened with change—intensifying their needs and desires in order to distract the initiate from the spiritual path. The Higher Powers who keep guard over certain magical currents can also place obstacles (both mental and physical) directly in the path of the student, not merely to discourage, but to test the mettle of the would-be initiate. (In a materialistic society, the pocketbook of the student is a favorite target of these guardians.) Those students who quickly crumble under the weight of such deterrents will inevitably fail, while those who bear the burden with tenacity and fortitude will triumph in the end. Indolence can play a role here as well, for the work of an initiate is not easy and requires much dedication and perseverance.

In deciding to write this book, we were faced with certain problems. How does a person initiate him/her self into a current of magic that calls for a complex ceremony performed by a team of competent initiators? How does someone who is not yet a Neophyte satisfactorily perform a ritual that is traditionally executed only by someone who holds the rank of Adept? It seemed like a Catch-22—an impossible scenario. Our solution was to supply the barebones of the rituals and provide step-by-step instruction in the necessary visualizations as they occur in the ceremonies. We revised the rituals so that they could be performed by a solitary individual. We also expanded and emphasized the role of the godform of Thmê (Mêet or Maat) as the Introducer and Mediator between the candidate and the other energies present during the initiation. It seemed only natural that the aspiring student who is working alone and unaided should call upon the reconciling attributions of Thmê to assist in his/her climb up the mountain of initiation. All advanced ritual gestures and techniques are carried out by the student only under the authority and dispensation of the Higher Self, not under the lower will or ego of the student. This is true of every initiation ceremony presented in this book, from Neophyte through the Portal grade; all of them are based upon this premise in order to circumvent, as much as possible, any tendency for ego-inflation (a primary scourge of many an unvigilant magician). Prior to any self-initiation, a dialogue must be established between the student and the godform of Thmê in order to set up a conscious link between the candidate (as the Lower Personality) and the goddess of Truth (as the Higher Self). A series of meditations for establishing this communication is given at the end of this introduction.

In designing these rituals we have tried as much as possible to give the student an initiatory experience that is as complete and fulfilling as any bestowed by an initiating team. We have chosen to retain certain long speeches in the Elemental grade ceremonies, due to the fact that reading them aloud insures that the student will focus on them and not simply skim over them.

One of the things that Israel Regardie was adamant about was that the occult student should seek out a course of psychotherapy as a safeguard against inflation of the ego and other problems that might possibly crop up as a result of the increased activation of the psyche through magical training. We also hold this view, but have found that it is not always possible for students to find a good therapist who is sympathetic to the magical arts. The solitary student is particularly at a disadvantage here, not having a group of temple-mates to consult if problems arise. Therefore we have liberally selected several good psychology books for suggested reading in each grade of this course.

We have already stated that magic is a spiritual science. The curriculum of the Golden Dawn represents, if you will, the academic program of one of the mostly highly acclaimed universities of that science. By the time a student reaches the end of the Portal grade in this course, s/he will have committed to memory the basics of Qabalah, Astrology, and spiritual Alchemy. The student will also know how to construct a natal or horary Astrology chart, perform divination by

Geomancy and Tarot, and understand the fundamental techniques of ritual, including vibration, visualization, skrying, and assumption of godforms.

Regardie's *The Golden Dawn*, although an excellent source book which contains much of the Order's teachings, is often too complex and overpowering for beginning students. All of the Golden Dawn's traditional Knowledge Lectures for the First Order are given here; expanded upon in a format designed to increase the student's comprehension of them. The Knowledge Lectures are not to be merely dismissed offhand as dry intellectual information. Study work is the foundation of the Hermetic science of magic. Just as a surgeon cannot be expected to perform an operation without having committed to memory the rudiments of medical knowledge, so too the magician cannot expect to perform an effective ceremony without understanding the fundamentals of magic. In this book, we have also incorporated much basic Astrological and Alchemical information in the Knowledge Lectures that is unavailable in Regardie's *The Golden Dawn*. In actual Golden Dawn temples, examinations are given to initiates before they can advance to the next grade. Here we have provided quizzes on the Knowledge Lectures and other materials, so that the student can test him/her self at a convenient pace. In addition, extensive ritual and meditative work is provided for each grade.

In Chapter One the reader will find a ritual detailing self-initiation into the grade of Neophyte in addition to gradework and examinations suitable to the $0^O=0^\square$. Chapters Two, Three, Four and Five cover the Elemental grades from Zelator through Philosophus. Chapter Six focuses on ritual and study work for the Portal grade, the apex of this course.

We suggest that the student who elects to assume the route of self-initiation first read the material at the beginning of the chapter appropriate to the grade about to be entered. Then the performance of the initiation ceremony can be undertaken. This ritual may be performed more than one time, since proficiency will increase with practice, and proficiency is, after all, what will determine the effectiveness of the initiation. After that, the Knowledge Lectures must be put to memory. A certain amount of time must be spent in each grade in order to absorb both the written knowledge as well as the initiation. This is especially important for the solitary student, who, without the support of an official temple and the help of peers, may have a tendency to rush through all of the work presented here in a ridiculously short period of time. Any reader thus disposed must remember that the process of spiritual growth is not a race, and it cannot be accomplished in a matter of weeks or months, but rather in terms of years and lifetimes. Keep in mind the old axiom of *Solvitur Ambulando*—solve your problems as you proceed. One does not have to rush through in order to prove one's intelligence or spiritual prowess. Because of this tendency to hurry through the grades, we recommend that solitary students in particular spend sufficient time in the various grades in order to fully assimilate the effects of each initiation. We suggest that the student of this course spend approximately four months as a probationer prior to any attempt at self-initiation into the Neophyte grade. The student should take this time to prepare for initiation by practicing the meditations and exercises given at the end of this introduction. Six months should be spent in the grade of Neophyte, and six months in each of the grades from Zelator through Practicus. Seven months should be spent in the Philosophus grade, while the duration of the Portal grade should be nine to twelve months. Ceremonial work provided in each grade is to be performed daily (though sometimes weekly depending upon the ritual). Finally the student can test his/her knowledge with the quizzes provided.

Although the main focus of this book is on the solitary practitioner, there is no reason why two people cannot undertake the same course of study and progress together. It is certainly easier for two people to study the Knowledge Lecture material and quiz each other. However, each person must spend the probationary period separately while establishing his/her own dialogue with the godform of Thmê. The initiation ceremonies presented here may be performed together so long as each person takes part in the visualizations and ritual gestures. The longer speeches may be divided between the two participants. Another technique which may prove helpful to one or two people undertaking this route is to pre-record some of the longer speeches and guided visualizations presented for later playback in the rituals. Hearing one's own voice speaking the words of the gods can have a powerful initiatory effect.

There is also no valid reason why students who may already belong to a Golden Dawn temple should not perform these self-initiatory rituals, for performance of them can only serve to increase the student's knowledge and proficiency. The Knowledge Lectures and meditations given here can also be used to supplement any student's existing gradework.

If the student perseveres through this study course and the rituals furnished here for self-attainment, we have no doubt that the result will be the birth of an initiate of the Golden Dawn tradition of magic. It is our sincerest hope that, through this book, individuals who previously have had no opportunity to do so may initiate themselves into the Western Mystery Tradition.✿

Preliminary Meditative Work

Daily Awareness Exercises:

Darkness Technique: Before the commencement of any meditation, breathe deeply and rhythmically. Cover your eyes with the palms of your hands; overlapping the fingers of one hand with the other. You should experience total darkness.

Sense Awareness Techniques: For the duration of a week, take a daily walk and make a mental note of everything you see, not focusing on anything in particular. Do not attempt to analyze or make judgments; merely observe. Keep a journal of your observations.

For the following week, take a daily walk and stop, deliberately focusing in on one particular object. Take note of everything concerning this object.

On the following week of daily walking, try to look for a single color each day. On Sunday look for orange; Monday—blue, Tuesday— red, Wednesday—yellow, Thursday—violet, Friday—green, Saturday—blue-violet (indigo).

For one week concentrate on the various sounds that are heard on the daily walk. Stop at certain times and close your eyes, so that the faculty of sight does not interfere with this exercise. Do not attempt to analyze or make judgments; merely take note.

For the following week, take a daily walk and stop, deliberately focusing in on one particular sound. Take note of everything concerning this sound.

For one week, take note of different tactile or touch sensations that you encounter during the course of a day. Stop at certain times and close your eyes, so that the faculty of sight does not interfere with this exercise.

For one week, take note of every taste that you encounter during the course of a day. Stop at certain times and close your eyes, so that the faculty of sight does not interfere with your sense of taste. For the following week, focus on one particular taste.

For one week, take note of every smell that you encounter. Stop at certain times and close your eyes, so that the faculty of sight does not interfere with your sense of smell. For the following week, focus on one particular smell.✿

Exercise:

It is vitally important that in the quest to exalt the health of the Spirit, the student does not neglect the health of the body. Physical well-being and endurance are essential to the magician who wishes to perform lengthy rituals as well as Astral work. During this probationary period, the student should begin a regular discipline of exercise to maintain physical fitness. We leave the choice of exercise to the individual student; swimming, biking, jogging, martial arts, aerobics, yoga or some other. Israel Regardie recommended that the student perform certain exercises that are designed to raise both the physical and psychic vitality of the practitioner. They are taken from a small pamphlet by Peter Kelder called *The Five Rites of Rejuvenation* or *The Eye of Revelation*. These exercises can also be found in Donald Michael Kraig's book *Modern Magick* (pages 222–229).

Whatever form of exercise is undertaken, the student should never overwork to the point of strain. If one is not used to exercise, begin slowly and gradually. If health concerns are an issue, consult a doctor before commencing any form of physical exertion.✿

Visualization Exercise:

Spend a few moments of each day in this exercise. Begin with the eyes closed and relax, breathing deeply and rhythmically. Then open your eyes and gaze into the palm of your left hand. Imagine a small yellow lump of a non-sticking substance formulating in your hand. It is somewhat clay-like and elastic in consistency. Cup your right hand over the other and press this yellow substance as if you were making a hamburger patty. Then begin to roll the substance between your hands as if you were making a meatball. When the image of the yellow ball of astral substance is very clear within your mind, place it somewhere near you. Repeat this technique three more times, forming next a red ball, a blue ball and finally a black ball.

When finished, place all four balls in a row. Visualize them strongly. Then concentrate on dissolving the balls one by one, starting with the black ball, followed by blue, red and finally yellow. See the area where the balls were placed as totally clear of the astral substance.✿

An Introduction to the Godform of Thmê

The next series of meditations is designed to open a working dialogue between the aspiring student and the archetypal part of the candidate's mind symbolized by the godform of Thmê (pronounced Tah-may). The Greek form of this deity is Themis, and in the Egyptian Pantheon, she is Mêet or Maat. This godform will act as the candidate's introducer and guide throughout all of his/her initiatory experiences in this course. Here Thmê acts as a portion of the candidate's own Higher Self, which conducts him/her along the initiatory path toward the eventual goal of full conversation with the Holy Guardian Angel. It is important that the aspirant establish a firm link of communication with Thmê before the act of self-initiation. We suggest that the student perform these meditations daily for a period of four months prior to self-initiation into the Neophyte grade. Meditation 1 is recommended for the first month, Mediation 2 is suggested for the second month, and Meditation 3 is to be performed during the remaining two months before initiation. If after four months the student still does not feel in touch with the godform, the entire series of meditations should be repeated for three additional months prior to self-initiation.

We should stress that at this early stage of development, the student is not asked to assume the godform of Thmê or any other godform. Assumption of godforms is not taught until much later in this course. The aspirant needs to concentrate instead on visualizing and becoming comfortable with the godform. A one-on-one dialog with the godform is encouraged but do not attempt to let the godform control your words or actions. (If the godform makes demands, asks you do something against your will, or simply gives you information which you know to be false, then you probably are not in dialogue with Thmê or your Higher Self—you are more than likely in touch with some lesser archetype that is playing games with you. In that case, banish the figure and start over.)✿

Vibration:

Certain names or *Words of Power* when properly vibrated or intoned attract certain energies which are associated with them. A technique known as the Vibratory Formula is a method by which divine names and words are spoken forcefully and with authority in a "vibration."

The student should first imagine a glowing white Light above the head, and then visualize this Light descending to the level of the heart. The letters of the name to be vibrated should be imagined in white within the heart center. Then the name is slowly pronounced so that the sound vibrates throughout the chest cavity and is felt throughout the entire body. The student should imagine that the sound reaches into every corner of the universe. The Vibratory Formula of pronouncing names normally produces a slight sense of fatigue combined with exhilaration if performed correctly. (Note: only Divine or Angelic names are to be vibrated in this fashion.)✡

First Month—Meditation 1: Themis

Take a ritual bath and perform a ritual of relaxation. Be seated comfortably in your temple space, bedroom or any other area where quiet and solitude may be maintained. Light a yellow candle in the center of your temple space. Burn incense or scented oil, preferably frankincense or cinnamon.

Perform the Lesser Banishing Ritual of the Pentagram, also known as the LBRP. (See Chapter One, pp. 82-84.)

Perform the Adoration to the Lord of the Universe. (See Chapter One, page 85.) Then give four knocks. Close your eyes and imagine yourself sitting in a violet ovoid shape. Say:

> *Through the Divine Name of Tetragrammaton, YHVH, (Yode-Heh-Vav-Heh) I, (state name) proclaim myself to be a humble seeker after the Light of Wisdom and the Splendor of the Divine. From this day forward I shall strive ever to prove myself a true and worthy candidate for initiation into the Mysteries. To this end I seek the guidance of the goddess THEMIS, that she might reveal herself to me and intercede on my behalf before the Guardians of the Sacred Knowledge.*

Again give the Battery of four knocks. Intone the name of the goddess THEMIS a number of times. As you do so, the violet ovoid shape surrounding you changes to brilliant yellow.

Visualize the form of a tall goddess standing before you. She has short, dark hair and dark eyes. Imagine this figure in flowing white Greek robes trimmed with yellow and violet. Her features are austere and her expression denotes seriousness. In her left hand she holds a pair of scales. In her right hand she holds a golden chalice. Visualize strongly the form before you. Say:

> *O thou radiant goddess of Wisdom and Oracles! THEMIS! Thou whose name means the Steadfast One! Thou Incorruptible One who defendeth those who are Just! Thou who presideth over the feasts of the gods on Olympus! Revealer of Laws! THEMIS! Thou who art the collective conscious and the Keeper of Order! Thou who art called the Lady of Justice and the Protectress. SOTEIRA! EUBOULOS! Thou who gives good counsel and advice! Interpreter of the Will of the gods! Let thine Oracle portray me in a favorable light. Thou goddess of the Scales! See thou that my heart is true, and that I am indeed a true Seeker after the Stone! Defend me as thou*

wouldst defend all worthy Aspirants on the Path of Wisdom! Speak on my behalf before the assembly of the gods! Counsel and guide me in my quest for the Light Divine! This I ask in the Name of the Ineffable One!

Visualize the form strongly. See it breathe with life. The goddess places her scales over your body—the two halves of the scales balancing from your right shoulder to your left shoulder. The scales are absorbed into your body—into your shoulders and arms—merging into the flesh. The balance point of the scales is absorbed into your heart center, becoming one with it. You feel strengthened by this blending.

The goddess Themis then hands you the golden chalice of nectar to drink from. You taste its pure sweet essence. A sensation of warm white Light washes over you. The drink invigorates you and leaves you with a feeling of calm and balance.

Meditate for a few moments on the godform of Themis before allowing her to fade gently from your sphere of awareness.

Slowly dissolve the yellow ovoid surrounding you. When you are ready, perform the Adoration to the Lord of the Universe, followed by the Battery of four knocks and the Lesser Banishing Ritual of the Pentagram.

Keep a written record of any impressions or insights gained during the meditation. ✿

Second Month—Meditation 2: Maat

Take a ritual bath and perform a ritual of relaxation. Be seated comfortably in your temple space. Light the yellow candle in the center of your temple space. Burn incense or scented oil, preferably frankincense or cinnamon.

Perform the Lesser Banishing Ritual of the Pentagram.

Perform the Adoration to the Lord of the Universe. Then sound the Battery of four knocks. Close your eyes and imagine yourself sitting in a violet ovoid shape. Say:

> *Through the Divine Name of Tetragrammaton, YHVH, (Yode-Heh-Vav-Heh) I, (state name) proclaim myself to be a humble seeker after the Light of Wisdom and the Splendor of the Divine. From this day forward I shall strive ever to prove myself a true and worthy candidate for initiation into the Mysteries. To this end I seek the guidance of Themis in her more ancient form as the goddess MAAT, that she might reveal herself to me and intercede on my behalf before the Guardians of the Sacred Knowledge.*

Again give the Battery of four knocks. Intone the name of the goddess MAAT a number of times. As you do so, the violet ovoid shape surrounding you changes to brilliant yellow.

Visualize the slender form of a goddess standing before you. Her black nemyss barely conceals her long dark hair. She is clothed in a glittering tunic of green and gold, with some flashing undertones of yellow, red and blue. Her collar is also composed of several colored beads and ornaments. Attached to her arms are a pair of great white wings, like those of an eagle. A red headband binds a large white ostrich feather to the crown of her head, atop her black nemyss. Her golden skin and darkly-painted eyes cannot hide the fact that she is one and the same as Themis of the Greeks. She holds a Lotus Wand in one hand, and an ankh in the other. Visualize strongly the form before you. Say:

> *O thou shining goddess of Justice and Truth! Thou who standeth between illusion and reality, between good and evil! Thou who replaced Chaos with Light! Thou who art upright and true! Thou who weighest the hearts of men and women in the Hall of Judgment! Thou Lady of Heaven and Queen of Earth! Thou mistress of the Underworld! Thou point of balance upon which the whole of the universe is poised! Hear my confession and judge me aright! Lady of the Feather, see thou that my heart is true, and that I am indeed a true Seeker after the Stone! Defend me as thou wouldst defend all worthy Aspirants on the Path of Wisdom! Speak on my behalf before the assembly of the gods! Counsel and guide me in my quest for the Light Divine! This I ask in the Divine Name of YHVH!*

Visualize the form strongly. See it breathe with life. The goddess Maat takes a white feather from one of her wings and presses it to the crown of your head. She points the head of the Lotus Wand at your forehead and, as she does so, the feather is absorbed into your flesh. Uniting with the feather of Maat brings you a sense of harmony and inner peace. The goddess then points the ankh at your head, base of your throat, heart, groin and feet in turn. As she focuses on each of these five points of your body, you are aware of an influx of Light-energy, followed by a gentle sense of balancing. The sensation reminds you of stones tossed into a pool of water—the ripples subsiding into delicate wave patterns. Once again, you feel strengthened by the encounter.

Meditate for a few moments more on the godform of Maat before allowing her to fade gently from your sphere of awareness. Slowly dissolve the yellow ovoid surrounding you. When you are ready, perform the Adoration to the Lord of the Universe, followed by the Battery of four knocks and the Lesser Banishing Ritual of the Pentagram.

As always, keep a written record of your impressions of this meditation whenever it is performed.✿

Third and Fourth Months—Meditation 3: Thmê

Take a ritual bath and perform a ritual of relaxation. Be seated comfortably in your temple space. Light the yellow candle in the center of your temple space. Burn incense or scented oil, preferably frankincense or cinnamon.

Perform the Lesser Banishing Ritual of the Pentagram.

Perform the Adoration to the Lord of the Universe. Then sound the Battery of four knocks. Close your eyes and imagine yourself sitting in a violet ovoid shape. Say:

> Through the Divine Name of Tetragrammaton, YHVH, (Yode-Heh-Vav-Heh) I, (state name) proclaim myself to be a humble seeker after the Light of Wisdom and the Splendor of the Divine. From this day forward I shall strive ever to prove myself a true and worthy candidate for initiation into the Mysteries. To this end I seek the guidance of the goddess of Balance in her Coptic form as THMÊ, the name by which she was known in the Graeco-Egyptian world. Grant that she might reveal herself to me and intercede on my behalf before the Guardians of the Sacred Knowledge.

Again give the Battery of four knocks. Intone the name of the goddess THMÊ a number of times. As you do so, the violet ovoid shape surrounding you changes to brilliant yellow.

Visualize the slender form of a golden-skinned goddess standing before you. At this stage of your dialogue with her, the goddess reveals her initial (simplified) form to you. Her nemyss is striped black and white, while her tunic has become pure glittering white. Her large pectoral collar is made of bands that are black and white. Her wristbands are similarly colored. She holds a yellow Phoenix Wand. Her painted eyes are the same as the eyes of Maat. Visualize the form strongly before you. Say:

> O Thou beautiful one of Truth, Balance and Order! Reconciler between the Darkness and the Light! Thou who art the Eye of Ra and the seat of Justice between the Pillars! Guardian of the Threshold and Preparer of the Way for the Enterer! Dweller in the Hall of Dual Manifestation—the Hall of Two Truths! Divine Mediator of opposites who breathest forth Equilibrium and Truth in the Reconciling Air! See thou that my heart is true, and that I am indeed a true Seeker after the Stone! Defend me as thou wouldst defend all worthy Aspirants on the Path of Wisdom! Speak on my behalf before the assembly of the gods! Counsel and guide me in my quest for the Light Divine! This I ask in the Divine Name of YHVH!

Visualize the form strongly. See it breathe with life. The goddess Thmê gestures for you to hold out both of your hands. You do so. The goddess places a small ceramic jar in your right hand as a symbol of your heart and your spiritual essence. In your left hand she places the white *shu* feather of Maat. She speaks:[10]

> My feather is that which is weighed against every human heart. Thy heart must be measured and judged to be true and just. Thy heart and thy soul must be made Maat. Let not thy scales tip either to the right or to the left, for either unbalanced is not good. Seek ever the center, for only the straight and narrow path between the Pillars can lead you to the Stone of the Wise. This is the great Truth which hath never been broken since the time of Osiris. Remember thou that God will judge the just.

The white *shu* feather and the ceramic heart are absorbed into the flesh of your hands. Thmê holds the yellow Phoenix Wand before you. The Wand bursts into flame within her hand. From the ashes of the Phoenix Wand a new Wand emerges. It is a red and yellow-gold Wand crowned by a split miter-head. A small red cross ornaments the head of the scepter. Thmê speaks:

> This is the Scepter of Wisdom which shall conduct thee always on the Path of Knowledge. It symbolizes religion and spiritual desire which guides and regulates life. Remember to hold all religions in reverence, for there is none but contains a ray of the ineffable Light that thou art seeking. Remember that the goddess who now stands before thee is a living symbol of those higher aspirations of the soul which should guide its action.

Meditate for a few moments more on the godform of Thmê before allowing her to fade gently from your sphere of awareness. Slowly dissolve the yellow ovoid shape surrounding you. When you are ready, perform the Adoration to the Lord of the Universe, followed by the Battery of four knocks and the Lesser Banishing Ritual of the Pentagram.✡

Bringing Down the Light

In all Golden Dawn ceremonies, the initiating Hierophant, acting as a living "channel" brings the Supernal Light down into the temple through a complex formula. The student of this course, acting as his/her own initiator, must use a greatly simplified method of bringing the Divine Light into the temple. A technique for accomplishing this is presented here. This exercise should be practiced for at least three months prior to self-initiation into the grade of Neophyte.

After taking a ritual bath, sit quietly for a few moments of meditation, facing the Eastern part of your temple space. When you feel ready, stand and place

---

[10] Please note that this ritual, as well as the initiation rites in the following chapters, contains passages which are set in a sans serif typeface, to indicate speeches that are "spoken" astrally by the godforms—not physically by the magician—and are "heard" internally.

both of your hands over your heart center, one hand crossing the other. Visualize a great brilliant Light which occupies a space that is both above you and beyond you in the East. As you contemplate this Light, visualize the figure of a white triangle traced in the brilliance before you. The white of the triangle shimmers and pulses iridescently.

When the vision is very strong, bring your right hand straight out in front of you and your left hand just in front of your heart area, palm outward. With your right hand, trace a large spiral in the air in front of you (begin at the outer left-hand edge of the spiral and go clockwise). Bring the spiral slowly in toward you as you trace it. When your right hand reaches your left hand, join both hands together with the fingers interlocking and turn them so that the knuckles of your hand touch your heart area, and the palms face outward. This is the Sign of the Spiraling Light. (Please note that this is not a traditional grade Sign of the Golden Dawn, but one that we have provided for the purpose of this course.) As you perform this, visualize the Divine Light spiraling in a funnel shape toward you. Say the words, *"Let the white brilliance of the Divine Spirit descend!"* As you do so, feel a flood of the Divine Light course through your entire body—from your head to your feet. The Light then centers itself at your heart area. Be aware of the connection that exists between your body and the universal Light. Equilibrate this Light through your body by performing the Qabalistic Cross.

Then say the words, *"Khabs Am Pekht, Konx Om Pax, Light in Extension."* Make three complete clockwise circuits around the boundaries of your temple space, all the while envisioning that you are carrying the Divine Light around the temple in a spiral of energy from the area of your heart. After completing the third circumambulation, return to the East and face West. Imagine the white triangle of Light firmly established in the center of your temple space. See it vividly.

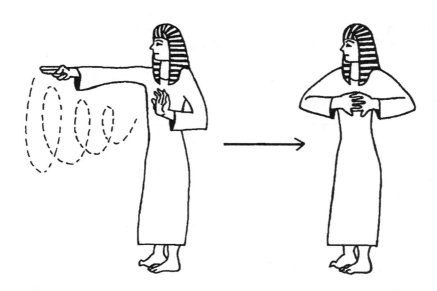

The Sign of the Spiraling Light

Continue meditating for as long as you like, but when you are finished, make three counter-clockwise circumambulations of the temple all the while envisioning the white triangle in the center of the room disintegrating. Imagine the Divine Light from the triangle flowing back through your heart center and up into the greater triangle of Light above you. At the end of the circumambulation, turn again toward the East and, with your hands interlocked over your heart, begin the Reverse Spiral of Light, which is simply the total reversal of the Sign of the Spiraling Light. Pause and perform again the Qabalistic Cross for equilibration. This ends the rite.

It is important to record all your meditations and ritual workings in every grade in order to have a tangible yardstick by which to measure your spiritual growth. It is equally important to record your perceptions of all your experiences within the grades, so that you may return to them time and time again for examination. In this course of study, as in many other aspects of life, you are the only one gauging your own progress.

In closing, there will always be some individuals who will simply read this book and fail to follow either the necessary workload or the minimal amounts of time suggested in each grade. Within a couple of months of having purchased this book, some will claim to have "done it all" and self-proclaim themselves as Adepts of this course. However, it will be far easier for such people to mislead and impress beginners than it will be for them to hoodwink those aspirants who truly undertake this work. It will be especially difficult for these individuals to fool their own Higher Selves. The Holy Guardian Angel will be able to tell the difference between bravado and true aspiration.

You have no one to blame but yourself if you fail to press onwards. But likewise, if you succeed, you have yourself to thank. The rewards are yours to enjoy.✿

Unto Thee Sole Wise, Sole Eternal,
and Sole Merciful One,
be the praise and glory forever.
Who hath permitted me,
who now standeth humbly before Thee,
to enter thus far into the sanctuary of thy mystery.
Not unto me, Adonai,
but unto thy name be the glory.
Let the influence of thy Divine ones
descend upon my head,
and teach me the value of self-sacrifice
so that I shrink not in the hour of trial.
But that thus my name may be written on high,
and my Genius stand
in the presence of the Holy One.
In that hour when the Son of Man is invoked
before the Lord of Spirits
and his Name before the Ancient of Days.

CHAPTER ONE

The Neophyte Grade

f all the initiation ceremonies of the Golden Dawn, the Neophyte Ritual stands apart from the rest. The Neophyte grade is called the $0^O = 0^\square$ grade because it is not attributed to any of the Sephiroth on the Tree of Life. This ceremony is a preliminary rite which contains all the fundamental magical formulae and techniques of the Order. It is based almost entirely around the idea of the Divine Light and the spiritual magnetism which draws that Light into the temple to be implanted in the aspirant's sphere of sensation. The word *Neophyte* comes from the Greek word *neophytos* or "newly planted."

In a traditional Neophyte Ceremony with a full initiating team, the Hierophant, the main officer of the ritual, acts on behalf of the Divine Self of humanity—the supreme spiritual Soul. As the physical embodiment of the godform of Ousiri (Osiris), he is stationed in the East, the place of the dawning sun and the symbolic direction of the Supernal Light of Kether. It is through Ousiri, represented by the Hierophant, that the Light is brought into the temple.

The Hegemon, who is the personification of the godform of Thmê, symbolizes the higher part of the candidate's mind—the highest part of the *Ruach* or reasoning mind working in combination with the *Neshamah*, the Divine Soul. The Keryx[11] represents the lower part of the Ruach functioning in obedience to the Will. The Hiereus is the active will of humanity, the guardian against evil. The Hegemon is the aspiring, compassionate and intuitive consciousness which seeks to bring about the Rise of the Light. (It is for this reason we have elaborated the role of godform of the Hegemon, Thmê, in the initiation rituals presented here.)

The primary objective of the student who wishes to initiate him/her self into the grade of Neophyte is twofold. First the Divine Light must be brought into the temple. Second, through a magnetic charge, this Light must be attracted to and implanted within the psyche of the aspirant. What must be remembered here is that the Higher Self rarely leaves its lofty abode, except when the Lower Self intentionally opens up to the Higher by an act of genuine aspiration or self-sacrifice. This action alone makes the descent of the Light into mind, heart and soul possible. Therefore the *self-initiated* must ever strive steadfastly in the utmost

---

[11] The old-fashioned spelling of this word was *kerux*, which transliterated the Greek letter upsilon as a "*u*." However this same letter is also transliterated as a "y" in such words as "mystery" and "sympathy," which are both of Greek origin.

desire for the Light. This spiritual energy can be magnetically attracted to the candidate through the disciplines of rhythmic breathing, vibration, sincere aspiration, prayer and many other methods.

All of the various symbols and movements in the Neophyte Ceremony are designed to enhance and reiterate the purpose of the ritual—the quest for the Light. Not all of the intricate symbolism is fully comprehended by the candidate, but that makes little difference in the long run, because the inherent value of such symbolism is that it has an auto-suggestive effect on the aspirant which is perceived at a deep subconscious level.

The objective of the Neophyte Ceremony as a whole is the purification of the personality. Purification and Consecration of both the temple and the candidate (who is the living temple) are a source of constant focus throughout the ritual. The Elements of Water and Fire are employed to this end until at length the aspirant is placed between the two Pillars of Light and Dark, in the position of Equilibrium, where a bond is formed between the Personality and the Higher and Divine Genius.

The ceremony of the $0^{\circ} = 0^{\square}$ symbolically occurs in the Hall of Judgment which is described in the 125th chapter of the Egyptian *Book of the Dead*. This depicts the "Weighing of the Soul" in which the deceased (who represents the Initiate) is brought into the Hall of Truth by Anubis, the god of the Underworld. After having undergone extensive interrogation and purification, the initiate makes the long negative confession and is asked to explain the complex symbolism of the Hall. The Soul of the initiate then watches the weighing of its actions on Earth against the feather of Truth in the mystical scales of Maat. The ibis-headed god Thoth records the judgment as a devouring beast stands ready to seize the soul if the initiate has led an unworthy life. When this ordeal has passed, Horus introduces the initiate to the god, Osiris, who sits enthroned within his shrine. Before him is a lotus flower, the emblem of metamorphosis. The deceased is then united with Osiris the Redeemer in an infinite Light. Thus the entire story of the Weighing of the Soul can be said to represent the advance and purification of the initiate in the Neophyte Hall.

Although many people respect the Neophyte Ceremony as a vital and sublime ritual replete with essential magical techniques, oftentimes these same individuals do not respect the Neophyte *grade*. No sooner do they become Neophytes and take that all-important first step into the current of the Golden Dawn than they wish to rush headlong into the $1^{\circ} = 10^{\square}$ grade of Zelator, as if the rank of Neophyte were somehow undesirable or demeaning compared to higher grades. We cannot overstate how foolish this supposition is. Advancement into the higher grades should not be likened to a race. It is a life-long commitment to complete the Great Work. A certain amount of time must be spent in each grade to thoroughly ingest and balance out the effects of initiation. Advancing through the grades too quickly is apt to result in imbalance and egotism. In the Western Mystery Tradition *we are all Neophytes* no matter what our outer rank might be. All of us have much to learn on the quest for spiritual growth. A suitable amount of time spent in the Neophyte grade (through self-initiation) should be approximately six to twelve months.

The aspirant will also need to choose a magical motto. A motto is usually a phrase that is descriptive of the magician's spiritual goal. It is rendered in Latin, Hebrew, or any language other than the aspirant's everyday speech, in order to set the magical name apart from secular life.

In the initiation ceremonies of the Golden Dawn, various participants known as officers assume certain godforms (i.e., take on the astral appearance and qualities of a god or goddess) who carry out specific duties in the ritual. True godform assumption should not be attempted by anyone who is not yet an Adept.[12] In a self-initiation rite these various godforms are built up in the imagination of the candidate where they represent different parts of the aspirant's psyche. These godforms are therefore microcosmic reflections of specific macrocosmic godforces to which they are linked. They are each called upon and orchestrated by the candidate's own Higher Self through the desire for the Light. The solitary aspirant does not actually assume the godforms created in the temple, but instead acts upon their behalf by taking on the various offices in the temple under the watchful guidance of the god-forces. An officer-form, so to speak, is a lesser extension of a godform which serves to carry out specific functions within the temple. It is the *officer-forms*, not the godforms themselves, that are assumed by the solitary aspirant of this course. When the officer-forms are not being assumed by the candidate, they are returned to the full authority of their respective godforms.

The combined activities in the ritual, especially the activities of the various godforms and officer-forms, symbolize the component parts of the candidate's own mind, which work together to effect initiation. However, preparation must be done prior to self-initiation into the Neophyte grade. It is very important for the student to have previously opened up a channel of dialogue with Thmê by practicing the exercises given in the introduction. We suggest that the aspirant study the section here entitled "The Godforms of the Visible Stations" and the diagrams of the temple provided for this rite. The reader is also advised to commit to memory the section of this chapter which describes the primary offices of the Neophyte grade and their officer-forms. All information required for the rise and circulation of the Light in the ritual, as well as the necessary visualizations, will be explained step-by-step in the ceremony given here.

The following manuscript describes the appearance of the various godforms of the Neophyte Hall, especially in terms of color. The colors of the Three Chiefs reflect their corresponding Sephiroth: Chesed, Geburah, and Tiphareth. The colors of these three officials are seen to "flash" with their respective vibratory energy.[13] Their high placement on the Tree of Life indicates the importance of these officers in guiding the current of magic from its source (the Supernal Triad) into the temple.

The remaining officers who do not occupy a seat on the Dais are each assigned two visible forms, the *initial form* and the *advanced form*. The initial forms

---

[12] Students who take on godforms before they are ready to do so may endanger themselves through psychic imbalance and deception.

[13] "Flashing Colors" are complimentary colors that are located directly opposite each other on a standard artist's color wheel. One of the two colors is active, the other passive. Two colors that "flash" are linked together with the same vibratory energy.

are appropriate for beginning students. The more advanced forms should not be envisioned until after the student has become proficient in the art of godform visualization.

The throne of each godform is also ornamented with the flashing pair of colors that reflect that officer's particular Elemental or Sephirotic affinity. Each throne is considered a receptacle or dwelling place for the Divine Powers of the god. They are batteries of specific energy forces.

The wands, swords and other implements associated with the various godforms in the Hall are also heavy with symbolic meaning. These items act to reinforce the respective potencies of the godforms.✿

The Godforms of the Visible Stations

Copyright © 1991 Adam P. Forrest

General Note

The human portions of the godforms follow the coloring conventions of Egyptian iconography in that the skin tone of women is represented as a rich yellow-gold and that of men as a warm reddish-brown.[14]

Above each of the godforms of the officers on the Dais may be envisioned a circled cross of white Light (like the lamen of the Hierophant) symbolic of the Inner Order, and above each of the other godforms of officers in the Hall may be envisioned a cross and triangle of white Light symbolic of the Outer Order. Above the godform of the Phylax[15] in the Pronaos may be envisioned a triangle of white Light (like the sash badge of the Neophyte) symbolic of the Light extended into the Darkness of the outer and uninitiated world.

The Godforms

Praemonstrator or Praemonstratrix

[Egyptian *Iset*, Coptic **ⲎⲤⲈ** Ȇse (Ay-say), Graeco-Egyptian *Isis*] Isis has a human head, and wears a nemyss striped blue and orange. Her linen gown is blue. Her

---

[14] The colors given here are different from those given in a manuscript published in Regardie's *The Golden Dawn*. That paper, entitled "The Egyptian Godforms of the Neophyte Grade" was written by someone in the Stella Matutina, and was never a part of the original Z documents by Mathers. The colors it assigns to the officers are in reality colors that apply only to the godforms in the game of Enochian Chess, and not to the godforms of the Neophyte Hall. It lists, for example, the colors of Nephthys as being primarily black—the color of Earth. In Enochian Chess Nephthys represents the Element of Earth, but in the Neophyte Hall she represents the Sephirah of Geburah and her colors would correspond to that sphere—primarily red. The other godforms would also be colored in accordance with their roles in the Neophyte Hall; the Hegemon's godform would be primarily yellow because of her role as the Reconciler.

[15] The Sentinel of the old G∴D∴ documents.

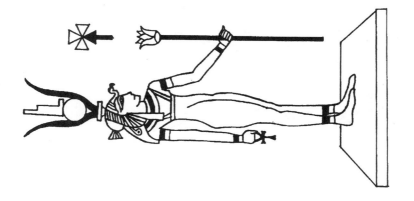

Isis

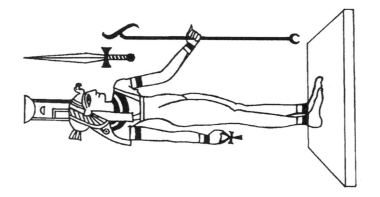

Nephthys

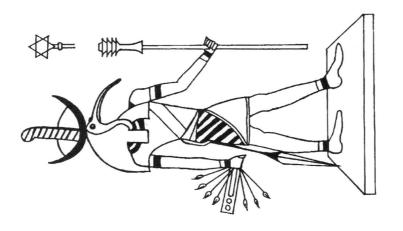

Thoth

7

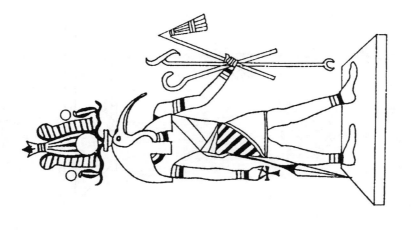

Thoth as the Three Chiefs

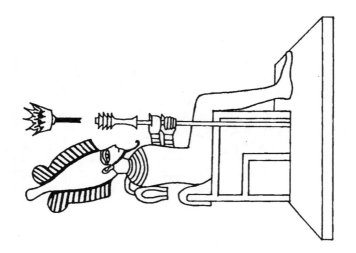

Osiris

Haroueris

8

Horus

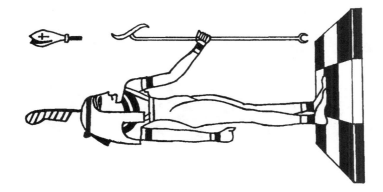

Thmê
(Mêet)

Neith

9

Auramoouth

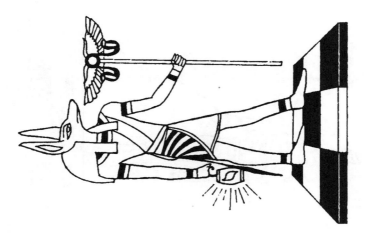

Anoubis

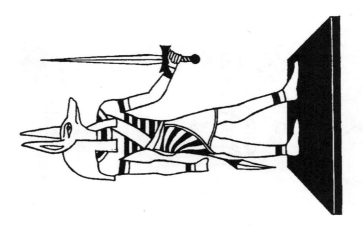

Ophois

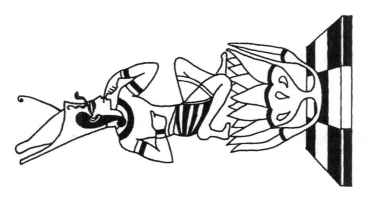

Ahathoor

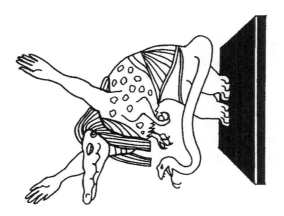

Hoor-peKroti
(Harparkrat)

Ouammoout peSatanas

11

pectoral collar is banded orange, blue, orange. Her wristbands are banded blue and orange.

Isis bears either a blue Lotus Wand or the blue wand of the Praemonstrator. The goddess sits upon a throne of blue ornamented in orange, which stands upon a white pavement.

Imperator or Imperatrix

[Egyptian and Coptic **ⲚⲈⲂⲐⲰ** *Nebethô* (Neb-et-ho), Graeco-Egyptian *Nephthys*] Nephthys has a human head, and wears a nemyss striped red and green. Her linen gown is red. Her pectoral collar is banded green, red, green. Her wristbands are banded red and green.

Nephthys bears either a red Phoenix Wand or the red sword of the Imperator. The goddess sits upon a throne of red ornamented in green, which stands upon a white pavement.

Cancellarius or Cancellaria

[Egyptian *Djehoti*, Coptic **ⲐⲰⲞⲨⲐ** *Thôouth* (Toh-oh-t) or (T'hoh-t), Graeco-Egyptian *Thôth*] Thoth has the head of a white ibis and wears a nemyss striped yellow and violet. His linen kilt is white, and his overkilt is striped yellow and violet. His pectoral collar is banded violet, yellow, violet. His wristbands are banded yellow and violet.

Thoth bears either a yellow Djed Wand or the yellow scepter of Cancellarius. He may also bear a yellow scribal pallet with brush-pens of the seven rainbow colors. The god sits upon a throne of yellow ornamented in violet, which stands upon a white pavement.

The Three Chiefs

[Egyptian *Djehoti*, Coptic **ⲐⲰⲞⲨⲐ** *Thôouth* (Toh-oh-t) or (T'hoh-t), Graeco-Egyptian *Thôth*] As the Z Rituals teach us, Thoth may also appear as the synthesis of the Three Chiefs.

As the synthesis of the Adept Triad, Thoth has the head of a white ibis and wears a nemyss striped yellow and white. His linen kilt is white, and his overkilt is striped yellow and white. His pectoral collar is banded red, yellow, blue. His wristbands are banded red, yellow, blue.

Thoth bears a yellow Phoenix Wand, a blue crook, and a red scourge. The god sits upon a throne of yellow ornamented in blue, red, and yellow, which stands upon a white pavement.

Hierophantês (Hierophant) or Hierophantissa

[Egyptian *Osir*, Coptic **ⲞⲨⲤⲒⲢⲒ** *Ousiri* (Oo-seer-ee), Graeco-Egyptian *Osiris*] *Form:* Osiris has a human head and wears a nemyss striped white and yellow, surmounted by the white *Stenu* crown of the Upper Regions. He is mummy-wrapped in white except for his head and hands. His pectoral collar is banded white, red, blue, yellow, black. His wristbands are banded yellow and white.

Osiris bears a white Djed Wand or a white crown-headed scepter of the Hierophant. The god sits upon a throne of white ornamented in yellow, which stands upon a white pavement.

Past Hierophant or Past Hierophantissa

[Egyptian *Hôr Wêr*, Coptic *Hôôr Ouer* ⳤⲱⲱⲣ ⲟⲩⲏⲣ (Hoor-wehr) or (Hoh-or-wehr), Graeco-Egyptian *Harouêris*] Haroueris has the head of a hawk, and wears a nemyss striped yellow and violet, surmounted by the dual red and white *Skhenet* (Graeco-Egyptian *Pschent*) crown of the Upper and Lower Realms. His linen kilt is white, and his overkilt is striped yellow and violet. His pectoral collar is banded violet, yellow, violet. His wristbands are banded yellow and violet.

Haroueris bears a red Phoenix Wand or the red crown-headed scepter of the Hierophant. The god stands upon a white pavement when upon the Dais and upon a black and white pavement when in the lower Hall. When seated, the god sits upon a throne of yellow ornamented in violet, which stands upon a white pavement.

Hiereus or Hiereia

[Egyptian *Hôr*, Coptic ⳤⲱⲱⲣ *Hôôr* (Hoor) or (Hoh-or), Graeco-Egyptian *Hôros*, Latinized Greek *Horus*] *Initial Form:* Hôros has the head of a hawk and wears a nemyss striped black and white. His linen kilt is white, and his overkilt is striped black and white. His pectoral collar is banded red, black, red. His wristbands are banded black and white.

Hôros bears a red sword. The god stands upon a black and white pavement. When seated, the god sits upon a throne of black ornamented in white, which stands upon a black and white pavement.

Advanced Form: Hôros has the head of a hawk, and wears a nemyss striped black and red, surmounted by the red *Desheret* crown of the Lower Realms. His linen kilt is white, and his overkilt is striped black and red. His pectoral collar is banded red, black, red. His wristbands are banded black and red.

Hôros bears a red lance or the red sword of Hiereus. The god stands upon a black and white pavement. Beneath his feet, he tramples a red dragon, serpent, or crocodile. When seated, the god sits upon a throne of black ornamented in red, which stands upon a black and white pavement.

Hêgemôn or Hêgemonê

[Egyptian *Mêet*, Coptic ⲑⲙⲏ *Thmê* (Tah-may), Greek *Themis*] *Initial Form:* Mêet has a human head and wears a nemyss striped black and white. Her linen gown is white. Her pectoral collar is banded black, white, black. Her wristbands are banded white and black.

Mêet bears a yellow Phoenix Wand or the miter-headed sceptre of Hegemon. The goddess stands upon a black and white pavement when in the Hall and on a black pavement when in the Pronaos. When seated, the goddess sits upon a throne of white ornamented in black, which stands upon a black and white pavement.

Advanced Form: Mêet has a human head and wears a nemyss striped yellow and violet. About her nemyss is bound a violet headband from which a white *shu* feather stands tall and straight. Her linen gown is yellow. Her pectoral collar is banded red, yellow, and blue. Her right wristband is banded yellow and blue, and her left wristband is banded yellow and red.

Mêet bears a yellow Phoenix Wand or the miter-headed scepter of Hegemon. The goddess stands upon a black and white pavement when in the Hall and on a black pavement when in the Pronaos. When seated, the goddess sits upon a throne of yellow ornamented in violet, which stands upon a black and white pavement.

Dadouchos or Dadouchê

[Egyptian *Neit*, Coptic **ⲑⲁⲧⲙ ⲏⲩ ⲛⲏⲓⲑ** *Thaum-Êsh-Nêith* (Thom-aesh-nay-eet), Graeco-Egyptian *Nêith*] *Initial Form:* Nêith has a human head and wears a nemyss striped black and white. Her linen gown is black. Her pectoral collar is banded white, black, white. Her wristbands are banded black and white.

Nêith bears a red censer. The goddess stands upon a black and white pavement. When seated, the goddess sits upon a black throne, which stands upon a black and white pavement.

Advanced Form: Nêith has a human head and wears a nemyss striped red and green. Her linen gown is red. Her pectoral collar is banded green, red, green. Her wristbands are banded red and green.

Nêith bears a red censer. The goddess stands upon a black and white pavement. When seated, the goddess sits upon a throne of red ornamented in green, which stands upon a black and white pavement.

Stolistês

[Egyptian *Mut*, Coptic **ⲁⲩⲣⲁⲙⲟⲟⲧⳛ** *Auramoouth* (Aura-maht) or (Ow-rah-maht), Graeco-Egyptian *Mouthis*] *Initial Form:* Auramoouth has a human head and wears a nemyss striped black and white. Her linen gown is black. Her pectoral collar is banded white, black, white. Her wristbands are banded black and white.

Auramoouth bears a blue cup. The goddess stands upon a black and white pavement. When seated, the goddess sits upon a black throne, which stands upon a black and white pavement.

Advanced Form: Auramoouth has a human head and wears a nemyss striped blue and orange. Her linen gown is blue. Her pectoral collar is banded orange, blue, orange. Her wristbands are banded blue and orange.

Auramoouth bears a blue cup. The goddess stands upon a black and white pavement. When seated, the goddess sits upon a throne of blue ornamented in orange, which stands upon a black and white pavement.

Kêryx or Kêrykissa

[Egyptian *Anup em Yebet*, Coptic **ⲁⲛⲟⲧⲡ ⲙⲡⲉⲓⲉⲃⲧ** *Anoup empelebet* (Anoup-em-pay-yeb-et), Graeco-Egyptian *Anoubis of the East*, Latinized Greek *Anubis*]. *Initial Form:* Anoubis has the head of a black jackal or wolf and wears a nemyss striped white and black. His linen kilt is white, and his overkilt is striped white and black. His pectoral collar is banded black, white, black. His wristbands are banded white and black.

Anoubis bears a Wand terminating in the *Khi* or *Wer Wadjeti* symbol (the winged solar Disk from which depend two uraei). He also bears a violet lamp whose flame burns in the form of a red Yod. The god stands upon a black and white pavement when in the Hall and on a black pavement when in the Pronaos. When seated, the god sits upon a black throne, which stands upon a black and white pavement.

Advanced Form: Anoubis has the head of a black jackal or wolf and wears a nemyss striped violet and yellow. His linen kilt is white, and his overkilt is striped violet and yellow. His pectoral collar is banded yellow, violet, yellow. His wristbands are banded violet and yellow.

Anoubis bears a wand terminating in the *Khi* or *Wer Wadjeti* symbol. He also bears a yellow lamp whose flame burns in the form of a white Yod.

The god stands upon a black and white pavement when in the Hall, and on a black pavement when seated in the Pronaos. When seated, the god sits upon a violet throne ornamented in yellow, which stands upon a black and white pavement.

Phylax or Phylakissa

[Egyptian *Opowet*, Coptic **Oϩⲟⲟⲩⲥ** *Ophooui* (Ah-paw-ee), Graeco-Egyptian *Ophois*; also Egyptian *Anup em Amenet*, Coptic **Ⲁⲛⲟⲩⲡ ⲙⲡⲉⲙⲛⲧ** *Anoup emp Emenet* (Anoup-em-pay-men-et), Graeco-Egyptian *Anoubis of the West*, Latinized Greek *Anubis*]. *Initial Form:* Ophois has the head of a black jackal or wolf and wears a black nemyss. His linen kilt is white, and his overkilt is black. His pectoral collar is banded black, white, black. His wristbands are black.

Ophois bears a red sword. The god stands upon a black pavement. When seated, the god sits upon a black throne, which stands upon a black pavement.

Advanced Form: Ophois has the head of a black jackal or wolf and wears a nemyss striped black and white. His linen kilt is striped black and white. His pectoral collar is banded white, black, white, and his overkilt is striped black and white. His pectoral collar is banded white, black, white. His wristbands are banded black and white.

Ophois bears a flaming red sword. The god stands upon a black pavement. When seated, the god sits upon a black throne ornamented in white, which stands upon a black pavement.✿ —APF

The Invisible Stations

It is not necessary for the student of this course to be preoccupied with the godforms of the invisible stations, since the study of these godforms comprises Adept-level work. However, we will list them here for later reference:

The Stations on the Path of Samekh

Ahathoor (A Great goddess)—stationed in the East of the Hall behind the throne of the Hierophant.

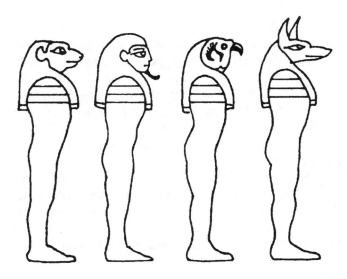

The Sons of Horus

Hoor-peKroti (god of Silence)—stationed in the exact center of the Hall.
Ouammooout peSatanas (The Evil Persona; Power of the Mouth of the Power of Destruction)—the devouring beast represented in the story of the Weighing of the Soul is stationed at the East of the Altar.

The Kerubim

Ahathoor (Human-headed) AIR—stationed in the East.
Tharpesh (Lion-headed) FIRE—stationed in the South.
Thoum Moou (Eagle-headed) WATER—stationed in the West.
Hap-Ouer (Bull-headed) EARTH—stationed in the North.

The Sons of Horus

Amset (Man-headed) AIR—stationed in the Northeast.
Toouamaautef (Jackal-headed) FIRE—stationed in the Southeast.
Kabehsonef (Hawk-headed)   WATER—stationed in the Southwest.
Ahaphi (Ape-headed) EARTH—stationed in the Northwest.

The Forty-Two Assessors

These forms are situated around the circumference of the room. They are the witnesses in the Hall of Judgment who make the Sign of the Enterer as the candidate passes by them. ✿

Kerub of Air

Kerub of Fire

Kerub of Water

Kerub of Earth

Primary Officers of the Outer Grades

This section defines the different officers in the Golden Dawn's current of magic. In all of the initiation rites presented in this book, the aspirant will have to assume some of the various officer-forms that correspond to these descriptions. The student should therefore commit these descriptions to memory.

The Three Chiefs[16]

Imperator (Latin meaning: commander, leader): The feminine form is *Imperatrix*. Purification by Fire. The lawgiver and figure of authority, who symbolizes the Element of Fire and the Sephirah of Geburah. The symbols and insignia of the Imperator are: the white robe, the red mantle (cloak or tabard) of Fire bearing a cross and triangle of white on the left breast, the red and green striped nemyss, a green collar from which hangs a red and green lamen depicting the circled cross, and red sword.

Praemonstrator (Latin meaning: a guide and/or one who prophesies): The feminine form is *Praemonstratrix*. Purification by Water. The teacher, who symbolizes the Element of Water and the Sephirah of Chesed. The symbols and insignia of the Praemonstrator are the white robe, the blue mantle (cloak or tabard) of Water bearing a cross and triangle of white on the left breast, the blue and orange striped nemyss, an orange collar from which hangs a blue and orange lamen depicting the circled cross, and the Maltese Cross Wand.

Cancellarius (Latin meaning: one who stands at the bar in a court, chancellor, or high official in a church or university): The feminine form is *Cancellaria*. Purification by Air. The keeper of records, who symbolizes the Element of Air and the Sephirah of Tiphareth. The symbols and insignia of the Cancellarius are the white robe, the yellow mantle (cloak or tabard) of Air bearing a cross and triangle of white on the left breast, the yellow and violet nemyss, a violet collar from which hangs a yellow and violet lamen depicting the circled cross, and the yellow hexagram-headed scepter.

Past Hierophant: Refer to the Hierophant.

Hierophant (Greek meaning: initiating priest, one who teaches spiritual matters, especially in regard to adorations and sacrifices): The feminine form is *Hierophantissa*. Expounder of the Mysteries in the Hall of Dual Manifestation of the goddess of Truth. The symbols and insignia of the Hierophant are the throne of the East, the red mantle (outer cloak or tabard) bearing a white cross on the left breast, a white collar from which hangs a red and green lamen depicting the circled cross, the crown-headed scepter, and the Banner of the East.

Hiereus (Greek meaning: priest, one who performs sacrifices in the temple): The feminine form is *Hiereia*. Avenger of the gods, Guardian of the Sacred Mysteries. The symbols and insignia of the Hiereus are the throne of the West, the black mantle

---

16 Students of this course will not be assuming the officer-forms of the Three Chiefs, who represent Potencies on a higher level of working. These forces act to direct the G∴D∴ current, but they are governed by even higher Powers. The descriptions of the Three Chiefs are provided here for the purpose of study only.

(outer cloak or tabard) bearing a white cross on the left breast, a red collar from which hangs a white and black lamen depicting a triangle, the Sword of Strength and Severity, and the Banner of the West.

Hegemon (Greek meaning: guide, leader, one who proceeds first on a path): The feminine form is *Hegemone*. Guardian of the Threshold of Entrance and Preparer of the Way for the Enterer. The symbols and insignia of the Hegemon are the white mantle (outer cloak or tabard) bearing a red cross on the left breast, a black collar from which hangs a black and white lamen depicting a cross, and the miter-headed scepter.

Keryx (Greek meaning: herald, one who announces, calls the meeting to order, and delivers messages): The feminine form is *Kerykissa*. Watcher for the gods. The Watcher within the temple. The symbols and insignia of the Keryx are the red lamp, a black collar from which hangs a white and black lamen depicting a Caduceus, and the Caduceus Wand.

Stolistes (Greek meaning: preparer, decorator, one who sees that all ritual clothing and ornamentation are in readiness. Comes from the root word *stolos* which indicates preparation of ships for war, by water): The feminine form is also *Stolistes*. The Affirmer of the Powers of Water. The Light shining through the Waters upon Earth. The symbols and insignia of the Stolistes are a black collar from which hangs a white and black lamen depicting a cup, and the chalice of Water.

Dadouchos (Greek meaning: torch bearer. In the Eleusinian Mysteries, the woman who holds the torch as a symbol of the way by which Demeter searched for her daughter): The feminine form is *Dadouche*. The Affirmer of the Powers of Fire. Perfection through Fire manifesting on Earth. The symbols and insignia of the Dadouchos are a black collar from which hangs a white and black lamen depicting a Swastika or Fylfot Cross, and the censer of incense.

Phylax (Greek meaning: sentinel, guardian): The feminine form is *Phylakissa*. The Watcher without the temple. The symbols and insignia of the Phylax are a black collar from which hangs a white and black lamen depicting an eye, and a sword.

The ceremonies in this book are challenging in the respect that a certain amount of the ritual work presented is physical and a certain amount is astral. Among the physical temple implements that the student will have to provide are the altar, cross and triangle, pillars,[17] banners, chalice, censer of incense, Elements for the altar, five candles in the Elemental colors, a sword, lamp, wands for the Hierophant, Hegemon, and Keryx, and the lamens of all the officers.[18]

The stations of all the officers are to be marked within the temple by the placement of the cardboard lamens. Most of the ritual work dealing with the officers and the godforms who govern them is done on the astral level. The aspirant will be

---

[17] At this stage in the student's spiritual development, it is not required that s/he construct a fully accurate set of pillars. The pillars may be simple large cardboard tubes, one black and the other white. The pillars may even be fashioned out of long single strips of cloth hung from the ceiling.

[18] The aspirant may elect to paint the symbols of the banners, cross and triangle, and lamens on sheets of posterboard or paper in the appropriate colors. The wands can be fashioned out of dowels with simple cardboard wand-heads. See our book *Secrets of a Golden Dawn Temple* for more information about making these implements.

AIR—East   WATER—West

Yellow

Violet

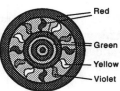

Blue

Orange

EARTH—North   FIRE—South

Russet   Citrine   White

Black   Olive

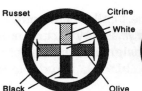

Red

Green

Yellow

Violet

Elemental Symbols for the
Four Quarters of the Temple

The Outer Order Lamens

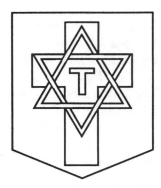

The Banner of the East
Field—white; Cross—gold;
Upper Triangle—red; Lower Tri-
angle—Blue; Tau Cross—White

The Banner of the West
Field—black; Triangle—white;
Cross—red; Outline of
Cross—gold

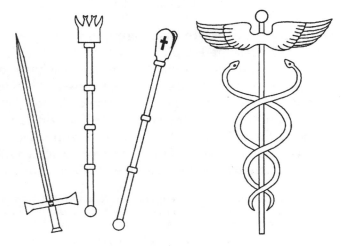

The Wands and the Sword

20

required to visualize each godform and be able to maintain the visualization for as long as it is called for. The student will also be required to visualize the various officer-forms within the temple—these forms are not the same as the godforms, although they are lesser extensions of them. (The officer-form of the Hierophant would appear as just that—a human being dressed in the robes and insignia of a Hierophant. The same is true for all of the officer-forms.) As stated earlier, it is the officer-forms who carry out specific functions within the temple, not the godforms themselves, that are assumed by the solitary initiate. When assuming an officer-form, the student inaugurates a separation of a particular godform and its corresponding officer-form. The two are clairvoyantly seen to be separated, although an etheric link between them remains. The officer-forms are returned to the dominion of their respective godforms when not in active use by the aspirant. When this is the case, the godform can be seen to absorb or overshadow the lesser form of the officer.

To summarize, a large part of the initiation rites in this book are to be carried out on a *physical level*, with actual temple symbolism (banners, lamens, altar, wands, etc.), to be constructed by the student. The *astral work* performed in these rituals revolve entirely around visualization of godforms, officer-forms and certain guided meditations.✿

THE NEOPHYTE CEREMONY

Temple Set-up: The aspirant will need to set up the Hall beforehand in accordance with the temple diagram. The black cubical altar is to be placed in the center of the room. Upon it are the symbols of the cross and triangle (the red cross is above the white triangle). The pillars are to be placed just East of the altar. The Banners of the East and West are placed in their respective quarters. A cup of Water should be placed in the North, and a censer of incense belongs in the South.

Around the circumference of the room are to be placed four candles: yellow in the East, red in the South, blue in the West, black in the North. In the Easternmost part of the temple should be placed a white candle. The aspirant should try to obtain glass candle holders which have two parts: a bottom which holds a colored votive candle and a glass cover (colored or opaque) with a hole in the top which acts to shade the candlelight.

A lantern should be placed in the Southwest. The four Elements of the Mystic Repast are to be placed on top of the altar near their respective quarters: a rose in the East, a red candle in the South, a chalice of wine in the West, and a paten of bread and salt in the North. The aspirant will need to have constructed beforehand the Hierophant's Wand, the Hegemon's Wand, and the Keryx's Wand. A convenient sword should also be procured for the station of Hiereus. The aspirant will need a finished Neophyte sash placed in the East of the temple. Elemental symbols may be placed in the four quarters. (See diagram.)

Ritual preparations: It is suggested that the aspirant fast for a period of 12 hours prior to the ritual. A ritual bath is required, after which the aspirant may put on the black Tau robe and red sandals or slippers. A black cord is to be wrapped three times around the waist. The aspirant must then spend a period of time (10 to 20 minutes) in a darkened room or antechamber to the temple seated in quiet mediation while wearing a hoodwink or blindfold. During this period of time, darkness and silence are to be maintained. The aspirant should imagine him/her self under the watch of Anubis of the West. After this period of silence, the hoodwink may be folded under the black cord tied around the waist. The aspirant may then enter the temple and begin the ritual. As you enter the temple, imagine that you are leaving your physical body outside as a sentinel to guard the temple—your spiritual self is free to receive initiation.

PART 1: The Opening

Enter the temple and walk clockwise to the East. With the sword, perform the Lesser Banishing Ritual of the Pentagram.

Give one knock with the pommel of the sword against the floor or altar and say *"HEKAS, HEKAS, ESTE BEBELOI!"* (Hey-kass, Hey-kass, es-tay Bee-beh-loi).

Put the sword aside and go to the West of the temple, facing East. Kneel down and invoke the godform of Thmê (pronounced Tah-may) as follows. Vibrate strongly:

> *THMÊ! THMÊ! THMÊ! Lady of the Feather by which all souls are measured! Thou daughter and eye of RA! Lady of Heaven, Queen of Earth and mistress of the Underworld! Great Lady of all the gods and goddesses. Thou whose name is MAAT! Lady of Truth! Goddess of Justice and Order! Mediator between Darkness and Light, Chaos and Order! THMÊ! THMÊ! THMÊ! Great Lady whose Name rules this temple—the Hall of the Dual Manifestation of MAAT, goddess of Truth! Thou who assesseth the heart of every man and woman in the Hall of Judgment before Ousiri and the assembly of the gods. Thou who art the eye and heart of balance! THMÊ! THMÊ! THMÊ! I invoke thee!*

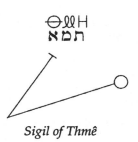

Sigil of Thmê

Visualize the image of the goddess Thmê before you, with human head and yellow-gold skin. She wears a black and white nemyss and a white linen gown. She carries the mitre-headed scepter of the Hegemon. Above her head is the glowing white outline of the cross and triangle, the symbol of the Outer Order of the G∴D∴.

East

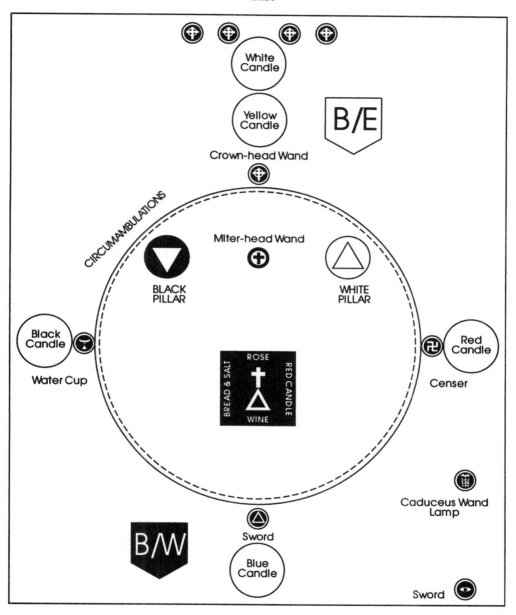

Neophyte Temple for Self-Initiation

23

Slowly and with much feeling, perform the Qabalistic Cross, drawing the light down from the Kether of the universe into the Kether at the crown of your head as you continue the QC (saying *"ATAH, MALKUTH, VE-GEBURAH, VE-GEDULAH, LE-OLAHM, AMEN"*). Strongly visualize the cross of Light you have formed in the center of your body. Trace within your heart the Hebrew letters of the name THMÊ in glowing white. Project a white ray of thought from your heart toward the image of Thmê you have created before you. See the figure breathe in life as your thought-ray animates it. Address the form:

> *THMÊ! Beautiful One of the Feather of Truth! I beseech thee to act upon my behalf in this my quest for the Light Divine! Guide me, O thou who art none other but my own Higher Self. Aid me and escort me in this Hall of Judgment. I am a true and willing Seeker of Light and Knowledge. Act as my overseer and reconciler. Speak for me amidst the assembly of the gods and the guardians of this temple. My intentions are honest. I am ready to undergo test and trial. I wish to be purified and consecrated to the Light. Grant that my heart is made MAAT! Grant that my Will is made MAAT! Merciful THME! Let me be judged aright! Grant that this humble aspirant before you be not turned away from that resplendent Light which resides in the East. Award me entrance into the Hall of Two Truths! Let me penetrate the Threshold in the Path of the Enterer!*

Thmê speaks to you in your own mind:

> I am the representative of your Higher and Holy Self. It is only through my intervention that thou canst even approach this sacred Hall. The Higher must arbitrate on behalf of the Lower, elevating it by virtue of association. In this Hall I am thy tongue, thy heart, and thy eye. Fear not, for I shall guide and conduct thee through the Hall of MAAT. Fear not, for I shall speak for thee in this assembly of the gods and the current of the Light.

Imagine the goddess Thmê communicating in silence with the energies in the East. She is the representative of your Higher Self, interceding on your behalf with the guardians of the Hall. You hear her voice as she calls out the names of other godforms in the East of the temple: ESE, NEBETHO, THOOUTH and another, HOOR OUER. You have a vague impression of four figures in the East, seated before a veil. As Thmê continues to address the figures, the scene becomes hazy, and it appears that the goddess stands not before the seated figures in the East, but before the gigantic form of Thoth—Djehoti—the ibis-headed god of Wisdom. Thmê continues a silent discussion with the god. After a few moments Thmê turns toward you, salutes with the Neophyte Signs toward the West and says silently:

> Thou mayest proceed, O aspirant; thou art MAAT.

(Rise and salute with the Projection [Enterer] Sign and say:) *I ask that the number of officers in this degree and the nature of their offices be proclaimed, that the Powers whose images they are may be reawakened in my sphere and in the sphere of this current—for by Names and Images are all Powers awakened and reawakened.* (Give the Sign of Silence.)

Thmê again gives the Signs. She then holds out the palm of her hand, upon which rests a single white feather. The goddess of Truth inhales sharply and breathes upon the feather, which drifts lightly through the air toward you. The feather is absorbed into your heart center. Say:

> *Breath is a symbol of Life. The letter "H" is a symbol of the ancient Greek aspirate or breathing, and breath is the evidence of Life. There are three chief officers in this grade, and they all commence with the letter "H": the Hierophant, the Hiereus, and the Hegemon. There are three lesser officers besides the Phylax; the Keryx, the Stolistes, and the Dadouchos.*

Thmê takes you by the hand and leads you clockwise to the North, where she traces the figure of the cross and triangle with the miter-headed wand. As she does so, you vibrate the name, *"AURAMOOUTH"* (ow-rah-maht). The beautiful astral form of Auramoouth takes shape before you. She bears a blue cup. Visualize the figure strongly. The godform of Auramoouth traces in the air before you the figure of a cup. She then hands you her chalice of Water. Picking up the Water cup in the North, you take on the office of Stolistes that the goddess has bestowed upon you and turn to face the altar. Say:

> *I am the Stolistes of the temple. My station is in the North to symbolize cold and moisture. My duties are to watch over the cup of lustral Water and to purify the Hall and the candidate with Water.*

THE NEOPHYTE SIGNS

The Projection Sign   *The Sign of Silence*

As the Stolistes, go clockwise to the East of the Hall. With the cup trace a cross in the air toward the East. Then sprinkle Water thrice in the form of an invoking Water triangle (tracing clockwise starting with the bottom point of the triangle). Trace this same figure in all four quarters, going clockwise around the room. Upon returning to the East hold the cup on high and say *"I purify with Water."* Return the cup to the North. Step out of the office of Stolistes and return the officer-form to the dominion of Auramoouth.

Thmê again takes you by the hand and leads you clockwise to the South. Once there she uses the miter-headed wand to trace the figure of the cross and triangle while you vibrate the name of, *"THAUM-ESH-NEITH"* (Thom-Aesh-Nay-eet). The goddess begins to formulate in the South. Neith bears a red censer. Visualize the figure strongly. The goddess Thaum-Esh-Neith traces in the air before you the figure of the swastika or Fylfot Cross. She then hands you her censer. Picking up the censer in the South, you take on the office of Dadouchos that the goddess has bestowed upon you and turn to face the altar. Say:

> I am the Dadouchos of the temple. My station is in the South to symbol-
> ize heat and dryness. My duty is to watch over the lamps and Fires of the
> temple, to watch over the censer and the incense, and to consecrate the
> Hall and the candidate with Fire.

As the Dadouchos, go clockwise to the East of the Hall. With the censer trace a cross in the air toward the East. Then wave the censer thrice in the form of an invoking Fire triangle (tracing clockwise starting with the top point of the trian-gle). Trace this same figure in all four quarters, going clockwise around the room. Upon returning to the East hold the censer on high and say *"I consecrate with Fire."* Return the censer to the South. Step out of the office of Dadouchos and return the officer-form to the dominion of Thaum-Esh-Neith.

Thmê again takes your hand and leads you clockwise to the Southwest. Once there she uses the wand to trace the figure of the cross and triangle while you vibrate the name of, *"ANOUP EMPEIEBET"* (Ah-noop-em-pay-yeh-bet). Anubis of the East begins to formulate there in the Southwest. The jackal-headed Anubis carries the *Khi* Wand or Caduceus and a violet lamp containing a red Yod of flame. Visualize the figure strongly. The god Anubis traces in the air before you the fig-ure of the Caduceus. He then hands you his wand and lamp. Picking up the Caduceus Wand and lantern in the Southwest, you take on the office of Keryx that the god has bestowed upon you, and turn to face the altar. Say:

> I am the Keryx of the temple. My place is within the portal. I am the
> guardian within as the Phylax who represents ANOUP EMPEMENET
> (Ah-noop-em-pay-men-et) is the guardian without. I watch over the recep-
> tion of the candidate. My duties are to lead all Mystic Circumambulations
> carrying the lamp of my office, and to make all reports and announcements.

> *My lamp is the symbol of the Hidden Knowledge and my wand is the symbol of its directing Power.*

Return the lamp and wand to the Southwest. Step out of the office of Keryx and return the officer-form to the dominion of Anubis.

Thmê takes you clockwise to her own station between the two pillars. Once again you vibrate the name of, *"THME"* as she makes the sign of the cross and triangle on herself. The goddess Thmê traces in the air before you the figure of a cross. She then hands you her miter-headed wand. Picking up the wand between the pillars, you take on the office of Hegemon that the goddess has bestowed upon you, and turn to face the altar. Say:

> *I am the Hegemon of the temple. My station is between the two Pillars of Hermes and Solomon and my face is towards the Cubical Altar of the Universe. My duty is to watch over the gateway of the Hidden Knowledge, for I am the reconciler between Light and Darkness. I watch over the preparation of the candidate and assist in his (her) reception and I lead him (her) in the path that conducts from Darkness to Light. The white color of my mantle is the color of purity, my ensign of office is a miter-headed scepter to symbolize religion which guides and regulates life, and my office symbolizes those higher aspirations of the soul which should guide its action.*

Return the wand. Step out of the office of Hegemon and return the officer-form to the dominion of Thmê. The goddess of Truth leads you clockwise to the West. Again she traces with her wand the figure of the cross and triangle as you vibrate the name of *"HOOR"* (Hoor or Hoh-or). Horus appears in the West. The hawk-headed god bears a red sword. Visualize the form strongly. The god traces in the air before you the figure of a triangle. He then hands you his sword. Picking up the sword and the banner of the West, you take on the office of Hiereus that the god Horus has bestowed upon you and turn to face the altar. Say:

> *I am the Hiereus of the temple. My station is on the throne of the West and is a symbol of increase of Darkness and decrease of Light, and I am the Master of Darkness. I keep the gateway of the West and watch over the reception of the candidate and over the lesser officers in the doing of their work. My black mantle is an image of the Darkness that was upon the Face of the Waters. I carry the Sword of Judgment and the banner of the evening twilight, which is the Banner of the West, and I am called Fortitude by the unhappy.*

Return the sword and the banner to the West and step out of the office of Hiereus. Thmê then takes you to the Eastern part of the Hall where she traces the symbol of the circled cross. Vibrate the name of *"OUSIRI"* (Oo-seer-ee) as the godform begins to formulate in the East. The mummy-wrapped Osiris wears a tall white *Stenu* crown and bears a white crown-headed scepter. Visualize the form strongly. The god traces in the air before you the figure of the cross and circle. He then hands you his scepter. Picking up the wand and the banner, you take on the office of Hiero-phant that Osiris has bestowed upon you, and turn to face the altar. Say:

> *I am the Hierophant of the temple. My station is on the throne of the East in the place where the Sun rises, and I am the Master of the Hall, govern-ing it according to the laws of the current, as he whose image I am is the Master of all who work for the Hidden Knowledge. My mantle is red because of uncreated Fire and created Fire, and I hold the banner of the morning light which is the Banner of the East. I am called Power and Mercy and Light in Abundance, and I am the Expounder of the Mysteries.*

The goddess Thmê returns to her place between the pillars as Hegemon. Replace the banner but retain the wand. Turn to face the East. Give the Sign of the Spiraling Light. Say, *"Let the white brilliance of the Divine Spirit Descend!"* Feel a flood of Divine Light course through your body from the Kether of the universe. Equilibrate this Light through your body by performing the Qabalistic Cross, loudly vibrating the Hebrew names. Then replace the crown-headed wand. Step out of the office of Hierophant and return the officer-form to the dominion of Osiris. Go clockwise to the Southwest and take up the lantern and wand there. Step into the office of Keryx. Walk deosil (clockwise) to the Northeast and say:

> *The visible Sun is the dispenser of Light to the Earth. Let me therefore form a vortex in this chamber that the invisible Sun of Spirit may shine therein from above.*

Circumambulate the temple three times, carrying the equilibrated light with you around the temple. Salute the banner of the East with the Neophyte Signs for each circumambulation. After the third pass, return to the West and give the Projection Sign at the symbols upon the altar. Visualize the Divine Light that you have circu-lated around the temple flowing from your heart center and entering the red cross and the white triangle—empowering them with the divine current. Say:

> *The Mystic Circumambulation symbolic of the Rise of Light is accomplished.*

Perform the Adoration to the Lord of the Universe, saluting after the first three lines with the Projection Sign. After the final line, give the Sign of Silence:

> *Holy art Thou, Lord of the Universe!* (Salute.)
> *Holy art Thou, Whom Nature hath not Formed!* (Salute.)
> *Holy art Thou, the Vast and the Mighty One!* (Salute.)
> *Lord of the Light and of the Darkness!* (Sign of Silence.)

Imagine the three astral officer/godforms of the Hierophant, Hiereus and the Hegemon, raising their implements in a salute to the Light and then slowly low-ering them.

Still in the office of the Keryx, go to the Northeast with wand and lamp. Hold the implements high and proclaim:

> *In the Name of the Lord of the Universe, who works in silence and whom naught but silence can express, I declare that the Sun has arisen and the shadows flee away!*

Return the implements to the Southwest and step out of the office of Keryx. Return control of the officer-form to Anubis. Walk to the West of the altar facing East. Give three knocks. Then repeat the following words, giving a knock before each word is spoken:

> *KHABS. AM. PEKHT. KONX. OM. PAX. LIGHT. IN. EXTENSION.*

Give the Neophyte Signs toward the altar.

PART 2: The Initiation

Before continuing, take the rose, red candle, cup of wine, and bread and salt off the altar and place them in their associated quarters. Visualize all the astral officer/godforms at their respective stations. Give one knock. Still standing West of the altar say: *"This candidate seeks for entrance."* Give a second knock and say:

> *I vow that within this mystic sphere, I shall henceforth lose my name and be known in this temple as (state magical motto). I am the inheritor of a dying world, arisen and entered into Darkness. The Mother of Darkness hath blinded me with her hair. The Father of Darkness hath hidden me under his wings. My limbs are still weary from the wars which were in Heaven.*

Anubis of the East speaks to you within your mind:

> Unpurified and unconsecrated, thou canst not enter our Sacred Hall.

Go clockwise to the station of Stolistes in the North. Visualize Auramoouth holding out the chalice of Water for you. She traces the sigil of the cup. Take up the cup and dip your thumb or index finger into the Water. Trace a cross upon your forehead. Then trace the Water triangle upon your brow, starting with the bottom point of the triangle. Say, *"I am purified with Water."* Return the cup.

Go clockwise to the station of Dadouchos in the South. Visualize Thaum-Esh-Neith holding out the censer for you. She traces the sigil of the Swastika. Take up the censer and trace with it a cross in front of your forehead. Then trace the Fire triangle in front of your brow, starting with the top point of the triangle. Say, *"I am consecrated with Fire."* Return the censer and walk to the West of the altar facing East.

Visualize the goddess Thmê appearing at your right side. Also imagine the god-form of Osiris in the East. In your mind you hear him ask:

> **Inheritor of a Dying World, why seekest thou to enter our Sacred Hall?**

> (You answer:) *My Soul wanders in Darkness and seeks the Light of the Hidden Knowledge. I believe that in this sacred temple of the Mysteries, knowledge of that Light may be obtained. I am truly willing to take a solemn obligation in the presence of this assembly to uphold the sacred Mysteries and the current of the Light.*

> *I understand that there is nothing contrary to my civil, moral or religious duties in this obligation. Although the magical virtues can indeed awaken into momentary life in the wicked and foolish hearts, they cannot reign in any heart that has not the natural virtues to be their throne.*

Osiris speaks to you:

> **He who is the fountain of the Spirit of man and of things, came not to break, but to fulfill the law. Are you ready to take this oath?**

Say: *"I am ready to take this oath."* Kneel down and place your right hand on the cross and triangle on the altar. Imagine the astral forms of the six primary officer/godforms gathering around you to form a hexagram. The Hegemon is already at your right. The Hierophant as Horus the Elder comes down from the East, pinning a black serpent under his foot as he comes to the East of the altar. Hiereus appears at your left. Behind you are Stolistes, Keryx and Dadouchos. The Hierophant, who has taken on the godform of HOOR OUER takes your left hand in his.

At this point in the ritual you are aware that the Hall seems much more crowded now with godforms than before—godforms that you can barely perceive. In the East the colossal form of Thoth remains in the Sign of the Enterer. Winged Kerubic deities mark the four cardinal points of the temple. Additional Egyptian figures are stationed at the sub-quarters. But you are mostly aware of forty-two silent figures who line all sides of the temple walls. However your attention is captured by the four colored candles which designate the boundaries of your temple circle. In their place are four enormous pillars of fire and cloud. The pillar to your right and the one in front of you are dual pillars of Light. The pillar to your left and the one behind you are the twin pillars of Darkness. After a pause, repeat the oath:

> *I (legal name) in the Presence of the Lord of the Universe, who works in silence and whom naught but silence can express, and in this Hall of the Neophytes of the current of the Golden Dawn, do, of my own free will, hereby and hereon, most solemnly promise by and on this holy symbol of the Light, to dedicate my life to the pursuit of the mysteries of the Golden*

Dawn tradition of magic and to the completion of the Great Work. I solemnly promise to persevere with courage and determination in the labors of the Divine Science, even as I shall persevere with courage and determination through this ceremony which is their image. I pledge from this day forward to strive with enthusiasm and devotion, in the study of the Hermetic Arts, seeing that such teachings are not given to those who wish only a cursory knowledge thereof.

I undertake to maintain a kindly and benevolent relation with all true seekers of the Light. I will respect all religions, seeing that all faiths contain a ray of the ineffable Light which I seek.

I pledge that I will not suffer myself to be placed in such a state of passivity, that any person, power, or being may cause me to lose control of my words, thoughts, or actions.

I vow that I will not debase my mystical knowledge in the labor of Evil magic at any time tried or under any temptation.

I solemnly promise not to flaunt or parade any knowledge I may acquire to those who are not seekers of the Light, lest our sacred Knowledge be profaned through my error, vanity, or neglect.

I swear upon this holy symbol to observe all these things without evasion, equivocation, or mental reservation. Furthermore, if I break this my magical obligation, I submit myself by own consent, to a punitive stream of power, set in motion by the Divine Guardians of this current, who live in the Light of their perfect justice, and before whom my soul now stands.

Hierophant, Hegemon and Hiereus officer/godforms whisper:

They journey upon the winds, they strike where no one strikes, they slay where no one slays....

(Say:) *And as I bow my neck under the sword of the Hiereus,* (visualize the sword on the nape of your neck) *so do I commit myself unto their hands for vengeance or reward. So help me my mighty and secret Soul, and the Creator of my Soul who works in silence and whom naught but silence can express.* (Give a knock.)

Rise Neophyte of the 0 = 0 grade of the Golden Dawn.

Visualize the officer/godforms returning to their stations. In the East the colossal figure of Thoth gives the Sign of Silence. Take up the cup of Water and the censer. Thmê takes your hand and leads you to the North facing East. Anubis comes forward with wand and lamp to the Northeast. Say:

The Voice of my undying and secret Soul said unto me—"Let me enter the path of Darkness and, peradventure, there shall I find the Light. I am the only being in an abyss of Darkness; from an abyss of Darkness came I forth ere my birth from the silence of a primal sleep."

And the Voice of Ages answered unto my Soul—"I am he who formulates in Darkness—the Light that shineth in Darkness, yet the Darkness comprehendeth it not."

Let the Mystical Circumambulation take place in the Path of Knowledge that leadeth unto the Light, with the lamp of Hidden Knowledge to guide me.

Visualize the Keryx and the Hegemon leading you sunwise around the temple. As you pass the Hierophant for the first time, imagine a loud knock and mentally intone the name of *"BINAH."* As you pass the Hiereus in the West, you also hear a loud knock. The second time you pass the Hierophant in the East, imagine a loud knock and mentally intone the name of *"CHOKMAH."* As you reach the South, the Keryx stops you. Anubis speaks:

Unpurified and unconsecrated, thou canst not enter the Path of the West!

Auramoouth steps forward and draws the sigil of the cup before you. With the Water, mark your forehead with the symbols of the cross and Water triangle as before. Say: *"I am purified with Water."*

Thaum-Esh-Neith steps forward and draws the sigil of the Swastika before you. Wave the censer in front of your forehead in the figures of the cross and Fire triangle. Say: *"I am consecrated with Fire."*

Thmê speaks:

Child of Earth, twice purified and twice consecrated, thou mayest approach the gateway of the West.

Continue to the West where the fierce form of the Hiereus stands. The fiery-eyed Horus with red sword and black banner bars your advance:

Thou canst not pass by me, sayeth the Guardian of the West, unless thou canst tell me my name.

(Say:) *Darkness is thy name, thou great one of the Paths of the Shades. Before all things are the Chaos and the Darkness and the gates of the land of Night. Thou art he whose name is Darkness. Thou art the Exorcist in the midst of the Exorcism. I stand before thee without trepidation, for fear is failure, and I am without fear.*

Horus speaks:

> Thou hast known me now, so pass thou on. Fear is truly failure, and
> he who trembles at the flame and at the flood and at the shadows
> of the Air, hath no part in God.

Give a knock. Visualize the Keryx and the Hegemon continuing to lead you in the
procession. As you pass the Hiereus in the West, imagine a loud knock. When you
pass the Hierophant, another knock is heard, and you mentally intone the name of
"KETHER." As you reach the North, the Keryx stops you again. Anubis speaks:

> Unpurified and unconsecrated, thou canst not enter the path of
> the East!

Auramoouth steps forward and traces the symbol of the cup in the air before you.
With the Water, mark your forehead with the symbols of the cross and Water triangle as before. Say: *"I am purified with Water."*

Thaum-Esh-Neith steps forward and traces the symbol of the Fylfot Cross in the
air before you. Wave the censer in front of your forehead in the figures of the cross
and Fire triangle. Say: *"I am consecrated with Fire."*

Thmê speaks:

> Child of Earth, thrice purified and thrice consecrated, thou mayest
> approach the gateway of the East.

Continue to the East where the form of the Hierophant stands. The great god
Osiris with crown-headed wand and white banner bars your advance:

> Thou canst not pass by me, sayeth the Guardian of the East,
> unless thou canst tell me my name.

> (Say:) *Light dawning in Darkness is thy Name, the Light of a Golden*
> *Day. After the formless and the Void and the Darkness, then cometh the*
> *knowledge of the Light. Thou art that Light which ariseth in Darkness.*
> *Thou art the Exorcist in the midst of the Exorcism. Unbalanced Power is*
> *the ebbing away of life. Unbalanced Mercy is weakness and the fading out*
> *of the Will. Unbalanced Severity is cruelty and the barrenness of mind.*
> *Thou art the wielder of the forces of Balance.*

Osiris speaks:

> Thou hast known me now, so pass thou on to the Cubical Altar of
> the Universe.

Return the cup and the censer to the stations in the North and South. Thmê leads you to the West of the altar facing East. She remains on your right side. Hiereus comes to your left side. Stolistes, Keryx and Dadouchos form a triangle behind you. The Hierophant descends from the East in the godform of HOOR OUER, Horus the Elder. He holds the crown-headed wand and the Banner of the East. As the godform advances between the pillars, say:

> *Come thou in the Power of the Light. Come Thou in the Light of Wisdom.*
> *Come Thou in the Mercy of the Light. The Light hath healing in its Wings.*

Kneel down and visualize all the officer/godforms except the Hierophant doing likewise. For a moment, close your eyes and visualize before you the godform of HOOR-PEKHROTI (Hoor-Pay-Khroh-tee) the child-god of Silence seated upon a white lotus. The Hierophant then gives a knock. Say the following invocation and imagine all the godforms repeating the invocation along with you:

> *Lord of the Universe—the Vast and the Mighty One! Ruler of the Light and*
> *the Darkness! We adore thee and we invoke thee! Look with favor upon this*
> *Neophyte who now kneeleth before thee. And grant thine aid unto the*
> *higher aspirations of his (her) soul, so that s/he may prove a true and faith-*
> *ful Frater (Soror) Neophyte. To the glory of Thine Ineffable Name. Amen.*

Rise and envision the officer/godforms doing likewise. Visualize the three main officers crossing their implements over your head. They speak:

> Inheritor of a dying world, we call thee to the living beauty. Wanderer
> in the wild Darkness, we call thee to the gentle Light. Long hast thou
> dwelt in Darkness—Quit the Night and seek the Day! We receive thee
> into the current of the Golden Dawn.

> (Say:) *KHABS. AM. PEKHT. KONX. OM. PAX. LIGHT. IN.*
> *EXTENSION.*

Feel a white Light forming over your head in the shape of a triangle. The officers take down their implements.

> (Say:) *In all my wandering the lamp of the Keryx went before me, though*
> *it was not seen by mine eyes. It is the symbol of the Light of the Hidden*
> *Knowledge.*

Thmê leads you to the East of the altar, where you visualize that you are tread-ing down a black serpent, a symbol of your own evil and unbalanced persona. Thmê remains on the outside of the white pillar. The astral form of Horus steps forward between the pillars to instruct you in the step, signs, grip, and words of a Neophyte.

Prompted by the godform, you give the step, by advancing your left foot a short space, as if entering a portal. Then give the First or Saluting Sign (Projection Sign) which alludes to your condition in a state of Darkness.

Give the Sign of Silence by placing the left forefinger on your lip, in the position of Harpocrates. (The First Sign is always answered by the Second.)

Exchange the grip or token with the officer/godform by advancing your left foot to touch his, toe and heel. Extend your hand to grasp his, fail and try again, succeeding in touching the fingers only (referring to your seeking guidance in Darkness). Give the Grand Word HAR-PAR-KRAT by whispering it to the astral officer, mouth to ear in exchanged syllables. It refers to the Egyptian god of Silence.

Horus then places you between the pillars. He takes up a position on the outside of the black pillar. You reach out to touch the columns. After a pause, say: *"Let the final consecration take place."*

Go to the station of the Stolistes. Auramoouth again traces the sigil of the cup before you. Take up the cup of Water. Return sunwise to the East of the temple and trace a cross in the Air with the implement. Sprinkle Water thrice towards the East in the form of the invoking Water triangle. Go clockwise around the temple and repeat in all four quarters. Upon returning to the East, step between the pillars and face East. Dipping into the Water, mark your forehead with the cross and Water triangle. Hold the cup high and say: *"I am purified with Water."*

Return the cup to the North and walk deosil to the South—the station of Dadouchos. Thaum-Esh-Neith traces the sigil of the Fylfot Cross before you. Take up the censer and walk to the East. With the censer, trace in the air the symbol of the cross and the invoking Fire triangle. Do this in all four quarters. Upon returning to the East, step between the pillars and face East. In front of your forehead, trace with the censer the symbols of the cross and the Fire triangle. Hold the censer high and say: *"I am consecrated with Fire."* Return the censer to the South and stand once more between the pillars. Visualize the four pillars surrounding you again, but this time they are strongly seen and felt.

Remove the black cord and hoodwink that was previously tied around your waist and throw them aside. Say: *"The last remaining symbols of the Path of Darkness are removed."* Pick up the Neophyte sash and put it on over your left shoulder. Say:

> *In and by the actions of my Higher and Divine Self, I hereby invest myself*
> *with the badge of this degree. It symbolizes Light dawning in Darkness.*
> *Let the Mystic Circumambulation take place in the pathway of Light.*

Visualize all the astral officer/godforms except the Hierophant (who stands holding wand and banner) lining up in the Northeast. The Hegemon takes you behind the black pillar to stand in the procession. Following the lead of the Keryx, the circumambulation begins. All salute with the Signs when passing the Banner of the East. As you pass the station of the Hierophant, imagine the figure of a red cross formulating above your head—over the white triangle formed upon your brow. The Hiereus drops out after one pass of the East, and the Hegemon drops out of the procession after two passes. You and the visualized forms of the others follow the Keryx in a third pass. All the astral officers return to their places.

At this point, you replace the rose, red candle, cup of wine, and bread and salt to the top of the altar. Stand West of the altar. Again imagine the godform of Hoor peKhroti. Repeat the following:

> *The threefold cord which was bound about my waist was an image of the threefold bondage of mortality, which amongst the initiated is called earthy or material inclination, that has bound into a narrow place the once far-wandering Soul; and the hoodwink was an image of the Darkness, of ignorance, of mortality that has blinded men and women to the happiness and beauty their eyes once looked upon.*

> *The Double Cubical Altar in the center of the Hall is an emblem of visible Nature or the Material Universe, concealing within herself the mysteries of all dimensions, while revealing her surface to the exterior senses. It is a double cube because, as the Emerald Tablet has said, "The things that are below are a reflection of the things that are above." The world of men and women created to unhappiness is a reflection of the world of Divine Beings created to happiness. It is described in the Sepher Yetzirah or The Book of Formation, as "An Abyss of Height" and "An Abyss of Depth," "An Abyss of the East" and "An Abyss of the West," "An Abyss of the North" and "An Abyss of the South." The Altar is black because, unlike Divine Beings who unfold in the Element of Light, the Fires of created Beings arise from Darkness and Obscurity.*

> *On the Altar is a white triangle to be the image of that immortal Light, the Triune Light, which moved in Darkness and formed the world of Darkness and out of Darkness. There are two contending forces and one always uniting them. And these three have their image in the threefold flame of our Being and in the threefold wave of the sensual world.*

Stand in the form of the Tau Cross and say: *"Glory be to thee, Father of the undying. For Thy glory flows out rejoicing, to the ends of the Earth!"* Put your arms down and continue the speech as before:

> *The red cross above the white triangle, is an image of him who was unfolded in the Light. At its East, South, West, and North angles are a rose, fire, cup of wine, and bread and salt. These allude to the four Elements, Air, Fire, Water, and Earth.*

The Mystical Words—KHABS AM PEKHT—are ancient Egyptian, and are the origin of the Greek "KONX OM PAX" which was uttered at the Eleusinian Mysteries. A literal translation would be "Light rushing out in one Ray," and they signify the same form of Light as that symbolized by the staff of the Keryx.

East of the Double Cubical Altar of created things are the Pillars of Hermes and of Solomon. On these are painted certain Hieroglyphics from the 17th and 125th chapters of the Book of the Dead. They are the symbols of the two powers of day and night, love and hate, work and rest, the subtle force of the lodestone and the eternal out-pouring and in-pouring of the Heart of God.

The lamps that burn, though with a veiled light, upon their summits show that the pathway to Hidden Knowledge, unlike the pathway of Nature— which is a continual undulation, the winding hither and thither of the Serpent—is the straight and narrow way between them.

It was because of this that I stepped between the Pillars to receive the Light and to receive the fourth and final consecration. Two contending Forces and one which unites them eternally. Two basal angles of the triangle and one which forms the apex. Such is the origin of Creation—it is the Triad of Life.

The throne of the Hierophant at the gate of the East is the place of the Guardian of the Dawning Sun. The throne of the Hiereus at the gate of the West is the place of the Guardian against the multitudes that sleep through the Light and awaken at the twilight. The throne of the Hegemon seated between the columns is the place of Balanced Power, between the ultimate Light and the ultimate Darkness.

The wand of the Keryx is the beam of Light from the Hidden Wisdom, and his lamp is an emblem of the ever-burning lamp of the Guardian of the Mysteries.

The seat of the Stolistes at the gate of the North is the place of the Guardian of the Cauldron and the well of Water—of cold and moisture. The seat of the Dadouchos at the gate of the South is the place of the Guardian of the Lake of Fire and the Burning Bush.

Go to the Southwest to face the astral figure of Anubis of the East. The god traces the sigil of the Caduceus before you. Take up the Caduceus Wand and the lantern. Walk deosil to the Northeast and say:

In the name of the Lord of the Universe, who works in silence and whom naught but silence can express, hear ye all, that I (give magical motto) proclaim to have duly initiated myself into the Golden Dawn current of magic as a Neophyte of the 0 = 0 grade.

Replace the wand and the lamp in the Southwest. Return to the West of the altar. Say:

> *I shall remember my obligations to keep secret this knowledge from those who are not Seekers of the Light—for strength is in silence, and the Seed of Wisdom is sown in silence and grows in darkness and mystery.*
>
> *I will hold all religions in reverence, for there is none but contains a ray from the ineffable Light which I seek. I will remember the penalty that awaits the breaker of the oath, and the mystery I have received, and that the secret of Wisdom can only be discerned from the place of Balanced Powers. I shall study well the Great Arcanum of the proper equilibrium of Severity and Mercy, for either unbalanced is not good. Unbalanced Severity is cruelty and oppression; unbalanced Mercy is but weakness and would permit Evil to exist unchecked, thus making itself, as it were, the accomplice of that Evil.*
>
> *I shall remember that things Divine are not attained by mortals who understand the body alone, for only those who are lightly armed can attain the summit.*
>
> *YHVH alone is our Light and the bestower of perfect Wisdom. No mortal power can do more than bring one to the pathway of that Wisdom, which he could if it so pleased him, put into the heart of a child. For as the whole is greater than the part, so are we but sparks from the insupportable Light which is in the Godhead. The ends of the Earth are swept by the borders of his garment of Flame—from him all things proceed and unto him all things return. Therefore I invoke him. Therefore even the Banner of the East falls in adoration before him.*

Visualize Horus coming around to the East of the altar. You hold out your right hand to him. Imagine that the godform pricks the tip of your finger with his sword, causing a small drop of blood to appear. Stand in the position of the Tau Cross and say:

> *If my oath be forgotten and my solemn pledge broken, let the hue of blood remind me that if I fail in this my oath, my blood may be poured out and my body broken, for heavy is the penalty exacted by the Guardians of the Hidden Knowledge from those who willfully betray their trust.*

PART 3: The Closing

Give one knock. Go to the Northeast and say: *"HEKAS, HEKAS, ESTE BEBELOI!"* Return to the West of the altar and give four knocks. Give the Neophyte Signs.

Walk to the station of Stolistes in the North where Auramoouth traces the sigil of the cup before you. Take on the office of the Stolistes. Pick up the cup of Water. Go clockwise to the East of the Hall. With the cup trace a cross in the air toward the East. Then sprinkle Water thrice in the form of an invoking Water triangle. Trace this same figure in all four quarters, going clockwise around the room. Upon returning to the East hold the cup on high and say *"I purify with Water."* Replace the cup in the North, and return control of the officer-form to Auramoouth.

Walk to the station of Dadouchos in the South where Thaum-Esh-Neith traces the sigil of the Fylfot Cross before you. Pick up the censer. Take on the office of Dadouchos. Go clockwise to the East of the Hall. With the censer trace a cross in the air toward the East. Then wave the censer thrice in the form of an invoking Fire triangle. Trace this same figure in all four quarters, going clockwise around the room. Upon returning to the East hold the censer on high and say *"I consecrate with Fire."* Replace the censer in the South and return control of the officer-form to Thaum-Esh-Neith. Stand once more by the West of the altar. Say:

> Let the Mystical Reverse Circumambulation take place in the pathway of the Light.

All of the astral officer/godforms except the Hierophant (who stands holding wand and banner) line up in the Southeast. The Hegemon takes you by the West and South to stand in the procession. Following the lead of the Keryx, the counterclockwise circumambulation begins. All salute with the Signs when passing the Banner of the East. Imagine the Light that had been drawn into the temple slowly beginning to fade. The Hiereus drops out after one pass of the East, and the Hegemon drops out of the procession after two passes. You and the others, follow the Keryx in a third pass. Perform the Reversal Sign of the Spiraling Light. All the astral officers return to their places.

When finished, return to the East. Osiris traces the sigil of the cross and circle in the air before you. You step into the office of Hierophant that Osiris has bestowed upon you and take up the crown-headed scepter. Imagine the Divine Light that you have brought into the temple being withdrawn from the symbol upon the altar—back into your heart center and toward the Kether of the Universe. Perform the Qabalistic Cross to equilibrate the energies within you. Say:

> The Mystical Reverse Circumambulation is accomplished. It is the symbol of the Fading Light.

Facing East, perform the Adoration to the Lord of the Universe, saluting after the first three lines with the Projection Sign. After the final line, give the Sign of Silence.

> Holy art Thou, Lord of the Universe! (Salute.)
> Holy art Thou, Whom Nature hath not Formed! (Salute.)

Holy art Thou, the Vast and the Mighty One! (Salute.)
Lord of the Light and of the Darkness! (Sign of Silence.)

Imagine the three officers (Hierophant, Hiereus, and the Hegemon) raising their implements in a salute to the Light and then slowly lowering them. Step out of the office of Hierophant, returning the officer-form to the authority of Osiris. Say:

Nothing now remains but to partake of the Mystic Repast, composed of the symbols of the Four Elements.

Go to the West of the altar, facing East. The goddess Thmê comes to the East of the altar, facing West. You give the Sign of the Enterer. Thmê answers with the Sign of Silence. Say:

I invite all Beings present to inhale with me the perfume of this Rose, as a symbol of Air. (Smell the rose.)

To feel with me the warmth of this sacred Fire. (Put your hand over the flame.)

To eat with me this bread and salt as types of Earth. (Dip the bread into the salt and eat.)

And finally to drink with me this wine, the consecrated emblem of Elemental Water. (Make a cross in the air with the cup and drink the wine.)

Once the wine is finished, place the cup upside-down between the cross and triangle. Say: *"It is finished!"* Thmê returns to her station between the pillars.

Give one knock and say, *"TETELESTAI!"* Give two more knocks. Then repeat the following words, giving a knock before each word is spoken: *"KHABS. AM. PEKHT. KONX. OM. PAX. LIGHT. IN. EXTENSION."* Give the Neophyte Signs toward the altar. Say:

May what I have partaken maintain me in my search for the Quintessence, the Stone of the Philosophers. True Wisdom, Perfect Happiness, the Summum Bonum.

Thmê comes to your side once more. The both of you walk to the South where Thmê traces the form of the cross and triangle. The godform of Thaum-Esh-Neith salutes with the Projection Sign, Thmê answers with the Sign of Silence. The godform of Thaum-Esh-Neith slowly fades away. In this same manner she releases all the astral godforms in the hall: Auramoouth, Anubis, and Horus. She releases Osiris, and even the great form of Thoth in the East by tracing the symbol of the circled cross. All the astral beings in the hall begin to fade from view.

Thmê herself is the last to dissolve. You thank the goddess for her beneficent guidance and trace the figures of the cross and triangle before her. She salutes you with the Projection Sign. You answer with the Sign of Silence. Withdraw the white ray which had activated Thmê back into your heart center. Perform the Qabalistic Cross to equilibrate the energy.

Take up the sword and perform the Lesser Banishing Ritual of the Pentagram. Say:

> *I now declare this temple duly closed. So mote it be!*✡

The First Knowledge Lecture

This is the work to be undertaken by the magician who has undergone the preceding initiation into the Neophyte grade. The lecture is divided up into six sections that make it easier for the reader to digest the knowledge. An examination for each section of the Knowledge Lecture is given at the end of this chapter.

SECTION 1: The Elements

There are four basic magical Elements: Fire, Water, Air, and Earth. (The final unifying Element of Spirit will be discussed in another chapter.) These four primary Elements are regarded as realms, kingdoms, or divisions of Nature. They are the basic modes of existence and action—the building blocks of everything in the universe. All that exists or has the potential to exist contains one or more of the these energies. (These Elements are not to be confused with the scientist's table of elements, which are only the most materialized expressions of the Elements in the physical plane.)

The four Elements of the ancients are assigned the dual combination of two of the four qualities of heat, cold, dryness, and moisture. They are:

Qualities	Name	Symbol
Heat and Dryness	FIRE	△
Cold and Moisture	WATER	▽
Heat and Moisture	AIR	△
Cold and Dryness	EARTH	▽

The Element of Fire

(Egyptian—*Ash* or *Ish*, Hebrew—*Asch*, Latin—*Ignis*, Greek—*Pyr*.) *Qualities of Fire:* active, masculine, spontaneous, quick, initiating, initializing, vitalizing, and energetic.

The most physical expression of Fire is the visible, active phase of combustion manifesting in heat and light. The Element of Fire was seen by the Alchemists as an Element which operates at the center of all things, as well as the "agent of transmutation" because all things are derived from and return to Fire. This Element is seen as the great Supernal Father energy—the "seed" force of the universe. It is an Element with two purposes: (1) it is an expression of spiritual energy and the determination of the Spirit, (2) it purifies, burns, and destroys the old so that the new may emerge. Thus it is a symbol of transformation and regeneration. There is a direct parallel between the concepts of Fire and Life. Fire is an image of energy found at the level of animal passions as well as on the plane of spiritual fortitude. Its action is quick and unpredictable. To pass through Fire is symbolic of transcending the human condition. The direction or cardinal point assigned to Fire is South.

The Element of Water

(Egyptian—*Mu*, Hebrew—*Maim*, Latin—*Aqua*, Greek—*Hydor*.) *Qualities of Water:* passive, feminine, receptive, sustaining, subconscious, creative, fluidic, and generative.

In a mundane physical sense, water is a liquid compound of hydrogen and oxygen molecules. In an esoteric sense, the concept of Water implies all liquid materials. Furthermore, the primeval Waters, the image of all primal matter, contain all solid bodies before they obtain rigidity and form. The so-called "fluid body" of man is translated by modern psychology as a symbol of the unconscious or the archetypal feminine side of the personality. Water is seen as a symbol of the Maternal, the Great Mother, as well as the great unfathomable and mysterious well of Wisdom contained within the subconscious mind. In short, Water symbolizes the infinite realm of possibilities, which precede all form and all creation. It is limitless and immortal—the Waters of Creation. Submersion in Water alludes to a return to the pre-formed state. Like the Element of Fire, Water also symbolizes the ideas of transfiguration and regeneration. The direction or cardinal point assigned to Water is West.

The Element of Air

(Egyptian—*Nef*, Hebrew—*Ruach*, Latin—*Aer*, Greek—*Aer*.) *Qualities of Air:* active, masculine, intellectual, ethereal, abstract, and communicative.

The physical expression of Air is that of a mixture of gases which forms the atmosphere of the Earth. Symbolically, Air is related to the creative breath of Life, and, therefore, speech. Light, flight, and weightlessness, as well as scent and smell are all related to the Element of Air. It is connected in many mythologies with the idea of creation and as a medium for movement and the emergence of life processes. Air is a volatile Element which is considered by the Qabalists to be the offspring of the Parental Elements of Fire and Water (thus creating steam). It is the Reconciler between the rival Elements of Fire (male) and Water (female)—balancing and equilibrating these two parental opposites. Air also alludes to the human intellect and thought processes, which are quick, changeable, and abstract. The direction or cardinal point assigned to Air is East.

The Element of Earth

(Egyptian—*Ta*, Hebrew—*Aretz*, Latin—*Terra*, Greek—*Ge*.) *Qualities of Earth:* passive, feminine, solid, materialization, physical, stable, slow-moving, and grounded.

In a technical sense, earth is the dry land surface of the planet, made up of solid organic and inorganic particles. Allegorically it is much more than that. Earth represents the physical, materialized universe in which we live. It is the tangible world around us that we can touch and feel. Earth is the Daughter of Fire and Water, just as Air is the Son. This Element encompasses all activities of productivity, fertility, growth, and regeneration. Earth is the fourth and final Element and the result of the actions of the other three. The direction or cardinal point assigned to Earth is North. ✿

SECTION 2: The Zodiac

What is Astrology and why is it important? Astrology is a science that examines the action of celestial bodies upon all living beings, non-living objects, and earthly conditions, as well as their reactions to such influences. The study of the stars is in fact one of the oldest sciences known to humankind, tracing its origins back to ancient Sumer and even earlier. The Astrological arts were also well known to the Egyptians, Hindus, Chinese, Persians, and the great civilizations of the ancient Americas.

Astrology is the progenitor of astronomy, and for many years the two existed as one science. Nowadays, astronomy is considered an "objective" science of distances, masses, speeds, etc., while Astrology is a "subjective" and intuitive science which not only deals with the astronomical delineation of horoscopes, but can also be called a *philosophy* which helps to explain the spiritual essence of life.

There are in reality two branches of Astrology. The first is *Exoteric Astrology* which includes the mathematics of the art involved with charting a horoscope and the predictive arts. The second is *Esoteric Astrology* which deals with mysteries of the universe itself, the spiritual, moral, intellectual and physical dynamics of the cosmos. Esoteric Astrology reveals the universal pattern of living and the means by which human beings can align themselves with the spiritual fabric and pattern of the universe. It is a system for understanding celestial energies and a method for viewing the universe as a symmetrical whole.

Of great importance to the art of Astrology is the *Zodiac*. This is a circle or belt, which anciently was said to extend eight or nine degrees on each side of the *ecliptic* (the Sun's apparent path around the Earth, or the orbit of the Earth as viewed from the Sun.) The Zodiacal "wheel" is a flat chart which is divided into twelve houses, each of which is said to be ruled by one of the twelve Signs.

The twelve Signs of the Zodiac are distributed among the four *Triplicities* (or sets of three Signs). Each of these triplicities is attributed to one of the four Elements, and they represent the operation of the Elements in the Zodiac. The twelve

Signs are also divided into three *Quadruplicities* (or groups of four Signs). Each of these Quadruplicities is attributed to one of the three qualities of Cardinal, Mutable, and Kerubic (Fixed).

The Triplicities (grouped by Element)

Fire Signs

Aries, Leo, and Sagittarius. *Positive traits:* fiery, impassioned, eager, spontaneous, independent, and enthusiastic. *Negative traits:* They can be too forceful, domineering, and overbearing.

Water Signs

Cancer, Scorpio, and Pisces. *Positive traits:* intuitive, receptive, emotional, sensitive, compassionate, and complex. *Negative traits:* They can be moody, easily influenced, self-pitying, and wavering.

Air Signs

Libra, Aquarius, and Gemini. *Positive traits:* able to communicate well, intellectual, logical, open-minded, idealistic, and objective. *Negative traits:* They can be cold, insensitive, and impractical.

Earth Signs

Capricorn, Taurus, and Virgo. *Positive traits:* stable, earthy, practical, dependable, conservative, and sensual. *Negative traits:* They can be dull, slow, possessive, and overly materialistic.

The Quadruplicities (grouped by quality)

Cardinal Signs

Aries, Cancer, Libra, and Capricorn. These Signs are known as Cardinal because they rule the change of seasons: Aries—spring; Cancer—Summer; Libra—Fall; and Capricorn—Winter. These Signs are also attributed to the four cardinal points of the compass: Aries—East; Cancer—North; Libra—West; and Capricorn—South. *Positive qualities:* Cardinal Signs are active, fervent, independent, enthusiastic, ambitious, and initiating. Mentally they are quick and insatiable. *Negative qualities:* They can be impetuous, domineering, thoughtless and without the ability to follow through with projects they have started.

Kerubic Signs

Leo, Scorpio, Aquarius, and Taurus. These *Fixed Signs* govern the middle month of each season. Unlike the Cardinal Signs which herald the transition between seasons, the Kerubic Signs are solidly established in the heart of each season. *Positive qualities:* These Signs are stable, determined, persevering, able to concentrate, and accumulative. Their goals are reached slowly but steadily. They are perceptive and have excellent memories. *Negative qualities:* They can be egotistical, obstinate and too firmly ingrained in their ways and opinions.

Mutable Signs

Sagittarius, Pisces, Gemini, and Virgo. These Signs rule the closing month of each season. Also called *Common Signs*, they govern the completion of the work of one season while looking ahead to the next season. *Positive qualities:* adaptable, versatile, changeable, subtle, intuitive, and understanding. Mentally, they are clever and flexible. *Negative qualities:* They can be unreliable, fickle, deceptive, and cunning.

To get a better understanding of each Sign, we will present a more in-depth look at each one in turn.

The Signs of the Zodiac

Symbol	Name	Image	Triplicity	Quadruplicity
♈	ARIES	the Ram	Fire	Cardinal
♉	TAURUS	the Bull	Earth	Kerubic
♊	GEMINI	the Twins	Air	Mutable
♋	CANCER	the Crab	Water	Cardinal
♌	LEO	the Lion	Fire	Kerubic
♍	VIRGO	the Virgin	Earth	Mutable
♎	LIBRA	the Scales	Air	Cardinal
♏	SCORPIO	the Scorpion	Water	Kerubic
♐	SAGITTARIUS	the Archer	Fire	Mutable
♑	CAPRICORN	the Sea Goat	Earth	Cardinal
♒	AQUARIUS	the Water-bearer	Air	Kerubic
♓	PISCES	the Two Fish	Water	Mutable

♈ ARIES (March 21–April 19)
Sigil: Ram's horns *Triplicity:* Fire *Quality:* Cardinal
Key phrase: I AM *Key word:* ACTIVITY

Positive traits:	*Negative traits:*
quick	quick-tempered
initiating	overbearing
pioneering	violent
executive	intolerant
eager	egotistical
courageous	impatient
independent	abrupt
dynamic	doesn't follow through
impulsive	hasty
competitive	"after ME"
lives in the present	

♉ TAURUS (April 20–May 20)
Sigil: Bull's head   *Triplicity:* Earth   *Quality:* Kerubic
Key phrase: I HAVE   *Key word:* STABILITY

Positive traits:	*Negative traits:*
stable	short-tempered
dependable	bull-headed
practical	slow-moving
thorough	quarrelsome
domestic	possessive
conventional	greedy
aesthetic	selfish
sensual	materialistic

♊ GEMINI (May 21–June 20)
Sigil: Roman Numeral 2   *Triplicity:* Air   *Quality:* Mutable
Key phrase: I THINK   *Key word:* VERSATILITY

Positive traits:	*Negative traits:*
versatile	changeable
adaptable	alternating
sociable	scatterbrained
dual	conniving
expressive	fidgety
inquisitive	short attention span
inventive	lacks follow-through
dexterous	lacks powers
intelligent	of concentration
literary	
quick-witted	

♋ CANCER (June 21–July 22)
Sigil: Crab's claws   *Triplicity:* Water   *Quality:* Cardinal
Key phrase: I FEEL   *Key word:* DEVOTION

Positive traits:	*Negative traits:*
nurturing	self-pitying
maternal	self-centered
domestic	moody
traditional	sulky
emotional	negative
sensitive	overcautious
understanding	indolent
supportive	manipulative
retentive	overly emotional
excellent memory	

♌ LEO (July 23–August 22)
Sigil: Lion's tail   *Triplicity:* Fire   *Quality:* Kerubic
Key phrase: I WILL   *Key word:* MAGNETISM

Positive traits:	*Negative traits:*
romantic	egotistical
charismatic	conceited
dramatic	bombastic
distinguished	pompous
proud	childish
ambitious	status conscious
enterprising	domineering
self-confident	cruel
idealistic	tyrant
charitable	

♍ VIRGO (August 23–September 22)
Sigil: Greek word for virgin   *Triplicity:* Earth   *Quality:* Mutable
Key phrase: I ANALYZE   *Key word:* PRACTICALITY

Positive traits:	*Negative traits:*
practical	faultfinding
analytical	critical
discriminating	picky
scientific	cynical
systematic	stuffy
exacting	snobbish
diligent	hypochondriac
industrious	self-centered
perfectionist	
neat	

♎ LIBRA (September 23–October 22)
Sigil: The scales   *Triplicity:* Air   *Quality:* Cardinal
Key phrase: I BALANCE   *Key word:* HARMONY

Positive traits:	*Negative traits:*
sociable	indecisive
tactful	ambivalent
amicable	inconsistent
cooperative	sulking
persuasive	easily deterred
peace-loving	lover of intrigue
sophisticated	peace at any cost
diplomatic	
fair	

♏ SCORPIO (October 23–November 21)
Sigil: Scorpion's Tail *Triplicity:* Water *Quality:* Kerubic
Key phrase: I DESIRE *Key word:* INTENSITY

Positive traits:	*Negative traits:*
intense	temperamental
profound	irritable
penetrating	intolerant
resolute	domineering
motivated	violent
resourceful	jealous
passionate	resentful
aware	distrustful
investigative	secretive

♐ SAGITTARIUS (November 22–December 21)
Sigil: Archer's arrow *Triplicity:* Fire *Quality:* Mutable
Key phrase: I UNDERSTAND *Key word:* VISUALIZATION

Positive traits:	*Negative traits:*
freedom-loving	exaggerating
honest	quarrelsome
straightforward	talks too much
open-minded	blunt
philosophical	tactless
religious	impatient
educated	procrastinating
ethical	self-indulgent
optimistic	pushy
enthusiastic	hot-headed
charitable	a risk-taker

♑ CAPRICORN (December 22–January 19)
Sigil: Sea-goat's horn and tail *Triplicity:* Earth *Quality:* Cardinal
Key phrase: I USE *Key word:* AMBITION

Positive traits:	*Negative traits:*
ambitious	stubborn
hardworking	sulking
serious	egotist
businesslike	status-conscious
conservative	overbearing
pragmatic	unforgiving
prudent	fatalistic
responsible	inhibited
scrupulous	mind over heart

♒ **AQUARIUS** (January 20–February 18)
Sigil: Waves of water   *Triplicity:* Air   *Quality:* Kerubic
Key phrase: I KNOW   *Key word:* IMAGINATION

Positive traits:	*Negative traits:*
imaginative	unemotional
inventive	aloof
progressive	dispassionate
independent	temperamental
scientific	unpredictable
intellectual	shy
logical	eccentric
individualistic	extremist
understanding	unruly
benevolent	fixed in opinions
philanthropic	

♓ **PISCES** (February 19–March 20)
Sigil: Two fish tied together   *Triplicity:* Water   *Quality:* Mutable
Key phrase: I BELIEVE   *Key word:* UNDERSTANDING

Positive traits:	*Negative traits:*
understanding	negative
intuitive	pessimistic
instinctive	melancholy
introspective	procrastinating
humanitarian	hesitating
compassionate	chatterbox
charitable	lazy
sympathetic	impractical
emotional	unrealistic
sacrificing	fearful
artistic	fainthearted
musical	feels misunderstood
sensitive	emotionally constrained

SECTION 3: The Seven Ancient Planets

To the Ancients, five Planets were known besides the luminaries of the Sun and the Moon. The Planets, like the Zodiacal Signs, each have a set of characteristics assigned to them. Each Planet is said to rule one or more of the Signs. The energy of a Planet is strong in the Sign(s) that it rules (the Sign of the Planet's *dignity*). In addition every Planet also has one Sign, aside from the one it rules, where it expresses itself in a compatible fashion (the Sign of the Planet's *exaltation*). When a Planet is in the Sign directly opposite to the one it rules, it is in the Sign of its *detriment*. Also, when a Planet is in the Sign opposite of its exaltation, it is in the Sign of its *fall*. Thus a Planet's dignity and its exaltation are harmonious with its energy, while its detriment and its fall are contrary to the Planet's energy. To get a better idea of the energies and associations of each Planet, the following explanations are provided:[20]

☽ **LUNA** (The Moon)
Rules: Cancer *Exaltation:* Taurus
Detriment: Capricorn *Fall:* Scorpio
Represents: domestic, nurturing urge
Key word: EMOTIONS

Luna is a Roman name identified with Diana, goddess of the Moon. The Moon embodies the primary female principle and women in general. It encompasses instincts, moods, feelings, habits, the subconscious, tides, phases, reflexes, reflections, alternations, and receptivity. Luna rules needs, desires, personal interests, magnetism, liquids, impressionability, fertility, and growth. The Moon's action changes and fluctuates.

☿ **MERCURY**
Rules: Gemini, Virgo *Exaltation:* Aquarius
Detriment: Sagittarius, Pisces *Fall:* Leo
Represents: intellectual, expressive urge
Key word: REASONING POWERS

Mercury is named after the fleet-footed Roman messenger god. Mercury governs communication, reason, intellect, rationalization, awareness, perceptions, adroitness, opinions, transmission, words, speaking, writing, mailings, and means of expression. In addition Mercury deals with family, children, siblings, social contacts, day-to-day activities, travel, and transportation. This Planet's action is rapid, unpredictable, and explosive.

♀ **VENUS**
Rules: Taurus, Libra *Exaltation:* Pisces
Detriment: Scorpio, Aries *Fall:* Virgo
Represents: social urge, values
Key word: AFFECTION

Venus, the Planet of Love, named after the Roman goddess, was in ancient times nicknamed the *Lesser Benefic*. It governs pleasure, natural love, sensuality, socia-

---

[20] Note that here the Planets are given in the order of their *speed*, whereas in most other Golden Dawn listings they are given in a reverse order according to their attribution to the Sephiroth descending the Tree of Life.

bility, attraction, interaction, art, music, poetry, drama, song, culture, beauty, possessions, jewelry, candy, sentiments, color, marriage, and unions. Its action is mild and harmonious.

☉ SOL (The Sun)
Rules: Leo *Exaltation:* Aries
Detriment: Aquarius *Fall:* Libra
Represents: Power urge, ego, personality
Key word: INNER SELF

Sol is the Roman name of the invincible Sun deity. It is the origin of the word "Solar." Sol represents the primary masculine principle and men in general. It is also the fundamental expression of the individual, displaying qualities of success and leadership. Sol governs health, vitality, personal fulfillment, energy, essential principles, authority, command, rank, office, title, advancement, identity, and capacity for experience. The Sun's action is energizing and stimulating.

♂ MARS
Rules: Aries (co-rules Scorpio) *Exaltation:* Capricorn
Detriment: Libra (Taurus) *Fall:* Cancer
Represents: Aggressive urge, initiative, action
Key word: ENERGY

The Planet Mars, named after the Roman god of war, was referred to by the Ancients as the *Lesser Malefic*. It governs desires, sexual energies, focused energies, dynamic action, animal nature, force, power, strife, strain, adversity, work, achievement, competition, and death. Mars also rules weapons, war, accidents, violence, surgery, tools, iron, and steel. The action of this Planet is sudden, forceful, and disruptive. The energy of Mars can be used violently and destructively or with valor and fortitude.

♃ JUPITER
Rules: Sagittarius (sub-rules Pisces) *Exaltation:* Cancer
Detriment: Gemini (Virgo) *Fall:* Capricorn
Represents: compassionate, protective urge
Key word: EXPANSION

Jupiter, named after the primary Roman god was called the *Greater Benefic* by the ancients. Jupiter is the lawmaker, the judge, and the benefactor of humankind. This Planet rules leisure time, wealth, growth, prosperity, opportunity, assimilation, indulgence, optimism, big business, morality, the higher (abstract) mind, higher education, ambitions, philosophy, and luck. Jupiter's action is orderly and efficient and fosters growth and increase.

♄ SATURN

Rules: Capricorn (sub-rules Aquarius) *Exaltation:* Libra
Detriment: Cancer (Leo)   *Fall:* Aries
Represents: security, safety urge
Key word: THE TEACHER

Saturn, named after the Roman god of agriculture, was called the *Greater Malefic* in earlier times. This Planet is known as the taskmaster of the horoscope. It rules organization, discipline, responsibility, structure, goals, career opportunities, limitations, conservatism, crystallized focus, restrictions, delays, theories, orthodoxy, tradition, depth, time, patience, truth, wisdom, aging, and solidification. Saturn's action is slow and enduring.

The Ancients also assigned certain Planetary values to the North and South Nodes of the Moon, that is, the points in celestial longitude where the Moon crosses over the ecliptic or path of the Sun. Luna's North Node is listed by its position in the ephemeris and the South Node is always its exact opposite, having the same number of degrees and minutes, but of the converse Sign. The Nodes of the Moon are called:

CAPUT DRACONIS *(The Head of the Dragon)* North Node ☊

CAUDA DRACONIS *(The Tail of the Dragon)* South Node ☋

The North Node is a point of gain, increase and added self-assurance. The South Node is a point of release, decrease, and letting go.

The Days of the week are attributed to and (in some cases) named after the seven ancient Planets and the gods who represented them. They are:

Norse	Latin	Saxon	English
	Sol	Sun's Day	Sunday
	Luna	Moon's Day	Monday
Tyr	Mars	Tiw's Day	Tuesday
Wotan	Mercury	Woden's Day	Wednesday
Thor	Jove (Jupiter)	Thor's Day	Thursday
Freya	Venus	Frigg's Day	Friday
	Saturn	Seterne's Day	Saturday

The New Planets

Uranus was discovered on March 13, 1782. Neptune was discovered on September 24, 1846, and Pluto on January 21, 1930. These outer Planets did not have a prominent place in early Order teachings, although the effect of Caput Draconis was said to be similar to that of Neptune, and the influence of Cauda Draconis was supposed to be similar to that of Uranus. Because these Planets are slow moving in their orbits around the Sun, they are regarded as symbols of eras. These Planets, which are also referred to as the *Transcendental Planets,* do not enter into the ancient sevenfold scheme of the Heptad of the Planets, which is a vital aspect of the Golden Dawn system of magic. Because of this, the outer Planets will rarely be referred to elsewhere in this book. They are mentioned here because it is important that today's student have a thorough grounding in the basics of modern Astrology.

♅ URANUS

Rules: Aquarius (with sub-ruler, Saturn) *Exaltation:* Scorpio
Detriment: Leo *Fall:* Taurus
Represents: Freedom urge ("divine discontent")
Key word: THE AWAKENER

Uranus was the god of the starlit sky, the progenitor of the gods. The Planet Uranus rules science, electricity, lightning, the stroke of genius, suddenness, magic, the occult, Astrology, x-rays, inventions, discoveries, originality, and psychology. It is intellectual, progressive, futuristic, humanitarian, egotistical, rebellious, eccentric, unorthodox, unconventional, and utopian. This Planet rules sudden change, individualism, independence, autonomy, and natural disasters. It is considered to be the upper octave of Mercury. Uranus's action is sudden, unforeseen, and usually violent.

♆ NEPTUNE

Rules: Pisces (with sub-ruler, Jupiter) *Exaltation:* ——
Detriment: Virgo *Fall:* ——
Represents: spiritual or escapist urge
Key word: INTUITION

The Planet Neptune is named for the Roman god of the Sea. It rules liquids, all marine activities, glamour, the stage, movies and television, the fantastic, dreams, psychic powers, intuition, illusion, delusion, mystique, spirituality, ideals, things we take for granted, fog, mystery, intangibles, immateriality, fragrances, trances, drugs, addictions, hypnosis, and sleep-walking. Neptune is said to be the upper octave of Venus. Its action is subtle and imperceptible, yet sometimes insidious.

♇ PLUTO

Rules: Scorpio (with co-ruler, Mars) *Exaltation:* ——
Detriment: Taurus *Fall:* ——
Represents: Fusion, destroying or reforming urge
Key word: TRANSFORMATION

The Planet Pluto was named after the god of the Underworld. It governs all things that are secret or hidden from view, such as the subconscious mind. Pluto also rules replication, conception, generation, regeneration, degeneration, birth and death, beginnings and endings, bacteria, viruses, slow growth, turmoil, rejuvenation, transfiguration, reorganization, phobias, obsessions, subversion, atomic power, crime, exposure, isolation, perspective, awareness of the masses, covert activities, and the exclusive. Many consider it to be the higher octave of Mars. Pluto's action is slow, ponderous and inescapable.

Finally, we must refer to the *Earth* which is not usually portrayed along with the other Planets. This is because the Earth as a Planet never leaves our sphere of experience. It is *terra firma*—a constant that is always with each of us, here and now, under our feet (so long as modern man does not destroy her). It represents the physical plane and mundane matters. In astrological terms the Earth is tentatively ruled by Taurus. Its Key word is *Reality*. In a horoscope, the Earth is always the exact opposite of the Sun by Sign, degree, and house placement. It alludes to the individual's mission in life.⊕

Table of Essential Dignities

Planet	Dignity	Detriment	Exaltation	Fall
Saturn	♑,♒	♋,♌	♎	♈
Jupiter	♐,♓	♊,♍	♋	♑
Mars	♈,♏	♎,♉	♑	♋
Sol	♌	♒	♈	♎
Venus	♉,♎	♏,♈	♓	♍
Mercury	♊,♍	♐,♓	♒	♌
Luna	♋	♑	♉	♏
Uranus	♒	♌	♏	♉
Neptune	♓	♍		
Pluto	♏	♉		

SECTION 4: The Qabalah

 Qabalah is a Hebrew word which means "tradition." It is derived from the root word *qibel*, meaning "to receive." This refers to the ancient custom of handing down esoteric knowledge by oral transmission. What the word *Qabalah* encompasses is an entire body of ancient Hebrew mystical principles that are the cornerstone and focus of the Western Esoteric Tradition. Virtually all Western spiritual systems can trace their roots to the Qabalistic Tree of Life. The exact origins of the Qabalah are unclear, but it certainly contains some vestiges of Egyptian, Greek, and Chaldean influence.

By its nature, mysticism is knowledge that cannot be communicated directly but may be expressed only through symbolism and metaphor. Like other esoteric systems, Qabalah also draws upon the mystic's awareness of the transcendence of the eternal deity. Another element of Qabalah is that it seeks to reveal the hidden mysteries of the Divine as well as the connection between the divine life on one hand and the life of humans on the other. The goal of the Qabalist is to discover and invent keys to the understanding of arcane symbols which reflect the eternal mysteries.

Israel Regardie stated that, "Qabalah is a trustworthy guide, leading to a comprehension of the universe and one's own self." It is all this and more. This "Tradition" was never restricted to instruction in the mystical path alone; it also includes ideas on the origins of the universe, of Angelic hierarchies, and the practice of magic. Qabalah is the foundation upon which the art of Western magic rests. Magic has been defined by Aleister Crowley as "the science and art of causing change to occur in conformity with Will." To this Dion Fortune added "changes in consciousness."

The Qabalah, which Dion Fortune called "the Yoga of the West" reveals the nature of certain physical and psychological phenomena. Once these are *rightly* understood, the student can use the principles of magic to exercise control over the conditions and circumstances of his/her life. Magic provides the practical application of the theories supplied by the Qabalah.

The Qabalah as it exists today is a vibrant, living and dynamic philosophy which includes ideas on the origin of the entire Cosmos, the eternal mind of God, and the spiritual development of humankind. It is a precise mystical system that describes universal laws and shows us how to utilize spiritual principles in everyday life. By firmly fixing Qabalistic symbols such as the Tree of Life in one's mind, the aspirant has access to a balanced group of archetypes that the Inner Self can more easily relate to, thus making true spiritual growth more readily attainable. As the Hermetic student begins to contemplate and experience the energies of the *Sephiroth* (the ten emanations of the Qabalistic Tree of Life) s/he will find that they develop into genuine Forces that become animated within the psyche. These newly awakened Forces will initiate a process of reorganization in the mind of the student, gathering up disjointed elements of the Divine Powers which lay dormant in the average person. They begin to structure themselves in accordance with the Sephiroth, permitting the student to tap into a previously unknown source of Divine Inspiration which is kept alive and prolific through meditation and active ritual work. The Qabalah has often been called the "Ladder of Lights" because it not only depicts Cosmic generation, which is the descent of the Divine into the physical, but also defines how the individual may employ it for spiritual ascent by purifying both body and mind through ceremony, contemplation, and prayer, until at length one achieves that pristine state of consciousness that is necessary to attain union with the Higher Self, which is the emissary to the Divine Self represented by the first Sephirah of Kether.

Some people who have a brief encounter with the Qabalah come away with the idea that it is a purely patriarchal or male-oriented philosophy simply because of its Hebrew origins. Nothing could be further from the truth. Take for example a word which is common throughout Qabalistic teachings, *"Elohim."* This a word formed from a feminine noun, *"Eloah"* and a masculine plural *"im."* You are left with a word that has both male and female characteristics which literally means "gods"—the creative principle formed from the perfect and equal union of

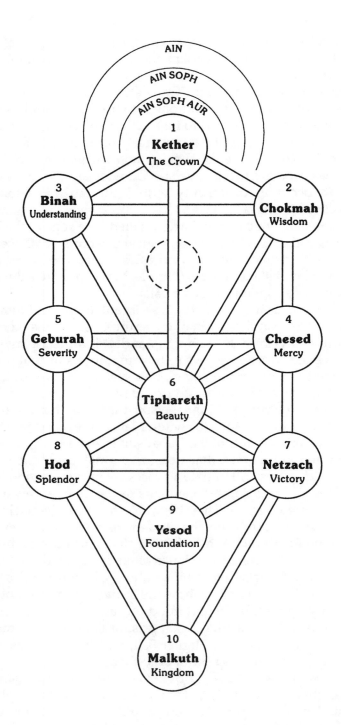

The Tree of Life

the divine male and the divine female principles. Read in this context, the Qabalistic origins of the first five books of the Old Testament (the *Pentateuch*) give an entirely new meaning. The first sentence of Genesis, which in Hebrew begins as "*Berashith bara Elohim Ath-ha-Shamaim w'Ath ha-Aretz,*" can be interpreted as "In the beginning, the gods (the united Male and Female aspects of the Divine) created the Heavens and the Earth." This idea of the equality of the divine male and divine female principles, although suppressed for centuries by male-dominated societies, is carefully hidden in Qabalistic doctrine, although at times it has slipped out unforeseen in almost all translations of the *Pentateuch*, such as in Genesis 1:26 and 1:27: "And God went on to say let *us* make man in *our* image, according to *our* likeness," "And God proceeded to create the man in his image, in God's image he created him; *male and female* he created them."

Another example is the word *Sephiroth,* which is used to describe the ten emanations of the Divine. Here we have a feminine noun *Sephirah* being joined to a feminine plural "*oth.*" This again points to the importance of the feminine in Qabalah. The Sephiroth themselves are generally considered feminine because they structure and give form to the emanations of deity. Thus anyone who seriously studies the Qabalah for any length of time will see that it is a very balanced system for spiritual growth.

The Qabalah is usually classified under four heads which overlap each other in some instances. They are:

1. THE DOGMATIC QABALAH—the study of ancient Qabalistic books such as the Written *Torah* also called the *Pentateuch,* the *Zohar,* the *Bahir,* and the *Sepher Yetzirah.*

2. THE PRACTICAL QABALAH—deals with the construction of talismans used in ceremonial magic.

3. THE LITERAL QABALAH—deals with *Gematria;* the relationships between numbers and the letters of the Hebrew alphabet, which yield many hidden meanings of Hebrew words and names.

4. THE UNWRITTEN QABALAH—refers to the correct knowledge of the sacred symbol known as the Tree of Life (*Etz-ha-Chayim*). This is the only branch of the Qabalah that the Neophyte of this course will need to study for now.

We will not at this time describe the long history and evolution of the Qabalah as espoused and elucidated by various teachers and sources down through the ages. To do so would be to place an undue burden upon the Neophyte. However, for ambitious students who like to take on burdens, we highly recommend a book by Gershom Scholem called simply *Kabbalah* published by Dorset Press (New York). This book gives an excellent and detailed account of the various schools of Qabalistic thought.

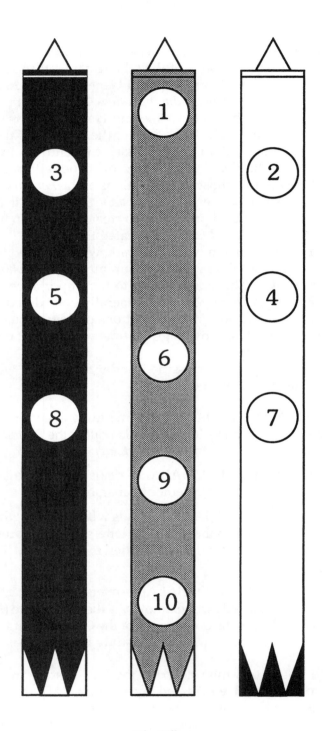

The Pillars

SECTION 5: The Sephiroth

 The Hebrew Qabalists referred the highest and most abstract ideas to ten emanations of deity which are called the *Sephiroth* (sef-eer-oth). Singularly they are called *Sephirah*. When arranged in a certain manner, the ten Sephiroth and the twenty-two paths which connect them form the *Tree of Life*. Together, the Ten Sephiroth and the Twenty-two Paths comprise what are called the *Thirty-two Paths of Wisdom*.

The Tree of Life is the single most important symbol of the Qabalah. Just a glance at its diagram will reveal it to be a system of perfect mathematics, symmetry, and beauty. It is represented as ten circles or orbs known as the *Sephiroth,* which is said to mean "Numbers," "Spheres" and "Emanations."[21] Some have seen the Sephiroth as divine powers or vessels. Others regard them as divine tools or instruments of the Eternal (although not separated from the Eternal like human tools are). All agree, however, that the Sephiroth express divine attributions or essences that are organized into an archetypal pattern which is the model for everything that has come into the manifest universe. The relationships implied in the Tree of Life underscore the whole of existence, and so the attributes of the Sephiroth may be found in any branch of knowledge. Although their basic definition confirms them as characteristics of the Divine, they can be described in terms of human experience because men and women are formed as stated before, in the image of the Divine.

One essential aspect of the Sephiroth is that they are placed upon the Tree of Life in perfect juxtaposition, so that each Sephirah counterbalances one on the opposite side of the Tree. The ten Sephiroth emanate from the *Three Negative Veils of Existence* (various abstract stages of "nothingness") in succession as if "one candle were lit from another without the Emanator being diminished in any way" and in a specific order. They are not seen as being separated from the Source. The Qabalists agree that there are ten because ten is a perfect number, one which includes every digit without repetition, and contains the total essence of all numbers. The number ten is therefore an all-embracing number. Outside of ten there exists no other such number, because what is beyond ten returns again to units.

The Pillars

The most important configuration which occurs on the Tree is that of three pillars formed by the natural succession of the Sephiroth. The left-hand pillar, also called the *Pillar of Severity*, consists of the spheres of Binah, Geburah, and Hod. The right-hand pillar, known as the *Pillar of Mercy*, is comprised of the spheres of Chokmah, Chesed, and Netzach. The central spheres of Kether, Tiphareth, Yesod, and Malkuth form the *Middle Pillar*, or the *Pillar of Mildness*.

The right-hand or white pillar is described as masculine, positive and active. It is also known as the *Pillar of Force*. The left-hand or black pillar is feminine, negative and passive. This pillar is called the *Pillar of Form*. The black and

---

[21] The word *Sephirah* is derived from the root word סבר, from which come *sepher*—"book," *siphar*—"number," *sippur*—"story," and *sipper*—"to tell."

white pillars represent the two great contending Forces in Nature, and their descriptions are not meant to imply that one is good and the other evil, but rather that magnetic energy exists between these two universal opposite forces. The whole of the cosmos depends upon the perfect balance of these energies.

The *Middle Pillar* is the pillar of balanced forces; the equilibrium of the other two columns. (In Golden Dawn temples only the left and right pillars are physically symbolized by actual pillars. The Middle Pillar is represented by the aspirant standing between the other two.)

Sexual Polarity on the Tree

There are numerous schools of Qabalistic thought that ascribe masculine or feminine attributes to each of the Sephiroth. Often times these various sources disagree with one another. Disagreements over Qabalah insure that the system is kept alive, dynamic, and expanding. (The minute everyone totally agrees with all the precepts of a specific esoteric system is the minute that system dies.) We too have often felt strongly about the sexual polarity of certain Sephiroth, only to change our minds later as our view of Tree of Life expanded. For the most part, each Sephirah is an abstraction that contains certain aspects which are characteristic of *both* sexual polarities. No one Sephirah is simply all masculine or all feminine. Here we will discuss the sexual polarities of the spheres as they relate to the three primary Elements of Fire, Water, and Air. As far as the spheres of the Tree are concerned, Fire is masculine, Water is feminine, and Air is neutral or androgynous.

The Ten Sephiroth

No.	Name	Transliteration	Hebrew	Translation
1.	**Kether**	KThR	כתר	The Crown
2.	**Chokmah**	ChKMH	חכמה	Wisdom
3.	**Binah**	BINH	בינה	Understanding
4.	**Chesed**	ChSD	חסד	Mercy
5.	**Geburah**	GBVRH	גבורה	Severity
6.	**Tiphareth**	ThPhARTh	תפארת	Beauty
7.	**Netzach**	NTzCh	נצח	Victory
8.	**Hod**	HVD	הוד	Splendor
9.	**Yesod**	YSVD	יסוד	Foundation
10.	**Malkuth**	MLKVTh	מלכות	The Kingdom

KETHER (Keh-ther or Kay-ther)
Translation: THE CROWN
Key word: SOURCE
Yetziratic Title: The ADMIRABLE or HIDDEN INTELLIGENCE
Physical Representation: The FIRST MOTION
Symbols: A Crown, a Point, a Swastika, or Fylfot Cross

The first Sephirah at the edge of the Three Negative Veils is Kether, the Crown. The number 1, which encloses within itself the remaining nine digits of the decimal scale, was described by Pythagoras as the undividable Monad. It cannot be divided, yet it can be defined. By the process of reflection (1 + 1 = 2; 1 + 2 = 3; etc.), the Monad defines and generates all the other numbers. Kether is the point; it is the moment that the universe as we know it was conceived. Kether is the initial Spark or first Breath of the Divine. This sphere is placed at the summit of the Middle Pillar on the Tree of Life, at the apex of Equilibrium.

The *Sepher Yetzirah*, or *Book of Formation*, says of Kether: "The First Path is called the Admirable or the Hidden Intelligence (the Highest Crown), for it is the Light giving the power of comprehension of that first principle which has no beginning; and it is the Primal Glory, for no created being can attain to its essence." The words "Hidden Intelligence" imply a hint of the unmanifest nature of Kether. The purest seeds of life (the Divine Spark) are found only at the level of the First Emanation, where they have always been—removed from the concept of having a "beginning point." The Divine Life Essence, as it descends the Tree of Life, is merely undergoing a process of transformation, from one form of energy to another (as explained in the teachings of Alchemy). The *Sepher Yetzirah* also indicates that no created being can hope to attain to the pure spiritual Light and Essence of Kether; that would be akin to an adult human being returning to the womb to become a fertilized egg. No being using a physical organism as its vehicle of consciousness can attain to the essence of Kether. However, if consciousness has been purified to the point where it transcends thought, it receives from the "Primal Glory" the power of comprehension of the First Principle.

Kether is the sphere that contains all that was, is, and will be—it is the place of first emanation and ultimate return. The Crown is the sphere of pure spiritual being; the point of absolute Unity without division—ultimate peace and oneness. Kether is the dwelling place of the Divine White Brilliance, the Godhead which is androgynous, but that which contains the purest potentials of both male and female. It is the Source of All and the Highest Divine Essence of which we can conceive; the Primum Mobile or First Whirlings of Manifestation—a phrase which aptly describes the activity of the cosmic energy at the time the universe was created. All comes from Kether and all will ultimately return to Kether.

CHOKMAH (Chohk-mah)
Translation: WISDOM
Key word: SUPERNAL FATHER
Yetziratic Title: The ILLUMINATING INTELLIGENCE
Physical Representation: The ZODIAC
Symbols: The Line, the Phallus, the Yod

Chokmah is the second Sephirah, and its name means Wisdom. Chokmah is almost an extension of Kether—the overflowing of the Divine into a second, which is a reflection of the First. From the Absolute Unity of the One now comes the Two, the first active expression of polarity and the balance of opposites which forms the matrix of the manifest universe.

According to the *Sepher Yetzirah:* "The Second Path is that of Illuminating Intelligence; it is the Crown of Creation, the Splendor of the Unity, equaling it, and it is exalted above every head, and named by the Qabalists the Second Glory." Chokmah is clearly confirmed here as the essence of Illumination; not the same as that Brilliant Spark of Kether which exists on a higher plane, but as Wisdom—perfect knowledge and understanding that has developed as a result of the reflection of Kether into a second sphere; a mirror of the First, enabling the Divine Spirit to both emanate from itself and behold itself. The "Crown of Creation" indicates that Chokmah was "created" from the Crown (Kether). Again we are presented with the idea that the Primal Spirit is not diminished in any way through the succession of the Sephiroth; "the Splendor of UNITY, equaling it." That, "it is exalted above every head," alludes to Chokmah's high position on the Tree along with the other Supernals above the Abyss.

As the first Sephirah to develop polarity, Chokmah is placed at the summit of the Pillar of Mercy or the right-hand pillar. If Kether can be described as a point, then Chokmah could be portrayed as a straight line, an extension of the point into space. The energy of Chokmah is dynamic and outpouring, for it is the great Stimulator of the universe. Within Chokmah lies the first masculine (Fire) expression as opposed to the androgynous expression of Kether. Whereas Kether is the calm center point of the universe, Chokmah is complete action and movement—the vital energizing element of existence. It is the archetypal Positive and the Great Supernal Father, *Abba*. However, Chokmah is not simply a masculine sexual energy, but rather the *root essence* of masculine or dynamic Force.

BINAH (Bee-nah)
Translation: UNDERSTANDING
Key word: SUPERNAL MOTHER
Yetziratic Title: The SANCTIFYING INTELLIGENCE
Physical Representation: The sphere of SATURN
Symbols: The Womb, the Cup, the Triangle, the letter Heh

Binah, the third Sephirah, whose name means "Understanding" is the feminine counterpart of Chokmah. This sphere is situated at the summit of the left-hand pillar on the Tree of Life. Binah is the Supernal Mother *Aima,* the Great Negative or Female (Water) Force. (By *negative* we mean *receptive* in a purely scientific way, like the positive and negative parts of an atom, not as a value judgment.) Positive and Negative are inseparable properties; one cannot properly function without the other. Receptivity is a feminine attribute, and just as in the case of Chokmah (masculinity), we are again referring to sexual functions in the most basic and unmanifested of concepts. Chokmah, the Sephirah of duality, by necessity overflows into a third sphere in order for another natural polarity to occur.

Binah, the number three, is a sphere which builds Form (another feminine function). Binah receives the overflow of the dynamic current of energy from Chokmah and organizes it for the first time under the concept of Form. *Force* and *Form* are respective male and female properties which occur over and over again on the Tree of Life, but this is where they begin. It must be remembered that at this level on the Tree, the concept of Form exists only as a polarity and as the merest essence of the capacity to build Form, stemming from the excess negative (receptive) energy that has spilled over from Chokmah. Binah as *Ama* is the Disciplining Mother, restricting and structuring the free-flowing energy from Chokmah into what will ultimately be borne into organized Form. The first letter of Binah is Beth, which means "house." Beth is also the archetypal symbol of all containers.

Together, Chokmah and Binah are the two polarizing facets of manifestation, the Supernal Father and the Supernal Mother, whose union results in the birth of the universe. Together, Chokmah and Binah are the "Elohim," the Creator gods referred to in Genesis. They are the two primal building blocks of Life, the archetypal proton and electron, that comprise the whole of creation.

The *Sepher Yetzirah* states this about Binah: "The Third Path is the Sanctifying Intelligence: it is the foundation of Primordial Wisdom, which is called the Creator of Faith, and its roots are AMN; and it is the parent of Faith, from which doth Faith emanate." Here the Yetziratic text implies that Binah is still in a hallowed or blessed state because it remains above the Abyss in an unmanifested condition. Sanctification expresses the idea of that which is holy and set apart. It is given the title, "Primordial Wisdom," because it is the primary source of organization at this stage of divine emanation where a distinct polarity has been defined on the Tree of Life. Binah is here referred to as the "Creator of Faith." Faith rests upon understanding, whose parent is Binah. Faith is also defined as belief and veneration, but in the light of mystical consciousness, faith can be defined as the conscious result of superconscious experience. The average personality is not aware of this faith, but is nonetheless effected and modified by it, possibly with great feeling and emotional intensity. The statement that the roots of Binah are in AMN (*Amen*— meaning "firm," "faithful," and "so be it") refers to Kether. This clearly indicates that, although Binah issues from Chokmah, the source of ultimate Faith or Truth is from the Crown of Kether.

Although Wisdom is the quality of Chokmah, Understanding is assigned to Binah. Wisdom alludes to complete and infinite knowledge, while Understanding imparts the notion of an ability to *grasp* the ideas that are intrinsic to Wisdom.

The Abyss

Between Binah and the rest of the Sephiroth is a great chasm known as the Abyss. This marks a distinct separation between the higher and lower parts of the Tree, a difference in levels of being. The three Supernals of Kether, Chokmah, and Binah symbolize higher states of consciousness that transcend human awareness. The lower Sephiroth operate within the realm of ideas and thus are the only ones we can comprehend with our normal consciousness. In order to understand the intangible essence of the Supernals, one must cross the Abyss, which means leaving the earthly personality and the physical body behind in order to reach the Divine Self. Within the gulf of the Abyss is what is known as the "Invisible Sephirah" of Daath, which is not a true Sephirah, but which can be likened to a passageway across the Abyss.

CHESED (Cheh-sed)
Translation: MERCY
(sometimes called *Gedulah* meaning "Greatness")
Key word: BUILDER
Yetziratic Title: The COHESIVE or RECEPTIVE INTELLIGENCE
Physical Representation: The sphere of JUPITER
Symbols: The Pyramid, the Square, the Orb, the Equal-armed Cross,
the Crook, the Scepter

Chesed is the fourth Sephirah; its name means "Mercy." This is the first sphere below the Abyss, the second Sephirah on the right-hand pillar. It is therefore the first sphere of our physical universe. In Chesed can be found the structural support of all that is manifested. Chesed receives the current of divine energy which has been modified and disciplined by Binah and gives it another influx of energy. This begins the process of materializing the abstract energies of the Supernals (Kether, Chokmah, and Binah). Chesed is the matrix upon which the archetypal ideas will later be built into tangible form. The fourth Sephirah is also the first sphere thus far that may be comprehended by the human mind, because it is the solidification of the abstract ideas formulated by the Three Supernals.

The patterns of the Tree of Life repeat themselves after the initial three spheres are formed; therefore Chesed is the same type of energy as Chokmah, but on a lower, more manifest level. While Chokmah may be likened to an All-Knowing, All-Powerful Father, Chesed is the benevolent, loving and protective Father, who is unselfish and forgiving. However the functions of Chesed are essentially feminine, the aptitude for form-building and materialization. This is because for the first time on the Tree, the idea of manifestation below the Abyss is beginning to coagulate, and the concepts of masculine and feminine (positive and negative) are here beginning to blend together as the process of evolution down the Tree continues. But it must be remembered that Chesed is a Water potency, and that it is the daughter of Chokmah and Binah. As such Chesed shares some similarities with Tiphareth, the offspring of Chesed and Geburah. The *Sepher Yetzirah* says: "The Fourth Path is named the Cohesive or Receptacular Intelligence; and it is so-called because it contains all the holy powers, and from it emanate all the spiritual virtues with the most exalted essences: they emanate one from the other by the power of the Primordial Emanation, the Highest Crown, Kether." The term *cohesive* again refers to Chesed's capacity to gather together all the unmanifested energies (the holy powers) it has received from the Supernals across the expanse of the Abyss. Again these powers or emanations are not in any way diminished as they descend the Tree and continue on the path of materialization.

GEBURAH (Geh-boo-rah or Geh-voo-rah)
Translation: SEVERITY / STRENGTH
Key word: ENERGY
Yetziratic Title: The RADICAL INTELLIGENCE
Physical Representation: The sphere of MARS
Symbols: The Pentagon, the Tudor Rose of Five Petals,
the Sword, the Spear, the Scourge

The fifth Sephirah, positioned below Binah on the left-hand pillar, is called Geburah, which translates as "Strength" or "Severity." Other titles given to this sphere are "Justice" and "Fear" (*Pachad*). Geburah is without a doubt the least understood and most feared Sephirah on the Tree. However, the natural order of the universe depends upon the concept of opposites in balance, thus the benevolence, mercy, and form-building qualities of Chesed are now equilibrated by the harsh, destructive actions of the fifth sphere. Geburah's duty is to break down the Form issued by Chesed and apply discipline in the manner of a purging Fire. Any energy that makes its way down the Tree of Life into the material world must be tested and tempered by the opposites of Mercy and Severity. It must be cleansed in the fires of Geburah. All impurities must be burned away, just as the blade of a strong sword must be tested by the fires of the metalsmith's furnace. Only in this way can the energy be fashioned as a sturdy vehicle for manifestation. Geburah is the strong arm of God, commanding respect and burning away all that is useless or outmoded. The harsh, destructive action of this sphere is absolutely vital to further evolution. The energy of Geburah is not an evil force unless its essence spills over from justice to cruelty. Geburah is essentially a conciliatory power which restricts the merciful love of Chesed. Without the powerful force of Geburah, the mercies of Chesed would deteriorate into frivolity and weakness.

Just as Chesed is the same energy as Chokmah on a lower level, Geburah is a lower form of Binah (the sphere which restricts and disciplines). However, Geburah displays Fire or masculine potency as opposed to Binah's Watery nature. On the other hand some sources insist that Geburah is primarily a feminine energy. It is only recently in our culture that the strength and determination of the feminine side are receiving notice and appreciation. (Nothing is more aggressive and ferocious than a Mother defending her child.) The same is true of Geburah, which aggressively deals with anything that corrupts the Divine current of energy from Kether. Again at this level on the Tree, the mixture of masculine and feminine traits in each sphere is becoming more and more evident. Geburah seems much more harsh and restrictive than Binah, simply because it is below the Abyss, and its effects are more easily seen by us in the manifest universe.

According to the *Sepher Yetzirah:* "The Fifth Path is called the Radical Intelligence, because it resembles the Unity, uniting itself to Binah or Intelligence which emanates from the Primordial depths of Wisdom or Chokmah." The word *radical* here implies basic or fundamental. Here the text tells us that Geburah, the Radical Intelligence, resembles Unity (one of the titles of Kether). Geburah's dynamic action overflowing into the world of form bears a close relationship to the overflowing force of Kether, which is the source of all manifestation. In addition, Unity also implies the uniting of a new and distinct polarity in the spheres of Chesed and Geburah. Geburah "unites itself with Binah" because it is the same restrictive feminine energy of Binah on a lower, more manifest level.

TIPHARETH (T'-fair-eth)
Translation: BEAUTY
Key word: MEDIATOR
Yetziratic Title: The MEDIATING INTELLIGENCE
Physical Representation: The sphere of SOL
Symbols: The Calvary Cross, the Rose Cross,
the Truncated Pyramid, the Cube, the letter Vav

The sixth Sephirah is called Tiphareth or "Beauty." Tiphareth lies at the very center of the Tree of Life on the Middle Pillar (the column of Equilibrium) and receives the powers of all the other Sephiroth. This sphere strikes the harmony between the Mercy of Chesed and the Severity of Geburah; therefore it contains the perfect balance of both benevolent and aggressive energies. Because of its position on the Tree, in line with Kether, Tiphareth mirrors much of the pureness of the Crown, but on a deeper, more manifest level. By the union of Mercy and Justice, Beauty is obtained.

The *Sepher Yetzirah* says: "The Sixth Path is called the Mediating Intelligence, because in it are multiplied the influxes of the emanations, for it causes that influence to flow into all the reservoirs of the Blessings, with which these themselves are united." This again refers to Tiphareth's position on the central pillar, mediating between the Pillars of Mercy and Severity. As a mediator, Tiphareth is also seen as a connecting link between higher and lower states of being (the Higher Self and the Lower Self). This sphere is a "two-way switch" which both receives the influxes of the emanations from above, and "causes that influence to flow into all the reservoirs of the blessings." Tiphareth's neutral position on the central pillar along with its androgynous nature allows the influences to combine, multiply and increase. It is the outward manifestation of the higher and subtler Sephiroth, as well as the spiritual principle behind the lower and more manifest spheres.

Until this point, we have described each Sephirah in abstract terms of Force and Form, Macrocosmic archetypes which are somewhat remote from us. But in Tiphareth, this changes, because the sixth Sephirah lies well within the range of human experience. The rest of the spheres from Tiphareth on down can be increasingly described by the effects they have on human consciousness, than by polarities alone, since the four lowest Sephiroth are symbolic of the Lower Self or Personality (at least on the level of the Microcosm in Malkuth of Assiah).[22]

The center of the Tree of Life is the place of the Reconciler or Redeemer. God-forms of this energy include Christ, Buddha, and Osiris. This is because Tiphareth mediates between the Godhead in Kether and the rest of the material universe. The sixth Sphere is a link or point of transition. It reconciles That Which is Above to That Which is Below. Tiphareth intercedes between these different levels of Being.

The sixth Sephirah is essentially a mystical sphere. The spiritual experience that takes place in Tiphareth is the Vision of the Harmony of Things. This is due to the fact that the Higher Self, or Holy Guardian Angel, of every individual sits in Tiphareth; referring again to Tiphareth as the mirror of Kether—the Divine Self. The goal of all spiritual experience is the search for the Light, which is obtained by devotion to the Great Work. Tiphareth is the sphere of Illumination and of Healing. This is why the so-called Christ-consciousness is placed here.

NETZACH (Net-zäch)
Translation: VICTORY
Key word: EMOTIONS
Yetziratic Title: The OCCULT INTELLIGENCE
Physical Representation: The sphere of VENUS
Symbols: The Girdle, the Rose, the Lamp

The Hebrew name of the seventh Sephirah is Netzach, which means "Victory." It is the final sphere on the right-hand pillar. As we have already stated, the lower spheres of the Tree can be described in terms of human consciousness and experience. This is especially true of the four remaining Sephiroth beginning with Netzach. The sphere of Netzach is the dwelling place of human instincts, emotions, and desires. It is the "feeling" side of the personality that can be likened to the right side of the human brain. This is where human creativity is born. Once again the idea of polarity comes into play, because Netzach is considered primarily a Fire (masculine) sphere which has an opposing (Water) Sephirah to balance it. But at this level on the Tree (in the world of Assiah), we are truly discussing negative and positive sides of the human mind.

Netzach is a dynamic force which inspires and drives us. This sphere is a reflection of the Fiery energy of Geburah, but at the level of the human personality, mediated by Tiphareth, Fire becomes desire and emotion. Art, music, dance, and poetry are all expressions of Netzach energy. In this sphere we find all expressions of beauty and love, but also the less understood emotions of anger and hate, because *all* emotions dwell here. It is for this reason that the energies of Netzach must be balanced by its opposite, Hod. The seventh sphere is the home of the "Group Mind," the storehouse of images and symbols in all of us, which inspires the artist, the dancer, and the musician.

---

[22] The level of humanity in the lowest Qabalistic World of Assiah. See Chapter Two for more information about the four Worlds of the Qabalah.

The *Sepher Yetzirah* says: "The Seventh Path is the Occult Intelligence, because it is the Refulgent Splendor of all the Intellectual virtues which are perceived by the eyes of the intellect, and by the contemplation of faith." The Occult Intelligence obviously refers to Hidden Intelligence. This is something hidden deep within ourselves that we must uncover—our Divine Nature that is kept hidden from us by mundane obstacles. The Refulgent or Brilliant Splendor of the intellectual virtues is the Divine White Light mediated through the prism of Tiphareth, reflected into many-rayed hues (aspects of manifestation). The One Light has been reduced to the many for the purpose of manifestation into form. The phrase "eyes of the intellect" alludes to the Wisdom of Chokmah at the apex of the Pillar of Mercy while the passage "contemplations of faith" refers to the act of devotion, the impetus behind all spiritual attainment.

HOD (Hohd)
Translation: SPLENDOR
Key word: INTELLECT
Yetziratic Title: The ABSOLUTE or PERFECT INTELLIGENCE
Physical Representation: The sphere of MERCURY
Symbols: Names of Power, the Apron (Masonic)

Hod is the eighth Sephirah, situated at the bottom of the Pillar of Severity. Its name means "Splendor" or "Glory." Just as Netzach symbolizes raw animal instincts, Hod represents the intellectual part of the mind to which the "left brain" can be assigned. It is the rational Mind which organizes and categorizes. All expressions of writing, language, communication, science, and magic are assigned to Hod. All words and Names of Power have their origins in this sphere. We also find the idea of the "Individual Mind" here, as opposed to the Group Mind, which is in Netzach. It is the Individual Mind of Hod which makes one aware of one's personal relationship to the Divine.

Hod is a lower form of the energy found in Chesed but mediated through Tiphareth. The energy of Hod is Watery (feminine) and fluidic. Hod and Netzach cannot function properly one without the other. The Eighth Sphere is where the emotions and instincts of Netzach take form and come into action. Intellect needs the balance of emotion to drive it; otherwise the words and science of Hod become mere rational labelings, dead and uninspired. Likewise, emotions need the discipline of intellect to stabilize and ground, to keep the dynamic energy from being squandered. The relationship between Hod and Netzach is symbiotic. In terms of the individual, the two spheres must be in harmony in order to maintain a healthy personality.

According to the *Sepher Yetzirah:* "The Eighth Path is called the Absolute or Perfect Intelligence, because it is the mean of the primordial, which has no root by which it can cleave, nor rest, except in the hidden places of Gedulah, Magnificence, from which emanates its own proper essence." It is the Perfect Intelligence because it is the mean (median) of the primordial. This implies a position halfway between two extremes: Force and Form. Hod is also the seat of the Intellect. To borrow the terms of Astrology, this correlates to the idea of Intellect being in the house of its "dignity"—a placement which is advantageous, or "perfect." Hod's root, from which it cannot be separated, is the watery sphere of Chesed, also called *Gedulah* or magnificence.

YESOD (Yeh-sohd)
Translation: FOUNDATION
Key word: ASTRAL LIGHT
Yetziratic Title: The PURE INTELLIGENCE
Physical Representation: The sphere of LUNA
Symbols: Perfume, Sandals

The ninth Sephirah, Yesod, whose name means "Foundation," is the third Sphere on the Middle Pillar. It is the result of the union between Netzach and Hod. The spiritual experience of Yesod is the vision of the machinery of the universe. What this implies is that Yesod is the sphere of the astral Light, also known as the *Akasha*. This is the etheric substance which underlies all dense matter. It is the astral matrix upon which the physical universe is built. Yesod is the receptacle of influences from all of the preceding Sephiroth, which are then combined into a type of blueprint made from the astral Light. This blueprint is the "Foundation" or Etheric Double upon which the earthly plane is constructed. All events, whether natural or man-made, occur in the aethers of Yesod *before* they occur in the physical world. The ninth Sephirah is that last push which activates the final manifestation of Form. In the same manner, all the Planets were born out of the mind of God, and all man-made inventions first appeared as ideas in the Yesodic part of the inventor's mind. Yesod is the seat of intuition in humankind. In addition, most magical operations take place in the sphere of Yesod, because the magician seeks to effect changes in the physical world by manipulating the subtle currents of the astral.

Like Kether and Tiphareth, Yesod is androgynous, yet the energy here is also sexual, because in Yesod the sexes are for the first time given the form that they will take in the Earthly plane. At this level on the Tree, Yesod is like a pregnant mother about to give birth. Sired by the whole of the Sephirotic influences above it, the child born is the manifest universe itself.

According to the *Sepher Yetzirah:* "The Ninth Path is the Pure Intelligence, so called because it purifies the Numerations, it proves and corrects the designing of their representation, and disposes their unity with which they are combined without diminution or division." The text states clearly that it is Yesod's duty to purify and correct the emanations. Although the emanations which flow down the Tree are intrinsically pure, they may need to be proven or corrected in order to fit them into a vehicle of dense matter. Yesod also disposes (orders) the unity of these emanations, so that only the most worthy manifested vehicles are designed for the reception of the divine energy, which is brought into the physical universe without becoming diminished in any way from its essential purity.

MALKUTH (Mahl-kooth)
Translation: KINGDOM
Key word: COMPLETION, STABILITY
Yetziratic Title: The RESPLENDENT INTELLIGENCE
Physical Representation: The sphere of the EARTH
Symbols: The Equal-armed Cross, the Mystic Circle,
the Triangle of Art (Evocation), Heh Final

Malkuth means "The Kingdom." It is the tenth and last sphere on the Tree of Life which is located at the bottom of the central pillar. This is the ultimate sphere of Form and of final manifestation, the material universe as we know it. Malkuth is essentially the sphere of humanity, and of sensation. The physical representation of Malkuth is the Planet Earth, our own *terra firma*. It is the seat of matter. Yet Malkuth is more than simply the ground beneath our feet, it is also the Sephirah in which all four Elements are based. Therefore when discussing Malkuth (in Assiah), we are really talking about the physical manifestations of Fire, Water, Air and Earth. There are three states of matter which correspond to the elements: solid—Earth, liquid—Water, and gas—Air. (Fire is assigned to the principle of electricity.) The sum of all physical phenomena are classified under the four Elements in order to comprehend their character. All of these Elements are used to describe the material nature of Malkuth.

Malkuth is the ultimate receptacle for the combined currents of energy on the entire Tree of Life. While the other Sephiroth are basically kinetic and mobile, Malkuth is the only sphere that has achieved stability and inertia (a period of rest). It is also the only sphere which is not a part of a triad. The tenth and final sphere receives the etheric framework of manifestation (the influences from Yesod) and completes the building process by grounding the energy in matter. Malkuth is the container for the emanations of the other nine Sephiroth.

As the absolute Sphere of Form and passivity, the fertile Malkuth is also known as the *Inferior Mother* (as opposed to the Great Mother, Binah), the Bride, and the Queen. Another title is the *Gate*, which implies that we as physical beings live out our lives in the realm of Malkuth, only to pass through the Gate upon leaving our bodies behind.

The tenth Sephirah is seen as the completion of the Tree of Life in one sense, and the beginning of a new Tree in another, because Malkuth is a lower reflection of Kether, and is in fact the Kether of another Tree.

According to the *Sepher Yetzirah:* "The Tenth Path is the Resplendent Intelligence, so called because it is exalted above every head, and sits on the throne of Binah. It illuminates the splendor of all the Lights, and causes an influence to emanate from the Prince of Countenances, the Angel of Kether." The title "Resplendent Intelligence" implies a close relationship between Malkuth and Kether, the first and last sphere of the Tree. At this point the emanations are completed and the result is the brilliance of the unified Tree of Life. Malkuth now becomes Kether of another Tree on another level. The mention of the throne of Binah implies another close relationship; Binah, the Great Mother, is the primordial giver of Form, while Malkuth, the Lesser Mother, is the final giver of Form.✿

SECTION 6: The Hebrew Alphabet

The Hebrew Alphabet was originally designed as a pictorial or hieroglyphic alphabet similar to that of the Egyptians. Each letter is a visual representation of an object. In addition to this however, Hebrew is the primary alphabet of Western magic. Not only does each letter have a literal meaning, but also an esoteric meaning, a numerical value, a color, a sound and various other hidden correspondences associated with it. The letters of the Hebrew Alphabet are sacred symbols which attract real forces that the magician can orchestrate by the techniques of visualization and vibration. These letters can also have a psychological influence on the aspirant who meditates upon them—affecting changes in consciousness. The importance of memorizing the Hebrew alphabet cannot be stressed enough, for it is one tool that the magician will use constantly throughout his/her ceremonial workings.

The twenty-two letters of the Hebrew alphabet correspond to the twenty-two Paths of the Tree of Life. Unlike English, Hebrew is written from right to left. In addition to this, all of the Hebrew letters are consonants; there are no vowels. At times the letters Yod and Vav may function as vowels, and the silent letters Aleph and Ayin can be used to indicate the position of a vowel, but again none of these letters *are* vowels. It was not until well into the Christian era that a system for indicating vowels with a *dagesh* (or *pointing*) was developed in order to standardize pronunciation. We will not enter into a discussion concerning the pointing system here, but such information is readily available in modern Hebrew texts.

Please note that five of the Letters (Kaph, Mem, Nun, Peh, and Tzaddi) have two forms associated with them. The second versions of these letters are called *Finals*, and they are used whenever the letter occurs at the end of a word. These Final letters also have different numeric values.

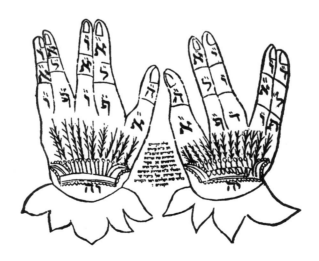

Letter	Power	Value	Final	Name	Meaning
א	A	1		Aleph	ox
ב	B	2		Beth	house
ג	G, Gh	3		Gimel	camel
ד	D, Dh	4		Daleth	door
ה	H	5		Heh	window
ו	O, U, V	6		Vav	pin, hook
ז	Z	7		Zayin	sword, armor
ח	Ch	8		Cheth	fence, enclosure
ט	T	9		Teth	serpent
י	I, Y	10		Yod	hand
כ	K, Kh	20—500	ך	Kaph	fist, palm of hand
ל	L	30		Lamed	ox goad
מ	M	40—600	ם	Mem	Water
נ	N	50—700	ן	Nun	fish
ס	S	60		Samekh	prop
ע	Aa	70		Ayin	eye
פ	P, Ph	80—800	ף	Peh	mouth
צ	Tz	90—900	ץ	Tzaddi	fishhook
ק	Q	100		Qoph	back of the head
ר	R	200		Resh	head
ש	S, Sh	300		Shin	tooth
ת	T, Th	400		Tau	cross

Concerning Pronunciation

During MacGregor Mathers' time, there were two principle dialects in the Hebrew language. They were the *Ashkenazic*, a dialect employed in Germany, Poland, and Russia, and *Sephardic*, which was used in Spain and the Mediterranean. The Golden Dawn teachings stress the Sephardic pronunciation.

      Hebrew words are almost never accented on the first syllable, but usually on the final syllable with secondary accents falling on every other syllable before the final one. The following chart shows the general pronunciations of transliterated Hebrew letters:[23]

Transliterated Letter	Usual transliteration of	Pronunciation
a	vowel point	a as in *Father* or a as in *cat*
b	Beth	b
c	Kaph	k
ch	Cheth (*sometimes Kaph*)	ch in German *nacht*
d	Daleth	d

---

[23] Adapted from information given in David Godwin's *Cabalistic Encyclopedia*, Third Edition (St. Paul: Llewellyn Publications, 1994, pgs. xxii–xxiii.)

dh	Daleth	th in *the* (hard th)
e	vowel point	e as in *met* or e as in *grey*, a as in *sofa*
f	Peh	f
g	Gimel	g as in *gamble* (never like j)
h	Heh *(sometimes Cheth)*	h
i	vowel point; Yod	i as in *fin* i as in *gasoline*; as a consonant, y
j	Yod	y
k	Kaph	k
kh	Kaph	ch in German *ich*
l	Lamed	l
m	Mem	m
n	Nun	n
o	vowel point, Vav	o as in *not* or o as in *obey* (as Vav always the latter)
p	Peh	p
ph	Peh	f
q	Qoph	k
r	Resh	r
s	Samekh, Shin	s
sh	Shin	sh
t	Teth, Tau	t
th	Tau	th as in *thin* (soft th)
ts	Tzaddi	ts as in *tsar, cats*
tz	Tzaddi	ts as in *tsar, cats*
u	vowel point, Vav	u as in *cut* or u as in *glue* (as Vav, always the latter)
v	Beth, Vav	v (or in the case of Vav, may be w)
w	Vav	w
x	—	not used
y	Yod	y
z	Zayin	z

As we have already stated, the letters of the Hebrew alphabet are both hieroglyphs and Holy Symbols which represent real forces. In addition to the literal meaning and numerical value of each letter, a brief investigation of the archetypes and abstract symbolism behind the Hebrew alphabet will yield many arcane insights:

ALEPH (Ah-lef) *meaning*—ox, *value* —1. Aleph is the dual principle that represents all that exists and all that does not exist, the positive and negative, life and death. It represents humanity as a collective unity and as the Ruler of the Earth. Aleph is the glyph of power and stability. The ideas that it expresses are those of unity and of the principle by which it is determined.

BETH (Beth) *meaning*—house, *value*—2. Beth is the symbol of all habitations and receptacles, of anything that "contains." It is virile and paternal; a glyph of active and interior action.

GIMEL (Gi-mel) *meaning*—camel, *value*—3. Gimel is the activity, the motion of contained, limited existence or nonexistence; it is Aleph in Beth. The throat. A canal. Gimel is an glyph which signifies organic development and produces all ideas originating from the corporeal organs and from their action.

DALETH (Dah-leth) *meaning*—door, *value*—4. Daleth is the archetype of physical existence. It is the glyph of nature, divisible and divided, expressing every idea that proceeds from the abundance born of division. The breast: every abundant, nutritive object: all division, all reciprocity.

HEH (Heh) *meaning*—window, *value*—5. Heh is the principle of universal life. Feminine. The breath; all that which animates: air, life, being.

VAV (Vahv, also Vah and Waw) *meaning*—pin or hook, *value*—6. Vav is the archetype of all fertilizing substances. It is the image of a knot which unites, or the point which separates nothingness and being. The Son. It is the universal, convertible glyph which makes a thing pass from one nature to another. The ear: all that is related to sound, noise, and wind.

ZAYIN (Zah-yeen) *meaning*—sword or armor, *value*—7. Zayin is the completed fertilizing act. Every object leading to an end. A symbol of luminous refraction. A staff or arrow.

CHETH (Chayth) *meaning*—fence or enclosure, *value*—8. Cheth is the enclosure of all unevolved cosmic energy. A field. An image of natural or elementary existence; all that which requires work, labor, and effort.

TETH (Tayth) *meaning*—serpent, *value*—9. Teth is the symbol of the initial female energy. A place of surety; a refuge, haven or shelter. An aim or goal. A glyph of resistance and protection.

YOD (Yode) *meaning*—hand, *value*—10. Yod is the opposite of Aleph; it is a steady state, continuity. The finger of a person, the extended hand. Masculinity. All that which indicates the directing power and which serves to manifest it. It is the image of potential manifestation, of spiritual duration, and of the eternity of time.

KAPH (Kahf) *meaning*—fist/palm of the hand, *value*—20 (Kaph Final—500). Kaph is the archetype of receivers. The hand of a person half closed and in the act of taking. An assimilative glyph which receives and makes all forms. Kaph Final is the cosmic final attainment of individual existences.

LAMED (Lah-med) *meaning*—ox goad, *value*—30. Lamed suggests everything which is extended, raised, or displayed. It is the glyph of expansive movement, including all ideas of extension, elevation, occupation, and possession. Lamed is the image of power derived from elevation.

MEM (Mem) *meaning*—Water, *value*—40 (Mem Final—600). Mem is the archetype of the maternal creative principle. Woman or femininity: all that which is fruitful and creative. An image of passive active. Mem Final is the cosmic state of fertility in humanity, both in mind and body.

NUN (noon) *meaning*—Fish, *value*—50 (Nun Final—700). Nun is the archetype of all individual and corporeal existences. The offspring of woman: a child, any fruit whatsoever, every produced or reflected being. Nun Final is the symbol of interplay of cosmic energies.

SAMEKH (Sah-mehk) *meaning*—prop or support, *value*—60. Samekh is the archetype of female fertility, the ovum. An image of all circumscription. It is a glyph of circular movement.

AYIN (Ah-yeen) *meaning*—eye, *value*—70. Ayin is the illuminating principle behind the act of impregnation. It is a glyph of material meaning and physical relations.

PEH (Pay) *meaning*—mouth, *value*—80 (Peh Final—800). The mouth of a person as an organ of speech. Anything relating to speech.

TZADDI (Tzah-dee) *meaning*—fish hook, *value*—90 (Tzaddi Final—900). Tzaddi is a symbol of womanhood in a social sense. Indicates movement toward an end or solution. Tzaddi Final is the archetype of womanhood in a mythical sense.

QOPH (Kohf) *meaning*—back of the head, *value*—100. Qoph is an exalted state of Aleph, transcending the negative or death aspect. A positive arm: all that which serves, defends or makes an effort for humanity. An image of restraint, compression and force.

RESH (Raysh) *meaning*—head, *value*—200. Resh is the archetype of universal or cosmic "containers." The head of a person. All that which possesses in itself a proper and determining movement. It is a glyph of all proper movement, good or bad: an image of the renewal of things and their movement.

SHIN (Sheen) *meaning*—tooth, *value*—300. Shin is the "spirit" of God. A glyph of relative duration and of movement connected therewith.

TAU (Tau) *meaning*—cross, *value*—400. Tau is the archetype of all cosmic existence. A symbol of symbols. An image of that which is mutual and reciprocal. Perfection.✿

Israel Regardie was adamant about the idea that Neophytes should be able to draw the Hebrew letters to the best of their ability. To this end he provided our temples with Hebrew practice sheets for students. Regardie suggested that the student use a calligraphy pen to draw the letters. For the sake of ease and simplicity, we suggest that the Neophyte use a writing instrument called a lettering pen or calligraphy marker. This type of marker has a felt tip which is wide along one edge. The marker can be held with the wide edge of the tip perpendicular to the lines on the practice sheets. The upward/downward and left-to-right movement of the marker across the page will result in the thin vertical lines and the thick horizontal lines.

Always remember that the Hebrew letters are holy symbols and as such they should be carefully and faithfully rendered. The letters are all the same height except for Lamed (which is taller than the other letters) and all of the Finals

Vav Heh Daleth Gimel Beth Aleph

Lamed Kaph Yod Teth Cheth Zayin

Tzaddi Peh Ayin Samekh Nun Mem

Tau Shin Resh Qoph

Tzaddi Final Peh Final Nun Final Mem Final Kaph Final

(except for Mem), which have tails that extend below the other letters. Mem Final is distinguished by being the only oblong letter, thicker in width than in depth. The general idea behind the Hebrew letters is the square formation. The letters should be drawn repeatedly until the student is proficient in recreating them.

On the previous page we have provided a chart that can be consulted when drawing the letters. We have also furnished a chart below that depicts a simple manner of drawing the Hebrew letters. This will prove useful to the student when a quick rendition of the letters is desired. We like to call this form *Simplified Hebrew*. ✿

Simplified Hebrew

Aleph	א	Lamed	ל
Beth	ב	Mem	מ ם
Gimel	ג	Nun	נ ן
Daleth	ד	Samekh	ס
Heh	ה	Ayin	ע
Vav	ו	Peh	פ ף
Zayin	ז	Tzaddi	צ ץ
Cheth	ח	Qoph	ק
Teth	ט	Resh	ר
Yod	י	Shin	ש
Kaph	כ ך	Tau	ת

This concludes the Knowledge Lecture. The information contained therein is to be put to memory. Examinations on the material covered in this section are given at the end of this chapter. The exams will include questions about the initiation ritual as well. ✿

An Additional Side Lecture
THE PILLARS

(from a manuscript lecture by MacGregor Mathers)[24]

In the explanation of the Symbols of the Grade of Neophyte, your attention has been directed to the general mystical meaning of the Two Pillars called in the Ritual the "Pillars of Hermes" of "Seth" and of "Solomon." In the 9th chapter of the Ritual of the Dead they are referred to as the "Pillars of Shu," the "Pillars of the Gods of the Dawning Light," and also as "the North and Southern Columns of the Gate of the Hall of Truth." In the 125th Chapter, they are represented by the sacred gateway, the door to which the aspirant is brought when he has completed the negative confession. The archaic pictures on the one Pillar are painted in black upon a white ground, and those on the other in white upon a black ground, in order to express the interchange and reconciliation of opposing forces and the eternal balance of Light and Darkness which gives force to visible nature.

The black cubical bases represent darkness and matter wherein the Spirit, the *Ruach Elohim*, began to formulate the Ineffable NAME, that Name which the ancient Rabbis have said "rushes through the universe," that Name before which the Darkness rolls back at the birth of time.

The flaming red triangular capitals which crown the summit of the Pillars represent the Triune manifestation of the Spirit of Life, the Three Mothers of the Sepher Yetsirah, the Three Alchemical Principles of Nature, the Sulphur, the Mercury and the Salt.

Each Pillar is surmounted by its own light-bearer veiled from the material world.

At the base of both Pillars rise the Lotus flowers, symbols of regeneration and metempsychosis. The archaic illustrations are taken from vignettes of the 17th and 125th chapter of the Ritual of the Dead, the Egyptian Book of the *Per-em-Hru* or the *Book of Coming Forth into the Day*, the oldest book in the world as yet discovered. The Recension of the Priests of ON is to be found in the walls of the pyramids of the Kings of the 5th and 6th Dynasties at Sakarah, the recension of the 11th and 12th Dynasties on the sarcophagi of that period, and the Theban recension of the 18th Dynasty and onward is found on papyri, both plain and illuminated. No satisfactory translation of these books is available, none having been yet attempted by a scholar having the qualifications of mystic as well as Egyptologist.

The Ritual of the Dead, generally speaking, is a collection of hymns and prayers in the form of a series of ceremonial Rituals to enable the man to unite himself with Osiris the Redeemer. After this union he is no longer called the man, but Osiris, with whom he is now symbolically identified. "That they also may be One of us," said Christ of the New Testament. "I am Osiris" said the purified and justified man, his soul luminous and washed from sin in the immortal and uncreated light, united to Osiris, and thereby justified, and the son of God; purified by

---

[24] From Regardie's *The Golden Dawn*.

suffering, strengthened by opposition, regenerate through self-sacrifice. Such is the subject of the great Egyptian Ritual.

The 17th Chapter of the Theban recension consists of a very ancient text with several commentaries, also extremely old, and some prayers, none of which come into the scheme of the original text. It has, together with the 12th chapter, been very carefully translated for the purpose of this lecture by the V.H. Frater M.W.T [Marcus Blackden], and V.H. Soror S.S.D.D. [Florence Farr] has made many valuable suggestions with regard to the interpretation. The Title and Preface of the 17th Chapter reads:

"Concerning the exaltation of the Glorified Ones, of Coming and Going forth in the Divine Domain, of the Genies of the Beautiful land of Amentet. Of Coming forth in the Light of Day in any form desired, of Hearing the Forces of Nature by being enshrined as a living Bai."

And the rubric is:

"The united with Osiris shall recite it when he has entered the Harbour. May glorious things be done thereby upon earth. May all the words of the Adept be fulfilled."

Owing to the complex use of symbols, the ritual translation of the Chapter can only be understood by perpetual reference to the ancient Egyptian commentaries, and therefore the following paraphrase has been put together to convey to modern minds as nearly as possible the ideas conceived by the old Egyptians in this glorious triumphal song of the Soul of Man made one with Osiris, the Redeemer.

"I am TUM made One with all things.

"I have become NU. I am RA in his rising ruling by right of his Power. I am the Great God self-begotten, even NU, who pronounced His Names, and thus the Circle of the Gods was created.

"I am Yesterday and Tomorrow. I can never more be overcome. I know the secret of Osiris, whose being is perpetually revered of RA. I have finished the work which was planned at the Beginning, I am the Spirit made manifest, and armed with two vast eagle's plumes. Isis and Nephthys are their names, made One with Osiris.

"I claim my inheritance. My sins have been uprooted and my passions overcome. I am Pure White. I dwell in Time. I live through Eternity, when Initiates make offering to the Everlasting Gods. I have passed along the Pathway. I know the Northern and the Southern Pillars, the two Columns at the Gateway of the Hall of Truth.

"Stretch unto me your hands, O ye Dwellers in the centre. For I am transformed to a God in your midst. Made One with Osiris, I have filled the eye socket in the day of the morning when Good and Evil fought together.

"I have lifted up the cloud-veil in the Sky of the Storm. Till I saw RA born again from out the Great Waters. His strength is my strength, and my strength in His strength. Homage to you, Lords of Truth, chiefs who Osiris rules. Granting release from Sin, Followers of Ma where rest is Glorious. Whose Throne Anubis built in the day when Osiris said:

"Lo! A man wins his way to Amentet. I come before you, to drive away my faults. As ye did to the Seven Glorious Ones who follow their Lord Osiris. I am that Spirit of Earth and Sun.

"Between the Two Pillars of Flame. I am RA when he fought beneath the Ashad Tree, destroying the enemies of the Ancient of Days. I am the Dweller in the Egg. I am he who turns in the Disc. I shine forth from the Horizon, as the gold from the mine. I float through the Pillars of SHU in the ether. Without a peer among the Gods. The Breath of my mouth is as a flame. I light upon the Earth with my glory. Eye cannot gaze on my darting beams, as they reach through the Heavens and lick up the Nile with tongues of flame. I am strong upon Earth with the strength of RA. I have come into Harbour as Osiris made perfect. Let priestly offerings be made to me as one in the train of the Ancient of Days. I brood as the Divine Spirit. I move in the firmness of my Strength. I undulate as the Waves that vibrate through Eternity. Osiris has been claimed with acclamation, and ordained to rule among the Gods. Enthroned in the Domain of Horus where the Spirit and the Body are united in the presence of the Ancient of Days. Blotted out are the sins of his body in passion. He has passed the Eternal Gate, and has received the New Year Feast with Incense, at the marriage of Earth with Heaven.

"TUM has built his Bridal Chamber. RURURET has founded his shrine. The Procession's completed. HORUS has purified, SET has consecrated, SHU made one with OSIRIS, has entered his heritage.

"As TUM he has entered the Kingdom to complete union with the Invisible. Thy Bride, O Osiris, is Isis, who mourned Thee when she found Thee slain. In Isis, thou art born again. From Nephthys is thy nourishment. They cleansed thee in thy Heavenly Birth. Youth waits upon thee, ardour is ready at thy hand. And their arms shall uphold thee for millions of years. Initiates surround Thee and Thine enemies are cast down. The Powers of Darkness are destroyed. The Companions of Thy Joys are with Thee. Thy Victories in the Battle await their reward in the Pillar. The Forces of Nature obey Thee. Thy Power is exceeding great. The Gods curse him that curseth Thee. Thine Aspirations are fulfilled. Thou are destroyed who barred Thy way."

The 125th Chapter is concerned with the entry of an Initiate into the Hall of the Two Columns of Justice, and commenced with a most beautiful and symbolic description of Death, as a journey from the barren wilderness of Earth, to the Glorious Land which lies beyond. The literal translation of the opening lines is as follows:

"I have come from afar to look upon thy beauties. My hands salute Thy Name of Justice. I have come from afar, where the Acacia Tree grew not. Where the tree thick with leaves is not born. Where there come not beams from herb or grass. I have entered the Place of Mystery. I have communed with Set. Sleep came upon me, I was wrapped therein, bowing down before the hidden things. I was ushered into the House of Osiris. I saw the marvels that were there. The Princes of the Gates in their Glory."

The illustrations in this chapter represent the Hall of Truth as seen through the open leaves of its door. The Hall is presided over by a God who holds his right hand over the cage of a hawk, and his left over the food of eternity. On each side of the God is a cornice crowned by a row of alternate feathers and Uraei symbolising justice and fiery power. The door leaf which completes the right hand of a stall is called "Possessor of Truth controlling the Feet," while that on the left is "Possessor of strength, binding the male and female animals." The 42 Judges of the Dead are represented as seated in a long row, and each of them has to be named, and the Sin over which he presided has been denied.

This chapter describes the introduction of the initiate into the Hall of truth by ANUBIS, who, having questioned the aspirant, receives from him an account of his initiation, and is satisfied by his right to enter. He states that he has been taken into the ante-chamber of the temple and there stripped and blind-folded, he had to grope for the entrance of the Hall, and having found it, he was reclothed and anointed in the presence of the Initiated. He is then asked for the Pass-words and demands that his Soul should be weighed in the Great Balance of the Hall of Truth, whereupon ANUBIS again interrogates him concerning the symbolism of the door of the Hall, and his answers being found correct, ANUBIS says: "Pass on, thou knowest it."

Among other things the Initiate states that he has been purified four times, the same number of times that the Neophyte is purified and consecrated in the ceremony of the Neophyte. He then makes the long Negative Confession, stating to each Judge in turn that he is innocent of that form of Sin over which he judges. Then he invokes the Judges to do him justice, and afterwards describes how he had washed in the washing place of the South, and rested in the North, in the place called "Son of the Deliverers" and he becomes the Dweller under the Olive Tree of Peace, and how he was given a tall flame of fire and a sceptre of cloud which he preserved in the salting tank in which mummies were swathed. And he found there another sceptre called "Giver of Breath" and with that he extinguished the flame and shattered the sceptre of cloud, and made a lake of it. The initiate is then brought to the actual Pillars, and has to name them and their parts under the symbol of the Scales of a Balance. He also has to name the Guardian of the Gateway, who prevents his passage, and when all these are propitiated, the plea of the Hall itself cries out against his steps, saying "Because I am silent, because I am pure," and it must know that his aspirations are pure enough and high enough for him to be allowed to tread upon it. He is then allowed to announce to Thoth that he is clean from all evil, and has overcome the influence of the planets, and THOTH says to him: "Who is He whose Pylons are of Flame, whose walls of Living Uraei, and the flames of whose House are streams of Water?" And the Initiate replies "Osiris!"

And it is immediately proclaimed: "Thy meat shall be from the Infinite, and thy drink from the Infinite. Thou art able to go forth to the sepulchral feasts on earth, for thou hast overcome."

Thus, these two chapters, which are represented by their illustrations upon the Pillars, represent the advance and purification of the Soul and its union with

Osiris, the Redeemer, in the Golden Dawn of the Infinite Light, in which the Soul is transfigured, knows all, and can do all, for it is made One with the Eternal God.

KHABS AM PEKHT. KONX OM PAX. LIGHT IN EXTENSION. ✥

Ritual Work for the Neophyte

Aside from the memorization of the First Knowledge Lecture, the Neophyte should begin regular practice of the rituals and meditative techniques provided here. These rites create a firm groundwork of ceremonial methods that the student will utilize throughout his/her entire magical life. They also serve as constant reminder of the goal of the path of an initiate.

The Outer Wand of Double Power

This is a simple wand that is employed in the basic Golden Dawn techniques of invoking and banishing. It consists of a dowel that is approximately 20" in length. Half of the wand is painted white for invoking and half is painted black for banishing. ✥

THE QABALISTIC CROSS (QC)

Stand and face East. Imagine a brilliant white Light touching the top of your head. Reach up with the index finger or blade of a dagger to connect with the Light and bring it to the forehead.

Touch the forehead and vibrate, "*ATAH*," (Ah-tah—meaning "*Thou art*").

Touch the breast and bring the dagger blade or index finger down till it covers the heart or abdominal area, pointing down to the ground. Imagine the Light descending from the forehead to the feet. Vibrate "*MALKUTH*," (Mahl-kooth—meaning "*The Kingdom*").

Touch the right shoulder and visualize a point of Light there. Vibrate "*VE-GEBU-RAH*," (v'ge-boo-rah—meaning "*and the Power*").

Touch the left shoulder and visualize a point of Light there. See the horizontal shaft of Light extending from the opposite shoulder to join this point of Light. Vibrate *"VE-GEDULAH,"* (v'ge-doo-lah—meaning *"and the Glory"*).

Imagine a completed cross of Light running from head to feet and shoulder to shoulder.

Bring the hands outward, away from the body, and finally bring them together again, clasped on the breast as if praying. Vibrate *"LE-OLAHM, AMEN,"* (lay-oh-lahm, ah-men—meaning *"Forever, unto the ages"*).✿

THE LESSER BANISHING RITUAL OF THE PENTAGRAM (LBRP)

Stand and face East. Perform the Qabalistic Cross.

Facing East, use the index finger of the right hand, a dagger, or the black end of the Outer Wand of Double Power to trace a large banishing pentagram of Earth. Thrust the dagger/wand tip or index finger through the center of the pentagram and vibrate *"YHVH."* (Yode-Heh-Vav-Heh). (Keep the right arm extended throughout; never let it drop. The pentagrams should be visualized in either a flaming blue or brilliant white Light.)

Turn to the South and trace the same pentagram there. Charge the figure as before, intoning *"ADONAI"* (Ah-doh-nye).

Turn to the West and trace the pentagram. Charge it with *"EHEIEH"* (Eh-hey-yay).

Turn to the North and draw the pentagram, intoning *"AGLA"* (Ah-gah-lah).

Keep the arm extended. Turn to face the East. Extend both arms out in the form of a cross and say, *"Before me RAPHAEL"* (Rah-fahy-el). Visualize before you the great Archangel of Air rising out of the clouds in flowing yellow and violet robes, carrying a Caduceus Wand.

Behind you visualize another figure and say *"Behind me GABRIEL"* (Gah-bree-el). See the Archangel stepping out of the sea like the goddess Venus, dressed in robes of blue and orange, with cup in hand.

See to your right another figure in flaming red and green robes carrying a sword. Say *"On my right hand MICHAEL"* (Mee-chai-el).

See another great Archangel at your left, who rises up from the vegetation of the Earth in robes of citrine, olive, russet, and black, holding stems of ripened wheat. Say, *"On my left hand URIEL"* (Ur-ee-el).

> (Say:) *"For about me flames the pentagram, and in the column shines the Six-rayed Star."*

Repeat the Qabalistic Cross. ✿

Uses of the Pentagram Ritual

This simple yet powerful cleansing ritual can be used as a protection against the impure magnetism of others. It is also a way to rid oneself of obsessing or disturbing thoughts. Give a mental image to your particular thought or disturbance and visualize it before you. Project it out of your aura with the Saluting Sign of a Neophyte, and when it is away from you, prevent its return with the Sign of Silence. Then imagine the form in the East and perform the LBRP. See the form dissolving on the outside of your ring of flaming pentagrams.

The LBRP can be used as an exercise in concentration. While seated or lying down, formulate yourself standing up in robes and holding a dagger. Place your consciousness in this astral form and go to the East. Make yourself "feel" there by touching the wall, opening your eyes, stamping on the floor, etc. Let your astral form perform the ritual, circumambulating the room and mentally vibrating the words. Finish in the East and try to see your results astrally, then walk back and stand behind your physical body and let your astral body be re-absorbed.

The LBRP is to be performed daily for no less than a period of six months. In fact, it should be practiced daily regardless of one's grade. The Golden Dawn manuscripts advocated doing the invoking form of this ritual in the morning and the banishing form at night. However we feel that the Neophyte needs to concentrate solely on the banishing form, since s/he has a tendency to light up on the astral and unknowingly attract all manner of Elementals at this early stage of the Work. It is far more important for the Neophyte to know how to *banish* rather than to invoke. Anyone can attract an Elemental or an energy. Getting rid of the same can be more difficult.✿

ADORATION TO THE LORD OF THE UNIVERSE

Face East and say, *"Holy art Thou, Lord of the Universe!"* Give the Projection Sign. Say, *"Holy art Thou, whom Nature hath not formed!"* Give the Projection Sign. Say, *"Holy art Thou, the Vast and the Mighty One!"* Give the Projection Sign. Say, *"Lord of the Light, and of the Darkness!"* Give the Sign of Silence. (Note: This affirmation should be done daily.)✿

MEDITATION

for the 0 = 0 grade of Neophyte[25]

Let the Neophyte consider a point as defined in mathematics—having position but no magnitude—and let him note the ideas to which this gives rise. Concentrating their faculties on this, as a focus, let him endeavour to realise the *Immanence* of the *Divine* throughout *Nature*, in all her aspects.

Begin by finding a position, balanced, but sufficiently comfortable. Breathe rhythmically until the body is still and the mind quiet. Keep this state for a few minutes at first—and for longer as you get more used to preventing the mind from wandering. Think now of the subject for meditation in a general way—then choose one thought or image and follow that to its conclusion.

The simplest rhythm for the beginner is the Fourfold Breath.

1. Empty the lungs and remain thus while counting 4.
2. Inhale, counting 4, so that you feel filled with breath to the throat.
3. Hold this breath while counting 4.
4. Exhale, counting 4 till the lungs are empty.

This should be practised, counting slowly or quickly till you obtain a rhythm that suits you—one that is comforting and stilling. Having attained this, count the breath thus for two or three minutes, till you feel quiet, and then proceed with the meditation. (Note: this should be done daily for no less than six months.)✿

---

[25] From Regardie's *The Golden Dawn.*

DAILY ADORATIONS

It is important for a magician to feel a link with the Divine Source of the universe every single day. In our modern secular society, human beings can easily become detached from that which is spiritual. In order to reaffirm our awareness of ourselves as beings who are a part of a greater Divine Self, it is important to make a ritual gesture confirming a link between the Eternal and ourselves. This Eternal Self is readily symbolized by the luminary of Sol, the Sun; the symbol of both Light and Life on Earth.

Although the Divine Self is encompassed by the idea of One, Sol, as a visible representation of the Divine is referred to four daily positions: East—Dawn, South—Noon, West—Sunset, and North—Midnight. Consequently, an adoration is directed towards Sol at each of these four positions.

Israel Regardie suggested that the student perform the four adorations from Aleister Crowley's *Liber Resh vel Helios*. We will present these adorations (adapted to include the Neophyte Signs in all four quarters) followed by our own alternative version, *Kheperu Nu Ra*. The choice of which adorations to use is left to the reader.✿

LIBER RESH VEL HELIOS

At Dawn, face East. Make the Sign of the Enterer and say:

> *Hail unto Thee who art Ra in Thy rising,*
> *Even unto Thee who art Ra in Thy strength,*
> *Who travelest over the Heavens in Thy bark*
> *At the Uprising of the Sun.*
> *Tahuti standeth in His splendor at the prow*
> *And Ra-Hoor abideth at the helm.*
> *Hail unto Thee from the Abodes of Night!*

Give the Sign of Silence and stamp the left foot on the ground. At Noon, face South. Give the same gestures as before.

> *Hail unto Thee who art Hathor in Thy triumphing,*
> *Even unto Thee who art Hathor in Thy beauty,*
> *Who travelest over the Heavens in Thy bark*
> *At the mid-course of the Sun.*
> *Tahuti standeth in His splendor at the prow*
> *And Ra-Hoor abideth at the helm.*
> *Hail unto Thee from the Abodes of Morning!*

Give the Sign of Silence. At Sunset, face West. Give the same ritual gestures as before.

Hail unto Thee who art Tum in Thy setting,
Even unto Thee who art Tum in Thy joy,
Who travelest over the Heavens in Thy bark
At the down-going of the Sun.
Tahuti standeth in His splendor at the prow
And Ra-Hoor abideth at the helm.
Hail unto Thee from the Abodes of Day!

Give the Sign of Silence. At Midnight or when retiring, face North. Give the same gestures as before.

Hail unto Thee who art Khephera in Thy hiding,
Even unto Thee who art Khephera in Thy silence,
Who travelest over the Heavens in Thy bark
At the Midnight Hour of the Sun.
Tahuti standeth in His splendor at the prow
And Ra-Hoor abideth at the helm.
Hail unto Thee from the Abodes of Evening!

Give the Sign of Silence. ✿

KHEPERU NU RA

The Evolutions of Ra

At Dawn, facing East, stand in the Sign of the Enterer.

Praise be to thee, O Khepera in thy rising,
Yet unto thee, O Khepera in thy birth,
Hail, thou Disk, Lord of Rays, Lord of Might!
Hail, thou Reborn One, Lord of Life, Lord of Light!
Isis and Nephthys salute thee
O Risen One of the Sky,
Homage to thee, O Khepera, who art the morning's Eye.

Give the Sign of Silence. At Noon, facing South, stand in the Sign of the Enterer.

Praise be to thee, O Ra in thy Zenith,
Yet unto thee, O Ra in thy Strength,
Hail, thou Disk, Lord of Rays, Lord of Might!
Hail, thou Shining One, Lord of Life, Lord of Light!

Isis and Nephthys salute thee
O Brilliant One of the Sky,
Homage to thee, O Ra, who art the Midday's Eye.

Give the Sign of Silence. At Sunset, facing West, stand in the Sign of the Enterer.

Praise be to thee, O Temu in thy setting,
Yet unto thee, O Temu in thy peace,
Hail, thou Disk, Lord of Rays, Lord of Might!
Hail, thou Subsiding One, Lord of Life, Lord of Light!
Isis and Nephthys salute thee
O Fading One of the Sky,
Homage to thee, O Temu, who art the Evening's Eye.

Give the Sign of Silence. At Midnight, facing North, stand in the Sign of the Enterer.

Praise be to thee, O Amon in thy hiding,
Yet unto thee, O Amon in thy veil,
Hail, thou Disk, Lord of Rays, Lord of Might!
Hail, thou Eternal One, Lord of Life, Lord of Light!
Isis and Nephthys salute thee
O Concealed One of the Sky,
Homage to thee, O Amon, who art the Midnight's Eye.

Give the Sign of Silence.✿

Whichever version of the four adorations you choose should be made a regular part of everyday life and practiced until it becomes second nature. Other exercises described in this book may be perform for varying periods of time, but the fourfold adorations are to be integrated permanently into the student's daily routine.✿

THE BERAKAH

(Blessing)

This is a rite of consecration for a meal or feast. The purpose for doing this short ritual is the same as that for the adorations; that is, to constantly remind one of the spiritual nature behind all aspects of life. It is to be performed before eating the main meal of the day. Here the rite is presented so that it may be performed by two people, but it may be just as conveniently performed by one person.

1st Person gives one knock.

2nd Person give one knock.

1st Person give a final knock.

> **1st:** *KHABS.*
>
> **2nd:** *AM.*
>
> **1st:** *PEKHT.*
>
> **2nd:** *KONX.*
>
> **1st:** *OM.*
>
> **2nd:** *PAX.*
>
> **1st:** *LIGHT.*
>
> **2nd:** *IN.*
>
> **1st:** *EXTENSION!*

1st person makes a cross over the meal with his/her right hand and says:

> *May this food, grown in the soil of the Kingdom, maintain our bodies and nourish our souls. Thus sustained, we reach ever toward the heights of Kether.*

2nd person makes a cross over the meal and says:

> *Thus sustained, may we follow the Path of Knowledge that leadeth unto the Light.*

1st Person gives one knock.

2nd Person give one knock.

1st Person give a final knock.

> **1st:** *KHABS.*
>
> **2nd:** *AM.*
>
> **1st:** *PEHKT.*

2nd: *KONX.*

1st: *OM.*

2nd: *PAX.*

1st: *LIGHT.*

2nd: *IN.*

1st: *EXTENSION!✡*

THE RITE OF ELEMENTAL EQUILIBRATION

One objective of the Outer Order is to bring to the initiate an awareness of the inner Elemental make-up of his/her own psyche. This awareness also includes the ability to experience the Elements and balance them in equal portion within the mind.

It is vitally important that the solitary student, working without the aid of an established temple, be able to consciously equilibrate those psychic Elements. Beginning with the Neophyte grade and especially in the higher grades of the Outer Order, the student must be constantly on guard against Elemental imbalance. The simple rite of the Qabalistic Cross is very useful for this purpose; however, we suggest that the student also perform the following Rite of Elemental Equilibration to actively combat such imbalances that may occur during the transformative process of self-initiation. This is a ritual that should be performed regularly, regardless of one's grade status.

Stand facing the East and perform the Fourfold Breath a number of times until you feel relaxed. Imagine a brilliant Light above your head. Reach up with your right hand as if to touch this Light and bring the Light down to your forehead. Imagine the yellow triangle of Air (apex up) superimposed over the upper part of your body. Vibrate, *"SHADDAI EL CHAI"* (Shah-dye El Chai).

Then picture the black triangle of Earth (apex down) covering the lower portion of your body. Bring your hand down as if pointing to the ground and vibrate, *"ADONAI HA-ARETZ"* (Ah-doh-nye Hah-Ah-retz).

Visualize the red triangle of Fire (apex up) superimposed over the right side of your body. Touch your right shoulder and intone, *"YHVH TZABAOTH"* (Yode-Heh-Vav-Heh Tzah-Bah-oth).

Imagine the blue triangle of Water (apex down) covering the left side of your body. Touch your left shoulder and intone, *"ELOHIM TZABAOTH"* (El-oh-heem Tzah-Bah-oth).[26]

Bring both hands together, interlocking the fingers, palms outward, and touch the area of your heart with the your knuckles. Imagine the sigil of the Spirit Wheel in white at the center of your body, uniting the four Elemental triangles. Imagine the Brilliant Light above your head connected with this sigil of Spirit. Vibrate, *"ETH."*

Continue the Four-fold breath and add the following visualizations:

> INHALE—imagine the Fire triangle.
> FULL HOLD—imagine the Water triangle.
> EXHALE—imagine the Air triangle.
> EMPTY HOLD—imagine the Earth triangle.

Strongly imagine all of the Elemental triangles within your aura balanced and in harmony under the guidance of Spirit.✿

BODY AWARENESS EXERCISE

One of the primary aims of any system of spiritual growth is the procurement of self awareness or perception. The only way to increase sensitivity is to become aware—aware of that which is within, as well as that which is without.

Sitting comfortably or lying down, merely attempt to observe what is happening with your own body. Simply watch your physical body and its various sensations. Do not do anything special; breathe normally and don't try to relax or control wandering thoughts. Just try to notice what happens.

After a few moments, find a comfortable position, then stay in it, without moving or consciously fidgeting in any way. Remain perfectly still. At first this exercise should be practiced for no more than ten minutes. Gradually increase the time spent in practice so that by the end of the student's time in the Neophyte grade, this exercise is extended to half an hour. Obviously, this exercise will be simple to some, terribly difficult to others. Any urge to wiggle and release tension should be resisted.

---

[26] This arrangement relates to the four colors of the sphere of Malkuth as projected onto the body of the aspirant. The Fire of Geburah (right shoulder) is reflected across the Tree to Netzach (YHVH Tzabaoth) and reflected back again into the russet quarter of Malkuth. Likewise the Water of Chesed (left shoulder) is reflected across the Tree to Hod (Elohim Tzabaoth) and reflected back again to the olive quarter of Malkuth.

The powers of concentration should also be developed as this awareness exercise is practiced. If the mind begins to wander, gently bring it back. Your powers of concentration will gradually but steadily become enhanced.

During this practice, you may become aware of itching sensations in various parts of your body. Do not attempt to scratch. Merely observe. Simply be aware of various body sensations without trying to alter or ignore them. Do not make judgments or criticisms about these sensations. Accept them as a part of you.

Sensations will come and go in different areas of the body. Study them. It is sometimes a good idea to verbally express what you are feeling or experiencing.

This exercise will result in a profound relaxation of nervous tension. Daily practice will heighten the function of self-awareness, something that is vital to the work of an initiate. All complex ceremonies and rituals actually begin with this heightening of self-awareness.

No special time period needs to be found to practice this. Lying in bed at night or in the morning is certainly an excellent time to rehearse body awareness. This exercise should be done twice daily while in the Neophyte grade. In addition to this, short periods of temporary pause from activity can be taken throughout the day during bathing, shaving or dressing, etc., in order to sharpen one's perceptions and observe what is happening within.✿

EXTRA SENSORY AWARENESS EXERCISE

Obtain a set of ESP cards such as those developed in the parapsychology laboratory at Duke University (for sale at most occult bookstores). The drawings on these cards are simple symbols—one symbol per card.

Shuffle the cards. Place the cards face down and place your hand upon the top card. Make your mind as blank as possible and attempt to guess what image is on the front of the card (square, circle, cross, waves, or star). Go through the entire deck in this fashion, at least once daily. Do not get discouraged if you do not often guess correctly. Record your results.✿

Suggested Reading

Introduction to the First Edition of *The Golden Dawn* by Israel Regardie

Introduction to the Second Edition of *The Golden Dawn* by Israel Regardie

A Garden of Pomegranates by Israel Regardie

The Mystical Qabalah by Dion Fortune

The Training and Work of an Initiate by Dion Fortune

The Kybalion by Three Initiates

"The ABC's of Qabalah" by Harvey Newstrom, published in *The Golden Dawn Journal, Book II, Qabalah, Theory and Magic*

"The Tree of Life, Jacob's Extending Ladder" by Gareth Knight, published in *The Golden Dawn Journal, Book II, Qabalah, Theory and Magic*

Introduction to *The Golden Dawn Journal, Book III, The Art of Hermes*

"Logos Revealed" by Madonna Compton, published in *The Golden Dawn Journal, Book III, The Art of Hermes*

Examinations

(Answers for all exams are given in the back of this book.)

QUIZ 0 *(The Ritual)*

1. Which officer carries the sword of Judgment?
2. What implement is carried by the Dadouchos?
3. Which officer is the Expounder of the Mysteries?
4. How many times is the candidate purified and consecrated?
5. What does the lamp of the Keryx symbolize?
6. What does "Konx Om Pax" mean?
7. What symbols are upon the altar?
8. What does the hoodwink symbolize?
9. What does the black cord symbolize?
10. Why is the altar a double cube?
11. What does the Mystic Circumambulation signify?
12. Which officer watches over the Gateway of the Hidden Knowledge?
13. Who is the Guardian of the Cauldron and the Well of Water?
14. What does the First or Saluting Sign refer to?
15. What do the two pillars represent?
16. The seed of _____ is sown in Silence and grows in darkness and mystery.
17. By _____ and _____ are all Powers awakened and reawakened.

18. Who is Har Par Krat?
19. What does the wand of the Keryx symbolize?
20. What does the Grip of the Neophyte refer to?
21. Which officer is the herald?
22. Which officer is called "Darkness" and "the Great One of the Path of the Shades?"
23. Which officer is referred to as "Light dawning in Darkness?"

QUIZ SECTIONS 1, 2, and 3 (*The Elements, the Zodiac, and the Planets*)

1. List the four Elements and draw their symbols.
2. What is the Element of Heat and Moisture?
3. What is the Element of Cold and Dryness?
4. What is the Element of Heat and Dryness?
5. What is the Element of Cold and Moisture?
6. What is the English name for the Element IGNIS?
7. What is the English name for the Element RUACH?
8. Which Element signifies the human intellect?
9. Which Element signifies the unconscious?
10. List the twelve Signs of the Zodiac and draw their symbols.
11. What is the Sign of Mutable Earth?
12. What is meant by the term "triplicity?"
13. A Quadruplicity of Signs is grouped by _____.
14. List the Signs of the Air Triplicity.
15. List the Signs of the Earth Triplicity.
16. What Signs rule the change of seasons?
17. List the Kerubic Signs.
18. What Signs are also called "Common" Signs?
19. What Signs are also called "Fixed" Signs?
20. Name the Sign whose Key word is Practicality.
21. Name the Sign whose Key word is Versatility.
22. Name the Sign whose Key word is Activity.
23. What is the Sign of Cardinal Air?
24. What is the Sign of Mutable Fire?
25. What Sign is dramatic, self-confident, and romantic?
26. What Sign is nurturing, maternal, and sensitive?
27. What Sign is intense, resourceful, passionate, and aware?
28. What Sign is introspective, charitable, intuitive, and artistic?
29. What is the Sign of Cardinal Earth?
30. What Sign is philosophical, open-minded, and straightforward?
31. List the seven ancient Planets and draw their sigils.
32. What is the Planet of emotions?
33. What is the Planet of expansion?
34. What Planet is known as the Lesser Malefic?
35. What Planet is known as the Greater Benefic?
36. What Planet's action is energizing and stimulating?

37. What Planet is known as "The Teacher?"
38. Give the appropriate sign for:
    a. Venus's exaltation
    b. Luna's detriment
    c. Mars's dignity
    d. Sol's exaltation
    e. Jupiter's fall
    f. Saturn's dignity
    g. Mercury's detriment
    h. Luna's exaltation
    i. Venus's dignity
    j. Uranus's detriment
    k. Neptune's dignity
    l. Pluto's detriment
39. What is the Planet of organization and discipline?
40. List the three "New" Planets and draw their symbols.
41. What is the Head of the Dragon?
42. What is the Planet of transformation?
43. What Planet is known as "The Awakener?"
44. What is the Planet of drug addiction and sleepwalking?
45. What is the Planet of the Inner Self?
46. Name the Planet whose action is sudden, forceful, and disruptive.
47. What is the Tail of the Dragon?
48. What Planet represents the primary feminine principle?
49. What Planet represents the primary masculine principle?
50. Which Element is called *hydor* in Greek?
51. Which Element was seen by the Alchemists as that which operates at the center of all things?
52. What is the English name for the Element MAIM?
53. What is the English name for the Element ARETZ?
54. Which Element signifies materialization?
55. Which Element is the "son" of Fire and Water?
56. What is the Sign of Kerubic Air?
57. List the Signs of the Water Triplicity.
58. List some of the characteristics of the Mutable Signs.
59. List some of the characteristics of the Kerubic Signs.
60. List some of the characteristics of the Cardinal Signs.
61. Which Planet rules the Sign of Virgo?
62. Which Planet rules the Sign of Libra?
63. Which Planet rules the Sign of Taurus?
64. What is the Planet of affection?
65. What is the Planet of competition?
66. Which Planet rules "Frigg's Day?"
67. Which Planet rules "Woden's Day?"
68. Which Planet rules "Tiw's Day?"

QUIZ: SECTIONS 4, 5, & 6:

(The Qabalah, the Sephiroth and the Hebrew Alphabet)

1. What does the word Qabalah mean?
2. The Qabalah is usually classified under four heads. What are they?
3. List the Ten Sephiroth and give their English translations. Also write out the names of the Sephiroth in Hebrew.
4. Which Sephirah is represented by the line, the phallus, and the Yod?
5. Which Sephirah is also called Gedulah?
6. Which is the Mediating Sephirah?
7. Name the Sephirah whose symbols are the Names of Power and the Apron.
8. Name the Sephirah whose physical representation is the Zodiac.
9. Name the Sephirah of the First Motion.
10. Name the Sephirah which represents the "left brain" and the Individual Mind.
11. Name the Sephirah which represents the "right brain" and the Group Mind.
12. Name the Sephirah whose keyword is energy.
13. Name the Sephirah of the astral Light.
14. Name the Sephirah whose physical representation is Sol.
15. Name the Sephirah of completion and stability.
16. Name the Sephirah whose symbols are the Calvary Cross and the cube.
17. Which Sephirah is also called Pachad?
18. Name the Sephirah whose physical representation is Luna.
19. Name the Sephirah whose symbol is the point.
20. Name the Sephirah whose physical representation is the sphere of Saturn.
21. Name the Sephiroth on the Pillar of Severity.
22. Name the Sephiroth on the Pillar of Mildness.
23. Name the Sephiroth on the Pillar of Mercy.
24. The Dogmatic Qabalah involves the study of the Torah. What is another name for the Torah?
25. Which two Hebrew letters have the power of "t?"
26. Which two Hebrew letters have the power of "s?"
27. Which Hebrew letter means "enclosure?"
28. Which Hebrew letter means "back of the head?"
29. Which Hebrew letter means "house?"
30. Name and draw the twenty-two letters of the Hebrew alphabet along with their English equivalents (powers). Also list their numeral values and literal meanings. Include the final letters.

CHAPTER TWO

The Zelator Grade

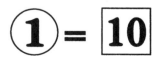

he four Elemental grades beyond Neophyte represent an understanding of the Elements within the psychological and spiritual makeup of the candidate. The initiation ceremonies of these Elemental grades are those of the Zelator, Theoricus, Practicus and Philosophus,[27] which are each referred to one of the four Elements of the Tetragrammaton: Earth, Air, Water and Fire. As a group, these four grades represent the essential work of the Golden Dawn, that is to equilibrate the Elemental forces within the psyche of the aspirant. These "inner Elements" can be characterized as distinct sections of the subconscious mind. The process undertaken by an initiate advancing through the grades is truly an alchemical one; the psychic mechanism of the candidate undergoes a kind of dissolution during the ceremony of the Neophyte. The integral Elements are awakened and purified through the Elemental grade ceremonies, until at length all of the base components are consecrated and integrated back into the psyche of the Initiate.

The first step is of course to awaken the Elemental portions, for unless their existence is realized, the work of alchemical transformation cannot take place. Through symbol and ceremony, the initiation rites of each grade summon forth the spirits and entities of a particular Element. Contact with a specific Elemental force produces a kind of magnetic attraction, whereby the corresponding Elemental energy is awakened within the sphere of the aspirant. Only then can further advancement and growth take place. Thus aroused, the Elemental portions of the mind become consecrated to union with the Higher Self and ultimately to the consummation of the Great Work. This process allows the initiate to bring vast amounts of energy and inspiration from the formerly untapped subconscious depths into the domain of the conscious mind where it can be utilized for further spiritual growth.

The Element offered for the act of transmutation in this grade is Earth—specifically the Earthy part of the aspirant's psyche. This ritual is the first to truly confer the title of *initiate* upon the candidate, symbolically launching his/her initial step onto the Tree of Life. Thus do the numbers 1 = 10 refer to this important first step onto the Tenth Sephirah, Malkuth. The Zelator Grade lays the foundation for all subsequent Elemental transmutations within the aspirant's sphere of sensation. The name *Zelator* comes from a Greek word for "zealot."

---

[27] All of these names, along with that of Neophyte, are titles of traditional Rosicrucian grades.

The only Planet assigned to this grade is *Terra Firma*, the Planet Earth beneath our feet. This is perhaps only one of the reasons why the Zelator grade has such a profound effect on those who attain it. The Zelator Ritual is also meant to ground the candidate firmly in the stabilizing Element of Earth. One of its primary functions is to strengthen the candidate in both mind and body for the difficult work of alchemical transformation which lies ahead. In fact the Zelator Ritual is often said to be the only true initiation ceremony out of all the Elemental grades—the rest being advancements which continue the process started in the 1 = 10. This is due to the fact that the Zelator ritual establishes the aspirant firmly in *Earth of Malkuth*, and the three grades beyond the 1 = 10 explore the other sub-Elements of Malkuth.

The task of a Golden Dawn magician is not an easy one—the very act of advancing through the grades will accelerate any stresses (physical, personal, or mental) that lie dormant within the candidate. Any such difficulties must be confronted and resolved before taking any further grade initiations. This is one of the reasons why we suggest that the student of this course spend a good deal of time in each grade.

The 1 = 10 is also well known as the grade that will separate the wheat from the chaff. Many of those individuals who reach this level, but whose primary motives for getting involved in magic are questionable (escapism, cravings for power or title, or adherence to the current magical "fad") will drop out because of the "filter" effect of the Zelator Ceremony. All of the Elemental grades act to screen out those who cannot bear the task of transformation, but the main thrust of this filtering effect will be felt in the 1 = 10 grade. Israel Regardie often stated that if a magician couldn't function in the Earthy material World of Malkuth, then he had no business attempting to reach the Higher Realms.

The ceremony of the Zelator can be briefly summarized as follows: As in all of the initiation ceremonies presented in this book, the goddess Thme, representative of the candidate's Higher Self, is called upon to safely arbitrate between the divine powers and the aspirant. (Note: A hexagram is formed by the positions of the astral officer/godforms twice in the ceremony, both at the opening and at the closing when the Elemental powers of Earth are being addressed.) After the forces of Elemental Earth are invoked, the candidate is tested on the secrets of the Neophyte grade. The aspirant then swears a further oath and is ceremonially brought to two stations—that of Evil and that of Good. At both of these stations, the Guardians of the Paths repel the unprepared candidate. The aspirant then takes the Middle Path of Equilibrium where s/he is again barred by the Guardians, but eventually the way is cleared by the Guardian of the Celestial Soul. It is during this journey along the path of balance that the stabilizing Element of Earth is established within the aura of the aspirant, so that eventually s/he may prove to be a worthy vessel of the Divine Spirit. The aspirant is at this point *a living cross of manifestation within the white triangle of art* formed by the officer/godforms and represented by the diagram at his/her feet.

In the beginning of this ritual the altar occupies a position much farther East than its previous position in the Neophyte Hall. The pillars are moved well toward the West of the temple. The officers' stations in the Zelator Hall are six in number: Hierophant, Hiereus, Hegemon, Keryx, Stolistes, and Dadouchos. (The station of the Phylax remains outside the Hall.) During the initial part of the ceremony, the stations of these six officers form a triangle, the emblem of Supernal revelation and the symbol of magical evocation. The three lesser officers compose the base, Hiereus and Hegemon (representatives of the opposing Light and Darkness) are beside the altar, and the Hierophant, who personifies the higher powers, is situated at the apex. This triangle, apex upwards, is also a triangle of Fire, which points out a curious relationship that exists between the letters Yod (Fire) and Heh Final (Earth) of Tetragrammaton. (Keep in mind that the group of Angels assigned to Malkuth is known as the Ashim, or the "Souls of Fire." The Admission Badge of this grade, the Fylfot Cross or Swastika, is another key to the puzzle, because it is formed from seventeen squares out of a square of twenty-five lesser squares. Twenty-five is also the number of squares attributed to the Qamea of Mars.) Thus initiation into the Earthy Zelator grade and the sphere of Malkuth indicates that a certain amount of Fire energy is also involved. Since advancement through the Elemental grades symbolizes an Alchemical process of examination and dissolution within the aspirant, it is no surprise that we find a fiery undercurrent infiltrating this initial step onto the Tree of Life.

In the next portion of the ceremony the candidate is then allowed to enter the sanctuary, where s/he symbolically treads the path of a Priest of the Hebrew mysteries. The symbolism of the ancient Tabernacle in the Wilderness, the first physical Qabalistic temple in Malkuth, is gradually revealed to the aspirant. This and other symbolism relating to the Earth grade are disclosed until finally the Earth powers are released.

During this segment in the ritual, the stations of the officers form a cross. The shaft of the cross is created by the three primary officer/godforms in alignment with the altar, while the stations of Stolistes and Dadouchos compose the crossbar. This cross formation stresses the four Elements as a balanced "whole" within the manifest universe, as well as the four sub-Elements of Malkuth. It also implies the need for the balance of psychic Elements within the candidate as well. (Note that the cross surrounded by a circle is the symbol of Malkuth.) The fact that the cross here is composed of five officers (not four or six) alludes to the pentagram, the number of man—the microcosm, and the initiate. But it also refers to the fifth Element of Spirit which surmounts and guides the other four.

Godforms of the Outer Order Grades

Unlike the Neophyte grade, the specific godforms to be employed in the remaining Outer Order grades *are not set and carved in stone*. In the Hermetic community there are differing opinions as to which godforms are present in the Elemental grades. For the purposes of *this* course, we have chosen to use the godforms first introduced in the Neophyte grade: Hierophant = Osiris, Hiereus = Horus, Hegemon = Thme, etc.

The Zelator initiation ceremony introduces three important Archangelic forms to the candidate. They can be visualized during the ritual using the following descriptions.

Archangelic Forms of the Zelator Grade

SAMAEL: (Hebrew meaning *poison of God*) Although described in the Zelator Ritual as an Archangel, Samael is more often described as an Archdemon, or as the Qlippotic force of the Sephirah of Hod on the black pillar. In this ritual Samael is portrayed as the guardian of the Path of Evil who prevents the candidate from journeying upon the Path of Darkness. Samael may be visualized as a black winged bird-like entity with glowing eyes. He wears a robe, tabard and nemyss, all black. He holds a large black sword.

    METATRON: (Hebrew. Possible Greek meaning: *near thy throne*) Metatron is usually described as the most powerful Archangel of Kether. In the Zelator ceremony, Metatron is the Guardian of the Path of Good, and the Kerub of the right-hand pillar. He bars the candidate from entering the Path of Good. Metatron is visualized as a horned male figure with dark hair and beard. He is dressed in a robe, tabard and nemyss, all white. He holds a miter-headed scepter.

    SANDALPHON: (Hebrew. Possible Greek meaning: *Lord of Height*) Sandalphon is described as the Archangel of Malkuth and the Kerub of the left-hand pillar. In the Zelator ceremony, she is the Reconciler for Earth, mediating between Good and Evil on behalf of the candidate. Sandalphon is visualized as a tall horned female figure dressed in a black robe. She wears a tabard in the four colors of Malkuth and a white nemyss. She bears a crown-headed scepter.

    In the months that follow the 1 = 10 initiation, the aspirant must strive to thoroughly absorb knowledge which relates to the Element of Earth. Much of this is presented in the Second Knowledge Lecture given in this chapter, along with other material for the Zelator to study, including sections on the Astrological houses, Alchemy, Geomancy, gemstones and metals, and the Qabalistic hierarchies. The task of the Zelator is to thoroughly assimilate this knowledge and to awaken the stabilizing Element of Earth within, so that further spiritual transmutation of the psychic Elements can take place. The aspirant must never forget the potent statement given in the Ceremony of the 1 = 10: *"Except Adonai build the house, their labor is but lost that build it..."*✿

THE ZELATOR CEREMONY

Temple setup: The aspirant will need to set up the Hall beforehand in accordance with the temple diagram. The black cubical altar is placed in the center of the room. Upon it are the symbols of the cross and triangle (the red cross is within the white triangle). A red lamp or candle is placed on the Eastern side of the altar. On the front of the altar should be a large diagram of the Flaming Sword and the Kerubim. Just in front of the altar on the floor should be a diagram of the cross within the triangle. The pillars are placed just West of the altar. The three Hebrew letters of Shin, Tau and Qoph are shown on large plaques in the East. In this ritual,

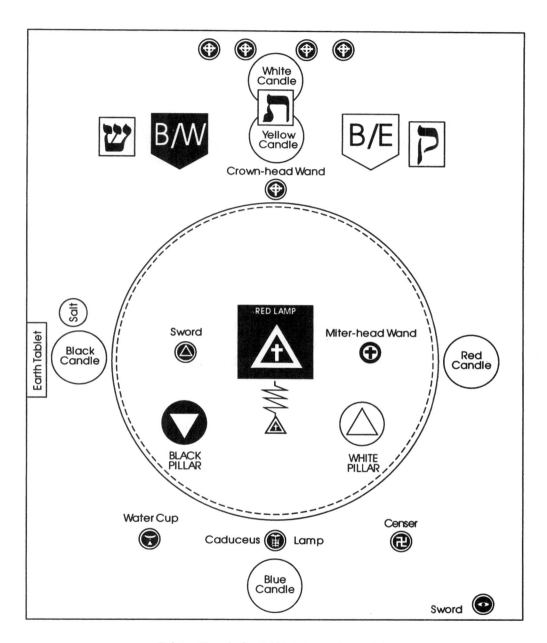

Zelator Temple for Self-Initiation: First Setup

both the Banners of the East and West are located in the East.[28] The Enochian Tablet of Earth is placed in the Northern section of the temple.[29] In front of the Tablet should be a platter of salt and a black lamp or candle for Earth. Place the lamens in accordance with the temple diagram, in the positions of the officer-forms. Place the implements of the officers, the wands, swords, cup and censer, next to the respective lamens.

As in the previous ritual, all of the Elemental candles should be placed around the circumference of the room, with a white candle in the East. The lights on the pillars should be unshaded.

Ritual preparations: As before, it is suggested that the aspirant fast for a period of 12 hours prior to the ritual. During this time the candidate should prepare a small piece of paper upon which is written a particular vice or failing that the aspirant wishes to be rid of. A ritual bath is required after which the aspirant may put on the black Tau robe and red slippers. The sash will need to be decorated with the Zelator designs, but it is not to be worn by the candidate at this time.[30] Place the sash inside the altar. Two diagrams will have to be on hand for the second part of the ritual. They are the *Seven-branched Candlestick* and the *Table of Shewbread*. (These diagrams can be found in the following pages of this chapter.)

The aspirant must meditate for a certain length of time on a drawing of the symbol of Earth—an Earth triangle (apex downward) in black. Next s/he must spend a period of time (20—30 minutes) in a darkened room or antechamber to the temple seated in quiet meditation while wearing a hoodwink or blindfold.) The Admission Badge for the grade of Zelator, the Fylfot Cross, should be held in the right hand throughout this period. A small candle is to be the only source of light in the room. During this time, darkness and silence are to be maintained. The aspirant should imagine him/her self under the watch of Anubis of the West. After this period of time, the hoodwink may be removed. The aspirant may then enter the temple and begin the ritual.

Upon entering the temple, imagine that you are leaving your physical body outside as a sentinel to guard the temple, so that your spiritual self has the freedom to accept initiation.

---

[28] The Banner of the West is shown in the East to block the energies of the three Paths from entering into the temple.

[29] Instructions on how to make this and the other Enochian Tablets are given in our book *Secrets of a Golden Dawn Temple*.

[30] The Aspirant should ornament his/her sash to reflect the Zelator grade. In our temple we have "generic" sashes that candidates may borrow (the Neophyte sash for the beginning of the Zelator grade, for example). At one point in the ritual the Neophyte sash is removed and the candidate is invested with his/her own newly embroidered Zelator sash. However, the solitary student can't afford to make different sashes for different grades. In this case the aspirant will have to forego wearing a sash at the beginning of the ceremony.

PART 0: The Opening

Enter the temple with the Admission Badge of the Fylfot Cross. Salute the Banner of the East with the Neophyte Signs. Leave the cross at the station of the Keryx. Once inside walk deosil to the East. With the Hiereus' sword, perform the LBRP.

Give one knock with the pommel of the sword against the floor or side of the chair and say *"HEKAS, HEKAS, ESTE BEBELOI!"*

Put the sword aside and go to the West of the temple, facing East. Kneel down and invoke the godform of Thmê as in the previous initiation. Vibrate strongly:

> *THMÊ! THMÊ! THMÊ! Thou daughter and eye of RA! Lady of Heaven, Queen of Earth and mistress of the Underworld! Great Lady of all the gods and goddesses. Thou whose name is MAAT! Lady of Truth! Goddess of Justice and Order! Mediator between Darkness and Light, Chaos and Order! THMÊ! THMÊ! THMÊ! Thou who assesseth the heart of every man and woman in the Hall of Judgment before Ousiri and the assembly of the gods. Thou who art the eye and heart of balance! THMÊ! THMÊ! THMÊ! I invoke thee!*

As in your previous initiation rite, visualize the image of the goddess Thmê before you, with human head and yellow-gold skin. She wears a black and white nemyss and a white linen gown. She carries the miter-headed scepter of the Hegemon. Above her head is the white glowing outline of the cross and triangle, symbolic of the outer magical current of the Golden Dawn.

Slowly and with much feeling, perform the Qabalistic Cross, drawing the Light down from the Kether of the universe into the Kether at the crown of your head as you continue the QC. Strongly visualize the cross of Light you have formed in the center of your body. Trace within your heart the Hebrew letters of the name THMÊ in glowing white. Project a white ray of thought from your heart toward the image of Thmê you have created before you. See the figure breathe in life as your thought-ray animates it. Address the form:

> *THMÊ! Beautiful One of the Feather of Truth! I beseech thee to act upon my behalf in this my quest for the Light Divine! Guide me, O thou who art none other but my own Higher Self. Aid me and escort me in this Tabernacle in the Wilderness. I am a true and willing Seeker of Light and Knowledge. Act as my overseer and reconciler in the temple of Malkuth. Speak for me amidst the assembly of the gods and the guardians of this sacred Hall. My intentions are honest. I am ready to undergo test and trial. I am willing to offer sacrifice in the Courtyard before the Holy Place! I wish to be purified and consecrated to the Light. Grant that my heart is made MAAT! Grant that my Will is made MAAT! Merciful THMÊ! Let*

me be judged aright! Grant that this humble aspirant before you be not turned away from that resplendent Light which resides in the East. Award me entrance into the Courtyard of the Sanctuary! Permit me to make an offering of atonement at the Brazen Altar! Grant that I may wash away all impurities in the Laver of Brass! Bestow upon me the right to offer incense upon the Golden Altar before the Veil of the Holy of Holies! Let me penetrate the Threshold in the Path of the Enterer!

Thmê speaks to you in your own mind.

Except Adonai build the house, their labor is but lost that build it. Except Adonai keep the City, the Watchman waketh in vain. I am the representative of your Higher and Holy Self. It is only through my arbitration that thou canst even approach the Sacred Tent. In this Hall I am thy tongue, thy heart and thy mind. Fear not, for I shall guide thee through the temple of Malkuth. I shall direct thee in the courtyard before the Tabernacle in the Wilderness! Fear not, for I shall speak for thee in this assembly of the gods before the powers of Adonai and the current of the Light.

Imagine the goddess Thmê communing in silence with the energies in the East. She speaks on your behalf to the divine guardians of the Hall. You hear her voice as she calls out the names of other godforms in the East of the temple: ESE, NEBETHO, THOOUTH and another, HOOR OUER. You have a vague impression of four figures in the East, seated before a veil. Thmê continues to address the figures, and the scene becomes hazy. It appears that the goddess stands not before the seated figures in the East, but once again before the gigantic form of Thoth—Djehoti—the ibis-headed god of Wisdom. Thmê continues a silent discussion with the god. After a few moments Thmê turns toward you, salutes with the Signs toward the West and says silently:

Thou mayest proceed, O aspirant; thou art MAAT.

Go the Northern side of the altar and make one loud knock with the sword of the Hiereus. Say:

Let the temple be consecrated and purified by Fire and by Water.

Thmê takes you by the hand and leads you clockwise to the Southwest, where she traces the figure of the cross and triangle with the miter-headed wand. As she does so, you vibrate the name *"THAUM-ESH-NEITH"* (Thom-Aesch-Nay-eet) The fiery form of Neith takes shape before you. She bears a red censer. Visualize the figure strongly. The godform of Thaum-Esh-Neith traces in the air before you the figure of a Fylfot Cross. She then hands you her censer. Picking up the censer in the Southwest, you take on the office of Dadouchos that the goddess has bestowed upon you and advance to the center of the Hall from the South side of the white pillar.

With the censer, trace a cross in the air. Then wave the implement thrice in the form of the invoking Fire triangle. Say: *"I consecrate with Fire."*

Return sunwise to the Southwest. Step out of the office of Dadouchos and return the officer-form to the dominion of Thaum-Esh-Neith. Thmê again takes your hand and leads you to the Northwest where she traces the figure of the cross and triangle with the miter-headed wand. As she does so, you vibrate the name *"AURAMOOUTH"* (ow-rah-maht). The beautiful form of Auramoouth takes shape before you. She bears a blue cup. Visualize the figure strongly. The godform of Auramoouth traces in the air before you the figure of a cup. She then hands you her chalice of water. Picking up the Water cup in the North, you take on the office of Stolistes that the goddess has bestowed upon you and advance to the center of the Hall from the North side of the black pillar.

With the cup, trace a cross in the air. Then sprinkle thrice in the form of the invoking Water triangle. Say: *"I purify with Water."*

Return sunwise to the Northwest. Step out of the office of Stolistes and return the officer-form to the dominion of Auramoouth.

Return clockwise to the West. There Thmê traces the figure of the cross and triangle with the miter-headed wand. As she does so, you vibrate the name *"ANOUP EMPEIEBET"* (Ah-noop-em-pay-yeh-bet). The Jackal-headed Anubis begins to formulate in the West. Visualize the figure strongly. Anubis traces in the air before you the symbol of the Caduceus of Hermes. He then hands you his wand and lamp. Picking up the wand and lamp in the West, you take on the office of Keryx that Anubis of the East has bestowed upon you and advance to the center of the Hall from between the two pillars. Say, *"The temple is cleansed."* Salute the Banner of the East with the Neophyte Signs.

Return sunwise to the West. Step out of the office of Keryx and return the officer-form to the dominion of Anubis.

Thmê goes to the station of the Hiereus and traces the figures of the cross and triangle. As she does so vibrate the name of *"HOOR"* (Hoor or Hoh-or). The Hawk-headed god takes shape.

Thmê goes to the South and traces the figures of the cross and triangle at her own station, the station of the Hegemon. She then walks clockwise to the East and traces the cross and triangle at the station of the Hierophant. As she does this you intone the name of *"OUSIRI"* (Oo-seer-ee). The figure of the reborn god formulates there.

Thmê leads you between the pillars. Say:

> *Let the Element of this grade be named that it may be awakened in my sphere, in the spheres of those beings who are present, and in the sphere of*

> *this magical current. The Element is EARTH. Let us adore the Lord and King of Earth!*

Visualize the symbol of the Earth triangle that you meditated on before entering the hall. Imagine its presence in your sphere of sensation around your feet and ankles. Imagine that this same image is activated in all the various officer-forms of the Hall. Then visualize a ball of white Light reflected into your Kether center—at the crown of your head.

Thmê leads you to the East of the temple. Visualize the mummy-wrapped form of Osiris strongly. The god traces in the air before you the figure of a cross and circle. He then hands you his crown-headed scepter. Picking up the Wand of Power, you take on the office of Hierophant that Osiris has bestowed upon you. Give the Sign of the Spiraling Light, then say, *"Let the white brilliance of the Divine Spirit Descend!"* Feel a flood of Divine Light flow through your body from the Kether of the universe. Equilibrate this Light through your body by performing the Qabalistic Cross, loudly vibrating the Hebrew names. Give one knock with the scepter. Say:

> *ADONAI HA-ARETZ. ADONAI MELEKH. Unto thee be the Kingdom and the Power and the Glory.* (Make the cross on yourself with the head of the wand.)

> *Malkuth, Geburah, Gedulah.* (Make the cross and circle in the air with the scepter as these names are spoken.) *The Rose of Sharon and the Lily of the Valley, Amen.*

As the Hierophant, go deosil to the North and sprinkle salt before the Tablet in the form of the invoking Earth triangle. Say: *"Let the Earth adore Adonai!"*

Stand facing the center of the Tablet. Visualize the rest of the astral officer/godforms (except for Keryx) falling into a hexagram position behind you. Hiereus takes his place to right and slightly behind you. Hegemon takes her place to the left and slightly behind you. Stolistes lines up behind Hiereus and Dadouchos lines up behind Hegemon. (Your own position marks the apex of the Fire triangle of the hexagram which points North, while the apex of the inverted Water triangle is marked by the position of the altar.)

Through the authority of the office of Hierophant bestowed upon you by Osiris, invoke the powers of the Earth Tablet. Give a knock, then trace with the scepter of Power a large circle in front of the Tablet. Then draw the invoking pentagram of Spirit Passive. As you do so, vibrate *"NANTA"* (en-nah-en-tah). Trace the sigil of the Spirit wheel in the center and intone *"AGLA"* (Ah-gah-lah). Give the Sign of the Spiraling Light. Then trace the invoking pentagram of Earth. As you do so, vibrate the name *"EMOR DIAL HECTEGA."* Draw the sigil of Taurus in the center and intone *"ADONAI."* Give the Sign of Zelator. Then say:

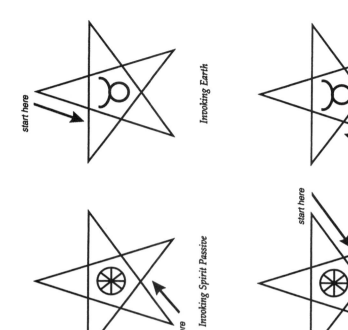

Invoking Earth

Banishing Earth

Invoking Spirit Passive

Banishing Spirit Passive

The Pentagrams of Earth

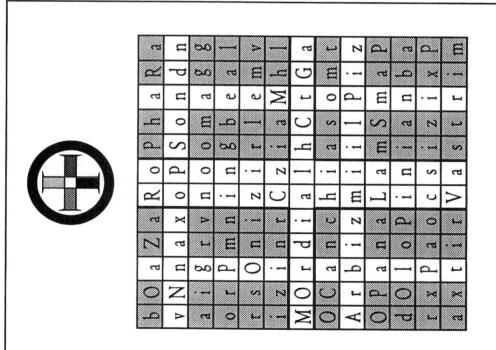

The Enochian Tablet of Earth

The Zelator Sign

And the Elohim said, "Let us make ADAM in our Image, after our likeness and let them have dominion over the fish of the sea and over the fowl of the air and over the cattle and over all the Earth, and over every creeping thing that creepeth over the Earth." And the Elohim created Eth-ha-Adam in their own Image, in the Image of the Elohim created they them. In the name of Adonai Melekh and of the Bride and the Queen of the Kingdom, Spirits of Earth adore Adonai!

Visualize the officer/godform of the Hiereus handing you his sword. Take up the sword of the Hiereus but remain in the officer-form of the Hierophant. Trace with it the sigil of Taurus in the center of the Tablet. Say:

> *In the Name of Uriel, the Great Archangel of Earth, and by the sign of the Head of the Ox—Spirits of Earth, adore Adonai!*

Return the sword. Visualize the officer/godform of the Hegemon handing you her scepter. Go clockwise to the station of Hegemon and take up the wand. Return to the Tablet and trace with the Hegemon's Wand the symbol of the cross. Say:

> *In the Names and Letters of the Great Northern Quadrangle, Spirits of Earth, adore Adonai!*

Return the Hegemon's Wand. Visualize the officer/godform of the Stolistes handing you her cup. Go clockwise to the station of Stolistes and take up the chalice. Return to the Tablet and trace with the cup the symbol of the cross. Then sprinkle thrice in the form of the invoking Water triangle. Say:

> *In the Three Great Secret Names of God, borne upon the banners of the North—EMOR DIAL HECTEGA—Spirits of Earth, adore Adonai!*

Return the cup. Visualize the officer/godform of the Dadouchos handing you her censer. Go clockwise to the station of Dadouchos and take up the censer of incense. Return to the Tablet and trace with the censer the symbol of the cross and wave the implement thrice in the form of the invoking Fire triangle. Say:

> *In the name of IC ZOD HEH HAL, Great King of the North, Spirits of Earth adore Adonai!*

Return the censer. Take up the Hierophant's Wand and return to the East to face West. Imagine all astral officer/godforms returning to their stations.

At this point visualize that the powers of Earth have been fully awakened in the temple, although they have not yet entered into your own sphere of sensation. The Earth energies remain vigilant and ready to follow the dictates of the Hierophant. Say:

> *In the name of ADONAI HA-ARETZ, I declare this temple duly opened in the 1 = 10 grade of Zelator.*

Give the following knocks with the pommel of the scepter: a set of four, followed by three, followed by another three. חוו חו חווו

Visualize the officer/godform of Hegemon repeating the Battery of knocks: 4—3—3. Visualize the officer/godform of Hiereus sounding the knocks: 4—3—3.

Step out of the office of Hierophant and return the officer-form to the dominion of Osiris. Go clockwise to the North and take up the platter of salt. Place it at the foot of the altar. The goddess Thmê leads you to the West of the temple.

PART 1: Advancement—First Segment

Visualize all of the officer/godforms at their respective stations. At this point, the temple has been opened under the guidance of the Guardians of the Hall. You have played an enormously active role in the opening of this Hall, more so than in the previous initiation, and you have already done a great deal of visualization needed to activate the Element of Earth in your sphere of sensation. However at this point, you should take a few moments to re-establish yourself as a candidate who seeks for entrance into this hall. Perform the Qabalistic Cross to maintain a psychic balance of all the Elements within your aura. Recall the experience in the antechamber, where you were blindfolded in the darkness. Restore the persona of the aspirant within you.

Take up the Fylfot Cross in your right hand. Give the Battery of knocks 4—3—3. Stand in the Western part of the temple, facing East and say:

> *This candidate seeks for entrance. I vow it to be true that I (state magical motto) have made such progress in the Paths of Occult Science to have enabled me to pass certain examinations in the required knowledge. Having accomplished this, I am now eligible for advancement to this grade. Let me enter the Portal of Wisdom.*
>
> *Except Adonai build the house, their labor is but lost that build it. Except Adonai keep the City, the Watchman waketh in vain. I seek admission to the 1 = 10 grade of Zelator in the current of the Golden Dawn by the guidance of Adonai, by the possession of the necessary knowledge, by the signs and tokens of the 0 = 0 grade, and by this symbol of the Hermetic Cross.*

Visualize the godform of the Keryx as he approaches you and gestures for the Fylfot Cross. You place it at his station. Osiris in the East speaks to you:

Give the Step and Signs of a Neophyte. (You do so.)

Anubis as the Keryx stands before you and says:

> Give me the Grip of the Neophyte.

You exchange the grip with the Keryx.

> Give me the Word.

You exchange the Grand Word of the Neophyte grade with the Keryx, in alternating syllables: *"HAR PAR KRAT."*

> Give me the Password. (You give the word you have chosen.)

The form of the Keryx turns toward the Hierophant and salutes. The goddess Thmê approaches you from her station and takes you by the right hand. She places you directly between the pillars facing the East. You hear the voice of Osiris:

> Are you ready to take this oath of the 1 = 10 grade?

> (You answer:) *I am ready to take this oath.* (Say:) *I (state magical motto) pledge to maintain and uphold the mysteries of this grade, just as I am pledged to maintain those of the 0 = 0 grade, never to flaunt or reveal them to those who are not true seekers of the Light Divine.*

Thmê assists you to kneel before the altar. Say: *"I swear by the Earth whereon I kneel."*

Still kneeling you take up the platter of salt at the foot of the altar. Take some of the salt in your left hand and cast it to the North and say: *"Let the Powers of Earth witness my pledge."*

Rise and replace the platter of salt in the North. Say: *"Let my pledge be confirmed with Water and with Fire."*

Thmê takes you by the hand and leads you clockwise to the Southwest, where Thaum-Esh-Neith traces in the air before you the figure of a Fylfot Cross. Picking up the censer, return to the threshold between the pillars. With the censer, trace a cross in the air before your own forehead. Then wave the implement thrice in the form of the invoking Fire triangle. Say: *"In the name of the Lord of the Universe who works in silence and whom naught but silence can express, I am consecrated with Fire."* Replace the censer.

Thmê leads you to the Northwest, where Auramoouth traces in the air before you the sigil of the cup. Picking up the chalice of Water, return to the threshold between the pillars. Dip your index finger into the water and mark your forehead with the symbol of the cross. Then sprinkle thrice in the form of the invoking Water triangle. Say: *"In the name of the Lord of the Universe who works in silence and whom naught but silence can express, I am purified with Water."* Replace the cup and return to a position between the pillars. Say:

The 0 = 0 grade of Neophyte is a preparation for other grades, a threshold before discipline, and it shows by its imagery the Light of the Hidden Knowledge dawning in the Darkness of Creation. I am now about to begin to analyze and comprehend the Nature of that Light. To this end I stand between the pillars, in the Gateway where the secrets of the 0 = 0 grade were communicated to me. I shall now prepare to enter the Immeasurable region.

And Tetragrammaton Elohim planted a garden Eastward in Eden, and out of the ground made Tetragrammaton Elohim to grow every tree that is pleasant to the sight and good for food; the Tree of Life also, in the midst of the Garden, and the Tree of Knowledge of Good and of Evil. This is the Tree that has two Paths, and it is the Tenth Sephirah Malkuth, and it has about it seven columns, and the Four Splendors whirl about it as in the Vision of the Merkabah of Ezekiel; and from Gedulah it derives and influx of Mercy, and from Geburah an influx of Severity, and the Tree of the Knowledge of Good and of Evil shall it be until it is united with the Supernals in Daath.

But the Good which is under it is called the Archangel Metatron, and the Evil is called the Archangel Samael, and between them lies the straight and narrow way where the Archangel Sandalphon keeps watch. The Souls and the Angels are above its branches, and the Qlippoth or Demons dwell under its roots.

The officer/form of the Hierophant speaks:

Let the Neophyte enter the Pathway of Evil.

The officer/godform of the Keryx steps in front of you and leads you in a North-Eastern direction to the station of the Hiereus. The form of the Hiereus rises up before you with a threatening attitude. He lunges between you and the Keryx—his sword at your chest. No longer does he have the appearance of Mighty Horus. He has instead taken on the countenance of a dark menacing bird-like being with flaming ruby colored eyes.

Whence comest Thou? (He snarls.)

(You answer:) *I come from between the two pillars and I seek the Light of the Hidden Knowledge in the Name of Adonai.*

The dark Angel seems somewhat appeased.

And the Great Angel Samael answered and said: I am the Prince of Darkness and of Night. The foolish and rebellious gaze upon the face of the created World, and find therein nothing but terror and obscurity. It is to them the Terror of Darkness and they are as drunken men stumbling in the Darkness. Return for thou canst not pass by.

Keryx leads you back the way you came. The voice of the Hierophant is again heard:

> Let the Neophyte enter the Pathway of Good.

The Keryx leads you in a Southeastern direction to the station of Hegemon. The figure of the Hegemon rises in a majestic attitude like the crest of a mighty wave. No longer do you recognize the familiar face of Thmê. The officer has taken on the appearance of a powerful and brilliant white being with horns of Light and velvet hair and beard. His miter-headed wand comes down between the Keryx and yourself like a wall of ice falling from a glacier.

> Whence comest thou? (He thunders.)

> (You answer:) *I come from between the pillars, and I seek the Light of the Hidden Knowledge in the Name of Adonai.*

> (The figure replies:) The Great Angel Metatron answered, and said: I am the Angel of the Presence Divine. The Wise gaze upon the created world and behold there the dazzling image of the Creator. Not yet can thine eyes bear that dazzling Image. Return for thou canst not pass by.

Keryx takes you back the way you came. The Hierophant speaks:

> Let the Neophyte enter the straight and narrow Pathway which turns neither to the right hand nor to the left hand.

Keryx leads you straight up the center of the hall. When Anubis is near the altar he stops and steps aside, leaving you to face the altar unobstructed. Stand upon the cardboard diagram of the cross and triangle on the floor as if you are the cross of the Elements which is to be evoked within the triangle of art.

The Hiereus and Hegemon as Samael and Metatron cross their weapons before the altar to bar you.

> Whence comest thou? (They demand.)

> (You reply:) *I come from between the pillars and I seek the Light of the Hidden Knowledge in the name of Adonai.*

Visualize the Hierophant advancing toward you. No longer do you recognize the face of Osiris. The officer has taken on the appearance of a very tall feminine Archangel with horns upon her head. She is dressed in the four colors of Malkuth. She approaches the altar and suddenly thrusts her scepter beneath the crossed implements of the Hiereus and the Hegemon. With a powerful upward motion, she raises her wand to an angle of 45 degrees, knocking the crossed implements of the other officers to either side. She speaks:

> But the Great Angel Sandalphon said, I am the reconciler for Earth, and the Celestial Soul therein. Form is alike in Darkness and in blinding Light. I am the left hand Kerub of the Ark and the Feminine Power, as Metatron is the right hand Kerub and the Masculine Power, and I prepare the way to the Celestial Light.

Imagine the forms of the Hiereus and the Hegemon stepping back respectively to the North and South of the altar.

The Archangel Sandalphon takes your right hand in her left hand and instructs you to examine the diagram on the front of the altar. As you do so say:

> *And Tetragrammaton placed Kerubim at the East of the Garden of Eden and a Flaming Sword which turned every way to keep the Path of the Tree of Life, for He has created Nature that humanity being cast out of Eden may not fall into the Void. He has bound Man with the Stars as with a chain. He allures him with scattered fragments of the Divine Body in bird and beast and flower, and he laments over him in the Wind and in the Sea and in the birds. When the times are ended, He will call the Kerubim from the East of the Garden, and all shall be consumed and become Infinite and Holy.*

Sandalphon comes around to the West of the altar to give you the secrets of the 1 = 10 grade. Prompted by the figure, you give the 6 x 6 step, which is similar to that of the Neophyte, but with the addition of bringing the right foot even with the left, showing that you have passed the Threshold. Then give the Zelator Sign by raising your right hand to an angle of 45 degrees. Sandalphon speaks:

> This was the Position in which I interposed for you between the Hiereus and the Hegemon. The Token is given by grasping fingers, the thumb touching thumb to form a triangle. It refers to the Ten Sephiroth.

You exchange the Token with the Archangel. She continues:

> The Grand Word is ADONAI HA-ARETZ, which means "the Lord of the Earth," to which Element this grade is allotted. The Mystic Number is 55, and from it is formed the Password Nun Heh. It means ornament, and when given is lettered separately.

> (You repeat the words:) *The Grand Word is ADONAI HA-ARETZ. The Mystic Number is 55. The password of the grade is NUN-HEH.*

> (Sandalphon continues:) The Badge of this grade is the sash of the Neophyte with the narrow white border, a red cross within the white

triangle, and the numbers one within a circle and ten within a square, also white, one on each side of the triangle.

Open the altar and remove the Zelator sash. As you put it on, visualize the Archangel Sandalphon investing you with the sash. She then points to the three Hebrew letters in the East of the Hall and says:

> The three Portals now facing you in the East are the Gates of the Paths which lead to the three further grades. They represent the Paths which connect the Tenth Sephirah Malkuth with the other Sephiroth. The letters Tau, Qoph and Shin make the word Qesheth—a Bow, the reflection of the Rainbow of Promise stretched over our Earth, and which is about the throne of God.

Visualize the Hegemon as she points out the diagram on the front of the altar. Examining it you say:

> *Before me is a drawing of the Flaming Sword of the Kerubim. It is a representation of the Guardians of the Gates of Eden, just as the Hiereus and the Hegemon symbolize the Two Paths of the Tree of the Knowledge of Good and of Evil.*

Imagine the form of the Hiereus gesturing at the emblems upon the altar. Observing it you say:

> *In this grade, the red cross is placed within the white triangle upon the Altar, and it is thus the symbol of the Banner of the West. The triangle refers to the Three Paths and the cross to the Hidden Knowledge. The cross and the triangle together represent Life and Light.*

The Hierophant as Sandalphon points out the Tablet of the North. She takes you by the hand and leads you to the North. As you inspect it say:

> *This grade is especially referred to the Element of Earth, and therefore, one of its principal emblems is the Great Watchtower or Terrestrial Tablet of the North. It is the Third or Great Northern Quadrangle or Earth Tablet, and it is one of the four Great Tablets of the Elements said to have been given to Enoch by the Great Angel Ave. It is divided within itself into four lesser angles. The mystic letters upon it form various Divine and Angelic Names, in what our tradition calls the Angelic secret language. From it are drawn the Three Holy Secret Names of God, EMOR DIAL HECTEGA, which are borne upon the banners of the North, and there are also numberless names of Angels, Archangels and Spirits ruling the Element of Earth.*

Go to the station of the Keryx and visualize the form of Anubis handing you the Fylfot Cross. Take up the cross and return with it to the West of the altar. Say:

The Hermetic Cross, which is also called Fylfot, Hammer of Thor, and Swastika, is formed of 17 squares out of a square of 25 lesser squares. These 17 represent the Sun, the four Elements, and the Twelve Signs of the Zodiac.

(Observe the pillars and say:) *In this grade the lights on the pillars are unshaded, showing that I have abandoned the Darkness of the outer world.*

Sandalphon returns to the East where she transforms once again into the godform of Osiris. The outer appearances of the Archangels Metatron and Samael are also shed to reveal the forms of Thmê and Horus. Thmê speaks to you:

> You have entered into the Immeasurable region where the Kerubim guard the Gates of Eden. Prepare this temple to reflect the ancient temple in the Wilderness, the Tabernacle of Adonai. Prepare thyself to pass through the Threshold of the Divine Wisdom.

Anubis leads you out into the antechamber where you spend a few moments rehearsing the Fourfold Breath and meditating on the image of the Flaming Sword. Perform the Qabalistic Cross to once again equilibrate the Elemental energies within your aura. When ready, set up the temple in accordance with the final part of the ritual.

Changes in the temple setup for the second segment of the ritual: pillars are moved to the West of the altar. Remove the diagram of the Flaming Sword. The diagram of the Table of Shewbread should be placed in the Northeastern part of the Hall, while that of the Seven-branched Candlestick belongs in the Southeast. Upon the altar should be the cross within the triangle, a cup of water to the left, a red candle or lamp to the right, and a censer of incense at the apex of the triangle. The station of the Hegemon is on the Western side of the altar. The station of the Hiereus is in the West of the temple. The station of the Stolistes is behind the black pillar. The station of Dadouchos is behind the white pillar. The station of the Keryx is in the Northwest. The Phylax is without the Hall. Leave the Water cup of Stolistes and the censer of Dadouchos in the West of the temple just inside the door. Have the piece of paper that you prepared earlier close at hand.

PART 2: Advancement—Second Segment

After setting up the hall, spend a few moments in relaxed meditation in the antechamber. Visualize the Earth triangle once more and perform the Qabalistic Cross. When finished, stand just outside the temple door and give the Battery of knocks: 4—3—3. Visualize all of the astral officer/godforms at their respective stations. Anubis bids you to enter. Remain just inside the door. The voice of Osiris speaks to you from the East:

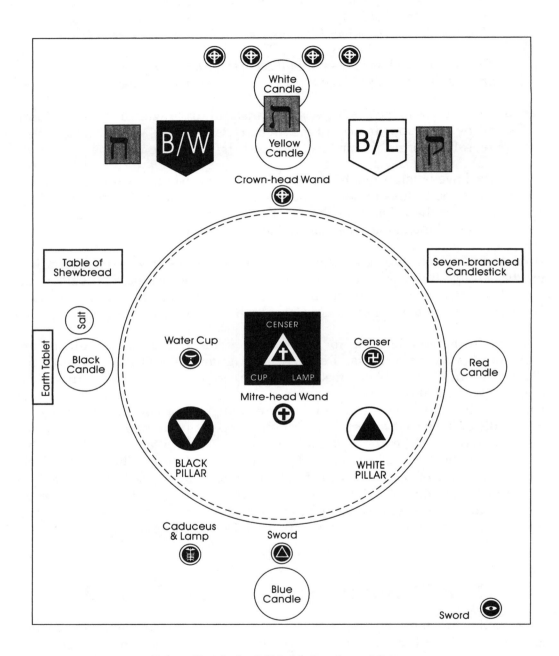

Zelator Temple for Self-Initiation: Second Setup

118

Frater/Soror _____, as in the grade of Neophyte, you came out of the world to the Gateway of Hidden Knowledge, so in this grade you pass through the Gateway and come into the Holy Place.

(Say:) *I am now in the Court of the Tabernacle, where stood the Altar of Burnt Offering, whereon were offered the sacrifices of animals, which symbolized the Qlippoth or Evil Demons who inhabit the plane contiguous to and below the Material Universe.*

Visualize the godform of Thaum-Esh-Neith leaving her station near the pillar. She approaches you and traces the symbol of the Fylfot Cross in the air before you. The goddess then hands you her censer. Picking up the censer you trace the symbol of a cross in front of your own forehead. Then trace the three points of the invoking Fire triangle.

At this point, picture in your mind's eye the Courtyard of the Tabernacle as it existed in the time of the ancient Hebrews. Take some time to imagine the following guided visualization:

The Courtyard is oblong in shape, approximately 150 by 75 feet in size. The walls of the Courtyard are composed of great curtains of blue, violet and red, supported by brass pillars with capitals of pure silver. There are twenty pillars running along each side of the courtyard's length, and ten pillars along the sides comprising the width. At the far end of the Courtyard is the Tabernacle or Sacred Tent of YHVH. But in the middle of the Court stands the Altar of Burnt Offering.

The altar is a large hollow case approximately seven and a half by four and a half feet in size. It is made of wood and overlaid with plates of brass. In the center of the top side of the altar is a grating of brass upon which several pieces of wood have been placed. At the four corners are projections known as "horns." On the sides of the altar are brass rings through which bars are placed to carry the altar.

Still watching with your mind's eye, you witness a Priest of the Hebrew mysteries about

The Courtyard of the Tabernacle

The Altar of Burnt Offering

to make the perfect sacrifice to the Almighty One on behalf of the entire congregation of the Camp. A bearded High Priest with a tall triple miter-headdress, jeweled breastplate and embroidered robes oversees the entire operation as several people lay their lands upon the garland-covered head of an ox, confessing their personal sins and shortcomings. At the appropriate time in the ceremony, the officiating priest slays the animal, and its blood is caught in basins by other attendant priests. The sight of the animal being slaughtered startles you—you are not accustomed to witnessing such archaic and bloody practices of worship. But you realize that what you are watching is something that happened ages ago when everything concerning human existence was a struggle, and often a bloody one. You are secure in the knowledge that today, in your own time, such blood sacrifices are no longer essential to spiritual beliefs that the idea of sacrifice is a symbolic one that can entail the sacrifice of one's lower personal desires to higher goals.

Prayers are recited continuously as the ox is cut into twelve pieces, all of which are placed upon the burning wood of the altar. The blood of the slain animal is sprinkled around the base of the brazen altar and smeared upon the four horns at the corners. The entire animal is consumed by the flames, as if sent to God on wings of fire. The flame burns continuously; never is it allowed to go out.

As you continue to meditate on the Altar of Burnt Offering, place your personal offering of paper into the censer of Dadouchos until it is wholly consumed. Contemplate this action as part of your desire to become more than human. Imagine yourself taking up a golden censer at the foot of the altar. See yourself taking some of the coals from the brazen altar and placing them within the censer along with some incense.

When you feel ready, bring your consciousness back to the Zelator Hall. Put down the censer of Dadouchos and say:

> *Between the Altar and the entrance to the Holy Place, stood the Laver of Brass wherein the Priests washed before entering the Tabernacle. It was the symbol of the Waters of Creation.*

Visualize the godform of Auramoouth leaving her
station near the pillar. She approaches you and traces
the symbol of the chalice in the air before you. The
goddess then hands you her cup. Picking up the
Water cup you dip your fingers into the fluid. Trace
the symbol of a cross on your own forehead. Then
trace the three points of the invoking Water triangle.

The Laver of Brass

At this point return in your mind's eye to the guided
visualization of the Courtyard of the Tabernacle in
the Wilderness and imagine the following:

> Past the brazen altar where the remains of the sacrifice are still
> burning, you see before you a huge Laver or vessel made of brass. It
> is quite large and round, standing upon a square brazen foot. The
> foot forms a hollow basin for receiving water which falls from sev-
> eral faucets on the main body of the Laver. The entire surface of the
> Laver is adorned with figures of Kerubic creatures and palm trees.
>
> As a new sacrifice is prepared for the altar, several priests
> come forward to wash pieces of the slain beast for a more perfect
> offering. Other priests use the water from the Laver's spigots to
> wash their feet and hands before entering the Holy Place. Their
> prayers are incessant, along with the sound of splashing water.
>
> As you continue to meditate on the Brazen Laver, dip your
> finger into the cup of Stolistes. Mark in succession a small cross on
> your forehead, breast, right shoulder and left shoulder while per-
> forming the Qabalistic Cross. (Think of this action as part of your
> desire to unite with the Divine Self.)

When you feel ready, bring your consciousness back to the Zelator Hall. Put down
the cup and say:

> *Having made offering at the Altar of Sacrifice, and having been cleansed at
> the Laver of Brass, the Priest then entered the Holy Place.*

The astral officer/godforms of Stolistes and Dadouchos return to their stations.
Anubis as the Keryx leads you to the West of the temple. He then leads you forward
toward the imposing figure of the Hiereus (Horus) who guards the Path between
the pillars and who now threatens you with his sword. Horus speaks:

> Thou canst not pass the Gateway which is between the pillars,
> unless thou canst give the Signs and Words of a Neophyte.

You give the Projection Sign and the Sign of Silence. Then you give the Step and
exchange the Neophyte Grip, along with the Grand Word *"HAR-PAR-KRAT"* with
the Hiereus. Satisfied with your performance, the Hiereus steps back to his posi-

tion in the West of the temple. Instructed by the Keryx, you advance between the pillars. The form of the Hegemon (Thmê) rises East of the pillars to bar your further progress into the temple with her scepter. Thmê speaks:

> **Thou canst not enter the Holy Place, unless thou canst give the Sign and Grip of a Zelator.**

You give the Zelator Sign and Step. You then exchange the Grip of the grade with the officer/godform. Thmê nods as Anubis returns to his station. She speaks:

> **Having made Offering at the brazen altar, having been cleansed at the Laver, and having passed the tests prescribed for thee, thou mayest enter the Holy Place.**

Take a step forward toward the altar. At this point return in your mind's eye to the guided visualization of the Courtyard of the Tabernacle in the Wilderness. Imagine the following:

> Past the Laver of Brass is the entrance to the Tabernacle. The structure itself is a large and magnificent tent supported by boards of wood overlaid with gold and silver. Four successive coverings of curtains cover the sides of the Tabernacle. The three outer curtains are constructed from goats' hair, badger skins and red-dyed ram skins. The entrance into the sanctuary is composed of curtains hung from seven mighty pillars.
>
> In your mind's eye you enter the outer chamber of the Tabernacle known as the Holy Place. The inner curtain is a sensuous linen embroidered with the figures of the Kerubim in blue, violet and red. Surrounded on all sides by such rich decorations, you notice that to your left is a low table of bread, to your right is a large candelabrum, and in the center of the room is a golden altar, beyond which is a curtain of sumptuous cloth that veils the innermost Sanctuary, as yet concealed from you. The scent of Frankincense fills the room.
>
> The officer/godform of the Hegemon takes you by the hand and leads you Northeast of the altar, where a diagram is located. In your mind's eye you picture an oblong golden table with legs. Upon this table are placed twelve

The Table of Shew-bread

cakes of bread in two rows of six each, with frankincense between each loaf. In addition to the Sabbath bread, there are golden bowls, vessels of wine and two small censers of burning incense.

Thmê brings your focus back to the diagram at hand. (See diagram page 196.) Examining it you say:

To the Northern side of the Holy Place stood the Table of Shew-bread. The drawing before me represents its occult meaning. On it twelve loaves were laid as emblems of the Bread of Life, and it is an image of the Mystery of the Rose of Creation. The twelve circles are the twelve Signs of the Zodiac, while the lamp in the Center is symbolic of the Sun, which is the source of heat and life. The Four triangles whose twelve angles each touch one of the twelve circles are those of Fire, Earth, Air, and Water, and allude to the four Triplicities of the Zodiacal Signs. The triangle inscribed within each of the twelve circles, alludes to the three Decanates, or phases of ten degrees of each Sign. On one side of each triangle is the permutation of the Divine Name, Yod Heh Vav Heh, which is referred to that particular Sign, while on the opposite side of it is the name of one of the Twelve Tribes which is also attributed to it.

The twenty-two sounds and letters of the Hebrew alphabet are the foundation of all things. Three Mothers, Seven Double and Twelve Simples. The Twelve Simple letters are allotted to the twelve directions in space, and those diverge to Infinity, and are in the arms of the Eternal. These Twelve letters He designed and combined, and formed with them the Twelve Celestial Constellations of the Zodiac. They are over the Universe as a King traversing his dominions, and they are in the heart of man as a King in warfare.

The Twelve loaves are the images of those ideas, and are the Outer Petals of the Rose, while within are the Four Archangels ruling over the Four Quarters, and the Kerubic emblems of the Lion, Man, Bull and Eagle.

Around the great central lamp which is an image of the Sun, is the Great Mother of Heaven, symbolized by the letter Heh, the first of the Simple Letters, and by its number five, the Pentagram, Malkah the Bride, ruling in her kingdom Malkuth, crowned with a crown of Twelve stars.

The twelve circles further represent the twelve Foundations of the Holy City of the Apocalypse, while in Christian symbolism the Sun and the twelve signs are referred to Christ and his Twelve Apostles.

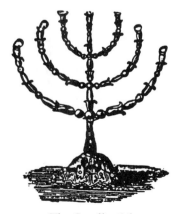

The Candlestick

The Hegemon leads you back to the officer/godform of the Hiereus in the West. The Hiereus then brings you Southeast of the altar to the diagram of the Seven-branched Candlestick. Continue the guided visualization of the Tabernacle as before. Imagine the following:

(In your mind's eye you return to the Holy Place where a large golden candelabrum is located opposite the Table of Shewbread. The implement is huge, nearly six feet in height and almost as wide, weighing about one hundred pounds. Made of beaten gold, the candlestick is composed of a base with a shaft rising out of it, six arms which come out by threes on opposite sides of the shaft. The arms and the shaft are ornamented with seventy-two almond-shaped cups, apples and flower blossoms. Each of its seven lamps ends in a cup-shaped depression supplied with cotton and olive-oil, enough to burn through the night until morning.)

The Hiereus brings your focus back to the diagram at hand. (See diagram on page 198.) Examining it you say:

> On the Southern side of the Holy Place stood the Seven-branched Candlestick, wherein was burned pure olive oil. It is an image of the Mystery of the Elohim, the Seven Creative Ideas. The symbolic drawing before me represents its occult meaning. The Seven circles which surround the Heptagram represent the Seven Planets and the Seven Qabalistic Palaces of Assiah, the Material World—which answer to the Seven Apocalyptic churches which are in Asia or Assiah—as these again allude to the Seven lamps before the throne on another Plane.
>
> Within each circle is a triangle to represent the Threefold Creative Idea operating in all things. On the right-hand side of each is the Hebrew Name of the Angel who governs the Planet, on the left-hand side is the Hebrew Name of the sphere of the Planet itself, while the Hebrew letter beneath the base is one of the duplicated letters of the Hebrew alphabet which refer to the Seven Planets.
>
> The Seven Double Letters of the Hebrew alphabet each have two sounds associated with them, one hard and one soft. They are called "Double" because each letter represents a contrary or permutation: Life and Death, Peace and War, Wisdom and Folly, Riches and Poverty, Grace and Indignity, Fertility and Solitude, Power and Servitude.
>
> The Seven letters point out seven localities, Zenith, Nadir, East, West, North, South, and the Place of Holiness in the midst sustaining all things. The Archetypal Creator designed, produced, combined and formed with them the Planets of the Universe, the Days of the Week, and in Man, the Gate of the Soul. He has loved and blessed the number seven more than all things under his throne. The powers of these seven letters are also shown

forth in the seven Palaces of Assiah, and the Seven Stars of that Vision are the seven Archangels who rule them.

The Hiereus leads you to the West of the altar facing East. The form of Osiris descends from the Dais and stands just East of the altar. He traces in the air before you the symbol of the circled cross, endowing you with the office of Hierophant.

You take up the censer from the altar and trace with it the symbol of the cross, and give three forward swings. Replace the censer. Continue the guided visualization of the Tabernacle. Imagine the following:

> In your mind's eye, return to the Holy Place in the Tabernacle, where you stand before a golden altar. This is the altar said to stand before Adonai in front of the Veil of the Most Holy Place. It is made of wood overlaid with pure gold and is in the shape of a double cube. Like the Altar of Burnt Offering, it has four horns at its corners which are of one piece with the rest of the altar. It has a top or roof on which the incense is laid and lighted. The altar also has a cornice of gold and four golden rings to receive wooden staves for carrying it. The incense burned thereupon every morning and evening is a sacred composition of spices. The scent of the perfumed smoke fills you with renewed vitality.

(Say:) Before the Veil of the Holy of Holies, stood the Altar of Incense, of which this Altar is an Image. It was of the form of a double cube, thus representing material form as a reflection and duplication of that which is spiritual. The sides of the Altar, together with the top and bottom, consist of ten squares, thus symbolizing the Ten Sephiroth of which the basal one is Malkuth, the realization of the rest upon the material plane, behind which the others are concealed. For if this cube were raised in the air immediately above my head, I would but see the single square forming the lowest side, the others from their position being concealed from me. Just so, behind the Material Universe, lies the concealed form of the Majesty of God.

The Altar of Incense was overlaid with Gold to represent the highest degree of purity, but the Altar before me is black to represent the terrestrial Earth. I must learn then to separate the pure

The Altar of Incense

from the impure, and refine the Gold of the Spirit from the Black Dragon, the corruptible body. Upon the Cubical Altar are Fire, Water and Incense, the Three Mother Letters of the Hebrew alphabet, Aleph, Mem and Shin. Mem is silent, Shin is sibilant, and Aleph is the tongue of a balance between these contraries in equilibrium, reconciling and mediating between them. In this is a great Mystery, very admirable and recondite. The Fire produced the Heavens, the Water, the Earth, and the Air is the reconciler between them. In the year, they bring forth the hot, the cold and the temperate seasons, and in man, they are imaged in the head, the chest, and the trunk.

Return to the guided visualization. See yourself in the Holy Place before the altar. Take the golden censer that you obtained at the Altar of Burnt Offering and pour out the coals and incense upon the golden altar. As you visualize this, perform the Qabalistic Cross.

Then direct your attention to the Most Holy Place beyond the Altar of Incense. This is the Holy of Holies—the most sacred portion of the Tabernacle. It is separated from the Holy Place by a Veil which is always kept closed and shrouded in darkness. The Veil is made from fine linen, richly embroidered with blue, violet, and red, and ornamented with figures of the Kerubim. Not yet are you permitted to enter this most sacred chamber—this privilege is granted but once a year on the Day of Atonement to the High Priest who has passed through the mysteries by right of initiation. However within your mind's eye, you are able to visualize the inner chamber, which contains only the Ark of the Covenant.

The Ark is an oblong chest of wood inlaid with gold, with a golden miter around the top. The upper side or lid is a plate of pure gold comprising the Mercy Seat. Two golden Kerubim are placed at either end of the lid. These beings are composite creatures who assume a stooping position over the Ark, overshadowing and protecting it with their expanded wings. They are the Right-hand and Left-hand Kerubim of the Ark, Sandalphon and Metatron. Within the Ark itself are the Stone Tablets of the Law, and above the whole arrangement the Glorious Light of God is said to reside.

As you meditate upon the Holy of Holies and its contents, imagine that you have now firmly established yourself as an initiate of the mysteries. The Light above the Cover of the Ark signifies that you have passed through the Threshold of the Enterer with your

The Ark of the Covenant

feet steadfastly anchored to the sphere of Malkuth in Assiah represented by the Tabernacle in the Wilderness. The Light of the Supernal Kether is reflected into your own Kether (Kether of Assiah), forming a connecting link. The sub-Element of Earth in Malkuth has been established within your aura and within your psyche.

Bring the focus of your conscious mind back to the Zelator Hall. Perform the Adoration to the Lord of the Universe toward the East. Return the office of Hierophant to the dominion of Osiris in the Eastern part of the Hall. Hear the voice of the god speaking to you:

> I now confer upon you the Mystic Title of Periclinus (Pericline)[31] de Faustis, which signifies that on this Earth you are in a Wilderness, far from the Garden of the Happy. And I give you the symbol of ARETZ which is the Hebrew name for Earth, to which the grade of Zelator is referred.

> (Visualize the triangle of Earth. Then say:) *The word Zelator is derived from the ancient Egyptian Zaruator, signifying "Searcher of Athor," goddess of Nature, but others assign to it the meaning of the Zealous student whose first duty was to blow the Athanor of Fire which heated the Crucible of the Alchemist.*

Go to the Southwest to face Anubis of the East. The god traces the sigil of the Caduceus before you. Take up the Caduceus Wand and the lantern. Walk to the Northwest and say:

> *In the Name of ADONAI MELEKH, hear ye all, that I* (state magical motto) *proclaim to have duly initiated myself to the 1 = 10 grade of Zelator, and that I have obtained the Mystic Title of Periclinus (Pericline) de Faustis and the symbol of Aretz.*

Replace the wand and the lamp in the Southwest. Return to the West of the altar and face East. Visualize the following:

> In your mind's eye see yourself standing and facing the Gate to the astral temple of Malkuth. A large door is in front of you. The door is divided into four colors: citrine, olive, russet, and black. The colors form triangles which come together in the center of the door. Carved into this door is the letter Mem painted in white. The two Archangels of Samael and Metatron stand before you, blocking your final passage into Malkuth with their implements. You hold up the Fylfot Cross and proclaim that you have received the Mystic Title of Periclinus de Faustis. The Archangel Sandalphon appears and knocks the

---

[31] Pericline is the feminine form.

implements of the other Archangels aside with her mighty scepter. She permits you final entrance into the Earthy temple of Malkuth. Astrally, you give the Neophyte Signs followed by the Sign of a Zelator and then step through the door into Malkuth.

The temple is a great ten-sided chamber with walls built from heavy earthen bricks. The floor is divided into black and white tiles. Enormous oak columns support the ceiling of pure rock crystal. On the Southern side of the temple is a great roaring hearth, and to the West is a fountain in the shape of an eagle—water flowing from its open mouth. To the North is a large black ox turning a mill which slowly grinds out crushed grain. In the East is a large brazier of incense. The scent of Dittany fills the air. In the middle of the chamber stands a black altar carved out of oak. It is covered by a cloth which is divided into the same colors as the door to the temple. The center of the altar top is white, and upon it is a bright burning flame.

The Archangel Sandalphon remains at your side. This is her abode. She is the guardian of the Gateway into the many unseen worlds. Sandalphon has brought you here and you instinctively know that you will see her many more times during your initiatory journeys.

Bring the focus of your conscious mind back to the Zelator Hall. Say the following:

In the Zelator grade, the symbolism of the Tenth Sephirah Malkuth is especially shown, as well as the Tenth Path of the Sepher Yetzirah. Among other Mystic Titles, Malkuth is called SHAAR, the Gate, which by metathesis becomes ASHUR, meaning the number ten. Also in Chaldee it is called THRAA, the Gate, which has the same number as the Great Name ADONAI, written in full: Aleph, Daleth, Nun, Yod, which both equal 671 in total numeration. It is also called the "Gate of Death," "The Gate of Tears," and the "Gate of Justice," the "Gate of Prayer," and "The Gate of the Daughter of the Mighty Ones." It is also called "The Gate of the Garden of Eden" and the Inferior Mother, and in Christian symbolism, it is connected with the Three Holy Women at the foot of the cross. The Tenth Path of the Sepher Yetzirah which answereth to Malkuth is called "The Resplendent Intelligence," because it exalts above every head and sitteth upon the throne of Binah. It illuminateth the Splendor of all the Lights—the ZOHAR ME-OUROTH—and causeth the current of the Divine Influx to descend from the Prince of Countenances, the Great Archangel Metatron.

PART 3: The Closing

Go to the Eastern part of the Hall. There the godform of Osiris traces before you the symbol of the circled cross, bestowing upon you the office of Hierophant. Taking on the officer-form of the Hierophant, you knock and say:

> *Let us adore the Lord and King of Earth.* (Turn to the East and visualize the Earth triangle. Say:) *ADONAI HA-ARETZ, ADONAI MELEKH, Blessed be Thy name unto the countless ages. Amen.* (Give the Sign of Zelator.)

Go Deosil to the North. Stand facing the center of the Earth Tablet. Visualize the rest of the officer/godforms falling into a hexagram position behind you. Hiereus takes his place to right and slightly behind you. Hegemon takes her place to the left and slightly behind you. Stolistes lines up behind Hiereus and Dadouchos lines up behind Hegemon. The Keryx is behind you. Recite the Prayer of the Gnomes or Earth Spirits:

> *O Invisible King, Who, taking the Earth for Foundation, didst hollow its depths to fill them with Thy Almighty Power. Thou whose Name shaketh the Arches of the World. Thou who causest the Seven Metals to flow in the veins of the rocks, King of the Seven Lights, Rewarder of the subterranean Workers, lead us into the desirable Air and into the Realm of Splendor. We watch and we labor unceasingly, we seek and we hope, by the twelve stones of the Holy City, by the buried talismans, by the Axis of the Lodestone which passes through the center of the Earth—O Lord, O Lord, O Lord! Have pity upon those who suffer. Expand our hearts, unbind and upraise our minds, enlarge our natures.*

> *O Stability and Motion! O Darkness veiled in Brilliance! O Day clothed in Night! O Master who never dost withhold the wages of Thy Workmen! O Silver Whiteness—O Golden Splendor! O Crown of Living and Harmonious Diamond! Thou who wearest the Heavens on Thy Finger like a ring of Sapphire! Thou Who hidest beneath the Earth in the Kingdom of Gems, the marvelous Seed of the Stars! Live, reign, and be Thou the Eternal Dispenser of the Treasures whereof Thou hast made us the Wardens.*

Through the authority of the office of Hierophant bestowed upon you by Osiris, banish the powers of the Earth Tablet. Trace with the Scepter of Power a large circle in front of the Tablet. Then draw the banishing pentagram of Spirit Passive. As you do so, vibrate *"NANTA"* (en-nah-en-tah). Trace the sigil of the Spirit wheel in the center and intone *"AGLA"* (Ah-gah-lah). Give the Reversal Sign of the Spiraling Light. Then trace the banishing pentagram of Earth. As you do so, vibrate the name *"EMOR DIAL HECTAGA"* (Ee-mor Dee-ahl Hect-tay-gah). Draw the sigil of Taurus in the center and intone *"ADONAI."* Give the Sign of Zelator.

(Give the License to Depart by saying:) *Depart ye in peace unto your abodes. May the blessing of Adonai be upon you. Let there be peace between us, and be ye ready to come when ye are called.* (Return the office of Hierophant to the godform of Osiris.)

The goddess Thmê comes to your side. Both of you walk to the station of Dadouchos where Thmê traces the figure of the cross and triangle. The godform of Thaum-Esh-Neith salutes with the Projection Sign—Thmê answers with the Sign of Silence. The godform of Thaum-Esh-Neith slowly fades from view. In this manner, Thmê releases all the godforms in the Hall: Auramoouth, Anubis, Horus, Osiris, and the godforms on the Dais. All the astral entities in the Hall begin to fade from view.

Thmê herself is once again the last godform to dissolve. You thank the goddess for guiding you in the Zelator Hall. You then trace the figures of the cross and triangle before her. She salutes you with the Projection Sign. You answer with the Sign of Silence. Withdraw the white ray which had activated the godform back into your heart center. Perform the Qabalistic Cross one last time to equilibrate all energies within your sphere of sensation.

Take up the sword and perform the Lesser Banishing Ritual of the Pentagram.

(Go to the East and say:) *In the Name of ADONAI MELEKH, I declare this temple to be duly closed in the grade of Zelator.* (Give the Battery of Knocks: 4—3—3. Go to the station of Hiereus and give the Battery: 4—3—3. Do the same at the station of Hegemon: 4—3—3. Give the Zelator Sign when exiting the temple.) The rite is finished. ✿

The Second Knowledge Lecture

SECTION 1: Basic Astrology—The Houses

 A "house" is an *arc* (a portion of a curved line) which is one-twelfth of the Zodiacal wheel. Spatially, the houses are 30 degrees each, one-twelfth of the 360 degree circle. Whereas the Signs in a horoscope are fixed divisions of the heavens, the houses are relative sections of the heavens which depend on the time and place of an individual's birth. The Earth's rotation causes the Planets and the Signs to pass daily through all of the twelve houses. The first house begins at 0° of the Ascendant.

A house symbolizes a basic area of activity. The interpretation of the houses varies when they are inhabited by Planets.[32] Each house is ruled by one of the Planets and is influenced by one of the Zodiacal Signs.

---

[32] Keep in mind that although a house may not always contain a planet, it does not mean that there is no activity in that region.

The Sign that is on the Eastern horizon at the time of birth is called the *Rising Sign* or the *Ascendant*. Since the houses never alter their position, with respect to the Earth, the Ascendant or first house cusp is always on the Eastern horizon, where Sol rises daily. The *Descendant* or seventh house cusp is always on the Western horizon where Sol sets.

The *Midheaven* (Latin: *medium coeli*), also called the *MC*, is the tenth house cusp at the top or Southern point of a Zodiacal chart. Opposite to this is the *IC* (from Latin: *imum coeli*, the lowest heavens) or fourth house cusp at the lowest or Northernmost point on the chart.

Cusp: A Cusp is an imaginary line which separates a Sign from adjoining Signs, and a house from its adjoining houses. It is a small arc in close proximity to the boundary line between neighboring Signs and houses, which causes uncertainty as to the Planet's location and influence at a particular moment. A Planet in a cusp between houses can be influenced by both houses (and Signs) affected by the cusp. A birth Planet is stronger in a cusp than in the later degrees of a house.

Decanate or *Decan:* A ten degree arc or subdivision of the Zodiacal wheel. A house contains three decanates, which are called the first, second and third decan. There are a total of 36 decanates in a Zodiacal wheel.

House Division by Element

Since each house is ascribed to one of the twelve signs, the houses can be categorized in accordance to the ruling Element of the signs:

Fire Houses

First, fifth and ninth houses. Individuals with several Planets in Fire houses are energetic, motivated, enthusiastic, spiritual and inspirational.

Water Houses

Fourth, eighth and twelfth houses. Individuals with several Planets in these houses are emotional, intuitive, and sensitive.

Air Houses

Third, seventh and eleventh houses. Individuals with several Planets in these houses are sociable, communicative, intelligent and interested in others.

Earth Houses

Second, sixth and tenth houses. Individuals with several Planets in these houses are stable, practical, and hardworking.

House Division by Quality

The houses, like the signs, can be defined by quality into three groups of four houses each. These qualities coniorm with those of the Cardinal, Kerubic and Mutable Signs, but in the houses they are called Angular, Succedent and Cadent.

Angular Houses

First, Fourth, Seventh and Tenth houses. These correspond to the Cardinal Signs. The "angles" refer to axes of the Horoscope or the four Cardinal Points (including the Ascendant, Descendant, MC and IC). When a Planet is in an Angular house, its influence is magnified and has great potential for vigorous action.

Succedent Houses

Second, Fifth, Eighth and Eleventh houses. The word "succedent" implies that they succeed or follow the Angular houses. Like the Kerubic Signs, they give steadiness and resolve. They are known as the Financial houses.

Cadent Houses

Third, Sixth, Ninth and Twelfth house. These correspond to the Mutable Signs. They are neither dynamic like the Angular houses nor stable like the Succedent houses, but are adaptable and accommodating. These are often labeled the Mental houses.

FIRST HOUSE
Element: Fire   *Quality:* Angular
Natural Sign: Aries   *Natural Ruler:* Mars
Key word: IDENTITY

The first house cusp is one of the most important points of a Natal chart. It is a house of beginnings and appearances. It shows natural disposition and personality, and represents the physical body and the primary outlook on life.

SECOND HOUSE
Element: Earth   *Quality:* Succedent
Natural Sign: Taurus   *Natural Ruler:* Venus
Key word: VALUES

The second house alludes to resources, possessions, values, earning ability and financial affairs. It refers to inner talents, self-worth, individual freedom and material gain or loss.

THIRD HOUSE
Element: Air   *Quality:* Cadent
Natural Sign: Gemini   *Natural Ruler:* Mercury
Key word: AWARENESS

The third house portrays communication, transportation, short trips, mental skills, learning ability, primary education, and brothers and sisters. It represents the conscious and objective portion of the mind.

FOURTH HOUSE
Element: Water   *Quality:* Angular
Natural Sign: Cancer   *Natural Ruler:* Luna
Key word: SECURITY

The fourth house depicts home, parents, character foundation, heritage and ancestry. It shows property, real estate, the parent who had the greater influence on an individual, the closing years of life, and endings.

FIFTH HOUSE
Element: Fire   *Quality:* Succedent
Natural Sign: Leo   *Natural Ruler:* Sol
Key word: CREATIVITY

The fifth house is the house of love given to another, romance, pleasure, love affairs, amusements, sports, speculations, originality and creativity. It shows children, social affairs, and artistic abilities.

SIXTH HOUSE
Element: Earth   *Quality:* Cadent
Natural Sign: Virgo   *Natural Ruler:* Mercury
Key word: DUTY

The sixth house characterizes work, service given, employment, health, diet, hygiene, clothing, and personal habits. It also shows dependents, pets, aunts and uncles.

SEVENTH HOUSE
Element: Air   *Quality:* Angular
Natural Sign: Libra   *Natural Ruler:* Venus
Key word: COOPERATION

The seventh house describes marriages, partnerships, contracts, agreements, and all dealings with the public. It shows cooperation or lack of cooperation with others, personal agents, open enemies and grandparents.

EIGHTH HOUSE
Element: Water   *Quality:* Succedent
Natural Sign: Scorpio   *Natural Ruler:* Pluto (and Mars)
Key word: REGENERATION

The eighth house delineates spiritual and physical regeneration, secrets, occult matters, hidden factors, sex, rebirth, degeneration and death. It shows moral, financial and spiritual support received from others, as well as inheritance, wills, trusts and partner's assets. It is known as the house of surgery and in conjunction with the Sixth house, it describes types of illness.

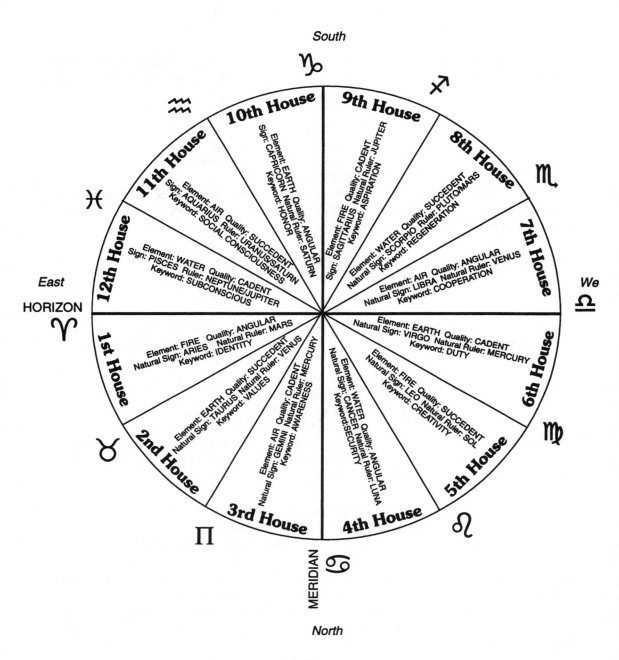

The Houses

NINTH HOUSE
Element: Fire   *Quality:* Cadent
Natural Sign: Sagittarius   *Natural Ruler:* Jupiter
Key word: ASPIRATION

The ninth house characterizes philosophy and the higher consciousness. It depicts ideals, ethics, religion, intuition, spirituality, visions, higher learning and mental study. It also portrays long-distance travel, grandchildren, in-laws and foreign affairs.

TENTH HOUSE
Element: Earth   *Quality:* Angular
Natural Sign: Capricorn   *Natural Ruler:* Saturn
Key word: HONOR

The tenth house reveals status, reputation, fame, profession and community standing. It portrays the ego, ambition, achievements, honors, promotion, influence, authorities, social and business activities. Here we find the parent other than the one indicated in the fourth house.

ELEVENTH HOUSE
Element: Air   *Quality:* Succedent
Natural Sign: Aquarius   *Natural Ruler:* Uranus (and Saturn)
Key word: SOCIAL CONSCIOUSNESS

The eleventh house indicates friends, acquaintances, all nonemotional relationships. It shows goals, desires, hopes and wishes, love received, humanitarian interests, foster children, organizations which relate to career, and circumstances beyond one's control.

TWELFTH HOUSE
Element: Water   *Quality:* Cadent
Natural Sign: Pisces   *Natural Ruler:* Neptune (and Jupiter)
Key word: SUBCONSCIOUS

The twelfth house depicts hidden strengths, dangers and weaknesses, as well as limitations, sorrows, secrets, hidden enemies, self-undoing, places of confinement and clandestine affairs. It is the house of the subconscious and of karmic debt. The Twelfth house is known as the dust-bin of the horoscope because it is here that people tend to hide their problems.

The Meridians

The meridians are lines drawn on a zodiacal chart which help to further interpret the Horoscope. The horizontal axis of the chart is known as the *horizon* or *equator*, and the vertical axis is known as the *meridian*. Each axis divides the chart in half.

The Horizon axis alludes to *awareness*. It separates the Horoscope into *Day* and *Night* sections, because it partitions the chart along the Dawn-Dusk (East-West) axis from 6 A.M. to 6 P.M. As a general rule, the Day half (upper half) of the chart symbolizes objectivity and extroverted tendencies, while the Night half alludes to instinct, subjectivity and introverted tendencies.

The Meridian or vertical axis refers to strength. It separates the chart into Eastern and Western sections from noon to midnight. This axis divides the Planets into *Rising Planets* and *Setting Planets*. A large number of rising Planets in the Eastern half denote a free and strong Will—it is the embodiment of a planting or sowing incarnation. Numerous setting Planets in the Western half indicate flexibility and involvement with the future of others —it is an indication of a harvesting incarnation.✧

SECTION 2: Basic Alchemy

 The word *Alchemy* is an Arabic term comprised of the article *al* and the noun *khemi*. The later word relates to *Khem* the Coptic name of Egypt. Alchemy thus means "that which pertains to Egypt." Thus the words Alchemy and chemistry are a reminder of the scientific legacy of Egypt. Another possible origin of the word is the Greek *cheo* which means "I pour" or "I cast": a word often used in reference to the ancient Greek metalworkers who used many Alchemical formulae.

Together, Alchemy and Astrology are two of the oldest sciences known to humanity. The specialized fields of herbalism, mineralogy, natural science, chemistry and medicine all evolved from the mother science known as Alchemy.

Legend has it that the god Hermes was the founder of Alchemy. The most significant early alchemical text was the *Emerald Tablet* of Hermes Trismegistus, also called the *Tabula Smaragdina*. No one is quite sure who the first alchemist was, although the first group to learn and work with the art were metalsmiths. Perhaps the best known of the alchemists was Paracelsus, who announced that the major goal of Alchemy should be to cure illness. He started what would later become the science of pharmacology.

The outer body of Alchemy is chemistry. It is in fact the ancestor of modern chemistry. But in addition to being a science, this ancient art is also a philosophy. Alchemy is a science that is based upon multiplication and the natural phenomenon of growth—it is the process of increasing and improving that which already exists. Alchemy is evolution—the raising of vibrations.

Practitioners of the art considered Nature to be the greatest alchemist of all, causing the latent seeds of all life to multiply and grow through the act of transmutation. One objective of the Alchemists was to carry out in the laboratory, as far as possible, the processes which Nature carries out in the Earth plane. Not only did they try to duplicate these natural operations, they tried to reproduce them in a comparatively short period of time—speeding up processes which Nature takes vast amounts of time to manifest.

The basic tenets of Alchemy are as follows:

1. The universe has a divine origin. The cosmos is an emanation of *One Absolute Divine Being*. Therefore All is One.

2. All physical manifestation exists by virtue of a *Law of Polarity or Duality*. Any concept can be sufficiently defined in relation to its opposite: male/female, sun/moon, spirit/body, etc.

3. All physical manifestation, whether Vegetable, Animal or Mineral (the so-called Three Kingdoms), is composed of Spirit, Soul, and Body: *the three Alchemic Principles.*

4. All Alchemical work, whether practical laboratory work or spiritual Alchemy, consists of three basic evolutionary processes: *Separation, Purification,* and *Cohobation* (or recombination). These three evolutionary processes are also the work of Nature.

5. All matter is composed of the *four Elements* of Fire (thermal energy), Water (liquid), Air (gas), and Earth (solid). The knowledge and skillful use of the four Elements is an essential part of Alchemical work.

6. The *Quintessence* or Fifth Essence is contained with the four Elements but is not one of them. It is one of the Three Essential Principles, also called the *Philosophic Mercury.*

7. Everything moves towards its *preordained state of perfection.*

In its popular (limited) definition, Alchemy is an empirical science which concerns itself with the transmutation of base metals into gold. For many the word *Alchemy* conjures up an image of a crude laboratory where foolhardy pseudo-scientists labor to turn lead into gold so that they may spend their lives living in a state of luxury. However Alchemy's true definition encompasses the doctrine of the transformation of humanity to a higher stage. The treatises of Alchemy are not only chemical in nature, but also mystical and magical. Certainly many Alchemists left behind a vast amount of information to prove the fact that one version of Alchemy was primarily practical and chemical in nature. On the other hand, the principal interest of many Alchemical philosophers was *spiritual.* These Alchemists did not look merely for the substance of gold, they sought to give the quality of gold to their own being—to transmute the base metals (gross and impure parts of their own nature) to spiritual gold (wisdom). To them gold, the metal which never tarnishes and cannot be corrupted by Fire or Water, was a symbol of illumination and salvation.

Alchemy is the Art and Science of transformation. This is not an easily understood art, because the primal medium of Alchemical expression is through the use of allegory and mythological symbols, which can be interpreted simultaneously both at a material and a spiritual level. The primary goal of Alchemy is to bring all things, including humanity, to its preordained state of perfection. To that end the Alchemical theory states that Eternal Wisdom remains latent, dormant and obscure in humanity so long as a mundane state of ignorance and superficiality exists. The objective of Alchemy is the uncovering of this Inner Wisdom and the removal of the veils and obstacles between the mind and its intrinsically pure Divine Source.

It is this spiritual Alchemy, as opposed to the purely chemical art, that the Golden Dawn stresses. The initiation of an aspiring magician into the Neophyte grade commences the spiritual Alchemical process. The Neophyte is the base material which is to be transmuted by the Work (or Art) of the Hermetic Path. Further initiations into the Elemental grades are analogous to the processes of separation and purification. Initiation into the Portal and Adept grades represents the cohobation or recombination of the Elemental constituents of the magician's psyche into a purified whole. However, the process does not end there. The Adept must incorporate the Quintessence into his/her being, an endeavor which may take a lifetime to achieve. This Great Work or quest for spiritual gold is a long undertaking. Although the goal may be distant, every step along the Path is infinitely rewarding.

The stages of the *philosophical process* of alchemical transmutation are symbolized by four different colors: *black* (guilt, origin, latent forces) for "Prime Matter," a symbol of the Soul in its original condition, or the Elementary organization of inherent possibilities, *white* (minor work, first transmutation, quicksilver), *red* (sulfur, passion), and finally *gold* (spiritual purity).

There are three fundamental substances in the science of Alchemy which exist in all things. The names and Alchemical symbols of these *Three Principles* (*Tria Principia*) of Nature are:

Sulfur   *Mercury*   *Salt*

These substances are not to be confused with ordinary substances of the same name. This triad of Principles may be considered as an undivided whole. However, this unified state exists only before the purification of the Alchemical art (the process of learning), one intention of which is to differentiate between these principles and their homogeneous base. The three components are then purified through the art and recombined into a more exalted whole.

The Principle of Sulfur

(Coptic—*Then*, Greek—*Theion*, Latin—*Sulfur*) This is the dynamic, expansive, volatile, acidic, unifying, masculine, paternal, and fiery principle. Sulfur is the emotional, feeling and passionate urge which motivates life. It is symbolic of the desire for positive change and of vital heat. The entire act of transmutation depends upon the correct application of this vibrant principle. Fire is the crucial Element in the science of Alchemy. Sulfur is the essential *Soul*.

In practical Alchemy, Sulfur is usually extracted from Mercury by distillation. Sulfur is the stabilizing aspect of Mercury, from which it is extracted and dissolved back into.

In mystical Alchemy, Sulfur is the crystallizing aspect of the inspiration commenced by Mercury.

The Principle of Salt

(Coptic—*Hemou*, Greek—*Hals*, Latin—*Sal*) This is the principle of substance or form, conceived of as a heavy, inert mineral body that is part of the nature of all metals. It is the hardening, fixed, contractive tendency, as well as crystallization. Salt refers to the vehicle in which the properties of Sulfur and Mercury are grounded. Salt is the essential corpus or *Body*. It is sometimes referred to as *Earth*.

The Principle of Mercury

(Coptic—*Thrim*, Greek—*Hydrargos*, Latin—*Mercurius*) It is sometimes called *Quicksilver*. This is a watery, feminine principle that relates to the concept of consciousness. Mercury is the universal Spirit or vital Lifeforce that permeates all living matter. This fluid and creative principle is symbolic of the act of transmutation—it is the transforming agent of the Alchemical process. Mercury is the essential *Spirit*, the most important of the Three Principles, which mediates between the other two, modifying their extreme tendencies.

In practical Alchemy, Mercury has two states, both of which are liquid. The first (*volatile*) state is prior to the removal of Sulfur. The second (*fixed*) state is after the Sulfur has been returned. This final and stabilized state is sometimes referred to as *the Secret Fire* or *Prepared Mercury*.

The Alchemical Elements

Primus—*TERRA:* The First Element of Earth. Life-essence. It is a product of Nature.
Secundus—*AQUA:* The Second Element of Water. Eternal life through the fourfold division of the universe.
Tertius—*AER:* The Third Element of Air. Power through a connection with the Element of Spirit.
Quartus—*IGNIS:* The Fourth Element of Fire. Transmutation of matter.

The Metals

The metals attributed to the Planets in Alchemy are as follows:[33]

Symbol	English	Latin	Planet
♄	**LEAD**	Plumbum	Saturn
♃	**TIN**	Stannum	Jupiter
♂	**IRON**	Ferrum	Mars
☉	**GOLD**	Sol	Sol
♀	**COPPER/BRASS**	Cuprum	Venus
☿	**QUICKSILVER**	Argentum Vivum	Mercury
☽	**SILVER**	Argentum	Luna

---

[33] The Alchemical sigils of the metals are the same as those of the planets.

The Alchemist's view on metals is very different from that of the metallurgist. The former sees metals as living things equal to animals and vegetables. And like all things in nature, they undergo natural evolution of birth, growth and increase. Metals contain their own "seed" for further growth. Under different conditions, this seed can be transformed, but only through *nature*. That is why in many Alchemical treatises, the practitioner is told time and time again to let the work of transformation proceed at various stages *naturally*, "without the laying on of hands."✿

Alchemical Terms and Symbols

ACETUM PHILOSOPHORUM: A synonym for "virgin's milk," Philosophic Mercury, or "Secret Fire."

ADAM: The archetypal man. The animus.

ADAMIC EARTH: The "Primal Element" or the "true oil of Gold" which is only once removed from the pure homogenous Element.

ADROP: Philosophic lead or antimony.

AERIS: Elemental Air.

AES HERMETIS: A term for Mercury. Said to be "the thing containing the thing contained."

AESCH MEZAREPH (Hebrew): "The Purifying Fire." An Alchemical/Qabalistic work collected from *The Kabalah Denudata* of Knorr Von Rosenroth.

AID: Steam or vapor.

AIR: In practical Alchemy this refers to the vapor arising from metals.

ALCHEMICAL MARRIAGE: The completion of the Great Work. The union of the King and Queen.

ALBEDO: A state where matter is stainless and no longer liable to decay.

ALKAHEST: Secret Fire. A universal liquid solvent.

ALEMBROTH: Philosophical Salt. Salt of Art. Part of the nature of metals.

ALLOY: Combination. The union of Fire and Water, male and female.

ALOOHOPH: The Earth Element in its incorporeal state. Also Earth of Spirit.

AMALGAM: Mixture of metals through fusion.

AMRITA: The First Matter transmuted.

AN: The Father, or Sulfur.

ANIMA: The feminine portion of the masculine psyche. The inner personality.

ANIMUS: The masculine portion of the feminine psyche.

ANSIR: The Son, or Mercury.

ANSIRARTO: The Holy Ghost of the Trinity, or Salt.

ANTIMONY: A poison which in certain doses acts as a powerful medicinal remedy. This substance is also a chemical paradox, having all the properties of a white metal while at times appearing as a non-metal. It is obtained from a sulphide known as Stibnite by heating it with iron. (There are four forms of antimony: a gray metal, a black soot, an unstable yellow and an explosive silver.)

APR (Hebrew): Powder or Ash.

AQUA: Elemental Water.

AQUA PERMANENS: The "Imperishable or Enduring Water." The Mercury of the Philosophers. Sol and Luna dissolved and united.

AQUA VITAE: Alcohol. Feminine secretions.

AQUILA PHILOSOPHORUM: The "Eagle of the Philosophers." The Mercury of metals described as a "metallic nature reduced to its First Matter."

ARCHAEUS: The hidden essence in the First Matter which must be drawn out.

ARGENT VIVE: "Secret Fire," Philosopher's Mercury; also called "living silver," the universal solvent of all metals.

ATTENUATED: Made thin.

AUR (Hebrew): Light.

AZOTH: The Universal Medicine to which all things are related, containing within itself all other medicines. It is also the term for the Mercury of any metallic body. Also considered as a living Spirit. The Quintessence. Water of Spirit.

AURUM ALBUM: White gold.

BAETYLUS: A living Stone containing a Spirit.

BALSAMUM VITAE (The Balsam of Life): A combination of natural heat and radical moisture. In mystical Alchemy it symbolizes compassion, love and revitalization.

BASILISK: A creature with the body of a serpent or dragon and the head and claws of a rooster. Symbolizes a dual nature or conflicting Elemental nature.

BAT: Androgyny. Double-natured.

BATH OF VENUS: Vagina.

BATHING: Purification through cleansing.

BEAR: The Nigredo of the First Matter.

BEE: Soul. Purity. Rebirth.

BEHEADING: Understanding which is forced on the Soul by nature through trial and suffering. Separation which surmounts the physical body.

BENNU: The Egyptian Phoenix. A symbol of the Philosopher's Stone.

BLACK DRAGON: Death, putrefaction, decay.

BLOOD: Spirit.

BLOOD OF THE RED LION: Masculine fluid.

BOOK: Universe.

BOW: Male and female combination. Crescent of Luna as the feminine, the issuing of the arrow as the masculine.

BREATH: Life-essence.

CADUCEUS: The power of transformation. Union of Opposites.

CAPUT MORTEM: The Tail end of the matter. Waste product.

CAUDA PAVONIS: The tail of the peacock.

CAULDRON (Kettle, cup or chalice): Fertility. The Womb. Transforming Power.

CHAIN: That which binds.

CHAOS: The Void. The fourfold division of the First Matter.

CHILD: Potential.

CHMO: Fermentation.

CHOL: Sand.

CINNABAR: The product of the productive interaction between the masculine and feminine principles. The Living Gold.

CLOUD: Gas or vapor.

COLEUM: Perfect living Being. Also called Virtus.

CONJUNCTIO SOLIS ET LUNA: The union of the Sun and the Moon. Union of opposites.

CORPOREAL STATE: Materiality or physical state of existence.

CORPUS: Alchemical substance. The unconscious.

CROSS: Descent of Spirit into matter. A balanced fourfold division. A symbol of man.

CROWN: Kingship or sovereignty.

CROWNED CHILD: The Stone of the Philosophers.

CROWNED ORB: The Philosopher's Stone.

CRUCIFIXION: Cleansing of all impurities.

CUPELLATION: Metallurgical process for testing Gold.

CYPRESS: Death. Male organ.

DAGGER: That which pierces and breaks down matter.

DIENECH: Fixed Water.

DOG: Philosophical Mercury.

DOG AND WOLF: The dual nature of Mercury.

DOUBLE-HEADED EAGLE: Masculine and feminine Mercury.

DOVE: Life Spirit.

DRAGON'S BLOOD: Cinnabar. Sulphide of Mercury.

DRYNESS: Solar Fire. Male Principle.

EAGLE (Also hawk or falcon): Sublimation. Mercury in its most exalted state. An emblem of knowledge, inspiration, and a sign of the completed Work.

EARTH: In practical Alchemy, metals are often referred to as Earth.

EGG: The sealed Hermetic Vessel wherein the work is completed. Symbol of creation.

ELECTRUM: A metal containing all the metals attributed to the seven Planets.

ELIXIR OF LIFE: Derived from the Philosopher's Stone, the Elixir is said to confer immortality and restore youth.

EMPEROR: The King. The active volatile principle.

EMPRESS: The passive, fixed principle.

EVE: The archetypal female. The anima.

FATHER: The Sun or male principle.

FILTH: The waste products and impurities extracted from the matter. Caput Mortem. The Gross.

FISH: Arcane substance.

FISH EYES: The stone in the early stages of evolution.

FLESH: Matter.

FLIGHT: The act of transcendence. Ascent to a higher level.

FLOWER OF GOLD: Spiritual rebirth. Elixir of Life.

FOETUS SPAGYRICUS: The stage of the alchemical process when matter inherits Spirit.

FORGE: The transmuting power of the sacred Fire of the furnace.

FOUNTAIN: The source of Eternal Life. Maternal source.

FRUIT: Essence. Immortality.

FROG: The First Matter. The origin of physical matter.

GARDEN: Paradise.

GIRDLE: That which binds.

GLUTEN: Feminine fluids.

GLUTINUM MUNDI: The glue of the world. That which unites body and mind.

GOAT: The male principle.

GOLD: The goal of the Great Work. Perfection and harmony. Complete balance of masculine and feminine.

GOOSE: Nature.

GRAIL: The Stone of the Philosophers. Immortality.

GRAIN (Barley, kernel, seed): The seed of life. The renewal of life. The core.

GREAT WORK: The attainment of the highest possible degree of perfection. The Union of the Smaller Universe with the Greater Universe (Microcosm and Macrocosm).

GREAT KING: The completion of the Magnum Opus. Attainment.

GREEN LION: The Stem and Root of the Radical Essence of the Metals. Raw and unpurified energy of nature. Symbol of the living force that must be sought in the First Matter. Relates to the Fire of Venus and Philosophic Mercury. The beginning of the work.

HAIR: Strength. Life Essence.

HERMAPHRODITE: Union of masculine and feminine.

HERMES: Mercury.

HIEROS GAMOS: Divine union. Conjunction.

HONEY: Initiation. Immortality.

HOURGLASS: Fleeting passage of time

HUMIDUM RADICALE: Radical Moisture. Moisture as a balsam.

HYDROLITH: Water Stone. The Philosopher's Stone.

HYLE: The Prima Materia or First Matter. The Primal substance from which the whole of the universe is created. It is a fusion of the four Elements and is regarded to be the same as the Philosopher's Stone.

INCREATUM: Self-generating.

IGNIS AQUA: Fiery Water. Alkahest.

IGNIS LEONIS: Elemental Fire or the "Fire of the Lion."

IGNIS ELEMENATARIS: Alchemical Sulfur.

JOY OF THE PHILOSOPHERS: Refers to that stage of the Great Work just prior to the victorious production of the Stone of the Wise. Success is virtually assured.

KIBRIC: The First Matter of Mercury and all fluids. That from which Mercury is derived.

KING: Red—The Qabalistic Son of the Supernal Father and Mother. The king is also known as Microprosopus or "Lesser Countenance" which is centered in Tiphareth. Analogous to Gold and the Sun. *(Relates to the Red Tincture.)*

LAC VIRGINIS: Virgin's milk. A term for Mercurial Water.

LAMP: A continuous spiritual Fire.

LANCE: Masculine energy.

LAPIS LUCIDUM ANGULARIS: "The cornerstone of Light." The supreme Essence.

LAPIS PHILOSOPHORUM: The Philosopher's Stone. In practical Alchemy this is a powder and not a stone.

LATON: The Matter of the work. The production of the Philosopher's Stone at the white stage.

LEO RUBEUS: The Red Lion.

LEO VIRDIS: The Ore of Hermes. The Blood from Sulfur. The first Mercury of Gold, altered by means of Luna. Sometimes called Green Water. Also sometimes refers to Vitriol.

LILY: The female principle.

LION: Heat and sulfurous action.

LUNA: The Planetary name for Silver (but in practical Alchemy this often refers to a mixture of antimony and iron).

LUNA PHILOSOPHORUM: The pure living Alchemical Spirit of Silver—the refined Essence of Heat and Moisture.

MAGNESIA: Sometimes used for talc, but often this term is used in reference to a mixture of metals.

MAGISTERIUM: A quality treated as a substance, or an operation to cultivate or emphasize a quality. (Example: The Magisterium of Principles—*Separation*. The Magisterium of Weight—*to exalt in weight*.)

MAGNUM OPUS: The Great Work or masterpiece. It is the goal of the Alchemic process—that is, to reach a purified state of spiritual perfection. The creation of the Philosopher's Stone. Illumination.

MARE NOSTRUM: Our Sea. The physical body.

MARRIAGE: Union. Conjunction.

MATER METALLORUM: The "Mother of Metals," also known as Living Silver.

MATERIA LAPIDIS: Tincture.

MATRIX: The place where a substance is developed. The womb. An essential component of realization, without which Spirit cannot be joined to matter.

MEDICINA CATHOLICA: Universal Medicine. The anima.

MENSTRUUM: That original material from which all metals are derived. This term is also used to describe Mercury wherein gold has been dissolved. Usually describes a solvent in the corporeal process of the purification of the gold. Any fluid that dissolves a solid, sometimes a catalyst. Constant mild heat that is continued for forty-two days.

MODERATE FIRE: Sexual passion.

MYSTERIUM: The Essence of the Interior Nature.

MYSTERIUM MAGNUM: The Great Mystery. The First Matter of All Things. The Mother of all finite living things.

NATURA ABSCONDITA: The Hidden Nature or Essence.

NITRE: Saltpeter.

OAK: A constituent of the Secret Fire.

OPUS: The work. To bring Order out of Chaos.

ORB: The world.

OUROBORUS: The serpent which bites its own tail. Indicates the cyclic quality of the Work.

PANACEA: The Universal Medicine obtained from the Stone.

PATER ET MATER REGIS: "The Father and Mother of the King." The combining of opposites required for the production of the Philosopher's Stone.

PEACOCK: A symbol which heralds the fact that transformation is occurring. The brilliant colors of the *peacock's tail* (Cauda Pavonis) mark the beginning of the process of integration, the formation of Philosophic Mercury. The varied colors that arise during the course of the work which resemble the colors of petroleum on a wet surface. (*Also a symbol of Elemental Air.*)

PELICAN: A symbol of the idea that the first matter contains within itself all that is needed for transformation and purification.[34] The sacrificial stage of the Alchemical process. A vessel used in the Work.

PHILOSOPHER'S STONE: Lapis Philosophorum. The Stone of the Wise. The Magnum Opus. The Celestial Ruby. Symbol of the transmutation of humanity's lower nature into the Higher Self. True spiritual attainment and illumination. The search for the Philosopher's Stone is the search for ultimate truth and purity. (*Also called the Elixir of Life, or Tincture.*) In physical Alchemy, the Stone is the manufacturing of Gold from a base metal. In mystical Alchemy it is the transmutation of the Lower into the Higher.

PHILOSOPHIC MERCURY: A brilliant clear liquid sometimes called Sophic Fire or "Our Mercury." It is described as "Water which does not wet the hands." Different from "vulgar" Mercury or common quicksilver. In practical Alchemy it is the vapor of antimony purified by iron. Also called Refined or Prepared Mercury.

PHILOSOPHIC SPERM: Masculine fluids.

PHILOSOPHIC SULFUR: The masculine principle.

PHOENIX: The bird of rebirth and recurrence. A symbol of alchemical resurrection. Indicates the preparation of the Red Tincture of the Solar forces, Philosophic Sulfur. (*Also a symbol of Elemental Fire.*)

POWDER OF PROJECTION: The goal of the Hermetic Work which, being projected upon metals, transforms them into Gold or Silver.

PRIMA MATERIA: The First Matter, the beginning of the Work, the base metal. The first state of unformed matter. The Elementary substance of inherent possibilities which contains the germs, seeds or potencies of all things. It is a fusion of the four Elements and is regarded to be the same as the Philosopher's Stone. Also called Hyle.

---

[34] Legend has it that the pelican feeds its young with blood from its own breast. This points to the Alchemical idea that the secret "water" is obtained from the original substance and then returned to it to initiate growth.

PRIMUM ENS: "The First Essence." Dividing the *Primum Ens* from the Prima Materia (First Matter) which provides a physical vehicle for the First Essence, is one of the primary goals of Alchemy. Spiritus Mundi.

PRINCIPIA CHYMIA: The three Alchemic Principles of Sulfur, Salt, and Mercury.

QUEEN: White—The Qabalistic Bride of Microprosopus, Malkuth—analogous to Silver and the Moon. *(Relates to the White Tincture.)*

QUINTESSENCE: The Fifth Essence. The most purified essence or essential life-giving force which permeates and sustains the body or matter. Spirit. Philosophic Mercury.

RAVEN or CROW: Initiation through blackness. Signifies the Nigredo or putrefaction of the first Material—the initial blackness that is necessary for further evolution. *(Also a symbol of Elemental Earth.)*

REBIS: "Two-Thing." The male (Solar) and female (Lunar) aspects of the substance usually represented by a being with two heads and one body or as two serpents. These two facets are not separated, but integrated. In practical Alchemy this describes two metals joined with the aid of a catalyst. Hermaphrodite.

RED LION: Sulfur (solar energy) combined with Mercury (Will). The force of nature under control. It the same as the Green Lion (Philosophic Mercury), but mixed with gold.

RED MAN: Iron or sulfur (sometimes "Our Gold" or copper).

REEZON: The Sulfur of the Philosophers when perfected at the red stage.

REGIMEN: State of temperature.

REGULUS: Two metals mixed by a natural heat that is bearable by humans. The two combined ingredients are counted as one principle.

SAL NITER: Saltpeter.

SANCUIS DRACONIS: Cinnabar.

SANDARACE: Fire of Spirit.

SANDUIFICATION: "Transforming food into blood." Creating the Philosopher's Stone.

SATURN: The Planetary name of Lead, often used to describe the blackening stage in Alchemy.

SECRET FIRE: The hidden or Elemental Fire. Philosophic Mercury, described as a "fiery water" or "Philosophic vinegar." It is the root of metals which harmonizes with them and is the medium which combines the tinctures. There are four divisions of the Secret Fire, each named after Zodiacal Signs: *Sun of Aries* (original stage), *Sun of Taurus* (black stage), *Sun of Gemini* (white stage), *and Sun of Leo* (red stage).

SICK KING: The king at the end of life. A state wherein the ego dominates.

SOL PHILOSOPHORUM: The pure living Alchemical Spirit of Gold—the refined Essence of Heat and Fire.

SOLUTION: Dissolving a solid into a liquid.

"SOLVE ET COAGULA": *"Dissolve and coagulate."* An axiom of Alchemical practice. The first work of the Alchemist was to reduce the solids in a liquid, then back into a solid. That which dissolves is *Spirit*, that which coagulates is *Body*.

SOPHIC FIRE: Secret Fire or Prepared Mercury.

SPAGIRUS: A person who can separate the true from the false, the good from the bad, the pure from the impure, yet reject duality and cleave to unity.

SPAGYRIC ART: "The separative art." A term for Alchemy, in which the fusion of duality is a constant theme.

SPIRITUS MUNDI: The Spirit of the World. Life-giving power. Archaeus. The hidden essence within the First Matter which must be extracted.

STIBNITE: A sulphide from which Antimony is obtained.

STREAMS OF THE PHILOSOPHERS: Arteries, veins.

SUNKEN KING: In the process of melting metal ores, the name used for clumps of metal formed beneath the slag.

TAPIS: Self-incubation.

TETARUS: Tarter. The bottom portion of the cooking vessel. The arcane substance which forms at the bottom of such a vessel.

TINCTURE: That part of a substance which is extracted by a solvent.

THUNDERBOLT OF JUPITER: The Fire of the Philosophers.

ULTIMA MATERIA: The Final Matter, the end of the Work.

UNICORN: Spirit.

UNIVERSAL MEDICINE: The powdered Stone of the Philosophers when diluted and taken as an oil or tincture.

UNIVERSAL SOLVENT: Secret Fire. Not to be taken literally as a solvent.

VITRIOL: Any of certain metallic sulphates. An acidic penetrating substance. Sulphuric acid is referred to as Oil of Vitriol. The name is an acronym of *Visita Interiora Terrae Rectificando Invenies Occultum Lapidem*, which means "Visit the interior of the Earth, in purifying you discover the hidden stone." The Stone or True Self, only found by seeking within.

VILITAS: Baseness.

VULGAR GOLD: Physical or natural Gold as we know it.

WASHING: Cleansing, preparing.

WATER: Philosophic Mercury. Any liquid substance.

WHITE EAGLE: Gluten.

WHITE SWAN or DOVE: Refers to the first instance of the "Soul" of matter being released—the matter having polarized into the black of the raven and the white of the more exalted bird. The white swan indicates the preparation of the white tincture of the Lunar forces, Philosophic Salt. (*Also a symbol of Elemental Water.*)

WHITE WIFE: A white metal. Sometimes referred to as "Our silver," Mercury or antimony.

WINGED DRAGON: The Volatile.

WINGLESS DRAGON: The Fixed.

SECTION 3: The Elementals

An *Elemental* is a nonphysical entity having a nature that is composed entirely of one of the four magical Elements. They are the invisible counterparts of visible Nature, or the spiritual essence of the Elements. Whereas humans, Angels, Archangels and higher spiritual beings have composite natures, Elementals are composed of only one etheric essence. In the spiritual realms, Elementals occupy a place between human beings and higher entities such as Angels and Archangels.[35] The *Four Orders* of the Elementals are:

1. *Gnomes*—The Spirits of Earth   2. *Sylphs*—The Spirits of Air
3. *Undines*—The Spirits of Water   4. *Salamanders*—The Spirits of Fire

These four Orders are the essential spiritual beings called upon to praise God in the *Benedicite Omnia Opera* (literal translation: "Blessed are his Works.")[36]

GNOMES: The name of these beings is derived from the Greek word *genomos*, meaning "Earth dweller." The gnomes work in an Element so close in vibration to the physical Earth that they have immense power over the rocks and vegetation, as well as the mineral Elements in the bodily makeup of humans and animals. They work with the stones, gems and metals and are said to be the guardians of hidden treasures. Various mythic traditions have depicted several types of Gnomes such as satyrs, brownies, elves and dryads. Gnomes are supposed to be patient and hardworking, but can be malicious and difficult. Because of their Earth nature, they are assigned to the North. The King of the Gnomes is called *Ghob*.[37]

SYLPHS: These beings dwell not in the physical atmosphere, but in the incorporeal spiritual substance which is similar to the Earth's atmosphere, although far more subtle. They are the highest group of Elementals because their Element has the highest vibrational rate. The wind and clouds are said to be their vehicle. Mythology usually depicts them as winged fayes or fairies. The Air Spirits are erratic, changeable creatures that move with the speed of lightning. They work through the ethers and gases of the Earth and indirectly with the human nervous system. Sylphs are beneficent, mirthful and inspirational to humans, especially artists and poets. They are assigned to the Eastern quarter. The King of the Sylphs, called *Paralda*, is said to dwell in the clouds surmounting the highest mountain peak.

UNDINES: These entities function in the incorporeal spiritual essence called humid or liquid ether. The vibratory rate of this substance is close to that of the Element of Water. Thus the Undines are able to control and manipulate the flow of Water in Nature. They also work with the vital fluids in plants, animals and humans. In mythology, Undines are given various forms, such as Water

---

[35] The Greeks assigned the name *daimon* or "spirit" to some of these beings. The Church lumped all elemental entities together under a corruption of this word, *demon*, which carries with it an evil connotation. This is an injustice, since Nature spirits are essentially no more malicious than are plants, animals and rocks.

[36] This is a reference to a passage from the Book of Revelation.

[37] In Medieval times, the subjects of Ghob were called *Goblins*.

nymphs, Water sprites, mermaids and nereids. They are said to be vital, graceful and generally beneficent to humans. The Queen of the Water spirits is called *Nichsa*. These beings are assigned to the Western quarter of creation.

SALAMANDERS: The strongest and most powerful of the Elementals, the Salamanders live in that spiritual ether which is the invisible Fire of Nature. Physical Fire and warmth cannot exist without them. The Salamanders work through the emotional nature of humans and animals by means of the blood-stream and body heat. They also exert influence over all fiery-tempered beings. They are said to be the most difficult of all Elementals to communicate with, owing to the incineratory nature of their Element. However the smoke of burning incense is a medium for their expression. Salamanders vary in size and appearance, from fiery balls or tongues of flame to mythological armored figures and fiery lizard-like creatures. In temperament they are dangerous and unpredictable. Their mighty King is an awe-inspiring flaming Spirit known as *Djin*. The Salamanders are assigned to the Southern quarter of creation.✿

SECTION 4: Tetragrammaton and the Kerubim

 *Tetragrammaton* is a Greek word that means "Four-Lettered Name." This alludes to the unknowable and unpronounceable name of God symbolized by the Hebrew letters *Yod Heh Vav Heh*.[38] Each of these four letters is assigned to one of the four Elements of Nature: *Yod*—Fire, *Heh*—Water, *Vav*—Air, and *Heh final* [or *Heh Sophith*]—Earth.

These letters portray the balance inherent to the Qabalistic system, for Yod-Fire and Vav-Air are *masculine, positive energies*, while Heh-Water and Heh Final-Earth are *feminine and negative potencies*. The Tetragrammaton is the cornerstone of the fourfold model of the manifest universe. It indicates that the Divine is a unified whole which contains within itself all opposites in balanced disposition. Legend has it that the proper understanding and pronunciation of this Supreme Name of God are the Keys to divine power.

The *Kerubim*, "the Strong Ones," are the living Powers of Tetragrammaton on the Material Plane and the Presidents of the four Elements. They operate through the *Fixed or Kerubic Signs* of the Zodiac:

> *Kerub of Fire:* **ARYEH**, the Lion, attributed to the Sign *LEO*
> *Kerub of Water:* **NESHER**, the Eagle, attributed to the Sign *SCORPIO*
> *Kerub of Air:* **ADAM**, the Man, attributed to the Sign *AQUARIUS*
> *Kerub of Earth:* **SHOR**, the Bull, attributed to the Sign *TAURUS*

The Kerubim are the guardians of the four Cardinal points and the four rivers which flow down the Tree of Life from the Creator. In Genesis the Kerubim were the Angels who hid the Garden of Eden from the sight of a fallen humanity. They were also the four creatures seen in Ezekiel's vision.✿

---

[38] The name *Jehovah* is a transcription of the Four-lettered name YHVH.

SECTION 5: Qabalah

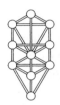

The *Sepher Yetzirah* divides the Hebrew alphabet into three classes: the *Mothers*, the *Doubles*, and the *Simples*. The *Three Mother Letters* are Aleph, Mem and Shin. These three letters are a trinity from which everything in the manifest universe arises. Aleph, Mem and Shin represent the ancient Elements of Air, Water, and Fire. Mem (Water) and Shin (Fire) are opposing forces while Aleph (Air) is the mediator and balancing force between them.

The *Seven Double Letters* are Beth, Gimel, Daleth, Kaph, Peh, Resh, Tau. The Seven Double Letters are called double because they each have a hard and a soft sound associated with them, in addition to a dual set of qualities attributed. Different sources attribute the following qualties to the Double Letters:

Beth—Wisdom and Folly	*Beth*—Life and Death
Gimel—Grace and Indignation	*Gimel*—Peace and War
Daleth—Fertility and Solitude	*Daleth*—Wisdom and Folly
Kaph—Life and Death	*Kaph*—Riches and Poverty
Peh—Power and Servitude	*Peh*—Grace and Indignation
Resh—Peace and War	*Resh*—Fertility and Solitude
Tau—Riches and Poverty	*Tau*—Power and Servitude

The Seven Double Letters represent the seven Planets of the ancients, the seven days of creation, seven orifices of perception in human beings, and seven directions in space.

The Twelve Simple (or Single) Letters: Heh, Vav, Zayin, Cheth, Teth, Yod, Lamed, Nun, Samekh, Ayin, Tzaddi, Qoph. The Twelve Simple Letters refer to the twelve Signs of the Zodiac, the twelve months of the year, and the twelve organs of a human being. The Twelve Simples are the foundations of twelve human properties:

Heh—Sight	*Lamed*—Work
Vav—Hearing	*Nun*—Movement
Zayin—Smell	*Samekh*—Anger
Cheth—Speech	*Ayin*—Mirth
Teth—Taste	*Tzaddi*—Imagination
Yod—Sexual Love	*Qoph*—Sleep

The *Holy Place* or *Tabernacle* as described in the Zelator Hall embraces the symbolism of the Twenty-two letters of the Hebrew alphabet: The Table of Shewbread represents the Twelve Single Letters. The Seven-Branched Candlestick alludes to the Seven Double Letters. The Altar of Incense refers to the Three Mother Letters.✿

The Three Mother Letters

א מ ש

Aleph, Mem, Shin

The Seven Double Letters

ת ר פ כ ד ג ב

Beth, Gimel, Daleth, Kaph, Peh, Resh, Tau

The Twelve Simple Letters

ה ו ז ח ט י ל נ ס ע צ ק

Heh, Vav, Zayin, Cheth, Teth, Yod, Lamed, Nun, Samekh, Ayin, Tzaddi, Qoph

The Four Worlds and the Ten Heavens

The Four Worlds

Qabalistic theory describes the universe as being separated into four distinct "Worlds." With the creation of the Sephiroth by the Path of the Flaming Sword, the Four Worlds came into being, each evolving from the one before it, becoming more substantial as they reached manifestation into physical form. Each of these worlds envelops its predecessor like the layers of an onion, the highest spiritual world at the center is progressively veiled from the lowest world that forms the outer layer.

In addition to this, each Qabalistic "World" is symbolized by one of the Hebrew letters of the Tetragrammaton, which once again reinforces the concept of the fourfold model of the universe. The Four Worlds of the Qabalah are:

> *Atziluth:* The Divine or Archetypal World (*Olam Atziluth*)
> *Briah:* The Archangelic or Creative World (*Olam ha-Briah*)
> *Yetzirah:* The Angelic or Formative World (*Olam ha-Yetzirah*)
> *Assiah:* The Material World or World of Action (*Olam ha-Assiah*)

ATZILUTH (אצילות) is the first and highest of the Four Worlds and is attributed to *Yod*, the first letter of Tetragrammaton. It is the World of pure deity and the domain of Primordial Fire. This world gave birth to the other three worlds, in a descending scale of Light. Some traditions assign it to the three Sephiroth of Kether, Chokmah, and Binah, while others ascribe to it only the sphere of Kether. (See the diagram.) For the purposes of this book, we will define Atziluth as containing only the first Sephirah. The so-called Secret Name of the World of Atziluth is *Aub*, which refers to "density, thicket, darkness and cloud."

BRIAH (בריאה) is the second World, the World of Creation. The second letter of Tetragrammaton, *Heh*, is ascribed to this World, marking it as the domain of Primordial Water. The Element of Water represents the fluid, inventive Mind, thus Briah is described as the World of Pure Intellect. It is known as the abode of the Archangels. Although some traditions assign the spheres of Chesed, Geburah, and

Tiphareth to this Realm, here we will employ only the Sephiroth of Chokmah and Binah to describe the World of Briah. The Secret Name of the Second World is *Seg*.

YETZIRAH (יצירה) is the third World or World of Formation. It is the abode of various orders of Angels. The third letter of Tetragrammaton, *Vav*, is assigned here, making Yetzirah the realm of Primordial Air. This world is approximate to the astral plane because the etheric framework behind the physical universe is found here. Some schools of thought assign only Netzach, Hod, and Yesod to this world, but here we will subscribe to the theory that places seven of the spheres from Chesed to Yesod in the Yetziratic World. The Secret Name of this Realm is *Mah*, which relates to the words "anything" or "something."

ASSIAH (עשיה) is the fourth and final World, the World of Action, consisting only of Malkuth.[39] The final letter, *Heh*, of Tetragrammaton is ascribed to Assiah, which is also the World of Primordial Earth. In Assiah the four Elements which make up the physical universe exist both in sensation and in the hidden properties of matter. This is the corporeal World where tangible activity can take place. It is the realm of matter and of humanity, yet it is also the world of "shells," made up of the denser Elements of the preceding three worlds. In addition, Assiah is the abode of evil demons, known to the Qabalists as the Qlippoth. The Secret Name of Assiah is *Ben*, which means "Son."

The Ten Heavens or Houses of Assiah

The Active and Material World of Assiah, the fourth and most manifest of the Qabalistic Worlds, has assigned to it the names of the heavenly spheres, which include the seven Planets of the ancients. These "Heavens" are physical manifestations attributed to each Sephirah. Some authors have termed these heavenly spheres "the ten mundane Chakras," likening these centers of manifestation to centers of energy that exist within the human body in Eastern mystical traditions. The Ten Heavens imply that each of the ten Sephiroth has some resemblance to the Divine Essence behind certain Planets or astronomical forces.

---

[39] The name "Asia" has associations with this World.

The Ten Heavens of Assiah are:

1. *Rashith ha-Gilgalim* (ראשית הגלגלים) [also known as the Primum Mobile] "The Beginning of Revolvings" or "The First Wirlings." Assigned to Kether.

2. *Mazloth* (מזלות) "The Stations." The Sphere of the Zodiac. Assigned to Chokmah.

3. *Shabbathai* (שבתאי) "the Seventh." The Sphere of Saturn. Assigned to Binah.

4. *Tzedek* (צדק) "The Righteous." Related to the word *tzaddik,* which means "holy person" or saint. The Sphere of Jupiter. Assigned to Chesed.

5. *Madim* (מדים) from the root word *mad* which means "Force" or "Might." The Sphere of Mars. Assigned to Geburah.

6. *Shemesh* (שמש) from Shamash, the name of the Sumerian Sun god. The Sphere of Sol. Assigned to Tiphareth.

7. *Nogah* (נוגה) "the Shiner." The Sphere of Venus. Assigned to the Sephirah of Netzach.

8. *Kokab* (כוכב) "Star." The Sphere of Mercury. Assigned to the Sephirah of Hod.

9. *Levannah* (לבנה) The Moon. The Sphere of Luna. Assigned to the Sephirah of Yesod.

10. *Olam Yesodoth*[40] (עולם יסודות) "The World of Foundations." The Sphere of the Elements. Assigned to Malkuth.✿

---

[40] According to Regardie, this has sometimes been rendered as *Cholem Yesodoth,* "The Breaker of Foundations." Regardie was of the opinion that this was a printer's error, and that *Olam,* not *Cholem* was the correct version.

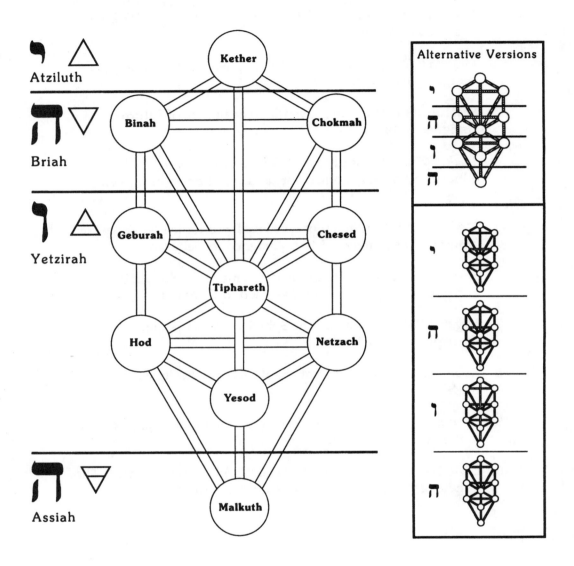

The Four Qabalistic Worlds

The Divine Names Attributed to the Sephiroth

Each of the Sephiroth has assigned to it various Divine Names known as the Hierarchies.[41] This list of Divine, Archangelic, and Angelic names is based upon the different divine levels of Being as defined by the Four Qabalistic Worlds.[42]

The Atziluthic or Divine Name represents the highest spiritual form of a specific Sephirah.

The Briatic Title is the name of an Archangel who organizes the forces intrinsic to a specific Sephirah and the direction of the activating forces that come under its authority. Archangels are actual beings without physical form, although representations of them in art come from the inventions of the human mind, which needs anthropomorphic images in order to enhance understanding. The true form of an Archangel would be similar to a great pillar of energy or a geometric shape that concurs with the individual Sephirah.

The Yetziratic Title is the name of a group of Angels who are responsible for the actual mechanics or workings of a Sephirah.

In magic these divisions can be likened to an army; at the top is the Commander-in-Chief, who holds a Divine (Atziluth) title. Under him is a general known as an Archangel (Briah) who commands various legions. These legions are made up of numerous footsoldiers known as Angels (Yetzirah). (Note: In the Golden Dawn's system of magic, if you want something done, you go straight to the top and petition the Divine or Atziluthic Name and work your way down the Hierarchy from there. The Highest must always be invoked first.)

Divine Names:

EHEIEH (אהיה): The deity name of Kether which means "I am." This name indicates the inhaling and exhaling of the breath, alluding to the idea that Kether is the root from which all begins and to which all returns. The letters of the name, *Aleph Heh Yod Heh* yield further meanings; Aleph indicates the beginning or initial outpouring of force, Heh is the stabilizing factor or receptacle, Yod symbolizes the fertilizing principle, and the final Heh is the stabilizing factor and resulting manifestation. The whole word thus encompasses the idea of increasing manifestation. It is the first and the last—the heart of everything—the first living breath of God and the last breath of Being.

---

[41] This part of the Knowledge Lecture was originally divided up and taught in the grades of Theoricus and Practicus. Today the Order includes this information (and the following section on the Planetary hierarchies) in the Zelator grade. In our own temple, we have divided these lists up—having parts of them distributed among the Knowledge Lectures of other grades: Zelator—Atziluthic (Divine) Names, Theoricus—Briatic (Archangelic) Names, and Practicus—Yetziratic (Angelic Choir) names. We have found that students take more easily to this approach; retaining the memorized names better, due to the fact that they automatically review the previous information concerning the Hierarchies for each new Knowledge Lecture. The reader of this book is free to choose whichever one of these approaches best suits his/her ability to learn the material, so long as in the end the list is committed to memory.

[42] Regardie suggested that the student draw several Trees of Life and place upon them the Divine Names in their proper order.

YAH: (יה) The deity name of Chokmah which means "The Lord." It is half of the Tetragrammaton, although some authors ascribe the full Name YHVH to this Sephirah. (YHVH signifies the idea "to be.") The name *Yah* implies explosive masculine power and fertilizing force (Yod). It is the great initiator of all action.

YHVH ELOHIM (יהוה אלהים): The deity name of Binah which has been translated as "The Lord God." However the word "Elohim" is a feminine noun (*Eloh*) with a masculine plural ending, implying a dual polarity of masculine and feminine. Since YHVH can be considered the action of the Divine in the Four Qabalistic Worlds, then *YHVH Elohim* presents the idea of the polarity principle (the perfect balance of masculine and feminine operating on all planes of existence) as the foundation of all form.

EL (or AL) (אל): The deity name of Chesed which means simply "God," but also implies *The Divine One* or *The Mighty One*. Whereas the name of *Ya* represented the primal masculine force of God, *El* refers to the primal feminine aspect of the deity. The name is composed of the letters Aleph and Lamed, whose letters mean respectively "Ox" and "Ox-goad," alluding to the idea of the primal motivating force under control. As the deity name of the first Sephirah below the Abyss, *Al* is the divine giver or benefactor of humanity, supplying us with the potential for the attainment of Divinity.

ELOHIM GIBOR (אלהים גבור): The deity name of Geburah which can be translated as "God of Battles" or as "Almighty God." This denotes that nothing can escape the might of the Divine and universal law. The essence of *Elohim Gibor* is Judgment that places the end before the means, striking quickly at the heart of a problem, even when the cure may be as harsh as the illness.

YHVH ELOAH VE-DAATH (יהוה אלוה ודעת): The deity name of Tiphareth which means "Lord God of Knowledge" but which might also be interpreted as "God made Manifest in the Sphere of the Mind." Once again we have the combined title of *YHVH Eloah*, indicating a perfect balance of masculine and feminine polarities. In addition, we have the idea that knowledge is power. *YHVH Eloah ve-Daath* is the Divine Mind within us that comprehends its own Divinity. In modern terms, it is the Universal Mind—that Mind which encompasses all minds.

YHVH TZABAOTH (יהוה צבאות): The deity name of Netzach which means "Lord of Hosts" (armies). This indicates the diffusing aspect of the sphere, which divides and distributes the Light from Tiphareth prismatically into the many splendid aspects of the lower worlds. As before, YHVH can be considered the action of the Divine in the Four Qabalistic Worlds. In addition to this *YHVH Tzabaoth* is the male-positive divine aspect of every living Soul.

ELOHIM TZABAOTH (אלהים צבאות): The deity name of Hod which means "God of Hosts." This name is similar to the deity name of Netzach. ELOHIM introduces the idea of polarity (balanced masculine and feminine principles). In Netzach, the "Hosts" are the many *forces* of the lower worlds, while in Hod they are the many *forms* which serve to house these forces. *Elohim Tzabaoth* is the female negative divine aspect of every living Soul.

SHADDAI EL CHAI (שדי אל הי): The deity name of Yesod which means "Almighty Living God." This also indicates the Supreme Lord of Life and of Lives. In this case, the "Life Power" is to be seen not only as a spiritual essence, but specifically as the driving force behind reproduction and regeneration. *Shaddai El Chai* is the God-aspect which is concerned with Life as a continuation of Itself.

ADONAI HA ARETZ (אדני הארץ): The deity name of Malkuth which means "The Lord of Earth." This signifies that, in Malkuth, we confront the Creator of all Matter as the Supreme Ruler thereof. Like *Eheieh, El* and *YHVH*, the name *Adonai* ("Lord") is considered a holy emanation of God. Therefore Malkuth is every bit as exalted as Kether, for both are holy aspects of the Divine. An additional deity name of Malkuth is *Adonai Melekh*, "The Lord and King," which stresses these same ideas.

Archangelic Names:[43]

METATRON (מטטרון): The Archangel of Kether. His Hebrew name has no clear etymological base and may in fact be a "channeled" name. The root word, *met*, may indicate downward (communicated) movement. Some authors have tried to provide a Greek etymology for it—and have translated the name as *meta ton thronos* or "near Thy throne." He is described as the Angel of the Presence and the World-Prince. Metatron alone sees the Eternal One face to face. He presides over the whole Tree of Life as well as Kether, and is considered the right-hand masculine Kerub of the Ark. Tradition has it that Metatron communicated the Qabalah to humankind. He has the additional titles of *Metatron Ketheriel, The Lesser YHVH, the King of Angels, the Great Scribe,* and the name *IOEL*—"I am God." Some Hebraic sources identify the patriarch Enoch with this Archangel. Metatron is responsible for presenting God and Human being to each other. He is the link between the human and the Divine, and is responsible for increasing the flow of Light to the initiate. His symbols include a crown, a lamp, and a white rose.

RAZIEL (רזיאל): The Archangel of Chokmah. His name in Hebrew means "the Herald or Sent Forth One of God." This denotes the Archangel as an envoy with a specific mission. The root word of his name, *raz*, indicates the secrets of Initiates—everything which is secret, mysterious or concealed. He is known as *Raziel Chokmael, Ophaniel* (as ruler of the Angelic host known as *Ophanim*), *Secret of God*, and *Angel of Mysteries*. It has been stated that Raziel is "the Angel of the secret regions and chief of the supreme mysteries." Raziel is the personification of the Divine Wisdom. The sapphire *Book of Raziel*, said to have been given to Adam and passed on to the great Hebrew teachers (including Solomon), was a book which held the secrets of the stars: the Zodiacal Signs, the courses of the Planets, and the effects they have on every aspect of Creation. (The prophet Enoch was said to come into

---

[43] Some of the material in this section is derived from the article, "This Holy Invisible Companionship: Angels in the Hermetic Qabalah of the Golden Dawn" by Adam P. Forrest in *The Golden Dawn Journal: Book II: Qabalah: Theory and Magic.*

possession of this book and consequently renamed it *The Book of Enoch*.) Raziel's duty is to make Wisdom available to all who are able to hear it. Raziel, as the teacher of Wisdom, stands atop the white pillar, sometimes envisioned as the Holy Mountain, proclaiming the secrets of the world in a great reverberating voice. He is the Archangel of creative force and energy. His symbols include a key, a book or scroll, an eye, and a lamp.

TZAPHQIEL (צפקיאל): The Archangel of Binah. Her name means "Beholder of God" or "the contemplation of God." Additional titles include *Binael* and *Tzaphqiel Erelel* (as the leader of the Angels known as the *Erelim*). She is the Eye of God, watching and observing, through which the Divine knows and sees all. Tzaphqiel governs meditation and contemplation. She is the Archangel of the archetypal temple, and is behind the formation of all mystical groups that have emanated from what is sometimes referred to as "the Great White Lodge."[44] The root word of her name, *tzaph*, indicates the overflowing of water. Tzaphqiel is also the Archangel of Primal Manifestation. Her symbols include an hourglass, a sickle, and a book.

TZADQIEL (צדקיאל): The Archangel of Chesed. His name means "Righteousness of God." This indicates a rightness by justification after the application of tests and tribulations. It implies one whose essence is essentially correct. The root word of this name, *tzad*, indicates the action of setting snares and hindrances (in order to test). Tzadqiel's duty is to direct everything to its best possible state of being, to make things perfect in order to assure that the ascent to the Divine is possible. Additional titles include *Tzadqiel Gedulael* and *Tzadqiel Chashmadel* (as the leader of the Angels known as *Chashmalim*). He is the Angel of benevolence, abundance, joy, mercy, and memory. His symbols include the rod or staff of guidance, a shepherd crook and an orb.

KHAMAEL (כמאל): The Archangel of Geburah. His name means "the Severity of God."[45] Khamael is the protector of the wronged, and also the Avenging Angel who pursues those who break both human and universal laws. He is associated with divine justice and severity. Khamael is sometimes called "The right hand of God"—meting out justice in order to restore a state of balance throughout the Tree of Life. He controls the aspects of burning and destroying in order to purify and

---

[44] Also referred to as the "Inner Council of Masters" or "Secret Chiefs." These are human beings who are said to have evolved spiritually beyond the need for physical bodies. They remain in the Earth plane to teach younger, less evolved initiates through direct inner communication.

[45] William Gray erroneously stated that the root of this name was *khab*, which meant to suffer, to feel pain or make war. However, prominent Golden Dawn scholar Adam P. Forrest has pieced together the true origin of this name. According to Forrest, the original Archangel of Mars was *Samael*—a name that MacGregor Mathers changed to *Zamael* in order to avoid confusion with the Qliphotic *Samael*. When the Qabalists began to assign Archangels to the Sephiroth, someone attributed a list of Planetary Archangels to their corresponding Sephiroth, and the martial *Samael* was naturally assigned to Geburah. At some point this list was copied into Greek. In late Greek writing, the letter Sigma (the first letter in *Samael*) came to be drawn in the shape of a "C." Still later, when the Greek list was copied into Latin, the copyist made the error of transliterating the Greek name of CAMAHL as "*Camael*" rather than "*Samael*." Even later, someone (perhaps a member of the Golden Dawn) back-transliterated *Camael* as כמאל and thus was *Khamael* born. And although it originated as an error in transliteration, it does help magicians distinguish between *Samael*, Archangel of Evil, *Zamael*, Archangel of Mars, and *Khamael*, Archangel of Geburah.

preserve. Khamael can be likened to a doctor who makes the necessary decision to cut off an infected limb in order to save the patient. Additional titles include *Khamael Gevurael* and *Khamael Seraphiel* (as the leader of the *Seraphim*). His symbols include a sword, a spear, a scourge and a shield.

RAPHAEL (רפאל): The Archangel of Tiphareth.[46] His name means "Healer of God," or "God has healed." *Raphael Tipharethel* is the Archangel specially appointed to heal the wounds (both physical and spiritual) of humankind. The root word of his name, *raph*, indicates medicine and healing as well as every kind of mediation, recovery and redemption. He is the Archangel attributed to the powers of the Divine Intellect as well as to the powers of love and self-esteem. Raphael is a teacher of the Hermetic Arts, thus pointing to his association with Tiphareth, the sphere whose deity name is "Lord God of Knowledge." An additional title is *Raphael Melakhiel* (as leader of the *Melakhim*). His symbols include the Caduceus of Hermes, an orb, a book or a seven-branched menorah.

HANIEL (האניאל): The Archangel of Netzach. Her name means "the glory or grace of God" or "one who sees God." Haniel brings an awareness of harmony and beauty into the lower worlds. She provides us with the opportunity to become aware of the Divine through feeling, emotion and the arts. It is her duty to give humanity a greater understanding of the interrelationships of all created things in the universe. Additional titles include *Haniel Netzachel* and *Haniel Elohel* (as leader of the Angels known as *Elohim*). (Her name has sometimes been misspelled as *Hamiel*.) The root word of her name, *ha*, indicates every evident, demonstrated and determined existence. Her symbols include a red rose, a mirror, a torch, a dove, a unicorn or a chalice.

MICHAEL (or MIKHAEL) (מיכאל): The Archangel of Hod. His name means "The Perfect of God" or "He who is like unto God." *Mikhael Hodael* helps to reveal the marvelous complexity of the universe. His duty is to engage the rational mind and powers of analysis. An additional title is *Mikhael Beniel* (as the leader of the *Beni Elohim*.) The root word of his name, *mi*, indicates water. His symbols include a book, a caduceus, or a staff, a lyre and an abacus.

GABRIEL: (גבריאל) The Archangel of Yesod. Her name means "The Strong One of God" or "the Strength of God." She is the Archangel of the Annunciation and the Resurrection. Gabriel is the divine messenger who relays information between the Divine and humanity. She gives us the powers of vision, hearing, and psychic abilities, as well as the powers of life, procreation and equilibration. Additional

---

[46] Some authors place Michael in Tiphareth and Raphael in Hod. Their reasoning for doing so is that in the Planetary Hierarchy of Angels, Michael is associated with Sol. However Israel Regardie stressed that Golden Dawn students should not confuse the Sephirotic, Planetary, and Elemental Hierarchies. Tiphareth (and not Hod) is the sphere of healing, and thus in the Sephirotic hierarchy Raphael is correctly associated with Tiphareth.

Also, different Angels, like different people, can have the same name. Therefore Raphael of Tiphareth (*Raphael Tipharethel*) will have duties, colors, and symbols which are different from those of either Raphael of Mercury (*Raphael Kokabiel*) or Raphael of Air (*Raphael Ruachel*).

titles include *Gabriel Yesodel* and *Gabriel Kerubiel* (as the leader of the *Kerubim*). The root word of her name, *gab*, indicates the idea of something placed or coming under another thing—something which is convex. Her symbols include a skrying crystal, a magic mirror, an orb or a lamp.

SANDALPHON (סנדלפון): The Archangel of Malkuth. Her Hebrew name has no clear etymological base and may in fact be a "channeled" name. The root word, *san*, may indicate something which is luminous. Some authors have tried to provide a Greek etymology for it—and have translated the name variously as "co-brother," "Lord of the extent of Height" or "the sound of sandals." An additional title is *Sandalphon Malkuthael*. Sandalphon is the twin of Metatron, and is in fact considered another form of Metatron. This points to the idea that Malkuth is the same as Kether, but after another manner. Sandalphon is the Archangel of the Earth sphere and the left-hand feminine Kerub of the Ark. Her duty is to mediate and sort out material energies which are to be brought forth into physical manifestation. She also conveys the power and beauty of the natural world to the Souls of humanity. Her symbols include a monolith, a stone circle, a horn of plenty and a crown of grape leaves.

Angelic Names:

CHAYOTH HA-QODESH (חיות הקדש): The group of Angels assigned to Kether. The name means "Holy Living Creatures." These are the only entities able to live in pure holiness next to the throne of the Eternal. They are the powers of the Eternal Elements whose duty is to uphold the universe and to create the primal matrix upon which the rest of existence is built. They help keep the focus of the initiate at all times on the Highest by increasing the flow of Light through the magician.

OPHANIM (אופנים): The group of Angels assigned to Chokmah. The name means "the Wheels." (This is derived from the root word *oph*, which means to surround or encircle.) The Ophanim are also known as the "many-eyed ones" and are sometimes called the *Galgalim* or "spheres." They are the wheels of the *Merkabah* or throne of God, and are sometimes pictured as wheels with spokes and wings. Their duty is to direct the flow of the divine force into form, thus keeping the cycles of manifestation in constant motion. They provide constant energy and motivation in magical work, and also aid in the manifestation of the divine masculine.

ERELIM (אראלים): The group of Angels assigned to Binah. The name means "the thrones." A throne is a seat of power, and in this case it indicates a focal point from which the divine power can effectively operate. The duty of the Erelim is to stabilize and provide support for the divine energy. They provide form and structure in magical work and are especially associated with the work of magical orders. In addition, they aid in the manifestation of the divine feminine.

CHASHMALIM (חשמלים): The group of Angels assigned to Chesed. The name means "The Shining Ones" or "the Brilliant Ones." They are fiery entities who bond the various parts of the cosmos together as a unified whole. The Chashmalim are sometimes referred to in certain texts as "the Dominations," and they also provide humanity with abundance, joy and the power of laughter.

SERAPHIM (שרפים): The group of Angels assigned to Geburah. The name means "Flaming Ones" and is derived from the root word *seraph*, which means to burn by fire. In certain texts the Seraphim are also known as "Fiery Serpents" or "the Powers." They are often pictured as winged serpents, or beings with six wings and many eyes. It is their duty to bring the principle of heat into the action of creation. They are the Angels of the purifying fire who burn away all that is not worthy of the Divine. The Seraphim provide focus in magical work through discipline, dedication and purification.

MELEKIM (מלכים): The group of Angels assigned to Tiphareth. The name means "the Kings," or "the Messengers." Certain texts refer to these Angels as "the Virtues." The Melekim are healing and life-giving entities. It is their duty to provide points of balance and stability amid the continuously evolving process of manifestation. They facilitate self-knowledge and self-understanding within the initiate.

ELOHIM (אלהים): The group of Angels assigned to Netzach. The name means simply "the gods." Some texts refer to them as "the Principles." The duty of these Angels is to provide stimulus (god-images, god-myths, or spiritual feelings) by which humanity can be made conscious of the Divine and be able to identify with it on a personal level. They engage the intuitive mind of the initiate in the Great Work and reveal the divine simplicity of the universe.

BENI ELOHIM (בני אלהים): The group of Angels assigned to Hod. The name means "Sons of the gods" or "Children of the gods." The Beni Elohim can be likened to polarized (masculine and feminine) units of divine consciousness which provide human intelligence and "god-awareness" in every individual. They are the stimulus that drives human beings in the search for knowledge. (The Elohim and Beni Elohim can be considered as the *Force* and *Form* aspects of all the numerous images of the gods created in the mind of humanity.) The Beni Elohim engage the rational mind of the initiate in the Great Work, and reveal the divine complexity of the universe.

KERUBIM (כרובים): The group of Angels assigned to Yesod. The name means "the Strong Ones" and is derived from the Akkadian word *karibu* which means "one who prays" or "one who intercedes." The Kerubim are the great formative powers of the Elements that are stationed in the sphere of Yesod, the etheric blueprint which supports the physical universe. As supporters of the universe, they can be considered reflections of the Holy Living Creatures in Kether. Their duty is to govern interaction between the inner and outer worlds and to serve as guardians of the portal between the worlds. They act as guides, heralds, or as agents of equilibration. The Kerubim are often pictured as winged humanoids with animal heads, or as sphinxes.

ASHIM (or ISHIM) (אשים): The group of Angels assigned to Malkuth. The name means "Souls of Fire." Said to be composed of snow and fire, these Angels are the forces which hold the atomic particles of physical matter together. Some consider the Ashim to be of human rather than Angelic origin—those individuals who are dedicated to the service of the Light and are messengers of the Spirit.

The Planetary Hierarchies

The Planets, like the Sephiroth, have certain Angelic names associated with them. Attributed to each of the Planets is an Archangelic name, an Intelligence name and a Spirit name. The workings of the Planetary hierarchies are somewhat similar to those of the Sephiroth: a Planetary Archangel governs a Planetary force in a similar fashion to a Sephirotic Archangel. Of the Intelligences and Spirits, tradition has it that the Spirits are evil and the Intelligences good. What this actually denotes, however, is that the Spirits of the Planets are blind forces in their most primal state. The Spirits of the Planets can be used for beneficial purposes, but they must always be employed in conjunction with, and under the presidency of their immediate superiors, the Intelligences, which serve to direct the blind and powerful Spirit forces in their operations.

(Note: many of the Planetary names, especially those of the Intelligences and Spirits, were specially created to add up to the sum of all the numbers on a given magical square or Qamea. Analysis of these names, however, still provides unique insights into the Planetary energies they represent.)

The Archangelic Names:

KASSIEL (כסיאל): The Archangel of Saturn. Ruler of Saturday. Said to be the Archangel of solitudes and tears who "shows forth the unity of the eternal kingdom." Kassiel is sometimes called an Angel of Temperance, and his name means "Speed of God." Kassiel can be envisioned in robes of either black or blue-violet (indigo) ornamented with the symbol of Saturn and holding a scythe or an hourglass. The root word of this name is *kas*, which indicates sum, accumulation, pinnacle or throne.

SACHIEL (סחיאל): The Archangel of Jupiter. Ruler of Thursday. His name means "Covering of God." Sachiel can be envisioned in robes of either violet or blue ornamented with the symbol of Jupiter and holding a royal scepter or a shepherd's staff. The root word of this name is *sach*, which indicates pouring out, purifying and cleansing.

ZAMAEL (זמאל): The Archangel of Mars and the Ruler of Tuesday. "The Severity of God." Zamael can be envisioned in robes and a helmet of red ornamented with the symbol of Mars and holding a sword, lance or shield. The root word of this name is *zam*, which indicates that which gives form or binds together the many into the one.

MICHAEL (or MIKHAEL) (מיכאל): "One who is as God." The Archangel of Sol and the Ruler of Sunday. (Also known as *Mikhael Shemeshel* in order to distinguish this Archangel from *Mikhael Hodael*.) Michael can be envisioned in robes of either orange or yellow ornamented with the symbol of Sol, wearing a sunburst diadem and breastplate.

ANAEL (אנאל):[47] "The Glory or Grace of God." The Archangel of Venus. Ruler of Friday. Anael can be envisioned in robes of green ornamented with the symbol of Venus

---

[47] This Angel has often been mistakenly spelled as *Hanael.*

wearing a girdle around her waist and a garland on her crown. Her symbols include a mirror, a necklace and a seashell. The root word of this name is *an*, which indicates the trials of the Soul, the sphere of moral activity and the body (or personality) of the individual.

RAPHAEL (רפאל): "The Healer of God." The Archangel of Mercury. Ruler of Wednesday. According to some, this Archangel was originally called *Labbiel*. In this hierarchy, Raphael is an Archangel of Science and knowledge. (Also known as *Raphael Kokabiel* in order to distinguish this Archangel from *Raphael Tipharethel*.) Raphael can be envisioned in robes of either yellow or orange ornamented with the symbol of Mercury and holding a Caduceus Wand, a stylus or a scroll.

GABRIEL (גבריאל): "The Strong One of God." The Archangel of Luna and the Ruler of Monday. (Also known as *Gabriel Levannael* in order to distinguish this Archangel from *Gabriel Yesodel*.) Gabriel can be envisioned in robes of either blue, violet, or silver ornamented with the symbol of Luna, crowned with the Lunar crescent and holding a bow.

The Intelligences:

AGIEL (אגיאל): The Intelligence of Saturn. The root of this name is *ag*, which indicates ignition and intense excitement. Similar in appearance to Kassiel.

IOPHIEL (יהפיאל):[48] The Intelligence of Jupiter. His name means "The Beauty of God." He is also invoked as an amulet Angel. Similar in appearance to Sachiel.

GRAPHIEL (גראפיאל): The Intelligence of Mars. His name means "the Might of God." Similar in appearance to Zamael.

NAKHIEL (נכיאל): The Intelligence of Sol. The root of the name is *na*, which means youth, beauty, and grace. It is also related to the root word *nak*, which denotes innocence and purity. Similar in appearance to Michael.

HAGIEL (הגיאל): The Intelligence of Venus. The root of this name is *hag*, which indicates movement, activity and pleasure. Similar in appearance to Anael.

TIRIEL (טיריאל): The Intelligence of Mercury. The root of this word is *ti*, which indicates reflection. (According to Budge, the names of Tiriel and Raphael were discovered on a ring amulet.) Similar in appearance to Raphael.

MALKAH BE TARSHISIM VE-AD RUACHOTH SCHECHALIM— (מלכא בתרשישים ועד רוחות שחלים): The Intelligence of the Intelligences of the Moon. This phrase is virtually untranslatable. According to David Godwin, the best translation of the phrase is "Queen of the Chrysolites and the Eternal Spirits of the Lions."

SHELACHEL[49] (שלחאל): An alternative Lunar Intelligence with a far more manageable name than the preceding one. Similar in appearance to Gabriel. The root

---

[48] This Hebrew spelling of Iophiel was designed to fit the Qamea system. יופיאל is the "traditional" way of spelling this name.

[49] Developed from the Qamea system by Adam Forrest.

of this name is *shel*, which indicates a straight line traced from one object to another—the connecting stroke which unites them. It expresses that which follows its laws, that which remains in its straight line, that which is in good order, in the way of salvation.

The Spirit Names:

ZAZEL (זאזל): The Spirit of Saturn. There is a strong correspondence here with the Hebrew letter Zayin, which means "sword." The root word *za* indicates a dart or an arrow.

HISMAEL (הסמאל): The Spirit of Jupiter. The root word of this name *his* expresses silence and calm.

BARTZABEL (ברצבאל): The Spirit of Mars. The root word of this name is *bar*, which indicates active power, potential emanation and the creative force of being.

SORATH (סורת): The Spirit of Sol. The root word of this name is *sor*, which denotes that which turns around or that which is directed.

QEDEMEL (קדמאל): The Spirit of Venus. The root word of this name is *qed*, which indicates a summit or pivotal point.

TAPHTHARTHARATH (תפתרתרת): The Spirit of Mercury. The root word of this name is *taph*, which expresses the noise of a drum.

SHAD BARSCHEMOTH HA-SHARTATHAN (שד ברשמעת השרתתן): The Spirit of the Spirits of Luna. This phrase is virtually untranslatable. According to David Godwin, the best translation of the phrase is "Demon, son of Shimeath, the Servant-Jackal."

CHASMODAI (חשמודאי): The Spirit of Luna (according to Paracelsus in his doctrine of Talismans). The root word of this name is *chash*, which indicates great movement, central fire, and inner passions which seek to extend themselves.

The Zodiacal Hierarchies

MALKHIDAEL (or MELCHIDAEL) (מלכידאל): Archangel of Aries. The name of this Angel means "fullness of God." Governing Angel of the month of March. Enoch referred to Malkhidiel as *Melkejal* saying, "he rises and rules in the beginning of the year." This Archangel can be envisioned in robes of red ornamented with the Aries symbol. The root word *mal* indicates continuity, plentitude and continued movement from the beginning to the end of a thing.

ASMODEL (אסמודאל): Archangel of Taurus. Angel of the month of April. Asmodel can be envisioned in robes of red-orange (or black) ornamented with the Taurus symbol. The root word *as* indicates the idea of basis as well as the earth.

AMBRIEL (אמבריאל): Archangel of Gemini. Angel of the month of May. The name of Ambriel was found engraved upon a Hebrew amulet for warding off evil. Ambriel can be envisioned in robes of orange (or yellow) ornamented with the

Gemini symbol. The root word *as* indicates origin, source, mother, formative faculty, measure and conditional possibility.

MURIEL (מוריאל): Archangel of Cancer. The name of Muriel comes from the Greek "myrrh." Angel of the month of June. Muriel can be envisioned in robes of yellow-orange (or blue) ornamented with the Cancer symbol. The root word *mur* indicates every variation or permutation.

VERKHIEL (ורכיאל): Archangel of Leo. Angel of the month of July. Verkhiel can be envisioned in robes of yellow (or red) ornamented with the Leo symbol. The root word *ver* indicates the noise of the wind, or that which is fanned.

HAMALIEL (המליאל): Archangel of Virgo. Angel of the month of August. Hamaliel can be envisioned in robes of yellow-green (or black) ornamented with the Virgo symbol. The root word *ham* indicates effort, labor, activity and contractile movement.

ZURIEL (זוריאל): Archangel of Libra. The name of Zuriel means "my rock is God." Angel of the month of September. One of the seventy childbed amulet Angels. Zuriel is also said to cure foolishness in man. In the Bible, Zuriel is described as "chief of the house of the father of the families of Merari." (Numbers 3:35.) Zuriel can be envisioned in robes of green (or yellow) ornamented with the Libra symbol. The root word *zur* indicates the idea of dispersion, radiation and dissemination, going out from the center, and manifesting Light.

BARKHIEL (ברכיאל): Archangel of Scorpio. The name of Barkhiel means "lightning of god." Barkhiel is the Angel of the month of October and he has dominion over lightning. At one time Barkhiel was invoked to bring success in games of chance. Barkhiel can be envisioned in robes of blue-green (or blue) ornamented with the Scorpio symbol. The root word *bar* indicates the idea of production with power, potential emanation or creation, fruit, offspring, and movement that tends to manifest exteriorly the creative force of being.

ADNAKHIEL (אדנכיאל):[50] Archangel of Sagittarius. Angel of the month of November. Adnakhiel can be envisioned in robes of blue (or red) ornamented with the Sagittarius symbol. The root word *ad* indicates the power of division, force, emanation, and individual distinction.

HANAEL (הניאל):[51] Archangel of Capricorn. Angel of the month of December. Hanael is invoked against evil. Hanael can be envisioned in robes of blue-violet (or black) ornamented with the Capricorn symbol. The root word *han* indicates the idea of actual and present existence, realities, and anything that can be perceived by the senses.

KAMBRIEL (or CAMBRIEL) (כמבריאל): Archangel of Aquarius. Angel of the month of January. Kambriel can be envisioned in robes of violet (or yellow)

---

[50] This name is usually incorrectly spelled as *Advachiel*.
[51] Not to be confused with *Haniel*, the Archangel of Netzach or *Anael*, the Archangel of Venus.

ornamented with the Aquarius symbol. The root word *kam* indicates the desire for assimilation.

AMNITZIEL (אמניציאל): Archangel of Pisces. Angel of the month of February. Amnitziel can be envisioned in robes of red-violet (or blue) ornamented with the Pisces symbol.✿

SECTION 6: Correspondences of Earth

 The 1 = 10 grade of Zelator is attributed to the Element of Earth. Earth symbolizes the stable, grounded part of the psyche. It is the Element of corporeal nature and physical manifestation. Earth is feminine, receptive, solid, and nurturing. The color given for Earth is black, the cardinal point is North. (Review all information on the Element of Earth given in Chapter One.)

The study of gemstones and minerals is some of the work to be undertaken by the Zelator. Stones were very useful to the ancients, serving as weapons, structural fortifications, markers, monuments, talismans, and even as necessary implements for creating fire. The early philosophers taught that the four Elements were present in the physiology of the human body; Fire corresponded to body heat, Water to the various body fluids, Air to the gases, and Earth to bones and flesh. Thus the stones and rocks themselves were symbolic of the bones of the gods in archaic worship. Stone worship, practiced all over the world, was probably the earliest type of religious expression known to humanity. The great monoliths erected by the ancients were venerated because of their agelessness and ability to resist the forces of decay and destruction that so plagued biological beings. These stones symbolized strength, unity and the very dwelling place of the eternal forces.

The material body of all things came to be represented as a rock. Eventually this symbolism evolved into the shape of a cube or pedestal, while the Spirit or essence of all things came to be symbolized by carved figures which surmounted the pedestal. Thus were the first altars and stone images of the gods created.

Gemstones and minerals also play an important role in the art of physical Alchemy. By definition, minerals are "a naturally occurring homogenous substance formed by inorganic processes and having a definite and limited range of physical properties, and a molecular structure usually expressed in crystalline form." In more general terms, minerals are "inorganic materials especially as distinguished from animal or vegetable matter." Minerals are the building blocks of the Earth's crust and of the very bedrock of the Planet.

To the Alchemist, there are three kingdoms or principalities: (1) vegetable, (2) animal, and (3) mineral. Each kingdom has its own essence. All three are evolved from the same original source, but each manifests under different *vibrations* in its respective realm. The vegetable kingdom has the lowest vibratory rate, while the mineral kingdom has the highest. Humanity is the highest part of the middle (animal) kingdom, which holds the balance between all three kingdoms. Thus humanity can partake of either the higher or lower kingdoms to its benefit through the art of Alchemy.

Certain stones and minerals (as well as metals) are attributed to different Planetary, Elemental, Zodiacal and Sephirotic energies. These various affiliations are based upon many factors: the stone's color, properties, chemical makeup, and vibratory rate.

It is therefore appropriate that the student of the 1 = 10 grade commit the following list of gemstone correspondences to memory:

Precious Stones and Minerals

The Sephiroth

1. Kether — Diamond
2. Chokmah — Star Ruby, Turquoise
3. Binah — Star Sapphire, Pearl
4. Chesed — Amethyst, Sapphire
5. Geburah — Ruby
6. Tiphareth — Topaz, Yellow Diamond
7. Netzach — Emerald
8. Hod — Opal, especially Fire Opal
9. Yesod — Quartz
10. Malkuth — Rock Crystal, Salt

The Zodiacal Signs[52]

Aries	—	Diamond, Red Jasper, Garnet
Taurus	—	Emerald, Red Coral, Lapis Lazuli
Gemini	—	Pearl, Agate, Alexandrite
Cancer	—	Ruby, Amber, Moonstone
Leo	—	Sardonyx, Cat's Eye, Chrysolite
Virgo	—	Sapphire, Peridot
Libra	—	Opal, Malachite, Emerald
Scorpio	—	Topaz, Obsidian, Bloodstone
Sagittarius	—	Turquoise, Blue Zircon
Capricorn	—	Garnet, Jet, Onyx
Aquarius	—	Amethyst, Aquamarine
Pisces	—	Bloodstone, Pearl

The Planets

Saturn	—	Onyx, Jet, Anthracite
Jupiter	—	Amethyst, Sapphire, Lapis Lazuli
Mars	—	Ruby, Garnet, Bloodstone
Sol	—	Topaz, Chrysolite, Heliodor, Zircon
Venus	—	Emerald, Turquoise, Jade, Malachite
Mercury	—	Opal, Fire Opal, Agate, Serpentine
Luna	—	Moonstone, Pearl, Quartz, Fluorspar

---

[52] Unfortunately there is little agreement as to the "correct" birthstones.

The Elements

Fire   —   Ruby, Fire Opal
Water   —   Aquamarine, Coral, Moonstone
Air   —   Topaz, Opal
Earth   —   Moss Agate, Rock Salt, Onyx, Galena

Hebrew and Other Names Connected with Earth

Element Name: ARETZ or OPHIR (ארץ or עָפִיר)
Outer Divine Name: ADONAI HA-ARETZ (אדני הארץ)
Cardinal Point: TZAPHON (North) (צפון)
Archangel: URIEL (אוריאל)
Angel: PHORLAKH (פורלאך)
Ruler: KERUB (כרוב)
Elementals: GNOMES
King of Gnomes: GHOB

A mythological Image of a Gnome

URIEL[53] is the great winged Archangel of Elemental Earth, whose name means "the Light of God." An additional title is *Uriel Aretziel.* Stationed in the North, Uriel is visualized as rising up from the vegetation of the Earth holding stems of ripened wheat and wearing robes of citrine, russet, olive and black.

SANDALPHON is the great feminine Archangel of the Planet Earth and the sphere of Malkuth. She is extremely tall and dark complected and is usually visualized in robes of the four colors of Malkuth.

Earth Deities

There are numerous deities associated with the Earth from different pantheons. The student should be familiar with several Earth deities from various Western traditions:

GEB (or SEB): The principle Earth god of the Egyptians and the father of Osiris, Isis, Nephthys, and Set. The Earth itself formed the body of Geb. He is usually depicted in the form of a man who wears upon his head the white crown or the crown of the North, to which is added the *Atef* crown. Geb is also depicted as a goose, of the particular species called *seb.* He is the god of the Earth's surface which gives rise to vegetation, and he is important to the mythology of the Underworld as well—having authority over the tombs of the dead. Geb figures prominently in the first act of creation, when the Earth god and the Sky goddess, Nut, were locked in a lovers' embrace. Geb's father Shu, the Air god, interceded and lifted

Geb

---

[53] Uriel is sometimes spelled as Auriel.

the starry body of Nut off that of the Earth god, thus forming the Earth, the starry heaven and the air between the two.

TAMMUZ (or DUMUZI): The principle Earth deity and harvest god of the Assyro-Babylonian pantheon. Tammuz was the lover of Ishtar, the primary goddess figure. However, like a ripened ear of corn, Tammuz was cut down—ravished by death in the fullness of youth and forced to descend into the underworld. Ishtar descended into the Earth and suffered death to save him. As a compromise, Tammuz was destined to spend half of the year ruling over the land during a season of growth and abundance. After harvest however, Tammuz entered a period of withdrawal back into the underworld. Thus were the seasonal cycles of the Earth created.

Other Babylonian Earth deities include a great Earth Mother who was worshiped under the various names of **NINHURSAG, NINMAH, NINTU** and **KI**. She was the pre-eminent Mother goddess, who, like the Gaea of the Greeks, represented the great creative principle.

GAEA (Equivalent to the Roman *Tellus Mater*): One of the most ancient of the Greek deities, Gaea was the deep-breasted and fertile Earth which appeared out of Chaos. From her was borne Uranus, the sky crowned with stars, followed by the mountains and the sea. Together, Gaea and Uranus produced the first race, the Titans. She is commonly represented in the form of a gigantic woman. In later times she became identified with the goddess, **RHEA**, whose name means "Earth."

CYBELE: Originally a Greek goddess of caverns, Cybele personified the Earth in its primitive and savage state. She exercised dominion over wild animals and was worshiped on the tops of mountains. Greek representations of Cybele retained an Asiatic character. She is usually depicted with the turreted crown of an Asian Mother-goddess, seated on a throne flanked by two lions, or else driving a chariot pulled by lions. **ATTIS** was the agricultural and vegetation god whose role in respect to Cybele was comparable to that of Tammuz to the Babylonian Ishtar (or **ADONIS** to the Phoenician Astarte).

DEMETER (Equivalent to the Roman *Ceres*): The Greek goddess of the fruitful Earth, Demeter represented the fertile and cultivated soil. She is above all a goddess of fruit trees and fields. Demeter was especially a corn-goddess, but wheat and barley were also sacred to her. She governed the harvest and all the agricultural activities. The goddess is usually represented dressed as a mature woman in a long robe and often wearing a veil that covers the back of her head. She is sometimes shown crowned with ears of corn or a ribbon, and she holds in her hand either a scepter, ears of corn, or a torch.

Demeter

PERSEPHONE (or *Kore* "girl"): The daughter of Demeter is the Greek goddess of harvest and fertility. Persephone was kidnapped by the God of the Underworld, Hades. At the loss of her daughter, Demeter set about making the Earth barren. The

Persephone

god Zeus persuaded Hades to release the young Kore, but tempted her to eat some pomegranate seeds first, which made their union indissoluble. To settle the matter, Zeus decided that Persephone would live with her husband in the Underworld for one-third of the year and spend the other two-thirds with her mother. Thus for part of the year, when Persephone joined Hades, the Earth became cold, sorrowful and unproductive, but when she returned in the Spring, the Earth resumed its warmth along with its mantle of flowering plants and fertile crops. Persephone is portrayed as maiden crowned and enthroned. She sometimes carries an ear of corn or a pomegranate.

Other Western Earth deities include numerous Celtic fertility goddesses or matres—Mother goddesses:

DANU or **DANA:** The companion of Bile. The descendants of Danu called themselves *Tuatha De Dannan* ("people of the goddess Dana" or "The children of Don").

Nerthus

BRIGIT: Celtic goddess of the seasons. Brigit's celebration *Imbolc*, a great festival of pagan purification, takes place on February 1st. (Incidentally, with the coming of Christianity, the goddess Brigit was transformed into a patron saint.)

Teutonic fertility goddesses include **GEFJON**, "the Giver" or "the Donor," and **NERTHUS**, the productive Earth Mother. Nerthus is pictured driving a chariot pulled by heifers.

EPONA: A Celtic goddess who was the protectress of horses, Epona also presided over the fertility of the soil.✪

SECTION 7: Divination and Geomancy

People who have no experience with Tarot and other forms of divination often think that these practices are little more than superstition and folklore. The truth is that those who study and practice divination believe that all things in the universe are *divine*. Nothing takes place in a divine universe by chance or coincidence. Nothing that exists within a divine universe is without meaning or significance.

The word *divination* is based on a Latin word which means "the faculty of foreseeing." The word comes from the Latin word for "divine power," or "of the gods." This indicates that the true meaning of the word *divination* is "to make divine."

Far from being a superstitious practice, the art of divination reveals itself as a spiritual science that seeks to discover the divine meaning behind "chance" events. Divination has existed as a tool for psychic well-being and spiritual health long before modern psychology was born, although the later science has often borrowed heavily from the former.

Ever since human beings first realized that there were Higher Powers beyond the Physical world, we have tried to communicate with these Forces. Prayers and invocations to the gods and goddesses developed out of the human desire to talk to the Divine—to worship them and ask them for guidance and intervention. Ritual trance and meditation developed out the human desire to let the gods talk to us—to enrich our lives with a higher form of Wisdom. Divination developed as a way to interact with the gods. It was a method by which humans could interpret and understand the Will of the Divine.

Divination can open up the mind of the *diviner* to wonders of the spiritual world and the invisible universe which is behind the visible universe. Also, the different methods of divination are good exercises for developing the student's powers of intuition and imagination.

The art of divination is a process of spiritual growth through which the diviner attempts to uncover what specific forces are at work in a given area of the astral realms. It is the art of acquiring psychic information with the help of physical accessories such as Tarot cards, skrying mirrors, crystals, pendulums or similar psychic aids. Properly done, divination can determine which underlying energies are at work in a specific region of the invisible universe. However, any information obtained in this manner is to be used as a guide or a road map only—not as an undeniable destiny carved into stone. Divination is an art that takes much practice in order to become proficient, yet practice is exactly what is needed in order to fine-tune the psychic powers of the diviner. The beginning student should not worry about whether or not the answers given in the divination are always correct. The important thing is that the student gradually increases his/her astral powers of perception with each reading.

One very important principle in any form of divination is the *Law of Correspondences*. This idea states that there is always a correspondence between the many planes of Being. The Hermetic Axiom states this idea in the words: *"As Above, so Below. As Below, so Above."* This Law is called into use whenever we apply symbols to mean certain things.

For example, in Tarot a cup is used to symbolize the Womb of the Divine Mother. A cup and a womb are definitely not the same thing. One is metal, the other is flesh and blood. Yet they both have the same essential quality of containing and nurturing life. In a sense, they have a similar cosmic reality.

Another example of the Law of Correspondences is when the metal gold is used to indicate the Sun, or silver for the Moon. It would not be right to say that gold is the same as the Sun or that silver is the same as the Moon. But the two metals and the two Planets are both symbols used to describe the same two divine realities.

The Law of Correspondences helps initiates apply various meanings to visible symbols, enabling us to better comprehend the divine nature of things which are not visible to us. Thus it is important that the student memorize the correspondences which apply to a system such as Geomancy or Tarot. All images and ideas associated with the system must become second-nature to the diviner, so that they can be recalled instantly in a reading.

Geomancy

The random generation of the Geomantic Tetragrams is called *Squilling*. Nowadays it is usually performed using pen and paper, by simply creating sixteen rows of dots with ink on paper or parchment. However, it was originally performed by poking holes into dirt or sand to obtain different symbols and figures.

Although this procedure can be done entirely using pen and paper, actual use of the Earth in the divination is a more powerful method of forming the magical link between the diviner and the Planetary Genius summoned.

To this end the student may wish to construct a wooden box specifically for Geomantic divinations. This box is to be filled with Earth and consecrated by a ritual. A wand is used for poking holes into the dirt and squilling the sixteen *Root Lines* which generate the Tetragrams.[54]

Geomancy can be performed using a variety of other techniques as well:[55]

Pebble-working: A bag of gemstones can be used for squilling the figures. The diviner draws a handful of stones from the bag and sets them aside in pairs until there are either one or two stones remaining, odd or even. This is done sixteen times to obtain the sixteen Root Lines needed.

Coin-Working: Flipping coins is an easy way to generate yes/no or odd/even responses. *I Ching* coins can easily be adapted for this purpose.

Dice-Working: The rolling of a dice will immediately give you an odd or even number.

Stone-Working: A set of Geomancy stones can be constructed out of oven-hardening clay (or wood) with the figures of the Tetragrams painted right on them. (Only ten stones are needed for a full set since many of the Tetragrams are reversed images of each other.) This is a quick way of squilling, since one only needs to pick out four completed Tetragrams rather than determining sixteen different Root Lines.

The Ruling Spirits of Geomancy

A successful divination using this method depends on the contact made with a Geomantic Spirit or *Genius*. These Spirits are collectively called *Genii*. They are the ruling Spirits of the Planetary energies invoked in a Geomantic reading. At the beginning of a reading, the *diviner* selects one of these ruling Spirits—whichever Spirit best reflects the Planetary nature of the question being asked. The diviner should take care to phrase the question clearly and concisely, because the answer is only going to reflect the most literal form of the question.

---

[54] The construction of the Geomancy Box is described in our book, *Secrets of a Golden Dawn Temple.*

[55] From Adam Forrest's article, "Mysteria Geomantica: Teachings in the Art of Geomancy," published in *The Golden Dawn Journal, Book 1: Divination.*

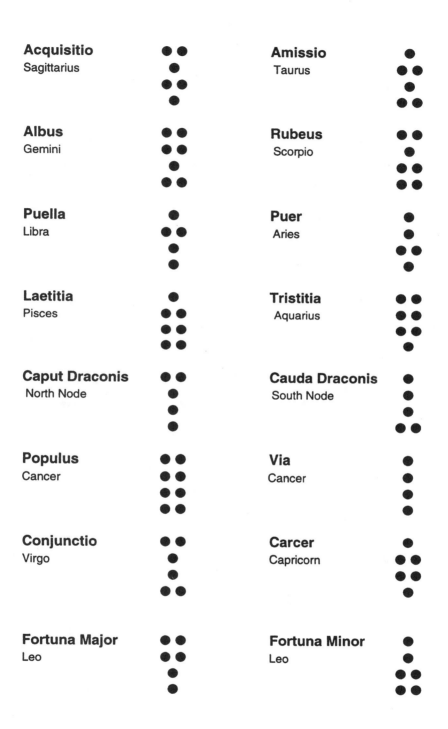

Acquisitio	Amissio
Sagittarius	Taurus
Albus	Rubeus
Gemini	Scorpio
Puella	Puer
Libra	Aries
Laetitia	Tristitia
Pisces	Aquarius
Caput Draconis	Cauda Draconis
North Node	South Node
Populus	Via
Cancer	Cancer
Conjunctio	Carcer
Virgo	Capricorn
Fortuna Major	Fortuna Minor
Leo	Leo

The Sixteen Tetragrams of Geomancy

The Tetragrams and their Genii

Geomantic Figure	Zodiacal Attribution	Name of Figure	Ruling Planet	Sigil of Genius	Ruler (Genius)
(dot figure)	♈	Puer	♂	(sigil)	Bartzabel
(dot figure)	♉	Amissio	♀	(sigil)	Kedemel
(dot figure)	♊	Albus	☿	(sigil)	Taphthartharath
(dot figure)	♋	Populus	☽	(sigil)	Chasmodai
(dot figure)	♋	Via	☽	(sigil)	Chasmodai
(dot figure)	♌	Fortuna Major	☉	(sigil)	Sorath
(dot figure)	♌	Fortuna Minor	☉	(sigil)	Sorath
(dot figure)	♍	Conjunctio	☿	(sigil)	Taphthartharath
(dot figure)	♎	Puella	♀	(sigil)	Kedemel
(dot figure)	♏	Rubeus	♂	(sigil)	Bartzabel
(dot figure)	♐	Acquisitio	♃	(sigil)	Hismael
(dot figure)	♑	Carcer	♄	(sigil)	Zazel
(dot figure)	♒	Tristitia	♄	(sigil)	Zazel
(dot figure)	♓	Laetitia	♃	(sigil)	Hismael
(dot figure)	☊	Caput Draconis	♀ ♃	(sigil)	Hismael and Kedemel
(dot figure)	☋	Cauda Draconis	♂ ♄	(sigil)	Zazel and Bartzabel

This system of divination is unlike others in that the psychic awareness of the diviner is of less importance than in a system such as Tarot. It is the diviner's ability to evoke the Spirit that becomes the focus of consideration for a successful Geomantic divination. This is the reason why Geomancy is perhaps a better method for individuals who have trouble visualizing or interpreting a reading.

The Mechanics of Geomancy

Using pen and paper: Formulate and state a question you wish to have answered in the divination.

Using a *Squilling sheet* or Geomancy chart especially created for Divination, trace an *invoking Pentagram of Earth* in the center of a circle. Inside the pentagram draw the sigil of the Planetary Genius who pertains to your question—the Genius of the Planet whose energy would be most receptive or helpful in the matter.

The diviner should recite a short invocation prior to tracing these magical symbols. First invoke the highest Divine Name for Elemental Earth, followed by the hierarchy of Angels associated with Earth, and finally enlist the help of the Planetary Genius who is involved in the working.

The following invocation, which procures the aid of the Genius *Hismael* is an example of such an invocation. The underlined names can be exchanged for whatever entities the Geomancer intends to work with.

> *In the Divine Name of ADONAI HA-ARETZ, I invoke the mighty and powerful Angel URIEL, come forth and invest this divination with Truth. I invoke thee, choir of Angels known as ASHIM, thou Souls of Flame, I invoke thee <u>SACHIEL</u>, thou Archangel of <u>TZEDEK</u> who rules the day and hour of the Planet <u>JUPITER</u>. Come forth IOPHIEL to manifest the Spirit of this working—the Spirit <u>HISMAEL</u>. Come forth I say and invest this working with the truth of what I perceive.*[56]

Next create the sixteen *Root Lines* required for judging the outcome by randomly squilling sixteen lines of ink dots as they fall into the sixteen different segments of the chart. (This process should take on somewhat of the nature of automatic writing, with the diviner *not consciously* aware of number of dots being put on the paper.) When finished, each of the sixteen sections should contain at least one dot. Then determine whether each line has either an odd or even number of dots. *If a line has an even number it is assigned two dots. If the number is odd, it receives one dot.*

The Mothers

The sixteen lines produce four *Mothers* known as figures 1—4 on the Squilling sheet. Each Mother is a figure formed from four of the sixteen Root Lines. Look at the first Mother Tetragram that you have constructed. Next to the top Root Line, write the word HEAD. Next to the second Root Line, write the word NECK. Next

---

[56] Adapted from an invocation from Mitch and Gail Henson's article "By the Signs of the Earth: Geomancy in the Golden Dawn," published in *The Golden Dawn Journal, Book 1: Divination*.

to the third Root Line, write the word BODY. And next to the bottom Root Line, write the word FEET.

The following is an example of the what the figures might look like:

Mothers	4	3	2	1
Head	●	● ●	●	● ●
Neck	●	●	● ●	● ●
Body	●	●	● ●	●
Feet	● ●	● ●	● ●	●

The Daughters

Once the four Mothers have been generated, the Geomancer must determine the four *Daughters*. The *Abacus Worksheet*[57] provides the easiest method for generating these figures. Transfer the first Mother into the vertical column labeled M1 on the Abacus worksheet. The four divisions of the column are for the separation of the Head, Neck, Body and Feet. The second Mother is placed in column M2, while Mothers 3 and 4 fall respectively into columns M3 and M4.

The first Daughter (D1) is formed from the *Heads* of all the Mothers from 1 to 4. placed on top of one another:

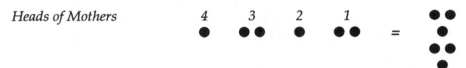

This is the first Daughter, or figure number 5.

Do the same with the Necks of the Mothers:

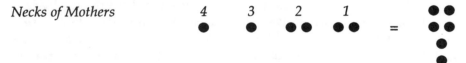

This is the second Daughter, or figure number 6.

Do the same with the Bodies of the Mothers:

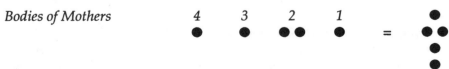

This is the third Daughter, or figure number 7.

---

[57] From Adam Forrest's article "Mysteria Geomantica: Teachings in the Art of Geomancy" published in *The Golden Dawn Journal, Book 1: Divination.*

An Astrologer Casting a Horoscope on a Square Chart

Do the same with the Feet of the Mothers:

Feet of Mothers

This is the fourth Daughter, or figure number 8.

On the Abacus worksheet, you will have formed the four figures of the Mothers (M1-M4) on the vertical columns, The four Daughters (D1-D4) will be formed from right to left on the horizontal rows of the Abacus.

The Nephews

The next group of four figures that the Geomancer must generate is known as the *Nephews*, sometimes called the *Resultants* (figures 9-12). The Nephews are generated in a somewhat different manner than were the Daughters. The first Nephew is formed by adding together the dots which compose the first and second Mothers (M1 + M2). By adding the dots of two figures together you will get an odd or even number. If the number were even you would put down two dots. If it were odd you would put down one dot. In our example to get Nephew 1, we will take Mothers 1 and 2, add together the two dots labeled *Heads*. This is the *Head* of the First Nephew (or figure 9).

Add together the dots labeled *Necks* of Mothers 1 and 2 using the same technique. The result will be the *Neck* of Nephew 1.

Add together the dots labeled *Bodies* of Mothers 1 and 2 using the same method. The result will be the *Body* of Nephew 1.

Add together the dots labeled *Feet* of Mothers 1 and 2 as before. The result will be the *Feet* of Nephew 1.

(The four inner side bars of the Abacus worksheet labeled N1-N4 are for generating the Nephews. Nephew 1 [N1] is located to the right of Mothers 1 and 2, so that the Geomancer can see the calculation clearly.)

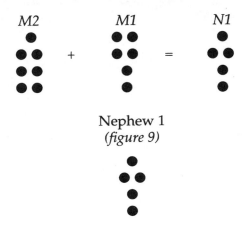

Nephew 1
(figure 9)

Following the same procedure with Mothers 3 and 4 you should be able to generate Nephew 2. (N2) is located to the left of Mothers 3 and 4 on the Abacus worksheet.

Nephew 2
(figure 10)

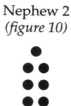

We now obtain Nephews 3 and 4 by following the same procedure with the two sets of Daughters. Nephew 3 is formed by adding together the first two daughters D1 + D2. Nephew 4 is formed by combining the final two daughters D3 + D4.

Nephew 4   Nephew 3
(figure 12)   *(figure 11)*

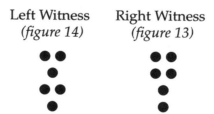

The Witnesses

Twelve Tetragrams have now been generated. Form the *Right Witness* (figure 13) by basic addition. Add together the first two Nephews (N1 + N2). Then form the *Left Witness* (figure 14) by adding the final two Nephews (N3 + N4).

Left Witness   Right Witness
(figure 14)   *(figure 13)*

The Judge

Form the *Judge* (figure 15) by adding together the two witnesses.

Judge
(figure 15)

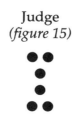

1. Access the general nature of the figure.

2. Interpret the figure in light of the house to which the question pertains. (Some relationships between the Judge and the house of the question will strengthen or weaken the impact of the Judge. Refer to the *Table of Essential Dignities* given in Chapter One.)

3. Interpret the Judge and the two Witnesses:
   A good Judge made of two good Witnesses is good.
   A bad Judge made of two bad Witnesses is bad.
   A good Judge made of mixed good & bad Witnesses means
       success, but delay and vexation.
   Two good Witnesses and a bad Judge, the result will be unfor-
       tunate in the end.
   First Witness is good and the second bad, the success will
       be very doubtful.
   First Witness bad and the second good, unfortunate beginning
       will take a good turn.

4. Check to see if the same Geomantic figure as the Judge actually turns up anywhere else.

At this point the Geomancer may have all that is necessary to obtain a quick answer by examining the three figures of the *Right Witness*, the *Left Witness* and the *Judge*. The Right Witness can be interpreted as the beginning of the matter, the Left Witness is the way in which the matter progresses, and the Judge is the conclusion of the Matter.

In our example, the Judge is the figure of Conjunctio, a positive Tetragram that indicates harmonious union and coming together. It is also the Tetragram of Virgo—an Earthy Sign. The Left Witness is Acquisitio— gain, which is attributed to Sagittarius—a Fire Sign. The Right Witness is Fortuna Major, a very positive figure associated with Leo, another Fire Sign. Overall, the results of such a reading depict a positive Fiery force grounding itself harmoniously into Earth or manifestation. A very good reading.

Of course the Geomancer may at this point decide to go further and explore the subtle nuances of the working. This is done more or less by reading the divination as one would read a Zodiacal chart.

The Part of Fortune

Calculate the *Part of Fortune* (especially helpful in questions of money). It is determined by adding together all the points of the first twelve tetragrams, then dividing this number by 12. The remaining number will indicate the house to which the Part of Fortune is allocated. Having found the house, the figure will provide, in context of its house, details concerning the Querent's financial position.

The Square Zodiacal Chart

Lay out the first twelve figures (Mothers, Daughters, and Nephews) on a chart provided for interpretation of houses. (This is to give greater detail to the answer of a complex question. A simple "yes/no" question will have been answered by this point.) The figures are placed as follows:

Figure 1 goes in the 10th house.　　Figure 2 goes in the 1st house.
Figure 3 goes in the 4th house.　　Figure 4 goes in the 7th house.
Figure 5 goes in the 11th house.　　Figure 6 goes in the 2nd house.
Figure 7 goes in the 5th house.　　Figure 8 goes in the 8th house.
Figure 9 goes in the 12th house.　　Figure 10 goes in the 3rd house.
Figure 11 goes in the 6th house.　　Figure 12 goes in the 9th house.

(*One of the old Medieval rules in Geomancy was to check to see if the *Rubeus* or *Cauda Draconis* fell in the first house. If either of these figures was present, the Geomancer was advised to destroy the chart and wait at least two hours before asking the question again. This old superstition is equivalent to teaching a Tarot reader to destroy a reading and thoroughly panic the Querent if the Tarot Trumps of the Devil or Death turned up as the Significator. Modern occultists no longer view the Sign of Scorpio or the South Node of the Moon as Evil. Therefore this particular rule should be disregarded.)

Determine which particular Zodiacal house relates to the question being asked. This figure will have great significance to the reading.

Write down the Zodiacal attributions of each figure in each house. (If the First house contains the figure of Amissio, which relates to Taurus, then the first house *starts with and is* Taurus. The rest of the houses follow in order, so that Figure 6 in the 2nd house is in the house of Gemini, even if the Figure happens to be Fortuna Minor, which relates to Leo. Thus as in Astrology, the ruling Planet of Leo, the Sun, is in Gemini.)

Determine the Planets of the Tetragrams, as they fall in each house; i.e., Puer equals Mars, Conjunctio equals Mercury. A normal Zodiacal chart showing the twelve houses in the circular chart or wheel form might be useful to write this information on. (A major difference between Geomancy and Astrology is that in a Geomantic chart, one Planet may occupy several different houses at the same time.)

Also determine the balance of Elements (Fire, Water, Air, Earth) in the chart. See if an imbalance of Elemental forces is apparent.

Estimate the *Accidental Dignity* of the figure. In modern Astrology, *Essential Dignity* relates to a Planet in a particular Sign. A Planet in a Sign in which it is strengthened is in one of its Essential Dignities. *Accidental Dignity* relates to a Planet in a particular house. A Planet in a house in which it is strengthened is in one of its Accidental Dignities. The Accidental Dignity of a figure in a particular house is a measure of its strength and the degree to which it will influence the judgment.) This brings us to the fact that *the Tetragrams are more strongly correlated to the Planets than they are to the Zodiacal Signs*, especially when they are placed in Zodiacal houses, such as on the Square Chart. It is for this reason that on the chart of *Accidental Dignities* certain Tetragrams can include two sets of Triplicity correspondences (in particular the Tetragrams assigned to Venus and Mercury).

A figure is *Strongest* when in what is called its house, *Very Strong* when in its Exaltation, *Strong* in its Triplicity, *Very Weak* in its Fall, *Weakest* of all in its Detriment. A figure is in its Fall when in a house opposite to that of its Exaltation, and in its Detriment when opposite to its own house. (Refer to the Table of Accidental Dignities. The numbers in this Table refer to the numbers of the Zodiacal houses; 1 = the first house, 2 = the second house, etc).

Aspects:

Consider the aspects[58] of the figure: *Opposition* would be the house directly opposite the house in question. The house in Question is known as the *Significator.*

Square—count four houses from and including the Significator in both directions. Both Opposition and Square are stressful.

Sextile—count three houses from and including the Significator in both directions. This is a mildly benevolent aspect.

Trine—count five houses from and including the Significator in both directions. Both Sextile and Trine ease the situation.

The directions are known as *Dexter* (clockwise) and *Sinister* (counterclockwise). Dexter is the more powerful of the two.

Meanings of the Tetragrams in the Houses

The following list contains brief summaries of the Geomantic figures in the Zodiacal houses. We suggest that the student substitute the word "unfavorable" for the Medieval term "evil."

ACQUISITIO

Generally good for profit and gain.

Ascendant	Happy, success in all things.
Second House	Very prosperous.
Third House	Favor and riches.
Fourth House	Good fortune and success.
Fifth House	Good success.
Sixth House	Good—especially if it agrees with the fifth.
Seventh House	Reasonably good.
Eighth House	Rather good, but not very. The sick shall die.
Ninth House	Good in all demands.
Tenth House	Good in suits.
Eleventh House	Good in all.
Twelfth House	Evil, pain and loss.

---

[58] Aspecting is explained in the Third Knowledge Lecture in Chapter Three of this book.

Diviner: _____

Querent: _____

Date: _____

Question:

House: ___ Planet: ____ Genius: _____

	Head
	Neck
	Body
	Feet

Mother 1
(figure 1)

	Head
	Neck
	Body
	Feet

Mother 2
(figure 2)

	Head
	Neck
	Body
	Feet

Mother 3
(figure 3)

	Head
	Neck
	Body
	Feet

Mother 4
(figure 4)

A Squilling Worksheet

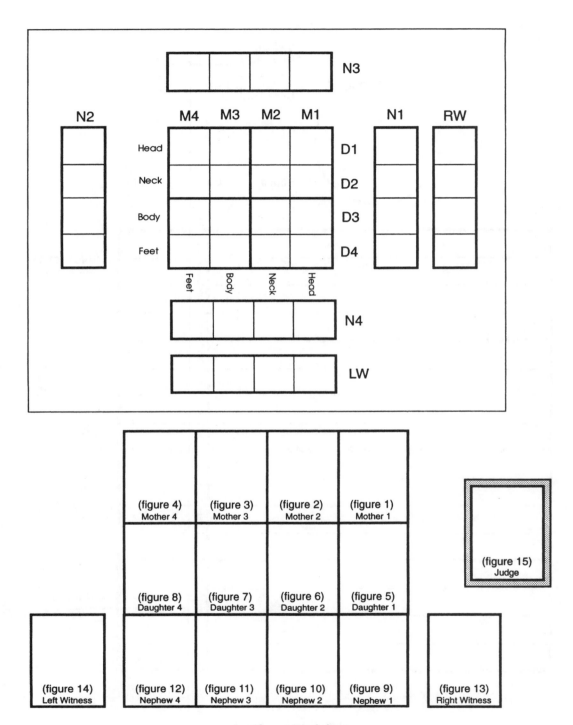

An Abacus Worksheet

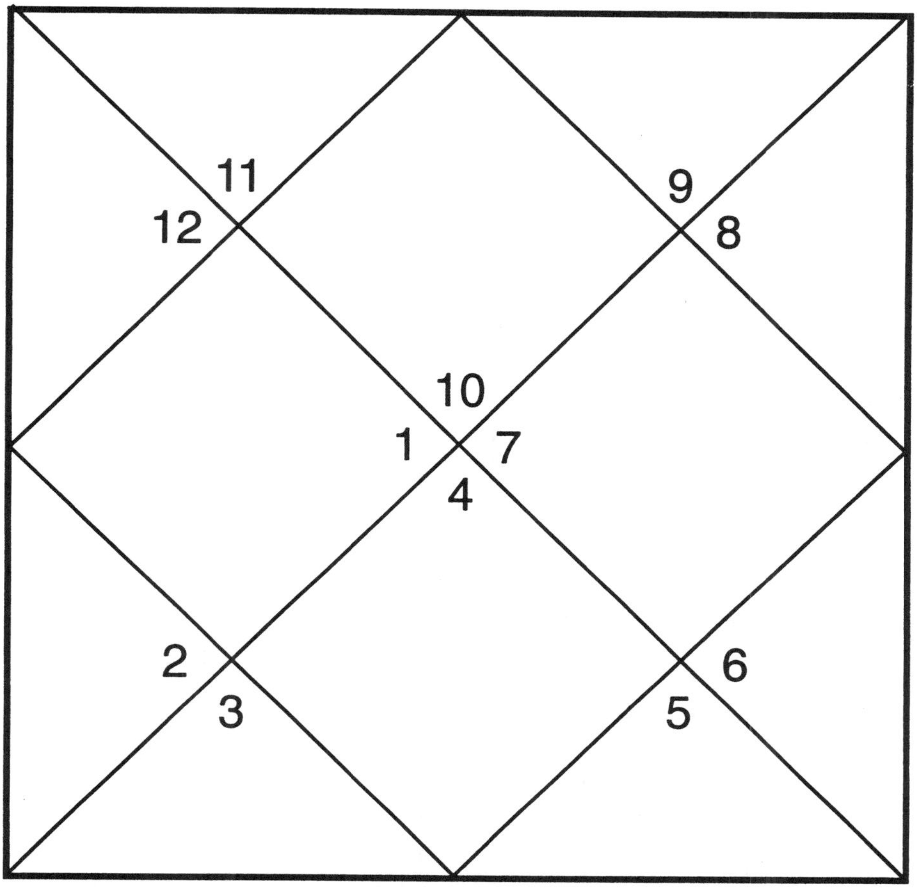

Significator: _____

Trines: _____

Squares: _____

Sextiles: _____

Oppositions: _____

4th House: _____

Fire: _____

Water: _____

Air: _____

Earth: _____

Interpretation:

A Square Zodiacal Chart
Representing the Twelve Houses

TABLE OF ACCIDENTAL DIGNITIES
Strengths and Weaknesses of the Tetragrams within the Houses

Geomantic Figure	Planet	Strongest: Ruler of	Very Strong: Exalted	Very Weak: Fall	Weakest: Detriment	Sign	Strong: Triplicity
Puer	Mars	1, 8	10	4	2, 7	Aries	5, 9
Amissio	Venus	2, 7	12	6	1, 8	Taurus	10
Albus	Mercury	3, 6	11	5	9, 12	Gemini	7, 11
Populus	Moon	4	2	8	10	Cancer	12
Fortuna Major	Sun	5	1	7	11	Leo	1, 9
Conjunctio	Mercury	3, 6	11	5	9, 12	Virgo	2, 10
Puella	Venus	2, 7	12	6	1, 8	Libra	3, 11
Rubeus	Mars	1, 8	10	4	2, 7	Scorpio	12
Acquisitio	Jupiter	9, 12	4	10	3, 6	Sagittarius	1, 5
Carcer	Saturn	10, 11	7	1	4, 5	Capricorn	2, 6
Tristitia	Saturn	10, 11	7	1	4, 5	Aquarius	3, 7
Laetitia	Jupiter	9, 12	4	10	3, 6	Pisces	4, 8
Cauda Draconis		8, 10, 11	10, 7	4, 1	2, 7, 4, 5		
Caput Draconis		2, 7, 9, 12	12, 4	6, 10	1, 8, 3, 6		
Fortuna Minor	Sun	5	1	7	11	Leo	1, 9
Via	Moon	4	2	8	10	Cancer	12

AMISSIO

Good for loss of substance and sometimes for love, but very bad for gain.

Ascendant	Ill in all things but for prisoners.
Second House	Very ill for money, but good for love.
Third House	Ill end—except for quarrels.
Fourth House	Ill in all.
Fifth House	Evil except for agriculture.
Sixth House	Rather evil for love.
Seventh House	Very good for love, otherwise evil.
Eighth House	Excellent in all questions.
Ninth House	Evil in all things.
Tenth House	Evil except for favor with women.
Eleventh House	Good for love, otherwise bad.
Twelfth House	Evil in all things.

FORTUNA MAJOR

Good for gain in all things where a person has hopes to win.

Ascendant	Good save in secrecy.
Second House	Good except in sad things.
Third House	Good in all.
Fourth House	Good in all, but melancholy.
Fifth House	Very good in all things.
Sixth House	Very good except for debauchery.
Seventh House	Good in all.
Eighth House	Moderately good.
Ninth House	Very good.
Tenth House	Exceedingly good. Go to superiors.
Eleventh House	Very good.
Twelfth House	Good in all.

FORTUNA MINOR

Good in any manner in which a person wishes to proceed quickly.

Ascendant	Speed in victory and in love, but choleric.
Second House	Very good.
Third House	Good—but wrathful.
Fourth House	Haste; rather evil except for peace.
Fifth House	Good in all things.
Sixth House	Medium in all.
Seventh House	Evil except for war or love.
Eighth House	Evil generally.
Ninth House	Good, but choleric.

Tenth House	Good, except for peace.
Eleventh House	Good, especially for love.
Twelfth House	Good, except for alternation, or for serving another.

LAETITIA

Good for joy, present or to come.

Ascendant	Good, except in war.
Second House	Sickly.
Third House	Ill.
Fourth House	Mainly good.
Fifth House	Excellently good.
Sixth House	Evil generally.
Seventh House	Indifferent.
Eighth House	Evil generally.
Ninth House	Very good.
Tenth House	Good, rather in war than in peace.
Eleventh House	Good in all.
Twelfth House	Evil generally.

TRISTITIA

Evil in almost all things.

Ascendant	Medium, but good for treasure and fortifying.
Second House	Medium, but good to fortify.
Third House	Evil in all.
Fourth House	Evil in all.
Fifth House	Very Evil.
Sixth House	Evil, except for debauchery.
Seventh House	Evil for inheritance and magic only.
Eighth House	Evil, but in secrecy good.
Ninth House	Evil except for magic.
Tenth House	Evil except for fortifications.
Eleventh House	Evil in all.
Twelfth House	Evil. But good for magic and treasure.

PUELLA

Good in all demands, especially in those things relating to women.

Ascendant	Good except in war.
Second House	Very good.
Third House	Good.
Fourth House	Indifferent.
Fifth House	Very good, but notice the aspects.

Sixth House	Good, but especially for debauchery.
Seventh House	Good except for war.
Eighth House	Good.
Ninth House	Good for music. Otherwise only medium.
Tenth House	Good for peace.
Eleventh House	Good, and love of ladies.
Twelfth House	Good in all.

PUER

Evil in most demands, except in those things relating to war or love.

Ascendant	Indifferent. Best in war.
Second House	Good, but with trouble.
Third House	Good fortune.
Fourth House	Evil, except in war and love.
Fifth House	Medium good.
Sixth House	Medium.
Seventh House	Evil, save in war.
Eighth House	Evil, save for love.
Ninth House	Evil except for war.
Tenth House	Rather evil. But good for love and war. Most other things medium.
Eleventh House	Medium; good favor.
Twelfth House	Very good in all.

RUBEUS

Evil in all that is good and good in all that is evil.

Ascendant	Destroy the figure if it falls here! It makes the judgment worthless.
Second House	Evil in all demands.
Third House	Evil except to let blood.
Fourth house	Evil except in war and Fire.
Fifth House	Evil save for love, and sowing seed.
Sixth House	Evil except for bloodletting.
Seventh House	Evil except for war and fire.
Eighth House	Evil.
Ninth House	Very Evil.
Tenth House	Dissolute. Love, fire.
Eleventh House	Evil, except to let blood.
Twelfth House	Evil in all things.

ALBUS

Good for profit and for entering into a place or undertaking.

Ascendant	Good for marriage. Mercurial. Peace.
Second House	Good in all.
Third House	Very good.
Fourth House	Very good except in war.
Fifth House	Good.
Sixth House	Good in all things.
Seventh House	Good except in all things.
Eighth House	Good.
Ninth House	A messenger brings a letter.
Tenth House	Excellent in all.
Eleventh House	Very good.
Twelfth House	Marvelously good.

CONJUNCTIO

Good with good, or evil with evil. Recovery from things lost.

Ascendant	Good with good, evil with evil.
Second House	Commonly good.
Third House	Good fortune.
Fourth House	Good save for health; see the eighth.
Fifth House	Medium.
Sixth House	Good for immorality only.
Seventh House	Rather good.
Eighth House	Evil, death.
Ninth House	Medium good.
Tenth House	For love, good. For sickness, evil.
Eleventh House	Good in all.
Twelfth House	Medium. Bad for prisoners.

CARCER

Generally evil. Delay, binding, bar, restriction.

Ascendant	Evil except to fortify a place.
Second House	Good in Saturnine questions; else evil.
Third House	Evil.
Fourth House	Good only for melancholy.
Fifth House	Receive a letter within three days. Evil.
Sixth House	Very evil.
Seventh House	Evil.
Eighth House	Very evil.
Ninth House	Evil in all.
Tenth House	Evil save in hidden treasure.

Eleventh House	Much anxiety.
Twelfth House	Rather good.

CAPUT DRACONIS

Good with good, evil with evil. Gives good issue for gain.

Ascendant	Good in all things.
Second House	Good.
Third House	Very good.
Fourth House	Good save in war.
Fifth House	Very good.
Sixth House	Good for immorality only.
Seventh House	Good especially for peace.
Eighth House	Good.
Ninth House	Very good.
Tenth House	Good in all.
Eleventh House	Good for the church and ecclesiastical gain.
Twelfth House	Not very good.

CAUDA DRACONIS

Good with evil, and evil with good. Good for loss,
and for passing out of an affair.

Ascendant	Destroy figure if it falls here! Makes judgment worthless.
Second House	Very evil.
Third House	Evil in all.
Fourth House	Good especially for conclusion of the matter.
Fifth House	Very evil.
Sixth House	Rather good.
Seventh House	Evil, war, and fire.
Eighth House	No good, except for magic.
Ninth House	Good for science only. Bad for journeys. Robbery.
Tenth House	Evil save in works of fire.
Eleventh House	Evil save for favors.
Twelfth House	Rather good.

VIA

Injurious to the goodness of other figures generally,
but good for journeys and voyages.

Ascendant	Evil except for prison.
Second House	Indifferent.
Third House	Very good in all.
Fourth House	Good in all save love.

Fifth House	Voyages good.
Sixth House	Evil.
Seventh House	Rather good, especially for voyages.
Eighth House	Evil.
Ninth House	Indifferent. good for journeys.
Tenth House	Good.
Eleventh House	Very good.
Twelfth House	Excellent.

POPULUS

Sometimes good and sometimes bad; good with good, and evil with evil.

Ascendant	Good in marriages.
Second House	Medium good.
Third House	Rather good than bad.
Fourth House	Good in all but love.
Fifth House	Good in most things.
Sixth House	Good.
Seventh House	In war good; else medium.
Eighth House	Evil.
Ninth House	Look for letters.
Tenth House	Good.
Eleventh House	Good in all.
Twelfth House	Very evil.

The Fourth House

After all is looked at, check the figure in the *fourth house,* which denotes the conclusion or outcome of the matter in question.

If you are still unsure at this point, construct the sixteenth and final figure of the *Reconciler,* by adding together the *first Mother and the Judge.* This will give a final reading. This figure is not to be constructed simply because you don't like the outcome. Generate this figure only you are still confused about the conclusion.

Israel Regardie was very fond of this system of divination and performed it regularly. We suggest that the student of this course prepare one Geomantic reading daily while in the grade of Zelator. Only by constant practice will the subtleties of this method be appreciated.

Geomantic Talismans

One unique aspect of the system of Geomancy is that numerous sigils or Talismanic emblems can be created from the Tetragrams, by tracing various lines from point to point. These characters are then attributed to their ruling Planets and ideas. Only a few of these possible sigils are shown in the accompanying diagram in the following page. Countless other sigils may be formed from the basic Geomantic Tetragrams. Each sigil thus formed may be used as a "door" for divining or skrying into.

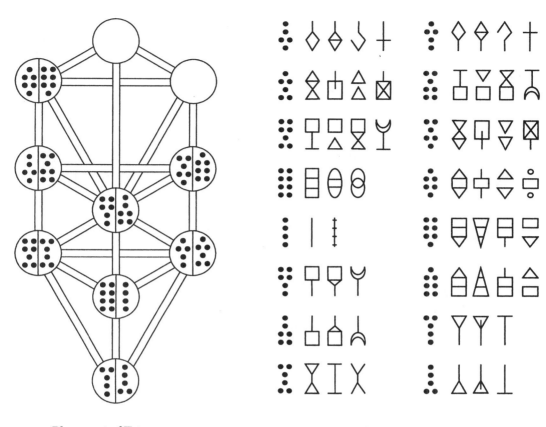

*Placement of Tetragrams
on the Tree of Life*

Geomantic Sigils

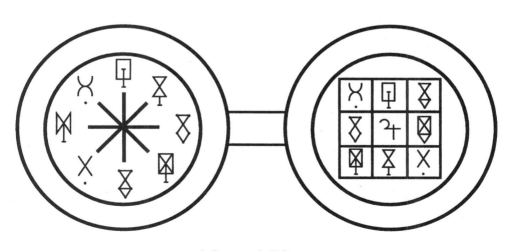

A Geomantic Talisman

A Talisman using the sigils may be constructed in the shape of a circle, placing the emblems at opposite ends of a wheel with eight spokes. A phrase or versicle which has meaning to the student may be written in a circle along the outer edge of the talisman. A square containing a given number of compartments may be used in place of the wheel or on the reverse side of the Talisman.✿

SECTION 8: Correspondences of Malkuth

The 1 = 10 grade of Zelator is attributed to the sphere of Malkuth on the Qabalistic Tree of Life. This is the first grade that actually places the aspiring magician on the Tree of Life. Malkuth has the additional titles of the *Gate*, and the *Inferior Mother*, and it is the ultimate Sephirah of form and manifestation. (Review all information on Malkuth given in Chapter 1.)

Name in English: The Kingdom
Divine (Atziluthic) Name: Adonai Ha-Aretz
Archangel (Briatic) Name: Sandalphon
Angelic (Yetziratic) Choir: Ashim
Planet or House of Assiah: Olam ha-Yesodoth
Spiritual experience: Vision of the Holy Guardian Angel
Qabalistic Number: Ten
Color (Briatic): Citrine, russet, olive, black
Element: Earth
Part of Anatomy: Feet
Tarot cards: The Four Tens
Magical Image: A young woman, crowned and throned
Incense: Dittany of Crete
Gemstone: Rock crystal, salt
Symbols: Double cube altar, equal-armed cross,
         the magick circle, the triangle of art
Lineal Figure: Dekagram
Virtue: Discrimination
Vice: Inertia

SECTION 9: Ritual Images and Diagrams

The Laver of Water of Purification refers to the Waters of Binah, the female power reflected in the Waters of Creation.
    The Altar of Burnt Offering for the sacrifice of animals symbolizes the Qlippoth or Evil Demons of the plane contiguous to and below the material universe. It points out that our passions should be sacrificed. *The Qlippoth* are the Evil Demons of Matter and the shells of the Dead.

The Altar of Incense in the Tabernacle was overlaid with gold. Ours is black to symbolize our work which is to separate the Philosophic Gold from the Black Dragon of Matter.

The Flaming Sword or *Lightning Flash* is formed by the natural order of the Sephiroth on the Tree of Life. It is the descending current of divine energy, and it resembles a flash of Lightning. The right-hand Kerub standing by the white pillar is Metatron, while the left-hand Kerub is Sandalphon, standing by the black pillar. The Kerubim are the guardians of the Garden of Eden. (See Color Plate 1.)

(Note: One fragment of a Babylonian text refers to the Sacred Grove of Anu, which corresponds to the Tree of Life. The Sacred Grove was guarded by a sword turning to all four points of the compass. Several other Babylonian legends allude to a sacred tree, grove or forest of the gods, which was often represented in ancient art as a tree attended by two winged Kerubim, one on each side of the sacred tree.)

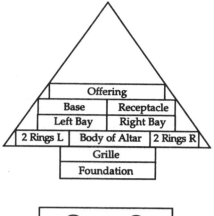
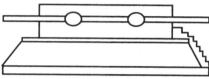

The Altar of Incense

The Sephiroth may be described as energy centers of God-consciousness, while the paths connecting them are conduits or energy channels. Together the Sephiroth and the Twenty-two Paths form the Thirty-two Paths of Wisdom as described in the *Sepher Yetzirah* or Book of Formation.

The Qabalah teaches that all manifestation is based upon the principle of polarity. *The two pillars* on either side of the altar represent the two great contending forces of the universe:

The Pillar of Mercy in the South: Its characteristics are: white, active, positive, masculine, force. It is a pillar of Light and Fire which is associated with the Biblical Adam and with Metatron who in this instance is the right-hand Kerub of the Tree of Life.

The Pillar of Severity in the North: Its characteristics are: black, passive, negative, feminine, form. It is a pillar of cloud which is associated with the Biblical Eve and with Sandalphon who in this case is the left-hand Kerub of the Tree of Life.

The Fylfot Cross is the Admission Badge to 1=10 grade of Zelator. It is also called the *Hermetic Cross*, the *Hammer of Thor*, the *Gammadion* and the *Swastika*. It is formed of seventeen squares out of a square of twenty-five lesser squares. These seventeen represent the Sun, the four Elements, and the twelve Signs of the Zodiac.

The Sacred Grove of the Gods

The Table of Shewbread

The symbol of the Sun is at the center of the cross at the point of stillness, while the Zodiacal Signs divided into the four Triplicities make up the arms of the cross. The Cardinal Signs all begin at the center of the cross, followed by the Fixed and Mutable Signs. The Arms terminate with the Elemental symbols of each Triplicity. The whole cross represents the center of the universe giving rise to the celestial Signs, which then formulate the Elements of the physical world.

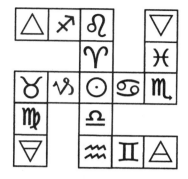

The Flyfot Cross

Since the Fylfot is originally formed out of twenty-five squares, this cross also has an affinity with Fire. Twenty-five is the number of squares forming the Qamea or magical square of Mars. According to J. E. Cirlot (*A Dictionary of Symbols*), all the words for "cross" (*crux, cruz, crowz, croaz, krois, krouz*) have a common etymological basis in *-ak, -ur*, or *-os*, signifying the "Light of the Great Fire." (This is also one reason why the lamen of the Dadouchos consists of this symbol.)

The Fylfot Cross is a symbol of an equal-armed cross with four arms appearing to rotate in the same direction around a central axis. During the Iron Age the Swastika represented the supreme deity. In the Middle Ages, the general interpretation of the figure was that it symbolized movement and the power of the Sun. This cross also signifies the action of the *origin* of the universe.

In addition, the Fylfot is a symbol attributed to the first Sephirah, Kether. Here it represents the four latent (Primal) Elements whose energies are united in Kether, activated by the Primum Mobile or First Whirlings. These energies are finally differentiated into the four base Elements of Fire, Water, Air and Earth upon reaching the level of Malkuth on the Tree. The Fylfot Cross, given to the candidate in the Zelator grade, points out a close relationship that exists between Kether and Malkuth.

The Table of Shewbread: In the Zelator Ritual, this diagram depicting the twelve Simple Letters of the Hebrew alphabet and their associated Zodiacal Signs is thoroughly explained. (Refer to the initiation ceremony.) The top of the dodekagram or twelve-sided figure points to Aries, and the letter Heh in the East, while the bottom tip of the figure points to Libra and the letter Lamed in the West. The Archangels and Kerubic emblems are shown in their proper quarters. The central pentagram which represents the Great Mother of Heaven through the letter Heh (5), points toward a position between the Signs of Aries and Pisces, thus referring to a point in the prismatic color wheel where red intersects red-violet. This is the point at which the invisible colors of infrared and ultraviolet are formed. The red color of Aries represents the beginning of the color wheel, whereas Pisces indicates the end (Alpha and Omega). The flames seen in the center of the Pentagram refer to the rays of the Sun.

The Seven-Branched Candlestick: This diagram which portrays the seven Double letters of the Hebrew alphabet along with their seven corresponding Planets is fully explained in the Zelator Ritual. However a couple of points concerning the diagram need to be mentioned. The heptagram in the center is the key to the

The Seven-Branched Candlestick

order of the days of the week—Sol (Sunday) is at the uppermost point of the heptagram. From the point of Sol the line leads to the Luna point (Monday) and on to the point of Mars (Tuesday) to Mercury (Wednesday) to Jupiter (Thursday) to Venus (Friday) to Saturn (Saturday) and back again to Sol.

Note: some previously published versions of this diagram have placed the Planets in a circular succession rather than following the natural order of the heptagram with regard to the days of the week.

Also, most published versions of this diagram list the Sephirotic Archangels rather than the Planetary Archangels which properly belong to this diagram. These points have been corrected here.✿

AN ADDITIONAL SIDE LECTURE
The Tribes of Israel and the Zodiacal Signs
(by MacGregor Mathers)[59]

The Twelve Tribes are thus attributed to the Twelve Zodiacal Signs and permutations of the Great and Holy Name of Tetragrammaton and the Angelic counterparts:

	Sign	*Permutation*	*Tribe*	*Angel*
♈	Aries	Yod Heh Vau Heh	Gad	Melchidael
♉	Taurus	Yod Heh Heh Vau	Ephraim	Asmodel
♊	Gemini	Yod Vau Heh Heh	Manasseh	Ambriel
♋	Cancer	Heh Vau Heh Yod	Issachar	Muriel
♌	Leo	Heh Vau Yod Heh	Judah	Verchiel
♍	Virgo	Heh Heh Vau Yod[60]	Naphthali	Hamaliel
♎	Libra	Vau Heh Yod Heh	Asshur	Zuriel
♏	Scorpio	Vau Heh Heh Yod	Dan	Barchiel
♐	Sagittarius	Vau Yod Heh Heh	Benjamin	Advachiel[61]
♑	Capricorn	Heh Yod Heh Vau	Zebulun	Hanael
♒	Aquarius	Heh Yod Vau Heh	Reuben	Cambriel
♓	Pisces	Heh Heh Yod Vau*	Simeon	Amnitziel

---

[59] This Lecture was originally given in the Philosophus Grade of the Golden Dawn and later in the Zelator Grade of the Stella Matutina. We have chosen to retain it in the Zelator Grade because of its relevance not only to the Table of Shewbread diagram but also to the ancient Hebrew Tabernacle in the Wilderness, which plays such an important role in the Zelator ritual of self-initiation.

[60] Unfortunately there is an error in this manuscript concerning the permutations of the Name for both Virgo and Pisces which should be switched. One of the Senior Adepts of our Order has determined that the error came about through a confusion between the letters Heh (Water) and Heh Sophith (Earth). The correct permutation of the Name for Virgo is HHYV and the Name for Pisces is HHVY.

[61] The name Advachiel is a centuries' old error. The true name of the Angel of Sagittarius is Adnakhiel. (See the article entitled "Mysteria Geomantica" by Adam Forrest in *The Golden Dawn Journal, Book 1: Divination*.

Of these, especially the Bull (Taurus), the Lion (Leo), the Scorpion (Scorpio, but in good symbolism the Eagle) and the Man (Aquarius) are to be noted as forming the Kerubic figures of Ezekiel and John. To these Signs are allotted the tribes of Ephraim, Judah, Dan and Reuben, who, as we shall presently see, encamped towards the Cardinal Points around the Tabernacle of the Congregation, and as the leaders of the others. The Signs of the Twins (Gemini), the Fishes (Pisces), and in a certain sense as a compounded figure, the Centaur (Sagittarius) armed with a bow, are also called bi-corporate, or double-bodied Signs. To these refer Manasseh (Gemini), Simeon (Pisces) and Benjamin (Sagittarius). Manasseh was divided into two half tribes with separate possessions (being the only tribe thus divided), and thus answers to the equal division of the Sign of the Twins, Castor and Pollux, the Great Twin Brethren. Simeon and Levi are classed together, like the two Fishes in the Sign, but Levi is withdrawn later, to form as it were the binding and connecting link of the Tribes, as the priestly caste. Benjamin is the younger brother of Joseph, for Rachael had only these two sons, and is the only one of the sons of Jacob who at his birth was called by two names, for Rachel called him "Ben oni," but his father Benjamin, and in the Sign of the two natures of Man and Horse are bound together in one symbol.

We shall find much light upon the connection between the Signs and the Tribes shown by the blessing of Jacob, and of Moses, from the former of which the Armorial bearings of the Twelve Tribes are derived. Let us note that as in the Tribes Levi was withdrawn, and the two Tribes of Ephraim and Manasseh substituted for the simple one of Joseph, so in the New Testament, Judas is withdrawn from the number of the twelve Apostles and his place filled by another, Matthias, who was chosen by lot to fill his place.

The following is the order by birth, of the children of Jacob: Leah bore Reuben (♒), Simeon (♓), Levi, afterwards withdrawn, and Judah (♌). Bilhah (Rachel's maid) bore Dan (♏), and Naphthali (♍), Zilpah (Leah's maid) bore Gad (♈) and Ashur (♎). Leah again bore Issachar (♋), Zebulun (♑) and Dinah (a daughter). Rachel bore Joseph, whose sons were Manasseh (♊) and Ephraim (♉), but died at the birth of Benjamin (♐), whom she wished to call Ben-oni.

In the Wilderness the Tabernacle was pitched in the midst, and immediately surrounding it were the tents of Levi. At a distance towards the four cardinal points were the standards of the Twelve Tribes erected there:

On the East:	JUDAH, Kerubic Sign of the Lion (♌) with *Issachar* (♋) and *Zebulun* (♑)
On the South:	REUBEN, Kerubic Sign of the Man (♒) with *Simeon* (♓) and *Gad* (♈)
On the West:	EPHRAIM, Kerubic Sign of the Bull (♉) with *Manasseh* (♊) and *Benjamin* (♐)
On the North:	DAN, Kerubic Sign of the Eagle (♏) with *Asher* (♎) and *Naphtali* (♍)

Save for the Kerubic emblems, the arrangement seems at first very confused; but when we notice the Maternal Ancestors of the Tribes, this confusion disperses, and we notice that at the East are three tribes descended from Leah, viz. Judah, Issachar and Zebulon. Opposite to them, towards the West, three tribes descended from Rachel, viz. Ephraim, Manasseh and Benjamin. At the South are two descended from Leah and one descended from Zilpah, viz. Reuben, Simeon and Gad, and at the North, two descended from Bilhah and one descended from Zilpah, viz. Dan, Naphthali and Asher. Here two tribes descended from Zilpah, Gad (Υ) and Asher (Ω), are the only ones separated, and placed in opposition to each other, for these are two signs of the Equinoxes.

The substitution of the two tribes of Ephraim and Manasseh for the single one of Joseph is given in Genesis 48, where Jacob blessed them prior to the general blessing of the Tribes, stating at the same time that Ephraim, though the younger, should take precedence over Manasseh: "And Jacob said unto Joseph... And now thy two sons, Ephraim and Manasseh, which were born unto thee in the land of Egypt before I came unto thee in Egypt, are mine; as Reuben and Simeon they shall be mine. And thy issue which thou begettest after them shall be thine and shall be called after the name of their brethren in their inheritance ... Moreover I have given unto thee one portion above of thy brethren."

Let us now notice the blessings of Jacob and Moses, and compare them with the Signs of the Zodiac attributed to each Tribe. We shall take them in the Zodiacal order.

Of Gad (Aries), Jacob says, "Gad, a troop shall overcome him, but he shall overcome at the last." Moses says, "Blessed be he that enlargeth Gad: he dwelleth as a lioness, and teareth the arm with the crown of the head, and he provideth the first part for himself because there, in a portion of the law-giver, was he sealed; and he came with the heads of the people, he executed the justice of the Lord, and his judgments with Israel." The armonial bearings of Gad are, white, a troop of cavalry. All this coincides well with the martial and dominant nature of Aries, the only one of the twelve signs in which the superior Planets alone bear sway, for it is the house of Mars, exaltation of the Sun and triplicity of Sun and Jupiter. The symbolism of the Lion is also proper to Aries on account of its solar, fiery and martial nature.

Of Ephraim and Manasseh (Taurus and Gemini), classed together under their father's name, Jacob says, "Joseph is a fruitful bough by a well, whose branches run over the wall; the archers have surely grieved him and shot at him, and hated him: but the arms of his hands were made strong by the hands of the mighty God of Jacob; (from thence is the shepherd, the stone of Israel:) Even by the God of thy father, who shall help thee, and by the Almighty who shall bless thee with the blessings of Heaven above, blessings of the deep that lieth under, blessings of the breasts and of the womb: the blessings of thy father have prevailed above the blessings of my progenitors unto the utmost bound of the everlasting hills: they shall be on the head of Joseph, and on the crown of the head of him who was separate from his brethren." Moses says, "Blessed of the Lord be his land, for the precious things of heaven, for the dew, and for the deep that coucheth beneath, and for the precious fruits brought forth by the Sun, and for the precious things put forth by the moon, and for the chief things of the lasting hills. And for the precious things of the Earth, and the fullness thereof, and for the good will of him that dwells in the bush: let the blessing come upon the head of Joseph, and upon the top of the head of him that was separate from his brethren. His glory is like the firstling of a bullock, and his horns are like the horns of unicorns: with them he shall push the people together to the ends of the Earth, and they are the ten thousands of Manasseh."

The Armorial Bearings of Ephraim are: Green, an Ox. Those of Mannesseh are flesh-color, a Vine by a Wall. All this refers to the natures of Taurus and Gemini, the firstling of the bullock and the Earthy nature of the Sign, shown by the hills, to Taurus while the archers over Manasseh, as Sagittarius, the Sign of the Archer, is in opposition to Gemini.

Of Issachar, (Cancer) Jacob says: "Issachar is a strong ass couching down between two burdens: and he saw the rest was good, and the land that it was pleasant, and he bowed his shoulder to bear, and became a servant under tribute." Moses says: "Rejoice Issachar, in thy tents ... and they shall suck of the abundance of the seas." The armorial bearings of Issachar are Blue, and an ass crouching beneath its burden. This coincides with the peaceful nature of the quiet and watery Sign of Cancer.

Of Judah (Leo) Jacob says: "Judah, thou art he whom thy brethren shall praise: thy hand shall be in the neck of thine enemies; thy father's children shall bow down before thee. Judah is a lion's whelp: from the prey, my son, thou art gone up; he stooped down, he crouched as a lion, and as an old lion; who shall rouse him up? The scepter shall not depart from Judah, nor a lawgiver from between his feet, until Shiloh come; and unto him shall the gathering of the people be. Binding his foal unto the vine, and his ass's colt unto the choice vine; he washed his garments in wine, and his clothes in the blood of grapes: his eyes shall be red with wine, and his teeth white with milk." Moses says, "This is the blessing of Judah, and he said, Hear, Lord, the voice of Judah, and bring him unto his people, let his hands be sufficient for him and be thou an help to him from his enemies." The armorial bearings of Judah are Scarlet, a lion rampant. All this well agrees with the regal and leonine nature of the Sign. "Binding the ass's colt unto the choice vine" may allude to the ass of Issachar, Cancer, lying between Judah, Leo, and the vine of Manasseh, Gemini.

Of Naphthali (Virgo) Jacob says, "Naphthali is a hind let loose, he giveth goodly words." Moses says, "O Naphthali satisfied with favor, and full with the blessings of the Lord, possess thou the West and the South." The armorial bearings of Naphthali are Blue, a hind.

Of Asher (Libra) Jacob says, "Out of Asher his bread shall be fat, and he shall yield royal dainties." Moses says, "Let Asher be blessed with children, let him be acceptable to his brethren, and let him dip his foot in oil. Thy shoes shall be iron and brass, and as thy days, so shall thy strength be." The armorial bearings of Asher are Purple, a Cup. All this coincides with the nature of Venus and Libra, while the feet refer to the Sign of Pisces, which rules the feet, and in which Venus is exalted. Iron and Brass are the metals of the friendly Planets of Mars and Venus.

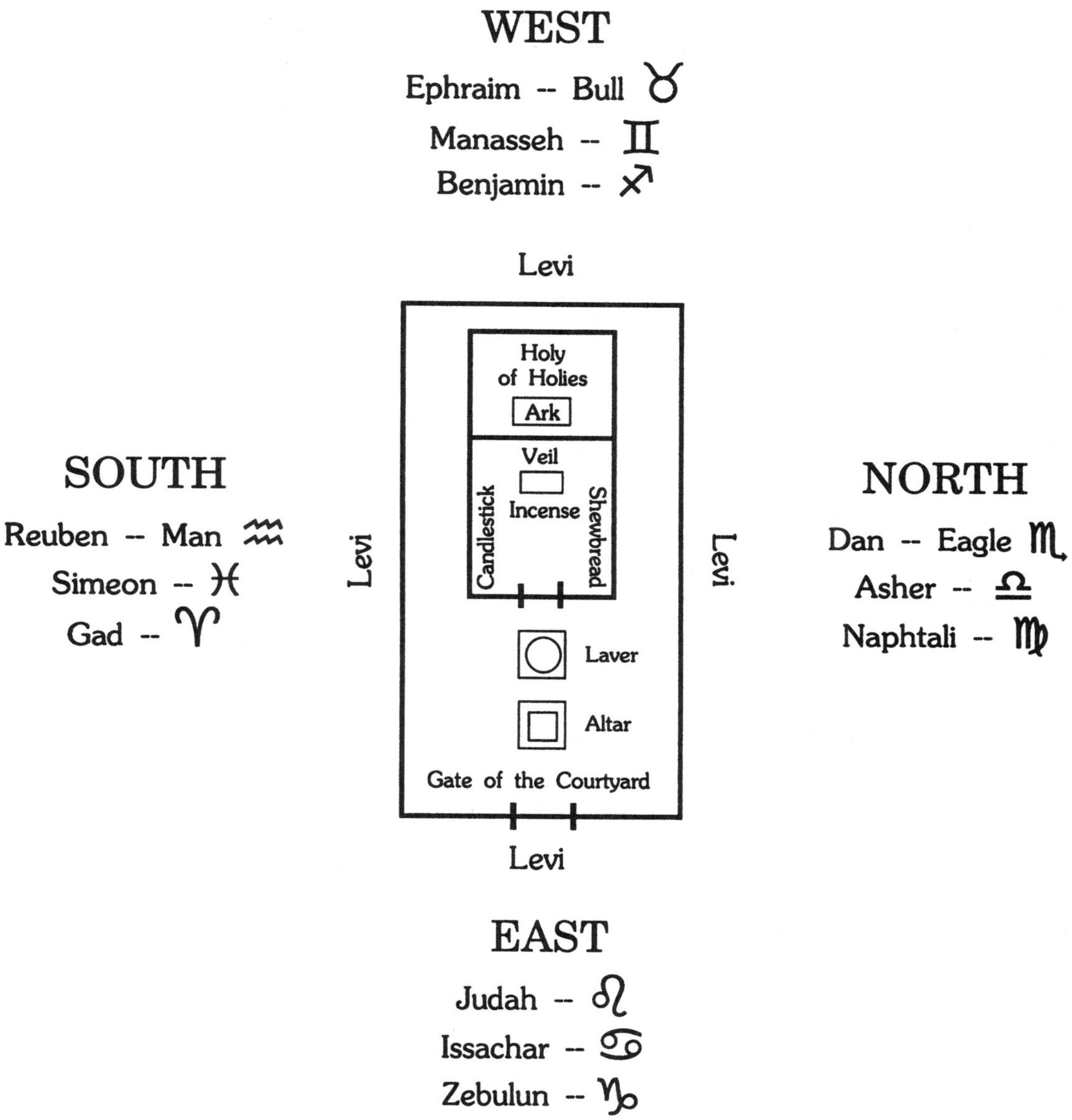

WEST

Ephraim -- Bull ♉

Manasseh -- ♊

Benjamin -- ♐

Levi

	Holy of Holies
	Ark

Veil

Candlestick | Incense | Shewbread

○ Laver

□ Altar

Gate of the Courtyard

Levi

SOUTH

Reuben -- Man ♒

Simeon -- ♓

Gad -- ♈

Levi

Levi

NORTH

Dan -- Eagle ♏

Asher -- ♎

Naphtali -- ♍

EAST

Judah -- ♌

Issachar -- ♋

Zebulun -- ♑

The Twelve Tribes

203

Of Dan (Scorpio) Jacob says: "Dan shall judge his people as one of the tribes of Israel. Dan shall be a serpent by the way, and adder in the path, that biteth the horse's heels, so that his rider shall fall backward. I have waited for thy salvation, O Lord." Moses says. "Dan is a lion's whelp, he shall leap from Bashan." The armorial bearings of Dan are Green, an Eagle. These things fit with the martial and fierce nature of this Sign in which Mars principally bears sway. To the Sign of Scorpio, the Egyptians attributed the Serpent, and also Typhon, the Slayer of Osiris, and on this account they call it the "Accursed Sign." In good symbolism it is generally represented by the Eagle. The horse's heels which the Serpent sometimes bites are found in the Centaur figure of Sagittarius which follows Scorpio in the Zodiac.

Of Benjamin (Sagittarius) Jacob says, "Benjamin shall ravin as a wolf: in the morning he shall devour the prey, and at night he shall divide the spoil." Moses says: "The beloved of the Lord shall dwell in safety by him; and the Lord shall cover him all the day long, and he shall dwell between his shoulders." The armorial bearings of Benjamin are Green, a Wolf. These suit the character of Sagittarius, partly keen, partly of the nature of Jupiter, and partly brutal.

Of Zebulon (Capricorn) Jacob says: "Zebulon shall dwell at the haven of the sea, and he shall be for a haven of ships, and his border shall be unto Sidon." Moses says: "Rejoice Zebulon in thy going out, and Issachar in thy tents, they shall call the people unto the mountain, there they shall offer sacrifices of righteousness, for they shall suck of the abundance of the sea, of the treasures hid in the sands." This suits well the tropical, Earthy and water signs of Capricorn and Cancer. The armorial bearings of Zebulon are Purple, a Ship.

Of Reuben (Aquarius) Jacob says: "Reuben, thou art my first-born, my might, and the beginning of my strength, the excellency of dignity and the excellency of power. Unstable as water, thou shalt not excel, because thou wentest up to thy father's bed, then defiledst thou it; he went up to my couch." Moses says: "Let Reuben live and not die, and let not his men be few." The armorial bearings of Reuben are Red, a Man. "Unstable as water" is still shown in the undulating hieroglyphic which marks this aerial and brilliant, but often superficial Sign of the Water-Bearer.

Of Simeon and Levi (Pisces) Jacob says: "Simeon and Levi are brethren; instruments of cruelty are in their habitations. O my Soul, come not thou into their secret, unto their assembly, mine honour, be not thou united: for in their anger they slew a man, and in their selfwill they digged down a wall. Cursed be their anger, for it was fierce; and their wrath, for it was cruel: I will divide them in Jacob, and scatter them in Israel." This alludes to their smiting Shalem, the city of Hamor and Shechem, and slaying the latter because they had carried off Dinah, the daughter of Leah. Moses says of them: "Let thy Thummim and thy Urim be with the Holy One, whom thou didst prove at Massah, and with whom thou didst strive at the water of Meribah; who said unto his father and mother, I have not seen him; neither did he acknowledge his brethren, nor knew his children; for they have observed thy word, and kept thy covenant. They shall teach Jacob thy judgments and Israel thy law: they shall put incense before thee, and whole burnt sacrifice upon thine altar. Bless, Lord, his substance, and accept the works of his hands; smite through the loins of them that rise against him, and of them that hate him, that they rise not again." The armorial bearings of Simeon are Yellow, a Sword.

These are the blessings of the twelve tribes of Israel, whose names were engraven upon the twelve stones of the High Priest's breastplate, upon which, according to some traditions, certain flashes of Light appeared playing over certain of the letters, and thus returning the answer of the deity to the consulter of the Oracle of the Urim.

By comparing these blessings with the nature of the Signs attributed to the particular tribes, we have thus been enabled to trace more or less clearly the connection between them, and also the derivation of the armorial bearings ascribed to them in Royal Arch Freemasonry.✿

This concludes the Knowledge Lecture. Examinations on the initiation ceremony as well as the material covered in this section are given at the end of this chapter.✿

Ritual Work for the Zelator

Continue the Fourfold breath technique as taught in the Neophyte grade. Add to this a visualization of the seasons as follows:

Inhale	—	Spring
Full Hold	—	Summer
Exhale	—	Autumn
Empty Hold	—	Winter

The Zelator should construct all of the following talismanic emblems to aid in meditation and ritual. All emblems should be painted white on a black background:

- A Square
- A Cube
- The Sigil of Elemental Earth
- The Sigil of Planet Earth
- The Sigil of Capricorn
- The Sigil of Taurus
- The Sigil of Virgo
- The Sigil of Salt
- The Number Ten
- The Name Adonai ha-Aretz in Hebrew
- The Dekagon & Dekangle (See Chapter Four)

MEDITATION

for the 1 = 10 grade of Zelator[62]

LET THE ZELATOR meditate on a straight line. Let him take a ruler or a pencil and by moving it a distance equal to its length, outline a square.

Having done this, after quieting his mind with the rhythmic breathing taught in the first meditation, let him mentally formulate a cube, and endeavor to discover the significance of this figure and its correspondences.

Let him meditate upon minerals and crystals, choosing especially a crystal of SALT, and entering into it, actually feel himself of crystalline formation.

Looking out on the Universe from this standpoint, let him identify himself with the EARTH SPIRITS in love and sympathy, recalling as far as he can their prayer as said in the closing of the Zelator grade.

Let him meditate upon the EARTH TRIPLICITY, visualizing the symbols of a BULL—a VIRGIN—a GOAT, which stand for KERUBIC EARTH—MUTABLE EARTH—CARDINAL EARTH.

For the above terms consult a simple Astrology manual. Make notes of the ideas and pictures which arise in your mind.✿

RELAXATION EXERCISE

The Sephirah of Malkuth is attributed to the Fourth Qabalistic World of Assiah, the World of Physical Matter. In one of the mediations given in the Neophyte grade, the student was encouraged to become more aware of the body's physical sensations. In the Zelator grade, the student should strive to learn how to use the techniques of relaxation to manipulate body sensations in a premeditated fashion, in order to cause certain changes that are both physical and psychological.

Relaxation is a crucial step in changing one's conscious awareness from the mundane events of the day to a more spiritual focus. It is also an essential procedure that will always be undertaken prior to more advanced techniques and rituals.

Before sitting or lying down, spend a minute or two engaged in physical exercise to increase the blood circulation and stimulate deep breathing. (One way to do this is to skip with an invisible rope in a stationary position.)

---

[62] From Regardie's *The Golden Dawn.*

Then stand upright with the legs slightly apart. Take a deep breath and exhale, expelling all of your air as you let yourself fall forward from the waist, completely relaxed, hands hanging near the feet for a moment. Allow yourself to be totally limp from the waist up. Inhale and bring yourself back to the full standing position. Repeat this process about a dozen times. Be aware only of the various body sensations.

The actual relaxation exercise which lasts approximately one half hour can now begin. Take some very deep breaths. Sit or lie down on the floor, and remain aware only of what the body is feeling.

Visualize your brain, just as you have seen the human brain in drawings—a large gray-white walnut shaped organ, divided into two hemispheres. Imagine it clearly. Concentrate. Do not allow your mind to wander from the visualization. If your mind wanders, gently bring it back. Hold the image of the brain in your mind until you begin to feel a warmth spreading out from the center of your head. Imagine yourself stimulating the flow of blood to the brain, relaxing the blood vessels there. You may be aware of a gentle tingling sensation. Picture the blood vessels within the brain, dilating enough to hold larger amounts of blood. This turns the brain pink, resulting in the sensation of warmth that you are experiencing.

Move on to the eyes, visualizing them as two balls held into place by muscles. Imagine the muscles become enlarged as you channel more blood to the area. This stimulates the feeling of warmth. Then relax, imagining the eyeballs sinking back gently into their sockets.

Follow this procedure for the rest of the head—visualizing the warming blood flowing into the blood vessels of the temples, cheeks, ears, nose, lips, tongue and chin. In all cases, feel the warmth and the tingling of the blood, gradually followed by the feeling of relaxation.

You should now be approximately ten minutes into the exercise. The time remaining should be spent visualizing the rest of the body in the same manner: The neck, shoulders and abdominal area. (The more you relax the abdomen, the more likely it is that the rest of the body will relax also.)

Finally imagine the current of blood separating into two mighty arterial rivers of blood which flow from the pelvis into the thighs, legs, feet and toes. Relax completely.

Once you have completed this cycle of relaxation, observe how you feel. Let a sense of total relaxation and fulfillment be permanently recorded in your mind. Feel the pleasure of the moment. Impress the image thoroughly and strongly upon your mind. If you are able to remember this experience clearly, it can be evoked at any time. Whether you are driving a car or riding on an airliner, you can remember the feeling of pleasurable relaxation and evoke the memory which will result in the tension leaving the muscles of your body.

If at any time you wish to relax, simply take a deep breath and imagine the word "relax" as you release the air from your lungs. Inhale deeply, and as you exhale, command yourself to relax. Remember the serenity of complete relaxation and it will be instantly brought back to you. Eventually this will become a conditioned reflex whose effects will be complete and automatic.

This exercise should be performed at least once a day. (Twice would be better—once in the morning and once in the evening.) Variations on this technique could also be used to help cure illnesses. One might imagine the stream of blood flowing though and breaking down a cancerous growth for elimination from the body—or the flow of blood may be seen to heal a wound.✿

A MEDITATION ON THE FOUR QABALISTIC WORLDS

For this meditation the Zelator will need a black robe and nemyss and the Outer Wand of Double Power. A Tarot deck should also be on hand. Prior to the meditation, remove all the Aces from the Tarot deck. Put the rest of the deck aside.

Perform a rite of relaxation. With the wand perform the LBRP.

Place the Aces on the altar or on the floor in front of you if you wish to be seated. Arrange the cards in a straight vertical line in descending order thus: The Ace of Wands should be farthest from you in the East. Then follow the Ace of Cups, the Ace of Swords, and the Ace of Pentacles which is the closest card to you.

See the cards before you as representations of the Four Worlds of the Qabalah: Atziluth, Briah, Yetzirah, and Assiah. Contemplate the cards for a few moments, observing their symbolism and coloring.

Close your eyes and begin breathing rhythmically after the manner of the Fourfold Breath. Continue breathing in this fashion through the following visualization:

As you inhale, see the Ace of Wands in your mind's eye. On the full hold, picture the Ace of Cups. When you exhale, visualize the Ace of Swords. On the empty hold, imagine the Ace of Pentacles. Keep breathing and visualizing while mentally intoning the name of each world represented by the Aces. (Wands—Atziluth; Cups—Briah; Swords—Yetzirah; Pentacles—Assiah.) Repeat this process a number of times, embellishing upon the symbolism of the cards in each rhythmic cycle. Feel the energy of each Elemental image until they become animated scenes moving within your imagination, proceeding from Fire to Water, Air and Earth in rhythmic progression. As the likeness of one card merges into that of the one that follows it, see how the energies flow into one another in the formula of the Tetragrammaton.

After some time is spent on the visualization, discontinue the Fourfold Breath and resume normal breathing.

Face the East and say, "*Unto thee, Tetragrammaton, be ascribed the Kingdom, and the Power and the Glory. Unto the ages, Amen.*"

Close the meditation by performing the Qabalistic Cross.✿

AN INVOCATION OF THE ELEMENT OF EARTH
For the grade of Zelator

For this ritual the Zelator will need a black robe, black and white striped nemyss, and the Outer Wand of Double Power. Upon the altar should be a black candle, a paten of bread and salt, and one of the talismanic emblems mentioned on page 205. The temple is to be arranged in accordance with the Zelator Hall (as in the second part of the initiation ceremony).

Relax for a few moments and perform the Fourfold Breath.

Go to the Northeast and say, "*HEKAS, HEKAS, ESTE BEBELOI!*"

With the black end of the wand, perform the LBRP.

> (Say the following invocation:) *Stoop not down into that darkly splendid world wherein continually lieth a faithless depth and Hades wrapped in gloom, delighting in unintelligible images, precipitous, winding, a black ever-rolling Abyss, ever espousing a body unluminous, formless and void.*

Go clockwise to the East. With the white end of the wand, trace the Lesser invoking Pentagram. Thrust the wand through the center of the figure and vibrate, "*AGLA!*" Do this also in the South, West, and finally in the North; drawing the same pentagram and intoning the same word in all four quarters.

> (Remain in the North and say:) *In the Divine Name ADONAI HA-ARETZ, I open this temple in the Element of Earth. May the Archangel*

Lesser Invoking Pentagram

Lesser Banishing Pentagram

The Forms of the Lesser Pentagram

URIEL look with favor upon this ceremony! May the Angel PHORLAKH and the ruler KERUB be also in attendance! I have gained admission to this temple through the Badge of the Hermetic Cross. Hear me! I am one who has received the Mystic Title of Periclinus de Faustis and the symbol of ARETZ. As a wanderer in the Wilderness, I invoke the powers of Earth to bear witness to my spiritual endeavor. Grant me the knowledge of the Element of Earth and the Active Realm, so that I may obtain greater understanding of Hidden Things and thereby advance in the Great Work.

Circumambulate the temple three times, saluting with the Neophyte Signs when passing the East. Go to the West and face East. Give the Adoration to the Lord of the Universe:

Holy art Thou, Lord of the Universe! (Projection Sign)
Holy art Thou, Whom Nature hath not formed! (PS)
Holy art Thou, the Vast and the Mighty One! (PS)
Lord of the Light, and of the Darkness! (Sign of Silence)

Go to the North and give the Zelator Sign. Recite the Prayer of the Gnomes:

O Invisible King, Who, taking the Earth for Foundation, didst hollow its depths to fill them with Thy Almighty Power. Thou whose Name shaketh the Arches of the World. Thou who causest the Seven Metals to flow in the veins of the rocks, King of the Seven Lights, Rewarder of the subterranean Workers, lead us into the desirable Air and into the Realm of Splendor. We watch and we labor unceasingly, we seek and we hope, by the twelve stones of the Holy City, by the buried talismans, by the Axis of the Lodestone which passes through the center of the Earth—O Lord, O Lord, O Lord! Have pity upon those who suffer. Expand our hearts, unbind and upraise our minds, enlarge our natures.

O Stability and Motion! O Darkness veiled in Brilliance! O Day clothed in Night! O Master who never dost withhold the wages of Thy Workmen!

O Silver Whiteness—O Golden Splendor! O Crown of Living and Harmonious Diamond! Thou who wearest the Heavens on Thy Finger like a ring of Sapphire! Thou Who hidest beneath the Earth in the Kingdom of Gems, the marvelous Seed of the Stars! Live, reign, and be Thou the Eternal Dispenser of the Treasures whereof Thou hast made us the Wardens.

Give the Zelator Sign. Go to the West of the altar. With the white end of the wand, trace the Lesser invoking Pentagram over the bread and salt. Place the wand aside.

Consume the bread and salt. As you consume the Repast of Earth, meditate on the chosen talismanic emblem for an extended period of time.

Take as much time as you need for the meditation. Perform the Reverse Circumambulation.

(Go to the East and say:) *I now release any Spirits that may have been imprisoned by this ceremony. Depart in peace to your abodes and habitations. Go with the blessings of ADONAI HA ARETZ!*

Perform the LBRP with the black end of the wand. Then say:

I now declare this temple duly closed. So mote it be.✡

Suggested Reading

Cunningham's Encyclopedia of Crystal, Gem & Metal Magic by Scott Cunningham (Note: Write a report on the book. Examine in particular the stones which are associated with the Sephiroth. Also try to find new associations of stones that you think could also be applied to the Sephiroth.)

The Philosopher's Stone by Israel Regardie

Divine Pymander attributed to Hermes Mercurius Trismegistus

Corpus Hermeticum edited by Walter Scott

Alchemy by Cherry Gilchrist

Alchemy by E.J. Holmyard

Alchemy by Titus Burckhardt

The Alchemist's Handbook by Frater Albertus

"Book 8: DIVINATION," from *The Golden Dawn* by Israel Regardie, (section on Geomancy, pages 523—539.)

"Invocation of Hermes Trismegistus and the Vision of the Poimandres: Two Ritual Pathworkings" by Oz—published in *The Golden Dawn Journal, Book III: The Art of Hermes.*

"By the Signs of the Earth: Geomancy in the Golden Dawn" by Mitch & Gail Henson—published in *The Golden Dawn Journal, Book I: Divination.*

"Mysteria Geomantica: Teachings on the Art of Geomancy" by Adam Forrest—published in *The Golden Dawn Journal, Book I: Divination.*

The Forgotten Books of Eden edited by Rutherford H. Platt, Jr.
    (Note: Read the section entitled "The Testaments of the Twelve Patriarchs.")

"Shebilim Bahirim (The Bright Paths)" by Mitch & Gail Henson—published in *The Golden Dawn Journal, Book II: Qabalah: Theory and Magic*

The Collected Works of C.G. Jung by Carl Gustave Jung
    Volume 12: Psychology and Alchemy
    Volume 13: Alchemical Studies
    Volume 14: Mysterium Conjunctionis

Psychosynthesis: A Manual of Principles and Techniques by Roberto Assagioli

Some Final Suggestions

- Make colored drawings of your own personal impressions of the various objects described in the Zelator Hall as belonging to the Tabernacle in the Wilderness (The Altar of Incense, the Candlestick, etc.)

- Draw your personal impression of a gnome.

- Construct a box for Geomantic Divination as described in our book *Secrets of a Golden Dawn Temple.*

- Perform a Geomantic Divination daily while in the grade of Zelator.

- Create several Geomantic sigils.

- Take note of where the Planet Earth falls in your own Zodiacal chart. (The Earth is always the exact opposite of the Sun by Sign, degree and house. This portrays how and where you approach the world and symbolizes your mission in life. It also relates to secular and physical matters.) Write a brief report on how you think you are affected by this.

- Take note of any Planets that are located in Earth signs in your own Zodiacal chart. Write a brief report on how you think you are affected by them.

- Make numerous copies of a blank Zodiacal wheel. Within each division of the wheel, fill in all pertinent information regarding the Zodiacal Sign that rules that division (the name of the house, the Sign, triplicity, quality, key phrase, key activity, the ruling Planet, etc.) Do this several times until the information becomes second nature to you.

- Make several more copies of the blank Zodiacal wheel. Within each division of the wheel, fill in all pertinent information regarding the houses (the name of the house, the natural Sign of the house, the natural ruler of the house, its quality, keyword, etc.) Do this several times until the information is thoroughly absorbed.

- Take regular excursions to a location that permits you to look out from a high position over the landscape. Observe how this perspective shifts your awareness from a limited to a wide perspective, enabling you see the expanded wholeness of your world and your environment.

- If possible take regular excursions to wilderness areas or parks and observe the natural world around you. Strive to become more aware of the Earth's ecology and your own role within it. Adopt recycling as an active way to curb pollution of the Earth.

- Take an excursion to any caverns that may be near your area.

- If possible, journey to a gemstone mine where you will be able to dig your own gemstones.

- Collect a number of various gemstones that correspond to the Planets. Use them as points of focus for daily meditations—one stone for each day of the week, employing the specific Planet that rules the day.

- Collect a handful of gemstones for your own personal talismans, based upon your birth Sign, Elemental affiliation, etc.

- Obtain a crystal growing kit and follow the instructions for creating crystals. Use this as talisman for focus while in the Zelator grade.

- Regularly perform the Rite of Elemental Equilibration given in Chapter One.

Examinations

(Answers for all exams are given in the back of this book.)

QUIZ 0 *(The Ritual)*

1. What is the Grand Word of the grade of Zelator?
2. What is the Mystic Number of the Zelator grade?
3. What is the password of the Zelator grade derived from the Mystic Number?
4. What is the Battery of knocks attributed to the Zelator grade?
5. What is the Step of the Zelator grade?
6. What is the Sign of the Zelator grade?
7. What is the Elemental symbol given to the Zelator?
8. List the name of the Element attributed to this grade (in English and in Hebrew.)
9. Which direction is associated with this Element?
10. What is the Mystic Title conferred upon a Zelator?
11. What does the Mystic Title mean?
12. Where does the name "Zelator" come from?
13. Which Sephirah is associated with this grade?
14. List two forms of the Divine (Atziluthic) Name of this Sephirah.
15. Name the Great Archangel of the Element of this grade.
16. Name the Kerubic Sign of this Element.
17. What are the Three Great Secret Names of God borne upon the Enochian banners of the Quarter?
18. Name the Great Enochian King of the Quarter.
19. How are the cross and triangle arranged on the altar?
20. What does the arrangement of the cross and triangle symbolize?
21. Where else in the temple does this arrangement of cross and triangle occur?
22. What does "1 = 10" signify?
23. What is the Admission Badge to the grade of Zelator? (Give several names for this Badge.)
24. The Admission Badge is identical to the lamen of which officer?
25. The distinct sections of a ritual are called "Points." Each grade ritual has at least three Points: an Opening, a Closing, and at least one Middle Point between the Opening and the Closing. How many Middle Points are there in the Zelator Ritual?
26. Briefly describe what happens in each of the Middle Points of this ritual.
27. During the Zelator oath, what gesture does the candidate make while swearing his/her oath to the Powers of the Element?
28. What Hebrew letters are associated with the three portals in the East of the temple?
29. What do these portals signify?
30. What is the name of the Great Archangel portrayed by the Hiereus?
31. What is the name of the Great Archangel portrayed by the Hegemon?
32. What is the name of the Great Archangel portrayed by the Hierophant?

33. Who guards the Pathway of Good?
34. Who guards the Pathway of Evil?
35. Who is the left-hand Kerub of the Ark and the feminine power?
36. Who is the right-hand Kerub of the Ark and the masculine power?
37. In this ceremony, the Zelator symbolically follows the Path of a Priest of the Hebrew mysteries. As the Priest progresses into the Tabernacle, he avails himself of three items concerned with purification and consecration.
    a. The first item is found within the Courtyard. What is it and what does it represent?
    b. The second item lies between the first item and the entrance to the Holy Place. What is it and what does it represent?
    c. The third item is in the Holy Place before the Veil of the Holy of Holies? What is it and what does it represent?
38. What item is seen by the Priest in the Northern side of the Holy Place? What does this item (represented by a diagram) symbolize?
39. What item is seen by the Priest in the Southern side of the Holy Place? What does this item (represented by a diagram) symbolize?

QUIZ—SECTION 1 (*Basic Astrology—The Houses*)

1. What is a Zodiacal "house?"
2. Each house is ruled by one of the _____ and is influenced by one of the _____.
3. The Sign that is on the Eastern horizon at the time of birth is known as what?
4. The Midheaven is also called the MC. What do these initials stand for?
5. What do the initials IC stand for?
6. If the Midheaven is the tenth house cusp, what is the IC?
7. If the Ascendant is the first house cusp, what is the Descendent?
8. The first, fifth, and ninth houses are known as Fire houses. True or False?
9. Name the three houses which are known as Earth houses.
10. Name the three houses which are known as Water houses.
11. Angular houses correspond to the Kerubic Signs. True or False?
12. The Succedent houses contain the Ascendant, Descendent, MC and IC. True or False?
13. The Cadent houses correspond to the Cardinal Signs. True or False?
14. The Succedent houses are known as the Financial houses. True or False?
15. The Cadent houses are known as the Mental houses. True or False?
16. Name the house whose Key word is Identity.
17. Name the house whose Key word is Honor.
18. Name the house whose Key word is Social Consciousness.
19. Name the house whose Key word is Awareness.
20. Name the house whose Key word is Security.
21. Which house reveals philosophy and the higher consciousness?
22. Which house shows hidden strengths, dangers and limitations?
23. Which house shows secrets, rebirth and regeneration?

24. Which house describes marriages, partnerships and agreements?
25. Which house reveals creativity, children and romance?
26. Which house alludes to values, self-worth and resources?
27. Luna rules which house?
28. Mercury rules which houses?
29. Jupiter rules which house?
30. Venus rules which houses?
31. Sol rules which house?
32. Neptune and Jupiter are the co-rulers of which house?
33. Uranus and Saturn of the co-rulers of which house?
34. The twelfth house is Cadent. True or False.
35. The ninth house is Cadent. True or False.
36. The third house is angular. True or False.
37. The fifth house is succedent. True or False.
38. The seventh house is succedent. True or False.
39. Scorpio is the natural Sign of what house?
40. Libra is the natural Sign of what house?
41. Cancer is the natural Sign of what house?
42. What are the Meridians?
43. What separates the horoscope into day and night sections?
44. What separates the horoscope into rising Planets and setting Planets?
45. If a person's natal chart has a large number of rising Planets in the Eastern half, what does it signify?
46. If a person's natal chart has a large number of setting Planets in the Western half, what does it signify?
47. What is an imaginary line which separates a house or a Sign from its neighbors called?
48. What is a ten degree arc or subdivision of the Zodiacal Wheel called?

QUIZ—SECTION 2 (Basic Alchemy)

1. What is the word "Alchemy" derived from?
2. Who is the legendary founder of Alchemy?
3. Who were the first Alchemists?
4. To Paracelsus, the major goal of Alchemy was what?
5. In addition to being a science Alchemy can also be described as what?
6. Alchemy was the ancestor of what modern science?
7. Practitioners of the art considered _____ the greatest Alchemist of all.
8. Name the Three Alchemic Principles.
9. Name the three basic evolutionary processes.
10. What is the Fifth Essence?
11. What is the primary goal of alchemy?
12. What does the color gold signify?
13. Which of the Three Alchemic Principles is described as dynamic and expansive?

14. Which of the Three Alchemic Principles is described as heavy and inert?
15. Which of the Three Alchemic Principles is described as fluid and creative?
16. List the seven metals along with the Planets that they are attributed to.
17. What term describes the refined essence of heat and moisture?
18. What term describes the refined essence of heat and fire?
19. What symbolic creature alludes to the force of nature under control of the Will?
20. What does the black dragon refer to?
21. What symbolic person is analogous to gold and the Sun?
22. What symbolic person is analogous to silver and the Moon?
23. What symbolic person is known as the "Lesser Countenance?"
24. What symbolic creature symbolizes the stem and root of the radical essence of the metals?
25. What words are used to describe the First matter?
26. What words are used to describe the Great Work?
27. What is another name for the Philosophic Mercury?
28. The search for the _____ is the search for ultimate truth and purity.
29. What is another name for Lapis Philosophorum?
30. What does the pelican symbolize?
31. What word describes "Two-thing?"
32. What does the Peacock symbolize?
33. What symbolic creature represents resurrection and Fire?
34. What color signifies the Prime Matter?
35. What substance acts like a metal but is not?
36. What term describes Mercury as "the thing containing the thing contained?"
37. What poison also acts as a powerful medicine?
38. What term describes a mixture of metals through fusion?
39. What term describes "The Imperishable or Enduring Water?"
40. What is the Universal Medicine; also considered as a living Spirit?
41. What term describes the Eagle of the Philosophers?
42. In Practical Alchemy, metals are often referred to as _____.
43. What symbolic creature signifies initiation through Blackness?
44. What term describes "the Fire of the Lion?"
45. What term describes the First Essence?
46. What term describes a metal which contains all the metals attributed to the seven Planets?
47. What term describes the Essence of Interior Nature?
48. What term describes Silver as the Mother of Metals?
49. What term describes a solvent and the original material from which all metals are derived?
50. What is the Red Man?
51. What term describes the First Matter of all things and the Mother of all finite living things?
52. What is the Secret Fire?
53. What other terms are used for the Secret Fire?

54. What is another name for the Celestial Ruby and the Elixir of Life?
55. What is the Spagyric Art?
56. What is a Tincture?
57. What is the *Principia Chymia*?
58. What term describes the end of the Work?
59. Describe "Solve et Coagula."
60. What term describes an acidic penetrating substance?
61. What does the white Swan symbolize?
62. Describe "Pater et Mater Regis" or "the Father and Mother of the King."
63. What is the "Spirit of Fire?"
64. What is "The cornerstone of Light" or the supreme Essence?
65. What does honey symbolize?
66. What does the goat symbolize?
67. What two animals symbolize the dual nature of Mercury?
68. What is the tailend of the matter?
69. What is Cauda Pavonis?
70. What is another name for white gold?
71. What is the Spirit of the World called?
72. What is another word for self-incubation?
73. What is symbolized by the Lily?

QUIZ—SECTIONS 3, 4 and 5 *(The Elementals, Tetragrammaton, The Hebrew Letters, the Four Worlds, the Divine Names)*

1. What is an Elemental?
2. Name the four orders of Elementals.
3. Which order of Elementals are said to be patient and hardworking?
4. Who is the king of the Air Spirits?
5. Who is the king of the Earth Spirits?
6. Which order of Elementals uses the smoke of burning incense as a medium for expression?
7. Which order of Elementals are especially inspirational to artists and poets?
8. Who is the Queen of the Water Spirits?
9. What does the word Tetragrammaton mean in Greek?
10. To what does the Tetragrammaton refer?
11. List the Hebrew letters of the Tetragrammaton along with their assigned Elements.
12. Which of the letters are masculine?
13. Which of the letters are feminine?
14. What does the name "Kerubim" mean?
15. The Kerubim operate through which Zodiacal Triplicity?
16. What is the name of the Lion Kerub? What is its Element?
17. What is the name of the Man Kerub? What is its Element?
18. What is the name of the Eagle Kerub? What is its Element?
19. What is the name of the Bull Kerub? What is its Element?

20. List the Three Mother Letters.
21. List the Seven Double Letters.
22. List the Twelve Simple Letters.
23. Why are the "Double Letters" so named?
24. The Seven Double Letters represent the __ _____ of the ancients.
25. What do the Three Mother Letters represent?
26. List the Four Worlds of the Qabalah. Give both English and Hebrew spellings.
27. Which World is the realm of Primordial Water?
28. Which World is the realm of Pure deity?
29. Which World is the realm of Primordial Fire?
30. Which World is approximate to the astral Plane?
31. Which World is assigned to the letter Heh Final?
32. Which World is assigned the secret name of Ben?
33. Which World is corporeal and dense?
34. Which World is assigned to the letter Vav?
35. Which World is assigned the secret name of Aub?
36. List the Ten Heavens of Assiah. Give both English and Hebrew spellings. Also list their Planetary correspondences.
37. List the Divine Atziluthic Names of the Sephiroth. Give both English and Hebrew spellings.
38. List the Archangelic Briatic Names of the Sephiroth. Give both English and Hebrew spellings.
39. List the Angelic Yetziratic Names of the Sephiroth. Give both English and Hebrew spellings.
40. What is the Hebrew Name for "God of Battles?"
41. What is the Hebrew Name for "I am?"
42. What is the Hebrew Name for "Lord God of Knowledge?"
43. What is the Hebrew Name for "God of Hosts?"
44. What is the Hebrew Name for "Almighty Living God?"
45. Identify the Archangel whose name means "near thy throne."
46. Identify the Archangel whose name means "The Severity of God."
47. Identify the Archangel whose name means "The Herald of God."
48. Identify the Archangel whose name means "The Healer of God."
49. Identify the Archangel whose name means "The Strong One of God."
50. Name the group of Angels known as "The Wheels."
51. Name the group of Angels known as "The Shining Ones."
52. Name the group of Angels known as "The Sons of the gods."
53. Name the group of Angels known as "The Souls of Fire."
54. Name the group of Angels known as "The Kings."
55. List the Planetary Angels. Give both English and Hebrew spellings.
56. List the Planetary Intelligences. Give both English and Hebrew spellings.
57. List the Planetary Spirits. Give both English and Hebrew spellings.
58. Identify the Planetary Archangel whose name means "Speed of God."
59. Identify the Planetary Archangel whose name means "Covering of God."

60. Identify the Planetary Intelligence whose name means "Beauty of God."
61. Identify the Planetary Intelligence whose name means "Might of God."
62. Give the name of an alternative Lunar Intelligence with a manageable name.
63. List the twelve Zodiacal Archangels next to their respective Signs. Give both English and Hebrew spellings.
64. Identify the Archangel whose name comes from the Greek "Myrrh."
65. Identify the Archangel whose name means "Lightning of God."
66. Who is the Archangel of Pisces?
67. Who is the Archangel of Leo?
68. Identify the Archangel whose name means "my rock is God."
69. What Archangel was referred to by Enoch as the one who rises and rules in the beginning of the year?
70. Who is the Archangel of Sagittarius?

QUIZ—SECTIONS 6 & 7 *(Earth Correspondences and Geomancy)*

1. List the precious stones which correspond to the Sephiroth.
2. List the precious stones which correspond to the Zodiacal Signs.
3. List the precious stones which correspond to the Planets.
4. List the precious stones which correspond to the Elements.
5. What are the two Hebrew names for Earth? Give both English and Hebrew spellings.
6. What is the Outer Divine Name of Earth in Hebrew? Give both English and Hebrew spellings.
7. What is the Hebrew name for the Cardinal Point of North? Give both English and Hebrew spellings.
8. What is the name of the Archangel of Earth? Give both English and Hebrew spellings.
9. What is the name of the Angel of Earth? Give both English and Hebrew spellings.
10. What is the name of the Ruler of Earth? Give both English and Hebrew spellings.
11. What is the name of the King of Earth Spirits?
12. What is the name of the Order of Elementals associated with Earth?
13. What is the name of the Egyptian deity associated with Earth?
14. What is the name of the Assyro-Babylonian deity associated with Earth?
15. What Greek goddess personified the primitive Earth and was also identified with caverns?
16. What Greek Earth goddess was the mother of the Titans?
17. What Greek Earth goddess was identified with the Underworld?
18. What Greek goddess governed the harvest and all agricultural activities?
19. Draw the sixteen Geomantic figures and give their names. Also list their corresponding Zodiacal Signs.
20. What are the first four figures that are derived from the sixteen lines of dots called?

21. What is the second set of four figures that are derived from the sixteen lines of dots called?
22. What is the third set of four figures that are derived from the sixteen lines of dots called?
23. What is another name for a Geomantic figure composed of four Root Lines?
24. How is the Judge formed?
25. How is the Left Witness formed?
26. The _____ is especially helpful in questions of money.
27. A figure is Very Strong when in a house opposite that of its Exaltation. True or False?
28. A figure is strongest when in its Exaltation. True or False?
29. A figure is Weakest of all in its Detriment. True or False?
30. A figure in its Exaltation when opposite its own house. True or False?
31. What is the house in question known as?
32. In aspecting the figures, Opposition would be the house directly opposite the house in question. True or False?
33. Both Opposition and Square are stressful. True or False?
34. Count three houses from and including the Significator in both directions to find the Trine. True or False?
35. What is another name for "clockwise?"
36. What is another name for "counterclockwise?"
37. Which house determines the conclusion or final outcome?
38. What is the name of the sixteenth and final figure that can be derived in order to give a final reading?
39. The random generation of Geomantic figures is called what?
40. What are the Resultants?
41. What is a Geomantic Spirit usually called?
42. What other hierarchy lists the Geomantic Spirits?
43. What is Essential Dignity?
44. What is Accidental Dignity?
45. With pen and paper, perform a divination by geomancy using all necessary figures and charts.

QUIZ—SECTION 8 *(Ritual Images and Diagrams)*

1. What object within the Tabernacle was overlaid with gold?
2. What object in the courtyard of the Tabernacle refers to the Waters of Binah?
3. What are the Qlippoth?
4. What object in the courtyard of the Tabernacle refers to the Qlippoth?
5. What symbolic image connects the Sephiroth on the Tree of Life?
6. What are the Thirty-two Paths of Wisdom?
7. Describe the Pillar of Severity.
8. Describe the Pillar of Mercy.
9. What is the Admission Badge to the 1=10 grade?
10. How many squares comprise this Badge?

11. How many squares was the Badge originally formed from?
12. What symbol is at the center of this Badge?
13. What symbols are depicted on the arms of this Badge?
14. List four other names for this Badge.
15. What does this Badge signify?
16. Describe the symbolism of the Table of Shewbread.
17. Describe the symbolism of the Seven-branched Candlestick.
18. List the twelve Tribes of Israel.
19. List the primary tribe of Israel whose standard was placed in the West.
20. List the primary tribe of Israel whose standard was placed in the South.
21. List the primary tribe of Israel whose standard was placed in the East.
22. List the primary tribe of Israel whose standard was placed in the North.

CHAPTER THREE

The Theoricus Grade

②=9

I n the previous chapter, we examined the Zelator grade which was the first grade to confer the title of *initiate* upon the aspirant, firmly placing him/her upon the initiatory Tree of Life. Once the candidate has attained the $1 = 10$ grade the groundwork for all ensuing Elemental transformation and equilibration within the aspirant's psyche has been built. In the $2 = 9$ grade the initiate takes the *second* Elemental initiation into the *ninth* Sephirah, Yesod, on the Qabalistic Tree, and the spiritual process of dissolution and integration continues.

There is one very important difference between the Zelator grade and the Grades of Theoricus, Practicus and Philosophus. The former initiation established the initial step onto the Sphere of Malkuth. The remaining grades (regardless of their respective Sephirotic correspondences) are in reality only further steps in the exploration of the *four sub-elements of Malkuth.*

The Element offered for the process of transmutation in this grade is Air, or rather the Airy portion of the aspirant's psyche (to be even more precise it is the *Air of Malkuth in Assiah*). As the grade of entry into the Sphere of Yesod,[62] the Theoricus grade also enjoys a special occult relationship with the Portal grade (as Yesod esoterically contains the "fifth" element—after the four elements of Malkuth).

The Planet assigned to this grade is Luna, the orb of reflected (and therefore sometimes illusionary) Light. The initiate approaching this grade had better make certain that s/he has fully assimilated the energies and knowledge of the Zelator grade. If not, the volatile astral winds of Yesod might well blow the aspirant off course. Sometimes students will experience the effects of the volatile Air grade as a general lack of focus or diminished ability to concentrate on one's studies. (Some have remarked that they "feel like an air-head" in this grade.) Like the previous grade, the $2 = 9$ is a filter which will screen out individuals who do not have what it takes to be a true and worthy initiate of the Hermetic mysteries.

The title of Theoricus is derived from a Greek word which means "beholder," "onlooker" or "student."

The ceremony of the Theoricus can be summed up as follows: After the standard (self-initiatory) rite of opening, the forces of Elemental Air are invoked. Then the candidate must prove that s/he has grasped the secrets of the Zelator

---

[62] The Theoricus grade deals specifically with *Yesod of Malkuth,* just as the Zelator grade placed the candidate in *Malkuth of Malkuth* (the Earth quarter of Malkuth.)

grade and swear an oath. Between the spheres of Malkuth and Yesod lies the 32nd Path of Tau, a journey through the subconscious mind and the astral plane, which the aspirant undertakes at this time. On this Path, the candidate is confronted by the four Kerubim, the group of Angels assigned to Yesod. (As the presidents of the Elemental forces, the four Kerubim are each assigned one of the letters of the Divine Name *YHVH*, and they operate in and through the four astral Elements in Yesod before these Elements are formulated into the physical world of Malkuth.) In the ritual, the Kerubim perform Elemental purifications on the aspirant, which aid the overall process of Alchemic transmutation. (Note: here the candidate also learns that the Elemental Spirits are to be invoked through the power and governance of the Kerubim and their Zodiacal symbols.) After completing the 32nd Path, the candidate is shown the Tarot card of The Universe and other symbolism. Equilibrium of the Elements is stressed.

The later half of the ritual involves the initiate's entry into the temple of Yesod. During this time the aspirant is shown further symbolism concerning the Garden of Eden and the Theoricus Hall. The secrets of the 2 = 9 grade are divulged, until at length, the Air Powers are released.

There are only four officers stationed in the Theoricus Hall (besides the Dais officers), including the three Middle Pillar officers and the Keryx. The Phylax, Dadouchos and Stolistes have been dropped at this point. The stations of the officers are symmetrically positioned at the four quarters. This harmonious arrangement suggests the reconciling Element of Air mediating between all the opposing energies within the Hall, resulting in perfect equilibrium. The number four, associated with the sphere of Chesed (the first Sephirah of manifestation below the Abyss) also refers to the firm foundation or matrix of the four Elements inherent within the sphere of Yesod—which later manifest in Malkuth during the course of the Qabalistic Lightning Flash. If you consider the central point of the Hall, the position of the altar, you obtain the number five, the fifth Element and the esoteric Lunar number.

Since the Kerubim play such an important role in this grade it is suggested that the student of this course become familiar with them:

The Kerubic Forms of the Theoricus Grade

The Kerubim listed here are given Hebrew names but their appearance is primarily Egyptian.

ADAM: (Hebrew meaning: *man*) Man-headed or rather *human*-headed. Often portrayed as feminine rather than masculine, Adam is the Kerub of Air. This Kerub is stationed in the East and is visualized as an upright winged figure wearing a nemyss and tunic in the colors of yellow and violet. Adam is crowned by the lunar crescent and the solar disk, and can be visualized as carrying either the Lotus Wand and ankh, or the yellow Air fan.

ARYEH: (Hebrew meaning: *lion*) Aryeh is the Kerub of Fire. This Kerub is stationed in the South and is visualized as an upright lion-headed winged figure wearing a nemyss and tunic in the colors of red and green. Aryeh can be visualized as carrying either the Lotus Wand and ankh, or the red lamp.

NESHER: (Hebrew meaning: *eagle*) Nesher is the Kerub of Water. This Kerub is stationed in the West and is visualized as an upright eagle-headed winged figure wearing a nemyss and tunic in the colors of blue and orange. Nesher can be visualized as wearing upon his head the disk encircled by a serpent and carrying either the Lotus Wand and ankh, or the cup of Water.

SHOR: (Hebrew meaning: *bull*) Shor is the Kerub of Earth. This Kerub is stationed in the West and is visualized as an upright bull-headed winged figure wearing a nemyss and tunic in the colors of black and white. Shor can be visualized as wearing upon his head the disk encircled by a serpent and carrying either the Crook and Scourge, or the platter of Salt.✿

Following the 2 = 9 initiation, the task of the Theoricus is to completely absorb all knowledge related to the Element of Air and the Planet Luna. The bulk of this is contained in the Third Knowledge Lecture, which also contains additional information on aspects, erecting a horoscope, plants, Alchemical processes and more. As in the previous chapter, ritual work and exercises are provided that are appropriate to the grade, including a pathworking visualization for the 32nd Path of Tau. We advise the student of the Theoricus grade to heed the statement given in the 2 = 9 ceremony: *"Quit the material and seek the Spiritual!"*✿

THE THEORICUS CEREMONY

Temple setup: The aspirant will need to set up the Hall beforehand in accordance with the temple diagram. The black cubical altar is placed in the center of the room. Upon it are a fan, platter of salt, red lamp or candle, and a cup of Water in their respective quarters. In the center of these items is the 21st Key of the Tarot, *The Universe.*[63] On the front of the altar should be a large diagram of the Flaming Sword and the Kerubim (from the Zelator grade). The pillars are placed just East of the altar. The three Hebrew letters of Shin, Tau and Qoph are shown on large plaques in the East. Both Banners of the East and West are located in the East as in the Zelator Ritual. The Enochian Tablet of Earth is placed in the North, and the Tablet of Air is situated in the East. A large pentagram is also to be located in the East behind the Hierophant. Place the lamens in accordance with the temple diagram, in the positions of the officer-forms. Arrange the implements of the officers next to their respective lamens.

As in the previous ritual, all of the Elemental candles should be placed around the circumference of the room, with a white candle in the East. The yellow Air candle is to be placed before the Enochian Tablet of the East. The lights on the pillars should be unshaded. A censer of burning incense should be placed in the South. The following diagrams are optional but may be employed if the candidate

---

[63] From *The New Golden Dawn Ritual Tarot.*

so desires: The Garden of Eden and the Holy City in the South and the diagram of Gehenna in the North.[64]

(Note: For the latter half of the ritual, the aspirant will also need plaques of the Hebrew letters Resh, Samekh and Tzaddi, as well as the Qamea, seal and sigils of Luna. [All the Qameoth and Planetary seals are found in Chapter Four.] The diagram of the Serpent on the Tree of Life, and the Caduceus Admission Badge are required, along with second red lamp and cup of Water. Have these items ready for when they are needed.)

Ritual preparations: As before, it is suggested that the aspirant fast for a period of 12 hours prior to the ritual. A ritual bath is required after which the aspirant may put on the black Tau robe, and red slippers. The sash will need to be decorated with the Theoricus emblems, but it is not to be worn by the candidate at this time. Place the sash inside the altar.

The aspirant must meditate for a certain length of time on a drawing of the symbol of Air—an Air triangle (apex upwards) in yellow. Next s/he must spend a period of time (20-30 minutes) in a darkened room or antechamber to the temple seated in quiet meditation while wearing a hoodwink or blindfold. The Admission Badge for the 32nd Path, the Greek Cubical Cross, should be held in the right hand throughout this period. A small yellow candle is to be the only source of light in the room. During this time, darkness and silence are to be maintained. The aspirant should imagine him/her self under the watchful eye of Anubis of the West. After this period of time, the hoodwink may be removed. The aspirant may then enter the temple and begin the ritual.

Upon entering the temple, imagine that you are leaving your physical body outside as a sentinel to guard the temple, so that your spiritual self has the freedom to accept initiation.

PART 0: The Opening

Enter the temple with the Admission Badge of the Cubical Cross. Salute the Banner of the East with the Neophyte Signs. Leave the cross in the Western part of the temple. Once inside walk deosil to the East. With the Hiereus' sword, perform the LBRP.

Give one knock with the pommel of the sword against the floor or side of the chair and say: "*HEKAS, HEKAS, ESTE BEBELOI!*"

Put the sword aside and go to the West of the temple, facing East. Kneel down and invoke the godform of Thmê as in the previous initiation. Vibrate strongly:

---

[64] Many diagrams that were used in the early days of the Order were later dropped from the grade ceremonies because they were considered nonessential. Some of them, such as the Altar of Incense diagram in the Zelator grade certainly are. However, the student may find some of these diagrams helpful and decide to utilize them in the initiation ceremonies. The diagram of Gehenna can be found in Chapter Five of this book.

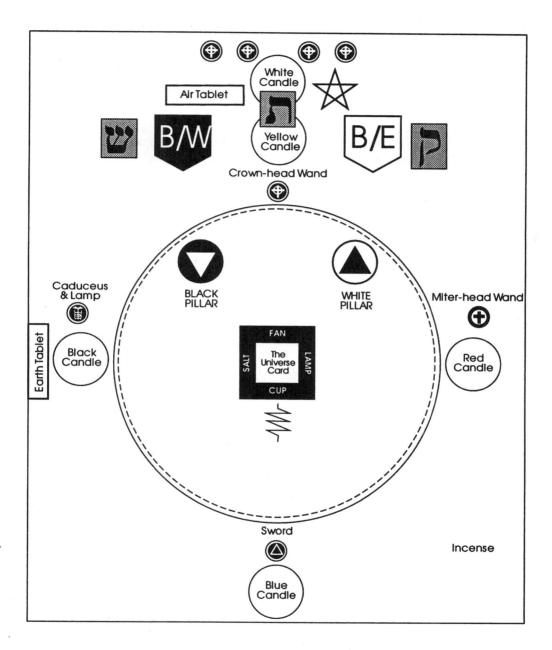

Theoricus Temple for Self-Initiation: First Setup

> *THMÊ! THMÊ! THMÊ! Thou daughter and eye of RA! Lady of Heaven, Queen of Earth and mistress of the Underworld! Great Lady of all the gods and goddesses. Thou whose name is MAAT! Lady of Truth! goddess of Justice and Order! Mediator between Darkness and Light, Chaos and Order! THMÊ! THMÊ! THMÊ! Thou who assesses the heart of every man and woman in the Hall of Judgment before Ousiri and the assembly of the gods. Thou who art the eye and heart of balance! THMÊ! THMÊ! THMÊ! I invoke thee!*

As in your previous initiation rite, visualize the image of the goddess Thmê before you, with human head and yellow-gold skin. She wears a black and white nemyss and a white linen gown. She carries the miter-headed scepter of the Hegemon. Above her head is the white glowing outline of the cross and triangle, symbolic of the outer magical current of the Golden Dawn.

Slowly and with much feeling, perform the Qabalistic Cross, drawing the Light down from the Kether of the universe into the Kether at the crown of your head as you continue the QC. Strongly visualize the cross of Light you have formed in the center of your body. Trace within your heart the Hebrew letters of the name THMÊ in glowing white. Project a white ray of thought from your heart toward the image of Thmê you have created before you. See the figure breathe in life as your thought-ray animates it. Address the form:

> *THMÊ! Beautiful One of the Feather of Truth! I beseech thee to act upon my behalf in this my quest for the Light Divine! Guide me, O thou who art none other but my own Higher Self. Aid me and escort me in this Astral Realm which is the invisible Foundation of the manifest universe. I am a true and willing Seeker of Light and Knowledge. Act as my overseer and reconciler in the temple of Yesod. Speak for me amidst the assembly of the gods and the guardians of this sacred Hall. My intentions are honest. I am ready to undergo test and trial. I am willing to be examined by the Kerubic Guardians! I wish to be purified and consecrated to the Light. Grant that my heart is made MAAT! Grant that my Will is made MAAT! Merciful THMÊ! Let me be judged aright! Grant that this humble Aspirant before you be not turned away from that resplendent Light which resides in the East. Permit me to rend the Veil of the Tabernacle! Award me a vision of the Garden of Paradise! Grant that I may pass the Gate of Eden. Let me penetrate the Threshold in the Path of the Enterer!*

Thmê speaks to you in your own mind.

> Quit the Material and seek the Spiritual! I am the representative of your Higher and Holy Self. It is only through my arbitration that thou canst even approach the Sacred Garden of Perfection. In this Hall I am thy tongue, thy heart and thy mind. Fear not, for I shall guide

thee through the terrible Abode of the Shells, and keep thee safe. Fear not, for I shall lead thee through the temple of Yesod. I shall direct thee in the Garden before the mighty Kerubim and the Flaming Sword! I shall speak for thee in this assembly of the gods before the powers of YHVH and the current of the Light.

Imagine the goddess Thmê communicating in silence with the energies in the East. She speaks on your behalf to the divine guardians of the Hall. You hear her voice as she calls out the names of other godforms in the East of the temple: ESE, NEBETHO, THOOUTH and another, HOOR OUER. You have a vague impression of four figures in the East, seated before a veil. Thmê continues to address the figures, and the scene becomes hazy. As in the previous rites, it appears that the goddess stands once again before the gigantic form of Djehoti, god of Wisdom. Thmê continues a silent discussion with the god. After a few moments Thmê turns toward you, salutes with the Signs toward the West and says silently:

Thou mayest proceed, O aspirant; thou art MAAT.

Thmê descends from the East. In regular progression, she traces with her scepter the figures of a cross and triangle in all four quarters where the officer/godforms are to be visualized, going from East to South, West, and North. As she does so in the East, vibrate the name *"OUSIRI"* (Oo-seer-ee) and visualize the figure of Osiris as he begins to formulate. Then she goes to the South and traces the figures at her own station, the station of the Hegemon. Thmê goes to the West to make the signs, as you vibrate the name *"HOOR"* (Hoor or Hoh-or) The god Horus commences to take shape. The goddess then goes North and you intone the name of *"ANOUP EMPEIEBET"* (Ah-noop-em-pay-yeh-bet). Anubis of the East appears at the station of the Keryx.

Thmê takes you by the hand, and leads you between the pillars. Say:

> The 2 = 9 grade of Theoricus is attributed to the Planet of Luna, and the 32nd Path of Tau which alludes to the universe as composed of the Four Elements—to the Kerubim, the Qlippoth and the Astral Plane, and the reflection of the sphere of Saturn. Let the Element of this grade be named that it may be awakened within my sphere, in the spheres of those beings who are present, and in the sphere of this magical current. The Element is AIR."

Visualize the symbol of the yellow Air triangle that you meditated on before entering the Hall. Imagine its presence in your sphere of sensation at the Tiphareth[65] area, the abdomen. Then visualize the triangle in violet reflected into your Yesod center—the groin. Imagine that these same images are activated in all of the various astral officer-forms of the Hall.

---

[65] The *Vav-Air* center of the Four Qabalistic Worlds.

Invoking Air

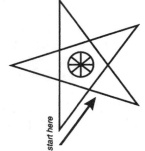

Banishing Air

Invoking Spirit Active

Banishing Spirit Active

The Pentagrams of Air

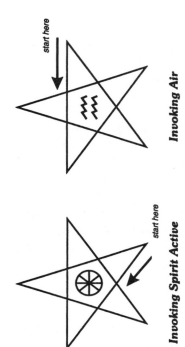

The Enochian Tablet of Air

Thmê leads you clockwise to the East, where she traces the figure of the cross and triangle with the miter-headed wand. As she does so, you vibrate the name *"OUSIRI."* The familiar image of the godform begins to grow stronger in the East. Visualize the mummy-wrapped form of the god strongly. Osiris traces in the air before you the figure of a cross and circle. He then hands you his crown-headed scepter. Picking up the Wand of Power, you take on the office of Hierophant that Osiris has bestowed

The Sign of Theoricus

upon you. Give the Sign of the Spiraling Light toward the East, then say, "Let the white brilliance of the Divine Spirit descend!" Feel a flood of Divine Light flow through your body from the Kether of the universe. Equilibrate this Light through your body by performing the Qabalistic Cross, vibrating the Hebrew names.

Give a knock and say, *"Let us adore the Lord and King of Air!"* Trace a circle toward the East with the scepter. Say, *"SHADDAI EL CHAI, Almighty and Ever-Lasting— Ever Living be Thy Name, Ever Magnified in the Life of All! Amen."* Salute with the Theoricus Sign.

Stand facing the Air Tablet. Visualize the rest of the astral officer/godforms leaving their stations to face East. Hiereus advances to just West of the altar. Hegemon and Keryx advance and stand at the outer sides of the pillars.

Through the authority of the office of Hierophant bestowed upon you by Osiris, invoke the powers of the Air Tablet. Give a knock, then trace with the wand a large circle in front of the Tablet. Then draw the invoking pentagram of Spirit Active. As you do so vibrate *"EXARP"* (Ex-ar-pay). Trace the sigil of Spirit in the center and intone *"EHEIEH"* (Eh-heh-yay). Give the Sign of the Spiraling Light. Then trace the invoking pentagram of Air. As you do so vibrate the name *"ORO IBAH AOZPI"* (Or-oh Ee-bah-hay Ah-oh-zohd-pee). Draw the sigil of Aquarius in the center and intone *"YHVH."* Give the Sign of Theoricus. Say:

> And the Elohim said, "Let us make ADAM in Our Image, after our likeness, and let them have dominion over the fowl of the Air." In the Name YOD HEH VAV HEH and in the Name of SHADDAI EL CHAI, Spirits of Air adore your Creator.

Take up the fan from the altar and return to the East. Trace with the fan the sigil of Aquarius before the Tablet.[66] Say:

---

[66] In Regardie's *The Golden Dawn*, the Hierophant uses a pentacle to trace these figures before the Tablet of the East. This is due to the fact that the number five is considered an esoteric Lunar number associated with Yesod, and it hints at a subtle correspondence that exists between the 2=9 grade and the Portal grade. However, we have always felt that the use of the pentacle to invoke the powers of Air was a bit too esoteric. For the sake of balance and cohesion with the tools used in the other Elemental grades, we have substituted the fan as the tool used to invoke Air.

In the Name of RAPHAEL, the Great Archangel of Air, and in the Sign of the head of the Man, Spirits of Air adore your Creator!"

Trace a cross with the fan. Say:

In the Names and Letters of the Great Eastern Quadrangle, revealed unto Enoch by the Great Angel AVE, Spirits of Air adore your Creator!

Hold the fan high and say:

In the Three Great Secret Names of God, borne upon the Banners of the East, ORO IBAH AOZPI, Spirits of Air adore your Creator! In the Name of BATAIVAH, Great King of the East, Spirits of Air, adore your Creator!

Replace the fan and return to the East facing West. Visualize all the officer/god-forms returning to their stations. Say:

In the Name of SHADDAI EL CHAI, I declare this temple opened in the 2 = 9 grade of Theoricus.

Give the following knocks with the pommel of the scepter: 111 111 111 (three sets of three knocks). Visualize the officer/godform of Hiereus repeating the Battery of knocks: 3—3—3. Visualize the officer/godform of Hegemon sounding the Battery: 3—3—3.

Step out of the office of Hierophant and return the officer-form to the dominion of Osiris, unto whom it rightly belongs. Place the fan by the station of the Hierophant, the red lamp or candle by the Hegemon, the cup by the Hiereus, and the salt next to the Keryx. The goddess Thmê then leads you to the West of the temple.

PART 1: Advancement in the 32nd Path of Tau

Visualize all of the astral officer/godforms at their respective stations. At this point, the temple has been opened under the guidance of the Guardians of the Hall, with your (very active) participation. You have already done much to activate the Element of Air within your sphere of sensation. As in the previous initiation ceremony, you must now take a few moments to reestablish yourself as a *candidate* who seeks for entrance into this Hall. Perform the Qabalistic Cross to maintain a psychic balance of all the Elements within your aura. Recall the experience in the antechamber, where you were blindfolded in the darkness. Restore the persona of the aspirant within you.

Take up the Greek Cubical Cross in your right hand. Give the Battery of knocks 3—3—3. Stand in the Western part of the Hall facing East and say:

This candidate seeks for entrance. I vow it to be true that I (magical motto) have made such progress in the Paths of Occult Science to have enabled me to pass certain examinations in the requisite knowledge. Having accomplished this, I am now eligible for advancement to the grade of Theoricus.

The goddess Thmê replies:

Quit the Material and seek the Spiritual!

She leads you between the pillars, and remains at your left side. Anubis is visualized standing at your right side. Osiris in the East speaks to you:

Give the Step and Sign of a Zelator. (You do so.)

Give me the Grip or Token.

You exchange the grip with the officer/godform in the East.

Give me the Grand Word of the 1 = 10 grade.

You give it: *"Adonai Ha-Aretz."*

Give me the Mystic Title of the 1 = 10 grade.

You give it: *"Periclinus de Faustis."*

Give me the Mystic Number of a Zelator.

You give it: *"55."*

What is the Password formed from the Mystic Number?—Osiris asks.

You answer: *"Nun Heh."*

Osiris returns to his station. You are very aware of the presence of Thmê on your left. You hear the voice of Osiris:

Periclinus de Faustis, are you ready to take this oath of the 2 = 9 grade?

You answer: *"I am ready to take this oath."* Standing between the pillars, say:

I (state magical motto) solemnly pledge to maintain and uphold the mysteries of the 32nd Path of the 2 = 9 grade of Theoricus, just as I am pledged to maintain those of the preceding grades.

Stretch out your right hand, holding the Cubical Cross toward the heavens as if giving the Zelator Sign and say: *"I swear by the Firmament of Heaven! Let the Powers of Air witness my pledge!"* Visualize Thmê returning to her station in the South. Anubis remains at your right side. Give one knock and say:

> *Before me are the Portals of the 31st, 32nd, and 29th Paths leading from the grade of Zelator to the three other grades which are beyond. The only Path now open to me, however, is the 32nd Path of Tau, which leads to the 2 = 9 grade of Theoricus, which I must traverse before claiming that grade.*

Osiris speaks:

> Take in your right hand the Cubical Cross and in your left the Banner of Light and follow your guide Anubis the Guardian, who leads you from the Material to the Spiritual.

Visualize the officer/godform of the Hierophant handing you the Banner of the East. Take up the Banner of East in your left hand. Anubis as Keryx speaks to you:

> Let us enter the Presence of the Lord of Truth. Arise and follow me.

Anubis with lantern and staff, turns to the right and leads you through the pillars, and very slowly around the Hall. As he does so, visualize the following:

> At this point, briefly imagine in your mind's eye that you are passing through a Gate marked with the Hebrew letter Tau, leaving the sphere of Malkuth behind and following your guide through a blue-violet tunnel or passageway. You are leaving the solid, material world behind as you begin to traverse the ethereal and sometimes illusory Path that connects the Active World with the astral plane. The Path is unfamiliar and unnerving, sometimes pressing in—other times expanding out to the edges of the universe. It is dark and full of shadows, but the powerful beam of light from the lamp of Anubis is there to guide and support you.

In the echoing distance you hear Horus speak:

> The Sphinx of Egypt spake and said: "I am the synthesis of the Elemental Forces. I am also the symbol of Man. I am Life and I am Death. I am the Child of the Night of Time."

Anubis leads you back around to the East to the station of the Hierophant. The figure of the Hierophant rises like a powerful gust of wind. No longer do you recognize the features of Osiris. The officer has taken on the appearance of a beautiful goddess figure with mighty clashing wings, dressed in a royal tunic of yellow and violet. She steps between you and your guide, barring your passage with the Banner of the West and the fan of Air. The figure speaks to you:

> The Priest with the mask of the Man spake and said: "Thou canst not pass the Gate of the Eastern Heaven unless thou canst tell me my name."

(You answer:) *Thou art NUET, goddess of the Firmament of Air. Thou art HARMACHIS, Lord of the Eastern Sun.*[67]

In what signs and symbols do ye come? (She demands.)

I come in the Letter ALEPH, in the Banner of Light, and the symbol of the Equated Forces. (You reply holding up the banner and the cross.)

Satisfied with your answers, the winged figure stands back and traces the sigil of Aquarius before you with the fan. A gentle breeze washes over you as she does so. Visualize the sigil at your heart center as your aura is filled temporarily with a yellow Light. Take up the fan at the station of the Hierophant and trace the sigil in the air before you. The figure speaks once more:

> In the sign of the Man and in the name of the Kerub ADAM, Child of Air, thou art purified. Pass thou on.

Anubis leads you once around the temple, through the blue-violet which colors the Path of Tau. After your experience with the Kerub, the shadows of the Path resume their play, yet they do not distract you from the light of the Keryx's lantern. Again you hear Horus speak:

> I am OSIRIS, the Soul in twin aspect, united to the Higher by purification, perfected by suffering, glorified through trial. I have come where the great gods are, through the Power of the Mighty Name.

Anubis leads you around to the South and the station of the Hegemon. The figure of the officer erupts forth like an explosive flame. No longer do you recognize the familiar features of Thmê. The officer has taken on the appearance of a fierce lion-headed figure with great wings, dressed in a royal tunic of red and green. He thrusts between you and Anubis, halting your passage with the Banner of the West and the red lamp. The majestic figure speaks to you:

---

[67] In the original Order Manuscripts, the names given here were *Nu* and *Hormaku*. *Nu* is a male Deity, whereas *Nuet* is the proper female divinity that is indicated here. *Hormaku* is simply a corrupted form of *Harmachis*. These mistakes and others have been amended here; all of the corrected god-names for this section of the ritual were provided by Adam P. Forrest.

The Priest with the mask of the Lion spake and said: "Thou canst not pass the Gate of the Southern Heaven unless thou canst tell me my name."

(You answer:) *MAU, the Lion, very powerful Lord of Fire, is Thy Name. Thou art RE, the Sun in his strength.*

In what signs and symbols do ye come? (He demands.)

I come in the Letter SHIN, in the Banner of the East, and the symbol of the Cubical Cross. (You reply holding up the banner and the cross.)

The Kerub stands back and traces the sigil of Leo before you with the lamp. A hot gust of air flows over you as he does so. Visualize the sigil at your heart center as your aura is filled briefly with a red Light. Take up the lamp at the station of the Hegemon and trace the sigil in the air before you.

The Kerub speaks once more:

In the sign of the Lion, and in the Name of the Kerub ARYEH, Child of Fire, thou art purified. Pass thou on.

Anubis turns to the station of Keryx in the North, leaving you under the charge of Thmê, who once again becomes your guide. Thmê leads you once around the temple, through the 32nd Path. (The blue-violet of the Tau is speckled with stars now, as if you were looking at the night sky.)

Again you hear Horus speak:

I have passed through the Gates of the Firmament. Give me your hands, for I am made as ye, Ye Lords of Truth! For Ye are the formers of the Soul.

Thmê leads you around to the South and the station of the Hiereus. The figure of the officer rises like the crest of a mighty ocean wave. No longer do you look upon the features of Horus, although the characteristics of this new deity are somewhat similar. The officer has taken on the appearance of a great hawk-headed figure with powerful clashing wings, dressed in a royal tunic of blue and orange. He steps in between you and Anubis, blocking your passage with the Banner of the West and the cup. The figure speaks to you:

The Priest with the mask of the Eagle spake and said: "Thou canst not pass the Gate of the Western Heaven unless thou canst tell me my name."

(You answer:) *"TEFNUT, goddess of the Waters, is Thy Name. Thou art TUM, the Sun in his setting."*

"In what signs and symbols do ye come?" (He asks.)

I come in the Letter MEM, in the Banner of Light, and the symbol of the Twenty-two Letters. (You reply holding up the banner and the cross.)

The Kerub stands back and traces the sigil of the Eagle's head (Scorpio) before you with the lamp. A cool sea breeze streams over you as he does so. Visualize the sigil at your heart center as your aura is filled momentarily with a blue Light. Take up the cup at the station of the Hiereus and trace the sigil in the air before you.

The Kerub speaks once more:

> In the sign of the Eagle, and in the Name of the Kerub NESHER, Child of Water, thou art purified. Pass thou on.

Thmê leads you once around the temple, through the dark Path of Tau. With each Elemental purification, the movements and whisperings of the shadows lessen until you are barely aware of them.

Horus speaks once more:

> Oh Lord of the Universe—Thou art above all things and Thy Name is in all things; and before Thee, the Shadows of Night roll back and the Darkness hasteneth away.

Thmê leads you around to the North and the station of the Keryx. The figure of the officer looms like an unyielding mountain. No longer can you make out the familiar features of Anubis. The officer has taken on the appearance of a mighty bull-headed figure with great wings, dressed in a royal tunic of black and white. He steps between you and Thmê, blocking your passage with the Banner of the West and the platter of Salt. The imposing figure speaks to you:

> The Priest with the mask of the Ox spake and said: "Thou canst not pass the Gate of the Northern Heaven unless thou canst tell me my name."

(You answer:) *SERAPIS, the mighty Bull of Earth is Thy Name. Thou art OSIRIS, the Sun at Night.*

In what signs and symbols do ye come? (He demands.)

I come in the Letters ALEPH, MEM and SHIN, in the symbols of Banner and cross. (Hold up the banner and the cross.)

The Kerub stands back and traces the sigil of Taurus before you with the Salt. A cool sense of physical stability envelopes you as he does so. Visualize the sigil at your heart center as your aura is filled temporarily with an Earthy black Light. Take up the Salt at the station of the Keryx and trace the sigil in the air before you.

The Kerub speaks once more:

> In the sign of the Ox, and in the name of the Kerub SHOR, Child of the Elements, thou art purified. Pass thou on.

Thmê leads you to the East where you replace the Banner of Light. She then leads you around the temple again, enabling you to replace all the Elements upon the altar as you circumambulate from East to South, West and North.

> Visualize all the great Kerubic forms that you have encountered on the Path of Tau. Like mighty pillars with outstretched wings they stand at the four quarters supporting the Vault of the Heavens, surrounded by a starry blue-violet tapestry. They are the guardians of the equilibrium and harmony of the universe and the stewards of the fourfold Name, balancing between the physical and the non-physical realms.

Return to between the pillars and strongly visualize all the officer/godforms at their stations as in the beginning of the ceremony. They have shed their outer appearance as the Kerubim. Hold the Admission Badge for the Path of Tau high and say:

> The Cubical Cross is a fitting emblem of the equilibrated and balanced forces of the Elements. It is composed of 22 squares externally, thus referring to the 22 letters that are placed thereon. Twenty-two are the letters of the Eternal Voice, in the Vault of Heaven, in the depth of Earth, in the Abyss of Water, in the All-Presence of Fire. Heaven cannot speak their fullness—Earth cannot utter it. Yet hath the Creator bound them in all things. He hath mingled them in Water. He hath whirled them aloft in Fire. He hath sealed them in the Air of Heaven. He hath distributed them through the Planets. He hath assigned unto them the Twelve Constellations of the universe.

Put the cross aside and focus your attention on the Tau plaque ahead of you. Say:

> The 32nd Path of the Sepher Yetzirah, which answereth unto Malkuth and the letter Tau, is called the Administrative Intelligence, and it is so-called because it directeth and associateth in all their operations, the Seven Planets, even all of them in their own due courses. To it therefore is attributed the due knowledge of the Seven Abodes of Assiah, the Material World, which are symbolized in the Apocalypse by the Seven Churches.

It refers to the universe as composed of the four Elements, to the Kerubim, to the Qlippoth, and to the Astral Plane. It is the Reflection of the Sphere of Saturn. It represents the connecting and binding link between the Material and Formative Worlds, Assiah and Yetzirah, and necessarily passes through the Astral Plane, the Abode of the Elementals and the Shells of the Dead. It is the Rending of the Veil of the Tabernacle, whereon the Kerubim and the Palm Trees are depicted. It is the passing of the Gate of Eden.

Go to the West of the altar and focus your attention on the Tarot Key of the Universe. Say:

These ideas are symbolically resumed in the representation of the Twenty-first Key of the Tarot. Within the oval formed of the 72 circles, is a female form, nude save for a scarf that floats round her. She is crowned with the Lunar Crescent of Isis, and holds in her hands, two wands. Her legs form a cross. She is the Bride of the Apocalypse, the Qabalistic Queen of the Canticles, the Egyptian Isis or great feminine Kerubic Angel Sandalphon on the left hand of the Mercy Seat of the Ark.

The Wands are the directing forces of the positive and negative currents. The Seven Pointed Heptagram or Star alludes to the Seven Palaces of Assiah, the crossed legs to the symbol of the Four Letters of the Name.

The surmounting crescent receives alike the influences of Geburah and Gedulah. She is the synthesis of the 32nd Path, uniting Malkuth to Yesod.

The oval of the 72 smaller circles refer to the Schem ha-Mephoresch, or Seventy-two fold Name of the Deity. The twelve larger circles refer to the Zodiac. At the angles are the four Kerubim which are the vivified powers of the letters of the Name Yod Heh Vav Heh operating in the Elements, through which I have just symbolically passed.

Take a few moments to contemplate the Tarot card and its description before continuing:

The Fan, Lamp, Cup and Salt represent the four Elements themselves whose inhabitants are the Sylphs, Salamanders, Undines and Gnomes.

Therefore I shall ever strive to be prompt and active like the Sylphs, but avoid frivolity and caprice. I shall endeavor to be energetic and strong like the Salamanders, but avoid irritability and ferocity. I shall be flexible and attentive to images, like the Undines, but avoid idleness and changeability. I shall be laborious and patient like the Gnomes, but avoid grossness and avarice.

So shall I gradually develop the powers of my Soul, and fit myself to command the Spirits of Elements.

The altar before me represents the material universe. On its right side is symbolically the Garden of Eden, represented by the Hegemon, while on its left side is symbolically Gehenna, the Abode of Shells, represented by the station of the Keryx."

Visualize the following:

Imagine that you are at the end of the starry indigo Path of Tau. The mighty winged Kerubim Adam and Aryeh are at your right side, while Nesher and Shor stand to your left. The Path in front of you remains unobstructed. In your mind's eye imagine that you now stand before the violet Gate that is the entrance leading to the temple of Yesod. Realize that your journey through the 32nd Path has taken you into the astral realm with sights both wondrous and terrifying. The lower astral symbolized by Gehenna is full of illusionary forms created and cast off by humanity, while the higher or upper astral symbolized by the Garden of Paradise is enriched with images Angelic and Divine. This journey has given you the keys to the universe including the four Elements, the seven Planetary influences, and the twelve Zodiacal Signs. It is now your responsibility to use these tools to traverse the universe with wisdom and true perception.

Osiris speaks to you:

I hereby confer on you the Title of Lord (Lady) of the 32nd Path.

(Say:) *I claim the Title of Lord (Lady) of the 32nd Path.*

Thmê speaks to you:

You have Passed the Gate of the Garden of Eden and penetrated the Threshold in the Path of the Enterer. Prepare this Hall to reflect the temple of Yesod. Prepare thyself to receive a vision of the Sanctum Sanctorum.

Anubis leads you out into the antechamber where you spend a few moments rehearsing the Fourfold Breath and meditating on the Universe card. Perform the Qabalistic Cross to once again equilibrate the Elemental energies within your aura. When ready, set up the temple in accordance with the final part of the ritual.

Changes in the temple setup for the remainder of the ritual—The temple of Yesod: pillars are moved so that they are slightly West of the altar. Remove the Tarot card of the Universe and the Elements (put the Elements back in their respective quarters). The Banner of the West is placed by the station of the Hiereus in the West.

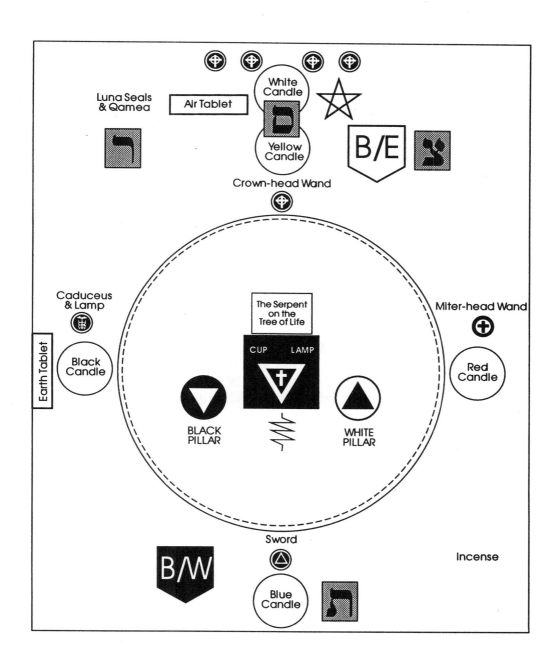

Theoricus Temple for Self-Initiation: Second Set-up

The plaque of the Hebrew letter Tau should be placed in the West behind the Hiereus. In the East should the letters Resh, Samekh and Tzaddi, along with the seal, Qamea, and sigils of Luna. On the front side of the altar should be the diagram of the Flaming Sword. On the top of the altar should be the red cross within the white triangle, apex downwards. Near the top right-hand point of the triangle a red lamp or candle should be placed. At the left-hand corner should be a cup of Water. Just East of the lamp, cup and triangle should be the diagram of the Serpent on the Tree of Life (on a diagram stand).

PART 2: Entry into Yesod

After setting up the Hall, spend a few moments more in relaxed meditation in the antechamber. Visualize the Air triangle once more and then perform the Qabalistic Cross. Take up the Caduceus Admission Badge. When ready, stand just outside the temple door and give the Battery of knocks: 3—3—3. Briefly visualize all of the astral officer/godforms at their respective stations. Then imagine Thmê and Anubis at the entrance facing you. Anubis bids you to enter. Remain just inside the door. You hear the voice of Osiris from the East:

> Frater Periclinus de Faustis (Soror Pericline de Faustis), as in the Zelator grade there were given the symbolic representations of the Tree of the Knowledge of Good and Evil, of the Gate of Eden and of the Holy Place, so in this grade of Theoricus, the Sanctum Sanctorum with the Ark and the Kerubim is shown, as well as the Garden of Eden with which it coincides; while in the 32nd Path leading hereunto, through which you have just symbolically passed the Kerubic Guardians are represented, and the Palm Trees or Trees of Progression in the Garden of Eden.

Thmê leads you to the West and places you before the Portal of the 32nd Path of Tau by which you have symbolically entered. She gestures for you to face the station of Hiereus. Horus questions you:

> By what symbol dost thou enter herein?

(You answer holding up the Admission Badge:) *I enter by the peculiar emblem of the Keryx, which is the Caduceus of Hermes. The Tree of Life and the Three Mother Letters are the Keys wherewith to unlock the Caduceus of Hermes. The upper point of the Wand rests on Kether, and the Wings stretch out to Chokmah and Binah, the Three Supernal Sephiroth. The lower seven are embraced by the Serpents, whose heads fall upon Chesed and Geburah. They are the Twin Serpents of Egypt—the currents of the Astral Light. Furthermore, the wings and top of the Wand form the letter SHIN, the symbol of Fire; the heads and upper halves of the Serpents form ALEPH, the symbol of Air; while their tails enclose MEM, the symbol of Water. The Fire of Life above, the Waters of Creation below, and the Air symbol vibrating between them.*

Thmê leads you to the West of the altar facing East. Still holding the Caduceus Badge, observe the emblems upon the altar for a few moments. Visualize the following:

In your mind's eye see yourself again at the end of the indigo Path of Tau, facing the Gate to the astral temple of Yesod. A large violet door is in front of you. Carved into it is the letter Yod painted in yellow. The winged Kerubim are at either side of you, blocking your final passage into Yesod with the Banner of the West. You hold up the Caduceus Lamen and proclaim that you have received the Title of Lord/Lady of the 32nd Path. The Banner of the West is removed and the Kerubim permit you final entrance into Yesod. Astrally, you give the Neophyte Signs followed by the Sign of a Theoricus and then step through the door into Yesod.

The temple is a nine-sided chamber colored in rich violet tones. A nine-sided polygon is etched into the floor, while quartz and ebony diagrams of the phases of the moon are etched into the ceiling. A hint of Jasmine is in the Air, and in the center of the room you notice a silver altar upon which is the sacred flame of the temple.

The mighty Kerubim are also here, but their appearance has also changed. They are now seen to have many wings and many eyes. Whereas before each Kerub had the face of one of the Elemental creatures (human, lion, eagle and bull), now each Kerub has the faces of all four. Two pairs of wings grace the bodies of each Kerub, two wings stretched upward and two outward, covering their sides. The glories surrounding the creatures are like sparkling ice, and a flaming light flickers back and forth between the creatures. Only the flashing colors of their tunics suggest which Element each individual Kerub is associated with.

The Archangel Gabriel is here as well, a dark-haired feminine Angel dressed in robes of blue and violet trimmed with orange and yellow. S/he leads you to a silver curtain at the far end of the temple. Giving the Sign of the Spiraling Light, you step through the curtain.

You step out into the Courtyard of the Tabernacle that you first encountered in the preceding initiation. You walk past the altar of Sacrifice and the Laver of Brass and enter the outer chamber of the Holy Place before the golden altar where you previously offered up incense. The familiar table of Shewbread and the Seven-branched Candlestick are in the North and South respectively. You still have some of the coals and incense from your previous journey to this place. Pouring them out upon the altar flame, you visualize yourself performing the Qabalistic Cross. You then approach the inner chamber of the Most Holy Place. The embroidered veil which separates the two chambers opens and you are afforded a view of the sacred Ark of the Covenant.

The long wooded chest inlaid with gold is just as you remember it. The golden winged Kerubs Sandalphon and Metatron stoop protectively over the Ark. Above the upper lid or Mercy Seat of the Ark is a brilliant glowing white Light, the glory of the Divine Presence or Shekinah. As you gaze into this Divine Light, you are permitted a glimpse of the Garden of Eden: from the brilliant crown of Kether flows a sparkling river of clear pure Water. This river nourishes the bountiful growth of all varieties of plant and animal life. Grains, wildflowers and various types of trees are found here. The shining river splits into four heads, which divide the Garden into four quarters of East (Air), West (Water), North (Earth) and South (Fire). There is a sudden flash of lightning in the Garden which activates a vision of the Tree of Life. In rapid succession the spheres are formed one after the other as the bolt of lightning animates them. Once formed, the Tree of Life in your vision of the Garden, divides into three parts: the spheres on the right-hand side form a pillar of brilliant Flame, the spheres on the left-hand side form a pillar of dark swirling clouds, and the spheres in the center of the Tree are calm and still. As you visualize the Tree, you notice a serpent slowly weaving its way up the branches of the Tree starting at the base of Malkuth, patiently exploring each upraised twig.

The entire vision gradually fades into the brilliant Light above the Mercy Seat of the Ark. The curtain before you closes and obscures once more the Ark and its attending Kerubim. You are once again in the astral temple of Yesod.

Bring the focus of your conscious mind back to the Theoricus Hall. Perform the Adoration to the Lord of the Universe. The officer-form of the Hierophant comes to the East of the altar to indicate the diagrams thereupon. When you are ready, direct your attention to the items on the altar and continue:

The symbols before me represent alike the Garden of Eden and the Holy of Holies. Before me stands the Tree of Life formed of the Sephiroth and their connecting Paths. It is the Key of all things when rightly understood. Upon each Sephirah are written in Hebrew letters, its Name, the Divine Names and those of Angels and Archangels attributed thereto. The connecting Paths are twenty-two in number and are distinguished by the Twenty-Two Letters of the Hebrew alphabet, making with the Ten Sephiroth themselves the Thirty-two Paths of Wisdom of the Sepher Yetzirah.

The course of the Hebrew letters, as placed on the Paths forms the symbol of the Serpent of Wisdom, while the natural succession of the Sephiroth forms the Flaming Sword and the course of the Lightning Flash.

The cross within the triangle, apex downwards, placed upon the altar at the base of the Tree of Life, refers to the Four Rivers of Paradise, while the angles of the triangles refer to the Three Sephiroth: Netzach, Hod and Yesod. The Two Pillars, right and left of the Tree are the symbols of active and passive, male and female, Adam and Eve. They also allude to the Pillars of Fire and Cloud which guided the Israelites in the wilderness, and the hot and moist natures are further marked by the Red Lamp and the Cup of Water.

The Pillars further represent the two Kerubim of the Ark—the right, METATRON, male—and the left, SANDALPHON, female. Above them ever burn the Lamps of their Spiritual Essence, of which they are partakers in the Eternal Uncreated One.

The form of the Hierophant in the East stands in the Sign of Theoricus. The voice of Osiris is heard:

Glory be unto Thee, Lord of the Land of Life, for Thy Splendor filleth the Universe.

Osiris comes around to the West of the altar to give you the secrets of the 2 = 9 grade:

The 2 = 9 grade of Theoricus is referred to Yesod, as the Zelator grade is to Malkuth. The Path between them is assigned to the letter Tau, whose portal in the West you have just symbolically passed.

Prompted by the figure, you exchange the grip of the First Order, which was revealed to you in the preceding grade. Osiris then prompts you to give the Sign of Theoricus and explains:

This Sign emulates a figure supporting a great weight. It represents you in the Path of Yesod, supporting the Pillars of Mercy and Severity. It is the Sign made by the Greek god Atlas, who supported the universe on his shoulders and whom Hercules was directed to emulate. It is the Isis of Nature, supporting the Heavens.

(The figure continues:) The Grand Word is a name of seven letters SHADDAI EL CHAI, which means the Almighty and Living One. The Mystic Number is 45, and from it is formed the Password which is Mem-Heh, the secret Name of the World of Formation. It should be lettered separately when given.

You repeat the words:

> *The Grand Word is SHADDAI EL CHAI. The Mystic Number is 45. The Password of this grade is MEM-HEH.*

> (You continue:) *"Unto this grade and unto the Sephirah Yesod, the Ninth Path of the Sepher Yetzirah is referred. It is called the Pure and Clear Intelligence, and it is so called because it purifieth and maketh clear the Sephiroth, proveth and amendeth the forming of their representation, and disposeth their duties or harmonies, wherein they combine, without mutilation or division.*

Osiris continues:

> The distinguishing Badge of this grade, which you are now entitled to wear is the sash of the Zelator, with the addition of a violet cross above the triangle and the numbers 2 and 9 in a circle and square respectively, left and right of its summit—and beneath the triangle, the number 32 between two narrow violet lines.

Open the altar and remove the Theoricus sash. As you put it on, visualize the god Osiris investing you with the sash as the mighty Kerubim look on. The figure then points to the three Hebrew letters in the East of the Hall and says:

> The three Portals facing you are the Gates of the Paths leading from this grade. That on the right connects with the grade of Philosophus, that on your left with the grade of Practicus, while the central one leads to the Portal.

Osiris as the Hierophant returns to his station. Thmê, the Hegemon takes your hand and leads you to the Enochian Tablet of the East. As you inspect the Tablet say:

> *This grade especially refers to the Element of Air, and therefore the Great Watch-Tower or Terrestrial Tablet of the East forms one of its principal emblems. It is one of the Four Great Tablets delivered unto Enoch by the Great Angel Ave. From it are drawn the Three Holy Secret names of God, ORO IBAH AOZPI, which are borne upon the Banners of the East, and numberless Divine and Angelic Names which appertain unto the Element of Air.*

Thmê brings your attention to the Qamea of Luna. You continue:

> *To the Moon, also, is this grade related. Its Qamea or Mystical Square is shown in the East, with Seals and Names appropriate thereto. It is also shown inscribed upon the Tree of Life, whereon its crescent in increase*

represents the side of Mercy—in decrease the side of Severity, while at the full it reflects the Sun of Tiphareth."

Thmê leads you back to the Western side of the altar, facing the East. Hear the voice of Osiris speaking to you:

I now congratulate you on having attained the grade of Theoricus and in recognition thereof, I confer upon you the Mystic Title of Poraios de Rejectis, which means "Brought from among the Rejected," and I give you the symbol of RUACH, which is the Hebrew name for Air.

Go to the North to face Anubis of the East. The god traces the sigil of the Caduceus before you. Take up the Caduceus Wand and the lantern. Give a knock. Turn to face the altar and say:

In the Name of SHADDAI EL CHAI, hear ye all, that I (state motto), having made sufficient progress in the study of Occult Science, now proclaim that I have duly advanced to the grade of 2 = 9 of Theoricus. I am Lord/Lady of the 32nd Path and I have received the Mystic Title of PORAIOS DE REJECTIS, and the symbol of RUACH."

Replace the wand and the lamp.

PART 3: The Closing

Go to the Eastern part of the Hall. There the godform of Osiris traces before you the symbol of the circled cross, bestowing upon you the office of Hierophant. Taking on the officer-form of the Hierophant, give a knock with the scepter and say:

Let us adore the Lord and King of Air.

Turn to face East and visualize the Air triangle. Knock and say:

SHADDAI EL CHAI, Almighty and Everliving, blessed be Thy Name unto the countless ages. Amen. (Give the Theoricus Sign.)

Stand facing the Air Tablet. Visualize the rest of the officer/godforms leaving their stations to face East. Hiereus advances to just West of the altar. Hegemon and Keryx advance and stand at the outer sides of the pillars. Give a knock with scepter and recite the Prayer of the Sylphs or Air Spirits:

Spirit of Life! Spirit of Wisdom! Whose breath giveth forth and withdraweth the form of all things: Thou, before Whom the life of beings is but a shadow which changeth, and a vapour which passeth: Thou, who mountest upon the clouds, and who walkest upon the Wings of the Wind. Thou, who breathest forth Thy Breath, and endless space is peopled: Thou, who drawest in Thy Breath, and all that cometh from Thee, returneth unto Thee!

Ceaseless Motion, in Eternal Stability, be Thou eternally blessed! We praise Thee and we bless Thee in the changeless Empire of Created Light, of Shades, of Reflections, and of Images. And we aspire without cessation unto Thy Immutable and Imperishable Brilliance.

Let the Ray of Thy Intelligence and the warmth of Thy Love penetrate even unto us! Then that which is Volatile shall be Fixed, the Shadow shall be a Body, the Spirit of Air shall be a Soul, the Dream shall be a Thought. And no more shall we be swept away by the Tempest, but we shall hold the bridles of the Winged Steeds of Dawn. And we shall direct the course of the Evening Breeze to fly before Thee!

O Spirit of Spirits! O Eternal Soul of Souls! O imperishable Breath of Life! O Creative Sigh! O Mouth which breathest forth and withdrawest the life of all beings, in the flux and reflux of Thine Eternal Word, which is the divine ocean of Movement and of Truth!"

Through the authority of the office of Hierophant bestowed upon you by Osiris, banish the powers of the Air Tablet. Trace with the Wand a large circle in front of the Tablet. Then draw the banishing pentagram of Spirit Active. As you do so vibrate *"EXARP"* (ex-ar-pay). Trace the sigil of Spirit in the center and intone *"EHEIEH"* (Eh-hey-yay). Give the Reversal Sign of the Spiraling Light. Then trace the banishing pentagram of Air. As you do so vibrate the name *"ORO IBAH AOZPI"* (Or-oh Ee-bah-hay Ah-oh-zohd-pee). Draw the sigil of Aquarius in the center and intone *"YHVH."* Give the Sign of Theoricus.

Give the License to Depart by saying:

Depart ye in peace unto your habitations. May the blessing of YOD HEH VAV HEH rest with ye. Be there peace between us, and be ye ready to come when ye are called. (Knock.)

Return the office of Hierophant to the dominion of Osiris in the Eastern part of the Hall.

The goddess Thmê comes to your side. She leads you to the station of the Keryx where she traces the figure of the cross and triangle in the Air. The godform of Anubis salutes with the Projection Sign—Thmê answers with the Sign of Silence. Anubis slowly fades from view. In this manner, Thmê releases the other godforms in the Hall: Horus, Osiris and the godforms on the Dais. All the astral entities in the Hall begin to fade from view.

Thmê herself is the last godform to dissolve. You thank the goddess for guiding you in the Theoricus Hall, and trace the figures of the cross and triangle before her. She salutes you with the Projection Sign. You answer with the Sign of Silence. Withdraw the white ray which had activated the goddess back into your heart center. Perform the Qabalistic Cross one last time to equilibrate all energies within your sphere of sensation.

Take up the sword and perform the Lesser Banishing Ritual of the Pentagram. Say, *"In the Name of SHADDAI EL CHAI, I declare this temple closed in the 2 = 9 grade of Theoricus."*

Give the Battery of knocks: 3—3—3. Go to the station of the Hiereus and repeat the Battery: 3—3—3. Go to the station of the Hegemon and repeat the Battery: 3—3—3. Give the Theoricus Sign before exiting the temple.☿

The Third Knowledge Lecture

SECTION 1: Basic Astrology—The Aspects

The last major subject that the student will need to know in order to be able to understand a horoscope is that of the aspects. Aspects help to determine how Planets interact within the Signs and houses. When Planets are located at a certain number of degrees away from one another, they are said to be in aspect. Some aspects are harmonious and congenial, while others are conflicting and challenging. The harmonious aspects are mild, benign and comfortable. The conflicting aspects are exciting, stress-producing and sometimes disagreeable.

It should be kept in mind that there is no such thing as a "good" or "bad" aspect. Too many harmonious aspects in a chart can often signify a boring personality. Too many conflicting aspects in a chart can make a person spiteful and mean-spirited. On the other hand a few challenging aspects can strengthen a person's character and make life more stimulating. In astrology, like Qabalah, the *middle* ground provides the strongest and best support.

The *orb* of an aspect is the number of degrees of difference from the exact angle that is permitted for each aspect. In other words, it is the number of degrees within which an aspect is judged to be effective. However, the strongest influence is

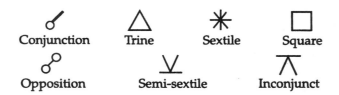

Conjunction	Trine	Sextile	Square
Opposition	Semi-sextile		Inconjunct

felt when the aspect is closer (or exact) in relation to the angle. An exact aspect is called *partile*. A wide or weak aspect is called *platic*.

Example of an orb in a horoscope: Mercury at 28º Aries conjunct Mars at 2º Taurus. An orb of 7º is allowable for the aspect of conjunction. In this instance the orb is 4º.

Some aspects are more important in delineating a horoscope than others. Here we will only be concerned with the seven *major aspects* of conjunction, sextile, square, trine, opposition, semi-sextile and inconjunct.[68] The following is a brief description of the aspects:

CONJUNCTION
Angle: 0º *Orb:* 7º
Considered: Favorable or Unfavorable
Key word: EMPHASIS

Conjunction occurs when two or three Planets are situated within an orb of 7 degrees. Normally Planets in a conjunction are all within the same Sign, however, they can sometimes be found in adjacent Signs.

This aspect gives more emphasis to a Sign. Its action is direct and obvious. The more Planets involved, the greater the emphasis. When two Planets are very close in proximity, their energies combine and become almost indistinguishable. Conjunctions are considered favorable or unfavorable depending on which Planets are involved, and whether or not those Planets are harmonious or opposite in character. Other words used to describe this aspect are intensification, fresh activity and concentration. (A conjunction of three or more Planets is called a *stellium*.)

SQUARE
Angle: 90º *Orb:* 7º
Considered: Unfavorable
Key word: CHALLENGE

A square occurs when two Planets are 90 degrees (or three Signs) apart. In this aspect, the energies of two Planets clash with one another, each trying to make the other conform to its manner of activity. Squares are the tension factors of a Zodiacal chart. Misunderstood, they can be difficult obstacles in one's path. Rightly understood they can be catalysts for decision and movement. Squares signify action: in Cardinal squares this action is swift, in Kerubic squares it is gradual and cautious, and in Mutable squares, the action is changeable and influenced by other factors.

(A *T-square* or *T-cross* occurs when three Planets are involved, two of which are in opposition. A *grand square* or *grand cross* occurs when four Planets are involved, with two pairs in opposition.)

---

[68] The minor aspects include: parallel, semi-sextile, nonagon, semi-square, septile, quintile, sesquisquare and biquintile. These do not impact the horoscope as strongly as the major aspects and are listed here only for future reference.

OPPOSITION
Angle: 180° *Orb:* 7°
Considered: Unfavorable
Key word: PERCEPTION

Opposition is the widest aspect. This aspect occurs when two Planets are 180 degrees (six Signs) apart. This results in a "stand off" or stalemate between two Planets. Opposition delineates rival factors in conflict, which if reconciled can balance each other through the virtue of their polarity. The inherent value of opposition is to cultivate awareness and understanding. This involves the recognition of imbalances within oneself and using the counterbalance of the two Signs involved to equilibrate the problem. Compromise between the polarized forces is achieved through cooperation.

TRINE
Angle: 120° *Orb:* 7°
Considered: Favorable
Key word: HARMONY

A trine occurs when two Planets are 120 degrees (four Signs) apart. This most favorable aspect allows easy interaction between the Planets involved, both of which when trined share a similarity of purpose. Trines allude to creativity, inspiration, balance, ease of movement, pleasure, and the natural flow of things. This is not always positive, however, since the lack of tension between Planets means that there is no obligation to use the Planets to one's advantage. This may result in complacency and the inclination to choose the path of least resistance.

(A *grand trine* occurs when three Planets are in trine with one another, all in the same triplicity or Element. An Example would be a *grand Water trine*, where the Planets involved would be positioned in all three Water Signs of Cancer, Scorpio and Pisces.)

INCONJUNCT
(quincunx)
Angle: 150° *Orb:* 5°
Considered: Unfavorable
Key word: ADAPTATION

The inconjunction occurs when two Planets are 150 degrees (five Signs) apart. The Signs involved within this aspect are totally unrelated to each other. They do not share the same element, quality or gender (active/passive). Since they have little in common, it is difficult to harmonize their energies.

Inconjunct is the most difficult aspect to understand because its effects are not as noticeable as those of the other "unfavorable" aspects. There is a perception of slight tension and disharmony that is hard for the conscious mind to grasp. False hopes and self-delusion can result. A person experiencing inconjunction often feels that some problem is about to be solved, yet the solution is constantly just out of reach.

This difficult yet challenging aspect calls for a change in attitude and old familiar routines. It signifies a necessity to adjust to the conditions dictated by the Planets and the houses involved.

SEXTILE
Angle: 60° *Orb:* 5°
Considered: Favorable
Key word: OPPORTUNITY

A sextile occurs when two Planets are 60 degrees (two Signs) apart. This aspect characterizes Signs that are of the same elemental "gender": active/positive Signs or passive/negative Signs.(Water and Earth Signs can sextile each other—Air and Fire Signs can do the same.)

The sextile promotes compatibility, affliation, communication, and exchange of understanding and expression between two Planets. It encourages a blending and integration between the Planetary energies resulting in cooperation. However, these qualities must be actively and consciously engaged in order to benefit from them.

SEMI-SEXTILE
Angle: 30° *Orb:* 1°
Considered: Favorable
Key word: SUPPORT

A semi-sextile occurs when two Planets are 30 degrees (one Sign) apart. This aspect is of mixed quality—it is rhythmically favorable, yet it involves Planets located in inharmonious Signs. The two Planets will support each other in an external sense, but will not share any true inner communication. This aspect is not considered to be very strong.✿

Erecting a Natal Chart

Once the student has committed to memory the astrological basics given in the previous chapters concerning the Signs, the Planets, the houses, and the aspects, the next step is to erect a birth chart. To accomplish this, the student will need to obtain certain natal information and additional books to aid in the mathematical calculations. For the purpose of this study course, we recommend that the reader begin by figuring out his/her own natal chart.

One essential fact that can never be overstated is the importance of keeping a written record of all your horoscope calculations. Of course the student should keep a record of all magical workings, meditations, grade work, and the like, but for accurate chart casting this is imperative.

Time of Birth:

It is important to know the exact time of birth. A copy of your Birth Certificate which can be found on file at the State Board of Health is the most accurate record of this. Other sources include baby books, hospital records or possibly the family Bible. A written record should always be sought out, if possible.

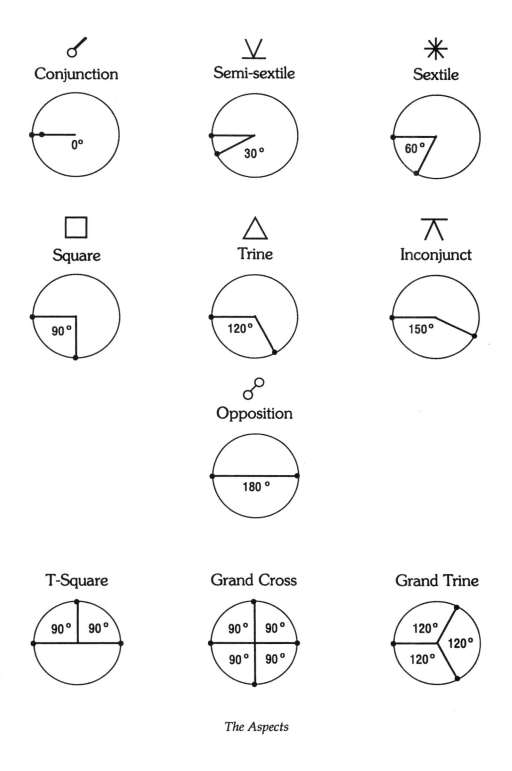

The Aspects

Mathematical Equivalents

The student should memorize the following information:

    12 Signs = 360°, the circumference of the Zodiacal wheel.
    30° (degrees) = 1 Zodiacal Sign.
    60' (minutes) = 1 degree or 1 hour.
    60" (seconds) = 1 minute.

Longitude and Latitude

It is important to know the longitude and latitude of the place of birth. For the purpose of geography, the Earth is sectioned by two theoretical sets of circles. The point of reference for the first set of circles is the *Equator*, while the focal point for the second set of circles is the *Prime Meridian*.

The *Equator* circles the middle of the globe from East to West and is used to calculate distances North or South of the Equator. Circles of geographic measurement which occupy fixed positions North and South of the Equator are called parallels of latitude.

The *Prime Meridian* circles the middle of the globe from North to South and is used to measure distance East or West of the Prime Meridian (the 0° mark at Greenwich, England). Circles of measurement located East and West of the Prime Meridian are called *meridians of longitude*.

For example: The City of Tampa, Florida is located at a latitude 27° (degrees) 57' (minutes) North of the Equator, and having a longitude of 82° (degrees) 27' (minutes) West of the Prime Meridian. Thus we would designate the exact location of Tampa, Florida as 82°W27' 27°N57'.

Time Abbreviations

In the science of Astrology, many abbreviated terms are used to indicate time. It would benefit the student to commit the following list to memory:

ST—Standard Time
DST—Daylight Saving Time
ST—Sidereal or Star Time
EDT—Eastern Daylight Time
CST—Central Daylight Time
MDT—Mountain Daylight Time
LTE—Longitude Time Equivalent
TCST—True Calculated Sidereal Time
TLT—True Local Time

WT—War Time
GMT—Greenwich Mean Time
EST—Eastern Standard Time
MST—Mountain Standard Time
PST—Pacific Standard Time
PDT—Pacific Daylight Time
PM—Prime Meridian
LMT—Local Mean Time

Essential Reference Tools

An *Ephemeris*—a book that provides the exact daily location of each Planet at noon or midnight for Greenwich, England (exactly 0° longitude). (Note: the examples given here were calculated with a noon Ephemeris.)

    A *U.S. Atlas*—which describes longitudes and latitudes in the U.S.

    An *International Atlas* which describes longitudes and latitudes outside the U.S.

Time Changes in the U.S.A. and *Time Changes outside the U.S.A.*—books which describe time zones, daylight savings time and wartime changes. (Note: some atlases already contain this information.)

A book on the *Tables of Houses*—there are several different books describing these tables. We recommend the *American Book of Tables*.

Calculating Time

Different time zones are established along the meridians of longitude. Therefore locations having the same longitude will have the same time, no matter how far North or South they are. However, even though two cities like Tampa and Miami are both in the Eastern Time zone and use that zone to *standardize* time, the distance between them in longitude (East—West) means that sunrise in Miami occurs earlier than sunrise in Tampa.

Local Mean Time

LMT or true local time is the actual time of a birth at a given location. It signifies the *actual* time as opposed to the clock time which is standardized for the entire time zone. LMT measures the time at the place of birth in relation to the longitude from 0° at Greenwich, England. In order to figure out the difference between LMT and the given clock time, *distance must be converted into time.*

The sun takes four minutes of time to travel 60 minutes or 1^O (degree) in longitude. (Although the exact rate of the sun's daily motion in the Zodiac can vary with the position of the earth in its orbit from as little as 57'06" up to as much as 62'30" in the Zodiac.) Remember that in converting distance into time, 1^O is equal to one hour or 60 minutes. In order to determine the LMT the *birthplace longitude must be multiplied by 4 and the result divided by 60.* (Later in this section, we will explain what is to be done once the LMT has been determined.)

Daylight Savings Time

Check a book of time changes to find out if the birth was in an area which was observing Daylight Savings Time (or War Time as it used to be called). DST sets the clock one hour ahead, so if the birth time occurred during DST, you must subtract one hour from the given time of birth before continuing with your calculations.

Steps in Erecting a Natal Chart

1. *Establish the date, time and place of birth.* (If the exact time is not known, use the closest known time. If no birth time is known, calculate from noon, although it will be impossible to determine either the Ascendant, Midheaven or house positions—thus limiting the horoscope.)

2. *Determine the Ascendant and Midheaven.* These calculations follow different lines for Eastern and Western longitudes, and for AM and PM birth times. For examples, we will use individuals born at 3:00, AM or PM, local time, occurring at longitudes both East and West of the Prime Meridian, Greenwich, England. (Note:

For Southern latitude births, continue as prescribed below until you have the local sidereal time at birth.)[69]

STAGE 1: Time Conversion

As you begin, you must convert the local birth time to Greenwich Mean Time (GMT). Check carefully to determine whether one or two hours had been added to the local standard time at the time of birth, as in the case of Daylight Savings Time or Summer Time. (The *Book of Time Changes* will list this information.) The extra hour or two added should be subtracted from the True Local Time (TLT) before continuing the calculations.

West of Prime Meridian		East of Prime Meridian	
Place of birth—Buffalo, NY (79° West—43° North)		*Place of birth*—Athens, Greece (24° East—38° North)	
3AM	**3PM**	**3AM**	**3PM**
To convert to GMT, 5 hours must be added—the difference between GMT and EST (Eastern Standard Time).		To convert to GMT, 2 hours must be subtracted—the difference between GMT and local time.	
3 AM EST plus 5 hours = **8 AM GMT**	3 PM EST plus 5 hours = **8 PM GMT**	3 AM Local Time minus 2 hours = **1 AM GMT**	3 PM Local Time minus 2 hours = **1 PM GMT**

STAGE 2: Finding Local Sidereal Time at Birth

After converting the birth time to Greenwich Mean Time, another conversion is needed. You must now calculate the *equivalent sidereal time at Greenwich. Sidereal Time* refers to the actual time taken by the Earth to complete a total revolution upon its axis, as opposed to the 24-hour divisions of the day that we use for a convenient measure of time.

To begin this calculation we must refer to the *Sidereal Time at Greenwich at noon on the date of birth.* This can be found by looking in an Ephemeris (It is usually described in the Ephemeris as *Sid. Time.* or *ST*) For our examples, we will assume that the date of birth was December 16, 1954. The Ephemeris tells us that the Sidereal Time at Greenwich at *noon* on that date was 17h 38m 23s, (17 hours 38 minutes 23 seconds). We must now find the interval between the GMT birth time and noon on that same date.

(Note: If your calculations have taken you into the day following the birth date, determine the interval between the GMT time and noon of that day, not the actual birthday. If your calculations have led you into the day prior to

---

[69] For individuals born in a Southern latitude, continue as follows: always add 12 hours to the local sidereal time. In Southern latitudes the order of the Signs must be reversed; therefore if the Table of Houses gives the Ascendant as Aries 15°12′ and the Midheaven as Capricorn 5°, the true Ascendant is Libra 15°12′ and the true Midheaven is Cancer 5°.

the birth date, find the interval between the GMT time and noon of that day, not the actual birthday.)

For our examples:

8 AM—GMT	**8 PM—GMT**	**1 AM—GMT**	**1 PM—GMT**
count ahead to noon	count back to noon	count ahead to noon	count back to noon
= 4 hours	= 8 hours	= 11 hours	= 1 hour

We have obtained the Sidereal Time (ST) at the Prime Meridian at noon on the date of birth. The next step is to discover the *Sidereal Time at Greenwich at the time of birth on the date of birth*. In order to do this we must employ the interval time just determined, adding to or subtracting from our Sidereal Time (In our example: 17h 38m 23s), for AM—subtract, for PM—add. (Remember that if your calculations have lead you into the days before or after the birth date, use the Sidereal Time at noon on that day and not that of the actual day of birth.)[70]

For our four examples:

ST at Greenwich for	ST at Greenwich for	ST at Greenwich for	ST at Greenwich for
noon on birthday =	noon on birthday =	noon on birthday =	noon on birthday =
17h 38m 23s AM	17h 38m 23s PM	17h 38m 23s AM	17h 38m 23s PM
- 4 hrs =	+ 8 hrs =	- 11 hrs =	+ 1 hr =
13h 38m 23s	**25h 38m 23s**	**6h 38m 23s**	**18h 38m 23s**

We must now make an adjustment to allow for the difference between Sidereal and regular time. This is called the *Acceleration on the Interval*. This is accomplished by adding or subtracting ten seconds for every hour and one second for every six minutes of interval time, always following the rule of subtracting for AM, adding for PM.

For our examples:

AM: subtract	**PM: add**	**AM: subtract**	**PM: add**
interval = 4 hrs.	interval = 8 hrs.	interval = 11 hrs	interval = 1 hr.
Accel on Inter.= **40s.**	*Accel on Inter.* = **80s.**	*Accel on Inter.* = **110s.**	*Accel on Inter.*= **10s.**
13h 37m 83s	25h 38m 23s	6h 36m 143s	18h 38m 23s
- 40s	+ 80s	- 110s	+10s
= **13h 37m 43s**	= **25h 39m 43s**	= **6h 36m 33s**	= **18h 38m 33s**
ST at Greenwich	ST at Greenwich	ST at Greenwich	ST at Greenwich

This tells us the *Sidereal Time at the Prime Meridian for the time of birth*. Next we must convert this to determine the Sidereal Time for the time of birth at the place of birth. The difference in time depends on the distance between Greenwich and the place of birth. This is known as the *Longitude Equivalent in Time*. To arrive at that figure we multiply the birthplace longitude by 4, naming the resulting numbers hours, minutes, and seconds; thus converting longitude distance into time:

---

[70] If your calculations ever leave you with a negative (minus) number for the ST at Greenwich, add 24 hours.

Buffalo, NY   **Athens, Greece**
Longitude = 79° West   Longitude = 24° East
79° x 4 = 316°   24° x 4 = 96°
Divided by 60   Divided by 60
= **5h 16m** *(in time)*   = **1h 36m** *(in time)*

The next step is to add or subtract the longitude equivalent in time to/from the Sidereal Time at Greenwich for the time of birth. For East we add, for West we subtract.

For our four examples:

ST at Greenwich =	ST at Greenwich =	ST at Greenwich =	ST at Greenwich =
13h 37m 43s	**25h 39m 43s**	**6h 36m 33s**	**18h 38m 33s**
West—subtract	*West—subtract*	*East—add*	*East—add*
- 5h 16m	- 5h 16m	+ 1h 36m	+ 1h 36m
= **8h 21m 43s**	= **20h 23m 43s**	= **8h 12m 33s**	= **20h 14m 33s**
LOCAL SID. TIME	LOCAL SID. TIME	LOCAL SID. TIME	LOCAL SID. TIME
AT BIRTH	AT BIRTH	AT BIRTH	AT BIRTH

The *Local Sidereal Time at birth and at the place of birth,* is a crucial factor for determining the Ascendant and the Midheaven. It is now a simple matter of referring to the Tables of Houses (listed in *The American Book of Tables*) which tabulate the Ascendant and Midheaven for various latitudes. Our four examples would show:

Asc = 27° ♎︎	Asc = 28° ♉︎	Asc = 27° ♎︎	Asc = 21° ♎︎
MC = 3° ♌︎	MC = 4° ♒︎	MC = 1° ♌︎	MC = 2° ♒︎

3. *Drawing up the Natal chart.* On a blank Zodiacal chart, like the one shown which is marked off into degrees, draw in the *Horizon line* using a straight edge and pencil. This will intersect the circle on the left and right (Zodiacal East and West). If the Ascending Sign is 27°, count 27° down from the cusp of the Ascendant or Rising Sign. Then count 27° up from the cusp of the Sign opposite the Ascendant. Draw the Horizon line connecting these two points on the chart. Draw in the symbol, degree and minute of the Ascendant Sign.

Mark off the degree of the Ascendant in each section of the chart, counter-clockwise around the chart, and join each marked point to its opposite on the other side of the circle. Number these twelve (30°) divisions counter-clockwise, with the first house situated immediately below the Ascendant.

Draw the symbols of the twelve Signs in the outer circle, in counter-clockwise order, beginning from the Ascendant Sign. (For example if the Ascendant Sign is 27° Libra, the next divisions reading counter-clockwise below Libra would be Scorpio, Sagittarius, etc.)

Place the Midheaven in the appropriate Sign, marking it with the letters MC, along with the degree and minute. The letters IC should be drawn at the opposite point on the Chart.

Short form for Erecting a Natal Chart

Name   _____

	Day	Month	Year
Birthdate			
Birthplace			
Latitude			
Longitude			

STAGE 1: Time Conversion

Birthtime as given *a.m., p.m.   _____

Zone Standard *(East -, West +)   _____

*Summer (or Double) Time (-)   _____

Greenwich Mean Time *a.m., p.m.   _____

Greenwich Mean Time date

(If altered by conversion)

	Day	Month	Year

STAGE 2: Finding Local Sidereal Time at Birth

	Hours	Minutes	Seconds
Sidereal Time noon G.M.T.			
Interval *to/from noon *a.m. -			
p.m. +			
Result			
Acceleration on interval *a.m. -			
p.m. +			
Sidereal Time at Greenwich at birth			
Longitude equivalent in time			
*East +			
*West -			
Local Sidereal Time at birth			
(subtract 24 hours if necessary)			

For southern latitudes add twelve hours and reverse signs.

*Delete whichever is not required.

261

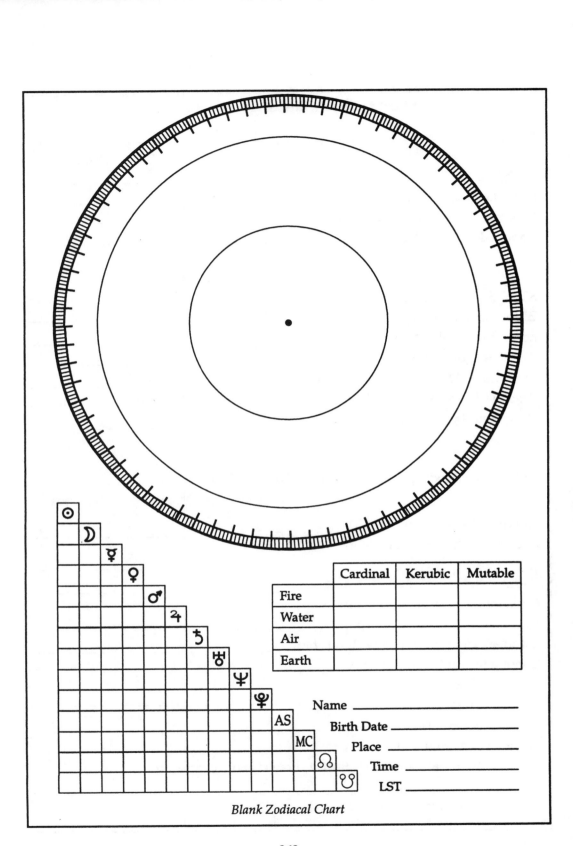

	Cardinal	Kerubic	Mutable
Fire			
Water			
Air			
Earth			

Name _____

Birth Date _____

Place _____

Time _____

LST _____

Blank Zodiacal Chart

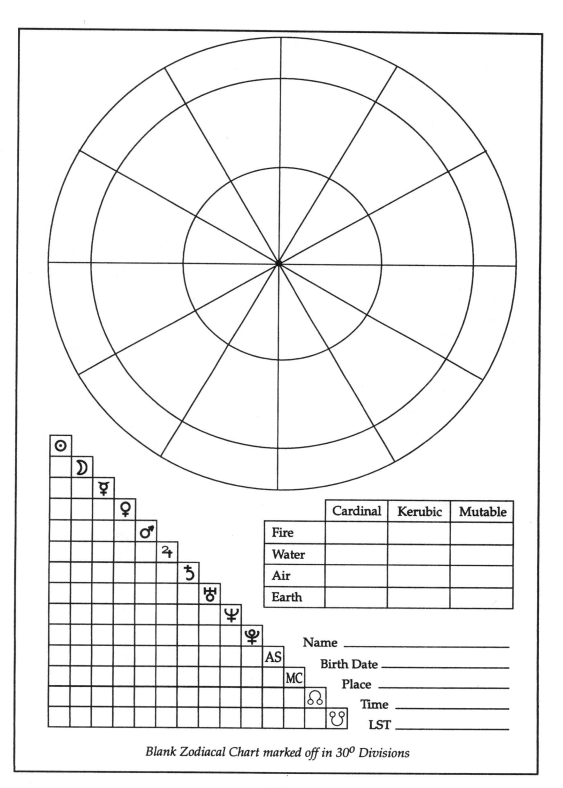

	Cardinal	Kerubic	Mutable
Fire			
Water			
Air			
Earth			

Name _____

Birth Date _____

Place _____

Time _____

LST _____

Blank Zodiacal Chart marked off in 30° Divisions

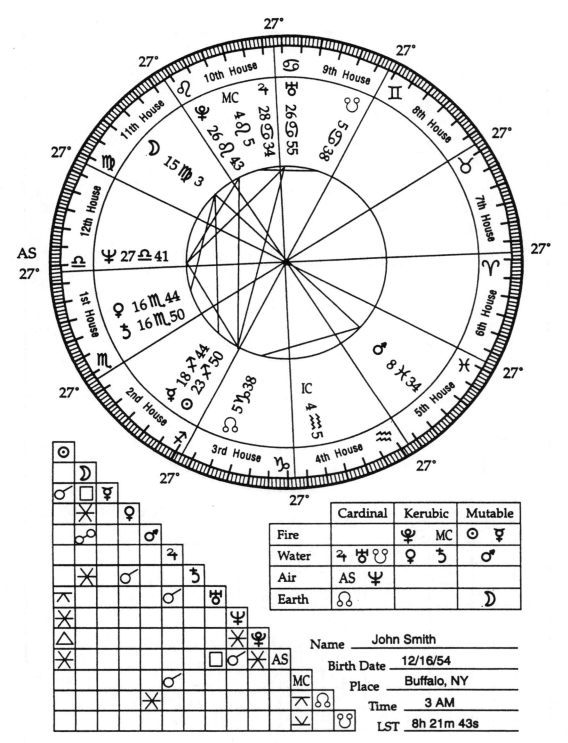

Sample Chart

Mark down the Planetary symbols in the appropriate Signs within the middle circle of the chart. (The degrees and minutes of the Planets are to be found by consulting an Ephemeris for the date of birth.)

Determine the aspects and place their symbols next to those of the appropriate Planets in the aspect grid. Within the inner circle of the chart, draw a series of marks opposite the marked positions of the Planets. (Do not mark the Ascendant or MC in this manner.) If two Planets are in aspect to each other (having the correct angle within the accepted orb), join the appropriate markings. Use lines of various colors to join different types of aspects, for example: a black line for squares and oppositions, a red line for trines and sextiles, and a green line for minor aspects. (Conjunctions are so close in proximity that they do not need to be marked.)

Refer to the Ephemeris for the locations of the Lunar nodes and mark their positions on the middle circle. (Remember that the South Node is always directly opposite the North Node.)

The Natal Chart is now complete and ready for interpretation. (Please note that the house system we have used here is the *Equal House* system, in which all twelve houses are of Equal size. Other Astrologers prefer either the *Placidus* system or the *Koch* system, in which the houses can be of various sizes. Once the student is thoroughly familar with the construction of a chart in the Equal house system, a Zodiacal wheel that has been previously marked off into 30° sections may be used.)✿

The previous method describing the erection of a Natal chart is sufficiently accurate for beginning student of this course. However, we have included a more detailed method which will have increased accuracy that may be needed for more detailed Astrological work, such as Progressed Charts, Solar Revolution Charts, Horary Astrology and divinatory work. This second technique includes directions for correcting the positions of the Planets—which can be especially useful in regards to fast-moving Planets, like the Moon. The *Alternate Method for Chart Erection* which follows may seem simpler to some, more complex to others. At any rate, we offer it here to those students who wish to obtain a more precise chart.

(Note: the Diurnal Tables of Planetary Motion can be purchased through the American Federation of Astrologers.)✿

Alternate Method for Chart Erection
(Noon-hour Ephemeris)

I. *Determine Birth Time* (Use Time Changes book)
    1. Note Time Zone (EST, CST, MST, PST, etc.) of birth.
    2. Note if Daylight Savings Time (DST) or War Time (WT) was in effect, and if so, *subtract* 1 hr. from Clock Time giving Birth Time. Otherwise, Birth Time is the same as Clock Time.
    3. Note at top of worksheet whether using noon or 0-hour Ephemeris.

II. *Determine True Local Time (TLT) and Greenwich Mean Time (GMT)*
    A. TLT (Use Longitudes-Latitudes book)

1. Find number of degrees birthplace is East or West (the difference in degrees of Longitude) of the Standard Time Meridian in use; *Multiply* this by 4 minutes.
2. If birthplace is East of meridian, *add* results to birth time.
   If birthplace is West of meridian, *subtract* results from birth time.

B. GMT
   1. Find number of degrees birthplace is from Greenwich (0° Long.); *multiply* this by 4 minutes.
   2. If birthplace is West Longitude (USA), *add* results to TLT.
      If birthplace is East Longitude (Europe), *subtract* results from TLT.
   3. (Short method:) *Add* to birth time—5 hours for EST, 6 hours for CST, 7 hours for MST, 8 hours for PST.

III. *Determine True Calculated Sidereal Time (TCST) and House Cusps*
   A. TCST (use Ephemeris)
      1. Note from Ephemeris of birth month and year the Sidereal Time (ST) of the day of the noon previous to TLT.
      2. *Add* 10" for each 15° of Longitude if West (USA) of Greenwich (EST—50", CST—60", MST—70", PST—80").
         Subtract 10" for each 15° of Longitude if East (Europe) of Greenwich.
      3. *Add* time elapsed (interval) between previous noon and TLT.
      4. *Add* 10" per hour interval found in the previous step (# 3).

   B. House Cusps (use Table of Houses)
      1. Find Latitude nearest that of birthplace.
      2. Find Nearest Sidereal Time (NST) to TCST and record cusps and degrees starting with 10th. (Opposite, remaining cusps are same degrees with opposite Signs.)

IV. *Determine Planetary positions at Birth Time* (use Diurnal Tables)
   1. Find interval between GMT and noon on GMT day.
   2. Find actual travel of Planets in 24 hours: *Subtract* positions on day of noon previous to GMT from those on noon following GMT (this is Daily Motion).
   3. Find correction or actual travel during interval (1.) using these rates (2.) and GMT interval (1.).
   4. If GMT is P.M.—*add* results to Planet's positions for noon on GMT day.
      If GMT is A.M.—*subtract* results from noon of GMT day.
      If planets are Retrograde, reverse this rule.

Supplement to Step IV: Determining the Planetary Positions at Birth

Bear in mind that the positions of the Planets listed in the Ephemeris will be accurate only for those born in Greenwich at Noon (if a Noon Ephemeris is used) or at Midnight (if a Midnight or 0-hour Ephemeris is used). Correcting for the difference in Longitude is accomplished by determining the ASC or MC and copying in the house cusps from a Table of Houses.

But one must also correct for the movement of the Planet from its listed position in the Ephemeris and the time which the person was actually born—which in the case of the Moon may be considerable. This is accomplished as follows using a Noon Ephemeris:

Step 1: Find the Interval between the Greenwich Mean Time (GMT) and NOON on the GMT DAY (which may be different from the date of birth). This is the GMT Interval.

Step 2: Find the actual travel of the Planets in 24 hours by subtracting the position listed for the Planet at Noon on the day *previous* to GMT from the position listed at Noon *following* GMT.

Step 3: Use the Interval found in Step one and the Rate found in Step 2 to determine the actual travel during the interval. Use the Tables of Diurnal Planetary Motion published by the American Federation of Astrologers.

Step 4: If the GMT is PM, *add* the results to the position of the Planet as listed for Noon on the GMT DAY. If GMT is in the AM, *subtract* the results from the position listed for GMT Day.

Example: A birth on January 2, 1953 in Oakland, California at clock time of 4:25 PM. The GMT will be 12:25 AM on GMT DAY (January 3).

Step 1.
    11:60   (eleven hours/sixty minutes or NOON)
  - 00:25   GMT (if GMT is 12 something, drop the 12.)
    11:35 = GMT Interval

Step 2. Find the actual travel of the Planets. In this example we will determine the daily motion for two of them, the Sun and the Moon.

	Sol			*Luna*	
D M S	Sign		D M	Sign	
12:49:58	♑		19:19	♌	
-11:48:49			-7:23		
1:01:09	= 61':09"		11:56	= Daily Motion	

Note that the Daily motion of the Sun is converted into minutes and seconds. This is because the table of Diurnal Planetary Motion for determining the Sun's position is formatted in that manner.

Step 3. Now we need to take these two bits of information and adjust the position shown in the Ephemeris for the actual time of birth.

First the Sun: Use *TABLE I* in the Diurnal Table for the Sun (and only the Sun). Across the top of the page of Diurnal Table I, find the description of Minutes and Seconds which is closest to the Daily Motion computed above in Step 2—(61'12"). (*Table I* has two separate columns of figures—one for Hours and one for minutes.)

Find the number of *Hours* of the GMT Interval and move to the right until you are in the column represented by the Daily Motion of 61':09" and record the resulting figure below on line A.

Short form for Erecting a Natal Chart (Alternate Method)

Hour Minute Seconds

_____ _____ _____ Clock Time

_____ _____ _____ Less DST or WT

_____ _____ _____ Birth Time

_____ _____ _____ +/- from Meridian

_____ _____ _____ TLT (AM or PM) Date _____

To Compute GMT

_____ _____ _____ TLT

_____ _____ _____ Hours from Greenwich

        (+ if West Long.)

        (- if East Long.)

_____ _____ _____ GMT (AM or PM) Date _____

To Determine ASC and House Cusps using Noon Ephemeris

_____ _____ _____ Sid. Time at the Noon previous to Birth.

        Sidereal Date _____

     _____ +/- 10 seconds for each 15 degree

        Long. (EST--50"; CST--60" etc.)

_____ _____ _____ TLT Interval (Time inverval from previous

        Noon to True Local Time.

     _____ 10" per Hour correction of TLT Interval

_____ _____ _____ Totals for each column

_____ _____ _____ (If totals above are in excess of 24 hrs.,

        subtract 24:00:00)

_____ _____ _____ True Calculated Sidereal Time

        (TCST) at Latitude

     _____ N_____ or _____ S _____

In a Table of Houses find the Sidereal Time nearest to the TCST and record the House Cusps listed for the Latitude of Birth. Generally only one half of the cusps are listed. Enter the opposite sign with the same degrees on the opposite house cusp.

Then find the number in the *Minutes* column listed under the closest Daily Motion, record it below on line B, and add the two together. Remember that you are adding minutes and seconds (base 60.)

$$
\begin{array}{ll}
A & 28':03'' \\
B & +\ \underline{1':29''} \\
 & 29':32''
\end{array}
$$

Then subtract this figure from the position listed in the Ephemeris on Noon of the GMT DAY if GMT is in the AM and add if it is PM. (Reverse this rule if Planet is retrograde.)

$$
\begin{array}{l}
12:49':58'' \\
\underline{-29':32''} \\
12:20':26''
\end{array}
$$

Sun in Capricorn 12°:20':26''. (Always compute down to the second for the Sun.)

Follow these four steps for the Moon using *Table II*. Table II is used for the correction of all Planet positions except the Sun.

Step 2	Step 3	Step 4	Moon's position
19° Leo 19'	5:28:10	19:19	
$-\ 7\quad\ 23$	$\underline{17:24}$	$-\ 5:46$	13° ♌ 53'
11 56	5:45:34	13:33	

(It is not necessary to calculate beyond degrees and minutes on Planets other than the Sun.) Use this formula to calculate the Planetary positions of Mercury, Venus and Mars. The remaining Planets move very slowly and need no correction.✿

Interpreting a Horoscope

Throughout the Knowledge Lectures, the student has been given the basic building blocks of Astrology. Once these principles are understood, the final step is to learn how to interpret or *delineate* all the information that comprises a horoscope. Much of this interpretive knowledge comes through reasoning, common sense and an understanding of human nature. It includes the ability to call to mind key phrases and words which are associated with each *Sign, Planet* and *house*.

No matter what Sign a Planet may be located in, the natural Sign of the house involved also lends its influence to the interpretation. For example: **Mercury in Taurus in the fifth house.** The key word for Mercury is *reasoning powers*. Other words describing Mercury include *communication* and *awareness*. The keyword for Taurus is *stability*. Other Taurean words include *practical* and *sensual*. The fifth house is the house of *creativity, love* and *pleasure*. Leo, the natural Sign of the fifth house is associated with the keywords *magnetism, charitable* and *self-confident*.

One can therefore summarize Mercury in Taurus in the fifth house (of Leo) in the sentence: *The stable and practical faculty of reason and awareness will be displayed creatively with self-confidence,* (or) *communication of pleasures and love will be given with charity and sensuality.*

For another example: **Jupiter in Cancer in the third house.** Important words for Jupiter are *expansion, philosophy,* and *prosperity.* Key words for Cancer are *devotion, nurturing,* and *sensitive.* The third house is the house of *conscious awareness* and *communication.* Gemini, the natural Sign of the third house is associated with the keywords *versatile, literary* and *inquisitive.*

Thus Jupiter in Cancer in the third house (of Gemini) can be described as: *The philosophical nurturing urge of this individual will be communicated with great versatility and skill,* (or) *Sensitive awareness and devotion to higher philosophical ideals will lead to expansion of literary pursuits.*

(Of course no Astrologer would use such convoluted language while talking to a Querent. In simpler terms, a person with this placement of Jupiter in the chart will tend to talk a lot about his/her feelings.)

Oftentimes house placement of a Planet will modify the influences of certain Signs in which the Planet is located. For instance **Venus in Aries in the tenth house** (Capricorn rules the tenth house). Aries is *Aggressive* and *Impulsive.* Venus symbolizes *affections,* and *social pursuits.* The tenth house refers to *honor, ambition,* and *profession.* Capricorn is *conservative* and *prudent.* One might conclude that this individual's professional and social pursuits would be approached in an aggressive fashion, however the prudent nature of Capricorn would serve to temper the impulsiveness of Aries.

A Planet will also function differently depending upon whether the house it is located in is Angular, Succedent or Cadent. An individual with Sun in Scorpio will be less temperamental and more easy-going when the Sun in Scorpio falls within a Cadent (Mutable) house rather than a Succedent (Kerubic or Fixed) house. An Angular (Cardinal) house placement might still indicate a temperament that is still volatile but not long lasting.

The houses are the constant variables in a horoscope. The Signs and the Planets do not change their basic characteristics; it is always the houses which are the various arenas for activity, and they are subject to change quite a bit.

The only way to truly learn how to interpret a Zodiacal chart is through *constant* practice. We highly recommend that the student obtain some good books on horoscope interpretation, including the series *The Only Way to Learn Astrology* (vol. 1-3) by Marion D. March and Joan McEvers.

A Zodiacal chart should bring questions to the Astrologer's mind. While interpreting the chart, the Astrologer should dialogue with the Querent and ask for answers to those questions in order to ground him/her self within the framework of the Querent's circumstances and worldview first. Then the Astrologer reads the possibilities which are apt to apply to the Querent.

Using the techniques mentioned here, the student is encouraged to look at *several* different horoscopes and try to delineate each one in accordance with the information s/he has accumulated through the Knowledge Lectures.

Aspecting

The influence of the aspects must also be examined when interpreting a chart. It is important to remember that aspects are calculated by counting Signs (not by counting houses), and each Sign has thirty degrees. In addition, if a Planet is in its dignity or exaltation, it can manage all aspects in a more harmonious fashion.

To find the aspects, take the degree position of each Planet, then proceed to add and subtract seven degrees, the widest possible orb permitted for most of the major aspects. (Some aspects have an orb of only five degrees or one degree.) Determine if any Planets form an aspect with each other within the allowed orb of degrees.

The following list includes two examples of aspects:

☿ 16° ♊ ☍ ♂ 11° ♐
♃ 4° ♌ □ ♄ 28° ♈

Example One: Mercury 16° Gemini is in opposition to Mars 11° Sagittarius. Example Two: Jupiter 4° Leo is square to Saturn 28° Aries.

The aspects can be interpreted using the same techniques mentioned above—the knowledge of keywords for the Signs, the Planets, the houses *and* the aspects. (Squares are always stressful and challenging, trines are always harmonious, etc.)

Aspects which encompass two different Signs can occur at the beginning or end of a Sign. This is an aspect *out of Sign,* so long as it is still within the permitted orb of degrees.

A *forming* or *applying* aspect occurs when one Planet is said to move toward another (toward an exact aspect). A *separating* or *waning* aspect occurs when one Planet is said to move beyond another (past an exact aspect). The forming aspect is the stronger of the two. The faster-moving Planet (active) is always listed before the slower-moving one (passive). A forming aspect indicates something that you are advancing towards. A separating aspect refers to something that has been recently experienced.

Solar aspects are very important to the character makeup of the individual. However all aspects shed light upon the personality, since they are in fact responsible for forming the individual's basic personality. The more exact the aspect, the more it helps to shape the essential character. Aspects indicate capabilities, inclinations and hindrances, rather than achievements. The birth chart alludes to a person's potential. However it is up to the individual to make use of that potential.☿

SECTION 2: Basic Alchemy Alchemical Operations

 The goal of Alchemy (both practical and mystical) is to obtain the Quintessence. This is accomplished in a number of stages. First, the material to undergo the process of transmutation exists with a state of *Chaos* (Void) which must be separated and categorized to fit into the fourfold model of the Elements. The alchemist then uses reason to apply this same fourfold model to the *First Matter*, intellectually structuring it into the divisions of the four Elements. The Spirit or *First Essence* (*Spiritus Mundi*) is then drawn out of the First Matter (implanted within the Alchemist s psyche). This Hidden Essence is then divided or broken down (through the *Unbodied Volatile*) into the Triad of the Alchemical Principles (Mercury, Salt and Sulfur). At length the Quintessence, which is the synthesis of these Three Principles as well as the sustaining Life Force, is obtained.

There are four colors associated with four distinct stages in alchemical transmutation of metals. In applied or practical Alchemy these stages are identified by the colors shown forth by the Prime Matter as it undergoes the process of transmutation. During these various levels the metals or materials used are said to undergo a drastic change in appearance, becoming a mud or slime and then a powder. These stages are also related to the four elements. In order they are:

> **MELANOSIS:** Blackening (Earth) also called *Nigredo*.
> **LEUKOSIS:** Whitening (Water) also called *Albedo*.
> **XANTHOSIS:** Yellowing (Air) also called *Citrinitas*.
> **IOSIS:** Reddening (Fire) also called *Rubedo*.

(Note: by the sixteenth century these colors were reduced to three the yellowing stage was dropped, resulting in a triad of colors: black, white and red.)

Melanosis is the first state, which is either present from the onset as a quality of the Prime Matter, or obtained from of a process of *separation, death, dissolution* or *putrefaction*. The next stage is *Leukosis,* which signifies a washing or cleansing process, a resurrection and the release of the pure essence. (This results in the white tincture or Lunar essence symbolized by the White Queen.) The final stage is *Iosis,* which results from the raising of heat to its highest intensity. (The Red King or Solar essence is the symbol here.)

Other colors may also be seen in the process. These additional colors represent *intermediate* states in the process. The four colors listed above are usually the only recognized colors in Alchemical work. After the black stage of Melanosis, the color blue may be seen, which is considered a feminine aspect, indicative of Height and Depth. After the red stage of Iosis, the color of violet may be seen to indicate the limit of the process.

The colors of Alchemy can be associated to the Planets in the following manner:

BLACK: Saturn (lead)
BLUE: Jupiter (tin)
PEACOCK'S TAIL: (multi-colored) Mercury (quicksilver)
WHITE: Luna (silver)
YELLOW: Venus (copper)
RED: Mars (iron)
VIOLET: Sol (gold)

In addition to the four color stages, there are different *gates* or *basic stages of process* used in applied Alchemy. Different Alchemists have divided the various stages of process into groups of five, seven, eight or twelve gates.

The following is one of the systems which employs seven gates:

1.	Calcination	— Mercury
2.	Sublimation	— Saturn
3.	Solution	— Jupiter
4.	Putrefaction	— Luna
5.	Distillation	— Mars
6.	Coagulation	— Venus
7.	Tincture	— Sol

Two Alchemical systems which list twelve gates are given below:

1.	Calcination	♈		1.	Calcination	♈
2.	Dissolution	♉		2.	Congealation	♉
3.	Separation	♊		3.	Fixation	♊
4.	Conjunction	♋		4.	Dissolution	♋
5.	Putrefaction	♌		5.	Digestion	♌
6.	Congelation	♍		6.	Distillation	♍
7.	Cibation	♎		7.	Sublimation	♎
8.	Sublimation	♏		8.	Separation	♏
9.	Fermentation	♐		9.	Incineration	♐
10.	Exaltation	♑		10.	Fermentation	♑
11.	Multiplication	♒		11.	Multiplication	♒
12.	Projection	♓		12.	Projection	♓

CALCINATION: Reducing the principles to atoms, but not by burning.
CIBATION: (or **IMBIBATION**) When the matter in the vessels appears dry, it is
wetted again. It provides a mild heat.
CIRCULATION: (This process may also include the processes of cohobation,
digestion, distillation and sublimation.) It is the betterment, progress or
Exaltation of a liquid through repeated dissolution and coagulation
(usually in the Pelican vessel) using heat. The liquid is brought by
repeated changes from liquid to vapor to liquid again.

COHOBATION: A number of repeated distillations of a solvent over a substance or substances which have been dissolved into it. The process loosens the structure of certain substances, volatilizing the solids which are thus loosened by the solvent.

CONGEALATION: Reducing the substance to liquid which then thickens. The liquefied matter congeals or solidifies.

CONJUNCTION: Joining the principles. Amalgamating the various elements.

DESPONSATION: The separation of liquids in a vessel.

DIGESTION: A mixture for the purpose of drawing out the Essence from the different substances.

DISSOLUTION: Dissolving the metals. Indicates letting time and nature do the work. A slow separation of a metal into its components in a liquid.

DISTILLATION: Also called *Circulation* or *Rectification* because it entails a continuous cycle (rising and falling). The process of boiling a liquid until it is vaporized, and then recondensed by cooling. The rising vapor is considered the Spirit of the substance. This process liberates the original metal from its corrupted state, while giving it new properties. The energy inherent in the rising vapors generates the multi-colors of the Peacock's tail. The substance is then heated more vigorously until it dries up into a grayish-black mass. When the color white is seen, it signifies that the process of coagulation is about to commence. (In mystical Alchemy, distillation entails the liberation of the Soul from the grip of the Lower Ego. This transformation implies that the ego has become purified and compliant to the Higher Self.)

EXALTATION: To elevate the Power of Virtue in the hope that the substance will transmute.

FERMENTATION: Adding the required precious metal as a yeast to the Philosopher's Stone enabling it to transmute base metals into this particular precious metal. It is associated with putrefaction and decay, but also the work of Transformation and regeneration—Death which leads to Life. (In mystical Alchemy, fermentation implies the liberation of intuitive powers and the creation of dreams.)

LIGATION: Separation in a sealed vessel.

MULTIPLICATION: Raising the quantity and quality of the powder or stone.

PROJECTION: The work of transmutation into gold and silver.

PUTREFACTION: The first change to be seen. The appearance of blackness.

ROTATION: Rhythmic cycling of the process of circulation. It entails the boiling of a liquid for a set period of time in a reflux system. The liquid is allowed to cool, reheated, and allowed to cool again, etc.

SEPARATION: Separating the light parts from the heavy parts. The slow separation of a body into its components in a liquid.

SOLUTION: Dissolving a solid into a liquid.

SUBLIMATION: Extraction by volatilization or distillation. This process entails forcing an extract upwards into the upper portion of a container where it is allowed to precipitate. Also called Rectification.

Sigils of Minerals and other Materials

Copper Chlate	Pulvis (dust)	Magnet, Lodestone
Antimony	Talc	Saltpeter
Oil	Volatile	Fixed
Tartarus	Dead Head	Urina (Urine)
Borax	Hematite	sugar
Black Ink	Roots	Iron Filings
Aluminum	Nitrum (soda)	Camphor
Vitriol	Ammonia	Crystals
Gold pigment	Arsenic	Wax
Mercury Solid	Refined Mercury	Orichalcum
Glass	Magnesia	Common Salt
Cinis (ashes)	Potash	Vinegar
Alcohol solution	Spirits of Wine	Lead Acetate
Quicksilver	Metal Oxide	Herb
Quick-sulphur	Red Lead Oxide	Quintessence
Powder	Sophic Sulphur	Liquor
Distilled Vinegar	Charcoal	Sand
Cinnabar	Chalk	Gum

Sigils of Operations

Sublimate	Precipitate	To Powder
Amalgamate	To Calcine	To Coagulate
Putrefaction	To Mix	To Fire
To liquefy	To Filter	To Dissolve
To Infuse	Extract	Evaporate
To Sublime	Digestion	To Rot
Layer on Layer	To Distill	To Boil
Solution	To Purify	Work Complete

SECTION 3: Spiritual Entities

 In the Zelator grade the student was made aware of the Qabalistic world of Assiah, the active World which encompasses the sphere of Malkuth. In the Theoricus grade the initiate is exposed to the Sephirah Yesod and the World of Formation known as *Yetzirah*. (Review the information given on Yetzirah in Chapter Two.) Yetzirah is the world of the astral plane, an immaterial realm close in proximity to our own. Both Angelic beings and the illusionary images given form by the mind of humanity are to be found there.

Astral Spirits

Astral Spirits are those belonging to the astral plane. Such are the false and illusionary forms, shells of the dead, and ghosts and phantoms. They are detached and nonconscious beings.

The human Soul is composed of several "layers." The outer layers govern a person's day-to-day habits, routines, spoken thoughts, and memories. After death, the higher parts of the Soul continue on the journey of spiritual evolution to the next level or plane of existence, while the lower parts usually dissipate. Occasionally, however, these outer shells are inhabited by an Elemental or similar astral being. This "ghost" then continues where it is and carries on with certain habits and routines.

Over time these phantoms will tend to disintegrate unless infused with fresh energy by a person or situation. Many people claim that they can be banished simply by telling these entities that their physical bodies have ceased to exist, and the remaining portion is free to leave.

Elemental Spirits

Elemental Spirits are those belonging to the nature of the Elements. Tradition has it that some are good and some are evil (although such labels don't really apply to Elementals). These beings (already discussed in Chapter Two) have hierarchies similar to those of Qabalistic Archangels and Angels. Elementals are thought to be childlike and innocent with respect to the human realm.

Angels and Archangels

An Angel is a pure and high Spirit of unmixed good in office and operation. In the Qabalah, Angels and Archangels are considered specific aspects of God, each with a particular purpose and jurisdiction. They are anthropomorphic symbols of what we believe to be good or holy. Nearly all of the Hebraic Angels have the suffixes "el" or "yah" at the end of their names, indicating that they are "of God." Powerful Angels which govern large groups or hosts of lesser Angels are known as Archangels.

The Soul

The difference between the *Soul* and the *Spirit* in humanity is as follows: The human Soul adjoins both the inner realm of Spirit from which it receives direct inspiration, and the physical or outer world from which it obtains impressions. A person who is not in touch with his/her inner spirituality but who instead routinely obeys the Will of the Ego or lower personal desires is living to one degree or another with a "dysfunctional" Soul. But as the individual steadily shifts his/her awareness to the knowledge of the Divine Light, the Soul undergoes purification that enables it to more easily connect with the Divine Spirit that is the source of all life. The Greeks referred to the Soul as the *Psyche* while the Egyptians referred to it as the *Ba*.

The Spirit

The Spirit (from the Latin *Spiritis*, meaning "breath") is the divine center in humanity. It is the material essence, animating key, or absolute pattern of an individual human life, which is eternal. The Greeks referred to this undying Spirit within each individual as *Nous*, the universal mind of God. Other Greek terms for Spirit include *daimon* and *pneuma* while the Egyptians refered to it as the *Khu*.

The Egyptian "Soul"

To the ancient Egyptians, there were several parts which made up the composite human being. The physical body was called the *Khat*, which implied something that was subject to decay. Attached to the *Khat* was the *Ka*. The *Ka* was the etheric double or "body of habits." It could be defined as an abstract personality endowed with the characteristics of a person, but which had an independent existance. The *Ka* was also supposed to have lived on after the body, so provisions were left for it in the tomb. (Some people equate the *Ka* with the astral body or Body of Light—the part of the Soul that can be used as a vehicle for ascending the astral planes.)

The *Ba* or Soul which dwelt in the *Ka*, was the seat of life in human beings. The word *Ba* implies something noble, sublime or mighty. Having the qualities of both substance and form, the *Ba* was free to leave the tomb and ascend to heaven. The *Ba* had the power to become corporeal or incorporeal at Will, and it was usually represented as a hawk with a human head.

The *Khu* was the immortal Spirit or spiritual intelligence of a human being. The word implies something shining or luminous and was symbolized by a plume of flame. The *Khu*, like the *Ka*, could be imprisoned in the tomb, so magical formulae were used to keep this from occurring.

The *Sekhem* (meaning: "to have mastery or power over something") was a person's vital force or strength personified. This part, like the *Khu*, also ascended to heaven.

The *Khaibit* or "shadow" was thought to be near a person's Soul.
Finally, the *Ren* or name was consider by the Egyptians to be very important, since a nameless person could not enter into the company of the gods. Preservation of the name insured immortality.

Planetary Intelligences and Spirits

In Planetary magic, an *Intelligence* is referred to as a guiding Angelic force which is directed in turn by a ruling Planetary Archangel. A *Planetary Spirit* is a blind force which can be used for good or ill. To insure that the Spirit is used for positive purposes, it should never be invoked without first invoking the Planetary Intelligence (or guiding principle).✿

SECTION 4: Qabalah—The Parts of the Soul

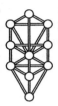 The Soul is divided by the Qabalists into three principal parts. These are the *Neshamah*, the *Ruach*, and the *Nephesh*. The **NESHAMAH** (נשמה) is the first and highest part, answering to the three Supernal Sephiroth of Kether, Chokmah and Binah. It corresponds to the highest aspirations of the Soul, and what Freud called the superego. The Neshamah is further subdivided into three parts. These are the *Yechidah* (יחידה), the *Chiah* (חיה), and the *Neshamah* (נשמה).

The *Yechidah* is centered in Kether. It is our true and immortal Divine Self. The *Chiah*, located in Chokmah is our inquisitive urge to become more than human—it is our True Will. Both the Yechidah and the Chiah are archetypal in essence and thus they are somewhat beyond the scope of our understanding. The final subdivision, the Neshamah is placed in Binah, although it lends its name to the other Supernals as being generally descriptive of the Soul's greatest aspirations. This is our true desire or highest state of consciousness—the intuitive power that connects humankind with the Divine. According to the ancient Qabalists, this part of the Soul remains dormant in the average person until s/he awakens spiritually and uncovers the powers of mystical comprehension. The descent of the Neshamah into the student's field of awareness occurs through the "holy union" of the "king" and "queen," (Tiphareth and Malkuth). A dialogue between the Higher Self and the Lower Self must be opened up for this descent to occur.

RUACH: (רוח) The middle part of the Soul is located in the five Sephiroth from Chesed to Yesod, although it is centered in Tiphareth. This is the conscious part of our being which is also known as the *Ego*. It is the mind and reasoning powers, as well as the seat of "outer" consciousness, where humanity becomes aware of thought-images and is able to fashion thoughts into actions. The Ruach represents an intermediate stage between the highest and lowest portions of the Soul where the ethical power to distinguish between good and evil is called into play. It is here where the individual can choose to focus either on secular and temporary desires, or on higher spiritual goals.

NEPHESH: (נפש) The lowest part of the human Soul resides in Yesod. This is the dark side or Shadow-self of the Soul, answering unto the animal vitality and primal instincts. It is however a very important part which ties humanity to the physical world of the elements and our animal ancestors. Entering the human body at birth, the Nephesh is the first part of the Soul to be activated in every human being.

The Nephesh represents those basic desires that run contrary to society and to our own ideals of behavior and personality. This is the dark underside of the consciousness that dwells in the Ruach—the human mind. However, there can be no Light without Darkness, no day without night. Proper use of the vital, stimulating Nephesh energy is important in some aspects of magic, but it must always remain under the firm control of the Ruach. The Lower Soul or Nephesh can arouse the Middle Soul (Ruach) which in turn can stimulate the Neshamah or Divine Soul. This triggers the descent of the Neshamah down through the lower portions of the Soul, bringing to the individual a conscious recognition of the Divine Self.

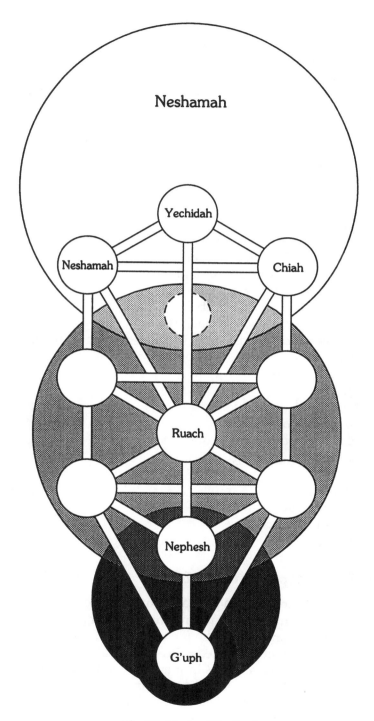

The Divisions of the Soul

279

Beyond this fivefold division of the human Soul, there is one more portion that is sometimes overlooked. This lowest part is called the **G'UPH** (ﻑﺞ). Centered in Malkuth, the G'uph is closely tied to the physical body and the total range of all psychophysical functions. It is a low level of the subconscious which communicates with the brain about the current condition of the human body.✿

SECTION 5: Correspondences of Yesod

The 2 = 9 grade is attributed to the sphere of Yesod on the Qabalistic Tree of Life. Yesod is the ninth Sephirah on the Tree and the second sphere encountered by the aspiring initiate. It is the realm of the Akasha or astral Light, as the substance which underlies all dense matter. (Review all information on Yesod given in Chapter One.)

Name in English: The Foundation
Divine (Atziluthic) Name: Shaddai El Chai
Archangel (Briatic) Name: Gabriel
Angelic (Yetziratic) Choir: Kerubim
Planet or House of Assiah: Levanah (Luna)
Spiritual experience: Vision of the Machinery of the Universe
Qabalistic Number: Nine
Color (Briatic): Violet
Element: Air
Part of Anatomy: Reproductive organs
Tarot cards: The four Nines
Magical Image: A beautiful strong naked man
Incense: Jasmine, Ginseng
Gemstone: Quartz
Symbols: Perfumes and sandals
Lineal Figure: Enneagram
Virtue: Independence
Vice: Idleness

SECTION 6: Correspondences of Air

The Theoricus grade is attributed to the Element of Air. Air symbolizes the intellectual and rational part of the psyche and the conscious mind. Air is the Element of balance and equilibration. It is the reconciler between Fire and Water. In the teachings of the Golden Dawn, Air is in many ways the most important Element for psychic growth and attainment. This Element is masculine, active, volatile, and abstract. The color given for Air is yellow, and the cardinal point is East. (Review all information on the Element of Air given in Chapter One.)

Incense has long been used by magicians and mystics to purify temples with fragrant smoke prior to ritual work. This helps to rid the surrounding area of any unwanted or negative energies. But more importantly the burning of incense helps to arouse the magician's mind toward an enhanced consciousness which enables him/her to tap into a well of personal energy. It helps promote the state of mind necessary for the successful practice of magic.

Some incenses are burned in order to attract particular energies to the magician. Like metals and gemstones, certain perfumes also attract the specific forces that correspond with them through vibration. However when incense is burned within a temple atmosphere it undergoes a transformation through the release of vibratory energy into the air. This released energy combined with the vitalized Will of the magician can have a potent effect upon the ritual. It is therefore appropriate that the student of the 2=9 grade commit the following list of incense correspondences to memory:

Perfumes and Incenses

The Sephiroth

1. Kether — Ambergris
2. Chokmah — Musk
3. Binah — Myrrh, Civet
4. Chesed — Cedar
5. Geburah — Tobacco
6. Tiphareth — Olibanum
7. Netzach — Benzoin, Rose, Red Sandal
8. Hod — Storax
9. Yesod — Jasmine, Ginseng
10. Malkuth — Dittany of Crete

The Zodiacal Signs

Aries — Dragon's Blood
Taurus — Storax
Gemini — Wormwood
Cancer — Onycha
Leo — Olibanum
Virgo — Narcissus
Libra — Galbanum
Scorpio — Siamese Benzoin, Opoponax
Sagittarius — Lign-Aloes (Wood-Aloe)
Capricorn — Musk, Civet
Aquarius — Galbanum
Pisces — Ambergris

The Planets

Saturn	—	Assafoetida, Scammony, Sulfur
Jupiter	—	Saffron
Mars	—	Pepper, Dragon's Blood
Sol	—	Olibanum, Cinnamon
Venus	—	Sandalwood, Myrtle
Mercury	—	Mastic, White Sandal, Mace, Storax
Luna	—	Camphor, Aloes

The Elements

Fire	—	Olibanum
Water	—	Onycha, Myrrh
Air	—	Galbanum
Earth	—	Storax

*Mythological Image
of a Sylph*

Hebrew and Other Names Connected with Air

Element Name: RUACH (רוח)
Outer Divine Name: SHADDAI EL CHAI (שדי אל חי)
Cardinal Point: MIZRACH (East) (מזרח)
Archangel: RAPHAEL (רפאל)
Angel: CHASSAN (חשן)
Ruler: ARAL (אראל)
Elementals: SYLPHS
King of Sylphs: PARALDA

RAPHAEL: (Specifically *Raphael Ruachel*) is the great winged Archangel of Elemental Air, whose name means "Healer of God." Stationed in the East, Raphael is visualized as a tall, fair figure standing upon the clouds in robes of yellow and violet. He holds the Caduceus of Hermes as a symbol of his healing powers of intellect.

ADAM: The name of the human-headed Kerub of Air in the East, symbolized by the Zodiacal Sign of Aquarius. A winged sphinx-like figure who wears a nemyss and tunic in the colors of yellow and violet.

Beings and Deities of Air and Sky

ANU: a supreme sky god of the Babylonians who reigned over the heavens. His name means "sky," and he resided in the uppermost region which was called the "sky of Anu." All other deities of the Assyro-Babylonian pantheon honored Anu as their "father" or chief. He symbolized power and justice. His royal emblems were the scepter, the diadem, the crown, and the staff of command. His army, which was used to destroy the wicked were the stars that he had created (called the "soldiers of Anu"). Never leaving the heavenly regions, he occasionally traversed a portion of the sky reserved only for him called "Anu's Way."

ENLIL: Babylonian god of the hurricane and Lord of the Air. His name means "Air god." This god is said to have separated Heaven and Earth with a pick-ax. He symbolized the forces of nature and was considered to be the master of humanity's fate. Like Anu, he had a reserved promenade in the heavens called "Enlil's Way" but his usual abode was the Great Mountain of the East.

VUL: Assyro-Babylonian god of the atmosphere between Heaven and Earth. Vul was a god of rain, storms and whirlwinds.

ADAD: A later Babylonian god who usurped Enlil's position as Lord of thunder and storm. Adad is usually depicted as standing upon a bull with a thunderbolt in each hand.

NUET: (or **NUT**) The Egyptian sky-goddess who was separated from her lover Geb (the Earth) by the Air-god Shu. She is often represented as a woman with an elongated body, who touches the earth with fingers and toes, while her star-spangled body is supported by Shu. She therefore forms the arc of the heavens. Nuet sometimes appears as a

Nuet

cow whose four legs are each held aloft by an appointed god. When in her human form, she often wears a round vase upon her head, the symbol of her name. Her maternal starry likeness was often painted on the inner lid of sarcophagi to watch over the deceased.

SHU: The Egyptian god of Air. His name means "to raise" or "he who holds up." Shu is the atmosphere which blankets the Earth. Equivalent to Atlas of Greek mythology, Shu is the one who supports the sky. The creation of Shu made possible a space between the Heavens and the Earth, into which the sun could shine. Because the sunlight immediately followed the creation of Shu, he is sometimes identified with Light. Acting upon orders from Ra, Shu slipped between Geb and Nut, separating Earth from sky. He is always represented in human form usually wearing an ostrich feather on his head.

HATHOR: An Egyptian sky-goddess whose name means "the dwelling of Horus." The Sun-god resided within her, being enclosed within her breast each dusk, to be born again each dawn. Sometimes represented as the celestial cow, but more often as a woman with a set of cow's horn atop her head. Hathor was the goddess of love and of joy. (Hathor is also the name given to the Kerub of the East in the Neophyte Hall.)

Shu

Hathor

Zeus

Hera

ZEUS (equivalent to the Roman *Jupiter*): Originally the Greek god of the sky and of all atmospheric phenomena, Zeus was the lord of winds, clouds, thunder and rain. The god is sometimes referred to as *Nephelgeretes* or "cloud-gatherer." He resided in the uppermost regions of the air and on mountain tops. Later Zeus took on the characteristics of a supreme god who was omnipotent and all-knowing. A wise leader of gods and men, he ruled all in accordance to the law of fate. Zeus is usually depicted as a robust mature man with a serious expression and deep set eyes. Thick hair and a curled beard frame his face and a crown of oak leaves adorns his head. Sometimes nude, but more often wearing a long mantle which uncovers his chest and right arm, the god holds a scepter in his left hand and a thunderbolt in his right. An eagle is sometime shown at his feet.

HERA (equivalent to the Roman *Juno*): Queen of the gods. Originally a Greek sky goddess, Hera became the wife of Zeus, and the cults of the two sky-deities merged. The noisy quarrels of Zeus and Hera were reflected in the storms and atmospheric disturbances. Hera also has a connection with the three phases of the moon. She is a champion of women and fecundity.

Greek Gods of the Winds:

BOREAS: The North Wind, harsh and destructive, represented as a winged mature man with hair floating in the wind.

ZEPHYRUS: The West Wind. Originally baleful, Zephyrus later became a sweet-scented and beneficial wind.

EURUS: The East Wind.

NOTUS: The South Wind.

AEOLUS: Guardian and father of the winds appointed by Zeus. He was the inventor of ships' sails, who could calm or arouse the fury of the winds at will.

THOR or **DONAR:** The Teutonic god of thunder and storm. Thor was the strongest of the gods and he is portrayed as a tall vigorous man with a red beard traversing across the heavens in a chariot pulled by goats. The Hammer of Thor, called *Mjollnir*, was a symbol of the thunderbolt. When his chariot rolled across the sky, it caused the sound of thunder. When lightning was seen, it was said to be Thor throwing his hammer down to Earth. Although he crushed his enemies with his hammer, Thor was considered benevolent to mankind.✿

SECTION 7: Correspondences of Luna

 The Planet attributed to the Theoricus grade is Luna. The Moon rules the subconscious mind, cycles and patterns, plant and animal life, the tides, and all instinctive processes in nature which are barren of personality. All of these are rhythmically connected with the cycles of the *moon*, or Levannah as it is known in Hebrew.

Luna is the closest "Planet" to the Earth and it moves rapidly through the Zodiac. It is considered a "feminine" and "moist" Planet. In an Astrological sense, Luna is said to be "cold" and "magnetic." The ancients described the Moon as the ruler of the period of life dominated by *growth* from the ages of 1 to 4 and symbolized by "the mewling babe."

In human anatomy, this Planet rules the breasts, the stomach, the body fluids, female organs and functions, the lymph glands, and digestion. Physical ailments associated with Luna include enflamed glands, defective eyesight, allergies, female disorders, mental instability, excess fluidity and depression.

Objects attributed to Luna include utensils used in the silversmith's trade, brewing and laundering; also soft smooth substances.

In magic, the days and hours of the Moon are used for femininity, alternation, change, receptivity, sleep, prophetic dreams, visions, messages, navigation, love, fertility, envoys, voyages, and the acquisition of merchandise by water.

The Lunar cycle takes approximately 28—29 days to complete, starting with the New Moon (completely Dark Moon), to the Full Moon (the fully illuminated Moon). This cycle is the result of a relationship that exists between the Sun, the Moon and the Earth. As the Moon makes one entire circuit around the Earth, it reflects the Solar light in various degrees, depending on the angle between Sol and Luna as seen from the Earth. This cycle is divided into four phases or quarters. These phases are as follows:

 The *First Quarter* commences when Sol and Luna are conjunct or in the same place (from the Earth's view). At first the Moon is not visible (New Moon), because it rises simultaneously with the Sun. However, toward the end of this phase, a sliver of Luna can be perceived just after sunset when the Moon follows the setting sun in the West.

The *Second Quarter* starts midway between the New Moon and the Full Moon, when Sol and Luna are at a 90 degree square to one another. At this time the waxing (increasing) Moon is seen as a half-moon which rises at noon and sets at midnight. It is seen in the West during the fist half of the night.

The *Third Quarter* commences with the Full Moon, when Sol and Luna are opposite each other and the light of Sol can illuminate the full sphere of Luna. During this phase the Moon is seen rising in the East at dusk, then rising a bit later each evening.

 The *Fourth Quarter* begins roughly midway between the Full Moon and the New Moon, when Sol and Luna are again at a 90 degree angle from each other. This waning (decreasing) Moon rises at Midnight, and can be seen in the East during the later half of the night.

The meaning of the Lunar symbol on the Tree of Life is thus: In its increase, it embraces the side of Mercy; in its decrease the side of Severity, and at the full, it reflects the Sun of Tiphareth. The following is a list of Lunar associations:

Hebrew Name: Levanah
Sephiroth: Yesod
Archangel: Gabriel
Day: Monday
Planetary Intelligence: Malkah be Tarshism
                      ve-ad Ruachoth Schechalim / Shelachiel
Planetary Spirit: Schad Barschemoth ha-Shartathan / Chasmodai
Olympic Planetary Spirit: Phul
Metal: Silver
Gemstones: Moonstone, pearl, quartz, fluorspar, beryl
Incenses: Camphor, aloes, jasmine
Trees: Willow, bay, hazel, papaya, coconut palm, almond
Herbs/plants: Lotus, opium, mushroom, poppy, gourds, moonwort
Animals: Cat, hare, dog, owl

Lunar Deities

SIN: The Babylonian Moon god was the chief among the astral triad which included Shamesh (the Sun) and Ishtar (the Planet Venus) who were his children. Sin was known as "He whose deep heart no god can penetrate" because of his mysterious transformations during the Moon's various phases. The full Moon was his crown, and thus he was known as the "Lord of the Diadem" and "the Shining Boat of Heaven." A very wise god, Sin was sometimes venerated under the name of *Nannar* and pictured as an old man with a long beard the color of lapis lazuli and wearing the full Moon as a crown. The bright crescent Moon was Sin's boat which navigated the night sky.

KHONSU or (KHENSU): The Egyptian god of the Moon whose name means "the Navigator" "the traveler" or "he who crosses the sky in a boat." Khonsu became the messenger of the great gods under the form of the Moon. Khonsu was later identified with Djehuti, another Moon god, and was called Khensu-Tehuti, the Twice Great. As the new Moon, Khonsu was likened to a mighty bull and as the full Moon, he was said to correspond to a gelded bull. As the crescent Moon, Khonsu shined his heavenly Light so that all female creatures would become fertile and conceive. He was thus the source of generation and reproduction. The god is sometimes portrayed with a hawk's head, but he is usually represented swathed in mummy cloth like Osiris and holding the scepters of crook, scourge, phoenix and *djed*. His head is shaven except for the heavy tress of a royal child on one side. He also wears a skullcap surmounted by a disk in a crescent Moon. Later he became known as an exorcist and a healer.

Khonsu

AAH-DJEHUTI: A form of the Egyptian god Thoth who was revered as a Moon god. He is the measurer of the seasons and the calculator of the different phases of the Moon. In the narrowest sense, this god symbolizes the new Moon (since Lunar calculations are based on the new Moon) but in truth he represents the Moon in all its phases. Aah-Djehuti is portrayed as a human-headed figure wrapped in mummy cloth holding the ankh, the djed, the crook, the scourge and the phoenix wand. He has the crescent and disk on his head, in addition to a lock of hair symbolic of youth. His head has two faces which represent the waxing and waning of the Moon.

Other Egyptian Deities associated with the Moon include the Great Mother goddess **ISIS** and the goddess **QETESH**.

ARTEMIS (equivalent to the Roman *Diana*): At first a Greek Moon goddess associated with Lunar light and the crescent Moon, (waning and waxing) she was later known as the goddess of the hunt and protectress of women who assisted in childbirth. Artemis is the goddess of untamed nature, "Lady of the Beasts." Fundamental to the worship of this goddess were vivacious dances and the Sacred Bough, which was probably derived from worship of the ancient Moon tree, considered a source of knowledge and immortality. At times she is depicted having many breasts, a reference to her powers of fertility. At other times she is depicted flanked by lions, dancing with a stag, or holding a slain deer in each hand.

SELENE (equivalent to the Roman *Luna*): The primary Greek goddess of the Moon, sister of Helios, the Sun. Particularly associated with the Full Moon, she was also called *Mene*, and her bright crown illuminated the dark night. Every evening, after the journey of Helios across the sky, Selene began her own excursion after bathing in the ocean. Then the broad-winged goddess would dress in fine robes and fly across the sky in a chariot drawn by radiant steeds or oxen. In early depictions, she is shown as a cow with the ancient horns of consecration—the crescent Moon. Selene is sometimes shown mounted on a horse, a bull or a mule.

Artemis

Hecate

HECATE: A powerful Greek Moon goddess who presided over navigation, enchantments and magic, and was referred to as the mother of witches. This goddess was particularly associated with the Dark New Moon. She later became known as a goddess of the underworld, ruling over ghosts and demons. Hecate was called the "Invincible Queen" who presided over purifications and expiations. Ritually prepared food was offered to appease the goddess, and her image was placed in front of homes to avert evil. Hecate is sometimes portrayed with three faces to represent the cycles of the Moon. She is often accompanied by wild hounds.

Complementary Planet: SATURN

In order to gain a better grasp of all the ancient Planets in the outer grades, it is necessary for the student to not only study the Planet assigned to the Sephirah of the grade, but also that Planet's complement. Complementary Planets are those Planets which are on opposite points of the Macrocosmic Hexagram on the Tree of Life. (See Chapter Five). Complementary Planets share similar characteristics and qualities.

Therefore in conjunction with the study material given on the Planet Luna, the student should review information supplied in Chapter One on Saturn, the Planet which complements Luna on the Macrocosmic Hexagram.

Saturn is the Planet of discipline, organization, time, restrictions, limitations, and solidification. It is attributed to the Great Mother goddess in all pantheons. This Planet also shares an occult correspondence with the Element of Earth. The energy of Saturn is slow, ponderous, and lasting.

In an astrological sense, Saturn is said to be "cold" and "barren." It is also thought of as a "malefic" Planet. The ancients described Saturn as the ruler of the period of life dominated by *resignation* from the ages 70 to 99 symbolized by "slippers."

In human anatomy, this Planet rules the teeth, bones and joints, the skin, the knees and the gall bladder. Physical ailments associated with Saturn include phobias, injuries from falls, melancholia, decayed teeth, malnutrition, skin disease, spinal ailments and arthritis.

In magic, the days and hours of Saturn are used for performing experiments, causing good or ill success to business, possessions, goods, seeds, fruits and similar things, in order to acquire learning, for destruction and discord, limitation, and organization. In addition to this Saturn is the "universal" Planet whose symbol and energy can be used to encompass all the other Planetary energies as a whole.[71] In the days of the week, Saturn rules Saturday.

---

[71] As in the Adept level *Lesser Banishing Ritual of the Hexagram.*

Deities associated with the Planet Saturn include: **PTAH** (Egyptian) **ISIS** (Egyptian), **CRONUS** (Greek), **HERA** (Greek), **RHEA** (Greek), **SATURNUS** (Roman) **EA** (Assyro-Babylonian) and **ISHTAR** (Assyro-Babylonian).

The following is list of Saturnian associations:

Hebrew Name: Shabbathai
Sephiroth: Binah
Archangel: Cassiel
Day: Saturday
Planetary Intelligence: Agiel
Planetary Spirit: Zazel
Olympic Planetary Spirit: Aratron
Metal: Lead, antimony
Gemstones: Onyx, jet, anthracite
Incenses: Assafoetida, scammony, sulfur
Trees: Yew, cypress
Herbs/plants: Ivy, hemlock, nightshade, amaranth, hemp
Animals: Crow, raven, chimera, spider

SECTION 8: Plants and Herbs

 The Vegetable Kingdom is closely affiliated with the Sephirah of Yesod and the Moon. All plants contain a high percentage of water which connects them to the Lunar energies. Plant life is quite literally *vital* to all animal life on earth. Plants make up the staple food of humanity throughout the world. It is only with great difficulty that human beings can adapt to areas where plants do not thrive. And without plants, there would be no oxygen—no air to breathe.

Plants are among the greatest Alchemists in nature, absorbing water and nutrients from the soil through a system of roots, soaking up sunlight into leaves, and converting both into food for growth and reproduction. Through respiration, plants take in carbon dioxide and release oxygen. But *photosynthesis* is the unique process of green plants, which manufacture their own food and food for all animal life from the Sun's energy (not unlike the sphere of Yesod which receives the reflected Solar light from Tiphareth and distributes it to the active sphere of Malkuth). The chlorophyll-bearing leaves are where the process of photosynthesis takes place. Sunlight is converted into sugar and starch grains. The final method by which plants convert carbohydrates, fats and proteins into protoplasm is called *assimilation*, the process of creating living material out of nonliving material. This mechanism is very close to the mystery of life itself.

The reproductive process of plants also depends heavily on the Air: Fertilization takes place when pollen is carried from one plant to another by the wind or by flying insects. Seeds containing young embryonic plants are dispersed by the winds or by birds and other creatures.

Growth is a characteristic of all life. This is especially vital for plants, because unlike animals, when plants cease to grow they die. And growth in plants is closely related to movement—in the slow upward search for light. Thus plants can also serve to teach humans about the search for the Light, for if we turn away from the divine quest, then our spiritual selves will cease to exist, and we will truly resemble the empty husks of spent plants.

The student should also take note of the deciduous and perennial plants that undergo a form of dormancy or apparent death during the cold season and are "reborn" with the warming winds of Spring, seeking light and air.

Plants have been venerated throughout history because their leaves, petals and flowers have been the source of various healing ointments, drugs, and visionary essences. The blossoming flower (especially the lotus and the rose) is a universal symbol of the creative mystery of life as well as spiritual enlightenment. The seed of a plant alludes to the *potential* for life expanding from a tiny germ. And of course the *tree* is one of the most essential of all traditional symbols, denoting: (1) wisdom and spiritual growth, (2) the mind of the Divine and the eternal life of the cosmos, (3) a connecting link between different worlds, represented by the different parts of the Tree, and (4) the life of humanity, the lesser cosmos.

Herbalism is the study of the medicinal uses of plants. *Herbal magic* is the use of plants to cause change in accordance with Will. Plants, like gemstones and metals, are associated with specific Powers: Planetary and Elemental. Each one of these substances has a *vibratory rate* that aligns it to one particular force or another. The vibratory rate of herbs, metals, and gems are determined by various factors: structural form, density, chemical makeup, etc. The Powers found in plants are ascertained by color, scent, form, habitat and other determinants. Related substances usually have similar vibratory rates.

The power of herbs is fairly easy to access because their magical energies are already present within the organic matter of the plants themselves. Herbs can be used in teas, incenses, sachets, ointments, baths and oils. However, the student who wishes to make use of herbs in magic must have a thorough knowledge of the properties of the plants s/he intends to use, because some herbs are poisonous and should not be ingested or rubbed on the skin. We suggest that the student obtain *Cunningham's Encyclopedia of Magical Herbs* to learn more about the proper uses of plants in magic.

Trees and Plants

Corresponding to the Planets

Saturn   — Ivy, yew, hemlock, nightshade, amaranth, hemp, aconite[72]
Jupiter   — Hyssop, fig, sage, star anise, nutmeg, sassafras
Mars   — Pine, wormwood, ginger, nettle, basil, radish, holly
Sol   — Sunflower, acacia, bay, marigold, saffron, rowan, peony
Venus   — Rose, myrtle, elder, geranium, hyacinth, thyme, licorice
Mercury   — Marjoram, fennel, mandrake, caraway, dill, pomegranate
Luna   — Willow, moonwort, lotus, lemon, gardenia, mushroom, poppy

Corresponding to the Elements

Fire   — Ash, mustard, cactus, pepper, garlic, onion, thistle
Water   — Most fruit trees, water plants, lotus, melon, orchid
Air   — Palm, mistletoe, dandelion, mint, lavender, goldenrod
Earth   — Oak, cypress, grains, potato, turnip, cotton, patchouli

Plant and Nature Spirits

NYMPHS: In Greek mythology, nymphs are a group of nature Spirits, who dwell within plants, trees, water, etc. There are many types of nymphs but all are usually depicted as beautiful maidens. Forest-nymphs, also known as *dryads* lived within trees and were the nature god Pan's cohorts in dance, music and pleasurable games. Of the other nymphs, *naiads* presided over brooks and fountains, *oreads* lived in mountains and grottos, *nereids* resided in the sea while *napaeae, auloniads, hylaeorae* and *alsaeids* inhabited the woods and valleys. These last types of nymphs were immortal, but the forest-nymphs were not. Their existence depended upon that of the trees. In Greek times it was a profane act to senselessly destroy a tree, and one which could result in severe punishment. Crowned with oak leaves the dryads were responsible for the well-being of trees, often dancing around the sacred oaks, guarding them with axes. Certain of the dryads, known as *hamadryads*, were even more closely related to the trees, of which they formed an essential part.

Pan and Olympos

SATYRS and **SILENI:** These Spirits are often confused with one another. *Satyrs* (equivalent to the Roman *fauns*), were deities of the woods, fields and mountains. They were a type of male forest genii thought to be the brothers of the nymphs. Satyrs were portrayed as being half man, half goat, with pointed ears and short sprouting horns on their heads. The lower half of their bodies ended with the legs, feet and tail of a goat. (Pan, the god of the woods, shepherd and flock, was often confused

---

[72] Many of these plants are poisonous.

with the satyrs, because of their shared physical appearance.) Satyrs delighted in chasing nymphs and and were attracted to the pursuit of pleasure. They were also the faithful companions of the god Dionysus.

The **SILENI** were rural genii of springs and rivers whose name appears to mean "water which bubbles as it flows." Unlike the satyrs, whose bodies were derived from he-goats, the bodies of the sileni were derived from horses, an animal symbolic of water. They possessed the ears, tail and hooves of horses.

PAN: The Greek god of the woods and forests, Pan is also the god of herds and wild places. He is depicted with the horns, haunches, legs and hooves of a goat. This god often carries the syrinx or panpipes.

Cernunnos

FLORA: The Roman goddess of Spring and vegetation.

CERNUNNOS: The Celtic horned god and universal Father-god. He is usually shown as a man with stag's horns, wearing a golden neck ring and sitting cross-legged. Cernunnos is sometimes portrayed as having three heads. At times he is accompanied by a horned serpent and a stag.✡

SECTION 9: Admission Badges and Diagrams

The Solid Greek Cubical Cross is the Admission Badge for the 32nd Path of Tau in the grade of Theoricus. It is composed of twenty-two external squares which refer to the twenty-two letters of the Hebrew alphabet. The cross is an emblem of the equilibrated and balanced powers of the Elements through the forces represented by the Hebrew letters. Upon the front of the cross are the Hebrew letters which correspond to the four Elements: Aleph—Air, Shin—Fire, Mem—Water, and Tau—Earth. In the center is the letter Resh, which is attributed to the Sun.

On the back of the cross are the Hebrew letters that represent the remaining Planets (minus Resh—Sol and Tau—Saturn). They are: Beth—Mercury, Peh—Mars, Gimel—Moon, Daleth—Venus with Kaph—Jupiter in the center.

The remaining three sides of the Aleph—Air arm contain the letters corresponding to Libra (Lamed), Aquarius (Tzaddi) and Gemini (Zayin). The sides of the Shin—Fire arm are covered by the letters which refer to Aries (Heh), Leo (Teth) and Sagittarius (Samekh). The Mem—Water arm includes the letters which are attributed to Cancer (Cheth), Scorpio (Nun) and Pisces (Qoph). The sides of the Tau—Earth arm include the letters corresponding to Capricorn (Ayin), Taurus (Vav) and Virgo (Yod).

The Cubical Cross combines the symbolism of the balanced Elements with the twenty-two letters (the powers of the Three Mothers, the seven Planets and the twelve Zodiacal Signs) to emphasize the eternal forces which are behind the base Elements of the physical universe.

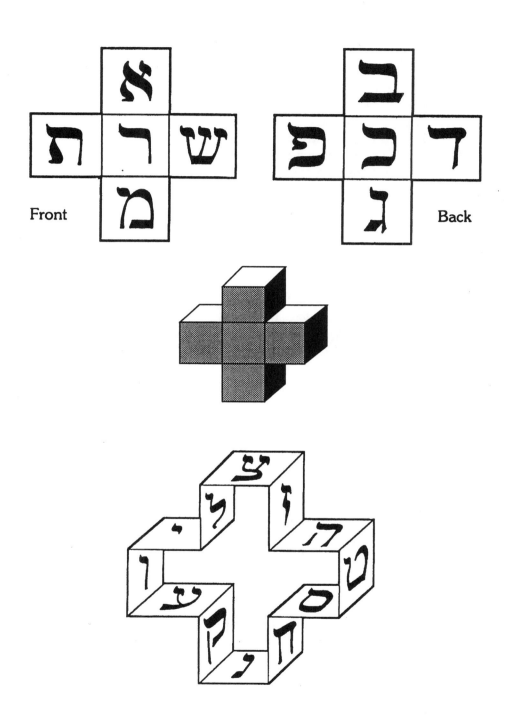

The Solid Greek Cubical Cross

The Caduceus of Hermes is the Admission Badge which grants the candidate entry into the temple of Yesod.

Legend has it that Hermes-Thoth, the god of Wisdom intervened in a fight between two serpents who then curled themselves around his wand. In ancient Mesopotamia, the intertwined serpents were a symbol of the god who cured all illnesses. The association of the Caduceus with the powers of healing was carried over into Greek culture and is still preserved today in medical emblems.

The Caduceus is an explicit representation of the of the same energies concealed within the wand and lamen of the Keryx. One form of the Caduceus is that of the Three Mother Letters placed one above the other in descending order thus: Shin, Aleph, Mem.

The Caduceus has another meaning on the Tree of Life. The upper point of the wand rests upon Kether, and the wings stretch out to Chokmah and Binah, thus completing the three Supernals. The lower seven Sephiroth are touched by the serpents whose heads rest upon Chesed and Geburah. The Wings and the top of the wand form the Hebrew letter Shin, the symbol of Fire. The upper parts of the serpent form the letter Aleph (Air), while the tails form the letter Mem.

The animals are the twin serpents of Egypt and the currents of the astral Light. The serpent on the left is Nekhebet, while that on the right is Uatchet. As a whole the Caduceus represents the balanced forces of Eternal Light working invisibly in the darkness.

The Flaming Sword with the Kerubim. This diagram was previously explained in the Zelator grade. (Refer to Chapter Two and Plate 1.)

The Serpent of Wisdom shows the Ten Sephiroth with all the connecting paths numbered and lettered, and the Serpent winding over every path. Around each Sephirah are written the names of the deity, Archangel and Angelic group attributed to it. The twenty-two paths are bound together by the Serpent of Wisdom. It

THE CADUCEUS BADGE

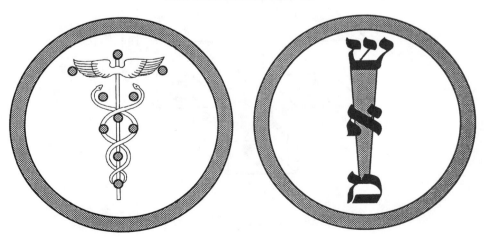

Front   Back

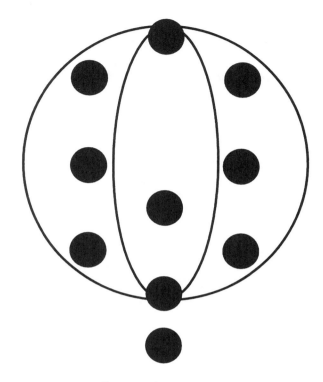

Luna on the Tree of Life

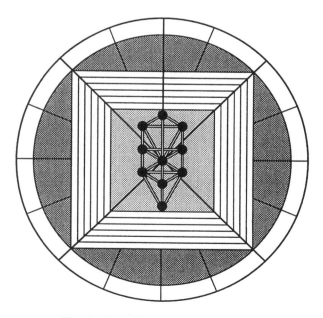

The Garden of Eden and the Holy City

295

unites the paths but does not touch any of the Sephiroth, which are linked by the Flaming Sword.

The Serpent of Wisdom is formed by the natural order of the twenty-two paths. It is the ascending reflux current of energy which aspires unto the Divine (whereas the *Flaming Sword* alludes to the rush of divine energy descending into manifestation). The Serpent also traces the path of an initiate of the mysteries who aspires unto the Hidden Knowledge. (See Plate 2.)

The Tarot Key of *The Universe* and the 32nd Path of the *Sepher Yetzirah* are fully described in the Theoricus Ritual. They are also explained in the next section entitled "Ritual Work for the Theoricus." ✿

This concludes the Knowledge Lecture. Examinations on the ritual as well as the material covered in this section are given at the end of this chapter.

ADDITIONAL SIDE LECTURE[73]
The Moon and the Tree of Life

As confusion is found to exist with regard to the Right and Left Pillars of the Sephiroth on the Tree of Life in relation to the right and left sides of a man, and as to the phases of the Moon—you must note:

That in every diagram and picture, the right hand side of the observer is next the Pillar of Mercy—Chokmah, Chesed, and Netzach; while the Pillar of Severity is on the observer's left hand. Yet when you apply the Tree of Life to yourself, your right side, arm, and leg represent the side of Strength and Severity, Binah, Geburah and Hod, and your left side refers to the Pillar of Mercy. So that when you look at a diagram, you are looking, as it were, at a man facing you, that your right side faces his left. His Merciful side forms the right hand Pillar in front of you, so that it is as if you looked at yourself in a mirror.

Just as the man looks at you, so does the Moon look at you and so you say that the Moon in her increase is on the side of Mercy, the right hand pillar of the Sephiroth; and in her decrease, the crescent is on the left hand Pillar of Severity.

A Diagram, then, is a picture of a Man or the Moon facing you. The temple pillars are similar:

Black Pillar	Severity	Left	North
White Pillar	Mercy	Right	South
Black Pillar	Boaz	Stolistes	
White Pillar	Jachin	Dadouchos	

That is, the white Mercy or Jachin Pillar is on your right hand as you approach the Altar from the West and from the Hiereus. (See Chronicles II. iii, 17.)

---

73 From Regardie's *The Golden Dawn*.

"And call the Name on the right hand (of him who enters) Jachin, and the Name of that on the left, Boaz."

Now Boaz = Strength, Severity, Binah, Black Pillar; and Jachin = White Pillar of Mercy.

So in making the Qabalistic Cross on your breast it is correct to touch the Forehead and say Atah—Thou art; the Heart—*Malkuth*; Right Shoulder—*ve-Geburah*; left shoulder *ve-Gedulah*, and with the fingers clasped on the breast say, *Le Olam Amen!*✿

Ritual Work for the Theoricus

The Theoricus should construct all of the following talismanic emblems to aid in meditation and ritual. These emblems should be painted violet on yellow.

- The sigil of Elemental Air
- The sigil of Luna
- The sigil of Libra
- The sigil of Aquarius
- The sigil of Gemini

The following symbols should be painted black on white:

- The pentagram and pentagon
- The number Nine
- The number Five
- The letter Tau
- The sigil of Saturn
- The name Shaddai El Chai in Hebrew
- The enneagram and enneangle

The following symbols should be painted silver on blue-violet:

- A Crescent
- The symbols for each of the Moon's phases

MEDITATION

for the 2 = 9 grade of Theoricus[74]

Let the Theoricus practice the Moon Breath, while saying mentally the word AUM: (Moon breath is through the left nostril only.)

Let him meditate upon the waxing and waning crescents, while visualizing a silver crescent upon an indigo background.

Let him now call before his mind the Signs of the Airy Triplicity ♊ ♎ ♒ and enclosed in these, let him meditate upon the numbers nine and five and therewith the form of the Pentagram and Pentangle.

Let him now rise in imagination above the mineral world into the world of trees and flowers and identify himself in love and sympathy with the Powers of the Elements behind these.

Let him realize the mental world where the mind rules over matter, and let him meditate upon the ideas of appearance and reality.✿

RHYTHMIC BREATHING

As stated in the Neophyte Ritual, "The letter 'H' is our mode of representing the ancient Greek aspirate or breathing, and breath is the evidence of Life." Once the procedures of body awareness and relaxation have been learned, the techniques of rhythmic breathing should be mastered. The previous exercises should have demonstrated to the student the fact that most of us have a massive amount of tension in our bodies. This tension can inhibit proper breathing. Improper breathing can in fact rob one of vitality and lifeforce. One of the goals of rhythmic breathing is to rid the body of neuromuscular tension, thus improving physical as well as magical vitality and energy.

If breath is indeed the evidence of *life*, then the initiate should proceed on the idea that the life of the universe exists everywhere and in fact pervades the atmosphere around us. Rhythmic breathing is based upon the precept that life is the active principle in the very air we breathe, and we as magical beings can draw upon this all-pervasive vitality.

---

[74] From Regardie's *The Golden Dawn*.

This exercise should be practiced at fixed periods of time every day. Twice a day is best, and for no more than ten minutes at one session. Do not force the breathing—all effort should be mild and unhurried. The entire process should be simple and enjoyable.

As the lungs attune to the rhythm, they gradually communicate it to the rest of the body. Within a short time the entire body will be felt to vibrate with the cadence, thus instilling a powerful current of spiritual energy with the body and mind.

In addition to this, rhythmic breathing is a discipline that trains the Will of the individual. Many students would like to skip over such simplistic yet laborious exercises as this, wishing to jump headlong into more advanced work. Perseverance and determination are required to comply with the curriculum presented here. It is precisely this type of exercise that pits the student against his/her own inertia and indolence. Those who persist will profit greatly in the long run.

The Fourfold Breath explained in Chapter One is an excellent example of a rhythmic breathing technique. The Theoricus can now expand on this method by adding certain visualizations:

Inhale	—	Waxing Moon
Full Hold	—	Full Moon
Exhale	—	Waning Moon
Empty Hold	—	Dark Moon

The student may wish to experiment with several different fourfold visualizations: the four quarters of the day (dawn, midday, dusk, midnight), the four seasons of the year, the four Elements, the four Qabalistic Worlds, the four letters of Tetragrammaton, etc., the list goes on.

It is essential that whatever rhythm the student chooses, be it the Fourfold Breath, a ten beat count, or any other, the practice should be maintained for the prescribed ten minutes. The rhythm itself is responsible for the assimilation of vital energy from without, and the augmentation of the divine life power within.

It might be helpful in the initial learning stages to employ an electric metronome attached to a timer. This can be adjusted to the correct length of the practice session, loudness and speed of the rhythmic beat.✿

THE PURIFYING BREATH

This simple exercise is an extension of the rhythmic breath and should be employed at the end of all meditations.

Take a deep full breath and hold it in for a few seconds. Then pucker the lips, leaving only a narrow opening in the mouth. Exhale the air strongly through the mouth, gradually and slowly forcing the air out through the small opening in the lips until all the air is gone.

Relax for a moment while maintaining the balance of the air, then repeat. This will impel an automatic rebound of the chest whenever the exhalation of breath is completed in this fashion. Repeat this technique over a long period of time until it can be executed easy and without discomfort.✡

MIND AWARENESS

The Sephirah of Yesod is attributed to the third Qabalistic world of Yetzirah, the formative World of primordial Air. This is the world of the astral plane and of subconscious images. In the Theoricus grade, the student is encouraged to raise the level of awareness from the body to the mind. The exercise employed for this purpose is a form of "free association" used by psychotherapists. It is performed by simply letting the mind wander as it may without obstruction.

Set a predetermined amount of time for the session beforehand and use an alarm clock or timer. (Twenty minutes or half an hour is appropriate.) At the end of the practice, stop immediately so that discipline is maintained.

Sit comfortably in a straight chair with a pillow for the back of the head. Keep the back straight, knees together, eyes closed, and hands in the lap. A tape recorder should be set up ahead of time to record the entire session.

Sitting in the position described above, calmly articulate any thought, idea, memory or feeling that happens to arise, into the microphone. Speak indiscriminately, without planning what to say next. At the end of the session, play back what has been recorded.

This practice will give the student a good idea of the hidden contents within the psyche. Some of it may seem shocking to the student who has not always been mentally "honest" with him/her self. The student may experience the opening of a floodgate of pent-up feelings or thoughts that been censored for years. However the simple act of becoming aware of these hidden thoughts is part of the process of being able to come to terms with them. The mental pressure and inner conflicts caused by these repressed thoughts will eventually dissipate, along with the number of "breaks" in concentration.

This method of mind awareness should be practiced continually while the student is in the grade of Theoricus. It should at least be practiced until the shock and anxiety usually encountered by the recognition of one's disturbing thoughts has vanished completely. What is most important about this exercise is that there should be no criticism, judgment or self-loathing concerning anything that might come up during the session. Your thoughts are a part of you, just like your arm or your leg. They are simply childlike parts of yourself that need training. With time and discipline the energies of these juvenile portions of the psyche can be directed toward higher pursuits.✿

SPEECH AWARENESS

During the course of a one week, be aware of everything that you say. Examine the thought that lies behind everything that you say.

During the following week, choose a specific hour each day (the same time each day) and maintain a period of total silence without talking (a temporary "vow of silence" if you will).

For one week, say nothing that is a negative value judgment. For the following week, refrain from making positive value judgment statements.

For one week try substituting the words "Thou" for "it." For the following week try substituting the word "it" for the word "I."✿

A SIMPLE CARD DIVINATION EXERCISE

Use the ESP cards obtained in the Neophyte grade to perform this exercise. Assign the following meanings to the simple images of the cards:

SQUARE: *Earth*—solid, manifestation, physical embodiment. Material environment. Completion. Also stubborn and slow to act. Resistant to change.

CROSS: *Fire*—Dynamic energy, active, initiating and stimulating force. Beginning of things. Movement. Masculine principle. Also impulsive and lacking in endurance.

WAVES: *Water*—Creative impluse, passive, fertility, instincts, passions, emotions, cycles. Feminine principle. Also unstable and lacking initiative or reason.

CIRCLE: *Air*—Intellectual, communicative, adaptable, changeable, mediating, reconciling. Health matters. Also indecisive and insensitive.

STAR: *Spirit*—Divine principle, spiritual guidance, inner strength. Illumination from within. Divine inspiration or assistance.

With these meanings in mind, shuffle the cards and formulate a question. Lay out three cards and put the rest away. (The first card is the central one. The second card is placed to the right of the first one, and the third card is placed to the left of the first.)

Card 1 represents the immediate influences upon the matter of the question. *Card 2* refers to the past influences which have shaped the matter. And *Card 3* symbolizes the completion of the matter or the influences that are needed to resolve the matter.

Keep in mind that two or three cards of the same Element may come up and serve to strengthen the Elemental qualities shown. Also remember that Fire and Water are opposing forces, as are Air and Earth. Air is compatible with Water and Fire, while Fire is compatible with Air and Earth. Compatible Cards will strengthen each other, while opposing cards will weaken each other and tend to emphasis the negative aspects of the Elements.✿

A MEDITATION ON THE PARTS OF THE SOUL

For this meditation, the Theoricus will need a black robe, nemyss, and the Outer Wand of Double Power. A Tarot deck should also be on hand. Prior to the meditation remove the following cards from the Tarot deck: *The Fool, The Magician, The Empress, Temperance* and *The Moon*.[75] Put the rest of the deck aside.

Perform a rite of relaxation. With the wand perform the LBRP.

Place the cards on the altar, or on the floor in front of you if you wish to be seated. The cards should be arranged thus: The farthest (Easternmost) card from you will be The Fool, below that will be two cards: The Magician and The Empress, to the right and left respectively. Below them is The Star. The final card, The Moon is at the bottom, closest to you.

---

[75] Refer to Chapter Four for additional information on these cards.

See the cards before you as representations of the parts of the Soul. Yechidah, Chiah, Neshamah, Ruach and Nephesh. (Your own physical body represents the G'uph.) Contemplate the cards for a few moments, observing their symbolism and coloring.

Close your eyes and begin breathing rhythmically after the manner of the Fourfold Breath. Continue breathing in this fashion for a few minutes before proceeding with the following visualization:

Picture The Fool card in your mind's eye. This is the card chosen to represent the *Yechidah,* centered in Kether. The 0 Key of the Tarot (also called the Spirit of Ether) is attributed to Aleph (the first Hebrew letter) which indicates absolute unity. The childlike innocence of The Fool represents extreme proximity to the Unmanifest; it is the *absolute beginning of all possibilities,* including the very root essence of spiritual nature. This is a glyph of the True, Immortal Self. Contemplate these ideas for a few minutes before continuing.

Visualize The Magician card before you. The First Key of the Tarot has been selected to represent the Chiah, located in Chokmah. The Magician or Magus of Power is an extension of The Fool. The Magician has the *ability to act* upon those thoughts created by the Fool. He represents the *True Will* and the inquisitive urge to become more than human. Spend some time contemplating these ideas.

Imagine The Empress card in front of you. The Third Tarot Key has been chosen to represent The Neshamah, stationed in Binah. The Empress symbolizes the Soul's True Aspiration or supreme state of consciousness—a higher universal love—the *intuitive power* that connects humanity with the Divine. She is the Key to the formation and unification of the universe. Meditate upon these concepts for a few moments.

Visualize these three cards together as generally representative of the highest aspirations of the Soul. Together, they comprise the "Superego," the "Oversoul" or the divine part of us which is eternal. As a group, all of these various parts of the greater Neshamah can be visualized by concentrating on the Tarot card of the Empress, the portion of the Triad which is closest to our conscious awareness.

Picture the Temperance card within your mind's eye. This card has been chosen to represent the *Ruach,* located in the five Sephiroth from Chesed to Yesod, but centered in Tiphareth. The Ruach symbolizes a middle stage between the Highest and lowest portions of the Soul where the ethical power to distinguish between good and evil is brought into operation. This conscious part of our being (intellect or ego) is the mind and reasoning powers where humanity is able to fashion thoughts into actions. The Temperance card alludes to a conscious exchange of energies between right and left, masculine and feminine and also between the higher and lower states of consciousness. It is therefore an important channel of communication between these various aspects of the Soul and of consciousness itself. Ponder this for a few moments before continuing.

Imagine The Moon card before you. This card has been selected to symbolize the *Nephesh*, centered in Yesod. The Key of the Moon represents both the subconscious mind and the lower astral, full of phantoms and illusions. It is also a card that depicts sexuality, wants, desires and instincts. This corresponds with the shadow-self of the Soul equivalent to the animal vitality and primal instincts. Meditate upon this.

Mentally embellish the symbolism of the cards in each rhythmic cycle. Feel the energy of each image until they become animated scenes moving within your imagination, proceeding from Nephesh to Yechidah and conversely from Yechidah to Nephesh in an alternating progression. As the likeness of one card merges into that of the one that follows it, see how the energies flow into one another. Also imagine the subconscious Moon, the Nephesh, collecting and reflecting impressions which stimulate the Ruach represented by Temperance—the cognizant decision-making aspect of the Soul. The Ruach transmits this consciously to the Neshamah or Divine Soul. This causes the descent of the Neshamah, symbolized by the Empress, into all portions of the Soul, bringing with it an awareness of the Divine Self. Continue this meditation for a short time.

After some time is spent on the visualizations, return to normal consciousness.

Face the East and say, *"Unto thee, Tetragrammaton, be ascribed the Kingdom, and the Power and the Glory. Unto the ages, Amen."*

Close the meditation by performing the Qabalistic Cross.✪

The 32nd Path of Tau

The *Sepher Yetzirah* or Book of Formation describes the 32nd Path as "The Administrative Intelligence, and it is so called because it directs and associates the motions of the seven Planets, directing all of them in their own proper courses." This is because the 32nd Path connects Malkuth (the Earth) with the balanced energies of the seven Planets, represented by the hexagram on the Tree of Life (from Yesod to Daath). The fact that it is described as the "Administrative Intelligence" shows that Spirit should be the directing Power behind the operation of all of the seven Planets and their corresponding attributes in the human vehicle.

The 32nd Path connects the physical world of Malkuth to Yesod, the universal subconscious realm and the astral blueprint which forms the foundation of material existence. It is a passage way from the material realm to the astral plane; a portal leading from sensory experience to inner examination. This Path is the point at which the student begins to explore the Tree of Life as well as his/her own inner makeup. The symbolism of the 32nd Path involves a descent into the Underworld or subconscious mind. This journey into the "unknown" realms of the mind includes the analysis of hidden fears and personal self-inflicted "demons" as well as an ascent to a new awareness of a higher state of consciousness. These shadows and ghosts of one's own making must be sufficiently dealt with before any further spiritual progress is made.

The 21st Key of the Tarot known as *The Universe* is attributed to this Path. The Magical Title of the this card is "The Great One of the Night of Time." Other symbols associated with this Path include the Hebrew letter Tau, the Planet Saturn (which also refers to the element of Earth) the seven-pointed star or heptagram, the Kerubim, the four Elements, and the twelve Signs of the Zodiac.

The letter Tau means "cross," which not only refers to a T-cross, but also to the four-armed cross of the Elements which are materialized in Malkuth. This cross also alludes to the inner Elements of the initiate's psyche which undergoes an intense process of introspection in the grades of Outer Order. Upon entering this Path, the student is fully immersed in an Alchemical process which began in the Zelator grade—that of *separation* into the various component parts of the mind. This can also be likened to an alimentary system of the human psyche, separating the gross from the refined, casting out impurities and reorganizing (cohobating) what remains, just as in Alchemy.

It must not be forgotten that this is also a Path of beginnings. The letters Aleph and Tau signify the beginning and the end, just as A to Z, or Alpha and Omega. And as with many things in Qabalah, the end of one thing is the beginning of another. The student on the Path of Tau is presented for the first time with all the tools necessary for further growth. The Elements, Planets and Signs presented in The Universe card are in fact the keys to the entire universe, which must be used intelligently in order to safely traverse the wonders of the cosmos. Whatever is encountered from this Path onward has its basis in how well one learns the lessons from the 32nd Path. In many ways, this Path summarizes the entire Qabalistic teachings—that balance and discrimination are essential to successfully scale the Tree of Life.✿

A JOURNEY ON THE 32nd PATH OF TAU[76]

For this ritual the Theoricus will need the robe, nemyss, red sandals, the Cubical Cross, and the Outer Wand of Double Power. The temple is to be arranged as in the Opening of the 2 = 9 grade. Upon the altar should be the Tarot Trump of the Universe. A comfortable place to sit and meditate should be arranged West of the altar.

---

[76] From our book *Secrets of a Golden Dawn Temple*.

After a period of relaxation has passed, go to the Northeast and say, *"HEKAS, HEKAS, ESTE BEBELOI! Far from this sacred place be the profane!"*

Go to the East. With the black end of the wand, perform the Lesser Banishing Ritual of the Pentagram.

Go the West of the altar. With the white end of the Wand of Double Power, trace a large letter TAU over the Tarot card. Visualize it in blue-violet (indigo). Intone the name of the letter twice. Give the Neophyte Signs toward the card. Put the wand aside, and take the Cubical Cross in your right hand.

With all your powers of concentration, look upon the card and comprehend it, consider all its meaning and symbolism. Give the Sign of the Zelator. At this point you may sit comfortably if you wish, but maintain a disassociation from the surrounding room. Behind the darkness of your closed eyelids, you begin to formulate the astral temple of the Sephirah Malkuth, as the journey begins:✿

From the complete blackness, a dim light appears which permits you to take in your surroundings. You are in the midst of a great temple with ten sides. The floor is divided into black and white tiles. The walls are built from large earthen bricks. Great oak columns support the ceiling which is pure rock crystal. In the Southern side of the temple is a great roaring hearth, whose fire warms the otherwise chill air within the temple. Behind you in the West is a great fountain of sculpted marble in the shape of an eagle with a fish in its claws—water spouts from the mouth of both creatures. In the Northern part of the temple are two enormous stones used for grinding wheat. A black ox is harnessed to the ancient milling device, slowly turning it as it crushes the hulls of the grain. At the East of the temple, is a large brazier of burning incense. The scent of Dittany of Crete fills the Air. At the center of the temple stands a black altar carved from solid oak. It is covered by a cloth divided into the four colors of Malkuth: citrine, russet, olive, and black. The top of the altar is white, and upon it is a bright burning flame.

Drawing nearer to the light, you intone the Divine Name of this temple, *Adonai ha-Aretz*. The flame burns brightly as you do so. Next intone the name of the Archangel who governs the Forces of this sphere, *Sandalphon*. Then vibrate the name of the Angelic order that operates in Malkuth, the *Ashim*, the Souls of Fire. Glowing embers dance around the central altar flame. Finally, you vibrate the name of the temple itself, *Malkuth*.

Within the swirling clouds of incense, a figure appears in the East. Appearing as a tall feminine form in robes of citrine, olive, russet and black is the archangel, Sandalphon with dark hair and compassionate brown eyes. Instinctively, you give the Sign of the Enterer. Sandalphon answers with the Sign of Silence. She speaks:

"You have entered the Immeasurable Region. This place is called THRAA, The Gate. It is the Gate of Justice, The Gate of Life and the Gate of Death. The Gate of Tears, and the Gate of Prayer. It is the Gate of the Garden of Eden and the Gate of the Daughter of the Mighty Ones. By what Sign have you entered herein?"

You answer by giving the Zelator Sign. She asks why you have come to this place. You hold up the Cubical Cross.

You face the Archangel across the light of the altar, as you prepare for your journey into the 32nd Path. Finally, Sandalphon turns toward the East where is a great wooden door which had previously been obscured by the smoke from the incense. The Tarot card of *The Universe* hangs like a veil in front of it. Sandalphon traces a cross in the air with her hand and the veil parts. A large metal Tau is now clearly seen on the heavy oak door. The Archangel moves aside after showing the way. It is up to you to open the door. Undaunted, you approach it and give the Sign of the Theoricus. Holding out the Cubical Cross, you trace with it a large letter Tau. The door slowly opens.

Beyond the door, you enter a lush meadow ablaze with flowers. To the North are snow-capped mountains and cool running streams. To the South is a low-lying desert. Before you in the East, the dawning Sun is breaking over the low rolling hills. This is the path you have chosen. Sandalphon leads the way.

Time and space seem distorted as they often do on astral journeys. You pass by many fields, farms, and villages, covering vast distances in what seems like a very short interval. The breeze is cool against your skin, and a hint of storax is in the air.

The path you are on leads into the hill country which has less trees than did the grassy meadow land before it. The clay beneath your feet has given way to sandy soil. The air is warmer and there is no breeze here. The trail leads straight into a hillside where there is a cavern leading into the earth. On either side of the jagged stone opening is a column cut from solid rock. The base of each pillar is carved into the shape of a lotus flower, while the capital is sculpted into the form of a pomegranate. Before each column stands a gigantic muscular figure with the head of a beast. Their human bodies are covered by tunics, but the black fur and pointed features of jackals stick out beneath their nemysses. The figure on the left holds a large sword, while the figure on the right holds a staff entwined with serpents in one hand, and a red lantern in the other.

Sandalphon tells you to continue onward. This is as far as she will take you. As you approach the Anubian guards, they lunge forward with a growl, crossing their implements to block your advance. "Whence comest Thou?" they demand to know.

You respond by giving the Sign of the Zelator and saying, "I have entered the Immeasurable Region. I have passed through the Gate of Life and the Gate of Death. I seek to journey upon the Path of Tau which leadeth between the pillars from the Kingdom to the Foundation."

"In what signs and symbols do ye come?" they ask.

You answer by standing in the Sign of the Theoricus. "In the divine name of *Shaddai El Chai*; in the word *Mem Heh* and in this symbol of the Solid Greek Cubical Cross, which contains the divine number, twenty-two."

The twin guards step back. Anubis of the East with lantern and staff, turns to enter the cave. You give the Signs of the Neophyte and follow him in.

Just inside the entrance is a small antechamber with a black and white tiled floor. Four large winged statues stare at you without emotion. All have human bodies, but with different heads. One has the head of lion. Another has the head of an eagle. There is also a bull, and finally the winged form of a man. You pass by these silent sentinels holding the cross high above you.

The light from outside of the cave soon fades as you descend deeper and deeper into the cave. Anubis leads silently on as the darkness closes in. The floor of the cave is rough, and you must feel the ground carefully with your feet to keep from stumbling. The ceiling presses in and you are forced to crouch at times. The path twists from one side to the other. At times you feel like you are climbing toward the surface again, only to follow your guide on another quick descent. Your sense of direction is gone—you quicken your pace to catch up to Anubis so that you won't get hopelessly lost. The light from his lantern makes strange and sinister shadows appear on the cavern walls. Voices from your past come to taunt you on this journey: school children calling you names, adults reprimanding you, peers telling you of your limitations. All the voices try to dissuade you from going deeper into the cave. "Go Back!" they warn. "You can't make it!" "It's too dangerous!" "You're too weak!" You know that the voices are merely echoes—ghosts—archetypes from your own mind that are uneasy at the prospect of being found out. You ignore them and press onward. The dark journey through the twisted rock seems to take forever.

Finally, a dim light ahead is a welcome sight. Your guide leads you into a large chamber where the smell of burning oil from torches fills the room. The walls and floor are plain and seem to have been cut completely out of solid rock with simple tools. From a great dark hole in one wall of the room, a slow-moving stream of water fills a gutter carved out of the floor and flows to the opposite wall. There it flows under a huge stone door. A small number of beings are in the room with you. Apes with jeweled collars hold the ropes that are attached to the two sides of the great door. Many celestial beings with both human and animal heads can be seen bearing all kinds of food, incense, weapons, staffs, jewels, jars of perfume and more. There are also a few men and women in all manner of Egyptian dress—some in fine silken clothes—others in simple tunics. Everyone in the room appears to be waiting for something.

"This is the *Arrit*," Anubis tells you," the antechamber of the *Tuat*—the Underworld. This is where I guide the Souls of the dead. This too, is where the dead Sun-god RA enters the Underworld from the West—for he is a dead god when the darkness of Night rules the sky. This is also *Amenet*, the Hidden Place. All assembled here wait for the coming of Ra. The Souls of the dead hope to be permitted to enter the Sektet Boat of Ra—to travel in safety through the terrors of the Tuat—and finally be reborn with him at the Dawning Light of the Eastern sky. Behold, it is time!"

The anticipation of the assembly grows and is rewarded by the sight of two long lines of priests pulling heavy ropes. Finally the long prow of a boat enters the chamber from the dark hole in the wall. The boat made from reeds, is light and slender. Thoth, the ibis-headed god of Wisdom stands at the bow, to guide the vessel. At the center of the craft is a shrine where the Sun-god sits enthroned. He has the body of a man with the tawny head and piercing eyes of a hawk. A large Solar disc crowns his nemyss, and he holds an ankh in one hand and a phoenix-headed staff in the other. The scarab, Khepera, surmounts the crown of the figure like a halo. But the god is old and has the pallor of death about him.

The god Horus stands at the rear of ship as an escort. At this marvelous sight, a roar of praise erupts from those assembled in the chamber.

At the center of the room, the boat stops and is boarded by the Souls who have stood waiting for it. Anubis leads you to the craft. "You must continue your journey under the protection of Ra," he tells you. "I must return to give guidance to the dead. Have courage. The Tuat is filled with sights both wondrous and terrible. Fear nothing and your strength shall see you through."

From the boat, a hand is offered. You take it and climb aboard, giving a final farewell to Anubis, who is already on his way back to the surface—the light from his lamp bobs through the cavern tunnel. Finding a seat with the other passengers, you settle in for the ride. The apes you saw earlier pull on the ropes which open the great stone doors leading to the Tuat. Slowly the Sektet boat moves forward and enters the underworld.

The place called the Tuat is so enormous that it is difficult to tell whether it is enclosed under the earth or if it exists at some point in space beyond the earth. The stream has widened into a river in the middle of a valley, on either side of which is a mountain range. It is a noisy place inhabited by many creatures. Monstrous beasts rummage about in the muddy shores. The Souls of the dead are everywhere, milling around along the river bank and swimming alongside the boat. A few are permitted to climb on board, but others are turned away, because each Soul must spend a certain amount of time in the underworld before re-entering the land of the Living.

The ship continues to travel through the twelve divisions of the Tuat, known as the twelve hours of the Night. Twin Pylons with serpent guardians mark each division. So many incredible sights appear that you can only sit and watch as gods battle hostile Spirits, evil serpents and crocodiles. There are great pits of fire that appear in the middle of the river. Hostile Spirits harangue the dead who walk along the shore. There are also benevolent and helpful creatures whose bodies are formed from many different animals. At times it seems like many lesser gods appear from nowhere to pull the ship forward with serpents instead of ropes. Sacred animals such as bulls, winged cobras and baboons join in the processions through the Underworld. And at one point, the great goddess Isis appears on the boat to utter magical words to repel the enemies of Ra.

At the sixth division of the Tuat, the Sektet boat stops at a great stone shrine topped with spearheads. Inside, the god Osiris is seated upon the summit of a flight of nine steps. He wears a double crown and holds in one hand a scepter and in the other an ankh, the symbol of Life. Before him is a pair of scales and a company of lesser gods. The Sektet boat pauses in homage to the god who reigns over the Underworld—Osiris, he who judges the dead. The Lord of Life, triumphant over Death.

After leaving the shrine, the journey continues as before, until eventually, the Sektet boat reaches the eleventh division of the Tuat—and the eleventh hour of the night. At this point, great pits of fire—each attended by a goddess—appear ahead of the boat, and the battle between gods and demons becomes decidedly more intense. The voices from your past which had earlier harassed you in the cave return to bother you now at this crucial moment. But you have already won over them in the knowledge that they are merely programmed archetypes within your own psyche, which do not wish to lose their position of prominence within your mind. In this last-ditch effort to force you to feel weak, inane, and guilty, the voices are desperate in the attempt to make you fail to complete this voyage.

The god Horus takes command of the vessel and orders all the demons and enemies of Ra to be consumed in the blazing fires. The attendant goddesses see that it is done. At this point, you also will your own personal demons into the purging flames. The ghostly voices are silenced. A sense of great relief and calm overtakes you, as the Sektet boat glides into the Twelfth Hour of the Night.

Twelve gods, all loyal servants of Ra, now pull the ship, which is no longer sailing on the river, but through the belly of a sacred serpent. In this surprisingly tranquil division of the Tuat, you hear in a whisper, the serpent's name, "Ka-en-Ankh-neteru, the Life of the gods." The circle of the Tuat is near its end, but there is utter darkness in the bowels of this serpent. There is also a feeling of nervous excitement among the Souls aboard the vessel. The horrors of the Tuat are in the past now, and a great transformation is about to take place.

As the ship enters the throat of the serpent, the enormous jaws begin to open. Beyond them is the indigo of the night sky, speckled with stars. As the boat slides off the tongue of the animal, the stars and Planets themselves erupt into a song of praise for the reborn Sun god. Twelve goddesses pull the ship into the sky. The Sektet boat of the night is no more. It is now the Matet boat of Day sailing into the Eastern part of the sky. Ra himself has transformed before your eyes. No longer pale and old, the god glows with the life of youth. His Solar disc lights up the countryside far below in all directions.

Of the fortunate Souls who have traversed the terrors of the Tuat in Ra's ship, some are rewarded with a new birth upon the earth, while others remain in the sky journeying at will through the universe. You, too, feel reborn and strengthened with the dawning of the sun upon the skies over the earth. The grass is wet and glistening with morning dew. Humans and animals below are just beginning to stir from their sleep and go about their daily activities. You realize that your journey upon the Path of Tau is nearing its end, but for the Sun god this journey is a nightly occurrence. Silently, you thank the god for helping you travel this path. The warmth of the Sun lulls you into a restful meditation.

When you open your eyes again, you see that an entire day has passed while you meditated. The last rays of light are fading as Ra's boat enters the Western sky. Under the earth, the ship again enters the dark Arrit, the antechamber to the Tuat. This is the end of your journey through the underworld. You realize that you will traverse this path again, perhaps many times. However you know that the journey will be easier each time. As the boat glides into the chamber, you see the familiar form of Anubis, who reaches out his hand to help you down from the vessel. With a final prayer of thanks to Ra, you turn and follow the jackal-headed god through the winding tunnel to the cave entrance. Once you are outside the cave, Anubis joins his twin and stands guard at the threshold. You salute them both with the Sign of the Theoricus.

Sandalphon is waiting on the path which leads to Malkuth. Following her, you return to the Tenth Sephirah. The Angel seals the great wooden door behind you after entering the temple. The flame upon the altar is a welcome sight after such an arduous adventure. The great fireplace, fountain and oaken walls are very familiar and comforting. Standing before the altar, you partake of the sacred flame a few moments before leaving the temple. Saying goodbye to Sandalphon, you salute with the Projection Sign. She answers with the Sign of Silence.✪

Bring your astral self back into your body and make yourself slowly aware of the physical room around you. Do not get up too quickly.

Perform the LBRP with the black end of the wand.

Say, *"I now declare this temple duly closed"*✪

AN INVOCATION OF THE ELEMENT OF AIR

For the grade of Theoricus

For this ritual the Theoricus will need a black Outer Order robe, black and white striped nemyss, the Outer Wand of Double Power. Upon the altar should be a yellow candle, a rose, and one or more of the talismanic emblems mentioned on page 297. The temple is to be arranged in accordance with the Theoricus Hall (as in the Second part of the initiation ceremony).

Relax for a few moments and perform the Fourfold Breath.

Go to the Northeast and say, *"HEKAS, HEKAS, ESTE BEBELOI!"*

With the black end of the wand, perform the Lesser Banishing Ritual of the Pentagram.

> (Say the following invocation:) *Such a Fire existeth, extending through the rushings of Air. Or even a Fire formless, whence cometh the Image of a Voice. Or even a flashing Light, abounding, revolving, whirling forth, crying aloud.*

Remain in the East. With the white end of the wand, trace the lesser invoking pentagram. Thrust the wand through the center of the figure and vibrate, *"YOD HEH VAV HEH!"* Do this same pentagram and intone the same name in all four quarters, going from East to South, West and North. Return to the East. Say:

> In the Divine Name SHADDAI EL CHAI, I open this temple in the element of Air. May the Archangel RAPHAEL look with favor upon this ceremony! May the Angel CHASSAN and the ruler ARAL be also in attendance! I have gained admission to this temple through the Badge of the Caduceus of Hermes. Hear me! I am one who has received the Mystic Title of Poraios De Rejectis and the symbol of RUACH. I have been brought from among the Rejected. As a Lord/Lady of the 32nd Path, I invoke the powers of Air to bear witness to my spiritual endeavor. Grant me the knowledge of the Element of Air and the Astral Realm, so that I may obtain Greater Understanding of Hidden Things and thereby advance in the Great Work.

Circumambulate the temple 3 times, saluting with the Neophyte Signs when passing the East.

Go to the West and face East. Give the Adoration to the Lord of the Universe:

> Holy art Thou, Lord of the Universe!
> Holy art Thou, Whom Nature hath not formed!
> Holy art Thou, the Vast and the Mighty One!
> Lord of the Light, and of the Darkness!

Go to the East and give the Theoricus Sign. Recite the Prayer of the Sylphs:

> Spirit of Life! Spirit of Wisdom! Whose breath giveth forth and withdraweth the form of all things: Thou, before Whom the life of beings is but a shadow which changeth, and a vapor which passeth: Thou, who mountest upon the clouds, and who walkest upon the wings of the wind.

> Thou, who breathest forth Thy Breath, and endless space is peopled: Thou, who drawest in Thy Breath, and all that cometh from Thee, returneth unto Thee! Ceaseless Motion, in Eternal stability, be Thou eternally blessed! We praise Thee and we bless Thee in the Changeless Empire of Created Light, of Shades, of Reflections, and of Images—

> And we aspire without cessation unto Thy Immutable and Imperishable Brilliance. Let the Ray of Thy Intelligence and the warmth of Thy Love penetrate even unto us!

> Then that which is volatile shall be fixed; the Shadow shall be a Body; the Spirit of Air shall be a Soul; the Dream shall be a Thought. And no more

shall we be swept away by the Tempest, but we shall hold the bridles of the Winged Steeds of Dawn. And we shall direct the course of the Evening Breeze to fly before Thee!

O Spirit of Spirits! O Eternal Soul of Souls! O Imperishable Breath of Life! O Creative Sigh! O Mouth which breathest forth and withdrawest the life of all beings, in the flux and reflux of Thine Eternal Word, which is the Divine Ocean of Movement and of Truth!

Give the Theoricus Sign. Go to the West of the altar. With the white end of the wand, trace the lesser invoking pentagram over the rose. Put the wand aside.

Inhale the fragrance of the rose. As you partake of the rose, meditate on the talismanic emblem you have chosen for an extended period of time. Take as much time as you need for the meditation.

Perform the Reverse Circumambulation. Then go to the East and Say:

I now release any Spirits that may have been imprisoned by this ceremony. Depart in peace to your abodes and habitations. Go with the blessings of SHADDAI EL CHAI!

Perform the LBRP with the black end of the wand.

(Say:) *I now declare this temple duly closed.* ✿

Suggested Reading

The Only Way to Learn Astrology, Volumes 1, 2, and 3 by Marion D. March and Joan McEvers. (An excellent trilogy of books which will help the magician become proficient in understanding the science of Astrology.)

The Complete Book of Incense, Oils & Brews by Scott Cunningham
(Note: Write a report on the book. Try to find new associations of incenses that you think could also be applied to the Sephiroth.)

Cunningham's Encyclopedia of Magical Herbs by Scott Cunningham
(Note: Write a report on the book. Try to find new associations of herbs that could be applied to the Sephiroth.)

The Secret Life of Plants by Christopher Bird and Peter Thompkins
(An intriguing look at the hidden powers of plants.)

"Images of Growth in the Hermetic Arts," by Gareth Knight—published in *The Golden Dawn Journal, Book 3: The Art of Hermes*

Outlines of the History of Greek Philosophy by Eduard Zeller

Porphyry's Launching Points to the Realm of Mind: An Introduction to the Neoplatonic Philosophy of Plotinus translated by Kenneth Guthrie

On the Mysteries by Iamblichus

The Science of Breath by Yogi Ramacharaka
(Although this book was written in the Esoteric Tradition of the East, many of the techniques described can also be applied to the Western Esoteric Tradition.)

Jungian Dream Interpretation: A Handbook of Theory and Practice by James A. Hall

Maps of the Mind by Charles Hampden-Turner

Toward a Psychology of Being by Abraham H. Maslow

The Rhizome and the Flower: The Perennial Philosophy, Yeats and Jung by James Olney

Some Final Suggestions

- Obtain a 8.5 x 11 black-and-white copy of the Tarot card THE UNIVERSE and paint it, or draw your own version of the card.

- Make colored drawings of the four Kerubim. Devise your own meditation for incorporating these figures.

- Draw your personal impression of a sylph.

- Draw your personal impression of a nature Spirit such as a nymph.

- Observe the phases of the Moon each and every night for one entire Lunar cycle (28 days). Note your observations in your magical diary. Also take note what Zodiacal Sign the Moon is in.

- Take note of where Luna falls in your own Zodiacal chart. Write a brief report on how you think you are affected by Luna's position in your natal chart.

- Take note of any Planets that are located in Air Signs in your own Zodiacal chart. Write a brief report on how you think you are effected by them.

- Erect fifty natal charts. (You may obtain natal information from people you know or from Astrology books that list such information on famous individuals.)

- Prepare your own mixture of incense for the Sephirah of Yesod, using your ingenuity and the source book listed on page 313.

- Prepare your own personal mixture of incense based upon your Zodiacal Sign, Elemental affiliation and other personal information or preferences.

- Find out how you can become personally involved in reducing Air pollution.

- Obtain a biology text book and write a report on the life cycle and growth of plants.

- Grow an herb or plant from a package of seeds. Incorporate the plant into your mediations while in the 2 = 9 grade.

- Take an active role in the welfare of plant life, be it the saving of a rain forest, or the landscaping of your front yard.

Examinations

(Answers for all exams are given in the back of this book.)

QUIZ 0 *(The Ritual)*

1. What is the Grand Word of the grade of Theoricus?
2. What is the Mystic Number of the Theoricus grade?
3. What is the Password of the Theoricus grade derived from the Mystic Number?
4. What is the Battery of knocks attributed to the Theoricus grade?
5. What is the Grip of the Theoricus grade?
6. What is the Sign of the Theoricus grade?
7. What is the Elemental symbol given to the Theoricus?
8. List the name of the Element attributed to this grade (in English and in Hebrew.)
9. Which direction is associated with this Element?
10. What is the Mystic Title conferred upon a Theoricus?
11. What does the Mystic Title mean?
12. Which Sephirah is associated with this grade?
13. List the Divine (Atziluthic) Name of this Sephirah.
14. Name the Great Archangel of the Element of this grade.

15. Name the Kerubic Sign of this Element.
16. What are the Three Great Secret Names of God borne upon the Enochian Banners of the Quarter?
17. Name the Great Enochian King of the Quarter.
18. How are the cross and triangle arranged on the altar?
19. What does the arrangement of the cross and triangle symbolize?
20. What does "2 = 9" signify?
21. What is the Admission Badge to the 32nd Path?
22. What is the Admission Badge to the temple of the 9th Sephirah of Yesod?
23. The Admission Badge is identical to the lamen of which officer?
24. The distinct sections of a ritual are called "Points." Each grade ritual has at least three Points: an opening, a closing, and at least one middle point between the opening and the closing. How many middle points are there in the Theoricus Ritual?
25. Briefly describe what happens in each of the middle points of this ritual.
26. During the Theoricus oath, what gesture does the candidate make in swearing his/her oath to the Powers of the Element?
27. What Hebrew letters are associated with the three portals in the East of the temple?
28. What do these portals signify?
29. List the four Kerubim encountered by the candidate in this ritual.
30. What is the name of the Kerub in the East? What Egyptian Air deity is associated with this Kerub? What Egyptian Solar deity is associated with this Kerub?
31. What is the name of the Kerub in the South? What Egyptian Fire deity is associated with this Kerub? What Egyptian Solar deity is associated with this Kerub?
32. What is the name of the Kerub in the West? What Egyptian Water deity is associated with this Kerub? What Egyptian Solar deity is associated with this Kerub?
33. What is the name of the Kerub in the North? What Egyptian Earth deity is associated with this Kerub? What Egyptian Solar deity is associated with this Kerub?
34. Describe the 21st Key of the Tarot.
35. In addition to the Tarot Key, what four items are found on the altar in the first part of the ritual?
36. In this grade, what does the station of the Hegemon symbolize?
37. In this grade, what does the station of the Keryx symbolize?
38. In addition to the Tarot Key and the Admission Badges, what diagrams are displayed in this grade?
39. What is the arrangement of the cross and triangle in this grade? What are the reasons for this?

QUIZ—SECTION 1 *(Basic Astrology—The Aspects; Erecting a Chart)*

1. The ____ of an aspect is the number of degrees of difference from the exact angle that is permitted for each aspect.
2. What is the angle of an Opposition?
3. What is the angle of a Sextile?
4. What is the most difficult aspect to understand?
5. What is a Grand Trine?
6. How many "Signs" apart are two Planets in Trine?
7. How many "Signs" apart are two Planets in Square?
8. Which is the widest aspect?
9. What is a wide or "weak" aspect called?
10. What is an exact aspect called?
11. What is the angle of a Conjunction?
12. What aspect indicates a stalemate or stand-off between Planetary energies?
13. How many "Signs" apart are two Planets in Sextile?
14. What is a Stellium?
15. Sextiles involve Signs of opposite gender. True or False?
16. Planets in Conjunction can sometimes be found in adjacent Signs. True or False?
17. Which aspect gives more emphasis to a Sign?
18. How many "Signs" apart are two Planets in Opposition?
19. Sextiles are the tension factors in a chart. True or False?
20. What is the angle of a square?
21. Conjunctions are always favorable. True or False?
22. What is a T-Cross?
23. What is another name for Inconjunct?
24. How many "Signs" apart are two Planets that are Inconjunct?
25. What is the angle of a Trine?
26. Having several Trines in the chart is always positive. True or False?
27. Inconjunct involves Signs that are totally unrelated to each other. True or False?
28. Trines indicate harmony, creativity and ease of movement. True or False?
29. A person experiencing Inconjunction often feels that the solution to a problem is just around the corner when in fact it isn't. True or false?
30. What is a Grand Cross?
31. Which aspect has to do with "perception?"
32. Inconjunction signifies action and challenge. True or False?
33. A Sextile promotes communication, cooperation and blending between Planets. True or False?
34. What is the angle of a Semi-Sextile?
35. How many degrees comprise the circumference of the Zodiacal Wheel?
36. How many degrees comprise one Zodiacal Sign?
37. What is the Prime Meridian?

38. Circles of geographic measurement which occupy fixed positions North and South of the Equator are called what?
39. Circles of geographic measurement which occupy fixed positions East and West of the Prime Meridian are called what?
40. What is GMT?
41. What is the actual time taken by the Earth to complete a total revolution upon its axis known as?
42. What is the adjustment between Sidereal and regular time called? How is it determined?
43. How does one determine the Longitude Equivalent in Time?
44. The Local Sidereal Time at birth and at the place of birth is crucial to determining what two factors of the Horoscope?
45. How does one determine the aspects when drawing up a Zodiacal chart?
46. What kind of aspect occurs when one Planet is said to move toward another?
47. What kind of aspect occurs when one Planet is said to move beyond another?

QUIZ—SECTION 2 (Basic Alchemy—Alchemical Operations)

1. Which of the four Alchemical stages is related to Fire?
2. Which of the four Alchemical stages is related to Air?
3. Which of the four Alchemical stages is related to Water?
4. Which of the four Alchemical stages is related to Earth?
5. What is another name for the "Whitening" stage?
6. What is another name for the "Reddening" stage?
7. What is another name for the "Blackening" stage?
8. What is another name for the "Yellowing" stage?
9. Which stage indicates a "washing" process?
10. Which stage was later dropped by fifteenth and sixteenth century Alchemists?
11. Which stage indicates the raising of heat to its highest intensity?
12. Which stage indicates putrefaction?
13. Which operation involves the amalgamation of the various elements?
14. Which operation involves adding precious metals as a "starter" material?
15. Which operation involves the "wetting" of dry material?
16. Which operation involves solidification?
17. Which operation involves extraction by volatilization or distillation?
18. Which operation involves the work of transmutation into silver and gold?
19. Which operation involves the first change to be seen?
20. Which operation involves reducing the principles to atoms, but not by burning?
21. Which operation involves raising the quantity and quality of the powder or stone?
22. Which operation involves raising the power or virtue of the stone enabling it to transmute?

23. Which operation involves separation in a sealed vessel?
24. Which operation involves rhythmic cycling of the process of circulation?
25. List the colors of Alchemy and the Planets that can be associated with them.
26. Which operation involves the separation of liquids in a vessel?
27. Which operation is also called Circulation or Rectification?
28. Which operation involves dissolving a solid into a liquid?

QUIZ—SECTIONS 3, 4, and 5 (*Spiritual Entities, Qabalah, Parts of the Soul, The Correspondences of Yesod*)

1. What is the English translation of the name "Yesod?"
2. What is the Magical Image of Yesod?
3. What is the Spiritual Experience of Yesod?
4. What is the Lineal figure associated with Yesod?
5. What are the symbols of Yesod?
6. What is the name of the Archangel of Yesod?
7. What is the Divine Atziluthic name of Yesod?
8. What is the name of the Angelic Choir of Yesod?
9. What is Yesod's Briatic color?
10. What part of the human anatomy does Yesod correspond to?
11. Yesod is attributed to which House of Assiah?
12. Name the Tarot cards associated with Yesod.
13. What is the Virtue associated with Yesod?
14. What is the Vice associated with Yesod?
15. To which of the four Qabalistic Worlds is Yesod assigned?
16. Elemental Spirits have hierarchies similar to that of Qabalistic Angels. True or False?
17. Angels and Archangels are considered specific aspects of God. True or False?
18. An astral Spirit is a pure and high Spirit of unmixed good in office and operation. True or False?
19. All Elemental Spirits are considered good. True or False?
20. Astral Spirits are anthropomorphic symbols of what we believe to be good or holy. True or False?
21. What are some Greek names for Spirit?
22. What is the Greek name for Soul?
23. The human Soul is the divine center in humanity. True or false?
24. List the three principle parts of the Soul as defined by the Qabalists. Give both English and Hebrew spellings.
25. Which part of the Soul is further divided into three parts answering to the three Supernals? Give both English and Hebrew spellings of these divisions.
26. Which part of the Soul is centered in Chokmah and represents the True Will?
27. Which part of the Soul remains dormant in the average person until awakened through spiritual growth?

28. Which part of the Soul is centered in Kether as the true, divine and immortal Self?
29. Which part of the Soul is the first part to be activated in every human being at birth?
30. Which part of the Soul corresponds to the Mind and reasoning powers?
31. Which part of the Soul corresponds to the dark side of the human Soul?
32. Which part of the Soul corresponds to the animal vitality and instincts?
33. Which part of the Soul corresponds to Binah?
34. Which part of the Soul corresponds to the intuitive power that connects humanity with the Divine?
35. Which part of the Soul corresponds to the ethical power to distinguish between good and evil?
36. What is the name of the additional portion of the Soul that is closely tied to the condition of the human body?

QUIZ—SECTION 6 *(The Correspondences of Air)*

1. List the incense(s) which correspond to the Sephiroth.
2. List the incense(s) which correspond to the Zodiacal Signs.
3. List the incense(s) which correspond to the Planets.
4. List the incense(s) which correspond to the Elements.
5. What is the Hebrew name for Air? Give both English and Hebrew spellings.
6. What is the Outer Divine Name of Air in Hebrew? Give both English and Hebrew spellings.
7. What is the Hebrew name for the Cardinal Point of East? Give both English and Hebrew spellings.
8. What is the name of the Archangel of Air? Give both English and Hebrew spellings.
9. What is the name of the Angel of Air? Give both English and Hebrew spellings.
10. What is the name of the Ruler of Air? Give both English and Hebrew spellings.
11. What is the name of the King of Air?
12. What is the name of the Order of Elementals associated with Air?
13. What is the name of the Assyro-Babylonian deity associated with Air whose name means "sky?"
14. List two Assyro-Babylonian deities associated with thunder and storm.
15. List two Egyptian deities associated with the sky.
16. What is the name of the Egyptian Air deity who was the equivalent of the Greek god Atlas?
17. What omnipotent Greek god was associated with the sky, thunder, and rain?
18. What Greek sky goddess was the champion of women?
19. List the Greek gods associated with the four winds.
20. Name the additional Greek wind god who was the inventor of ships' sails.
21. What was the name of the Teutonic god of thunder?

QUIZ—SECTION 7 (*The Correspondences of Luna*)

1. List some of the things that are ruled by the Moon.
2. List some of the things that the days and hours of Luna are used for in magic.
3. Approximately how many days does it take to complete the Lunar cycle?
4. Which Phase(s) or Quarter(s) of the Moon's cycle takes effect when Sol and Luna are at a 90 degree square to one another?
5. Which Phase(s) or Quarter(s) of the Moon's cycle takes effect when Sol and Luna are opposite each other?
6. Which Phase(s) or Quarter(s) of the Moon's cycle takes effect when Sol and Luna are conjunct?
7. Which Quarter represents the waning Moon?
8. Which Quarter represents the waxing Moon?
9. Which Quarter commences with the Full Moon?
10. Which Quarter commences with the New Moon?
11. What is the meaning of the Lunar symbol on the Tree of Life?
12. What is the Hebrew name of Luna?
13. What is the name of the Archangel of Luna?
14. What is the day associated with Luna?
15. What is the name of the Planetary Intelligence of Luna?
16. What is the name of the Planetary Spirit of Luna?
17. What is the name of the Olympic Planetary Spirit of Luna?
18. What metal is associated with Luna?
19. Name some of the gemstones associated with Luna.
20. Name some of the Trees associated with Luna.
21. Name some of the Herbs/Plants associated with Luna.
22. Name some of the animals associated with Luna.
23. What is the name of the Assyro-Babylonian god of the Moon?
24. What is the name of the Egyptian Moon god who is known as "The Navigator?"
25. Name the Greek goddess of magic and enchantments.
26. Name the Egyptian Moon god who is a form of Thoth.
27. What is the name of the Greek goddess of the Full Moon?
28. What is the name of the Greek Moon goddess who is know as the "Lady of the Beasts?"
29. What is the name of the Greek goddess of the New Moon?
30. What Planet complements Luna on the Macrocosmic Hexagram? List some characteristics that these two Planets share. Name some of the deities associated with this Planet.

QUIZ—SECTIONS 8 and 9 (*Plants and Herbs, Admission Badges, and Diagrams*)

1. What is the name of the process used by plants to manufacture food?
2. What is the name of the process used by plants to covert living material out of nonliving material?
3. The reproductive processes of plants depend heavily on the _____.
4. What happens when plants cease to grow?
5. Blossoming flowers are universal symbols of what?
6. What type of plant is a universal symbol of wisdom and spiritual growth?
7. Why should a student have a thorough knowledge of the properties of plants before using them in herbal magic?
8. What are some of the factors used to ascertain the powers and correspondences of plants and herbs?
9. List some of the plants which correspond to the seven Planets.
10. List some of the plants which correspond to the four elements.
11. What are nature Spirits called in Greek mythology?
12. Which form of these nature Spirits are said to preside over brooks and streams?
13. Which form of these nature Spirits are said to preside over forests?
14. Which form of these nature Spirits are said to be mortal?
15. Which form of these nature Spirits are said to preside over mountains and grottos?
16. Which four types of these nature Spirits are said to preside over the woods and valleys?
17. Which form of these nature Spirits is most closely related to trees?
18. In Greek mythology, a group of rural Spirits presided over springs and rivers. What were these horse-like creatures called?
19. What were a group of goat-like forest Spirits called in Greek mythology?
20. Name the Admission Badge for the 32nd Path of Tau.
21. What does this Badge symbolize?
22. The Admission Badge for the 32nd Path contains the 22 letters of the Hebrew alphabet. As a whole, what do the letters on the front of Badge refer to? Name these letters.
23. What letter is placed in the center and what does it refer to?
24. What do the letters on the back of the Badge refer to? Name these letters.
25. Symbolically, what two letters are missing from the back of the Badge and why?
26. What three letters cover the remaining three sides of the Mem-arm? What do these letters represent?
27. What three letters cover the remaining three sides of the Tau-arm? What do these letters represent?
28. What three letters cover the remaining three sides of the Aleph-arm? What do these letters represent?

29. What three letters cover the remaining three sides of the Shin-arm? What do these letters represent?
30. What is the Admission Badge to the temple of Yesod?
31. Describe this Admission Badge as it relates to the Tree of Life.
32. As a whole, what does this symbol represent?
33. What are the names of the animals on this Badge and what do they represent?

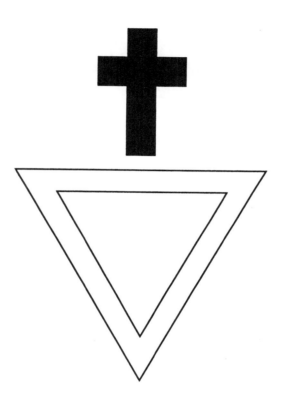

CHAPTER FOUR

The Practicus Grade

③=8

I n the 3 = 8 grade the initiate takes the *third* Elemental initiation into the *eighth* Sephirah, Hod, on the Qabalistic Tree, continuing the process of spiritual Alchemy within the aspirant's psyche. For the first time the initiate is faced with the prospect of stepping off the relative "safety" of the Middle Pillar and onto the Black Pillar of Severity. The Practicus grade thus represents a point in the initiate's spiritual growth where more weight is theoretically placed on one side of the aspirant's psychic scales of balance. It is important to remember that once the student begins on this path of Elemental introspection, *all four* Elemental Initiations should be completed. Even if the student decides in the middle of this course that the Golden Dawn System is not his/her spiritual path, all of the Elements should still be equilibrated within the mind for the sake of harmony. One should not be left hanging off balance on one pillar or the other.

The title of Practicus is derived from the Greek word for "practitioner." The Element offered for the process of transmutation in this grade is Water, or rather the watery portion of the aspirant's psyche (in actuality it is the *Water of Malkuth in Assiah*).[77]

Initiates of this grade usually experience a sense of ease and relief at having passed through the astral turbulence of Yesod (Although the initiation ceremony itself can sometimes prove to be quite eventful.) In fact the nurturing Waters of Hod can feel truly comforting to those initiates who have experienced firsthand the harmful effects of an unbalanced materialistic society. The problem is that sometimes students are reluctant to leave the Water temple for the Fire grade of Philosophus. There is also an increased awareness of student's own creative faculties, some of which may have remained dormant until this time. The Planet assigned to this grade is Mercury, the orb of the Intellect, communication and expression.

The 3 = 8 ceremony can be summed up as follows: After the standard (self-initiatory) rite of opening, the forces of Elemental Water are invoked. Then the candidate must prove that s/he has grasped the secrets of the Theoricus grade and swear an oath. Between the spheres of Malkuth and Hod lies the 31st Path of Shin, a journey of psychic purification and consecration through Elemental Fire. On this path, the candidate is confronted by three figures known as the *Kabiri*, or godforms from the Samothracian Mysteries. These figures symbolize the various

---

[77] And also *Hod of Malkuth*.

aspects and attributes of Elemental Fire. On the path of Shin the Kabiri expose the candidate to the different energies of Fire which are used to purge the aspirant of psychic impurities before the Water temple is entered. After completing the 31st Path, the candidate is shown the Tarot card of Judgment.

Next the mysteries of the 30th Path of Resh are revealed to the candidate by the Kabiri who take on various Solar and seasonal aspects. The Path of Resh is a journey of intellectual awareness where the student is exposed to the Higher Powers that have gone into the formation of his/her own personality. (Whereas the 31st Path is a journey of purification, the 30th Path is one of consecration.) When the journey on the Path of Resh is finished, the candidate is shown the Tarot card of The Sun.

The later part of the ritual, involves the initiate's entry into the temple of Hod. During this time the aspirant is shown symbolism concerning the Garden of Eden before the Fall and the Practicus Hall. The secrets of the 3 = 8 grade are divulged, until at length, the Powers of Water are released.

It is important to note that in this grade, two fiery paths are traversed in order to arrive at a watery Sephirah. This shows the constant equilibration which is inherent to the G∴D∴ system. Fire and Water, the two primary opposing Elements, are always counterbalanced one against the other so that neither is allowed to overpower the energies of the other. Water is maternal and nurturing, while Fire is paternal and inseminating. The aspirant is led to the receptive Waters of Hod by way of the vitalizing energies of Fire. Thus the union of the two is the only possible route to building a firm creative base for spiritual attainment. The Waters of Intellect must never be allowed to become stagnant and insensitive; they must be ever excited by the passionate Fires of Emotion.

There are only three officers stationed in the Practicus Hall besides the Dais officers—these are the three Middle Pillar officers only—the Keryx is no longer present. This leaves three officers who form an approximate equilateral triangle. The triangle, whose apex is marked by the station of Hierophant, refers to the Fire triangle and the Fiery nature of the 31st and 30th Paths in relation to the Tree of Life. The placement of the pillars in the Northeastern part of the Hall suggests the actual location of these paths on the diagram of the Tree. In the final part of the ritual the Hierophant takes up a temporary position West of the altar, forming a Water triangle with the other two officers (like that indicated by the items on the altar).

Many of the speeches in the 3 = 8 grade are symbolically given by the Samothracian Kabiri, but are in actuality taken from excepts of the Chaldean Oracles, a body of work which is from a much later time period than the Samothracian mysteries.✿

The Samothracian Mysteries

Samothrace was the name given to a Greek island in the Northeast portion of the Aegean Sea that was the center of the oldest of the Greek mystery cults. This island was said to be settled by the ancient Pelasgi, early Asiatic colonists in Greece. The esteem shown the Samothracian Mysteries by ancient literary sources proved that they once ranked alongside the Eleusinian Mysteries in importance and popularity. This stormy, mountainous and wooded island was renowned as the home of the mysterious gods known as the *Kabiri* (or *Corybantes*, as they are sometimes referred to). So great was the respect for the mystery rites of Samothrace that the island itself was considered *sacred*, a sanctuary to be respected by all nations.

Not much is now known of the Kabiri or "great gods" whose name is derived from the Kabira mountains or Phrygia.[78] The rituals are immersed in profound secrecy. It is certain though that great festivals were held to worship these gods and initiate new candidates into their mystery rites.

The mysteries of Samothrace included the rites of the Kabiri and the rites of Hecate. Hecate's secret mysteries were said to have taken place in the cave of *Zerynthia*, called the *Grotto of Hecate*, where a nocturnal ritual was performed by torch-bearing participants who sacrificed dogs to honor the goddess of the Underworld.

Near the door of the temple of the Kabiri on Samothrace, there were two bronze statues (it is unclear whether they were both masculine or if one was feminine). They represented the Heavens and the Earth—the two primary portions into which the world is divided—the active and passive principles of universal generation. Within the temple were three altars dedicated to the Kabiri, the Great gods of Samothrace: the *Great*, the *Powerful* and the *Influential* (or Helpful).[79]

Some claim that there were a total of seven Kabiri and referred them to the seven Planets. Others spoke of them as the seven Spirits of Fire before the throne of Saturn. Some ancient writers say there were but two Kabiri who represented Zeus the Elder and Dionysus the younger. At Samothrace the Kabiri were thought of as lesser gods who were sworn to the service of greater deities such as Rhea. At Thebes they were allied with the cult of Demeter and Kore, for their temple was located near a grove sacred to these deities. At Lemnos the Kabiri originated as benevolent gods or genii of volcanic (Fiery) Earth. They were either the sons of Hephaestus or the sons of Zeus and Calliope. These first metal-workers were said to be the noisy and never-resting assistants of Hephaestus at his forge. They would at times shake the earth with their tumultuous rumbling. At Thessaly there was a legend of a Kabir who was killed by his brothers and buried at the foot of Mt. Olympus. It is this Kabiric myth in particular which relates to the Practicus ritual of the Golden Dawn.

Initiation into the Kabiric mysteries at Samothrace concerned four of these "great gods." Their names were *Axieros, Axiokersa*, and *Axiokersos*. Axieros was associated with Demeter, Axiokersa with Persephone, and Axiokersos with Hades. The fourth Kabir, known as *Kasmillos*, was attributed to Hermes.[80]

The names of the first three Kabiri bear a resemblance to the Greek word *axioma* which means something worthy or something that is self-evident. The name Kasmillos is based upon the word *camilla* which refers to a handmaiden

---

[78] The name "Kabiri" has also been associated with the Phoenician word *qabirim* which means "the powerful." The word *Cabar* "great" can be traced to Hebrew, Phoenician and Arabic languages.

[79] The Kabiri were later adopted into Roman mythology as the *Penates*.

[80] The Samothracians derived their doctrines concerning the Kabiri and Hermes from the Pelasgians.

assistant who aids in matters of a secret nature. A *camillus* was an assistant at a wedding who carried a basket of unknown contents during the service.[81] In the Samothracian mysteries, the name *Kasmillos* is used to describe a divinity who attends upon the greater gods.

In *Secret Teaching of All Ages*, Manly P. Hall also examined the mysteries of the Samothracian Kabiri:

> *While a vast number of deities are associated with the Samothracian Mysteries, the ritualistic drama centers around four brothers. The first three—Aschieros, Achiochersus, and Achiochersa—attack and murder the fourth—Cashmala (or Cadmillus). Dionysidorus, however, identifies Aschieros with Demeter, Achiochersus with Pluto, Achiochersa with Persephone, and Cashmala with Hermes. Alexander Wilder notes that in the Samothracian ritual "Cadmillus is made to include the Theban Serpent-God, Cadmus, the Thoth of Egypt, the Hermes of the Greeks, and the Aesculapius of the Alexandrians and Phoenicians." Here again is a repetition of the story of Osiris, Bacchus, Adonis, Balder, and Hiram Abiff.[82] The worship of Atys and Cybele was also involved in the Samothracian Mysteries. In the rituals of the Cabiri is to be traced a form of pine-tree worship, for this tree, sacred to Atys, was first trimmed into the form of a cross and then cut down in honor of the murdered god whose body was discovered at its foot.*
>
> *"If you wish to inspect the orgies of the Corybantes," writes Clement, "then know that, having killed their third brother, they covered the head of the body with a purple cloth, crowned it, and carrying it on the point of a spear, buried it under the roots of Olympus. These mysteries are in short, murders and funerals. (This ante-Nicene Father in his efforts to defame the pagan rites apparently ignores the fact that like the Cabirian martyr, Jesus Christ was foully betrayed, tortured, and finally murdered!) And the priests of these rites, who were called kings of the sacred rites by those whose business it is to name them, give additional strangeness to the tragic occurrence, by forbidding parsley with the roots from being placed on the table, for they think that parsley grew from the Corybantic blood that flowed forth; just as the women, in celebrating the Thesmorphoria,[83] abstain from eating the seeds of the pomegranate, which have fallen on the ground, from the idea that pomegranates sprang from the drops of the blood of Dionysus. Those Corybantes also they call Cabiric; and the ceremony itself they announced as the Cabiric mystery."*

---

[81] Children employed in the temples were called *Mercuries* or *Casmilli*.

[82] In Masonic legend, Hiram Abiff was the architect of King Solomon's temple, who was killed by three of his workers who were also brothers. The body was buried at the foot of a mountain and an acacia tree was planted over it. This legend is re-enacted in the Third Degree of the Master Mason.

[83] A festival of the Eleusinian Mysteries which celebrated the departure of Kore into the underworld.

The Mysteries of the Cabiri were divided into three degrees, the first of which celebrated the death of Cashmala at the hands of his three brothers; the second, the discovery of his mutilated body, the parts of which had been found and gathered after much rejoicing and happiness—his resurrection and the consequent salvation of the world. The temple of the Cabiri at Samothrace contained a number of curious divinities, many of them misshapen creatures representing the Elemental powers of Nature, possibly the Bacchic Titans. Children were initiated into the Cabiric cult with the same dignity as adults, and criminals who had reached the sanctuary were safe from pursuit. The Samothracian rites were particularly concerned with navigation, the Dioscuri[84]—Castor and Pollux, or the gods of navigation—being among those propitiated by members of that cult. The Argonautic expedition, listening to the advice of Orpheus, stopped at the island of Samothrace for the purpose of having its members initiated into the Cabiric rites.[85]

Herodotus relates that when Cambyses entered the temple of the Cabiri he was unable to restrain his mirth at seeing before him the figure of a man standing upright and, facing the man, the figure of a woman standing on her head. Had Cambyses been acquainted with the principles of divine astronomy, he would have realized that he was then in the presence of the key to universal equilibrium. "'I ask,' says Voltaire, 'who were these Hierophants, these sacred Freemasons, who celebrated their Ancient Mysteries of Samothracia, and whence came they and their gods Cabiri?" (See Mackey's Encyclopedia of Freemasonry.) Clement speaks of the Mysteries of the Cabiri as "the sacred mystery of a brother slain by his brethren," and the "Cabiric death" was one of the secret symbols of antiquity. Thus the allegory of the Self murdered by the not-self is perpetuated through the religious mysticism of all peoples. The Philosophic Death and the Philosophic Resurrection are the Lesser and the Greater Mysteries respectively."[86]

One version says that the ceremonies of Samothrace represented the death of the youngest of the Kabiri at the hand of his brothers, who fled to Etruria, carrying with them the ark that contained the genitals of the slain Kabir. The Phallus and the sacred ark that contained it were revered by the Samothracian initiates.[87]

The great annual festival of the Samothracian mysteries took place at midsummer and lasted for three days. There were nightly processions to the cave of Zerynthia where initiations took place. The priests of the rites were known as *sai*

---

[84] The Twins of Gemini.

[85] With a storm arising, Orpheus, an initiate of the mysteries, counselled the Argonauts to land at Samothrace and be initiated into the sacred rites. When they set sail again, they were assured of a safe voyage.

[86] Hall, Manly P. *Secret Teachings of All Ages* (Los Angeles: The Philosophical Research Society, Inc., 1977), p 36.

[87] This is reminiscent of the story of the dismembering of Osiris.

who are said to have been famed for leading a type of armed war dance which included leaping, the stamping of feet, drumming, the clashing of cymbals, the playing of flutes, torches, and the outcry of the mysteries—"EUAH!" Perhaps this was meant to imitate the noisy forges of the volcanic Kabiri.

Purifications played a very important role in these rites, including moral purification of initiates. One type of priest at the Kabiri rites was known as a *koies*, or a cleanser of sins. The historian Plutarch recounts that one initiate who was called Antalcidas was asked by an initiating priest what especially dreadful thing he had committed during his lifetime. Apparently, Antalcidas replied that if he had committed a terrible crime, the gods themselves would be aware of it. Initiates were consecrated to the Deities and pledged to virtue. They would then be assured of those rewards which the justice of the gods reserve for initiates after death.

The ceremony included an invocation of the Kabiri to appear and protect the initiates. Those righteous individuals who became initiates were said to have been protected from danger and storms—particularly mishaps at sea and other marine disasters.[88] Sacred robes and fillets or ribbons of violet cloth were worn about the abdomen by these initiates. A crown of olive graced their brows.

As a final note of interest, a type of fish known as the pompilus[89] fish was sacred to the Samothracian gods. The fish is a symbol of spiritual fecundity and by virtue of its association with the Sign of Scorpio, it is also an emblem of regeneration and transformation.

Godforms of the Kabiri

It is necessary for the student who seeks to self-initiate into the grade of Practicus to envision the gods of the Samothracian mysteries. Although these godforms are obscure, they can nevertheless be constructed specifically for the 3=8 grade in the mind of the aspirant using the following visualizations:

AXIEROS: The First Kabir is a mature bearded man with olive skin and thick wavy hair. He wears golden sandals, a golden tunic and an orange cloak. Upon his brow is an emblem of the Sun attached to a crown of oak leaves. In one hand he holds a lamp and the thunderbolt of Zeus, and in the other a golden scepter surmounted by an ear of corn, sacred to Demeter.

AXIOKERSOS: The Second Kabir is a robust dark-bearded warrior in red Greek armor and crested helmet. A black cloak hangs from his shoulders and black sandals are upon his feet. The symbol of an anvil is upon his brow. In one hand he holds a flaming torch (of Hades) and in the other a spear.

AXIOKERSA: The third Kabir is an olive-skinned woman with thick dark hair. She wears a green tunic, a yellow cloak and green sandals. Upon her brow is a white crocus flower, attached to a yellow strophion or headband. In one hand she bears a candle flame and in the other a scepter surmounted by a pomegranate, sacred to Persephone.

---

[88] The Argonauts were supposed to have become initiates in order that they might sail more safely.

[89] In mythology, Pompilus was a ferryman who was turned into a fish by Apollo.

KASMILLOS: The candidate (and the Fourth Kabir) is a youth who wears a black tunic and black sandals. On his brow he wears the emblem of an acorn attached to a white strophion and he bears a covered basket made from reeds.✿

The Chaldean Oracles

The Chaldean Oracles are all that remain of a rather lengthy text that was said to have been brought to Rome by Julianus the Chaldean Theurgist (magician) in the Second Century A.D. These fragments, reputed to have been written by Zoroaster, contain sacred doctrines and philosophies of ancient Babylonian priests, which have come down to us through Greek translations. Paraphrased in Neoplatonic literature and philosophy, the Chaldean Oracles form an important part of the Western Esoteric Tradition.

Although the Chaldeans had an Oracle that was as highly regarded as the Delphic Oracle, the word *Oracles* was probably imparted to these fragments to imply the idea that they were of a highly profound and spiritual nature. The emphasis of these scraps of knowledge is on non-objective realities that Platonists call "the intelligible world." In order to understand this realm, the intellect can be employed to understand the various concepts which flow from it, but not their origin. In order to comprehend the nature of the source of the universe, the Oracles strongly imply that the practice of Theurgy is required. (Theurgy means "god-working"—it is a word used to indicate highly philosophical magical workings.) While philosophy can steer one's thoughts to the contemplation of the Divine, Theurgy is a method of securing union with the Divine. The focus of Chaldean Oracles is therefore a description of the spiritual scheme of the universe and a portrayal of the practices used in Theurgy to contact and unite with the Divine Source of the universe.

According to the Oracles, a human being is composed of Three Souls (or *Vehicles*) which clothe the physical body. The first is the *Intelligible* or *Divine* part of the Soul or the "radiant vehicle." The second is the *Intellect* or *Rational* part of the Soul. The third is the *Irrational* or *Passionate* part of the Soul (which approximates the astral body). The first is immortal, the third is perishable, and the second may be attracted and assimilated to either the first or the last.

The Oracles describe a threefold pattern of cosmic realities. The first principle is a self-manifesting eternal and *Intellectual Fire* called the "Father of the gods." The second principle is the feminine *World-Soul* or living power called *Hecate*. It is she who flows eternally and sustains all the worlds. The third principle is the second Intellect, *Apollo*, who constructs the various realms and sends his perceptions into them. In describing these principles, the Oracles use the word "Intelligible" to portray a power which transcends all human intellectual comprehension.

It is these three principles that the Theurgist or high magician attempts to contact and make psychic union with—requiring abilities beyond that of the human intellect. The Oracles indicate that several prefatory purifications are needed to perform the sacred rites, but only the *divine vehicle* of the Soul can withstand the *Intellectual Fire* of the Divine. However the Theurgist must also gain awareness of his/her own personal Angelic guide prior to any important magical working.

After all the necessary purifications are performed the Theurgist must invoke certain deities who are associated with the time of the ritual. In this way the Supreme god of Time may be invoked and entreated to assist the magician and reveal the names of even greater deities. The Chaldean Oracles explain that there are in reality two sets of divine names to be used by the Theurgist: one is spoken verbally to link the magician with that which the name symbolizes, the other is an unspoken name or "watchword." This name has been "forgotten" by the conscious mind of the individual by the descending of the Soul into matter. It can only be revealed to the practitioner by the Angelic guide or invoked deities.

The purpose of the rite is then stated clearly: namely the rising of the Theurgist's Soul into union with the Godhead. Sacrifice and total commitment to the Higher are essential on the part of the magician. Thus the totality of the Theurgist's being is focused like a laser beam on the work at hand. Next, according to the Oracles, the gods themselves appear, from the lowest Elementals to Hecate herself—the second principle of the World Soul. The details are scarce but at this point the exaltation of the magician's Soul is accomplished, though it is summarized as a type of battle wherein the Soul fights off obstacles and pushes upwards toward the heavenly Light symbolized by Apollo, the third principle. The Solar Fire then plunges downward to join with the upward rushing human Soul, resulting in a glorious union with the Divine.

After the marriage of human with divinity, the Soul returns the way it came, but preserving a full memory of the transforming experience. Ancient magicians believed that given enough practice with this technique, it could be employed at the time of death as a means of gaining immediate ascension to the Divine Light. Thus the whole Theurgic experience described in the Oracles could be summed up as a conscious transformation (both physical and psychological) designed to activate a spiritual current of energy which brings the magician closer to the divine eternal principles of the universe.

These are also the ideas referred to in the Practicus Ritual as spoken by the Samothracian Kabiri. ✿

Following the 3 = 8 initiation, the task of the Practicus is to thoroughly assimilate all knowledge related to the Element of Water and the Planet Mercury. Most of this information is contained in the Fourth Knowledge Lecture, which also contains additional information on Literal Qabalah, and the Tarot. Ceremonial work and exercises appropriate to the grade, are also included.

The Task of the Practicus is to bear in mind the perfect Alchemical equilibrium of the two Primary Elements and always recall the phrase, *"Except ye be born of Water and the Spirit ye cannot enter the Kingdom of heaven."* ✿

THE INITIATION CEREMONY

Temple setup: The aspirant will need to set up the Hall beforehand in accordance with the temple diagram. The black cubical altar is placed in the center of the room. Upon it should be placed the Tarot card of *Judgment*. Two large candle holders complete with candles[90] flank the Northern and Southern sides of the altar. (If you do not own such large candle holders, an average pair of candles and candle holders can be placed on top of the altar on either side of the Tarot card.) The pillars are placed in the Northeast part of the Hall before the Dais. The Hebrew letter Shin is shown on a large plaque in the Northeast. The letter Tau is directly East, while the letter Qoph is in the Southeast. The Banners of the East and West are located near their respective officers. The Enochian Tablet of Water is placed in the West, and Tablets of Earth and Air are also shown. A cup of Water is also needed in the West. Place the lamens and implements in accordance with the temple diagram, in the positions of the officer-forms. The station of Hierophant is located in the East, while the Hiereus and Hegemon are stationed in the Northwest and Southwest respectively. In addition, you will need three red lamps or candles to be placed by each officer's station.

As in the previous ritual, all of the Elemental candles should be placed around the circumference of the room, with a white candle in the East. The Blue Water candle is to be placed before the Enochian Tablet of the West. The lights on the pillars should be unshaded. A censer of burning incense should be placed in the South.

(Note: For other segments of the ritual, the aspirant will need the following items close at hand: plaques of the Hebrew letters Resh, Mem, Ayin, and Peh, as well as the Qamea, seal and sigils of Mercury, the Tarot card of *The Sun*, and the diagram of the *Garden of Eden before the Fall* [see Plate 3]. You will need three Admission Badges for this ceremony: the Pyramid of Flame, the Solar Greek Cross of Thirteen Squares, and the Cup of Stolistes Badge.)

Ritual preparations: The aspirant should fast for a period of 12 hours prior to the ritual. A ritual bath is required after which the aspirant may put on the black Tau robe, and red slippers. The sash will need to be decorated with the Practicus emblems, but it is not to be worn by the candidate at this time. Place the sash inside the altar.

The aspirant must meditate for a certain length of time on a drawing of the symbol of Water—a Water triangle (apex downward) in blue. Next s/he must spend a period of time (20-30 minutes) in a darkened room or antechamber to the temple seated in quiet meditation while wearing a hoodwink or blindfold. The Admission Badge for the 31st Path, the Pyramid of Flame, should be held in the right hand throughout this period. A small blue candle is to be the only source of light in the room. During this time, darkness and silence are to be maintained. The aspirant should imagine him/her self under the watchful eye of Anubis of the

---

[90] You may use one white and one black candle, or both may be white.

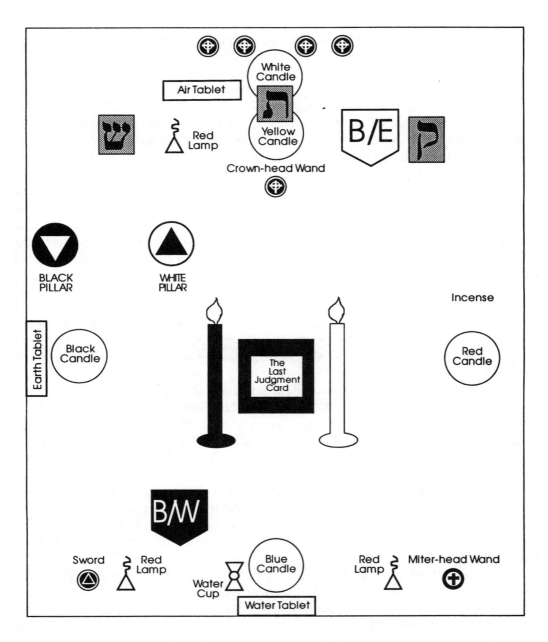

Practicus Temple for Self-Initiation: First Setup

West. After this period of time, the hoodwink may be removed. The aspirant may then enter the temple and begin the ritual.

Upon entering the temple, imagine that you are leaving your physical body outside as a sentinel to guard the temple, so that your spiritual self has the freedom to accept initiation.

PART 0: The Opening

Enter the temple with the Admission Badge of the Pyramid of Flame. Salute the Banner of the East with the Neophyte Signs. Leave the Pyramid in the Western part of the temple. Once inside walk deosil to the East. With the Hiereus' sword perform the LBRP.

Give one knock with the pommel of the sword against the floor or side of the chair and say: *"HEKAS, HEKAS, ESTE BEBELOI!"*

Put the sword aside and go to the West of the temple, facing East. Kneel down and invoke the godform of Thmê as in the previous initiation. Vibrate strongly:

> *THMÊ! THMÊ! THMÊ! Thou daughter and eye of RA! Lady of Heaven, Queen of Earth and mistress of the Underworld! Great Lady of all the gods and goddesses. Thou whose name is MAAT! Lady of Truth! Goddess of Justice and Order! Mediator between Darkness and Light, Chaos and Order! THMÊ! THMÊ! THMÊ! Thou who assesseth the heart of every man and woman in the Hall of Judgment before Ousiri and the assembly of the gods. Thou who art the eye and heart of balance! THMÊ! THMÊ! THMÊ! I invoke thee!*

Visualize the familiar image of the goddess Thmê before you, with human head and yellow-gold skin. She wears a black and white nemyss and a white linen gown. She carries the miter-headed scepter of the Hegemon. Above her head is the white glowing outline of the cross and triangle, symbolic of the outer magical current of the Golden Dawn.

Slowly and with feeling, perform the Qabalistic Cross, drawing the Light down from the Kether of the universe into the Kether at the crown of your head as you continue the QC. Strongly visualize the cross of Light you have formed in the center of your body. Trace within your heart the Hebrew letters of the name THMÊ in glowing white. Project a white ray of thought from your heart toward the image of Thmê you have created before you. See the figure breathe in life as your thought-ray animates it. Address the form:

THMÊ! Beautiful One of the Feather of Truth! I beseech thee to act upon my behalf in this my quest for the Light Divine! Guide me, O thou who art none other but my own Higher Self. Aid me and escort me in this Mercurial Realm which is the intellectual power of the manifest universe. I am a true and willing Seeker of Light and Knowledge. Act as my overseer and reconciler on the paths and in the temple of Hod. Speak for me amidst the assembly of the gods and the guardians of this sacred Hall. My intentions are honest. I am ready to undergo test and trial. I am willing to be examined by the Samothracian Kabiri! I wish to be purified and consecrated to the Light. Grant that my heart is made MAAT! Grant that my Will is made MAAT! Merciful THMÊ! Let me be judged aright! Grant that this humble aspirant before you be not turned away from that resplendent Light which resides in the East. Permit me to tread the fiery paths that lead to the watery temple of Hod. Award me a vision of the mysteries of ancient Samothrace! Grant that I may safely digress from the middle path; and grant me the ability to return to that stable pillar! Permit me to enter the Mercurial Sphere! Let me penetrate the Threshold in the path of the Enterer!"

Thmê speaks to you in your own mind:

He hath filled me with words of Truth, that I may speak the same. And like the flow of Waters flows Truth from my mouth, and my lips show forth his fruit. I am the representative of your Higher and Holy Self. It is only through my arbitration that thou canst even approach the sphere of Splendor. In this Hall I am thy tongue, thy heart and thy mind. Fear not, for I shall guide thee through the paths of Flame and scorching heat, and I shall keep thee safe. Fear not, for I shall lead thee through the watery temple of Hod. I shall direct thee in the temple before the mighty Kabiri! I shall speak for thee in this assembly of the gods before the powers of AL and the current of the Light.

Visualize the goddess Thmê communicating in silence with the energies in the East. She speaks on your behalf to the divine guardians of the Hall. Once again you hear her voice as she calls out the names of other godforms in the East of the temple: ESE, NEBETHO, THOOUTH and another, HOOR OUER. You have a vague impression of four figures in the East, seated before a veil. Thmê continues to address the figures, and the scene becomes hazy. The goddess stands once more before the gigantic form of Djehoti, god of Wisdom. Thmê carries on a silent discussion with Thoth. After a few moments Thmê turns toward you, salutes with the Signs toward the West, and says silently:

Thou mayest proceed, O aspirant; thou art MAAT.

Thmê descends from the East and walks to her own station of Hegemon in the Southwest where she traces the figures of a cross and triangle with her scepter. She then goes to the Northwest and traces the figures at the station of the Hiereus. As she does so, vibrate the name *"HOOR"* (Hoor or Hoh-or) The figure of Horus begins to formulate rapidly. She returns to the East and traces the figures at the station of Hierophant. As she does this, intone the name *"OUSIRI"* (Oo-seer-ee) The mummy-wrapped form of Osiris commences to take shape.

Thmê takes you by the hand, and leads you to the East of the altar. Say:

> *The 3 = 8 grade of Practicus is attributed to the Planet of Mercury and the 31st and 30th Paths. The 31st Path of SHIN refers to the reflection of the Sphere of Fire and the 30th Path of RESH alludes to the reflection of the Sphere of the SUN. Let the Element of this grade be named that it may be awakened within my sphere, in the spheres of those beings who are present, and in the sphere of this magical current. The Element is WATER.*

Visualize the symbol of the blue Water triangle that you meditated on before entering the Hall. Imagine its presence in your sphere of sensation at your Chokmah-Binah[91] area—the left and right temples of the forehead. (Note: You should become aware of a feeling of harmonic resonance between the Water triangle and your Chesed sphere—the left shoulder. Then visualize the triangle in orange reflected into your Hod center—the right hip.) Imagine that these same images are activated in all of the various officer-forms of the Hall.

Thmê leads you to the figure of Osiris in the East. The god traces in the air before you the figure of a cross and circle. He then hands you his crown-headed scepter. Picking up the Wand of Power, you take on the office of Hierophant that Osiris has bestowed upon you. Give the Sign of the Spiraling Light toward the East, and then say, *"Let the white brilliance of the Divine Spirit descend!"* Feel a flood of Divine Light flow through your body from the Kether of the universe. Equilibrate this Light through your body by performing the Qabalistic Cross, vibrating the Hebrew names.

Give a knock and say, *"Let us adore the Lord and King of Water!"* Turn to the East and continue: *"ELOHIM TZABAOTH—Elohim of Hosts! Glory be unto the RUACH ELOHIM who moved upon the Face of the Waters of Creation! Amen."* Salute with the Sign of Practicus.

Go clockwise to the West and stand before the Water Tablet. Visualize the other astral officer-forms facing West also.

Through the authority of the office of Hierophant bestowed upon you by Osiris, invoke the powers of the Water Tablet. Give a knock, then trace with the Wand a large circle in front of the Tablet. Then draw the invoking pentagram of Spirit Passive. As you do so vibrate *"HCOMA"* (Hay-koh-mah). Trace the sigil of Spirit in the center and intone *"AGLA"* (Ah-gah-lah). Give the Sign of the Spiraling Light. Then

---

[91] The *Heh-Water* area of the Four Qabalistic Worlds.

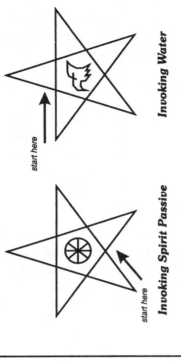

The Enochian Tablet of Water

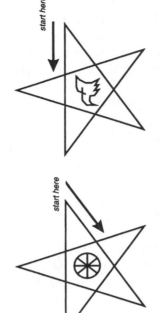

Invoking Water

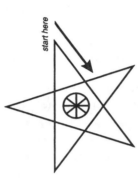

Banishing Water

Invoking Spirit Passive

Banishing Spirit Passive

The Pentagrams of Water

trace the invoking pentagram of Water. As you do so vibrate the name *"EMPEH ARSEL GAIOL"* (Em-pay Ar-sell Gah-ee-ohl). Draw the sigil of the eagle in the center and intone *"Aleph Lamed, AL."* Give the Sign of Practicus. Say:

> *And the Elohim said, "Let us make ADAM in our Image, after our likeness and let them have domin-ion over the Fish of the Sea. In the Name of AL strong and powerful, and in the name of ELOHIM TZABAOTH, Spirits of Water adore your Creator!*

The Practicus Sign

Take up the cup of Water and with it trace the Sign of the Eagle before the Tablet. Say:

> *In the Name of GABRIEL, the Great Archangel of Water, and in the Sign of the Eagle, Spirits of Water, adore your Creator!*

Trace a cross with the cup and say:

> *In the Name and Letters of the great Western Quadrangle revealed unto Enoch by the Great Angel Ave, Spirits of Water adore your Creator!*

Hold the cup high and say:

> *In the Three Great Secret Names of God, born upon the banners of the West, EMPEH ARSEL GAIOL, Spirits of Water adore your Creator! In the Name RA-AGIOSEL, Great King of the West, Spirits of Water adore your Creator!*

Replace the cup and return to the station of the Hierophant to face West. Visualize the other astral officers at their stations facing East. Say:

> *In the Name of ELOHIM TZABAOTH, I declare the temple opened in the 3 = 8 grade of Practicus.*

Give the following knocks with the pommel of the scepter: ו וו ו וו (1—3—1—3). Visualize the officer/godform of the Hiereus repeating the Battery of knocks: 1—3—1—3. Visualize the officer/godform of the Hegemon repeating the Battery of knocks: 1—3—1—3.

Step out of the office of Hierophant and return it to the dominion of Osiris. The goddess Thmê then leads you to the West of the temple.

PART 1: Advancement in the 31st Path of Shin

Visualize all of the officer/godforms at their respective stations. At this point, the temple has been opened under the guidance of the Guardians of the Hall, with your very active participation. You have already done much to activate the Element of Water within your sphere of sensation. Just as in the past you must now take a few moments to re-establish yourself as a candidate who seeks for entrance into this Hall. Perform the Qabalistic Cross to maintain a psychic balance of all the Elements within your aura. Recall the experience in the antechamber, where you were blindfolded in the darkness. Restore the persona of the aspirant within you.

Take up the Pyramid of Flame in your right hand. Give the Battery of knocks: 1—3—1—3. Stand in the Western part of the Hall facing East and say:

> *This candidate seeks for entrance. I vow it to be true that I (magical motto) have made such progress in the paths of Occult Science to have enabled me to pass certain examinations in the requisite knowledge. Having accomplished this, I am now eligible for advancement to the grade of Practicus.*

The goddess Thmê replies:

> His Throne was like a Fiery Flame and the Wheels as Burning Fire.

She leads you before the station of the Hiereus and faces you toward the godform of Horus, who demands the 2 = 9 Signs and words from you:

> Give me the Sign of the grade of Theoricus. (You give it.)

> Give me the Grip or Token.

You exchange the Outer Order Grip with the hawk-headed god.

> Give me the Grand Word of the 2 = 9 grade.

You give it: *"Shaddai El Chai."*

> Give me the Mystic Number of the 2 = 9 grade.

You give it: *"45."*

> What is the Password formed from the Mystic Number?—Horus asks.

You answer: *"Mem-Heh."*

> What is the Mystic Title of the 2 = 9 grade?

You give it: *"Poraios de Rejectis."*

What symbol did you receive in that grade?

You give it: *"Ruach."* Behind you, you hear the voice of Osiris speak:

Poraios de Rejectis, are you ready to take this oath of the 3 = 8 grade?

You answer: *"I am ready to take this oath."* Face the Water Tablet and say:

> I (state magical motto) *solemnly pledge to maintain and uphold the mysteries of the 31st and 30th Paths and of the grade of Practicus, just as I am pledged to maintain those of the preceding grades.*

Give the Saluting Sign of a Neophyte and say: *"I swear by the Abyss of the Waters."* Take up the cup that is before the Tablet of the West. With your fingers, sprinkle Water thrice in front of the Tablet and say: *"Let the powers of Water witness my pledge."*

Thmê as Hegemon leads you between the pillars in the Northeast. She remains at the outer side of the white pillar. Give a knock and say:

> *Before me are the Portals of the 31st, 32nd, and 29th Paths. Of these, the central one leads to the grade of Theoricus from that of Zelator. The one on my left now open to me, is the 31st, which leads from the 1 = 10 of Zelator to the 3 = 8 grade of Practicus.*

Osiris speaks:

Take in your right hand the Pyramid of Flame, and follow your guide, AXIOKERSA, the Kabir, who leads you through the path of Fire.

The Hegemon turns to the right. You pass between the pillars and follow her as she leads you slowly around the Hall. Take time however to visualize the following:

> At this point, briefly imagine in your mind's eye that you are passing through a Gate marked with the Hebrew letter Shin; leaving the sphere of Malkuth behind and following your guide through a bright red tunnel or passageway. You are leaving the material world behind as you begin to traverse the fiery path of initiation that connects the Active World with the Realm of the Intellect. The energy of the path is electric and pulsating, as if you have walked into an active volcano.
>
> You have a vision that you are in a mountain grove surrounded by a large gathering of people who are reveling in celebration. It is mid-evening and already the revelry has continued for three days, yet the participants show no sign of fatigue. The purple-cloaked

Priests known as the *Sai* seem obsessed as they dance in leaping spirals armed with shields and javelins. Warriors, sailors, shepherds, women and even children take to the dance stamping their bare feet in the soil of Demeter's sacred grove with offerings of grain, bread and wine to the goddess. The sound of reed pipes, drums, chants and cymbals is raised to a deafening uproar which continues until dusk.

With the coming of nightfall, the celebration turns more somber. Pine torches are passed out among the participants to be lighted from the hestia or public hearth fire. Then single file, the group proceeds up a well worn hillside path. Past rocky outcroppings and stunted trees, the procession eventually winds through the darkness to the stony side of a cliff where the mouth of a large cavern is flanked by the carved images of two dogs holding great torches. This is the Grotto of Hecate, the dark goddess of the Moon and the Underworld. One by one the celebrants file into the gaping mouth of the earth.

Your ears pick up the sound of a foundry—hammers striking iron —the tearing sound of steam as flaming hot metal strikes water. The image of the burly smith god Hephaestus standing over an anvil pounding red-hot metal with a hammer appears before you. The piece of hot metal he is working seems to be triangular. The god holds the metal on the anvil with iron tongs. The sweat of the god forms fiery droplets at his brow. The air is hot and humid with steam and sparks, but your mysterious guide leads you onward.

After one circumambulation around the Hall, the Hegemon leads you to the Hierophant's throne. The officer-form of the Hierophant rises, but you no longer recognize the figure of Osiris; in his place is a mature bearded figure crowned with oak leaves and dressed in a golden Greek tunic. Holding a red lamp, the figure approaches you and begins to speak:

> AXIEROS, the First Kabir, spake unto Kasmillos the candidate, and said: "I am the apex of the Pyramid of Flame. I am the Solar Fire pouring forth its beams upon the lower World—Life-giving, Light-producing. By what symbol dost thou seek to pass by?"

Hold up the Admission Badge and say: *"I seek to pass by bearing the symbol of the Pyramid of Flame."* The Hierophant speaks:

> Hear Thou the voice of AXIEROS, the First Kabir: "The Mind of the Father whirled forth in reechoing roar—comprehending by invincible Will, ideas omniform, which flying forth from that One Fountain issued. For, from the Father alike were the Will and the End, by which yet they are connected with the Father, according to alternating Life through varying vehicles."

You take up the red lamp at the station of Hierophant and continue the speech of the Kabir:

> *"But as they were divided asunder, being by Intellectual Fire distributed into other Intellectuals. For the King of all previously placed before the polymorphus World, by which the universe shines forth decked with ideas all various, of which the Foundation is One and Alone. From this: the others rush forth distributed and separated through the various bodies of the universe and are borne in swarms through its vast Abysses, ever whirling forth in Illimitable Radiation.*
>
> *They are Intellectual Conceptions from the Paternal Fountain, partaking abundantly of the Brilliance of Fire in the culmination of Unresting Time.*
>
> *But the Primary, Self-Perfect Fountain of the Father pours forth these Primogenial Ideas. These being many, ascend flashingly into the Shining World and in them are contained the Three Supernals—because it is the Operator— because it filleth the Life-producing Bosom of Hecate[92]—and it instilleth into the Synoches,[93] the enlivening strength of Fire, endued with Mighty Power."*

The figure of the Kabir continues the speech:

> "The Creator of all, Self-operating, formed the World, and there was a certain mass of Fire, and all these self-operating He produced, so that the Cosmic Body might be completely conformed—that the Cosmos might be manifest and not appear membranous.
>
> And he fixed a vast multitude of in-wandering stars, not by a strain laborious and hurtful, but to uphold them with stability, void of movement—forcing Fire forward into Fire." Hereunto is the speech of AXIEROS.

Replace the lamp. After hearing the Kabir's speech, the Path of Shin seems to glow scarlet with the warming rays of the Sun after the end of a long winter. The Hegemon leads you round to the station of the Hiereus, who rises at your approach with red lamp in hand. No longer do you perceive the hawk-headed god, Horus. The features of the Hiereus are now that of a fierce Greek warrior in red armor and helmet. The figure speaks to you:

> AXIOKERSOS, the Second Kabir, spake to Kasmillos the candidate and said: "I am the left basal angle of the triangle or Flame. I

---

[92] The Chaldeans considered Hecate as a Goddess of central rank; she therefore possessed the center of all the Powers. At her right hand was the Fountain of Souls, while at her left hand was the Fountain of Virtues.

[93] The Chaldean Oracles list the *Synoches* as one of three Intellectual species of spiritual Powers which are attributed to the Second Mind or the Empyraean World. In the Qabalistic scheme, this world would correspond to Briah.

am the Fire Volcanic and Terrestrial, flashingly flaming the Abysses of Earth—Fire rending—Fire penetrating—tearing asunder the curtain of Matter—Fire constrained—Fire tormented—raging and whirling in lurid storm. By what sign dost thou seek to pass by?"

(Hold up the Admission Badge and say:) *"I seek to pass by bearing the symbol of the Pyramid of Flame."*

Your guide leaves you in the care of the Hiereus who continues:

Hear thou the voice of AXIOKERSOS, the Second Kabir: "For not in Matter did the Fire which is in the Beyond First enclose His Powers in acts, but in MIND!"

You take up the red lamp at the station of Hiereus and continue the speech of the Kabir:

"For the Former of the Fiery World is the Mind of Mind, Who first sprang from Mind, clothing the one Fire with the other Fire, binding them together so that He might mingle the fountainous craters while preserving unsullied the brilliance of His own Fire—and thence a Fiery Whirlwind drawing down the brilliance of the Flashing Flame—penetrating the Abysses of the Universe; thence-from downward all extend their wondrous rays, abundantly animating Light, Fire, Aether and the Universe."

The figure of the Kabir continues:

"From Him leap forth all relentless thunders, and the whirlwind-wrapped, storm-enrolled Bosom of the All-splendid Strength of Hecate, Father-begotten, and He who encircleth the Brilliance of Fire and the strong Spirit of the Poles, all fiery beyond." Hereunto is the speech of AXIOKERSOS.

Replace the lamp. You feel as if the heat of the path has increased greatly, as though you were walking through the molten bowels of the Earth. You can almost smell the acrid odor of lava and liquefied steel. The atmosphere of the path has suddenly become volatile and explosive. Beneath your feet the earth seems to rumble with pangs of volcanic pressure. The officer-form of the Hiereus leads you round to the station of the Hegemon, who rises with a red lamp. The face of Thmê is gone; in its place is the face of a dark-complected woman in a green Greek tunic. The figure speaks to you:

AXIOKERSA, the Third Kabir, spake to Kasmillos the candidate, and said: "I am the Right Basal Angle of the triangle of Flame. I am the Fire astral and fluid, winding and coruscating through the

Firmament. I am the Life of beings—the vital heat of existence. By what sign dost thou seek to pass by?"

Hold up the Admission Badge and say: *"I seek to pass by bearing the symbol of the Pyramid of Flame."* The figure continues:

Hear thou the voice of AXIOKERSA, the Third Kabir: "The Father hath withdrawn Himself but hath not shut up His Own Fire in His Intellectual Power. All things are sprung from that One Fire."

You take up the red lamp at the station of Hegemon and continue the speech of the Kabir:

For all things did the Father of all things perfect, and delivered them over to the Second Mind Whom all races of men call First. The Mind of the Father riding on the subtle girders which glitter with the tracings of inflexible and relentless Fire.

The figure continues:

"The Soul, being a brilliant Fire, by the Power of the Father remaineth immortal and is Mistress of Life, and filleth up the many recesses of the Bosom of the World, the channels being inter-mixed, wherein she performeth the works of Incorruptible Fire." Hereunto is the speech of AXIOKERSA.

The "feel" of the path remains fiery, yet it is now a nourishing Fire—the Fire of the hearth which provides heat and warmth. It is the Fire of Life moving unseen through all aspects of Creation—a vibration and electrical charge of energy. You receive an image of Samothracian priests pouring water from a vase onto your forehead and anointing your hands and feet in ritual purification. Other priests fan clouds of scented smoke over you.

The Hegemon leads you to the West of the altar facing East. The first Kabir at the station of Hierophant speaks to you:

Stoop not down unto the darkly splendid World wherein continually lieth a faithless Depth, and Hades wrapped in clouds delighting in unintelligible images, precipitous, winding, a black ever-rolling Abyss, ever espousing a Body, unluminous, formless and void.

You continue the speech of the Kabir:

Nature persuadeth us that there are pure daemons and that even the evil germs of Matter may alike become useful and good. But these are Myster-ies which are evolved in the profound abyss of the Mind.

The First Kabir continues:

> Such a Fire existeth extending through the rushings of Air or even
> a Fire formless whence cometh the Image of a Voice, or even a
> flashing Light, abounding, revolving, whirling forth, crying aloud.

You continue the speech:

> *Also there is the vision of the Fire-flashing Courser of Light, or of a Child*
> *borne aloft on the shoulders of the Celestial Steed, fiery or clothed in gold,*
> *or naked and shooting with a bow, shafts of Light, and standing on the*
> *shoulders of a horse.*[94]

> *But if I prolong this meditation, I shall unite all these symbols in the form*
> *of a Lion.*[95]

> *When the Vault of the Heavens and the Mass of the Earth are no longer*
> *visible to me; when unto my sight the Stars have lost their light and the*
> *lamp of the Moon is veiled; when the Earth abideth not and around me is*
> *the Lightning Flame—then I will not call before myself the Visible Image*
> *of the Soul of Nature, for no matter the temptation to do so, I must not*
> *behold it ere my body is purged by the Sacred Rites—since ever dragging*
> *down the Soul and leading it from the Sacred Things, from the confines of*
> *Matter, arise the terrible Dog-faced Demons, never showing true image*
> *unto mortal gaze.*

The First Kabir continues the speech:

> So therefore first the priest who governeth the works of Fire must
> sprinkle with the lustral Water of the Loud, Resounding Sea.

You continue the speech:

> *I shall labor around the Strophalos*[96] *of Hecate. Whenever a terrestrial*
> *Demon approaches, I shall cry aloud and sacrifice the Stone MNI-*
> *ZOURIN.*[97]

---

[94] A reference to Sagittarius, the Sign of Mutable Fire.

[95] Leo, the Sign of Fixed or Kerubic Fire.

[96] A golden ball dedicated to Hecate bearing a sapphire in its center. Around it is a leather thong inscribed with various sacred characters. Holding the leather thong the Chaldeans whipped this orb into the air around their heads as they invoked the *Iynges* or Intellectual Spirit Powers associated with the Second Mind and the Empyraean World.

[97] Because of their proximity to matter, Terrestrial Spirits are notorious for giving falsehoods. The stone *Mnizourin* was said to have the power of evoking Superior Spirits that would reveal the Truth to the magician. According to the Oracle, the evocation of a superior Spirit went hand-in-hand with the sacrificing of the stone.

I shall not change the barbarous Names of Evocation, for they are Names Divine, having in the Sacred Rites a power ineffable."

The First Kabir continues the speech:

And when, after all the phantoms have been banished, thou shalt see that Holy and Formless Fire—that Fire which darts and flashes through the Hidden Depths of the Universe, Hear thou the Voice of Fire. Hereunto is the speech of the Kabir.

Visualize all of the astral officer/godforms shedding their outer appearance as the Kabiri and assuming their regular demeanor. Hold the Admission Badge for the Path of Shin high and say:

The Solid Triangular Pyramid is an appropriate hieroglyph of Fire. It is formed of four triangles, three visible and one concealed, which yet is the synthesis of the rest. The three visible triangles represent Fire, Solar, Volcanic, and Astral, while the fourth represents the latent Heat; AUD—active, AUB—passive, AUR—equilibrated, while Asch is the name of Fire.

Put the Pyramid aside and focus your attention on the plaque of the letter Shin. Say:

The Thirty-first Path of the Sepher Yetzirah which answereth unto the Letter Shin is called the Perpetual Intelligence, and it is so-called because it regulateth the proper motion of the Sun and the Moon in their proper order, each in an orbit convenient for it.

It is therefore a reflection of the Sphere of Fire, and of the path connecting the Material Universe as depicted in Malkuth with the Pillar of Severity and the side of Geburah, through the Sephirah Hod.

Focus your attention on the Tarot Key of Judgment and say:

The Twentieth Key of the Tarot symbolically represents these ideas. To the uninitiated eye it apparently represents The Last Judgment with an Angel blowing a trumpet and the Dead rising from their tombs—but its meaning is far more recondite than this, for it is a glyph of the powers of Fire.

The Angel encircled by the rainbow, whence leap coruscations of Fire, and crowned with the Sun, represents MICHAEL, the Great Archangel, the Ruler of Solar Fire.

The Serpents which lead in the rainbow are symbols of the Fiery Seraphim. The Trumpet represents the influence of the Spirit descending from Binah, while the Banner with the Cross refers to the Four Rivers of Paradise and the Letters of the Holy Name.

He is also AXERIOS, the first of the Samothracian Kabiri, as well as Zeus and Osiris. The left hand figure below, rising from the Earth is SAMAEL, the Ruler of Volcanic Fire. He is also AXIOKERSOS, the Second Kabir, Pluto and Typhon.

The right hand figure below is ANAEL, the Ruler of Astral Light. She is also AXIOKERSA, the Third Kabir, Ceres and Persephone, Isis and Nephthys. She is, therefore, represented in duplicate form, and rising from the waters. Around both these figures dart flashes of Lightning.

These three principle figures form the Fire triangle, and further represent Fire operating in the other Three Elements of Earth, Air, and Water.

The central lower figure with his back turned, and his arms in the Sign of the Two equals Nine, is ARIEL, the Ruler of latent heat. He is rising from the Earth as if to receive the properties of the other three. He is also KASMILLOS, the candidate in the Samothracian Mysteries, and the Horus of Egypt. He rises from the rock-hewn cubical Tomb and he also alludes to the candidate who traverses the path of Fire. The lower figures represent the Hebrew letter Shin, to which Fire is especially referred. The seven Hebrew Yods allude to the Sephiroth operating in each of the Planets and to the Schem ha-Mephoresh.

Visualize the following:

Imagine that you are at the end of the blazing reddish Path of Shin leading from the bowels of the Earth up to a vast ocean above you. A priest of the mysteries comes forward and places a hot brand against your forehead. The pain is minimal, replaced by a feeling of elation. The branding iron of Hephaestus leaves a red triangle-shaped mark on your skin. The priests then clothe you in a violet cloak.

In your mind's eye imagine that you now stand before the orange Gate that is the entrance leading to the Water temple of Hod. You realize that your journey through the 31st Path has been a primary step in your spiritual initiation. For the first time you have traversed a path which has veered off the security of the Middle Pillar. You have been baptized in and through the Element of Fire as a balancing stage prerequisite for immersion into the Water temple of Hod. All the psychic impurities within yourself which would block your spiritual progress must be burned away utterly. You must be reborn through spiritual Fire like the phoenix. You are the fourth side of the Pyramid of Flame, receiving the properties of the other three sides—within your Soul is the latent or Hidden Fire of Nature which courses through all things in the manifest universe that are touched by the Divine. And you are more aware than ever of a Higher Presence—a force that moves through the universe and through your very essence. On this path the divine powers have descended into materialization—into Fire—and have left their brand upon you, marking you as an initiate of the mysteries.

Osiris speaks to you:

I hereby confer on you the Title of Lord (Lady) of the Thirty-First Path.

(Say:) *I claim the Title of Lord (Lady) of the 31st Path.*

Thmê speaks to you:

You have passed the Gate of the Path of Shin in the footsteps of an initiate. Prepare this Hall to reflect the 30th Path of Resh. Prepare thyself for passage into the Path of the Sun.

The goddess leads you out into the antechamber where you spend a few moments rehearsing the Fourfold Breath and meditating on the Judgment Card. Perform the Qabalistic Cross to once again equilibrate the Elemental energies within your Aura. When ready, set the temple in accordance with Part 2 of the ritual.

Changes in the temple setup for the second part of the ritual—the 30th Path: Replace the plaque of the letter Shin in the Northeast with the letter Resh. Replace the letter Tau with Samekh. Replace the letter Qoph with Tzaddi. Also replace the Tarot card of Judgment with that of The Sun. All other temple furnishings remain as they are.

PART 2: Advancement in the 30th Path of Resh

Spend a few moments in the antechamber in a state of relaxed meditation. Perform the Qabalistic Cross. Take up the Admission Badge of the Greek Cross of Thirteen Squares. Visualize all of the astral officer/godforms at their respective stations. Take a few moments to re-establish yourself as a candidate who seeks for entrance into this Hall.

With the Greek Cross in your right hand, stand in the Western part of the Hall facing East.

The goddess Thmê comes to your side and says:

Behold, He hath placed His Tabernacle in the Sun.

Thmê as Hegemon leads you between the pillars in the Northeast. She remains at the outer side of the white pillar. Give a knock and say:

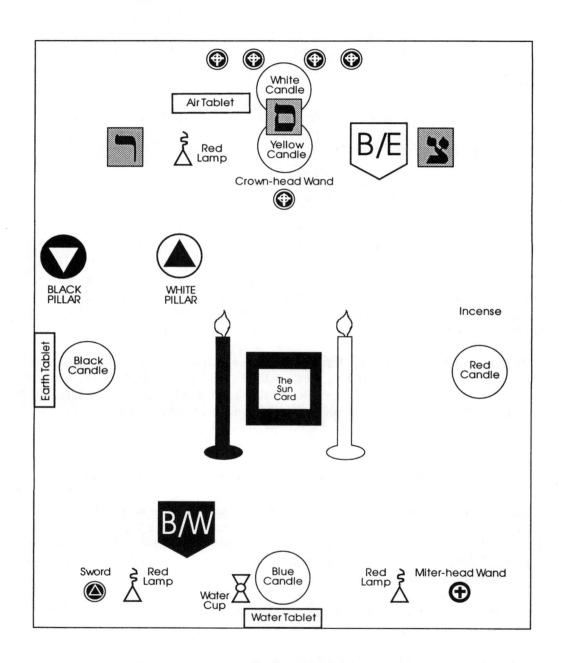

The Practicus Temple for Self-Initiation: Second Setup

Before me are the Portals of the 30th, 25th, and 28th Paths leading from the 2 = 9 grade of Theoricus to those grades which are beyond. Of these, the only one now open to me is the 30th which leads to the 3 = 8 grade of Practicus.

Osiris speaks:

Take in your right hand the Solar Greek Cross, and follow your guide, through the pathway of the Sun.

(Say:) *"Before the Intellectual Whirlings of Intellectual Fire, all things are subservient through the Will of the Creator of All."*

The Hegemon turns to the right. You pass between the pillars and follow her as she leads you slowly around the Hall. During this time visualize the following:

At this point, briefly imagine in your mind's eye that you are passing through a Gate marked with the Hebrew letter Resh, leaving the sphere of Yesod behind and following your guide through a bright orange tunnel or passageway. You are leaving the astral sphere behind as you begin to traverse the fiery Solar path of the individual human mind that connects the sphere of Foundation with the Realm of the Intellect. The energy of the path is warming and pulsating, as if you have walked out into a bright Summer's day which has stirred the creative process in your mind and arouses your awareness of a higher presence that moves through all aspects of the universe. The image of a ship comes to your mind—a ship which carries you across the Aegean Sea. Above you is the chariot of Helios, the god of the Sun. Your mysterious guide leads you onward.

After one circumambulation around the Hall, the Hegemon leads you to the Hierophant's throne. The officer-form of the Hierophant rises, and again you see before you a mighty bearded figure clothed in a golden tunic. Holding a red lamp, the figure approaches you and begins to speak:

AXIEROS, the First Kabir, spake unto Kasmillos the candidate, and said: "I am the Sun in greatest elevation, bringing upon Earth the ripening heat—fructifying all things—urging forward the growth of vegetable nature, Life-giving, Life-producing—crowning summer with golden harvest, and filling the lap of plenteous Autumn with the purple vintage of the Vine." Thus far the voice of AXIEROS!

Visualize the following:

After hearing the Kabir's speech, the Path of Resh seems to glow orange with the brilliant Solar rays of the midday Summer Sun—

the rays of Apollo. The air is hot and humid. You can feel the Sun's heat on your arms and face, and you can feel its life-blood in the sap of the plants. The warmth seems to have a stimulating effect on your mind, which quickens with new creativity and insight. It is as though a new channel of communication has been opened between your individual human mind and the greater divine Mind. Instinctively you know that you will gradually be privileged to gain intellectual knowledge from that Greater Mind, but only through an inner communication which needs no words, only symbols.

The Hegemon leads you round to the station of the Hiereus, who rises at your approach with red lamp in hand. The fierce figure in red armor appears to you once more. The scarlet warrior speaks:

> AXIOKERSOS, the Second Kabir, spake to Kasmillos the candidate and said: "I am the Sun in greatest depression beneath the Equator when cold is greatest and heat is least—withdrawing his light in darkening winter, the Dweller in mist and storm." Thus far the voice of AXIOKERSOS!

Visualize the following:

> You feel as if the warming heat of the path has been snuffed out, replaced by a chill wind. The sense of intellectual creativity that you enjoyed a few brief moments ago has given way to the realization of possible barrenness and abuse of mental powers. You understand now that the energy of this path, can be quite harsh if used incorrectly, or without balance.
>
> In your mind's eye you again see a vision of your ship in the Aegean Sea. Storm clouds have blotted out the sun and the fury of the waves crashes down upon the bow of the boat. Against the wrath of the tempest, you stand firm, focusing on the singular purpose of all your spiritual quest. Your power as an initiate of the mysteries will see you through.

The officer-form of the Hegemon leads you round to her station, where she takes up the red lamp. Her face is again that of a woman in a green tunic. The figure speaks:

> AXIOKERSA, the Third Kabir, spake to Kasmillos the candidate, and said: "I am the Sun in Equinox, initiating Summer or heralding Winter—mild and genial in operation, giving forth or withdrawing the vital heat of life." Thus far the voice of AXIOKERSA!

Visualize the following:

The energy of the path now seems curiously calm and balanced, as if you stood in the center of a hurricane, in total equilibrium, while turbulence is all around you. You are at the pivotal point of Solar energy, which is peaceful yet potent. Above all you have a powerful sense of consciousness and purpose.

The Hegemon leads you to the West of the altar facing East. The First Kabir at the station of Hierophant speaks to you:

> The Creator of All congregated the Seven Firmaments of the Cosmos, circumscribing the Heaven with convex form. He constituted a Septenary of Wandering Existences, suspending their disorder in well-disposed zones.

You continue the speech of the Kabir:

> *He made them six in number and for the seventh, he cast into the midst thereof the Fire of the SUN—into that Center from which all lines are equal—that the swift Sun may come around that center eagerly urging itself towards that Center of Resounding Light. As rays of Light, His locks flow forth, stretching to the confines of Space, and of the Solar Circles, and of the Lunar flashings and of the Aerial Recesses, the Melody of the Aether and of the Sun and of the Passages of the Moon and of the Air.*

> *The wholeness of the Sun is in the supermundane orders, for therein a Solar World and endless Light subsist. The Sun more true measureth all things by time, for He is the Time of Time, and his disc is in the Starless above the inerratic Sphere, and he is the center of the Triple World. The Sun is Fire and the Dispenser of Fire. He is also the channel for the Higher Fire.*

The First Kabir continues the speech:

> O Aether, Sun and Spirit of the Moon, ye are the Leaders of Air. And the great goddess bringeth forth the vast Sun and the brilliant Moon and wide Air, and the Lunar Course and the Solar Pole. She collecteth it, receiving the melody of the Aether and of the Sun and of the Moon, and of whatever is contained in Air.

> Unwearied doth Nature rule over the Worlds and Works, so that the Period of all things may be accomplished. And above the shoulders of the great goddess, is Nature in her vastness exalted. Thus far the voice of the Kabiri.

Visualize all of the astral officer/godforms shedding their outer appearance as the Kabiri and assuming their regular demeanor.

Hold the Admission Badge for the Path of Resh high and say:

> The Solar Greek Cross is formed of thirteen squares which fitly refer to the Sun's motion through the Zodiac, these Signs being further arranged in the arms of the cross according to the four Elements with the Sun in the Center and representing that luminary as the center of the whole.

Put the Badge aside and focus your attention on the plaque of the letter Resh. Say:

> The 30th Path of the Sepher Yetzirah which answereth to the letter Resh is called the Collecting Intelligence, and it is so called because from it the Astrologers deduce the judgment of the Stars, and of the Celestial Signs, and the perfections of their science according to the rules of their resolutions. It is therefore the Reflection of the Sphere of the Sun and the path connecting Yesod with Hod—Foundation with Splendor.

Focus your attention on the Tarot Key of The Sun and say:

> The Nineteenth Key of Tarot symbolically resumes these ideas. The Sun has twelve principal rays which represent the Twelve Signs of the Zodiac. They are alternately waved and salient as symbolizing the alternation of the masculine and feminine natures. These again are subdivided into the 36 Decanates or sets of ten degrees in the Zodiac, and these again into 72, typifying the 72 quinances or sets of five, and the 72-fold Name Schem ha-Mephoresh. Thus the Sun embraces the whole of creation in its rays.

> The seven Hebrew Yods on each side, falling through the air, refer to the Solar influence descending. The Wall is the Circle of the Zodiac, and the stones are its various degrees and divisions.

> The two children standing respectively on Water and Earth represent the generating influence of both, brought into action by the rays of the Sun. They are the two passive Elements, as the Sun and Air above them are the active Elements of Fire and Air. Furthermore, these two children resemble the Sign Gemini which unites the Earthy Sign of Taurus with the Watery Sign Cancer, and this Sign was, by the Greeks and Romans, referred to Apollo and the Sun.

Visualize the following:

> Imagine that you are at the end of the orange Path of Resh. In your mind's eye imagine that you now stand before the orange Gate that is the entrance leading to the Water temple of Hod. You realize that your journey through the 30th Path has been a personal one of inner communication with the Divine Mind. Your mind is like that of a small child, and you must be taught in order to grow wise. You

are the fourth Sun in the path—the latent Sun—yet to rise in the East as the child of the great gods. You have stepped off the safety of the central path, so you must proceed with caution and knowledge. This knowledge can only be taught from the voiceless mouth of the Divine within. In this path there is much wisdom and intellectual learning to be gained, but you must walk with discretion, because the knowledge is powerful, yet it can easily be abused. The life-giving rays of the Sun can just as easily scorch the vegetation and create a desert wasteland. Knowledge is a sacred gift.

Osiris speaks to you:

> I hereby confer on you the Title of Lord (Lady) of the Thirtieth Path.

(Say:) *"I claim the Title of Lord (Lady) of the 30th Path."*

Thmê speaks to you:

> You have passed the Gate of the Path of Resh in the unfolding rays of the Sun. Prepare this Hall to reflect the Water temple of Hod. Prepare thyself for advancement into the 3 = 8 grade of Practicus.

The goddess leads you out into the antechamber where you spend a few moments rehearsing the Fourfold Breath and meditating on the Sun Card. Perform the Qabalistic Cross to once again equilibrate the Elemental energies within your Aura. When ready, set the temple in accordance with the final part of the ritual.

Changes in the temple setup for the remainder of the ritual—the temple of Hod: Place the pillars slightly West of the altar. Just East of the altar should be a diagram stand with the diagram of *The Garden of Eden before the Fall* placed thereon. Upon the altar itself the cross should be placed above the triangle with a cup of Water in the center, separating the two. The triangle is pointed apex downward, and its three points are surrounded by the three red lamps which had accompanied the officers in the previous part of the ritual.

The station of Hiereus is situated North of the altar, while the station of Hegemon is located South of the altar. The station of the Hierophant should temporarily be imagined just West of the altar, (although it is not necessary to move the Hierophant's lamen or scepter from the East). The plaques of the Hebrew letters are needed as follows: East—Mem, Southeast—Ayin, South—Peh, Southwest—Resh, Northwest—Shin. In the East should be the Qamea of Mercury, along with the Mercurial sigils and the symbol of Mercury on the Tree of Life.

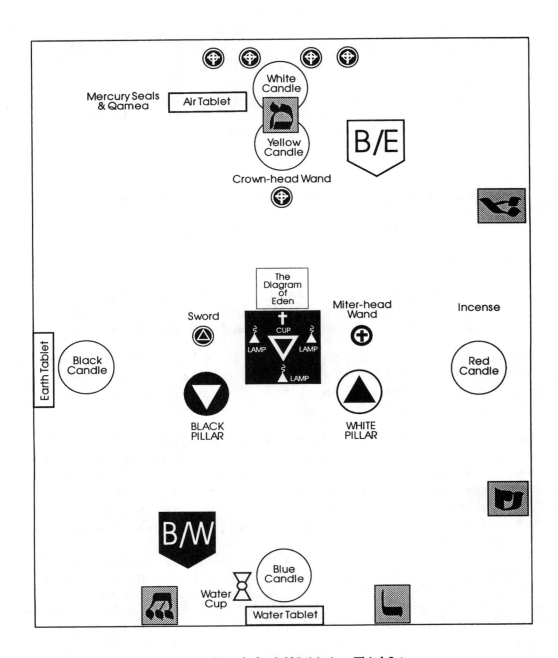

The Practicus Temple for Self-Initiation: Third Setup

PART 3: Entry into Hod

After setting up the Hall, spend a few additional moments in relaxed meditation in the antechamber. Visualize the Water triangle once more and then perform the Qabalistic Cross. Take up the Admission Badge to the temple of Hod—the cup of Stolistes Lamen. When finished, stand just outside the temple door and give the Battery of knocks: 1—3—1—3. Briefly visualize all of the officer/godforms at their respective stations. Then imagine Thmê at the entrance facing you. The goddess motions for you to enter and places you before the plaque of the Hebrew letter Resh, by which you have symbolically entered this grade from the 2 = 9 grade of Theoricus. She leads you forward to the figure of the Hiereus. Horus inquires:

By what symbol dost thou enter herein?

(You answer:) *I enter by the peculiar emblem of the Stolistes, the Cup of Water, which partakes in part of the symbolism of the Laver of Moses and the Sea of Solomon. On the Tree of Life it embraces nine of the Sephiroth, exclusive of Kether. Yesod and Malkuth form the triangle below, the former the apex, the latter the base. Like the Caduceus, it further represents the Three Elements of Water, Air, and Fire. The Crescent is the Water which is above the Firmament, the Circle is the Firmament, and the triangle the consuming Fire below, which is opposed to the Celestial Fire symbolized by the upper part of the Caduceus.*

Thmê leads you to the position of the Hierophant, just West of the altar. All three astral officer/godforms turn inward to face the altar. Visualize the following:

In your mind's eye see yourself standing at the end of the orange path of Resh, facing the Gate to the astral temple of Hod. A large orange door is in front of you. Carved into this door is the letter Heh painted in blue. The three Samothracian Kabiri stand before you, holding up their red lamps and blocking your final passage into Hod with the Banner of the West. You hold up the Stolistes' lamen and proclaim that you have received the Title of Lord/Lady of the 31st and 30th Paths. The Banner of the West is withdrawn and the Kabiri permit you final entrance into the Water temple of Hod. Astrally, you give the Neophyte Signs followed by the Sign of a Practicus and then step through the door into Hod.

The temple is an eight-sided chamber draped in curtains of orange silk. Embedded into the floor is a figure of an octagon made from fire opals. The scent of storax is in the Air, and the ceiling is ornamented with a large blue sigil of Mercury. Eight columns surround the blue central altar, upon which are a temple flame, a chalice of Water, and the Book of Knowledge.

The Archangel Michael is also here, a noble winged warrior in red armor who wields a large sword. He leads you to a curtain at the far end of the temple. Giving the Sign of the Spiraling Light, you step through the curtain.

Again you find yourself in the familiar Courtyard of the Tabernacle. Briskly you walk past the brazen altar and the Laver, entering the outer chamber of the Holy Place before the golden altar. As in your previous visit, you offer up coals and incense and perform the Qabalistic Cross. Then crossing the chamber, the veil before you separates and you stand again before the sacred Ark.

You gaze into the Divine Light that is perched atop the golden Mercy Seat between the two winged Kerubim. Another vision of the Garden of Eden presents itself to you:

You see before you the Tree of Life, completely formed through the action of the Lightning Bolt which you witnessed in the Theoricus grade. On the right is the pillar of brilliant flame, while on the left is the dark pillar of swirling clouds. At the Summit of the Tree is a great and beautiful goddess with long dark hair and the sculptured face of an Egyptian. She is AIMA, the Supreme and everlasting Mother who resides within the realm of the Three Supernals. The goddess is the shining image of divinity and her face is full of grace and compassion. She wears a gleaming crown of stars and her ethereal white robe is ornamented with the golden orb of the Sun. She stands upon a silver dais which is the Crescent Moon itself.

You are aware of a divine name which enters your mind, YOD HEH VAV HEH ELOHIM. The combination of the masculine god YAH with the feminine goddess ELOAH results in a unified masculine/feminine deity—YHVH ELOHIM, who is both male and female, yet who transcends both of these terms. YHVH ELOHIM is the essence of masculine vitality and feminine creativity. However the outer appearance that this Being presents to the world below the Supernals is feminine—the great Mother AIMA.

And from her Supernal feet flows a perpetual stream of water, the mighty river Naher, the Never-failing waters which nourish the bountiful supply of plant and animal life in the Garden of Eden. The river Naher contains the Waters of Life, clear as crystal bringing forth all living things and inanimate objects which comprise the manifest universe. The river flows from the feet of the goddess to the sphere of Daath, where it is separated into the four rivers which divide the Garden into the four Cardinal Points of East, West, North, and South.

The combined rivers water the Garden of Eden, the Tree of Life, and all of Creation in its primal splendor. Before your eyes the rivers form an equal-armed cross. Beneath the surface of the flowing waters you can make out the mighty form of a man who wears a kingly crown, his arms spread out in the form of a Tau Cross under the currents of the Northern and Southern rivers—his head in the Eastern river, while his feet lie in the Western waters. His hands stretch out as if to grasp the spheres of Chesed and Geburah, while his torso is centered at Tiphareth.

In Malkuth stands the mighty crowned goddess Eve, who supports the entire Tree of Life with her delicate yet strong arms. She single-handedly holds up the two great opposing pillars of Fire and Cloud, Light and Darkness. She stands fearlessly in the realm of matter, sustaining the universe by completing and solidifying the Tree of Life in the physical world. Beneath her feet, under the very soil and stones and burrowing earth creatures, is a great and terrible dragon coiled in sleep. This beast has seven heads and ten horns, the Seven Infernal Palaces and the Ten Averse Sephiroth. It is the inverted and evil Tree which mirrors the Tree of Life. The abode of the Dragon is the kingdom of shells (cast-off forms and shadows) that lies directly below Malkuth.

At the feet of the goddess Eve grows another Tree, the tree of the knowledge of Good and of Evil, which is between the Tree of Life and the Kingdom of Shells. The upper branches of this Tree reach upwards to the seven lower Sephiroth, but the lower branches reach downward to the seven Infernal Palaces of the Qlippoth. The fruit carried on the upper branches of the Tree (good) is sweet and without blemish, while the fruit on the lower branches (evil) is bruised and poisonous. This implies that knowledge can be used for the purposes of good, or it can equally be abused for the purposes of evil. In this lies an important truth, as well as a great responsibility.

Gradually, this vision of the Garden of Eden fades once more into the brilliant Light above the mercy Seat of the Ark. The curtain before you closes and obscures the Ark and its guardians. You are again in the astral temple of Hod.

Bring the focus of your conscious mind back to the Practicus Hall. Perform the adoration to the Lord of the universe. The officer-form of the Hierophant at your side directs your attention to the diagram of the Garden of Eden East of the altar. When you are ready, continue and say:

> *Before me is represented the symbolism of the Garden of Eden. At the summit is the Supernal Eden, containing the Three Supernal Sephiroth, summed up and contained in Aima Elohim, the Mother Supernal, the Woman of the twelfth chapter of the Apocalypse, crowned with the Sun and the Moon under her feet, and upon her head the Crown of Twelve Stars—Kether. And whereas the Name YOD HEH VAV HEH, is joined to the name Elohim, when it is said Tetragrammaton Elohim planted a*

Garden Eastward in Eden, so this represents the power of the Father joined thereto in the Glory from the Face of the Ancient of Days. And in the Garden was the tree of the Knowledge of Good and of Evil, which latter is from Malkuth, which is the lowest Sephirah between the rest of the Sephiroth and the Kingdom of Shells, which latter is represented by the Great Red Dragon coiled beneath, having Seven Heads (the Seven Infernal Palaces) and Ten Horns—(The Ten Averse Sephiroth of Evil, contained in the Seven Palaces).

The a River Naher went forth out of Eden, namely from the Supernal Triad, to water the Garden (the rest of the Sephiroth), and from thence it was divided into Four Heads in Daath, whence it is said "In Daath the Depths are broken up and the clouds drop down dew." The first Head is PISON, which flows into Geburah (whence there is Gold). It is the River of Fire. The Second Head is GIHON, the River of Waters, flowing into Chesed. The Third is HIDDEKEL, the River of Air, flowing into Tiphareth, and the Fourth River is PHRATH, Euphrates, which floweth down upon the Earth.

This river going forth out of Eden is the River of the Apocalypse, the Waters of Life, clear as crystal proceeding out of the Throne of God and the Lamb, on either side of which was the Tree of Life, bearing Twelve manner of fruits. And thus do the Rivers of Eden form a cross, and on that cross the Great ADAM, the Son who was to rule the nations with a Rod of Iron, is extended from Tiphareth and his arms stretch out to Gedulah and Geburah, and in Malkuth is Eve, Mother of all, the Completion of all, and above the Universe she supporteth with her hands the Eternal Pillars of the Sephiroth. As it was said in the 30th Path, "And above the shoulders of that great goddess is Nature in her vastness exalted."

The officer-form of the Hierophant captures your attention to give you the secrets of the grade. You hear the voice of Osiris:

> The 3 = 8 grade of Practicus is referred to the Sephirah Hod and the 30th and 31st Paths—those of Resh and Shin are bound thereto.

Osiris then prompts you to give the Sign of Practicus and explains:

> This Sign is given with the hands together, raising the arms until the elbows are level with the shoulders. The thumbs and fore-fingers make a triangle over the breast—a triangle apex downward. This represents the Element of Water, to which this grade is attributed.

> The Grip or Token is the general Grip of the First Order. The Grand Word is a Name of ten letters, ELOHIM TZABAOTH, which means Lord of Hosts. The Mystic Number is 36, and from it is formed the

Password of this grade which is ELOAH, one of the Divine Names. It should be lettered separately when given thus—ALEPH, LAMED, HEH.

You repeat the words:

> *The Grand Word of this grade is ELOHIM TZABAOTH. The Mystic Number is 36. The Password of the grade is ELOAH—ALEPH, LAMED, HEH.*

> (You continue:) *Unto this grade and unto the Sephirah Hod, the Eighth Path of the Sepher Yetzirah is referred. It is called the absolute or perfect Path, because it is the means of the Primordial, which hath no root to which it may be established, except in the penetralia of that Gedulah or Magnificence which emanate from the subsisting properties thereof.*

Osiris continues:

> The distinguishing Badge of this grade, which you are now entitled to wear is the sash of the Theoricus with the addition of an orange cross above the violet cross and the number 3 and 8 in a circle and square respectively, left and right of its summit—and below the 32, the numbers 30 and 31 in orange between two narrow orange lines.

Open the altar and remove the Practicus sash. As you put it on, visualize the god Osiris investing you with the sash. The god then points out the Enochian Tablet of the West behind you. As you inspect the Tablet say:

> *This grade is especially referred to the Element of Water and therefore the Great Watchtower or Tablet of the West forms one of its principal emblems. It is known as the Second or Great Western Quadrangle or Tablet of Water, and it is one of the Four Great Tablets delivered unto Enoch by the Great Angel Ave. From it are drawn the Three Holy Secret Names of God—EMPEH ARSEL GAIOL—which are borne upon the Banners of the West, and numberless Divine and Angelic Names which appertain unto the Element of Water.*

The officer-form of the Hierophant indicates the cross and triangle upon the altar. Say:

> *The cross above the triangle represents the power of the Spirit of Life rising above the triangle of the Waters and reflecting the Triune therein, as further marked by the lamps at the angles. While the Cup of Water placed at the junction of the cross and triangle represents the maternal Letter MEM.*

The officer-form of the Hierophant returns to his throne in the East. Osiris speaks, pointing to the Hebrew letter plaques:

> The Portals in the East and South East are those of the paths which conduct to higher grades, while that in the South leads to the 4 = 7 grade of Philosophus, the highest grade in the First Order.

Osiris directs your attention to the Qamea of Mercury. You continue:

> *The grade of Practicus is especially related to the Planet Mercury, whose Qamea or Mystical Square, together with Seals and Names formed from it, is shown in the East. The symbol of Mercury when inscribed on the Tree of Life is also shown. It embraces all but Kether. The horns spring from DAATH, which is not properly a Sephirah, but rather the conjunction of Chokmah and Binah.*

Hear the voice of Osiris speaking to you:

> I now congratulate you on having passed through the ceremony of the 3 = 8 grade of Practicus, and in recognition thereof, I confer upon you the Mystic Title of Monocris de Astris, which means "Unicorn from the Stars," and I give you the symbol of MAIM which is the Hebrew name for Water.

Go to the East and face the godform of Osiris. The god traces the sigil of the cross and circle before you. Take up the crown-headed scepter and turn to face the East. Taking on the officer-form of the Hierophant, give a knock and say:

> *In the Name of ELOHIM TZABAOTH, hear ye all, that I (state magical motto) proclaim that I have been duly advanced to the grade of 3 = 8 of Practicus, Lord (Lady) of the 30th and 31st Paths, and that I have received the Mystic Title of MONOCRIS DE ASTRIS and the symbol of MAIM.*

PART 4: The Closing

Give a knock and say: *"Let us adore the Lord and King of Water!"* Knock again. Face the East and visualize the Water triangle. Say, *"Let ELOHIM TZABAOTH be praised unto the Countless Ages of Time, Amen!"*

Go to the West of the temple facing the Enochian Tablet of Water. Visualize the astral officer/godforms standing at their stations, facing West also. Give a knock with the scepter and recite the Prayer of the Undines or Water Spirits:

Terrible King of the Sea, Thou who holdest the Keys of the Cataracts of Heaven, and who enclosest the subterranean Waters in the cavernous hollows of Earth. King of the Deluge and of the Rains of Spring. Thou who openest the sources of the rivers and of the fountains; Thou who commandest moisture which is, as it were, the Blood of the Earth, to become the sap of the plants. We adore Thee and we invoke Thee. Speak Thou unto us, Thy changeful creatures, in the Great Tempests, and we shall tremble before Thee. Speak to us also in the murmur of the limpid Waters, and we shall desire Thy love.

O Vastness! Wherein all the rivers of Being seek to lose themselves — which renew themselves ever in Thee! O Thou Ocean of Infinite Perfection! O Height which reflectest Thyself in the Depth! O Depth which exaltest into the Height! Lead us into the true life, through intelligence, through love! Lead us unto immortality through sacrifice, that we may be found worthy to offer one day unto Thee, the Water, the Blood and the Tears, for the Remission of Sins! Amen.

Through the authority of the office of Hierophant bestowed upon you by Osiris, banish the powers of the Water Tablet. Trace with the wand a large circle in front of the Tablet. Then draw the banishing pentagram of Spirit Passive. As you do so vibrate "HCOMA" (Hey-coh-mah). Trace the sigil of Spirit in the center and intone "AGLA" (Ah-gah-lah). Give the Reversal Sign of the Spiraling Light. Then trace the banishing pentagram of Water. As you do so vibrate the Name "EMPEH ARSEL GAIOL" (Em-pay Ar-sel Gah-ee-ohl). Draw the sigil of the eagle's head in the center and intone "Aleph Lamed, AL." Give the Sign of Practicus.

Give the License to Depart by saying:

Depart ye in peace unto your habitations. May the blessing of ELOHIM TZABAOTH be upon you. Be there peace between us, and be ready to come when ye are called! (Give a knock.)

Return the office of Hierophant to the dominion of Osiris in the Eastern part of the Hall.

The goddess Thmê comes to your side. She leads you to the station of the Hiereus where she traces the figure of the cross and triangle in the Air. The godform of Horus salutes with the Projection Sign—Thmê answers with the Sign of Silence. Horus slowly fades from view. In this manner, Thmê releases the other godforms in the Hall, Osiris and the godforms on the Dais. All the astral entities in the Hall begin to fade from view.

Thmê herself is the last godform to dissolve. You thank the goddess for guiding you in the Practicus Hall, and trace the figures of the cross and triangle before her.

She salutes you with the Projection Sign. You answer with the Sign of Silence. Withdraw the white ray which had activated the godform back into your heart center. Perform the Qabalistic Cross one last time to equilibrate all energies within your sphere of sensation.

Take up the sword and perform the Lesser Banishing Ritual of the Pentagram. Then go to the East and say: *"In the Name of ELOHIM TZABAOTH, I declare this temple closed in the 3 = 8 grade of Practicus."*

Give the Battery of knocks: 1-3-1-3. Go to the station of the of Hiereus and repeat the Battery: 1-3-1-3. Go to the station of Hegemon and repeat the Battery: 1-3-1-3. Give the Practicus Sign before exiting the temple.✿

The Fourth Knowledge Lecture

SECTION 1: Admission Badges and Diagrams

 The Solid Triangle, Tetrahedron or *Pyramid of Fire*, is the Admission Badge for the Path of Shin in the 3 = 8 grade. It is an appropriate symbol of Fire, representing the simple Fire of Nature and the Latent or Hidden Fire. It is formed of four triangles, three visible and one concealed, which yet is the synthesis of the rest. The three upper triangles represent Solar Fire, Volcanic Fire, and Astral Fire, while the fourth and basal triangle represents latent heat. Active Fire is AUD, passive Fire is AUB, equilibrated Fire is AUR, while the name of Fire itself is ASCH.

The Greek Cross of 13 Squares, is the Admission Badge to the Path of Resh in the 3 = 8 grade. It is formed of 13 squares which fitly refer to the Sun's motion through the Zodiac. The Celestial Signs are further arranged in the arms of the cross according to the four Elements with the Sun in the center and representing that luminary as the center of the whole figure.

The Cup of Stolistes, is the Admission Badge to the Water temple of Hod in the Practicus grade. Based upon the lamen of the Stolistes, this Badge is an explicit representation of the same energies utilized by that officer. This Badge partakes to some extent of the symbolism of the Laver of Moses and the Sea of Solomon.

On the Tree of Life, it embraces nine of the Sephiroth, exclusive of Kether. Yesod and Malkuth form the triangle below, the former the apex, the latter the base. Like the Caduceus, it further represents the three primary Elements of Water, Air, and Fire. The crescent is the Water which is above the Firmament, the circle is the Firmament, and the triangle is the consuming Fire below, which is opposed to the Celestial Fire symbolized by the upper part of the Caduceus. The cup is a symbol of spiritual receptiveness.

The Symbol of Mercury on the Tree of Life embraces all but Kether. The horns spring from Daath (knowledge) which is not, properly speaking, a Sephirah, but rather a conjunction of Chokmah and Binah.

The Unification of the Planets in Mercury[98] represents a glyph of the Planets combined in a Mercurial figure. Descending in order are the symbols of Luna, Mars, Sol, Venus, Jupiter and Saturn.

The Garden of Eden Before the Fall (see Plate 3). This diagram is described in the Practicus Ritual. It shows in a glyph the teaching proper to the Practicus on entering the Sephirah Hod which he has reached by the Paths of Shin and Resh from Malkuth and Yesod respectively.

At the summit are the Three Supernal Sephiroth summed up into One *Aima Elohim*, the Mother Supernal The Woman of the Apocalypse clothed with the Sun, the Moon under her feet, and on her head the Crown of Twelve Stars.

It is written So the Name Jehovah is joined to the Name Elohim, for Jehovah planted a Garden Eastward in Eden.

From the Three Supernals follow the other Sephiroth of the Tree of Life. Below the Tree, proceeding from Malkuth is The Tree of Knowledge of Good and of Evil which is between the Tree of Life and the World of Assiah or Shells, represented by the Coiled up Dragon with Seven Heads and Ten Horns being the Seven Infernal Palaces and the Ten Averse Sephiroth.

The River **NAHAR** (נהר) flows forth from the Supernal Eden and in Daath it is divided into Four Heads:

PISON (פישון): Fire flowing to Geburah where there is Gold.
GIHON (גיהון): Water the Waters of Mercy, flowing into Chesed.
HIDDIKEL (הדקל): Air flowing into Tiphareth.
PHRATH (Euphrates) (פרת): Earth flowing into Malkuth.

It is written In Daath the Depths are broken up and the Clouds drop down dew.

The word *Nahar* has the meaning perennial stream never failing waters as opposed to other words meaning Torrent or Brook.

The River going out of Eden is the River of the Apocalypse, the Waters of Life, clear as crystal proceeding from the Throne, on either side of the Tree of Life, bearing all manner of Fruit.

Thus the Rivers form a Cross and on it The Great Adam, the Son who is to rule the Nations, was extended from Tiphareth and his arms stretch out to Geburah and Gedulah, and Malkuth is Eve, supporting with her hands the Two Pillars.[99]

As a important note of interest, archeologists have recently theorized that the land called Eden was once a fertile plain in a region now covered by the waters of the Persian Gulf. The words Eden and Adam are pre-Sumerian words for fertile plain, and settlement on the plain. The names of the rivers Hiddekel, Gihon, Pison, and Euphrates are probably linguistic remnants of a people who lived in the area before the Sumerians appeared. The Rivers Phrath (Euphrates) and Hiddekel (Tigris) still flow today. But scientists have recently discovered, via pictures from space, images of a fossil river which once flowed

---

[98] Optional Diagram.
[99] The above section is from Regardie s *The Golden Dawn*.

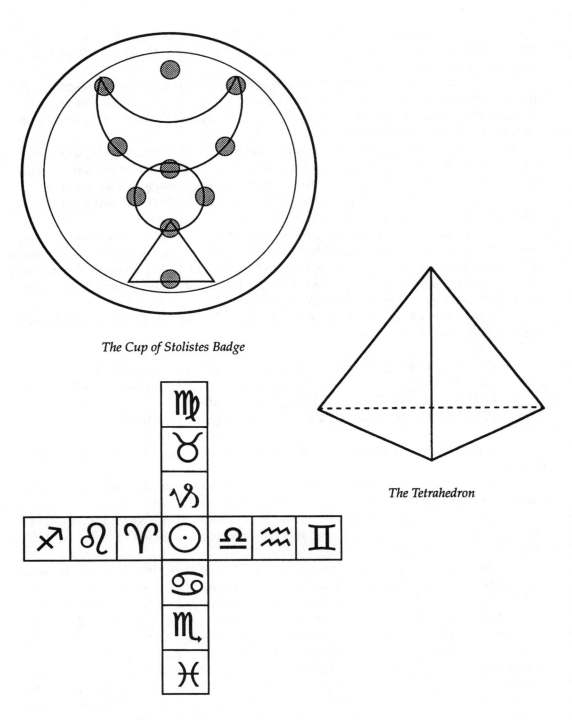

The Cup of Stolistes Badge

The Tetrahedron

The Greek Cross of 13 Squares

through dry river beds in northern Arabia now called the Wadi Batin and the Wadi Rimah (Pison). Some archeologists now believe that the Karun river which rises in Iran and flows southwest to the Gulf was in fact the ancient river Gihon.

The river Gihon brings up the geographical problem in that it is supposed to "encompass the whole land of Ethiopia." The Hebrew script refers to it as the land of Kush. Seventeenth-century translators of the King James Bible rendered this as "Ethiopia." Kush could in fact refer instead to Kashshu and the Kashshites, a people who occupied Mesopotamia from 1500 to 900 BCE. All of these ancient rivers could have joined a single river that once ran through a rich fertile area (Eden) which was flooded by the Persian Gulf in approximately 5000 to 4000 BCE, when a sudden rise in sea levels occurred around the world. Thus the Genesis passage referring to the river of Eden dividing and forming four heads, is rooted in geography as well as in spiritual legend.

The diagram of the Garden of Eden, along with its counterpart in the following grade, holds the keys to many psychological and spiritual dilemmas which besiege the aspirant. In fact both diagrams taken together can be said to outline the entire magical philosophy.

The diagram of Eden before the Fall is a pictorial embodiment of the three basic principles in humanity; the three Qabalistic parts of the Soul. Each principle is seemingly independent from and oblivious to the others. An early evolutionary stage in the history of the human race is symbolized here—a time when humans were not sentient beings—there was no such thing as self-consciousness. It was to coin a phrase, an age of innocence, when peace and tranquillity reigned by right of birth not by toil.

Bear in mind that what is meant by peace here is psychological peace rather than a peaceful environment. Certainly the first human-creatures on Earth did not often have peaceful surroundings. But since self-consciousness (*sentience*) had not yet been born into the mind of humanity, there were no psychological conflicts such as those which torture so many Souls today. The diagram is revealed in the 3 = 8 Grade because the Element of Water is an appropriate expression of this tranquil existence.

At the top of the drawing is a great goddess with a diadem of twelve stars and clothed with the glory of the Sun who stands upon the crescent moon. Her symbolism refers to the archetypal or Supernal mind-state, thus she is a glyph of the Neshamah or Highest Self of the Soul. At the bottom of the Tree is Eve, the symbol of the Nephesh, standing in *balanced opposition* to the Divine Self. The goddess Eve is the dark and extremely ancient terrestrial feminine principle of passions and instincts, which dates back to the primeval origins of human physiology. Reconciling between these two goddesses is Adam, sustained by the might of Eve. Adam represents the Ruach not yet aware its own latent power and potential. Moreover, he symbolizes humankind as a whole; he is a personified glyph of the collective creative principle or manifesting Light incarnating into humanity; touching upon the Divine above him and the instinctive below him. Adam can also be said to represent the aspirant of the mysteries

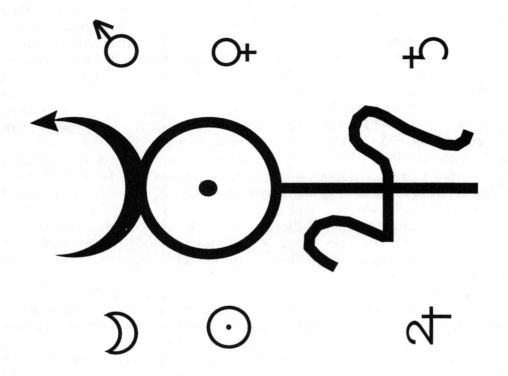

Unification of the Planets in Mercury

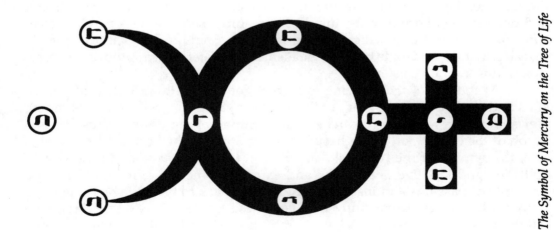

The Symbol of Mercury on the Tree of Life

at a point in time preceding the arousal of any "personal demons" buried deep within the modern subconscious mind.

The slumbering dragon beneath is a symbol of the latent magical abilities within humanity—vast in power but neutral; neither good nor evil in and of themselves.

The Tarot Keys of *Judgment* and *The Sun* along with the 31st and 30th paths of the *Sepher Yetzirah* are fully described in the Practicus Ritual. They are further delineated in the section describing "Ritual Work for the Practicus."✿

The Tree of the Knowledge of Good and Evil

SECTION 2: Lineal Figures and Magical Squares

As stated earlier, one of the most pervasive ideas behind the science of magic is the Law of Correspondences. In addition to to colors, musical notes, incenses, gemstones, metals, and other items, the various Sephirotic and Planetary energies are also correlated (first and foremost) to the idea of numerical value. The numbers and lineal figures appropriate to Planets are:

Saturn	—	3	—	Triangle
Jupiter	—	4	—	Square
Mars	—	5	—	Pentagram
Sun	—	6	—	Hexagram
Venus	—	7	—	Heptagram
Mercury	—	8	—	Octagram
Moon	—	9	—	Enneagram

Additional lineal figures that the Practicus should be aware of are the Rhombus and the Vesica.

A *Rhombus* is an equilateral parallelogram (or four-sided figure whose opposing sides are parallel and equal) with no right angles. In such a figure, each side is identical to the side opposite it. A diagonal line drawn between two opposite points on the rhomboid would form two congruent triangles. The figure of a rhombus is very similar to that the vesica.

A *Vesica* is a pointed oval formed by the intersection of two circles. It is the "common ground" shared by both circles, and is often used to symbolize a state of transition, transference or transcendence. (The *vesica piscis* or pointed oval aureole was used by medieval artists to enclose holy figures.)✿

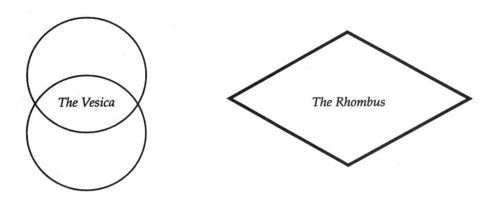

The Vesica

The Rhombus

Polygons and Polygrams[100]

The Point within the Circle represents the operation of Kether in general, and the Cross within the Circle that of Chokmah, for therein are the roots of Wisdom. In using these lineal figures in the formation of Talismans under the Sephiroth, remember that:

> *The Point within the Circle*—Kether
> *The Cross within the Circle*—Chokmah
> *The Triangle within the Circle*—Binah
> *The Square within the Circle*—Chesed,

and that the remaining Sephiroth should have the double, treble or quadruple forms of their lineal figures bound together in their Talismans. For example, in the Heptangle for Netzach, the Heptagon and the two forms of the Heptagram should be united in the same Talisman, the extremities of the angles coinciding.

The Endekangle is attributed to the Qlippoth, the Dodekangle to Zodiacal Forces in Malkuth. Kether hath the Primum Mobile, Chokmah the Sphere of the Zodiac in command, and Malkuth that of the elements.

And many other meanings are bound together in the lineal figures besides those which are given in this book. Two or more different lineal figures may be bound together in the same Talisman.

The *Triangle* is the only lineal figure into which all surfaces can be reduced, for every Polygon can be divided into triangles by drawing lines from its angles to its center; and the triangle is the first and simplest of all lineal figures. It refers to the Triad operating in all things, to the Three Supernal Sephiroth and to Binah, the Third Sephirah, in particular.

Among the Planets it is especially referred to Saturn, and among the Elements to Fire, and, as the color of Saturn is black, and that of Fire red, the black Triangle will represent Saturn, and the red, Fire.

---

[100] From an abridged Order Document in Regardie's *The Golden Dawn*.

The Three Angles also symbolize the three Alchemical Principles of Nature: Salt, Sulphur and Mercury.

The *Square* is an important lineal figure, which naturally represents stability and equation. It includes the idea of surface and superficial measurement. It refers to the Quaternary in all things, and to the Tetrad of the Holy Name YHVH operating through the four Elements of Fire, Water, Air and Earth. It is allotted to Chesed, the 4th Sephirah, and among the Planets to Jupiter. And as representing the Four Elements, it represents their ultimation in the Material Form.

The *Pentangle* can be traced in two ways: reflected from every second point, when it is called the *Pentagon*; and reflected from every third point when it is called the *Pentagram*. The Pentangle as a whole is referred to the Fifth Sephirah, Geburah. The Pentagon naturally represents the power of the Pentad, operating in Nature by the dispersal of the Spirit and the four Elements through it.

The Pentagram with a single point upwards is called the "Sign of the Microcosm," and is a good symbol, representing man with his arms and legs extended adoring his Creator, and especially the dominion of the Spirit over the four Elements, and consequently of reason over matter.

But with the single point downwards it is a very evil symbol. The Head of the Goat, or Demon's Head, representing the abasement of reason beneath the blind forces of matter, the elevation of anarchy above order, and of conflicting forces driven by chance above God.

It represents the concentrated force of the Spirit and the four Elements governed by the five letters of the Name of the Restorer of all things YHShVH, and it is especially attributed to the Planet Mars. It also shows the Kerubim and the Wheel of the Spirit. It is a symbol of tremendous force, and of HEH, the letter of the Great Supernal Mother AIMA.

The *Hexangle* can be traced in two ways as a complete symbol: viz, reflected from every 2nd point, when it is called the *Hexagon*, and reflected from every 3rd point when it is called the *Hexagram*. The Hexangle as a whole is referred to the 6th Sephirah, Tiphareth. The Hexangle naturally represents the powers of the Hexad operating in Nature, by the dispersal of the rays of the Planets, and of the Zodiac emanating from the Sun. The number of degrees of a great circle cut off between its angles is sixty, forming the astrological sextile aspect, powerful for good. It is not so consonant to the Sun nature as the Hexagram, and remember thou, that the *'Gon signifieth dispersion, distribution, and radiation of a force; but the 'Gram concentration*. Hence use thou the 'Gon for spreading, and the 'Gram for concentration and sealing; and when there is need, thou canst compare, interpose and combine them; but the 'Gon initiateth the whirl.

The Hexagram with a single point uppermost is called the *Sign of the Macrocosm*, or greater world, because its six angles fitly represent the six days or periods of Creation evolved from the manifestation of the Triune; while its synthesis forms the seventh day, a period of rest, summed up in the hexagonal center.

It represents especially the concentrated force of the Planets, acting through the Signs of the Zodiac, and thus sealing the Astral Image of Nature

Kether

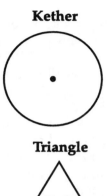

Chokmah

Binah

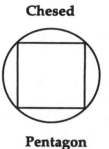

Chesed

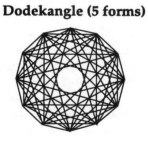

Triangle

Binah.
The
Supernal
Triad.

Square

Chesed.
The
Tetrad.
YHVH

Pentangle (2 forms)

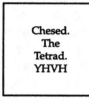

Pentagon

Geburah.
The
Five
Elements.

Pentagram

Hexangle (2 forms)

Heptangle (3 forms)

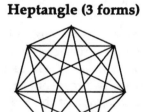

Octangle (3 forms)

Enneangle (4 forms)

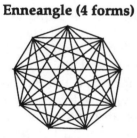

Dekangle (4 forms)

Endekangle (5 forms)

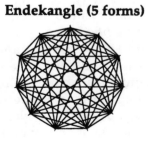

Dodekangle (5 forms)

Polygons and Polygrams

Hexagon

Tiphareth
The 7 Planets &
The 12 Signs

Hexagram

Two Triangles
Tiphareth
7 Planets

Heptagram

Netzach.
The
7 Planets

Continuous,
reflected at
every 3rd point.

Heptagram
Star of Venus

Continuous,
reflected at
every 4th point.

Octogram

Hod.
The 8
Lettered
Name.

Two squares
reflected at
every 3rd point.

Octogram
The Star of Mercury

Continuous
reflected at
every 4th point.

Enneagram

Triple
Ternary
of 7 Planets
with Lunar
Nodes

Continuous
reflected at
every 3rd point.

Enneagram

Triple
Ternany

Three Triangles
reflected at
every 4th point.

Enneagram
The Star of Luna

Continuous
reflected at
every 5th point.

Dekagram

Malkuth

Two Pentagons
reflected at
every 3rd point.

Dekagram

The
Ten
Sephiroth

Continuous
reflected at
every 4th point.

Dekagram
Duplicated letter Heh

Two Pentagrams
reflected at
every 5th point.

Endekagram

Evil Triad,
Dukes of
Edom

Continuous
reflected at
every 3rd point.

Endekagram

Restriction
of Evil

Continuous
reflected at
every 4th point.

Endekagram
The Qlippoth

Continuous
reflected at
every 5th point.

Endekagram
Qlippotic Princes

Continuous
reflected at
every 6th point.

Dodekagram

Masculine
& Feminine
Signs of the
Zodiac

Two Hexagons
reflected at
every 3rd point.

Dodekagram

The Three
Quadru-
plicities

Three squares
reflected at
every 4th point.

Dodekagram

The 4
Tripli-
cities

Four triangles
reflected at
every 5th point.

Dodekagram

Continuous
reflected at
every 6th point.

Polygons and Polygrams

under the presidency of the Sephiroth; and also the 7 Palaces of the same. It is especially attributable to the Sun.

It is a symbol of great strength and power, forming with the Cross and the Pentagram, a triad of potent and good symbols, which are in harmony with each other.

The *Heptangle* as a whole is referred to the 7th Sephirah, Netzach. The *Heptagon* naturally represents the dispersal of the powers of the seven planets through the week, and through the year. It alludes to the power of the Septenary acting through all things, as exemplified by the seven colors of the rainbow.

The *Heptagram* reflected from every 3rd point yieldeth 7 triangles at the apices thereof; fitly representing the Triad operating in each Planet, and the Planets themselves in the week and the year.

The Heptagram is the *Star of Venus*, and is especially applicable to her nature. And as the Heptagram is the lineal figure of the Seven Planets, so is Venus as it were their Gate or entrance, the fitting symbol of the Isis of Nature, and of the seven lower Sephiroth of the Bride.

The *Octangle* as a whole is referred to the Eighth Sephirah, Hod. The Octangle naturally represents the power of the Ogdoad, and the *Octagon* showeth the Ogdoad operating in Nature by the dispersal of the rays of the Elements in their dual aspect under the presidency of the 8 letters of the name.

The *Octagram* reflected from every 3rd point yieldeth 8 triangles at the apices thereof; fitly representing the Triad operating in each element in its dual form, i.e., of Positive and Negative, under the powers of the Name YHVH ADONAI or as it is written bound together IAHDONHI.

This Octagram reflected from every fourth point is the *Star of Mercury*, and is especially applicable to his nature. It is further a potent symbol, representing the binding together of the concentrated Positive and Negative Forces of the Elements under the Name of IAHDONHI. And forget not that ADONAI is the key of YHVH.

The *Enneangle* as a whole is referred to the 9th Sephirah Yesod. It naturally representeth the power of the Ennead, and the *Enneagon* showeth the Ennead operating in Nature by the dispersal of the rays of the seven Planets and of the Head and Tail of the Dragon of the Moon.

The *Enneagram* reflected from every 3rd point representeth the Triple Ternary operating both in the 7 Planets with the Caput and Cauda Draconis of the Moon, and with the Alchemical principles counterchanged and interwoven. It is not so consonant with the Nature of Luna as the Enneagram reflected from every 5th Point.

The Enneagram is the *Star of Luna*, and is especially applicable to her nature. It represents her as the administratrix to the Earth of the virtues of the Solar System under the Sephiroth.

The Enneagram reflected from every fourth point is composed of three triangles united within a circle, and alludes to the Triple Ternary of the three alchemical principles themselves. It is not so consonant with the nature of Luna as the next Form.

The *Dekangle* as a whole is referred to the Tenth Sephirah—Malkuth. The Dekangle naturally represents the power of the Dekad, and the *Dekagon* showeth the Dekad operating in nature by the dispersal of the rays of the ten Sephiroth therein. The number of degrees of a Great Circle cut off between its angles is 36, the half of the Quintile astrological aspect.

The *Dekagram* reflected from every 3rd point is especially consonant with Malkuth, and shows the Triad operating through the angle of the two Pentagons within a circle, of which it is composed. It alludes to the combination of the three Alchemical Principles with the Spirit and the Four Elements in their Positive and Negative form, under the presidency of the Ten Sephiroth themselves.

The Dekagram reflected from every 5th point is composed of two Pentagrams within a circle. It shows the operation of the duplicated Heh of the Tetragrammaton, and the concentration of the Positive and Negative forces of the Spirit and of the four Elements under the presidency of the potencies of the Five in Binah; the Revolutions of the Forces under Aima, the Great Mother.

The *Endekangle* (and *Endekad*) as a general rule is referred to the Qlippoth: of its forms however, the one reflected from every 4th point represents their restriction, and therefore it is not altogether to be classed with those that represent their operations in Nature. The Endekangle naturally represents the evil and imperfect nature of the Endekad, and the *Endekagon* represents the dispersal of the eleven curses of Mount Ebal through the Universe (Deut. XXVII).(Though they are paraphrased as 12 in the English Bible, in the Hebrew version they are paragraphed as eleven, two being classed together.)

The *Dodekangle* as a general rule is referred to the Zodiac, and naturally represents the power of the Dodekad.

The *Dodekagon* shows the dispersal of the influence of the Zodiac through nature, the Dodekagram its concentration. The number of degrees of a Great Circle cut off between its angles is 30, forming the weak astrological semi-Sextile aspect, good in nature and operation.✿

Magic Squares

The *Qameoth* or magical squares of the Planets, are both diagrams as well as potent mystical pentacles which relate to the Planets and to specific Planetary energies. The word *Qamea* comes from a Hebrew root word meaning talisman or amulet, but the word also has connections with the English word "cameo." Although the magic squares are best known through the works of such magicians as Cornelius Agrippa (*Occult Philosophy*) and Peter De Abano (*The Heptameron*), they are undoubtedly of ancient and probably Persian origin.

The magical squares of the Planets are formed of the squares of the number of the Planet, arranged so as to yield the same number each way (horizontal, vertical and diagonal). The number of the sum of each column of figures and the number of the total of all the numbers of the square, are also numbers especially attached to the Planet. The number of lesser squares or units on each side of the Qamea determines which Planet it is associated with through correspondence of the number of the appropriate Sephirah. Thus the number of the Planet *Saturn* is 3 (Binah), square 9, sum of all columns vertical, horizontal and diagonal—15; total sum of all numbers—45. Thus one can easily see from this example that there are many numbers contained in each Qamea which are designated as Planetary numbers. These numbers are then formed into Divine and Spirit names (and sigils) which correlate to certain Planetary energies.

The Planetary energies are said to include *Archangels, Intelligences* and *Spirits*. The Names of these beings are themselves derived from the primary numbers of the square. The administrative force is the Planetary Archangel. The Intelligence of a Planet is seen as an evolutionary, nurturing, inspiring or guiding entity, while the Spirit is traditionally viewed as a blind or "raw" energy force without guidance or intelligence. The Spirit must always be guided by the Planetary Intelligence, under the control of the Archangel.

A *sigil* or *seal* is a magical symbol that contains the seed or essence of a spirit or deity. The word is derived from the Latin word *sigillum*, which means a sign or signature. It is the magical glyph that is derived from a name or magic formula by a process of numerical conversion the result of which is traced upon a Qamea (or similar device). The method of Gematria known as *Aiq Beker* is very important to the drawing of sigils on a Qamea (Refer to the section on *Aiq Beker*.)

The *Planetary seal* or sigil of the Planet is a symbol designed in such a manner that its traced lines touch every number or unit square of the Qamea. The seal is used in talismanic magic to represent the Qamea or act as a governing force for it.

The Qameoth are very important in the designing of *talismans;* magical objects which are ceremonially consecrated to attract a particular Planetary, Sephirotic, Zodiacal or Elemental force. Designing such talismans is part of the gradework of an Adept. However, many published versions of the Qameoth as well as their corresponding Planetary Sigils often contain mistakes. The student would be well advised to never trust a sigil to be correct simply because it is published. The magician should always work sigils out for him/her self.

Some of the most important numbers associated with the Qameoth are given here. The "units" represent the total number of lesser squares in a given Qamea. The initials **MC** stand for *magic constant*, which represents the sum of the numbers of any given row, column or diagonal line of the Qamea. The initials **GT** allude to the *grand total* or the total sum of all the numbers that appear on a Qamea.

SATURN

Sephirah: 3   *Units:* 9   *MC:* 15   *GT:* 45
Intelligence: Agiel = 45   *Spirit:* Zazel = 45

JUPITER

Sephirah: 4   *Units:* 16   *MC:* 34   *GT:* 136
Intelligence: Iophiel = 136   *Spirit:* Hismael = 136

MARS

Sephirah: 5   *Units:* 25   *MC:* 65   *GT:* 325
Intelligence: Graphiel = 325   *Spirit:* Bartzabel = 325

SOL

Sephirah: 6   *Units:* 36   *MC:* 111   *GT:* 666
Intelligence: Nakhiel = 111   *Spirit:* Sorath = 666

VENUS

Sephirah: 7   *Units:* 49   *MC:* 175   *GT:* 1225
Intelligence: Hagiel = 49   *Spirit:* Kedemel = 175

MERCURY

Sephirah: 8   *Units:* 64   *MC:* 260   *GT:* 2080
Intelligence: Tiriel = 260   *Spirit:* Taphthartharath = 2080

LUNA

Sephirah: 9   *Units:* 81   *MC:* 369   *GT:* 3321
Intelligence: Shelachel = 369   *Spirit:* Chashmodai = 369
Intelligences: Malkah be-Tarshism ve-ad Ruachoth Shechalim = 3321
Spirit of the Spirits: Shad Barshemoth Ha-Shartathan = 3321

4	9	2
3	5	7
8	1	6

Qamea

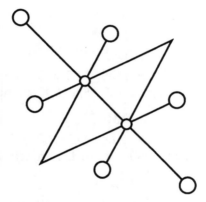

Planetary Seal

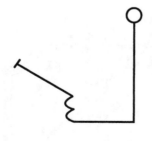

Archangel
CASSIEL
כסיאל

Intelligence
AGIEL
אגיאל

Spirit
ZAZEL
זאזל

The Qamea and Sigils of Saturn

4	14	15	1
9	7	6	12
5	11	10	8
16	2	3	13

Qamea

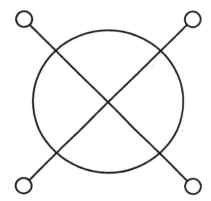

Planetary Seal

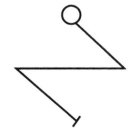

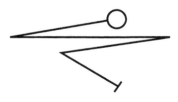

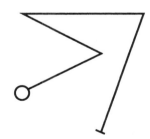

Archangel
SACHIEL
סחיאל

Intelligence
IOPHIEL
יהפיאל

Spirit
HISMAEL
הסמאל

The Qamea and Sigils of Jupiter

11	24	7	20	3
4	12	25	8	16
17	5	13	21	9
10	18	1	14	22
23	6	19	2	15

Qamea

ג	כ	ז	כד	יא
יי	ח	כה	יב	ד
טו	כא	יג	ה	יז
כב	יד	א	יח	י
יה	ב	יט	ו	כג

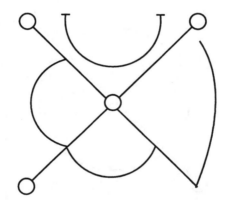

Planetary Seal

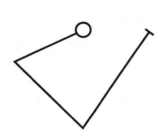

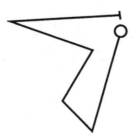

Archangel
ZAMAEL
זמאל

Intelligence
GRAPHIEL
גראפיאל

Spirit
BARTZABEL
ברצבאל

The Qamea and Sigils of Mars

6	32	3	34	35	1
7	11	27	28	8	30
19	14	16	15	23	24
18	20	22	21	17	13
25	29	10	9	26	12
36	5	33	4	2	31

Qamea

Planetary Seal

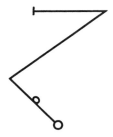

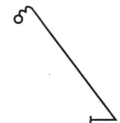

Archangel	Intelligence	Spirit
MICHAEL	**NAKHIEL**	**SORATH**
מיכאל	**נכיאל**	**סורת**

The Qamea and Sigils of Sol

22	47	16	41	10	35	4
5	23	48	17	42	11	29
30	6	24	49	18	36	12
13	31	7	25	43	19	37
38	14	32	1	26	44	20
21	39	8	33	2	27	45
46	15	40	9	34	3	28

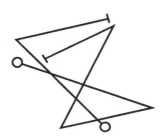

♀

Qamea

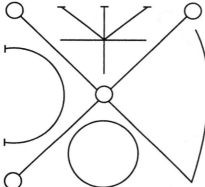

Planetary Seal

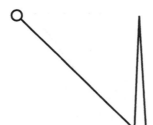

Intelligences
BENI SERAPHIM
בני שרפים

Archangel
ANAEL
אנאל

Intelligence
HAGIEL
הגיאל

Spirit
QEDEMEL
קדמאל

The Qamea and Sigils of Venus

8	58	59	5	4	62	63	1
49	15	14	52	53	11	10	56
41	23	22	44	45	19	18	48
32	34	35	29	28	38	39	25
40	26	27	37	36	30	31	33
17	47	46	20	21	43	42	24
9	55	54	12	13	51	50	16
64	2	3	61	60	6	7	57

Qamea

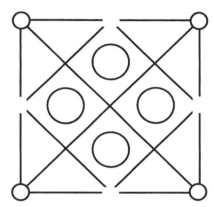

Planetary Seal

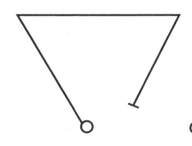

Archangel	Intelligence	Spirit
RAPHAEL	**TIRIEL**	**TAPHTHARTHARATH**
רפאל	**טיריאל**	**תפתרתרת**

The Qamea and Sigils of Mercury

385

37	78	29	70	21	62	13	54	5
6	38	79	30	71	22	63	14	46
47	7	39	80	31	72	23	55	15
16	48	8	40	81	32	64	24	56
57	17	49	9	41	73	33	65	25
26	58	18	50	1	42	74	34	66
67	27	59	10	51	2	43	75	35
36	68	19	60	11	52	3	44	76
77	28	69	20	61	12	53	4	45

Qamea

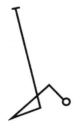

Archangel
GABRIEL

גבריאל

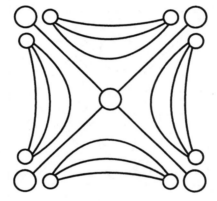

Planetary Seal

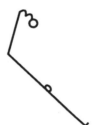

Intelligence
SHELACHEL

שלחאל

Spirit
CHASHMODAI

חשמודאי

Alternative Sigil
CHASHMODAI

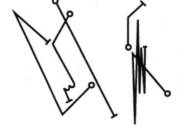

Intelligence of the Intelligences
MALKAH BE TARSHISM VE-AD
RUACHOTH SCHECHALIM

Golden Dawn Spelling מלכא בתרשישים ועד רוחות שחלים

Agrippa Spelling מלכא בתרשיתים עד ברוח שחקים

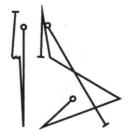

Spirit of the Spirits
SHAD BARSCHEMOTH
HA-SHARTATHAN

Golden Dawn Spelling שד ברשמעת חשרתתן

Agrippa Spelling שד ברשהמעת שרתתן

The Qamea and Sigils of Luna

It is easy to see how the *grand total* of each Qamea is arrived at, since it is simply the total sum of all the numbers on a given magic square. However, this is not true of the magic constant. Although many occultists know what the magic constant (or mystical number) of a Qamea is, they often do not know how it is arrived at. A mathematical formula is needed to determine the magic constant of each Qamea. The formula for finding the magic constant of any given Qamea is:

$$\frac{N^3 + N}{2}$$

In all of these formulas, "N" stands for the number of the Sephirah that corresponds to the Planet involved. For example in the case of the Saturn square, N = 3. The formula for finding the MC would follow:

$$\frac{N^3+N}{2} = \frac{3 \times 3 \times 3+3}{2} = \frac{27+3}{2} = \frac{30}{2} = 15$$

The magic constant of the Saturn square is 15. To find the MC of the Jupiter square we would use the same formula, the only difference is that in this case N = 4.

$$\frac{N^3+N}{2} = \frac{4 \times 4 \times 4+4}{2} = \frac{64+4}{2} = \frac{68}{2} = 34$$

The magic constant of the Jupiter square is 34.

Besides the magic constant and the grand total, there is another Planetary number that is crucial to the understanding of magic squares, the *arcane compliment*.

The arcane compliment (AC) is a hidden number which controls how the numbers are placed on a Qamea. It is a number which determines the arrangement of *all* the numbers on the magic square. There are two different formulas for finding the arcane complement—one for odd-numbered magic squares, the other for even-numbered Qameoth.

Odd Squares:

The formula for finding the AC of an odd square is:

$$\frac{N^2 + 1}{2}$$

Remember that in the case of Saturn, N = 3, the number of Binah. The formula is worked out as follows:

$$\frac{N^2+1}{2} = \frac{3 \times 3+1}{2} = \frac{9+1}{2} = \frac{10}{2} = 5$$

The arcane compliment of the Saturn square is 5. And on all of the odd-numbered Qameoth, the AC is *always placed* in the exact center of the square. The numbering of the lesser squares or units starts immediately below the arcane compliment, beginning with the number 1.

To place the remaining numbers on the square, one must not think of the Qamea as just a flat surface with numbers. The magic square must be visualized as being cylindrical or spherical. If the paper Qamea was rolled into a tube, the right and left columns of numbers would then touch each other. Had the tube been rolled the other way, the top and bottom rows of numbers would touch each other. Either way, the columns and rows of numbers on the Qamea should be imagined as being connected on all sides. (The best way for the student to learn the method of number placement, is to draw up a blank Saturn square.)

The remaining numbers after 1 then begin in a downward progression to the right. The number 2 would be placed on a unit below the lower right-hand corner of the Qamea, but since there is no square there to place the number, the 2 would be placed in the next available space at the top of the next column. The downward progression to the right would continue, so that the next number, 3, is placed in the middle of the first column.

The next number, 4, encounters a problem, in that it would normally fall into a space that is already occupied by another number—1. When a number's natural progression is blocked by another number, the rule is to drop the new number straight down (in its original column) by two spaces. Since in our Qamea, the bottom row is imagined to touch the top row, the number 4 will drop down two spaces and end up in the upper left-hand corner of the square.

The number 5 is the arcane compliment, which has already been placed in its proper position at the center of the Qamea. The following number 6, continues the downward progression to the right. The number 7 is blocked by the number 4, so it drops two spaces down and falls into the unit in the middle of the right-hand column. The numbers 8 and 9 then follow the usual progression.

This is the complete formula for figuring out the arcane complement and the placement of numbers on all of the odd-numbered squares.

Even Squares:

The formula for the arcane complement of any even square is:

$$N^2 + 1$$

Remember that in the case of Jupiter, N = 4, the number of Chesed. The formula is worked out as follows:

$$N^2 + 1 = 4 \times 4 + 1 = 16 + 1 = 17$$

The AC of the Jupiter square is 17. But in order to place all of the numbers on an even square, a different method is called for.

Using the Jupiter square as the example, one must first draw a blank Qamea that is composed of 16 units (4 x 4). The squares are then numbered in progression starting from the upper right-hand corner, going from right to left—1, 2, 3, 4, etc., until all 16 squares are numbered. Then draw a large "X" through the Qamea from corner to corner.

Then a second blank Qamea is drawn. This new Qamea is then filled in with numbers from the previous one, but only with the numbers that are touched by the "X."

The remaining (untouched) numbers from the first Qamea are then subtracted from the arcane complement (17). The final numbers arrived at are then placed into the remaining blank squares of the second Qamea. This is how the numbers on the Jupiter square are obtained.[101]

SECTION 3: Literal Qabalah

The *Literal Qabalah,* one of the four branches of the ancient Hebrew mystical Qabalah, concerns the relationship between the numbers and letters of the Hebrew alphabet. It exists primarily in three forms which have been of great value to magicians throughout the ages. These include *Gematria, Notariqon,* and *Temurah.*

Gematria

The method of assigning numbers to each of the Hebrew letters is known as *Gematria.* The ancient Hebrews did not have a separate set of figures to describe numbers. Instead they used the letters of their alphabet. Gematria developed as a process of ascribing *meaning* to numbers and determining the meanings of words from their numerical value. This is usually accomplished by converting words into their numeral values and comparing them to the values of other words in order to acquire a new perspective on the original meaning. Words which share the same numerical value are said to have a significant relationship to one another.

For example the name *Ruach Elohim* (the Spirit of the gods) in Hebrew has a numeral value of 300 (Ruach = *Resh:* 200, *Vav:* 6, *Cheth:* 8 = 214—Elohim = *Aleph:* 1, *Lamed:* 30, *Heh:* 5, *Yod:* 10, *Mem:* 40 = 86). 300 is the same as the value of the Hebrew letter *Shin,* which incidentally is the symbol of the Ruach Elohim.

(Note: The student could take this one step further by lopping off the two zeros. This would leave 3, the number of *Gimel,* thus pointing to a relationship between the Ruach Elohim and the Tarot card of The High Priestess.)

In another case, the Hebrew word *Achad* which means "one" or "unity" has the numeral value of 13, the same value as the word *Ahevah,* "love." Therefore a relationship exists between these Hebrew words. In a final example, 26 is the number given to the Tetragrammaton—YHVH— the most sacred name of the Divine (*Yod:* 10 + *Heh:* 5 + *Vav:* 6 + *Heh:* 5 = 26). Twenty-six is also the number of the Middle Pillar on the Tree of Life (counting the value of the Sephiroth: 1+6+9+10=26).

(Note: In the study of Gematria one will find numerous cases of sublime names and concepts sharing numerical values with low and demonic ones. The student is advised to consider this as an example of the Hermetic axiom "As above, so below." Even the highest heavens have their equivalents in the lowly abode of shells.)

---

[101] Many of the other even-numbered squares follow increasingly complex methods of numerical arrangement that we will not explore here. However these formulas will be examined in depth in a forthcoming book by Adam Forrest, who has also published two new magic squares (the Qamea of the Elements and that of Mazzaloth or the Zodiac) in Book 1 of *The Golden Dawn Journal.*

300 30 3	200 20 2	100 10 1
שׁ ל ג	ר כ ב	ק י א
600 60 6	500 50 5	400 40 4
ם ס ו	ך נ ה	ד מ ת
900 90 9	800 80 8	700 70 7
ץ צ ט	ף פ ח	ן ע ז

300 30 3	100 10 1	200 20 2
BINAH	KETHER	CHOKMAH
שׁ ל ג	ק י א	ר כ ב
500 50 5	600 60 6	400 40 4
GEBURAH	TIPHARETH	CHESED
ך נ ה	ם ס ו	ד מ ת
800 80 8	900 90 9	700 70 7
HOD	YESOD	NETZACH
ף פ ח	ץ צ ט	ן ע ז

Aiq Beker—The Qabalah of Nine Chambers

Aiq Beker:

The method known as *Aiq Beker* is an important tool of Gematria used not only to convert letters into numbers, but also to create sigils and talismans. In order to trace the sigil of an Angel or Spirit name on a magic square, it is important to first *reduce* the name to the lowest possible numerical value that will fit on a given Qamea. This is done by using an ancient Qabalistic technique known as Aiq Beker or the *Qabalah of Nine Chambers.* This is a diagram that shows three rows and three columns (a total of nine chambers) of numbers which are grouped together according to the similarity of their numbers. (For example in one chamber, *Gimel, Lamed* and *Shin* are placed because of their numbers 3, 30, and 300.) The numbers in this diagram, from 1 to 900 are read from right to left, in the same manner that Hebrew is read. The name Aiq Beker comes from reading the Hebrew letters in the first two chambers from 1 to 200: *Aleph, Yod, Qoph,* and *Beth, Kaph, Resh.*

(Note: a second form of the diagram shows the chambers arranged in accordance with the Sephiroth on the Tree of Life.)

For example, if one wanted to trace the sigil of the Intelligence of Saturn, AGIEL, on the Saturn square, the numerical value of each Hebrew letter of the name would have to be reduced to nine or less than nine (nine is the highest number on the Saturn square). The letters in the name are *Aleph*—1, *Gimel*—3, *Yod*—10, *Aleph*—1, and *Lamed*—30. The only letters which need to be reduced in this case are *Yod* and *Lamed,* which can be reduced to 1 and 3 using the Aiq Beker chart. The numbers obtained which can be used to trace the sigil on the square are 1, 3, 1, 1, 3.

Tracing a Sigil:

When tracing a sigil on a Qamea, the first number of the name is marked with a small circle. From there a line is drawn following the progression of the numbers. When the final number of the name is reached, a short line is drawn to indicate the completion of the sigil.

Variations in Tracing sigils:

If two letters of the same kind such as two *Beths* or two *Gimels* are side-by-side within a name, this is represented in the sigil by a wave or crook in the line at that point. If there is a letter in the name through which the line of the sigil passes straight through to meet another letter, a loop or noose is formed at that point to indicate that the letter is indeed a part of the name.

(Note: Another way of using Aiq Beker is to take one of the three letters in any given section of the Aiq Beker diagram and exchange it for one of the other two letters in that section. Thus in the first box, the letter Qoph could be substituted for either the letter *Aleph* or the letter *Yod.* This manner of using Aiq Beker falls somewhat under the category of *Temurah.*)

Although not a part of the Qabalistic system of Gematria, the *Pythagorean Table* is worth mentioning in conjunction with Aiq Beker. This Greek-based table shows how our own alphabet can be reduced to numbers:

The Pythagorean Table

1	2	3	4	5	6	7	8	9
A	B	C	D	E	F	G	H	I
J	K	L	M	N	O	P	Q	R
S	T	U	V	W	X	Y	Z	

Notariqon

This aspect of the Literal Qabalah derives its name from the Latin word for "short-hand writer," *notarius*. This is a method for finding acronyms.

The first form of Notariqon is *expansive*, meaning that every letter in a single word is used to create the initial letter of another word in a sentence. For an example, take the word *Berashith*, the first word in Genesis. Every letter of this word can be made an abbreviation of another word, yielding the sentence *Berashith Rahi Elohim Sheyequebelo Israel Torah*, which means "In the Beginning the gods saw that Israel would accept the law."

The second form of Notariqon is *contractive*—a complete reversal of the first form. In this case the first letter of each word in a sentence is taken to create a single word which is the synthesis of the entire sentence. One example of this a word found in the Lesser Banishing Ritual of the Pentagram, *AGLA*. The letters of this word are taken from the sentence *Atah Gibor Le-Olahm Adonai*, which means "Thou art great forever, my Lord." Another example is the word *ARARITA* which is constructed from the sentence *Achad Rosh Achdotho Rosh Ichudo Temurahzo Achad*,[102] meaning "One is his beginning, One is his individuality, his permutation is One."

For another example we shall cite a word that is commonly used by several religions, but with little true understanding of its meaning. AMEN is written in Hebrew as *Aleph, Mem, Nun*, which stands for the phrase *Adonai Melekh Na'amon* or "Lord, Faithful King."

As a note of interest, one of the names given to the Qabalah is *Chokmah Nestorah* or the "secret wisdom." The initial letters of this phrase are *Cheth* and *Nun*, which form the Hebrew word *chen* meaning "grace." Thus the Qabalists maintain that certain Biblical passages that refer to God granting His *grace* to someone are really implying that what he granted was in fact the secret wisdom of the Qabalah.

Notariqons may also be formed using letters other than the initial ones, such as the final or middle letters of words.

Temurah

The word *Temurah* means "permutation." It is a method of transposing letters similar to crytography. Using this system, each letter of a word is replaced by another letter, usually in accordance with a chart or table. This can result in a new word which can be compared to the original one in order to provide new interpreta-

---

[102] Israel Regardie gave the wording of this sentence as *Achad Raysheethoh; Achad Resh Yechidathoh; Temurathoh Achod.*

tions. Temurah is important for interpreting Qabalistic texts such as the Torah, and for creating talismans.

Avgad: A simple form of Temurah in which any letter in a word is replaced by the letter which follows it in the alphabet. Thus the letter Beth could be substituted for Aleph, Daleth for Gimel, etc.

Thashrag: The method of writing a word backwards.

Boustrophedon: A method of writing in alternating lines, one from right to left, and the other from left to right. (The *Shem ha-Mephoresh* was derived from Biblical chapter of Exodus using this method.)

Tziruph: A method of folding the Hebrew alphabet back upon itself so that one half may be exchanged for the other half. Then by alternately changing the first letter or first two letters at the beginning of the second line, twenty-four combinations are obtained. These are the known collectively as the *Table of the Combinations of Tziruph.* (See Appendix II for the complete table.)

For an example we will use the first of the twenty-four combinations known as *Albath:*

11	*10*	*9*	*8*	*7*	*6*	*5*	*4*	*3*	*2*	*1*
K	I	T	Ch	Z	V	H	D	G	B	A
M	N	S	O	P	Tz	Q	R	Sh	Th	L

Each combination from the *Table of the Combinations of Tziruph* derives its name from the first two pairs of letters from both lines (ALBTh). These letters are the key to the makeup of the system, since either letter in one of the pairs is substituted for the other. Therefore using the method of *Albath,* the word *Ruach* (RVCh) would be transformed into *Detzau* (DTzO).

There are four other tables used in Tziruph called the *Rational Table, the Right Table, the Averse Table* and the *Irregular Table.* We will not go into detail about these tables except to say that they are each formed from a square containing 484 lesser squares (22 x 22). The *Right Table* places the letters of the Hebrew alphabet into these squares in their natural succession starting from the upper right-hand corner going from right to left and from top to bottom. The *Averse Table* begins the natural succession of the letters starting from the upper left-hand corner of the square from left to right, but also from the lower right-hand corner of the square from bottom to top.

Alternate Methods

Some Qabalists also add hidden meanings to Hebrew words by placing the final form of a letter in the middle of a word, or by not using the usual final form of the letter at the end of a word. (Both would change the numerical value of the entire word.)

There are also ways of encoding esoteric meanings into words by using odd-sized letters or upside-down letters. Meanings may also be obtained by meditating on the shape of the Hebrew letters.✿

SECTION 4: Correspondences of Hod

 The Practicus grade is attributed to the sphere of Hod on the Qabalistic Tree of Life. Hod is the eighth Sephirah on the Tree and the third sphere encountered by the aspiring initiate. It is the sphere of the intellect, communication, science, the Element of Water, and the Individual Mind. (Review all information on Hod given in Chapter One.)

Name in English: Splendor
Divine (Atziluthic) Name: Elohim Tzabaoth
Archangel (Briatic) Name: Michael
Angelic (Yetziratic) Choir: Beni Elohim
Planet or House of Assiah: Kokab (Mercury)
Spiritual experience: Vision of Splendor
Qabalistic Number: Eight
Color (Briatic): Orange
Element: Water
Part of Anatomy: Right hip
Tarot cards: The four Eights
Magical Image: Hermaphrodite
Incense: Storax
Gemstone: Opal, fire opal
Symbols: Names, versicles, apron
Lineal Figure: Octagram
Virtue: Truthfulness
Vice: Dishonesty

SECTION 5: Correspondences of Water

 Water symbolizes the creative and fertile part of the psyche and the subconscious mind. It is the Element of transmutation and regeneration. Water is feminine, receptive, nurturing, and eternal. The color given for Water is blue, and the cardinal point is West. (Review all information on the Element of Water given in Chapter One.) The correspondences of perfumes and incenses listed in Chapter Three can be used in liquid form such as in essential oils, herbal baths or inks. These can be employed by the magician as symbolic forms of Elemental Water.

Hebrew and Other Names Connected with Water

Element Name: Maim (מים)
Outer Divine Name: Elohim Tzabaoth (אלהים צבאות)
Cardinal Point: Maarab (West) (מערב)
Archangel: Gabriel (גבריאל)
Angel: Taliahad (טליהד)
Ruler: Tharsis (תרשים)
Elemental: Undines
Queen of Undines: Nichsa

Mythological Image of an Undine

GABRIEL: (Specifically *Gabriel Maimel*) is the great winged Archangel of Elemental Water, whose name means "Strong One of God." Stationed in the West, Gabriel is visualized as a feminine Archangel standing upon the Waters of the sea wearing robes of blue and orange. She holds a chalice of Water as a symbol of her creative and fertile powers of consciousness in all its forms.

NESHER: The name of the Kerub of Water symbolized by the Zodiacal Sign of Scorpio, or by the head of an eagle. Nesher is visualized as a powerful winged sphinx-like figure with a human body and eagle's head. His colors are primarily blue and orange.

Beings and Deities of Water

According to the Assyro-Babylonian pantheon, in the beginning of the universe there existed only the god **APSU**, the primordial ocean of fertile fresh Water and the goddess **TIAMAT**, the tumultuous and salty Sea. From the mingling of their Waters came **MUMMU**, the tumult of the waves, and a pair of monstrous serpents, who in turn gave birth to both the celestial world and the terrestrial world, followed by the gods. Tiamat is sometimes depicted as a great dragon. She was slain by the god Marduk and from her body was fashioned the Heavens and the Earth.

In Assyro-Babylonian mythology, the rivers were deified. Not only were they seen as the creators of all things, but also as devices of the gods' justice.

NAMMU: The Sumerian goddess whose name was expressed by the ideogram for "sea." She was described as "the mother who gave birth to Heaven and Earth" and as "the mother of Enki." She is very similar to the cosmic sea personified by the Babylonian Tiamat.

EA (or HEA): An Assyro-Babylonian deity whose name means "house of Water." He was the main divinity of the liquid elements. Ea's domain was the Apsu—the fresh Water that surrounded the Earth (and in which the Earth was suspended). The springs and rivers came from the Apsu, which when spread over the Earth were a source

Tiamat

Oannes

of abundance, mines, treasures, and happiness as well as the source of all knowledge and wisdom. He is the lord of gifts, of fishermen, and sailers. In Sumer, Ea's name was **ENKI** "Lord of the Earth," and he was also known as a god of Wisdom and of the Underworld. Ea is often represented as a goat with a fish's tail, although sometimes he is portrayed as man with waves springing from his shoulders or from a vase which he holds. Sometimes the serpent is mentioned as one of his emblems. Ea's wife was called *Davkina,* consort of the deep.

OANNES: An Assyro-Babylonian deity of the sea who was depicted with the body of a man underneath the body of a fish. Oannes came from the sea to teach humans language, sciences, arts, agriculture, construction, laws and the principles of geometrical knowledge. By this action, he enabled humans to soften their manners and organize their lives for the better. When he had finished instructing humanity, the god returned to the sea.

NANSHE: The daughter of Ea who was known as the goddess of springs and canals. Worship of Nanshe included an annual procession of boats to escort the sacred barge in which the goddess rode. Her symbol was a vase containing a swimming fish.

NUN or **NU:** The Egyptian god of the great primordial Ocean (or Chaos) which contained the germs of all things before the Creation. Often called "the Father of the gods," he was conceived of more as an intellectual concept—having neither temples nor worshippers. Nun is represented as a figure standing waist-high in Water, holding his arms up to support his offspring—the gods.

TEFNUT: This Egyptian goddess was also more of a theological concept rather than a person. She is the sister and wife of Shu, who she helps to support the sky. Tefnut is the goddess of the dew and the rain. Each morning Shu and Tefnut receive the newborn sun as it breaks free from the mountains of the East. She is depicted as a lioness or a woman with the head of a lion.

Khnemu

KHNEMU: An Egyptian god portrayed as a ram-headed man with long wavy horns. Like most of the ram-headed gods, Khnemu was a god of the river Nile, who was worshiped to provide fertility to the Earth, making it fruitful. This god watched over the sources of the Nile and over the formation of children in their mother's womb. His name means "the Molder" and it was he who fashioned the world-egg on his potter's wheel. He is called "the potter who shaped men and

modeled the gods,"—the procreator who engendered the
gods and human beings. Khnemu is said to have molded
the limbs of Osiris.

HAPI: The Egyptian god who personified the river Nile.
To the Egyptians, the Waters of the Nile flowed from
Nun, the primordial ocean which fed the visible as well
the invisible worlds. Hapi was said to reside in a cavern
where he poured Water from urns to the heaven and the
Earth. Every June the Nile would rise and the worshippers of Osiris affirmed that the inundation (whose height
was dictated by the year's prosperity) was caused by the
goddess Isis weeping for her slain husband Osiris. In
order that the Waters of the Nile should attain a suitable
height (sixteen cubits), offerings were made to Hapi,

Hapi

often accompanied by the singing of poetic hymns. Hapi is depicted as a vital but
somewhat fat man with hanging breasts. He is dressed in the clothes of a fisherman
with a narrow belt which supports his huge belly. On his head he wears a crown of
Water plants—either lotuses or papyri.

POSEIDON (Equivalent to the Roman *Neptune*): Poseidon was the Greek god of
the Sea. His name is derived from a root word which means "to be master." It is
likely that he was once a celestial god as his symbol, the trident (a form of the
thunderbolt) would seem to indicate. Although he was the equal of his brother
Zeus in dignity and birth, he was nonetheless subject to Zeus' power and authority. In addition to being the Lord of the Sea, Poseidon was also the master of lakes
and rivers. He could shake the Earth at will, and would often split mountains with
his trident and roll them into the sea to make islands. His palace was located in the
depths of the Aegean Sea. Whenever the god left his palace, he would don golden
armor, harness swift golden-maned horses to his chariot, and race across the
watery plain with whip in hand. Sea monsters would pay homage to him and
frolic in the waves as he passed by. The very sea would open up before him as he
sped lightly across the waves. The appearance of Poseidon coincided with fierce
storms at sea, a sign of the god's rage.

AMPHITRITE: This Greek goddess was the wife of
Poseidon and the female personification of the sea. The
reluctant goddess was brought to Poseidon by a faithful
dolphin. From then on however, she shared his kingdom
and his chariot which was at times drawn by tritons
(Water beings) blowing on conch shells. She is at times
portrayed as holding a trident.

PONTUS: The oldest Greek Water god who personified
the sea itself.

OCEANUS: One of the Greek Titans who was considered the River Ocean which surrounded the universe

Poseidon

Triton

beyond the seas of the Earth. He was seen as one of those primal forces which had contributed to the manifestation of the world and in power he was second only to Zeus. Oceanus is the one who gave birth to all the rivers, the seas and all the Waters of the Earth. With his sister-wife **TETHYS** (the goddess who personified the fertility of the sea), Oceanus lived in a palace in the West of the world. Together they sired three thousand rivers. Later the role of Oceanus was greatly diminished as Poseidon became the reigning lord of the sea and the rivers. The daughters of Oceanus were sea nymphs known as the Oceanids.

NEREUS: A Greek god who was the son of Pontus and Gaea. Often called "The Old Man of the Sea," he is pictured as a kindly and helpful old man with a long gray beard. Known as "he who is true and lies not" this just and gentle god was always true to the laws of righteousness. His abode was in the Aegean Sea and he was known for coming to the aid of sailors. Nereus possessed the gift of prophecy and was the father of the Nereids (sea nymphs).

PROTEUS: The son of Oceanus and Tethys, and who was also an "Old Man of the Sea." It was his duty to guard Poseidon's herd of seals. He had the ability to see into the future as well as the talent to change shape at will.

PHORCYS: The son of Pontus and Gaea. Phorcys is referred to as "The Old man who rules the waves." His name indicates the white foam upon the crest of the waves, and the god is seen as the personification of the treacherous and tempestuous sea.

GLAUCUS: The legend concerning this Greek god says that he was once a humble fisherman who became immortal by eating a mysterious herb that grew near the sea. Like many of the marine gods, he had the gift of prophecy. He often appeared to sailors, with his thin body covered with seaweed and seashells, predicting ominous events. Another ocean divinity of human origin who is often confused with Glaucus is **Melicertes Palaemon**, usually represented as a child carried by dolphins.

TRITON: The son of Poseidon and Amphitrite, this god was half man, half fish. A benevolent and helpful god who saved the Argonauts from a tempest, Triton also had the gift of prophecy. He could raise or quiet the waves, and he personified the mighty roar of the ocean as well as its movement. Triton was imaged riding the waves on a chariot drawn by horses whose hooves were the claws of crayfish. By blowing on a conch shell, he assumed the powerful voice of the sea. Eventually the name of this god was used to describe a whole race of marine genii, the tritons: half man, half fish who frolicked around the chariot of Amphitrite, blowing on conch shells and cavorting with the Nereids. Some of these creatures, who were supplied with a pair of horse's legs were known as *Centaur-Tritons*.

ACHELOUS: In ancient Greece, the rivers were also ruled by divine beings.[103] These fresh Water gods were portrayed as vigorous men with long beards and a pair of horns on their brow which symbolized their great strength. The most famous of these was Achelous. In a fight with the hero Hercules, one of the god's horns was torn off (which became the *Horn of Plenty*). Six rivers were named after him, and he was invoked whenever oaths were taken.

Achelous

WATER NYMPHS: In Greek mythology, every river had a god. But in addition to this, every stream, brook and pond had a lesser Spirit known as a nymph (see Chapter Three). Water nymphs were classified according to their abode. *Potamids* resided in rivers and streams, *Naiads* were found in brooks and fountains, *Crenae* or *Pegae* were the Spirits of springs, and *Limnads* were the nymphs of stagnant Waters. Like many Water entities, they had the gift of prophecy and could deliver oracles. Though generally benevolent, they could occasionally become dangerous to those mortals who attracted their affections.

MANANNAN: The Celtic Lord of the Sea which lay beyond and above *Tir na nOc* (Land of Youth), the Celtic Underworld. Manannan was one of the most colorful of the gods—dressed in mail, a golden helmet and carrying a sword which never failed. He traveled in a boat that needed no sails nor oars, propelled only by the will of the god. The sea god played an important role in the well-being of all the gods, for his pigs were killed and eaten daily by them, only to return to life as a never-failing supply of divine food.

LLYR: Celtic god of the Sea.

AEGIR: A Teutonic Giant[104] who was known as the Lord of the Sea. Treasures swallowed up by the sea were said to adorn his marine palace. His wife was the goddess **RAN**, who frequently drowned sailors only to reward them with great feasts in the afterlife.

MIMIR: Another Teutonic Water giant whose name means "he who thinks." His domain was limited to springs, pools, and lakes. Like Aegir, this giant was on friendly terms with the Teutonic gods. The fountain of Mimir near the roots of the ash tree *Yggdrasil*, was the hiding place of all wisdom and knowledge. He was the wise counselor of the god, Odin.

---

[103] Other river gods included: Asopus, Inachus, Cephissus, Peneius, Ladon, Alpheius, Xanthus, and Maeander.

[104] In Northern mythology, giants were the personification of great natural forces.

NIX: The Teutonic form of an Undine or Water sprite, similar to the Water nymph of the Greeks. Like the nymphs, the *nixies* were said to be nature Spirits in the form of beautiful maidens who inhabited springs and rivers. Unlike the Greek nymphs, however, the nixies were frequently malevolent.✿

PART 6: Correspondences of Mercury

The planet attributed to the Practicus grade is Mercury. Mercury rules the conscious mind, thoughts, ideas, memory, communications, intellect, logic, abstractions, reason, language, learning, reading, writing, the magical Arts, awareness, perceptions, and expression. Mercury governs the rational, thinking part of the human mind as well as that part of us that wishes to communicate with others and express our ideas. It is the "left-brain" part that seeks to learn, advance our skills, create, and teach others. The energy of Mercury is active, dexterous, quick, unpredictable and volatile.

The planet Mercury takes 88 days to complete one orbit of the sun, and it is never located more than 28° from the sun. It is considered an "androgynous" or "neuter" Planet. In an astrological sense, Mercury is said to be "cold" and "magnetic." The ancients described Mercury as the ruler of the period life dominated by education from the ages 5 to 14.

In human anatomy, this planet rules the thyroid gland, the brain, the nervous system, the sense of sight, the respiratory system, the tongue and the organs of speech, and the arms and hands as instruments of intelligence and communication. Physical ailments associated with Mercury include nervous disorders, stress, overwork, headaches, loss of memory and impaired respiration.

Objects attributed to Mercury include legal documents, books, papers connected with money, pictures, writing materials, and anything connected with education and communications. All flowing and veined substances are attributed to this Planet.

In magic, the days and hours of Mercury are used for science and divination, eloquence and intelligence, skill in business, wonders, apparitions, writings, deceit, theft and merchandise. In the days of the week, Mercury rules Wednesday.

The symbol of Mercury on the Tree of Life embraces all of the Sephiroth except for Kether. The horns spring out from *Daath* (Knowledge) which is not, properly speaking, a Sephirah, but rather *a conjunction of Chokmah and Binah.*

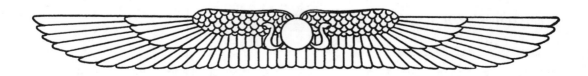

Hebrew Name: Kokab
Sephirah: Hod
Archangel: Raphael
Day: Wednesday
Planetary Intelligence: Tiriel
Planetary Spirit: Taphthartharath
Olympic Planetary Spirit: Ophiel
Metal: Quicksilver
Gemstones: Opal, fire opal, agate, serpentine
Incenses: Mastic, white sandal, mace, storax
Trees: Birch, aspen, mulberry
Herbs/plants: Marjoram, fennel, mandrake, lavender, caraway, dill
Animals: Jackal, ibis, ape, swallow, twin serpents

Mercurial Deities *(Gods and Goddesses of Wisdom)*

ENKI: The Sumerian deity who was one and the same with the god **Ea**. As Enki he was "Lord of the Earth," the supreme god of Wisdom. He was sometimes referred to as *Ninigiku*, "Lord of the Sacred Eye" and "He from whom nothing escapes." Enki presided over magical incantations—often the gods themselves consulted him. As the god of Knowledge, Enki spoke oracularly, and was invoked in incantations. However, he also presided over the work of humans. He was the patron god of stone cutters, carpenters and metalsmiths. Enki was sometimes regarded as the creator of the human race, fashioning mankind from clay. As stated earlier Enki (Ea) is often represented as a goat with a fish's tail, or as a man with waves springing from his shoulders or from a vase which he holds.

NABU: The Assyro-Babylonian god who presided over intellectual activities. He was the divine scribe of the gods who engraved the decisions of the deities on the sacred tablets. Nabu could increase or decrease the number of days allotted to each human being. He was declared secretary to the gods because both he and his wife, **TASHMETUM**, had invented writing. He is depicted with a chisel and engraving tablet, and his emblem (like that of his father, Marduk) is the serpent-headed dragon.

DJEHOTI (THOTH or TAHUTI): The Egyptian god who is the patron of wisdom and inventions, science and literature. He is the spokesman of the gods, as well as the divine scribe or record-keeper. It was he who invented all the arts and sciences: geometry, arithmetic, astronomy, surveying, medicine, music, drawing, and writing. He is also the god of magic and the world's first magician. The disciples of Djehoti claimed to have access to magical books of Thoth. When deciphered, these formulas could command all the forces of nature and subdue the gods themselves. This infinite power of Djehoti is the reason why his followers

Djehoti

Seshat

called him Thoth—three times very, very great (translated by the Greeks as Hermes Trismegistus). Djehoti is the one who divided time into months, years, seasons and aeons. He is the divine calculator, arbiter, chief historian and keeper of the divine archives. Herald of the gods, he also served as their clerk and scribe. Djehoti is pictured as a human figure with the head of an ibis, wearing the kilt, collar and headdress (sometimes with the Lunar disc and crescent) of the Old Kingdom. He holds in his hands the tablet and writing stylus of a scribe.

SESHAT: The spouse of Djehoti, goddess of writing, record-keeping and history. Known as "The Mistress of the house of books" and "Mistress of the house of architects," she was the foundress of temples, helping to determine the axis of a new sanctuary through the judgment of the stars. Seshat was a stellar divinity who measured time and along with her mate, invented the letters of the alphabet. She is sometimes portrayed as a woman wearing a headdress upon which is a star inscribed within a reversed crescent, surmounted by two long feathers (an ideogram of her name which means "the secretary.") She holds the Tablet and stylus of a scribe.

HERMES (equivalent to the Roman *Mercury*): The Greek god who was the messenger of Zeus. It is his duty to bring the dictates of the gods to Earth. Primarily a god of travelers, Hermes guided those who were journeying. And because most journeys undertaken were for commercial reasons, Hermes became known as the god of commerce and eloquence. He was also charged with the task of conducting the Souls of the dead to the underworld. He is often represented as an athletic god, sometimes bearded, who wears a winged helmet and winged sandals. Hermes holds a winged staff around which are two twining serpents—the Caduceus.

Hermes

IRIS: A Greek divinity who like Hermes was a messenger of the gods, particularly Zeus and Hera, whose orders she delivered to both gods and humans. Iris personified the rainbow, and she was often depicted with golden wings which graced her shoulders. Like Hermes, she occasionally wears winged sandals upon her feet.

ATHENE (equivalent to the Roman *Minerva*): This Greek warrior goddess was formidable in war but benevolent in peace. Her functions were many—her skills in battle rivaled those of Ares, but she was also known as a goddess of the arts and of intelligence. Protectress of various industries, Athene was the patron of sculptors, architects, spinners and weavers. Her renowned wisdom and valuable service to humanity earned her the titles of *Pronoia*, "the foreseeing," as well as counselor and goddess of the Assembly. She taught the skills of horsemanship, charioteering, pottery, cloth weaving and embroidery. Athene was at times known for her healing arts and for her role as protectress of both individuals and

entire cities. The goddess is usually depicted dressed in tight drap-
ing robes and wearing a helmet. In one hand she holds a spear and
in the other a shield. Her symbol is the owl.

ASCLEPIUS: A Greek god of light, medicine and healing. He is
sometimes represented as a serpent, but more often as a kindly
middle-aged man with a staff around which one serpent was
twined. (It was probably this staff which was intended to be a
modern symbol of medicine, rather than the Caduceus of Hermes.) His daughter **HYGIEIA**, was the goddess of health. The cult
of Asclepius was both a religion and a system of therapeutics. The
priests of this god had a wide knowledge of the medical arts.

Asclepius

LUG: The Celtic god who was known as "the many skilled one."
When asked to state his craft in order to be admitted to the assembly of gods, Lug replied that he was adept in carpentry, warfare,
smith-craft, knowledge of history, music, poetry, heroics, magic and
other pursuits. Lug was often depicted armed with spear and
sling—highly specialized and accurate weapons which delineated
the god's adroitness.

ODIN (Equivalent to the German *Woden*): The god who was the
supreme divinity of Teutonic mythology as well as the god of war
and wisdom. He was a magician-god, the deity of spiritual life,
ruling by magic—thus it is only natural that the Romans compared him to their Mercury. Odin spoke with eloquence and liked
to express himself in verse. He was the god of poetry because he
had the cunning and dexterity to steal the "Poet's mead" which
was of divine origin. He had the power to change himself into any
shape he desired, and it was he who ordained the laws which
ruled human society. Odin often intermingled in human affairs,
assuming the guise of a lowly traveler. He was helpful and benev-

Athena

olent, offering wise counsel and magic formulas to cure illness. Odin was also the
Lord of the Runes—characters carved on stones or wood which had magical
meanings and power. He is often portrayed as a handsome, robust warrior armed
with a shining breastplate, a golden helmet, his spear (which was called *Gungnir*)
which nothing could deflect. His steed *Sleipnir*, had eight hooves and was the
swiftest of all stallions.

Complementary Planet: JUPITER

In conjunction with the study material given on the Planet Mercury, the student
should review information supplied in Chapter One on Jupiter, the planet which
complements Mercury on the Macrocosmic Hexagram.

Jupiter is the planet of expansion, aspiration, higher education, philosophic reasoning, justice, law and sovereignty. The energy of Jupiter is orderly,
benevolent and helpful.

In an Astrological sense, Jupiter is said to be "warm" and "moist" and it is associated with Water. It is also thought of as a "masculine" planet. The ancients described Jupiter as the ruler of the period life dominated by reflection from the ages 58 to 69 symbolized by *"the judge."*

In human anatomy, this Planet rules the liver, arterial blood circulation, thighs, hips, and fatty tissues of the body. Physical ailments associated with Jupiter include abnormal blood pressure, chronic acidity and diseases associated with excess.

In magic, the days and hours of Jupiter are used for obtaining honors, acquiring money or other desired commodities, contracting friendships and preserving health. In the days of the week, Jupiter rules Thursday.

Deities associated with the planet Jupiter include: **AMON-RA** (Egyptian) **MAAT** (Egyptian), **ZEUS** (Greek), **POSEIDON** (Greek) **ATHENE** (Greek), **MARDUK** (Assyro-Babylonian) and **ADAD** (Assyro-Babylonian).

The following is a list of Jupiterian associations:

Hebrew Name: Tzedek
Sephirah: Chesed
Archangel: Sachiel
Day: Thursday
Planetary Intelligence: Iophiel
Planetary Spirit: Hismael
Olympic Planetary Spirit: Bethor
Metal: Tin
Gemstones: Amethyst, sapphire, lapis lazuli
Incenses: Saffron
Trees: Fig, oak, cedar, chestnut
Herbs/plants: Sage, nutmeg, hyssop
Animals: Unicorn, eagle, swan, whale

SECTION 7: The Olympic Planetary Spirits

The Olympic Planetary Spirits are described in *The Arbatel of Magic* which dates to 1575. This book originally consisted of nine sections, each containing a different branch of magic. Unfortunately, most of the book, including sections on Hermetic magic, Pythagorean magic and Olympic magic, has been lost. Only the introduction seems to have survived. Part of the Introduction contains a summary of the now lost section on Olympic magic.

It is likely that certain books dealing with Olympic magic existed before the *Arbatel* was written (as indicated by the author himself). The *Arbatel* has a Christian rather than Judaic emphasis, therefore its author must have been a Christian magician who was schooled in a variety of magical traditions. Whoever he was, he clearly believed that the greatest magical teachings were to be procured through an Angelic teacher sent to the Theurgist from the Divine.

The *Arbatel* states that there are seven Olympic Spirits which rule over 196 Olympic Provinces or divisions of Heaven; each Spirit governing alternately for 490 years. (490 is the sum of consecutive multiples of seven.) Bethor was supposed to have ruled 60 years before the birth of Christ, until 430 AD when the rule of Phaleg was implemented. This rule ended in 920 AD when the rule of Och began. Haggith began her rule in 1410 and ended it in 1900. (Following the author's reasoning, Ophiel would be the reigning Olympic Spirit today.)

According to the author of the *Arbatel*, the names and sigils of the Olympic Spirits have no power or virtue in and of themselves, and the only divine names of power to be used are given to the theurgist by these Spirits, but even then, the potency of the names only lasts for 40 years. The Olympic Planetary Spirits are:

ARATRON—the Spirit of Saturn. Aratron governs all things ascribed to Saturn. He teaches alchemy, magic and medicine. He is said to have the power to make one invisible, to convert objects to stone or treasure, and the power to make the barren fruitful. Aratron governs the subterranean Spirits.

BETHOR—the Spirit of Jupiter. Bethor governs all things ascribed to Jupiter. He teaches medicine and has the power to open treasures, governs the spirits of Air into giving true answers, and he can also bestow longevity.

PHALEGH—the Spirit of Mars. Phalegh governs all things ascribed to Mars.

OCH—the Spirit of Sol. Och governs all things ascribed to the Sun. He bestows wisdom and health, converts things into gold, reconciles with the highest Spirits and teaches medicine.

HAGITH—the Spirit of Venus. Hagith governs all things ascribed to Venus. He has the knowledge of beauty and can transmute metals. Hagith reconciles between faithful Spirits and humans.

OPHIEL—the Spirit of Mercury. Ophiel governs all things ascribed to Mercury. He teaches the magical Arts.

PHUL—the Spirit of Luna. Phul governs all things ascribed to the Moon. He turns all metals into silver, and governs all Water Spirits. ✿

VNVS DEVS, VNVS CONCILIATOR DEI ET HOMINV, HOMO CHRISTVS IESVS, QVI DEDIT SEMETIPSVM PRECIVM REDEMPTIONIS PRO OMNIBVS

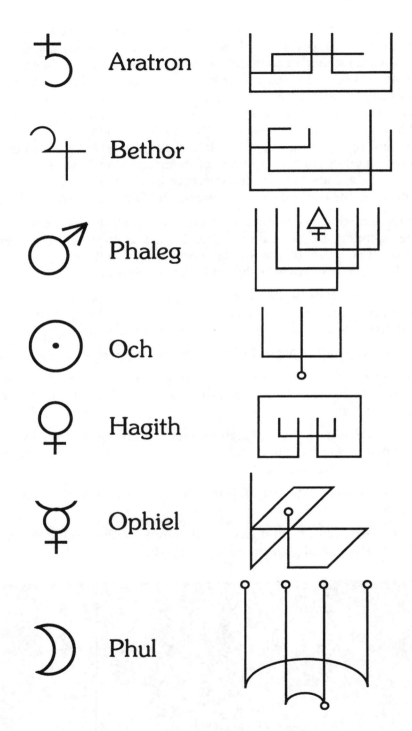

Names and Sigils of the Olympic Planetary Spirits

SECTION 8: The Tarot

 The Tarot or "Book T" as it is sometimes called, is a pictorial book of ageless, esoteric wisdom. For centuries it has been used by magicians, occultists, and mystics for the purposes of divination and meditation. Like the Qabalah, the Tarot is a complete and elaborate system for describing the hidden forces behind the manifest universe. Not only is it the key to all occult science, but also a map for uncovering the various parts of the human psyche. Some have called the cards of the Tarot the "hieroglyphs of the Western Mystery Tradition."

The origin of the Tarot remains a mystery. Various theories abound, including the speculations that: (1) the Tarot is of Egyptian origin, (2) that it was created by a group of Adepts to insure the survival of a persecuted esoteric philosophy by concealing it in a deck of playing cards, and (3) that it was invented by the gypsies (Bohemians) to protect its hidden wisdom under the exterior disguise of gambling and fortune telling. However the first known Tarot decks can only be documented with certainty as having been developed in the late fourteenth century during the reign of Charles VI of France. Some of the earliest decks include: the Tarot of Jacquemin Gringonneur, the Tarot of the Visconti-Sforza family, and the Tarocchi of Mantegna.

During the first part of the fifteenth century, the Tarot was used exclusively at the European courts of nobility—it had become a pastime reserved for the aristocracy. The invention of the printing press made the cards more common. In 1781, interest in the Tarot gained momentum when the Court de Gibelin, a freemason and Protestant minister claimed that the Tarot's Trump cards were from a secret Egyptian book called *The Book of Thoth*.

Qabalistic Associations of the Tarot

However, it was not until 1856 that Eliphas Levi, (whose real name was Alphonse Louis Constant) a noted figure in the Occult Revival of the 19th century, established an undeniable parallel between the twenty-two Trumps of the Tarot and the twenty-two letters of the Hebrew alphabet. The Occult Revival ushered in serious study of the Tarot and its Qabalistic associations. Whether or not the original inventors of the Tarot deliberately placed Qabalistic symbolism into the cards is unimportant. The fact remains that the two systems of Qabalah and Tarot are so strikingly similar that they easily compliment and describe each other. At the end of the 19th century, the Hermetic Order of the Golden Dawn, spearheaded by MacGregor Mathers, formulated some of the most comprehensive teachings of the Qabalistic Tarot ever devised.

The traditional Tarot consists of a pack of seventy-eight cards made up of four suits of fourteen cards each, together with twenty-two Trumps, or Major Arcana, which tell the story of the Soul. (The Major Arcana contains twenty-two cards, while the Minor Arcana has a total of fifty-six cards.) The twenty-two Trump cards are each referred to one of the twenty-two paths that connect the Sephiroth on the Tree of Life. They also correspond to the twenty-two letters of the Hebrew alphabet.

Within the Minor Arcana each Tarot suit consists of ten numbered cards, as in the modern playing cards, but there are four instead of three Royal (Court) cards: King, Queen, Prince and Princess. Thus there are a total of sixteen Court cards. (Note: in some decks these cards are referred to as Knight, Queen, Emperor, and Knave or Page.) The four suits of the Tarot are:

1. **WANDS** (or scepters) comparable to *Clubs*.[105]
2. **CUPS** (or chalices) comparable to *Hearts*.
3. **SWORDS** comparable to *Spades*.
4. **PENTACLES** (or coins) comparable to *Diamonds*.

In the Tarot, the ten small cards of each suit refer to the ten Sephiroth. The four suits refer to the letters of Tetragrammaton thus: wands to Yod, cups to Heh, swords to Vav, pentacles to Heh (final).

The four suits also refer to the Four Worlds of the Qabalah thus: wands to Atziluth, cups to Briah, swords to Yetzirah, pentacles to Assiah.

The sixteen court cards (or honors as they are sometimes called) are the Vice-gerants of the Great Name, in the Qabalistic World to which each suit is referred. They allude to the fourfold Tetragrammaton and also symbolize the following:

1. **KING**—Father, Birth
2. **QUEEN**—Mother, Life
3. **PRINCE**—Son, Death
4. **PRINCESS**—Daughter, Resurrection

The Sephiroth, as represented by the Minor Arcana cards which accompany them, symbolize *objective* centers of energy emanating from the Divine. They are static and fixed points of force whose qualities are impartial and immobile. These cards allude to the unchangeable parts of the human psyche—those components which are inherent to the human mind.

The twenty-two paths and their corresponding Trump cards, on the other hand, are active and moving. They are *subjective* conduits or energy channels that run between the Sephiroth, connecting the spheres. These cards represent our own mutable experiences as we travel the pathways on the Tree of Life, encountering the differences that occur between one Sephirah and the next.

The Twenty-two Trumps

The twenty-two cards of the Major Arcana are also called the Trumps, Keys or Atus[106] of Tahuti. They are attributed to the twenty-two letters of the Hebrew alphabet as well as the twenty-two paths which connect the ten Sephiroth on the Tree of Life.

---

[105] In Regardie's *The Golden Dawn*, the attributions for wands and pentacles are reversed: wands = diamonds, pentacles = clubs. However, those attributions have never seemed like the correct ones to us.

[106] According to Mathers, the word *atu* comes from the Egyptian word *aat*, meaning "Mansion." E.A. Wallis Budge lists the word as *aait*, meaning "house," "abode," or "chamber."

They represent the energies of the Planets, the Signs of the Zodiac and the Elements of the ancients. These paths, numbered 11 through 32 are dynamic, subjective conduits of karmic energy. They symbolize forces in transit and allude to the Powers of consciousness in illustrated form. Their place on the Tree of Life is imaged by the winding path of the Serpent of Wisdom. Unlike the cards of the Minor Arcana, the Trump cards are considered true initiatory forces—having both an esoteric or spiritual meaning as well as an exoteric or mundane meaning which is used in divination.

Yetziratic Attribution of the Trumps

The twenty-two paths (symbolized by the Trumps) and the ten Sephiroth combined form the *Thirty-two Paths of Wisdom*. Since the Tarot Trumps correspond to the Hebrew letters, they can also be grouped in accordance with the three classes of letters described in the *Sepher Yetzirah*:

Elemental—The Three Mother Letters

THE FOOL (Air—*Aleph*)
THE HANGED MAN (Water—*Mem*)
JUDGMENT (Fire—*Shin*)

Planetary—The Seven Double Letters

THE MAGICIAN (Mercury—*Beth*)
THE HIGH PRIESTESS (Luna—*Gimel*)
THE EMPRESS (Venus—*Daleth*)
THE WHEEL OF FORTUNE (Jupiter—*Kaph*)
THE TOWER (Mars—*Peh*)
THE SUN (Sol—*Resh*)
THE UNIVERSE (Saturn—*Tau*)

Zodiacal—The Twelve Simple Letters

THE EMPEROR (Aries—*Heh*)
THE HIEROPHANT (Taurus—*Vav*)
THE LOVERS (Gemini—*Zayin*)
THE CHARIOT (Cancer—*Cheth*)
STRENGTH (Leo—*Teth*)
THE HERMIT (Virgo—*Yod*)
JUSTICE (Libra—*Lamed*)
DEATH (Scorpio—*Nun*)
TEMPERANCE (Sagittarius—*Samekh*)
THE DEVIL (Capricorn—*Ayin*)
THE STAR (Aquarius — *Tzaddi*)
THE MOON (Pisces—*Qoph*)

The Yetziratic attributions of the Hebrew alphabet make it possible to signify certain divine names and words by employing their Elemental, Planetary, or Zodiacal symbols. This can result in some curious hieroglyphic symbolism. For example the name YOD HEH VAV HEH can be written from right to left using the symbolic counterpart of each letter thus, ♈ ♉ ♈ ♍. The name EHEIEH, *Aleph Heh Yod Heh*, can be transliterated as—♈ ♍ ♈ △ . YEHESHUAH, the Qabalistic spelling of Jesus, *Yod Heh Shin Vav Heh*, would be listed as ♈ ♉ △ ♈ ♍. (Virgo—born of a Virgin, Aries—the Sacrificial Lamb, Fire—the Fire of the Holy Spirit, Taurus—the Ox of the Earth in whose Manger He was laid, and lastly Aries—the flocks of sheep whose Herdsmen came to worship Him.) ELOHIM, *Aleph Lamed Heh Yod Mem*, ▽ ♍ ♈ ♎ △ . (Elohim yields Air, Libra, Aries, Virgo, Water—the Firmament, the Balanced Forces, the Fire of the Spirit [For Aries is a fiery Sign], operating in the Zodiac, the Fire goddess, and the Waters of Creation.)

The Attribution of the Tarot Trumps

Path	No.	Tarot Trump	Letter	Symbol
11	0	The Fool	א	△
12	1	The Magician	ב	☿
13	2	The High Priestess	ג	☽
14	3	The Empress	ד	♀
15	4	The Emperor	ה	♈
16	5	The Hierophant	ו	♉
17	6	The Lovers	ז	♊
18	7	The Chariot	ח	♋
19	8	Strength	ט	♌
20	9	The Hermit	י	♍
21	10	The Wheel of Fortune	כ	♃
22	11	Justice	ל	♎
23	12	The Hanged Man	מ	▽
24	13	Death	נ	♏
25	14	Temperance	ס	♐
26	15	The Devil	ע	♑
27	16	The Tower	פ	♂
28	17	The Star	צ	♒
29	18	The Moon	ק	♓
30	19	The Sun	ר	☉
31	20	Judgment	ש	△
32	21	The Universe	ת	♄

THE FOOL
Key: 0   *Yetziratic Path:* 11   *Letter:* Aleph   *Attribution:* Air
Esoteric Title: The Spirit of Ether
Connecting Sephiroth: Kether to Chokmah
Key word: POTENTIALITY

Related ideas: The fiery Intelligence. The first current of potential Vibration. Possibility. Precursor of the first thought. The Unmanifest. Absolute Unity. The first Breath. The first thought of manifestation. Innocence. Spirituality. Baptism of Air. The number 0 represents the circle of the universe and the mathematical beginning point. *Images:* An innocent child. Harpocrates, the god of Silence. A dangerous wolf on a leash. A tree bearing yellow roses. *Interpretation in a Tarot Reading:* Idea, thought, spirituality. (If the question concerns the material this card is not good: showing folly, instability, stupidity.)

THE MAGICIAN
Key: 1   *Yetziratic Path:* 12   *Letter:* Beth   *Attribution:* Mercury
Esoteric Title: The Magus of Power
Connecting Sephiroth: Kether to Binah
Key word: DIRECTION

Related ideas: The act of experience. Energy. Invocation. Director of energy. Organization of thought. Thought becoming manifest. Wisdom. Skill. Occult power. *Images:* The magician, Hermes-Thoth. The altar. The four Elemental Weapons. Caduceus Wand. The Infinity sign. *Interpretation in a Tarot Reading:* Skill, wisdom, adaptation, craft, cunning, dexterity, occult wisdom.

THE HIGH PRIESTESS
Key: 2   *Yetziratic Path:* 13   *Letter:* Gimel   *Attribution:* Luna
Esoteric Title: The Priestess of the Silver Star
Connecting Sephiroth: Kether to Tiphareth
Key word: CONSCIOUSNESS

Related ideas: Root essence of consciousness. Ultimate expression and source of Water. Regulator of the flow and direction of vibration. Fluctuation. *Images:* The High Priestess veiled and crowned with the crescent Moon. The cup of Water. *Interpretation in a Tarot Reading:* Wisdom, knowledge, change, alteration, increase and decrease. Fluctuation.

THE EMPRESS

Key: 3   *Yetziratic Path:* 14   *Letter:* Daleth   *Attribution:* Venus
Esoteric Title: Daughter of the Mighty Ones
Connecting Sephiroth: Chokmah to Binah
Key word: UNITY

Related ideas: Union of the two opposing powers of force and form. Union of masculine and feminine. The universal Mother. The universal power of love. Fertility. Builder of form. The womb of manifestation. The root essence of pure emotion. The divine feminine power. *Images:* The Empress enthroned. The ankh or Venus symbol. The royal scepter. The dove. *Interpretation in a Tarot Reading:* Beauty, happiness, pleasure movement. (If extremely ill-dignified: luxury, dissipation.)

THE EMPEROR

Key: 4   *Yetziratic Path:* 15   *Letter:* Heh   *Attribution:* Aries
Esoteric Title: Son of the Morning; Chief among the Mighty
Connecting Sephiroth: Chokmah to Tiphareth
Key word: ENERGY

Related ideas: Initiation of energy. Creative force. Stimulation of a dynamic current. Cycle of rebirth. The divine masculine power. *Images:* The Emperor enthroned. The horned crown. The ram. The ram-headed scepter. The golden orb. *Interpretation in a Tarot Reading:* War, conquest, victory, strife, ambition, realization, development.

THE HIEROPHANT

Key: 5   *Yetziratic Path:* 16   *Letter:* Vav   *Attribution:* Taurus
Esoteric Title: Magus of the Eternal Gods
Connecting Sephiroth: Chokmah to Chesed
Key word: ILLUMINATION

Related ideas: Connecting That which is Above to That which is Below. Channel for spiritual instruction. Expounder of the Mysteries. The great Teacher. Inner illumination. *Images:* The Hierophant enthroned. The bull. The triple crown. The Crook of Mercy. The scroll containing the Logos (the word of creation). *Interpretation in a Tarot Reading:* Divine Wisdom, mercy, manifestation, explanation, teaching, occult wisdom.

THE LOVERS
Key: 6   *Yetziratic Path:* 17   *Letter:* Zayin   *Attribution:* Gemini
Esoteric Title: Children of the Voice Divine;
The Oracles of the Mighty Gods.
Connecting Sephiroth: Binah to Tiphareth
Key word: LIBERATION

Related ideas: Integration of the Higher and the Lower. The joining of the two great contending forces. Personality uniting with the Higher Self. Divine Love. Freedom through unity. Fusion. Bonding. *Images:* Perseus and Andromeda. The rock and chains of material bondage. The sword and the shield. The sea monster. *Interpretation in a Tarot Reading:* Inspiration (passive and in some cases mediumistic). Motive, power and action, arising from inspiration and impulse.

THE CHARIOT
Key: 7   *Yetziratic Path:* 18   *Letter:* Cheth   *Attribution:* Cancer
Esoteric Title: Child of the Power of the Waters;
Lord of the Triumph of Light
Connecting Sephiroth: Binah to Geburah
Key word: SUBLIMATION

Related ideas: Conqueror. Exaltation. Vision of unseen energies. Guidance of the Lower by Spirit. Descent of the Spirit into the world of manifestation. Movement through all planes of existence. *Images:* Armored figure enthroned in a chariot. Two horses, one black one white. Eagle's head. *Interpretation in a Tarot Reading:* Triumph, victory, overcoming obstacles, health, success (though not always enduring).

STRENGTH
Key: 8   *Yetziratic Path:* 19   *Letter:* Teth   *Attribution:* Leo
Esoteric Title: Daughter of the Flaming Sword;
Leader of the Lion
Connecting Sephiroth: Chesed to Geburah
Key word: CONTROLLED POWER

Related ideas: Fortitude. Mastery of the Lower by the Higher. Harnessed force. Passions under the control of the Will. Kinetic energy. Resolve. *Images:* A veiled woman. A red lion. *Interpretation in a Tarot Reading:* Courage, strength, might, fortitude. Power not arrested as in the act of judgment, but passing on to further action. (Sometimes obstinacy and abuse of power.)

THE HERMIT

Key: 9   *Yetziratic Path:* 20   *Letter:* Yod   *Attribution:* Virgo
Esoteric Title: The Magus of the Voice of Light;
The Prophet of the Gods
Connecting Sephiroth: Chesed to Tiphareth
Key word: DIVINE INTERVENTION

Related ideas: The Light bearer. Message from the Higher. Divine Wisdom. Vibration. The word of power. The Supreme Will. Help and inspiration from the Higher. *Images:* Old and wise master magician concealed in a hooded cloak. The lamp of Light. The Staff. *Interpretation in a Tarot Reading:* Wisdom sought for and obtained from above. Divine inspiration, prudence, deliberation.

THE WHEEL OF FORTUNE

Key: 10   *Yetziratic Path:* 21   *Letter:* Kaph   *Attribution:* Jupiter
Esoteric Title: The Lord of the Forces of Life.
Connecting Sephiroth: Chesed to Netzach
Key word: KARMA

Related ideas: Time. Destiny. Fluctuation. The rotation and cycling of human incarnation. Perpetual motion. Karma—bringing past deeds into the present and on into the future. *Images:* The Wheel of Fortune. The Sphinx. The Cynocephalus (dog-faced ape). *Interpretation in a Tarot Reading:* Good fortune and happiness (If ill-dignified: intoxication with success or ill-fortune and failure.)

JUSTICE

Key: 11   *Yetziratic Path:* 22   *Letter:* Lamed   *Attribution:* Libra
Esoteric Title: Daughter of the Lord of Truth;
The Holder of the Balances
Connecting Sephiroth: Geburah to Tiphareth
Key word: EQUILIBRATION

Related ideas: Necessary adjustment. Equilibrating action. Compensation. Keeper of balance. Perpetuator of harmony and forward movement. Law and truth. *Images:* The goddess Maat. The Scales of Balance. The double-edged sword. The jackal. The two pillars. *Interpretation in a Tarot Reading:* Eternal justice and balance, equilibrium. Strength and force, but arrested as in the act of judgment. Also legal proceedings. (If ill-dignified: severity and bias.)

THE HANGED MAN
Key: 12   *Yetziratic Path:* 23   *Letter:* Mem   *Attribution:* Water
Esoteric Title: The Spirit of the Mighty Waters
Connecting Sephiroth: Geburah to Hod
Key word: SACRIFICE

Related ideas: Crucifixion. Self-sacrifice. Self-denial. Suspended animation. Trance-state. Period of withdrawal. Reversal. Submergence of the Higher into the Lower in order to sublimate the Lower. Descent of Spirit into matter, for the sake of transcendence. Baptism of Water. *Images:* A man hanging upside-down from a tree over Water. His legs are crossed and his hands are bound behind his back. *Interpretation in a Tarot Reading:* Enforced sacrifice. Punishment. Loss. Suffering generally. Sacrifice that is not always voluntary.

DEATH
Key: 13   *Yetziratic Path:* 24   *Letter:* Nun   *Attribution:* Scorpio
Esoteric Title: The Child of the Great Transformers;
Lord of the Gates of Death.
Connecting Sephiroth: Tiphareth to Netzach
Key word: TRANSFORMATION

Related ideas: Transmutation. Transition. Change of one form for another. Cycle of death and rebirth. Purification. *Images:* The skeleton of Death. The scythe. The parts of corpses. The darkened sun. The serpent. The eagle. *Interpretation in a Tarot Reading:* Time. Ages. Transformation. Alteration. Involuntary change.

TEMPERANCE
Key: 14   *Yetziratic Path:* 25   *Letter:* Samekh   *Attribution:* Sagittarius
Esoteric Title: Daughter of the Reconcilers;
The Bringer Forth of Life
Connecting Sephiroth: Yesod to Tiphareth
Key word: RECONCILIATION

Related ideas: Tempering of opposites. Combination. Mediation. Arbitration. Necessary trial and temptation for the sake of balance and union. *Images:* A great feminine Angel standing on Earth and Water, mixing Water and Fire from two vases. A volcano. The sun. The yellow square of Chesed. *Interpretation in a Tarot Reading:* Combination of Forces. Realization. Uniting. Material action. (Effect either for good or ill.)

THE DEVIL

Key: 15   *Yetziratic Path:* 26   *Letter:* Ayin   *Attribution:* Capricorn
Esoteric Title: Lord of the Gates of Matter;
Child of the Forces of Time
Connecting Sephiroth: Tiphareth to Hod
Key word: MATERIALITY

Related ideas: Natural generative force. The powers of Nature. Sexual force and natural reproduction. Also illusion and distorted perceptions. Mirth. *Images:* The grotesque image of the Devil made up from several animal parts. The horn and the torch. The altar of materiality. Two smaller demons chained. *Interpretation in a Tarot Reading:* Materiality. Material Force. Material temptation or obsession.

THE TOWER

Key: 16   *Yetziratic Path:* 27   *Letter:* Peh   *Attribution:* Mars
Esoteric Title: Lord of the Hosts of the Mighty
Connecting Sephiroth: Netzach to Hod
Key word: RESTRUCTURING

Related ideas: Destruction of the old in order to rebuild the new. Demolition of outmoded beliefs. Sudden involuntary illumination. Dramatic realization. Remodeling of obsolete ideas. *Images:* A brick tower with its summit sheared off. The lightning bolt of Mars. Two figures falling from the Tower. The Tree of Life. The reversed or Qlippotic Tree. *Interpretation in a Tarot Reading:* Ambition, fighting, strife, war, courage. (If ill-dignified: destruction, ruin, danger.)

THE STAR

Key: 17   *Yetziratic Path:* 28   *Letter:* Tzaddi   *Attribution:* Aquarius
Esoteric Title: Daughter of the Firmament;
Dweller between the Waters
Connecting Sephiroth: Netzach to Yesod
Key word: MEDITATION

Related ideas: Meditation. Listening to the Inner Voice. Using knowledge and imagination to receive information from within. Contemplation. Delving into pure consciousness. The upper astral. *Images:* A nude goddess pouring Water into a river from two vases. A large seven-pointed star. Seven lesser stars. The Tree of Life. The Tree of the Knowledge of Good and of Evil. An ibis. *Interpretation in a Tarot Reading:* Hope, faith, unexpected help. (If ill-dignified: dreaminess, deceived hope.)

THE MOON

Key: 18   *Yetziratic Path:* 29   *Letter:* Qoph   *Attribution:* Pisces
Esoteric Title: Ruler of Flux and Reflux;
Child of the Sons of the Mighty
Connecting Sephiroth: Netzach to Malkuth
Key word: SUBCONSCIOUS MIND

Related ideas: Unconscious influences and impulses. Repressed ideas and desires. Personal demons and self-created phantoms. The reptilian brain. Evolution. Progression. *Images:* A crayfish in Water, starting to journey up the path onto land. Two fierce dogs. Two towers in the distance. The waxing Moon containing a face. Four Hebrew Yods. *Interpretation in a Tarot Reading:* Dissatisfaction, voluntary change, error, lying, falsity, deception.(Depending much on dignity.)

THE SUN

Key: 19   *Yetziratic Path:* 30   *Letter:* Resh   *Attribution:* Sol
Esoteric Title: Lord of the Fire of the World
Connecting Sephiroth: Hod to Yesod
Key word: CONSCIOUS MIND

Related ideas: The intellectual mind. Active awareness of the Divine. The power of knowledge. Increased perception. The knowledge of existence of Higher realms of being. Inner spiritual communication made available to the lower self. *Images:* A large and brilliant Sun. Two children playing in the Water and on the Earth. A stone fence surrounding the children in the garden. Two groups of seven Hebrew Yods falling on either side of the Sun. *Interpretation in a Tarot Reading:* Glory, gain, riches, happiness, joy. (If ill-dignified vanity, arrogance and display.)

JUDGMENT

Key: 20   *Yetziratic Path:* 31   *Letter:* Shin   *Attribution:* Fire (or Spirit)
Esoteric Title: The Spirit of the Primal Fire
Connecting Sephiroth: Hod to Malkuth
Key word: INITIATION

Related ideas: The act of initiation. Receiving an infusion of divine energy (Spirit). The first awareness of the Divine. Spirit descending into physical matter in an act of consecration. Consecration through Fire. Baptism of Fire. *Images:* The Archangel Michael descending. The candidate rising from the tomb. The Hebrew letter Shin. The rainbow. The fiery serpents (Seraphim). The triangle of flame. The two figures of Samael and Anael. The final figure of Ariel. *Interpretation in a Tarot Reading:* Final decision, judgment, sentence, result, determination of a matter without appeal on its plane. (If ill-dignified: postponement.)

THE UNIVERSE
Key: 21   *Yetziratic Path:* 32   *Letter:* Tau   *Attribution:* Saturn (or Earth)
Esoteric Title: The Great One of the Night of Time
Connecting Sephiroth: Yesod to Malkuth
Key word: EXPLORATION

Related ideas: The exploration of the invisible universe. Investigation of one's inner psychic makeup. Inquiry into the unconscious. A journey into the Underworld. The beginning and the end. The keys to the Universe. *Images:* The goddess Isis crowned with a crescent and surrounded by a floating scarf. The two wands of positive and negative power. The twelve circles of the Zodiacal Signs. The ring of seventy-two smaller circles (the Schem ha-Mephoresh). The four Kerubim. The night sky. *Interpretation in a Tarot Reading:* The matter itself, synthesis, completion, reward. (Usually denotes the actual subject of the question and therefore depends entirely on accompanying cards.)✿

Notes on the Tarot[107]

In the Tree of Life in the Tarot, each path forms the connecting link between two of the Sephiroth. The King and Queen are the correlations of the *Abba* and the *Aima* in that suit; the Knave or Prince answers to *Microprosopus*, and the Knave or Princess which was anciently a female figure, is referred to the Bride, *Kallah* or *Malkuth*. Combining, then, the material attributions of the Sephiroth and the Path, it results that:

0. Fool = The Crown of Wisdom, the Primum Mobile, acting through the Air on the Zodiac.
1. The Juggler[108] = The Crown of Understanding, the beginning of material production, the Primum Mobile acting through the Philosophic Mercury on Saturn.
2. High Priestess = The Crown of Beauty, the beginning of Sovereignty and Beauty, the Primum Mobile, acting through the Moon on the Sun.
3. Empress = The Wisdom of Understanding, the Union of the powers of Origination and Production; the Sphere of the Zodiac acting through Venus upon Saturn.
4. Emperor= The Wisdom of Sovereignty and Beauty, and the originator of them; the Sphere of the Zodiac acting through Aries upon the Sun, and initiating Spring.
5. Hierophant = The Wisdom and fountain of Mercy, the Sphere of the Zodiac acting through Taurus upon Jupiter.

---

[107] This section was written by Frater S.R.M.D. (Mathers) and was originally published in Regardie's *The Golden Dawn.*

[108] Better known as "The Magician."

6. The Lovers = The Understanding of Beauty and Production of Beauty and Sovereignty. Saturn acting through Gemini upon Sol.
7. Chariot = Understanding acting upon Severity. Saturn acting through Cancer upon Mars.
8. Strength = Fortitude. Mercy tempering Severity. The Glory of Strength. Jupiter acting through Leo upon Mars.
9. Hermit = The Mercy of Beauty, the Magnificence of Sovereignty, Jupiter acting through Virgo upon Sol.
10. Wheel of Fortune = The Mercy and Magnificence of Victory. Jupiter acting through Jupiter direct upon Venus.
11. Justice = The Severity of Beauty and Sovereignty. Mars acting through Libra upon Sol.
12. The Hanged Man = The Severity of Splendor. Execution of Judgment. Mars acting through Water upon Mercury.
13. Death = The Sovereignty and result of Victory. Sol acting through Scorpio upon Venus, or Osiris under the destroying power of Typhon afflicting Isis.
14. Temperance = The Beauty of a firm Basis. The Sovereignty of Fundamental Power. Sol acting through Sagittarius upon Luna.
15. The Devil = The Sovereignty and Beauty of Material (and therefore false) Splendor. Sol acting through Capricorn upon Mercury.
16. The Tower = The Victory over Splendor. Venus acting through Mars upon Mercury. Avenging force.
17. Star = The Victory of Fundamental Strength. Venus acting through Aquarius upon Luna. Hope.
18. Moon = The Victory of the Material. Venus acting through Pisces upon the Cosmic Elements, deceptive effect of the apparent power of Material Forces.
19. Sun = The Splendor of the Material World.[109] Mercury acting through the Sun upon the Moon.
20. Judgment = The Splendor of the Spiritual World. Mercury acting through Fire upon the Cosmic Elements.
21. Universe = The Foundation of the Cosmic Elements and of the Material World. Luna acting through Saturn upon the Elements.✿

The Minor Arcana

The Minor Arcana is composed of forty small (or numbered) cards plus sixteen court cards. The small cards are numbered Aces through tens and are divided into the four suits (wands, cups, swords, and pentacles) which allude to the four Elements, the Tetragrammaton and the Four Worlds of the Qabalah. Every Small card is attributed by its number to one of the Sephiroth. *Therefore each Small card represents one of the Ten Sephiroth in one of the Four Qabalistic Worlds.* In addition to this, each small card is assigned one of the decanates of the Zodiac (one of the 36 divisions of 10 degrees on a Zodiacal chart).

---

[109] This could also be interpreted as "The Splendor of a firm Foundation."

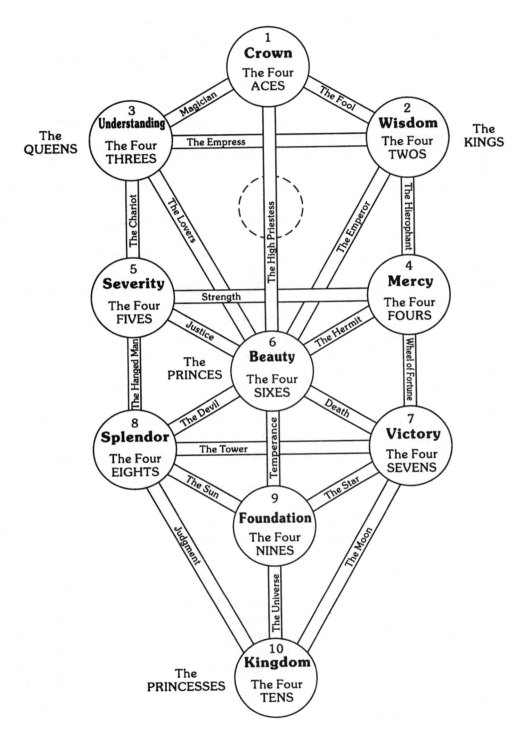

The Tarot on the Tree of Life

The Suit of Wands

The first suit of the Tarot represents the Yod-Force of Tetragrammaton, the Element of Fire and the Qabalistic World of Atziluth. In general, wands indicate great energy and dynamic power. They also allude to the great masculine power as the first stimulating spark of energy which begins life and sets everything in motion.

The Suit of Cups

The second suit in the deck symbolizes the Heh-Force of the Four-lettered Name of God, the Element of Water and the Qabalistic World of Briah. Cups refer to the form-building capacity of the great feminine power.

The Suit of Swords

The third Tarot suit alludes to the Vav-Force of Tetragrammaton, the Element of Air and the Qabalistic World of Yetzirah. Swords indicate intellect, communication, mental faculties and sometimes trouble. This suit is the son, the first offspring of the marriage of the primary Elements represented by the two preceding suits.

The Suit of Pentacles

The fourth and final suit of the Tarot refers to the Heh-Final Force of the Four-lettered Name, the Element of Earth and the Qabalistic World of Assiah. For the most part, pentacles or disks suggest material or worldly affairs, business or money. This suit is the daughter of the first two (wands and cups) implying that their combined energies have manifested in this final suit.

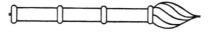

THE ACE OF WANDS
Decan: —
Associated Sephirah: Kether   *World:* Atziluth
Key word/Esoteric Title: THE ROOT OF THE POWERS OF FIRE

Image: Angelic hand issuing from clouds grasping a heavy club with three branches ending in ten flames. Twenty-two flaming Yods surrounding. *Interpretation:* Force, strength, rush, vigor, energy. Natural force as opposed to invoked force.

THE TWO OF WANDS
Decan: Mars in Aries, 1°—10°
Associated Sephirah: Chokmah   *World:* Atziluth
Key word/Esoteric Title: DOMINION

Image: Angelic hand issuing from clouds grasping two wands. *Interpretation:* Influence over others, authority, power, dominion, boldness, courage. Sometimes obstinate and unforgiving.

THE THREE OF WANDS
Decan: Sun in Aries, 10°—20°
Associated Sephirah: Binah   *World:* Atziluth
Key word/Esoteric Title: ESTABLISHED STRENGTH

Image: Angelic hand issuing from clouds grasping three wands—two crossed and one upright. *Interpretation:* Established strength and force. Success of the struggle. Self-assertion. Sometimes obstinate and rude.

THE FOUR OF WANDS
Decan: Venus in Aries, 20°—30°
Associated Sephirah: Chesed   *World:* Atziluth
Key word/Esoteric Title: PERFECTED WORK

Image: Two hands issuing from clouds clasped in the center with the First Order grip, holding four wands crossed. *Interpretation:* Settlement, arrangement, completion, perfection, success. Rest after labor.

THE FIVE OF WANDS
Decan: Saturn in Leo, 1°—10°
Associated Sephirah: Geburah   *World:* Atziluth
Key word/Esoteric Title: STRIFE

Image: Two hands issuing from clouds clasped in the center with the First Order grip, holding four wands crossed plus one upright in center. *Interpretation:* Quarreling and fighting, strife and contest, cruelty, rashness.

THE SIX OF WANDS
Decan: Jupiter in Leo, 10°—20°
Associated Sephirah: Tiphareth   *World:* Atziluth
Key word/Esoteric Title: VICTORY

Image: Two hands issuing from clouds clasped in the center with the First Order grip, holding six wands. Flames at point of junction. *Interpretation:* Gain, victory after strife, pleasure gained by labor, success through energy and perseverance.

THE SEVEN OF WANDS
Decan: Mars in Leo, 20°—30°
Associated Sephirah: Netzach   *World:* Atziluth
Key word/Esoteric Title: VALOR

Image: Two hands issuing from clouds clasped in the center with the First Order grip, holding six wands crossed. A third hand at bottom holding a seventh upright wand. *Interpretation:* Courage in the face of opposition, possible victory depending upon the energy and courage exercised.

THE EIGHT OF WANDS
Decan: Mercury in Sagittarius, 1º—10º
Associated Sephirah: Hod   *World:* Atziluth
Key word/Esoteric Title: SWIFTNESS

Image: Four hands issuing from clouds clasped in two pairs in the center with the First Order grip, holding eight wands crossed four and four. *Interpretation:* Hasty communication, swiftness, rapidity, too much force applied too suddenly. Very rapid rush but too quickly expended. Violent but not lasting.

THE NINE OF WANDS
Decan: Moon in Sagittarius, 10º—20º
Associated Sephirah: Yesod   *World:* Atziluth
Key word/Esoteric Title: GREAT STRENGTH

Image: Four hands as before holding eight wands crossed four and four. A fifth hand at bottom holding a ninth wand upright. *Interpretation:* Strength, power, health, tremendous and steady force. Great success after strife.

THE TEN OF WANDS
Decan: Saturn in Sagittarius, 20º—30º
Associated Sephirah: Malkuth   *World:* Atziluth
Key word/Esoteric Title: OPPRESSION

Image: Four hands as before holding eight wands crossed four and four. A fifth hand at bottom holding two additional upright wands. *Interpretation:* Cruelty, malice, revenge, injustice, cruel and overbearing force. Selfishness.

THE ACE OF CUPS
Decan: —
Associated Sephirah: Kether   *World:* Briah
Key word/Esoteric Title: THE ROOT OF THE POWERS OF WATER

Image: Angelic hand issuing from clouds supporting on the palm a cup from which rises a fountain of clear Water cascading on all sides. Calm Water below contains lotus and Water lilies. *Interpretation:* Fertility, productiveness, beauty, happiness, pleasure.

THE TWO OF CUPS
Decan: Venus in Cancer, 1°—10°
Associated Sephirah: Chokmah   *World:* Briah
Key word/Esoteric Title: LOVE

Image: Angelic hand issuing from clouds holding two lotuses. A lotus flower rises above the Water and the hand. From this lotus springs the stem of another lotus from which Water gushes. Crossed on the stem of the top flower are two dolphins, one gold and one silver. The Water flows in two streams of gold and silver over the animals into two cups which overflow. *Interpretation:* Pleasure, love, home, marriage, harmony unity. (Sometimes folly and waste depending on dignity.)

THE THREE OF CUPS
Decan: Mercury in Cancer, 10°—20°
Associated Sephirah: Binah   *World:* Briah
Key word/Esoteric Title: ABUNDANCE

Image: A hand holding a group of lotus flowers, two flowers hang over the central cup, filling it with Water. Other flowers pour Water into the two side cups. All cups overflow with Water. *Interpretation:* Plenty, abundance, success, bounty, pleasure.

THE FOUR OF CUPS
Decan: Moon in Cancer, 20°—30°
Associated Sephirah: Chesed   *World:* Briah
Key word/Esoteric Title: BLENDED PLEASURE

Image: Two upper cups overflow into two lower cups which do not overflow. A hand grasps the stem of a single flower card from which the Water issues. The stem and two leaves at the center form a cross between the cups. *Interpretation:* Mixed blessings, receiving pleasure but with some drawbacks, and anxieties.

THE FIVE OF CUPS
Decan: Mars in Scorpio, 1°—10°
Associated Sephirah: Geburah   *World:* Briah
Key word/Esoteric Title: LOSS IN PLEASURE

Image: A hand holding the stem of five lotus flowers which overhang five cups. No Water is shown. *Interpretation:* End of pleasure, disappointment, sorrow and loss, treachery, troubles, anxieties, loss of friendship.

THE SIX OF CUPS
Decan: Sun in Scorpio, 10º—20º
Associated Sephirah: Tiphareth   *World:* Briah
Key word/Esoteric Title: PLEASURE

Image: A hand holding the stem of six lotus flowers which overhang six cups. Water flows from each flower into one of the cups but they are not overflowing. *Interpretation:* Beginning of happiness, pleasure, success or enjoyment. Commencement of steady increase. (Sometimes vanity and presumptuousness, according to dignity.)

THE SEVEN OF CUPS
Decan: Venus in Scorpio, 20º—30º
Associated Sephirah: Netzach   *World:* Briah
Key word/Esoteric Title: ILLUSIONARY SUCCESS

Image: A hand holding the stem of six lotus flowers which overhang seven cups. The hand in the middle, just above the lower central cup which has no flower. No Water is shown and all the cups are empty. *Interpretation:* Promises unfulfilled, illusion, error, deception in the face of apparent success.

THE EIGHT OF CUPS
Decan: Saturn in Pisces, 1º—10º
Associated Sephirah: Hod   *World:* Briah
Key word/Esoteric Title: ABANDONED SUCCESS

Image: A hand holding the stem of two lotus flowers. Eight cups are shown but the flowers overhang and pour Water only into the middle two cups. Only two other cups on the bottom receive Water. *Interpretation:* Success abandoned, decline of interest, temporary success that is not followed up, indolence in accomplishments.

THE NINE OF CUPS
Decan: Jupiter in Pisces, 10º—20º
Associated Sephirah: Yesod   *World:* Briah
Key word/Esoteric Title: MATERIAL HAPPINESS

Image: A hand holding the stem of nine lotus flowers which overhang and pour Water into nine cups. All cups overflow. *Interpretation:* Complete success, perfect realization of pleasure and happiness, wish fulfilled, a generous and lovable nature.

THE TEN OF CUPS
Decan: Mars in Scorpio, 20⁰—30⁰
Associated Sephirah: Malkuth   *World:* Briah
Key word/Esoteric Title: PERFECTED SUCCESS

Image: A hand holding the stem of ten lotus flowers which overhang nine cups. A single flower at the top is the source of all the Water. It pours Water into the topmost cup, which is held sideways by another hand. All the cups are filled and overflowing. *Interpretation:* Complete good fortune, permanent success, pleasure, true happiness that is inspired from above. (Possible debauchery and wastefulness, depending on dignity.)

THE ACE OF SWORDS
Decan: —
Associated Sephirah: Kether   *World:* Yetzirah
Key word/Esoteric Title: THE ROOT OF THE POWERS OF AIR

Image: A hand issuing from clouds grasping the hilt of a great sword which is surmounted by a radiant crown. On the right of the crown is the olive branch of peace, while on the left is the palm branch of suffering. Six Vavs fall from the point of the sword. *Interpretation:* Great power for good or evil, whirling force, the double-edged sword of Justice. Always represents invoked force rather than natural force. True Will.

THE TWO OF SWORDS
Decan: Moon in Libra, 1⁰—10⁰
Associated Sephirah: Chokmah   *World:* Yetzirah
Key word/Esoteric Title: PEACE RESTORED

Image: Two crossed swords each held by an Angelic hand issuing from clouds. At the point where the swords cross is a large red rose of five petals. *Interpretation:* Quarrels resolved, yet tensions remain. Pleasure after pain, sacrifice and trouble but strength resulting. Peace restored, truce, arrangement of differences. Contradictory characteristics in the same nature.

THE THREE OF SWORDS
Decan: Saturn in Libra, 10⁰—20⁰
Associated Sephirah: Binah   *World:* Yetzirah
Key word/Esoteric Title: SORROW

Image: Three hands holding three swords upright. The central sword cuts apart the five-petaled rose. *Interpretation:* Unhappiness, sorrow, quarreling, deceit, disruption, sowing of discord and strife.

THE FOUR OF SWORDS
Decan: Jupiter in Libra, 20⁰—30⁰
Associated Sephirah: Chesed   *World:* Yetzirah
Key word/Esoteric Title: REST FROM STRIFE

Image: Two hands each holding two swords which four cross in the center. The red rose of five petals is reinstated on the point of intersection. *Interpretation:* Peace after war, rest from sorrow, relaxation of anxiety, recovery from sickness, change for the better.

THE FIVE OF SWORDS
Decan: Venus in Aquarius, 1⁰—10⁰
Associated Sephirah: Geburah   *World:* Yetzirah
Key word/Esoteric Title: DEFEAT

Image: Two hands each holding two swords upright but tilted away from each other. A third hand holds a sword upright in the center. The petals of the rose are torn apart. *Interpretation:* Defeat, loss, failure, trouble, malice, spite, slander. Clever yet cruel.

THE SIX OF SWORDS
Decan: Mercury in Aquarius, 10⁰—20⁰
Associated Sephirah: Tiphareth   *World:* Yetzirah
Key word/Esoteric Title: EARNED SUCCESS

Image: Two hands each holding three swords which six cross in the center. The red rose of five petals is reinstated on the point of intersection. *Interpretation:* Success after anxiety and trouble, dominion, labor, patience.

THE SEVEN OF SWORDS
Decan: Moon in Aquarius, 20°—30°
Associated Sephirah: Netzach   *World:* Yetzirah
Key word/Esoteric Title: UNSTABLE EFFORT

Image: Two hands each holding three swords whose points touch at the tips. A third hand holds the seventh sword upright in the center. The red rose of five petals is held by the central hand. *Interpretation:* Partial success, yielding when victory is within grasp, as if the last reserves of strength were used up. Inclination to lose on the point of gaining through not continuing the effort. Vacillating and unreliable.

THE EIGHT OF SWORDS
Decan: Jupiter in Gemini, 1°—10°
Associated Sephirah: Hod   *World:* Yetzirah
Key word/Esoteric Title: SHORTENED FORCE

Image: Four hands each holding two swords, all eight of which point upward and inward. The rose of five petals is re-established at the tips of the swords. *Interpretation:* Too much attention to details at the expense of more important principles. Patience in detail of study undermined by disorder in other things. Narrow attention. (If ill-dignified: malice, pettiness and domineering qualities.)

THE NINE OF SWORDS
Decan: Mars in Gemini, 10°—20°
Associated Sephirah: Yesod   *World:* Yetzirah
Key word/Esoteric Title: DESPAIR AND CRUELTY

Image: Four hands each holding a pair of swords upright which are tipped away from each other. A fifth hand holds a ninth sword upright in the center. No rose is shown. *Interpretation:* Mental cruelty, despair, pitilessness, malice, suffering loss, burden, oppression. (Yet also patience and unselfishness, according to dignity.)

THE TEN OF SWORDS
Decan: Sun in Gemini, 20°—30°
Associated Sephirah: Malkuth   *World:* Yetzirah
Key word/Esoteric Title: RUIN

Image: Four hands each holding a pair of swords upright but tipped away from each other. Two more hands hold two large swords which cross in the center. No rose is shown. *Interpretation:* Ruin, death, defeat, disruption, failure, a spoiler. (Sometimes clever and eloquent depending on dignity.)

THE ACE OF PENTACLES
Decan: —
Associated Sephirah: Kether   *World:* Assiah
Key word/Esoteric Title: THE ROOT OF THE POWERS OF THE EARTH

Image: An Angelic hand holding a branch of a rose tree which supports a large pentacle, formed of five concentric circles. The innermost circle is white, charged with a red Greek Cross. From the white center, twelve white rays issue. Above the whole figure is a small winged circle in the center of which is a Maltese Cross. Four roses and two buds are shown. *Interpretation:* Materiality in all senses, good and evil. Material gain, labor, power, wealth. (Sometimes illusionary.)

THE TWO OF PENTACLES
Decan: Jupiter in Capricorn, 1⁰—10⁰
Associated Sephirah: Chokmah   *World:* Assiah
Key word/Esoteric Title: HARMONIOUS CHANGE

Image: Two pentacles united by a serpent which is bound about them like a figure eight, holding its tail in its mouth. *Interpretation:* Pleasant change, alteration of gain and loss, variable, inconsistent, flux and reflux.

THE THREE OF PENTACLES
Decan: Mars in Capricorn, 10⁰—20⁰
Associated Sephirah: Binah   *World:* Assiah
Key word/Esoteric Title: MATERIAL WORKS

Image: An Angelic hand holding a branch of a rose tree, on which two white rosebuds touch and surmount the topmost pentacle. All three pentacles are in triangular formation. *Interpretation:* Business, paid employment, commercial transactions. Constructive force, building, increase in material matters, cleverness in business. (Sometimes narrow and prejudiced, depending on dignity.)

THE FOUR OF PENTACLES
Decan: Sun in Capricorn, 20°—30°
Associated Sephirah: Chesed   *World:* Assiah
Key word/Esoteric Title: EARTHLY POWER

Image: A hand holding a branch of a rose tree that is without flowers or buds except for a large central white rose. Four pentacles surround the flower. *Interpretation:* Gain of money or influence, a gift, assured material gain, success, rank, dominion, earthly power completed but nothing beyond. Careful and orderly but with little originality.

THE FIVE OF PENTACLES
Decan: Mercury in Taurus, 1°—10°
Associated Sephirah: Geburah   *World:* Assiah
Key word/Esoteric Title: MATERIAL TROUBLE

Image: A hand holding the branch of a white rose tree, from which roses are falling to pieces. Five pentacles are shown, one central and four surrounding. *Interpretation:* Loss of money, loss of profession or position, monetary troubles, poverty, harshness.

THE SIX OF PENTACLES
Decan: Moon in Taurus, 10°—20°
Associated Sephirah: Tiphareth   *World:* Assiah
Key word/Esoteric Title: MATERIAL SUCCESS

Image: A hand holding a rose branch with six roses, six buds, and six pentacles. *Interpretation:* Success and gain in material things, prosperity in business, gain in rank and influence. (If ill-dignified: wasteful and insolent due to success.)

THE SEVEN OF PENTACLES
Decan: Saturn in Taurus, 20°—30°
Associated Sephirah: Netzach   *World:* Assiah
Key word/Esoteric Title: SUCCESS UNFULFILLED

Image: A hand holding a rose branch with seven pentacles (in the formation of Rubeus). Five rose buds touch the upper five pentacles only. *Interpretation:* Unprofitable speculation and employment, promises of success unfulfilled, disappointment. Loss of apparently promising future. Hoped deceived and crushed. Little gain for much labor.

THE EIGHT OF PENTACLES
Decan: Sun in Virgo, 1°—10°
Associated Sephirah: Hod   *World:* Assiah
Key word/Esoteric Title: PRUDENCE

Image: A hand holding a rose branch with eight pentacles (arranged in the figure of Populus). Four white roses are shown which touch only the lower four pentacles. *Interpretation:* Prudence, cunning, skill, industrious. Over-cautious in small things at the expense of more important things. "Penny wise and pound-foolish."

THE NINE OF PENTACLES
Decan: Venus in Virgo, 10°—20°
Associated Sephirah: Yesod   *World:* Assiah
Key word/Esoteric Title: MATERIAL GAIN

Image: A hand holding a rose branch with nine pentacles—four above, four below and one in the center. Each pentacle has a rose next to it, while the central one also has two buds. *Interpretation:* Much increase of goods, complete realization of material gain, inheritance. (Sometimes covetousness and theft, according to dignity.)

THE TEN OF PENTACLES
Decan: Mercury in Virgo, 20°—30°
Associated Sephirah: Malkuth   *World:* Assiah
Key word/Esoteric Title: WEALTH

Image: A hand holding a rose branch with ten pentacles, in two groups of five. Each pentacle is touched by one of ten roses. *Interpretation:* Riches and wealth, prosperity in money transaction, completion of material gain and fortune, but nothing beyond. (Sometimes slothfulness and dullness of mind, depending on dignity.)

The Court Cards

The sixteen Court cards, like the forty other cards of the Minor Arcana, are based upon the Fourfold Name of God, the Tetragrammaton. The foundation here again is four and four. (The four suits of the Tarot further divided into four persons of Royalty.)

The four suits indicate the Elements and the Four Qabalistic Worlds. The four royal individuals that are contained within a particular suit embody the characteristics of a specific Element in all four Qabalistic planes of existence. Each Court card thus represents what is called a *Sub-Element*, such as Fire of Water, Air of Earth, etc.

The Royal cards also have a somewhat more humanistic feel to them compared to the forty small or numbered cards, which are more objective, static and impersonal.

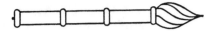

THE KING OF WANDS

Primary Element: Fire   *Qabalistic World:* Atziluth (Yod/Fire)
Sub-Element designation: Fire of Fire
Esoteric Title: The Lord of the Flame and the Lightning;
King of the Spirits of Fire
Associated Sephirah: Chokmah
Key word: DYNAMIC FORCE

Image: A winged warrior clothed in red armor riding a charging black horse over a ground of flames. He holds a burning club like that of the Ace of Wands. His emblem is a winged horse's head. *Interpretation:* Dynamic and uncontrollable force. Initiating. Volcanic force which is swift but not lasting. Energy like that of a *Flash Fire.* A mature man who is active, generous, fierce and impetuous. (If ill-dignified: he is cruel, brutal and bigoted.)

THE QUEEN OF WANDS

Primary Element: Fire   *Qabalistic World:* Briah (Heh/Water)
Sub-Element designation: Water of Fire
Esoteric Title: Queen of the Thrones of Flame
Associated Sephirah: Binah
Key word: STEADY FORCE

Image: A crowned Queen seated upon a throne with steady flames beneath. She wears mail and holds a conical-headed wand. A leopard is at her side. Her emblem is a winged leopard's head. *Interpretation:* Adaptable, steady force. Energy that is not so swift but enduring. Creative and persistent energy. Energy like that of a *steady burning flame.* Authority and power of command. A mature woman who is kind, assertive, self-assured, kind-hearted and generous. (If ill-dignified: she is domineering, tyrannical and revengeful.)

THE PRINCE OF WANDS
Primary Element: Fire   *Qabalistic World:* Yetzirah (Vav / Air)
Sub-Element designation: Air of Fire
Esoteric Title: The Prince of the Chariot of Fire
Associated Sephirah: Tiphareth
Key word: SWIFT FORCE

Image: A young winged man holding a wand in a chariot drawn by a lion. Flames dance under the wheels of the vehicle. The emblem of the Prince is a winged lion's head. *Interpretation:* A force that is swift and enduring although not especially strong. Energy like that of a *fire fed by wind.* A young man who is quick, strong, hasty, noble, rather violent, but just and generous. (If ill-dignified: he is cruel, intolerant, prejudiced and ill-natured.)

THE PRINCESS OF WANDS
Primary Element: Fire   *Qabalistic World:* Assiah (Heh / Earth)
Sub-Element designation: Earth of Fire
Esoteric Title: The Princess of the Shining Flame;
The Rose of the Palace of Fire
Associated Sephirah: Malkuth
Key word: EXPLOSIVE FORCE

Image: An Amazon warrior, wearing the skin of a tiger and brandishing a flaming club. Her other hand rests upon a fiery altar. Flames are all around. The emblem of the Princess is a winged tiger's head. *Interpretation:* Violently strong and enduring force. Manifesting Force. Energy like that of *combustion, an explosive backdraft.* A young woman who is brilliant, courageous, enthusiastic, daring, captivating and vigorous. (If ill-dignified: she is domineering, cruel, theatrical, unstable, irrational, violent and unforgiving.)

THE KING OF CUPS
Primary Element: Water   *Qabalistic World:* Atziluth (Yod/Fire)
Sub-Element designation: Fire of Water
Esoteric Title: The Lord of the Waves and the Waters;
King of the Hosts of the Sea
Associated Sephirah: Chokmah
Key word: CREATIVE FORCE

Image: A winged warrior clothed in armor riding a charging white horse over the waves of the sea. He holds a chalice from which issues a crab. His emblem is a peacock with opened wings. *Interpretation:* Energy that is swift but not enduring. Creative energy which gives rise to multiple forms. Energy like that of *a sudden rain or flash flood.* A mature man who is noble, gallant, sensitive, quick and enthusiastic. (If ill-dignified, he can be shallow and cursory.)

THE QUEEN OF CUPS
Primary Element: Water   *Qabalistic World:* Briah (Heh/Water)
Sub-Element designation: Water of Water
Esoteric Title: Queen of the Thrones of the Waters
Associated Sephirah: Binah
Key word: REFLECTIVE FORCE

Image: A crowned Queen seated upon a throne with flowing Water beneath. In one hand she holds a cup containing a crab. Her other hand holds a lotus and is placed on the head of an ibis. Her emblem is an ibis with opened wings. *Interpretation:* Reflective force, which mirrors the surrounding energy. Transmitting force which casts back the nearby influences while remaining unaffected. An energy conduit. Energy like that of *a clear still pool.* A mature woman who is imaginative, creative, dreamy, poetic, kind, good-natured and tranquil. (If ill-dignified: she is deceptive and ungrounded.)

THE PRINCE OF CUPS
Primary Element: Water   *Qabalistic World:* Yetzirah (Vav / Air)
Sub-Element designation: Air of Water
Esoteric Title: The Prince of the Chariot of the Waters
Associated Sephirah: Tiphareth
Key word: INTENSE FORCE

Image: A young winged man in a chariot drawn by an eagle. Calm Water is under the wheels of the vehicle. He holds a cup from which issues a serpent. The emblem of the Prince is an eagle with opened wings. *Interpretation:* A force that is volatile, changeable and mysterious. Erratic energy that can be both sublime and destructive. Energy like that of *steam or mist*. A young man who is subtle, violent, craft, secretive, clever and intense. A fierce nature with a calm exterior. (If ill-dignified: he is intensely evil and merciless.)

THE PRINCESS OF CUPS
Primary Element: Water   *Qabalistic World:* Assiah (Heh / Earth)
Sub-Element designation: Earth of Water
Esoteric Title: The Princess of the Waters; Lotus of the Palace of the Floods
Associated Sephirah: Malkuth
Key word: IMAGINATIVE FORCE

Image: A beautiful young Amazon standing on the foam of the sea. In one hand she holds a lotus, in the other a cup from which issues a turtle. The emblem of the Princess is a swan with open wings. *Interpretation:* Creative, fertile energy that has the power to take on substance or form. Unceasing power to generate images and ideas. Energy like that of *a Waterfall*. A young woman who is gentle, kind, poetic, imaginative, artistic, and dreamy. (If ill-dignified: she is indolent, selfish and luxurious.)

THE KING OF SWORDS
Primary Element: Air   *Qabalistic World:* Atziluth (Yod / Fire)
Sub-Element designation: Fire of Air
Esoteric Title: The Lord of the Winds and Breezes; King of the Spirits of Air
Associated Sephirah: Chokmah
Key word: UNSTABLE FORCE

Image: A winged warrior clothed in armor riding a brown horse over dark clouds. He holds a drawn sword and his emblem is a winged six-pointed star. *Interpretation:* Violent, fiery energy that is unstable and extremely volatile. Swift and agitated energy that is unpredictable. Energy like that of *a hurricane*. A mature man who is clever, subtle, aggressive, skillful and courageous. (If ill-dignified: he is tyrannical, crafty, domineering and deceitful.)

THE QUEEN OF SWORDS
Primary Element: Air   *Qabalistic World:* Briah (Heh/Water)
Sub-Element designation: Water of Air
Esoteric Title: Queen of the Thrones of Air
Associated Sephirah: Binah
Key word: SEVERE FORCE

Image: A stern, crowned Queen seated upon a throne with cumulus clouds beneath. In one hand she holds a sword and in the other the severed head of a man. Her emblem is a winged head of a child. *Interpretation:* Creative, enduring and elastic energy. A rational, sharp and severe force that enacts harsh measures for good results. Energy like that of *a storm driven by fierce winds.* A mature woman who is intensely perceptive, intelligent, subtle, quick, accurate and decisive. (If ill-dignified: she is malicious, deadly, cruel, sly and unreliable.)

THE PRINCE OF SWORDS
Primary Element: Air   *Qabalistic World:* Yetzirah (Vav/Air)
Sub-Element designation: Air of Air
Esoteric Title: The Prince of the Chariot of the Winds
Associated Sephirah: Tiphareth
Key word: INTELLECTUAL FORCE

Image: A young winged man holding a sword in one hand and a sickle in the other. He is seated above the clouds in a chariot drawn by two archons or Arch Fairies. The emblem of the Prince is a winged Angel's head. *Interpretation:* Intellectual force that destroys ideas as quickly as they are created. A harsh force that is too volatile to be enduring. Energy like that of *a random whirlwind.* A young man who is full of ideas, thoughts and designs. He is suspicious, loyal, and impractical. (If ill-dignified: he is harsh, malicious, obstinate, and unreliable.)

THE PRINCESS OF SWORDS
Primary Element: Air   *Qabalistic World:* Assiah (Heh/Earth)
Sub-Element designation: Earth of Air
Esoteric Title: The Princess of the Rushing Winds;
Lotus of the Palace of Air
Associated Sephirah: Malkuth
Key word: AVENGING FORCE

Image: An Amazon warrior, standing on the clouds and brandishing a sword in one hand. Her other hand rests upon a smoldering altar. The emblem of the Princess is the head of Medusa. *Interpretation:* Decisive, stabilizing force in an erratic environment. Harsh and severe energy coming into manifestation. Energy like that of *a deadly tornado.* A young woman who is aggressive, wise, strong, subtle, skillful and graceful. (If ill-dignified: she is deadly wrathful, avenging, cunning and frivolous.)

THE KING OF PENTACLES
Primary Element: Earth   *Qabalistic World:* Atziluth (Yod/Fire)
Sub-Element designation: Fire of Earth
Esoteric Title: The Lord of the Wild and Fertile Land;
King of the Spirits of Earth
Associated Sephirah: Chokmah
Key word: STIMULATING FORCE

Image: A dark winged warrior clothed in armor seated on a light brown horse which stands in a fertile field. He holds a pentacle and his emblem is the winged head of a stag. *Interpretation:* Stimulating and fertilizing energy that causes growth and material production. Expansive force. Energy like that of *a fertile mountain slope.* A mature man who is laborious, domestic, a good worker and a sturdy provider. (If ill-dignified, he can be dull, unintelligent, greedy, jealous and cowardly.)

THE QUEEN OF PENTACLES
Primary Element: Earth   *Qabalistic World:* Briah (Heh/Water)
Sub-Element designation: Water of Earth
Esoteric Title: Queen of the Thrones of Earth
Associated Sephirah: Binah
Key word: REGENERATIVE FORCE

Image: A crowned Queen seated upon a throne beneath which is barren soil. In one hand she holds a scepter surmounted by a cube, in the other she holds a golden orb with a cross. Behind her throne is a goat. Her emblem is a winged goat's head. *Interpretation:* Receptive, germinating force which carries out the process of regeneration. Energy like that of *a desert receiving a nourishing rain.* A mature woman who is impetuous, kind, charming, great-hearted, intelligent, and truthful. (If ill-dignified: she is moody, changeable, timid and melancholy.)

THE PRINCE OF PENTACLES
Primary Element: Earth   *Qabalistic World:* Yetzirah (Vav/Air)
Sub-Element designation: Air of Earth
Esoteric Title: The Prince of the Chariot of the Earth
Associated Sephirah: Tiphareth
Key word: RESOLUTE FORCE

Image: A young winged man in a chariot drawn by a bull. A grassy plain is under the wheels of the vehicle. He holds a golden orb and cross in one hand and in the other a scepter surmounted by an orb and cross. The emblem of the Prince is a winged bull's head. *Interpretation:* An energy that is slow but steady. Unstoppable and patient force that is fertile and productive. Energy like that of *a fertile, cultivated field.* A young man who is clever, capable, steady, reliable, thoughtful, energetic and practical. Violent-tempered if pushed to extremes. (If ill-dignified: he is material, dull and insensitive.)

THE PRINCESS OF PENTACLES
Primary Element: Earth   *Qabalistic World:* Assiah (Heh/Earth)
Sub-Element designation: Earth of Earth
Esoteric Title: The Princess of the Echoing Hills
Rose of the Palace of Earth
Associated Sephirah: Malkuth
Key word: MANIFESTING FORCE

Image: A young Amazon standing in a fertile field near a grove of trees. In one hand she holds a scepter surmounted by a disc, while in the other she bears a pentacle. Her emblem is a winged ram's head. *Interpretation:* Force manifesting into physical form. Energy acquiring density. Materialization. Energy like that of *a dense forest or jungle.* A young woman who is generous, kind, diligent, benevolent, careful, mysterious, courageous and strong. (If ill-dignified: she is wasteful and prodigal.)✿

This concludes the Knowledge Lecture. Examinations on the initiation ceremony as well as the material covered in this section are given at the end of this chapter.✿

AN ADDITIONAL SIDE LECTURE
On the General Guidance and Purification of the Soul[110]

Learn first, O Practicus of our Ancient Order, that true Equilibrium is the basis of the Soul. If thou thyself hast not a sure foundation, whereon wilt thou stand to direct the forces of Nature?

Know then that as Man is born into this world amidst the darkness of Nature and the strife of contending forces, so must his first endeavor be to seek the Light through their reconciliation. Thus, thou who hast trial and trouble of this life, rejoice because of them, for in them is strength, and by their means is a pathway opened unto that Light Divine.

How should it be otherwise, O man, whose life is but a day in Eternity, a drop in the Ocean of Time? How, if thy trials were not many, couldst thou purge thy soul from the dross of Earth?

Is it but now that the higher life is beset with dangers and difficulties; hath it not been ever thus with the Sages and Hierophants of the Past? They have been persecuted and reviled, they have been tormented of men, yet through this has their glory increased. Rejoice, therefore, O Initiate, for the greater thy trial, the brighter thy triumph. When men shall revile thee and speak against thee falsely, hath not the Master said "Blessed art thou." Yet, O Practicus, let thy victories bring thee not vanity, for with increase of knowledge should come increase of wisdom. He who knows little, thinketh he knows much; but he who knoweth much hath learned his own ignorance. Seest thou a Man wise in his own conceit? There is more hope of a fool than of him.

Be not hasty to condemn other's sin. How knowest thou that in their place thou couldst have resisted the temptation? And even were it so, why shouldst thou despise one who is weaker than thyself? Be thou well sure of this, that in slander and self-righteousness is sin. Pardon therefore the sinner, but encourage not the sin. The Master condemned not the adulterous woman, but neither did he encourage her to commit the sin.

Thou therefore who desirest magical gifts, be sure that thy soul is firm and steadfast, for it is by flattering thy weakness that the Evil One will gain power over thee. Humble thyself before thy God, yet fear neither man nor spirit. Fear is failure and the forerunner of failure; and courage is the beginning of virtue. Therefore fear not the Spirits, but be firm and courteous with them, for thou hast no right either to despise or to revile them, and this too may lead thee into sin. Command and banish the Evil ones. Curse them by the Great Names of God, if need be; but neither mock nor revile them, for so assuredly thou wilt be led into error.

A man is what he maketh himself within the limits fixed by his inherited destiny; he is a part of mankind. His actions affect not himself only, but also those with whom he is brought into contact, either for good or for evil.

---

[110] From Regardie's *The Golden Dawn*. (Note that Crowley "borrowed" heavily from this lecture and renamed it *Liber Librae, the Book of Balance,—The Equinox*, Vol. 1, No. 1).

Neither worship nor neglect the physical body, which is thy temporary connection with the outer and material world. Therefore let thy mental equilibrium be above disturbances by material events. Restrain the animal passions and nourish the higher aspirations; the emotions are purified by suffering. Do good unto others for God's sake, not for reward, not for gratitude from them, not for sympathy. If thou art generous, thou wilt not long for thine ears to be tickled by expressions of gratitude. Remember that unbalanced force is evil, that unbalanced severity is but cruelty and oppression, but that also unbalanced Mercy is but weakness which would allow and abet evil.

True prayer is as much action as Word; it is Will. The Gods will not do for man what his Higher Powers can do for himself, if he cultivate Will and Wisdom. Remember that this Earth is but an atom in the Universe, and thou thyself but an atom thereon. And that even couldst thou become the God of this Earth whereon thou crawlest and grovellest, thou wouldst even then be but an atom and one among many. Nevertheless, have the greatest self-respect, and to that end sin not against thyself. The sin which is unpardonable is knowingly and willfully to reject spiritual truth, but every sin and act leaveth its effect.

To obtain magical Power, learn to control thought. Admit only true ideas which are in harmony with the end desired, and not every stray and contradictory idea that presents itself. Fixed thought is a means to an end; therefore pay attention to the power of silent thought and meditation. The material act is but the outward expression of the thought, and therefore it hath been said that "the thought of foolishness is sin." Thought therefore is the commencement of action, and if a chance thought can produce much effect, what cannot fixed thought do? Therefore, as has been already said, establish thyself firmly in the Equilibrium of Forces, in the center of the cross of the elements, that Cross from whose center the creative word issued in the birth of the dawning universe.

As it was said unto thee in the grade of Theoricus: "Be thou therefore prompt and active as the Sylphs, but avoid frivolity and caprice. Be energetic and strong like the Salamanders, but avoid irritability and ferocity. Be flexible and attentive to images like the Undines, but avoid idleness and changeability. Be laborious and patient like the Gnomes, but avoid grossness and avarice." So shalt thou gradually develop the powers of thy Soul and fit thyself to command the spirits of the elements.

For wert thou to summon the Gnomes to pander to thy avarice, thou wouldst no longer command them, but they would command thee. Wouldst thou abuse the pure creatures of God's creation to fill thy coffers and to satisfy thy lust for Gold? Wouldst thou defile the Spirits of driving Fire to serve thy wrath and hatred? Wouldst thou violate the purity of the Souls of the Water to pander to thy lust and debauchery? Wouldst thou force the Spirits of the evening breeze to minister to thy folly and caprice?

Know that with such desires thou canst but attract the evil and not the good, and in that can the evil will have power over thee.

In true religion there is no sect. Therefore take heed that thou blaspheme not the name by which another knoweth his God for if thou doest this thing in Jupiter, thou wilt blaspheme YHVH; and in Osiris YEHESHUAH.

"Ask of God and ye shall have,
Seek and ye shall find.
Knock, and it shall be opened unto you."✿

Ritual Work for the Practicus

Continue the Fourfold breath technique as taught in the Neophyte grade. Add to this the following visualizations:

Inhale	—	I KNOW (Air)
Full Hold	—	I WILL (Fire)
Exhale	—	I DARE (Water)
Empty Hold	—	I KEEP SILENT (Earth)

The Practicus should construct all of the following talismanic emblems to aid in meditation and ritual. These emblems should be painted orange on blue.

- The sigil of Elemental Water
- The sigil of Mercury
- The sigil of Cancer
- The sigil of Scorpio
- The sigil of Pisces

The following symbols should be painted black on white:

- The number eight
- The letter Shin
- The letter Resh
- The name Elohim Tzabaoth in Hebrew
- The octagram and octangle

MEDITATION

for the 3 = 8 grade of Practicus[111]

Let the Practicus meditate upon the Symbols of the Rhomboid and the Vesica. Let him seek out their meaning and correspondences. Let him contemplate the Symbol of Mercury and the number eight.

Let him now learn to control his emotions, on no account giving way to anger, hatred and jealousy, but to turn the force he hitherto expended in these directions towards the attainment of perfection, that the malarial marsh of his nature may become a clear and limpid lake, reflecting the Divine Nature truly and without distortion.

Let him identify himself with the Powers of Water, considering the Water Triplicity in all its aspects, with its attributions and correspondences.✡

CONCENTRATION AND MANTRA

The exercises of relaxation, rhythmic breathing and mind awareness given in the previous grades should have by this time instilled within the student a high degree of sensitivity, peace and awareness. The next step is to introduce the faculty of concentration.

The Sephirah of Hod is the sphere of the intellectual mind—the part of the human psyche which consciously observes, examines and reflects on images and ideas. The mind must be trained to open up and receive an influx of Divine Spirit. And the only way to train the mind to concentrate is through practice.

There are two important side-effects which arise from developing the faculty of concentration. These include (1) the development of the Will and (2) the development of the imagination, both of which will prove to be essential in the aspirant's spiritual growth.

The first step in this training is to set up more frequent and shorter periods of time each day for the exercise. Though at first it may seem to the student that s/he is not progressing during these first periods of concentration training, discouragement must not be allowed to lead one into failure. What we are teaching here is a discipline, and the student should not expect immediate results. Also, the mind must never be forced into compliance by trying to block out thoughts, which is of course impossible. Patience is a prerequisite.

---

[111] From Regardie's *The Golden Dawn.*

The exercises already undertaken by the student of this course will have given the student the opportunity to observe the physical sensations followed by the wanderings of the mind, neither of which can be ignored or subdued. Efforts to fight them will only give them power. However, the mere observation of them will gradually lessen their strength and occurrence. Once this happens the concentration training can begin.

The next step is to break out of old habits and construct new habits or behavior patterns which will better aid the process of concentration. Choose a specific time of day for the exercise and make it a daily routine. Eventually this habit of concentration practice will become second-nature to you, much like the time of day that you wake up every morning.

Candles, incense, and ritual oils will help the student create the proper spiritual awareness for the exercise, although they should never be thought of as crucial to one's practice. The only essential element in this exercise is the Mantra which is a mechanical aid to the practice of concentration.

A *mantra* is a word or phrase (usually devotional) which is repeated over and over, audibly or astrally, until the mantra itself remains the only thing that the mind is aware of. A mantra can be a sound or a word which is connected with a spiritual force or concept, intended to bring about changes in one's inner and outer realities. By constant repetition, the astral body of the practitioner attunes itself to the energy which is inherent within the mantra.

Mantras which are most suitable for the student of this course include those that are derived from the Golden Dawn tradition. Five such mantras are:

Khabs Am Pekht
Konx Om Pax

—

Yod Heh Vav Heh
Adonai

—

Kether
Malkuth

—

Ve-Geburah
Ve-Gedulah

—

Eheieh
Agla

The mantra is to be memorized and recited mentally in time with the breathing. The first line of the mantra is repeated with the inhalation, and the second line is recited on the exhalation. With a little time this practice becomes simple and automatic. When this occurs the aspirant can contemplate the meaning of the phrase, and what it invokes within. Emotional force can be applied to the mantra, directing the mind toward the support of the mantra until the focus of concentration is an undeniable fact. The mechanical repetition of the words eventually subdues the wayward mind, inducing a deep state of contemplation. In due time this faculty of concentration can be summoned and dismissed at Will.

This exercise is to be maintained throughout the entire length of time that the student is in the grade of Practicus. If more time is needed to master the method and attain a state of true concentration, then by all means take more time to practice it.✿

PSYCHIC DEVELOPMENT

Exercise 1

This exercise is designed to develop the student's sensitivity. Obtain a deck of Tarot cards and remove all the Trump cards. Shuffle the remaining Minor Arcana cards thoroughly. Take the time to instill some of your own personal magnetism into the cards. Shuffle them again and place the deck on the table before you, face down. Place your hand upon the top card and spend a few moments trying to visualize what Tarot suit (or Trump card) it is. Let your intuitive powers have total rein and do not be the least concerned if you find that you have guessed wrong. Go on to the next card. Practice often and keep a written record of your progress, (what your guess was, and what the actual card was). With time and practice your degree of accuracy will improve. For the first two months, concentrate only on trying to determine the suit of the cards.

Exercise 2

Repeat the method stated above, but this time instead of trying to determine the card suit, try to visualize what number (or Sephirah) is associated with each card of the Minor Arcana. Practice this for the next two months.

Exercise 3

Repeat the previous technique, but now try to determine both the suit and number of the card. (Keep in mind that the two positive masculine suits are compatible with each other, as are the two negative feminine suits, therefore their energies will feel similar.) Practice this exercise for the remaining time in the grade, and as always, record your findings.✿

The 31st Path of Shin

The *Sepher Yetzirah* calls the 31st Path (from Malkuth to Hod) the Perpetual Intelligence, because it regulates the motions of the Sun and Moon in their proper order, each in an orbit convenient for it. For the initiate traveling this path, the key word is "perpetual." This is the persistent regulation of the progress of the initiate's Personality toward the cosmic consciousness. The Angelic powers, called forth by the student journeying upon the Tree, determine what aspects of the initiate are unsuitable for his/her spiritual growth. These undesirable qualities are slowly burned away by the purging Fire of Shin. This permits the "Sun and Moon" of the initiate (i.e., the positive and negative sides of the student) to work "each in their proper order."

The 20th Key of the Tarot *Judgment,* is attributed to this path. The Magical Title of this card is "The Spirit of the Primal Fire." The path of Judgment connects Hod to Malkuth, and it is known as "The Splendor of the Material World. Mercury acting through Fire upon the Cosmic Elements." In other words this path serves to awaken the Intellectual center (Mercury) in the psyche (Cosmic elements) of the initiate using fiery *Yod* energy.

This is the first path undertaken by the aspiring student which is off the Middle Pillar and the relative "safety" of the center Column of the Tree. It can be quite a jolt to the initiate as s/he journeys along this path, which can be best described as a Baptism into the Primal Element of Fire. The 31st Path is also the path which best represents the act of Initiation. On this path the initiate first becomes aware of the divine forces which guide and implant much-needed spiritual energy into the Lower Personality. Shin, the Hebrew letter associated with this path means "tooth," suggesting the breaking down and ingesting of food (energy). Shin is not only attributed to the Element of Fire, but also to the Fifth Element of Spirit. Thus the experience of traversing the 31st Path is that of the divine spiritual energy plunging into physical matter. This spiritual force descends from Hod (by way of Binah and the Black Pillar) and infuses the aspirant with the Fiery Shin energy. The ingesting of this spiritual "food" awakens the initiate for the first time to the Divine Presence working internally. The "Judgment" indicated on this path, is that which is undertaken by the Personality of the initiate as s/he becomes more aware of a Greater Reality, which serves to equilibrate his/her own imbalances. The Shin of Judgment is a consecrating and purifying Fire which perpetually burns away the gross, leaving only the balanced and the pure.

Symbols included within the Tarot card of Judgment are: the Archangel Michael descending, the candidate rising from the tomb, and the two figures of Samael and Anael (all personifications of Fire and Heat), the Hebrew letter Shin, the rainbow of Promise, the fiery serpents (Seraphim) and the triangle of flame. The figure in the foreground is Kasmillos, a representation of the initiate of the mysteries, standing in the Theoricus Sign, indicating that he has received the redeeming Fire of Shin from the actions of the other figures (the three Kabiri) who have tested and tried him in order to burn away all his impurities. He now stands in the Sign of Air as the Reconciler while the other three figures herald his triumphant rebirth. He welcomes an influx of Spirit descending through the ether into his physical form.✿

A JOURNEY ON THE 31ST PATH OF SHIN[112]

For this ritual the Practicus will need the robe, nemyss, red sandals, the Tetrahedron, and the Outer Wand of Double Power. The temple is to be arranged as in the Opening of the 3 = 8 grade. Upon the altar should be the Tarot Trump of *Judgment*. A comfortable place to sit and meditate should be arranged West of the pillars.

After a period of relaxation has passed, go to the Northeast and say, *"HEKAS, HEKAS, ESTE BEBELOI! Far from this sacred place be the profane!"*

Go to the East. With the black end of the wand, perform the Lesser Banishing Ritual of the Pentagram.

Go the West of the altar. With the white end of the Wand of Double Power, trace a large letter *Shin* over the Tarot card. Visualize it in Red. Intone the name of the letter thrice. Give the Neophyte Signs toward the card. Put the wand aside, and take the Tetrahedron in your right hand.

With all your powers of concentration, look upon the card and comprehend it—consider all its meaning and symbolism. Give the Sign of the Practicus. At this point you may sit comfortably if you wish, but maintain a disassociation from the surrounding room. Behind the darkness of your closed eyelids, you begin to formulate the astral temple of the Sephirah Malkuth, as the journey begins:

Astrally, you give the Sign of the Zelator. Once again the ten-sided temple of Malkuth formulates around you with its black-and-white tiled floor and rough-hewn oak walls. The sacred flame burns brightly upon the central altar. The brazier of incense, fireplace, fountain, and mill stones are familiar sights to you now.

You intone the divine name of this temple, *Adonai ha-Aretz*, and call upon its archangel *Sandalphon*, and the choir of Angels the *Ashim*. Finally you vibrate the name of the temple, *Malkuth*.

From the clouds of incense in the East, Sandalphon appears. You salute her with the Sign of the Enterer, and she answers with the Sign of Silence. She speaks: "You have entered the Kingdom of Malkah, the Queen. What symbol do you bring to define what you seek?" You hold out the Pyramid of Flame.

Sandalphon leads you to a door in the Northeast part of the temple. Before the door is a veil made from the tarot trump of *Judgment*. The archangel traces a Fire triangle and the veil parts and vanishes. The door leading to the 31st Path is carved from pure fire opal and painted upon it is the Hebrew letter, Shin. Giving the Sign of Practicus, you then hold out the Solid Triangle and trace with it the letter, Shin. The door opens outward.

---

[112] From our book, *Secrets of a Golden Dawn Temple*.

You and your guide step out onto the craggy side of a cliff. You can just make out the mountain tops which seem to rise above a valley below, whose subtleties are hidden to your view. Sandalphon leads you on a narrow descending path which seems more suited to the hooves of a mountain goat than to your feet.

By the time you reach the valley floor, it is mid-afternoon. The climate is moderate, but chill. Ahead, you hear a commotion—the sounds of people shouting and the bellowing of some great beast. This distraction causes you to step on a stinging nettle, but you ignore the pain. Sandalphon gestures for you to continue on the path without her.

Just over a hill, you discover the source of the disturbance. A primitive looking group of men have cornered a mammoth and driven it over the edge of a small ravine. The huge animal was carefully trapped by the hunters who used torches and dugout pits of fire to maneuver the beast in the direction they wanted it to go—toward the ravine. Now, with the huge animal trapped, they kill it with heavy spears and rocks. When the mammoth is dead, the hunters give great shouts of joy which bring even more people onto the scene of the drama.

A woman and small boy who have come to help cut up the meat with stone knives notice you standing there. Puzzled, they approach. When they see the Pyramid of flame in your hand, they smile and point to markings tattooed on the palms of their hands, which is that of a red triangle. This is the mark of the Tribe. They are the Clan of Fire.

With great efficiency, the animal is skinned, butchered and hauled away to a nearby village. You follow, and appear to be accepted by these people and their strange and primitive ways. The main shelter of the encampment is an enormous cave, but a few simple lodges, made from Mammoth bone and hide stand just a short distance from the cave entrance. From one of these shelters, a wise old medicine woman brings a bag of ointments and herbs to tend the wounds of some of the hunters. The entire village, women and children, young and old, help with the storing of meat and the curing of strips of hide. Chunks of meat are skewered to cook over several small fires around the camp. Everyone is hungry from all the work. Food including meat, flat bread, fruit and a spicy drink is passed around to all, including you. In the center of the village, and in front of the cavern entrance, burns a great bonfire. After they have eaten, the hunters are led in a ceremony by an old shaman dressed in mammoth wool and a helmet carved from bone. They perform a sacred dance reenacting the hunt to thank the Spirit of the mammoth for giving its life to feed the Clan. The celebration continues well into the evening. There is laughter around the Fire, as well as talk of brave deeds, Spirits, and gossip. The Fire is the life of the village—it brings food, warmth, security, and protection to the tribe. It also brings them together as a human community, setting them apart from the animals in the valley.

Finally the festivity winds down and you feel the urge to press on with your journey. As you bid goodbye, some of the clan members give you small sacred objects: a lion carved from stone, a spearhead, and the tooth of a bear. You thank them and continue on the 31st Path.

The setting sun is hanging low in the sky behind you as you continue Northeast of the valley. The land opens out into a wide sandy plateau with stunted trees and desert scrub. Off in the distance, you see the outline of a great pyramid against the evening sky. Two smaller pyramids loom on either side of the main one. Wanting to reach the structure before dark, you quicken your pace.

As you approach the great pyramid, its beauty becomes evident. Constructed from enormous red stones, many hieroglyphs and relief sculptures are carved into its surface. At the main entrance into the pyramid are two enormous goddesses enthroned before a pair of columns whose capitals end in carved lotus flowers. Both goddesses are lion-headed and each bears a lotus staff in one hand and an ankh in the other. The goddess on the left wears a green tunic, while her twin is dressed in red. An uraeus sits atop the nemysses of both, surmounted by the Solar disc. As you draw near, the figures stand and bar your path with their staffs. They speak: "Thou canst not enter the Pyramid of Flame unless thou canst tell us our names."

"Thou art the sister goddesses of the West and East." You direct your answer to the figure in red. "Thou art Sekhet, lady of flame, beloved of Ptah. Thou art the fierce and scorching aspect of Fire, destroyer of the enemies of Ra, who consumes the wicked and the unbalanced." You turn toward the form in green. "Thou art the goddess Bast, the eye of Ra, whose name means "Fire." Thou art the power of the heat of the Sun as it warms the Earth and causes the growth of plants and the bearing of seeds."

"In what signs and symbols do ye come?" they whisper.

Standing in the Sign of the Practicus you state, "In the divine name of *Elohim Tzabaoth*, in the name *Eloah*, and in this symbol of Pyramid of Flame."

The figures step back. The goddess Bast traces the sigil of Leo before you with her lotus staff. "In the Sign of the Lion," she says, "Thou art purified."

The goddess Sekhet traces the letter Shin before you. "In the letter of Initiation and of Judgment, Thou art consecrated. Pass Thou on."

Entering the pyramid, you give the Neophyte Signs. You step into a great hall with a black and white tiled floor. Two great pillars, one black and one white, resembling the feet of two goddesses dominate the hall. You recognize this chamber as the Hall of Dual Manifestation, the place of the Weighing of the Soul. You had to pass through its physical representation on Earth when you were initiated as a Neophyte. Here you see it in its astral and original form. The scales of the goddess Maat are at the center of the temple—their balance is tested and watched over by the jackal-headed Anubis. Thoth, the ibis-headed god of wisdom acts as a scribe, ready with stylus and clay tablet to record the judgment. A fierce-looking beast crouches menacingly behind Thoth—part hippopotamus, part leopard, and part crocodile. Forty-two lesser gods sit in silence on all sides of the room.

A goddess with a sistrum acts as your guide—the gentle sound of her implement is soothing. With the strength of conviction, you step forward and face the assembly of gods. You place the Tetrahedron upon the scales as a symbol of your heart and your deepest spiritual aspirations. The goddess Maat, governess of truth, places her feather in the scale also, weighing it against the purity of your heart. Anubis questions you with the determination of a prosecuting attorney. He asks you to describe all the symbols in the hall in detail. Luckily you are familiar with these symbols from your studies, and you satisfactorily answer all question. The forty-two lesser gods each question you in turn:

"Hast thou given due thought to the body inhabited by thee?"

"Hast thou spoken unjustly in anger?"

"Hast thou been undiligent in work?"

"Hast Thou lived in the Light?"

"Hast Thou faced the mirror of Self?"

Their questions are hard, but you answer all of them truthfully to the best of your ability. At the end of their questioning, you are tired, but relieved, as if the negative confession had unburdened your Soul. Thoth beckons you forward and asks one final question. "Who is He whose Pylons are of flame, whose walls of Living Uraei, and the flames of whose house are streams of Water?"

"Osiris!" you reply.

The god records your answer approvingly. "Pass on, thou knowest it," is his answer. The Hawk-headed god Horus, who has witnessed all of the proceedings, takes your hand in his and leads you past the Devouring Beast, to a shrine in the Eastern part of the hall. He instructs you to kneel before an altar in front of the shrine. There upon the Dais the god Osiris sits enthroned. He wears the tall white crown of the South flanked by two plumes. From his chin hangs the royal beard of authority and judgment, and he holds the Scourge of Severity, the Crook of Mercy and the Phoenix Wand. The Children of Horus are at his feet and the goddesses of the two pillars, Isis and Nephthys stand behind him.

Upon the altar before the god, you place the bear's tooth and the spearhead from the clan as an offering to the god of Judgment. He reaches out and touches the crown of your head with the Phoenix Wand. The god speaks: "Thy meat shall be from the Infinite, and Thy drink from the Infinite. Thou art able to go forth to the initiatory feasts on Earth, for thou hast overcome."

A lion-headed goddess, Tharpesh, bids you to rise and follow her. She leads you to a chamber where a statue of Ptah, the creator god stands with an iron knife in one hand and a hammer in the other. Ptah, the greatest of the old gods is known as the architect of the universe, and the patron of craftsmen, metalsmiths, and workmen. Next to the statue is a triangular portal whose edges are ringed with flames. The goddess gestures for you to enter the portal. Giving the Sign of the Practicus, you do so.

The heat of the flames is all around you. You no longer seem to be walking forward. Instead you are rising upward, like smoke. Sweating from the hot blast of Air. Your black robe is incinerated, but you feel no pain as this baptism of Fire continues. There is no fear, only the desire to rise like a phoenix into a new state of being through the initiating power of Fire. The sounds of a trumpet are heard somewhere above you.

Suddenly the roaring flames propel you upward through a square opening in the rocks above. There is no time to react. Naked, you rise to find yourself standing leg-high in a black stone tomb which juts out of the bare Earth. Before you is a cool, placid lake covered by a layer of mist and steam. Above the mist is a truly glorious vision. The Archangel of Fire, Michael surrounded by a fireball of red, orange, and green flames. His wings are sheer and translucent, formed from white-hot vapors at the center of the flame. Threads of Fire weave up and down his bare skin, disturbing not a single hair. The golden disc of Sol sits atop his dark-haired crown, and he blows a long summoning note upon a trumpet from which hangs a banner of white with a central red cross. Behind the figure is a rainbow formed from living creatures. The Seraphim, fiery serpents coruscate in a blazing stream within the bow of promise. The entire horizon beyond this vision is ignited with burning Yods. At the point where the flames meet the Waters of the lake, great clouds of steam are formed.

As if this sight were not enough, you notice a movement to your left. A swarthy masculine figure rises from the dark Earth in a halo of Fire. This is Samael—ruler of volcanic Fire—erupting from the belly of the Earth. To your right, a female form breaks forth from the Waters. She is Anael, ruler of the astral Light. Her etheric twin rises at her side. You realize that you are in the presence of the three living powers of Fire: Solar, Volcanic and Astral—the three tongues of flame. Within you is the Hidden Fire, waiting to be ignited by a spark. Instinctively, you raise your arms in the Sign of Theoricus and the Element of the Redeemer. As you do so, three fiery Yods from the crown of Michael come together, forming a flaming letter Shin, which drifts downwards. It is absorbed into your heart center. Another letter Shin is formed which hovers over the top of your head where it turns brilliant white. A feeling of calm elation overtakes you. You truly feel that you have become a part of something which is greater than yourself. From this day forward, you will strive to become more than human, and rise from the ashes of your old self.

An Adoration escapes from your lips, "There is no part of me that is not of the gods!"

After a moment of contemplation, you silently thank the beings of flame. Turning you step out of the tomb and are surprised to see the smiling face of Sandalphon. She carries a velvet black robe to replace the one that you sacrificed on the Path of Fire. With tenderness, she helps you into it.

The journey back is swift. It is now morning, and the dawning sun forms a magnificent backdrop for the three pyramids in the desert. In the valley at the mountain foothills, the Clan of Fire is just starting to stir. Smoke drifts upward from many cooking pits.

The treacherous path leading up the side of the cliff is the same, but your adventure has left you as nimble as an Alpine sheep. With no exertion, you are soon at the opal door at the temple of Malkuth. Once inside, Sandalphon seals the portal.

Standing at the altar flame, you feel totally rejuvenated. In fact you feel so strengthened that you are quite willing to rush headlong on to the 30th Path. Sandalphon persuades you otherwise. Bidding her farewell, you salute with the Neophyte Sign. She in turn gives the answering Sign.

At this point bring your astral body back to the physical temple around you. Do not rush.

Perform the LBRP with the black end of the wand.

Say, *"I now declare the temple duly closed."* ✡

The 30th Path of Resh

The Thirtieth Path of Resh is called the Collecting Intelligence, because from it the Astrologers deduce the judgment of the Stars, and of the Celestial Signs, and the perfections of their science according to the rules of their resolutions. It is therefore the reflection of the sphere of the Sun and the path connecting Yesod with Hod, Foundation with Splendor.

This path, which connects the sphere of Yesod to that of Hod, is described as the "Collecting Intelligence" because it governs many integral factors in the makeup of the individual Personality—specifically, the Signs of the Zodiac, which are vessels of Planetary influence. A person's Sun Sign is central to both his/her present and past incarnations. The 30th Path signifies a *collecting of knowledge* on every level. On this path, the "collected" parts of the student's Personality are given an infusion of the Sun's intellectual qualities of warmth and Light. Here the student also begins to perceive the Higher forces which have formed his/her own personality.

The 30th Path connects Yesod, the astral foundation behind all materialized forms, to Hod, the seat of the Intellect. It is also the first path of the astral triangle (the Personality) that the aspirant confronts when scaling the Tree. This path is the conductor of the thought process or intellectual energy. Resh, the Hebrew letter assigned to this card means "head" which further reveals its function as the "Collecting Intelligence," collecting and assembling information and experiences which the Personality can use in its quest for Higher Knowledge. On this path, the initiate attempts to reconcile his spiritual mind with his/her raw animal instincts. It is thus the first path of many which deals with equilibration—the weighing and balancing of the "collected" information.

The 19th Key of *The Sun* is attributed to this path. The Magical Title of this card is "The Lord of the Fire of the World." Images and symbols associated with this card include: a large Sun, two children playing in the Water and on the Earth, a stone fence, and two groups of seven Hebrew Yods.

The Sun is the center of our world and the giver of light and warmth to the planet. Yet too much sun (like too much intellect without emotion) is harmful and can scorch the Earth, creating deserts. This points to the importance of balance on this path. The Sun seen in the 19th Key has a head and face (Resh) but with no mouth, signifying that humanity, for all its intellectual achievements, cannot communicate with the Divine Being through human speech. Language is far too inadequate to even describe a true spiritual experience. When communicating with the Higher Mind, no words are needed—they are in fact obsolete under such circumstances.

The wall of stones which surrounds the two children is the circle of the Zodiac. It is wall of knowledge which acts as a boundary, keeping the children within the garden because they know not how to unlock its secrets. Once they learn this knowledge, they are free to climb over the wall. This knowledge used wisely can enable the children to leap effortlessly over the wall. Used unwisely, the stones of the wall can come crashing down on their heads.✿

A JOURNEY ON THE 30TH PATH OF RESH[113]

For this ritual the Practicus will need the robe, nemyss, red sandals, the Greek Cross and the Outer Wand of Double Power. The temple is to be arranged as in the Second Part of the 3 = 8 grade. Upon the altar should be the Tarot Trump of *The Sun*. A comfortable place to sit and meditate should be arranged West of the pillars.

After a period of relaxation has passed, go to the Northeast and say, *"HEKAS, HEKAS, ESTE BEBELOI! Far from this sacred place be the profane!"*

Go to the East. With the black end of the wand, perform the Lesser Banishing Ritual of the Pentagram.

Go the West of the altar. With the white end of the Wand of Double Power, trace a large letter *Resh* over the Tarot card. Visualize it in orange. Intone the name of the letter thrice. Give the Neophyte Signs toward the card. Put the wand aside, and take the Greek Cross in your right hand.

With all your powers of concentration, look upon the card and comprehend it, consider all its meaning and symbolism. Give the Sign of the Practicus. At this point you may sit comfortably if you wish, but maintain a disassociation from the surrounding room. Behind the darkness of your closed eyelids, you begin to formulate the astral temple of the Sephirah Malkuth, as the journey begins:

Astrally, you give the Sign of the Zelator. The now familiar temple of Malkuth formulates around you. The central flame burns brightly with a renewed passion upon the central altar.

As before you intone the names which call forth the inhabitants of this temple, *Adonai ha-Aretz, Sandalphon, Ashim,* and finally, *Malkuth*. Sandalphon appears as

---

[113] From our book, *Secrets of a Golden Dawn Temple.*

in your previous journeys and you exchange the usual Signs. This time you hold up the Solar Cross for the Archangel to see. She takes you swiftly through the portal of Tau directly in the East of the temple. Within a short time you are at the entrance to the temple of Yesod. You enter without Sandalphon, giving the Neophyte Signs.

Nine walls form the inner chamber which is a rich violet color. The figure of an enneangle or nine-sided polygon graces the floor. In each of the nine corners of the room, a brazier of incense hangs, scenting the room with the smell of jasmine. Around the ceiling are depicted the various phases of the moon inlaid with quartz and ebony. The central altar is surrounded by four large statues, each with four faces: that of a man, a lion, and eagle, and a bull. The altar itself is cast in silver and covered with a velvet indigo cloth. The temple flame burns from a silver bowl supported by three crescents.

The feel of this temple is quite different from that of Malkuth. No sensations of security or solidity are evoked here. There is an ethereal quality to everything here. You almost feel as if your hand would pass right through the kerubic statues if you tried to touch them. There is also a sense of excitement akin to sexual awareness. This temple is the dwelling place of the serpent power or kundalini. You can feel its power tingling certain nerves along your spine—stirred slightly by your entrance into Yesod.

With a sense of exhilaration, you vibrate the divine name of this sphere, *Shaddai El Chai*. You then call upon the Archangel *Gabriel* for guidance, and the order of Angels known as the *Kerubim*. Finally, you intone the name of the temple itself, *Yesod*.

From the jasmine mists, the Archangel starts to formulate. Taking on a material form before you, Gabriel is dressed in robes of violet trimmed with yellow. His features are breathtaking—a fine oval-shaped face framed by shoulder-length dark brown hair. His green eyes are large and sensual. The wings from his shoulders are very large and white. Somehow, you get the feeling that Gabriel could have just as easily appeared as a beautiful young girl—so slight and delicate is his appearance. He speaks:

"Behold around you, the Vision of the Machinery of the Universe. You have entered the Treasure House of Images and the sphere of Maya, Illusion. By what Sign hast thou entered into the Mirror of the Cosmos?"

You answer by giving the Sign of the Theoricus.

"Why have you come to the house of the Almighty Living One?" he inquires. You hold up the Greek Solar Cross.

Satisfied, Gabriel takes you to the central altar where he anoints you with a perfumed oil and gestures to a pair of violet leather sandals on the floor in front of the altar. He instructs you to wear these sandals on every path leading from the sphere of Yesod—that you may always tread upon a firm foundation in your journeys. The Archangel then takes you to a curtain in the Northeast upon which is depicted the Tarot card of *The Sun*. He traces the sigil of Sol and the veil parts, revealing a door carved from crysoleth. Upon the door is the Hebrew letter *Resh* in orange. Stepping forward, you hold up the Solar Cross and trace with it the letter Resh. The door opens and you and your guide start out on the 30th Path.

It is noon and the sun is at its zenith overhead. The ground you are walking along is rich and fertile—black soil that is perfect for most vegetation. Heliotrope and sunflowers abound. Groves of laurel trees cover the low rolling hills. A cool stream, full of fish meanders its way along the path. Butterflies chase each other from flower to flower, causing you to wonder if any place on Earth could be more perfect than this.

Gabriel sets a steady pace that covers much ground. Eventually, you come upon a clearing where a drama is about to take place. The Sun god, Ra is sitting upon the ground clutching the bleeding heel of his foot. A deadly viper, caught in the act, slithers away from the scene of the crime. The god is enraged with pain—his bellowing frightens all creatures within earshot. As the venom starts to work, the color drains from the deity's face and limbs. The Solar disc on his headdress dims. Crying out against his impending death, Ra calls for Isis to heal his wound.

The great goddess appears quickly, for it was she who created the poisonous serpent—fashioning the creature from dust and Ra's own spittle. Isis is compassionate but firm. She will not heal Ra until he reveals unto her his most hidden name. The god is reluctant to do so, for it would mean that Isis would have power over him. Ra is proud and stubborn. At last when the fingers of death begin to steal the life away from him, he whispers his secret name to her.

Great Isis, skilled in the arts of magick, then utters the Words of Power taught to her by Thoth. As soon as the words are spoken, the poison is driven out of the body of Ra, and the color of life returns to him. With the help of the ibis-headed one, Isis now possesses the words of power as well as the knowledge of how to pronounce and vibrate them. In this skirmish, the great Sun god has been outwitted by the lady of the moon through intellect.

Gabriel gestures that it is time to move on. You continue on the Path of Resh until at length you come to a great city of shining stone buildings at the edge of the sea. On a 400 foot cliff overlooking the ocean is one of the Seven Wonders of the World, the great stone Pharos, the 100 foot tall lighthouse which guides ships into the port of Alexandria, the great cosmopolitan city which is the apex of knowledge and education in the ancient world.

The city was built according to a strict geometric design, with public buildings of marble, a huge gymnasium, and even an artificial hill dedicated to the god Pan. Walking along the city's main street which is over 3 miles long and 100 feet wide, you are impressed by the people and their culture, which is neither Greek nor Egyptian, but contains the best of both. At the center of the city is a plaza dominated by two adjoining buildings—great columned structures set high atop marble steps. You and your guide enter the first building, the museum of Alexandria founded by Ptolemy. It is the first university and scientific institute in history.

There are many chambers to explore. In one room, the dissection of bodies provides anatomic studies for a group learning the art of medicine. Other rooms are set aside for zoological and botanical collections. You pass by one chamber where the Hellenistic mathematician Euclid is teaching his axioms of geometry to a number of students. In another room, the astronomer Aristarchus is espousing the conclusion that the sun, not the Earth is the center of our universe. There are many studio chambers for artists, scientists and craftsmen.

Gabriel then leads you to the huge library where uncounted numbers of scrolls and tablets of clay, stone, and even wax tablets of writing are carefully stored and studied by historians, poets, astronomers and scholars from all over the ancient world. It was here that writing was for the first time divided into "books," these being determined by the length of the papyrus. A bronze statue of Hermes stands at the center of the great hall. The ceiling is covered by a circular fresco depicting a reproduction of the famous Zodiac of Dendera. There are many tables where the intellectuals of Alexandria are busy copying manuscripts of Greek literature. One of the books you see lying upon a table is Ptolemy's *Syntaxis*, an ancient book of maps which carefully explains the motions of the Sun, Moon and Planets, giving a celestial latitude and longitude for each of them. *The Emerald Tablet*, and the *Divine Pymander* as well as the forty other works of Hermes Trismegistus can be found here.

Your guide leads you through a maze of books to a chamber deep within the library walls. At this point Gabriel tells you to continue on without him. The door into the chamber is guarded by a seated figure completely shrouded from head to foot in an unimpressive looking old cloak. A grizzled hand poking out of the robe grasps a staff adorned with the carved serpents. Another hand is raised to stop you from entering. "In what Signs and symbols do you come?" the form croaks.

You answer by giving the Sign of the Practicus. "In the divine name of *Elohim Tzabaoth*, in the word *Eloah* and in this symbol of the Solar Greek Cross which refers to the sun in the twelve Signs of the Zodiac."

"Thou canst not enter the temple of the Logos unless thou canst tell me my name." the form replies.

"Thou art Tahuti, Lord of divine words. Thoth, the self-created counter of the stars and measurer of Earth art Thou. Hermes, the Thrice Great—god of writing, science and magic."

The cloak and the illusion of age is suddenly cast aside to reveal the god of knowledge in his Greek persona with winged helmet and sandals. His skin is bronze and his youthful eyes sparkle with mischief. He seems delighted at the quickness of your reply, but his only response is to give the Sign of Silence as he opens the door for you. You step out into the bright sunlight.

Before you is a hill with a stone wall at its summit. The mound is divided into two halves, one side of Earth, and one of Water—the two receptive elements. The stones which comprise the wall are carved with various Zodiacal and Astrological sigils. A pair of children are playing joyfully on the knoll. The young boy tumbles in the grass while the girl splashes him with Water. In the sky above them is the sun, a huge and brilliant orange disc. It is surrounded by 12 rays, half of which are waved and feminine and half of which are salient and masculine. Seven Hebrew Yods falling from either side of the disc contain within them the sigils of the Planets of the ancients. In the center of the sun are the suggestions of a face, but without a mouth. The head of this Solar being stirs feelings of awareness and recognition within you. You know that the countenance before you is the emissary of a Higher Mind, greater than anything you have yet encountered. Longing for an opportunity to have conversation with this higher consciousness, you give the Sign of the Practicus, the receptive cup.

A white *Yod* begins to formulate where the Solar mouth would be. It floats down toward you and is absorbed into the crown of your head. The first link of inner communication is established between you and the divine teacher. It is a warm and loving feeling of spirituality that you simply cannot describe. No words can do it justice. No human can adequately recount it to another. No tongue can own it.

You salute with the Sign of Silence and a gesture of thanks. Before leaving this idyllic scene, you stop to play a momentary game of tag with the children, who both run laughing into the Water, splashing at you. In turning, you see Gabriel, amused by your behavior. It is time to be heading back.

The mid-afternoon sun is hot during the trek back, and you are thankful that Gabriel came to get you when he did, before you ended up with a nasty burn. Some animal bones bleached white by the side of the road testify to the potential destructiveness of the Solar energy if not balanced by cool weather and rainfall.

Soon you are at the temple of Yesod where you return the violet sandals to the foot of the altar. The cool air of the chamber is refreshing after such a hot journey. The Archangel then guides you back to the temple of Malkuth. Sandalphon closes the portal behind you. She goes to the fountain in the West and returns with a wooden chalice of Water for you to drink from. Finally, bidding her farewell, you salute with the Neophyte Sign. She in turn gives the Sign of Silence.

At this point bring your astral body back to the physical temple around you. Do not hurry.

Perform the LBRP with the black end of the wand.

Say, *"I now declare the temple duly closed."*✿

AN INVOCATION OF THE ELEMENT OF WATER

For the grade of Practicus

For this ritual the Practicus will need a black Outer Order robe, black and white striped nemyss, and the Outer Wand of Double Power. Upon the altar should be a blue candle, a cup of wine, and one or more of the talismanic emblems mentioned earlier on page 441. The temple is to be arranged in accordance with the Practicus Hall (as in the final part of the initiation ceremony).

Relax for a few moments and perform the Fourfold Breath.

Go to the Northeast and say, *"HEKAS, HEKAS, ESTE BEBELOI!"*

With the black end of the Outer Wand of Double Power, perform the Lesser Banishing Ritual of the Pentagram.

> (Say the following invocation:) *So therefore first the Priest who governs the works of Fire must sprinkle with the Lustral Waters of the loud resounding sea.*

Go to the East. With the white end of the wand, trace the lesser invoking pentagram. Thrust the wand through the center of the figure and vibrate, *"EHEIEH!"* Trace this same figure and intone the same name in all four quarters, going from East to South, West and North. Return to the East. Say:

> *In the Divine Name ELOHIM TZABAOTH, I open this temple in the Element of Water. May the Archangel GABRIEL look with favor upon this ceremony! May the Angel TALIAHAD and the ruler THARSIS be also in attendance! I have gained admission to this temple through the Badge of the Cup of Stolistes. Hear me! I am one who has received the Mystic Title of Monocris de Astris and the symbol of MAIM. As a Unicorn of the Stars I invoke the powers of Water to bear witness to my spiritual endeavor. Grant me the knowledge of the Element of Water and the Creative Realm, so that I may obtain Greater Understanding of Hidden Things and thereby advance in the Great Work.*

Circumambulate the temple three times, saluting with the Neophyte Signs when passing the East.

Go to the West and face East. Give the Adoration to the Lord of the Universe:

> *Holy art Thou, Lord of the Universe!*
> *Holy art Thou, Whom Nature hath not formed!*
> *Holy art Thou, the Vast and the Mighty One!*
> *Lord of the Light, and of the Darkness!*

Go to the West and give the Practicus Sign. Recite the Prayer of the Undines:

> *Terrible King of the Sea, Thou who holdest the Keys of the Cataracts of Heaven, and who enclosest the subterranean Waters in the cavernous hollows of Earth. King of the Deluge and the Rains of Spring. Thou who openest the sources of the rivers and of the fountains; Thou who commandest moisture which is, as it were, the Blood of the Earth, to become the sap of the plants. We adore Thee and we invoke Thee. Speak Thou unto us, Thy Mobile and changeful creatures, in the Great Tempests, and we shall tremble before Thee. Speak to us also in the murmur of the limpid Waters, and we shall desire Thy love.*

> *O Vastness! Wherein all the rivers of Being seek to lose themselves—which renew themselves ever in Thee! O Thou Ocean of Infinite Perfection! O Height which reflectest Thyself in the Depth! O Depth which exaltest into the Height! Lead us into the true life, through intelligence, through love! Lead us into immortality through sacrifice, that we may be found worthy to offer one day unto Thee, the Water, the Blood and Tears, for Remission of Sins! Amen.*

Give the Practicus Sign. Go to the West of the altar. With the white end of the wand, trace the lesser invoking pentagram over the cup of wine. Place the Wand of Double Power aside.

Drink the wine. As you partake of the Element, meditate on the talismanic emblem you have chosen. Take as much time as you need for the meditation.

Perform the Reverse Circumambulation. Go to the East and say:

> *I now release any Spirits that may have been imprisoned by this ceremony. Depart in peace to your abodes and habitations. Go with the blessings of ELOHIM TZABAOTH!*

Perform the LBRP with the black end of the wand.

Say: *I now declare this temple duly closed.*✡

Suggested Reading

The New Golden Dawn Ritual Tarot (Book) by Chic Cicero and Sandra Tabatha Cicero (Note: Write a report on the book. Try to find personal insights into each card of the Tarot.)

The New Golden Dawn Ritual Tarot (Deck) by Sandra Tabatha Cicero

Archetypes on the Tree of Life by Madonna Compton
(Note: Perform the meditations and exercises suggested in this book and keep a written record of your experiences with them.)

The Chaldean Oracles by Julianus, translated by Thomas Stanley
(Note: Write a report on the book. Examine in particular the passages which can be found in the Practicus Ceremony. Also explore how the Chaldean scheme of the universe is similar to the Qabalistic scheme of the universe.)

Greek Magical Papyri in Translation edited by Hans Dieter Betz
    (This is a collection of rituals dating from the second to the fifth century A.D. They are the closest existing rituals that parallel the rites described in the *Chaldean Oracles*.)

Divination in the Græco-Egyptian Magical Papyri by M. Isidora Forrest—published in *The Golden Dawn Journal, Book 1: Divination*.
    (Note: Perform the divination ritual suggested in the article and write a report on your experience and results.)

Egyptian Magic by E.A. Wallis Budge
    (Note: Write a report on the book. Contrast and compare "High" Egyptian magic with "Low" forms of Egyptian magic. Also examine the parallels between Egyptian magic and that which is described in the Chaldean Oracles or the Greek Magical Papyri.)

The Rose Cross and the Goddess by Gareth Knight
    (Contains a good modern account of the mysteries of Isis according to Apuleius.)

Godwin's Cabalistic Encyclopedia by David Godwin
    (A reliable reference book for Gematria which also contains good all-around Qabalistic information.)

The Hero Within: Six Archetypes We Live By by Carol Pearson

The Symbolic Quest: Basic Concepts of Analytical Psychology by Edward C. Whitmont

What We May Be by Piero Ferrucci

Some Final Suggestions

- Obtain a black-and-white 8.5 x 11 copy of the Tarot card of *Judgment* and paint it, or draw your own version of the card.

- Obtain a black-and-white 8.5 x 11 copy of the Tarot card of *The Sun* and paint it, or draw your own version of the card.

- Take a Tarot deck and place each card before you in the form of the Tree of Life with the Minor cards in the positions of the Sephiroth and the Trumps in their proper place as connecting paths. Do this several times until it becomes second nature to you. Study their relationships.

- Make colored drawings of the Three Kabiri and well as a sketch of Kasmillos the candidate. Devise your own meditation for incorporating these figures.

- Create numerous sigils from the Qameoth using the lists of divine and Planetary Names given in Chapter Two.

- Create several examples of Temurah and Notariqon as explained in this chapter.

- For the course of a week, take a daily walk and try to focus on finding geometric shapes when they occur within your surroundings.

- Draw your personal impression of an undine.

- Practice divination by Hydromancy. (See the introduction of *The Golden Dawn Journal, Book 1: Divination*.)

- Take periodic observations of the planet Mercury (at both dawn and dusk) Also take note of what Zodiacal Sign the Planet is in.

- Take note of where Mercury falls in your own Zodiacal chart. Write a brief report on how you think you are affected by Mercury's position in your natal chart.

- Take note of any Planets that are located in Water Signs in your own Zodiacal chart. Write a brief report on how you think you are affected by them.

- Prepare your own mixture of perfumed oils, herbal baths, magic inks or herbal teas for the Sephirah of Mercury, using your ingenuity and the source book *The Complete Book of Incense, Oils and Brews* by Scot Cunningham.

- Prepare your own personal mixture of oils, herbal baths, magic inks or herbal teas based upon your Zodiacal Sign, Elemental affiliation and other personal information or preferences. Use the source book listed above.

- Examine the various cards of the Tarot and try to come up with new words and phrases which describe the qualities and/or meanings of each individual card. These interpretations can be highly personalized or perhaps reflect some meaningful prose or poetry.

- Take periodic nature walks which bring you close to a body of Water (ocean, lake or river). Meditate on the importance of the Water Element to all aspects of Life on this planet.

- Find out how you can become personally involved in Water ecosystem cleanup and protection of wetlands.

Examinations

(Answers for all exams are given in the back of this book.)

QUIZ 0 *(The Ritual)*

1. What is the Grand Word of the grade of Practicus?
2. What is the Mystic Number of the Practicus grade?
3. What is the password of the Practicus grade derived from the Mystic Number?
4. What is the Battery of knocks attributed to the Practicus grade?
5. What is the Grip of the Practicus grade?
6. What is the Sign of the Practicus grade?
7. What is the Elemental symbol given to the Practicus?
8. List the name of the Element attributed to this grade (in English and in Hebrew.)
9. Which direction is associated with this Element?
10. What is the Mystic Title conferred upon a Practicus?
11. What does the Mystic Title mean?
12. Which Sephirah is associated with this grade?
13. List the Divine (Atziluthic) Name of this Sephirah.
14. Name the Great Archangel of the Element of this grade.
15. Name the Kerubic Sign of this Element.
16. What are the Three Great Secret Names of God borne upon the Enochian Banners of the Quarter?
17. Name the Great Enochian King of the Quarter.
18. How are the cross and triangle arranged on the altar?
19. What does the arrangement of the cross and triangle symbolize?
20. What does "3 = 8" signify?
21. What is the Admission Badge to the 31st Path?
22. What is the Admission Badge to the 30th Path?
23. What is the Admission Badge to the temple of the 8th Sephirah of Hod?
24. The Admission Badge is identical to the lamen of which officer?
25. The distinct sections of a ritual are called "points." Each grade ritual has at least three points: an opening, a closing, and at least one middle point between the opening and the closing. How many middle points are there in the Practicus Ritual?
26. Briefly describe what happens in each of the middle points of this ritual.
27. During the Practicus oath, what gesture does the candidate make in swearing his/her oath to the Powers of the Element?
28. List the names of the Kabiri encountered by the candidate in this ritual.
29. What is the name of the Kabir in the Southwest? What type of Fire is associated with this figure? What type of Solar energy is associated with this figure?

30. What is the name of the Kabir in the East? What type of Fire is associated with this figure? What type of Solar energy is associated with this figure?
31. What is the name of the Kabir in the Northwest? What type of Fire is associated with this figure? What type of Solar energy is associated with this figure?
32. Describe the 20th Key of the Tarot.
33. Describe the 19th Key of the Tarot.
34. In addition to the Tarot Keys and the Admission Badges, what diagrams are displayed in this grade?

QUIZ—SECTIONS 1, 2, and 3 (*Admission Badges, Diagrams, Lineal Figures and Magical Squares, Literal Qabalah*)

1. Describe the Admission Badge for the 31st Path. What do the various sides of this Badge represent?
2. Describe the Admission Badge for the 30th Path.
3. What is another name for active Fire?
4. What is another name for equilibrated Fire?
5. What is another name for passive Fire?
6. What is the name of Fire itself?
7. Describe the Admission Badge to the temple of Hod.
8. How does the symbol of Mercury fit on the Tree of Life?
9. Who is the figure shown at the top of the diagram of the Garden of Eden before the Fall?
10. What is the name of the river that flows from the Supernal Eden? What does this name mean?
11. What is the River of Air? What Sephirah does it flow into?
12. What is the River of Fire? What Sephirah does it flow into?
13. What is the River of Earth? What Sephirah does it flow into?
14. What is the River of Water? What Sephirah does it flow into?
15. Who is the figure supporting the pillars in the Eden diagram? What does she represent?
16. Who is the figure extended from Tiphareth? His arms stretch from _____ to _____. What does he represent?
17. What does the Eden diagram symbolize?
18. What is another name for an equilateral parallelogram?
19. What is a pointed oval formed from two intersecting circles called?
20. What is the only lineal figure into which all surfaces can be reduced?
21. List the seven lineal figures that are associated with the seven Planets.
22. What Sephirah is associated with the cross within the circle?
23. What Sephirah is associated with the point within the circle?
24. What Sephirah is associated with the square within the circle?
25. What lineal figure is associated with the Alchemical principles of Nature?
26. What lineal figure is associated with the Qlippoth?
27. What lineal figure is associated with the letters YHVH?

28. What lineal figure is known as the Sign of the Microcosm?
29. What lineal figure is associated with the Supernal Mother AIMA?
30. What lineal figure is associated with the Kerubim and the Wheel of the Spirit?
31. What lineal figure is known as the Sign of the Macrocosm?
32. True or False. A hexagram signifies radiation.
33. True or False. A hexagon signifies concentration.
34. What lineal figure is a fitting symbol for the Isis of Nature?
35. What lineal figure is a fitting symbol for the concentrated positive and negative forces of the Elements under the name YHVH ADONAI?
36. What is the meaning of IAHDONAI?
37. What lineal figure is associated with the Planets and the Lunar Nodes?
38. What lineal figure is associated with Malkuth?
39. What lineal figure is associated with the Zodiac?
40. What does the word "Qamea" refer to?
41. The word "sigil" is derived from what Latin word? What does this word mean?
42. What are the names of the Planetary energies (beings) derived from?
43. The Planetary _____ is seen as a blind force or "raw" energy force without intelligence.
44. The Planetary _____ is a guiding entity.
45. What symbol is designed in such a manner that its line touches every number on a magical square?
46. What number represents the total number of lesser squares in any given row, column or central diagonal line of a Qamea?
47. What number represents the total sum of all the numbers that appear on a Qamea?
48. What is used to represent the Qamea in Talismanic magic?
49. What is the mathematical formula for finding the magic constant?
50. What is the arcane compliment?
51. What is the mathematical formula for finding the arcane compliment of an odd square?
52. What is the mathematical formula for finding the arcane compliment of an even square?
53. What is the method of converting Hebrew words into their numeric values called?
54. What is another name for the Qabalah of Nine Chambers?
55. What Greek-based Table shows the English alphabet reduced to numbers?
56. What method of Literal Qabalah uses acronyms?
57. What method of Literal Qabalah means "permutation?"
58. What method of Literal Qabalah means "shorthand writer?"
59. What method of Literal Qabalah involves transposing a letter with the letter that follows it?
60. What method of Literal Qabalah involves writing a word backwards?

61. What method of Literal Qabalah involves folding the Hebrew alphabet back upon itself so that one half may be exchanged for the other half?

QUIZ—SECTIONS 4, 5, 6, and 7 (*Correspondences of Hod, Water, Mercury, the Olympic Planetary Spirits*)

1. What is the English translation of the name "Hod?"
2. What is the Magical Image of Hod?
3. What is the Spiritual experience of Hod?
4. What is the Lineal figure associated with Hod?
5. What are the symbols of Hod?
6. What is the name of the Archangel of Hod?
7. What is the Divine Atziluthic name of Hod?
8. What is the name of the Angelic Choir of Hod?
9. What is Hod's Briatic color?
10. What part of the human anatomy does Hod correspond to?
11. Hod is attributed to which House of Assiah?
12. Name the Tarot cards associated with Hod.
13. What is the Virtue associated with Hod?
14. What is the Vice associated with Hod?
15. What is the Hebrew name for Water? Give both English and Hebrew spellings.
16. What is the Outer Divine Name of Water in Hebrew? Give both English and Hebrew spellings.
17. What is the Hebrew name for the Cardinal Point of West? Give both English and Hebrew spellings.
18. What is the name of the Archangel of Water? Give both English and Hebrew spellings.
19. What is the name of the Angel of Water? Give both English and Hebrew spellings.
20. What is the name of the Ruler of Water? Give both English and Hebrew spellings.
21. What is the name of the King of Water?
22. What is the name of the Order of Elementals associated with Water?
23. What is the name of the Assyro-Babylonian deity associated with the primordial fresh-Water Ocean?
24. What is the name of the Assyro-Babylonian deity associated with the tumultuous and salty sea?
25. What Sumerian deity's name means "sea?"
26. What Assyro-Babylonian deity's name means "house of Water?" What is the Sumerian name of this god?
27. Name the Assyro-Babylonian deity whose worship included an annual procession of boats.

28. Name the Assyro-Babylonian deity whose symbol was a vase containing a swimming fish.
29. Name the Egyptian deity of the Great Primordial Ocean and the "Father of the gods."
30. Name the Egyptian deity of dew and rain (who also supports the sky).
31. Name the ram-headed Egyptian deity who watched over the sources of the Nile.
32. Name the Egyptian god of the Nile.
33. Name the Greek god who was "Lord of the Sea" and the brother of Zeus.
34. Name the Greek goddess who was the female personification of the Sea.
35. Name the oldest Greek Water god.
36. Name the Greek Titan who gave birth to the rivers.
37. Name the Greek god who was "the Old Man of the Sea" and the father of Sea nymphs.
38. Name the Greek sea god who has half man, half fish.
39. Name the most famous of the Greek river gods (often portrayed as a vigorous bearded man with horns).
40. Greek Water deities often had the gift of _____.
41. Name the Celtic Lord of the Sea who supplied food for the gods.
42. Name the Teutonic giant whose fountain was near the roots of the ash tree, Yggdrasil.
43. Name the Teutonic goddess who drowned Sailors only to reward them in the afterlife.
44. Name the Teutonic Undines.
45. Mercury is said to rule the period of life dominated by _____ from ages ____ to ____.
46. What part of the human mind is governed by Mercury?
47. Describe the energy of Mercury.
48. Describe the symbol of Mercury on the Tree of Life.
49. List some of the things that the days and hours of Mercury are used for in magic.
50. What is the Hebrew name for Mercury?
51. What is the name of the Archangel of Mercury?
52. What is the day associated with Mercury?
53. What is the name of the Planetary Intelligence of Mercury?
54. What is the name of the Planetary Spirit of Mercury?
55. What is the name of the Olympic Planetary Spirit of Mercury?
56. What metal is associated with Mercury?
57. Name some of the gemstones associated with Mercury.
58. Name some of the Trees associated with Mercury.
59. Name some of the Herbs/Plants associated with Mercury.
60. Name some of the animals associated with Mercury.
61. What Planet complements Mercury on the Macrocosmic Hexagram? List some characteristics that these two Planets share. List some deities associated with this complementary Planet.

62. Name the Sumerian Lord of magic and incantations.
63. Name the Assyro-Babylonian deity who was the divine scribe and god of the Intellect.
64. Name the Egyptian god of wisdom, magic and science.
65. Name the Assyro-Babylonian goddess who invented writing.
66. Name the Egyptian "Mistress of the house of books."
67. Name the Greek god of travelers and commerce.
68. Name the Greek messenger goddess.
69. Name the Greek goddess of the arts, industry and healing.
70. Name the Greek goddess whose title was Pronoia or "the foreseeing."
71. Name the Greek goddess symbolized by the owl.
72. Name the Greek goddess symbolized by the rainbow.
73. Name the Greek god of Light, medicine and healing (sometimes represented as a serpent.)
74. Name the Celtic god known as "the many-skilled one," whose symbols were the spear and the sling.
75. Name the supreme Teutonic deity who was a god of war and wisdom.
76. Name the Teutonic Lord of the Runes.
77. Name the Egyptian deity called "the Molder."
78. Name the Greek god of sea foam and stormy seas.
79. Name the Teutonic Water giant whose name means "he who thinks" and whose fountain was the hiding place of all wisdom and knowledge.
80. Name the Sumerian deity often represented as a goat with a fish's tail.
81. Name the Egyptian deity who is portrayed as a woman wearing a star within a crescent surmounted by two long feathers.
82. Name the messenger god of Zeus.
83. Name the Greek goddess of health.
84. List the Olympic Spirits of the seven Planets.

QUIZ—SECTION 8 *(The Tarot)*

1. How many cards are there in a traditional Tarot Deck?
2. How many Major Arcana (Trump) cards are there?
3. How many Minor Arcana cards are there?
4. List the four Tarot suits next to the four suits of a traditional deck of playing cards (to which they correspond).
5. How are the letters of the Tetragrammaton assigned to the Suits of the Tarot?
6. How are the Four Worlds of the Qabalah assigned to the suits of the Tarot?
7. What do the ten Sephiroth and the Minor Arcana cards represent in terms of the human psyche?
8. What do the Twenty-two Paths and the Trump cards represent in terms of the human psyche?
9. Why are there Twenty-two Trumps cards?
10. List the other types of energies (3 in all) that are represented by the Trumps.
11. What are the Thirty-two Paths of Wisdom?

12. List the Twenty-two Trump cards along with their Yetziratic attributions.
13. By employing the Yetziratic attributions of the Tarot, the name EHEIEH can be written as _____.
14. By employing the Yetziratic attributions of the Tarot, the name ELOHIM can be written as _____.
15. What Tarot Trump embodies "energy, creative force and masculine power?"
16. What Tarot Trump embodies "potentiality and innocence?"
17. What Tarot Trump embodies "inner illumination and spiritual instruction?"
18. What Tarot Trump embodies "consciousness and fluctuation?"
19. What Tarot Trump embodies "direction, skill and invocation?"
20. What Tarot Trump embodies "unity, manifestation and feminine power?"
21. What Tarot Trump embodies "exploration and journey into the Underworld?"
22. What Tarot Trump embodies "liberation, integration and bonding?"
23. What Tarot Trump embodies "initiation and consecration by Fire?"
24. What Tarot Trump embodies "sublimation, guidance and descent of Spirit?"
25. What Tarot Trump embodies "the conscious mind and the power of knowledge?"
26. What Tarot Trump embodies "controlled power and fortitude?"
27. What Tarot Trump embodies "meditation and contemplation?"
28. What Tarot Trump embodies "divine intervention, wisdom and vibration?"
29. What Tarot Trump embodies "restructuring and sudden involuntary illumination?"
30. What Tarot Trump embodies "karma?"
31. What Tarot Trump embodies "equilibration and adjustment?"
32. What Tarot Trump embodies "materiality and generative force?"
33. What Tarot Trump embodies "sacrifice and reversal?"
34. What Tarot Trump embodies "transformation and rebirth?"
35. What Tarot Trump embodies "reconciliation and combination?"
36. What Trump card is assigned to the path that runs between Geburah and Tiphareth?
37. What Trump card is assigned to the path that runs between Yesod and Netzach?
38. What Trump card is assigned to the path that runs between Chokmah and Tiphareth?
39. What Trump card is assigned to the path that runs between Chokmah and Chesed?
40. What Trump card is assigned to the path that runs between Hod and Yesod?
41. What Trump card is assigned to the path that runs between Binah and Chokmah?
42. What Trump card is assigned to the path that runs between Tiphareth and Netzach?
43. What Trump card is assigned to the path that runs between Binah and Tiphareth?

44. What Trump card is assigned to the path that runs between Geburah and Hod?
45. What Trump card is assigned to the path that runs between Tiphareth and Yesod?
46. The Hermit card represents the Planet _____ acting through _____ upon _____.
47. The Hierophant card represents the _____ acting through _____ upon _____.
48. The Star card represents the Planet _____ acting through _____ upon _____.
49. The Judgment card represents the Planet _____ acting through _____ upon _____.
50. The Chariot card represents the Planet _____ acting through _____ upon _____.
51. Each numbered card of the Minor Arcana represents one of the _____ in one of the ____ _____.
52. Describe the energy of the suit of wands.
53. Describe the energy of the suit of pentacles.
54. Describe the energy of the suit of cups.
55. Describe the energy of the suit of swords.
56. In addition to the Elemental and Sephirotic correspondences, each Minor card is assigned what Zodiacal attribute?
57. What Minor card represents "Dominion?"
58. What Minor card represents Chesed in Atziluth?
59. What Minor card represents "Established Strength?"
60. What Minor card represents "Swiftness?"
61. What Minor card represents Tiphareth in Atziluth?
62. What Minor card represents "Love?"
63. What Minor card represents "Abundance?"
64. What Minor card represents Geburah in Briah?
65. What Minor card represents "Illusionary Success?"
66. What Minor card represents "Peace Restored?"
67. What Minor card represents Binah in Yetzirah?
68. What Minor card represents "Earned Success?"
69. What Minor card represents "Despair and Cruelty?"
70. What Minor card represents Malkuth in Yetzirah?
71. What Minor card represents "Harmonious Change?"
72. What Minor card represents Netzach in Assiah?
73. What Minor card represents "Material Success?"
74. What Minor card represents "Prudence?"
75. What Minor card represents "Ruin?"
76. What Minor card represents "Perfected Success?"
77. What Minor card represents "Valor?"
78. What Minor card represents Fire of Fire?
79. What Minor card represents Water of Air?

80. What Minor card represents Air of Water?
81. What Minor card represents Earth of Fire?
82. What Court Card represents "Manifesting Force?"
83. What Court card represents "Creative Force?"
84. What Court card represents "Explosive Force?"
85. What Court card represents "Intellectual Force?"
86. What Court card represents "Regenerative Force?"
87. What Court card represents "Severe Force?"

CHAPTER FIVE

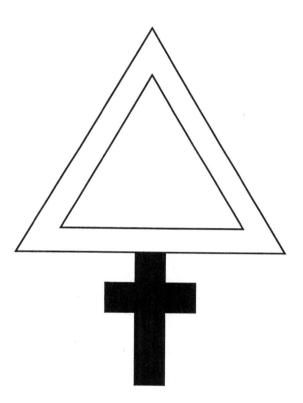

The Philosophus Grade

④=7

I n the 4 = 7 grade the initiate takes the *fourth* Elemental initiation into the *seventh* Sephirah, Netzach, on the Tree of Life—advancing the psycho-alchemical process of Inner growth. Once again the initiate deliberately veers off the security of the middle course, this time on the side of the white pillar. This action is necessary to balance out the previous initiation which took the aspirant to the black pillar. In fact the two grade initiations of Practicus and Philosophus compliment and balance each other so completely, that it is difficult to adequately describe one without describing the other.

The Element offered for the process of transmutation in this grade is Fire. It is the Fiery section of the aspirant's psyche (*Fire of Malkuth in Assiah*).[114] Once again the two primary opposing and parental Elements are counterbalanced one against the other so that neither is allowed to overwhelm the other. Two of the paths leading to this grade are watery in Nature, therefore the two primary Elements of Water and Fire are both encountered in this grade, as in the preceding one. However in the 4 = 7 grade their order and potency are reversed. In the Practicus grade the Element of Water was predominant. In the Philosophus grade the Fire Element now swirls in fury, though it is only able to safely manifest upon the complimentary Element of Water.

The 4 = 7 ceremony can be summarized as follows: After the standard (self-initiatory) rite of opening, the forces of Elemental Fire are invoked. Then the candidate must prove that s/he has grasped the secrets of the Practicus grade and swear an oath. Between the spheres of Malkuth and Netzach lies the 29th Path of Qoph, a journey of psychic evolution and the conquering of fears and illusions. On this path, the candidate is confronted by the three Egyptian godforms of Osiris, Horus and Isis. These figures symbolize the various attributes of Elemental Water and the different aspects of time. After completing the 29th Path, the candidate is shown the Tarot card of *The Moon*.

Next the mysteries of the 28th Path of Tzaddi are revealed to the candidate by a different triad of godforms: Isis, Nephthys and Hathor. These godforms expose the initiate to the different aspects of Celestial Water—the Waters of Creation and the Waters of Life. The Path of Tzaddi is a journey of intuitive awareness where the student learns how to tap into the deep well of knowledge within the

---

[114] It is also *Netzach of Malkuth*.

subconscious mind through meditation and imagination. A further description from *The Chaldean Oracles* on the Monad, Duad and Triad is revealed to the aspirant. When the journey on the Path of Tzaddi is finished, the candidate is shown the Tarot card of *The Star*.

The mysteries of the 27th Path of Peh are then revealed to the candidate. This is a Martial path which unveils the Biblical story of the death of the Kings of Edom (Chaos). The Path of Peh is a difficult but very necessary journey which includes the fiery destruction of the old and outmoded in favor of the new. It is the removal of all that is base and low within the mind of the candidate in favor of that which is Divine. This journey symbolizes the beginning phase of the reconstruction of the aspirant's psyche. When the pilgrimage on the Path of Peh is completed, the candidate is shown the Tarot card of *The Tower*.

The later part of the ritual involves the initiate's entry into the temple of Netzach. During this time the aspirant is shown symbolism concerning the Garden of Eden after the Fall and the Philosophus Hall itself. The secrets of the 4 = 7 grade are disclosed, until at length, the Powers of Fire are released.

The three officers stationed in the Practicus Hall (in addition to the Dais officers) are the Hierophant, the Hiereus, and the Hegemon. Initially they form the figure of the Water triangle with the station of the Hiereus marking the apex in the West. This alludes to the Watery nature of the 29th and 28th Paths of Qoph and Tzaddi, which the candidate traverses in this grade. The pillars are placed in the Southeast, indicating the exact placement of these paths on the Tree. In the fourth segment of the ceremony, which marks the candidate's entrance into the 27th Path of Peh, all three officers are stationed in the East—the Hiereus and the Hegemon on either side of the Hierophant. This points out the direction of the 27th Path on the Tree of Life as a reciprocal path—one which straddles all three columns on the Tree. Finally in the fifth segment of the ceremony, the officers are positioned in the form of a Fire triangle, the symbol of the Fiery nature of the Sephirah Netzach, into which the aspirant has achieved entry.

The two Elements of Fire and Water, when sensibly directed and creatively engaged can lead to the reconstruction of the Garden of Eden from the chaos into which it had plunged. The Divine Light cannot dwell within humanity until disorder has been transformed into the harmony of total realization and illumination. Human beings cannot claim inner peace and tranquillity until order and balance has been restored to the lower Elements of Malkuth.

The 27th Path in particular heralds the beginning of this process in the initiate. Through the stimulation of the fiery and watery Elements within the mind, the aspirant begins to realize the chaotic state of his/her own existence and the confusion that reigns within the psyche as a result of spiritual denial and stagnation. Although these Elements naturally call forth that which is high and sublime within the Soul, they also awaken that which is gross and low. Consequently, the first step in the process of reconstruction is a leveling or unbalancing—the tearing down in an analytical progression, of all that was previously held in high esteem. The result is of course disorder and darkness, an undesirable state, but one that is absolutely necessary if one wishes to transcend chaos and make progress toward true spiritual growth. From the ashes of the old Tower of Edom, the new Tower of Light may be constructed.

The symbolism encountered on the Path of Peh serves two purposes. First of all, it serves to awaken those long forgotten root memories inherent within the very cells of our bodies—what could be termed *Macrocosmic memories* of the primordial evolution of Creation itself. In addition, the symbols also refer to the *Microcosmic experiences* of chaos and reconstruction which occur on a personal level within the initiate.

To the aspirant, the stimulation of the magical Elements along with the process of introspection is analogous to causing a small earthquake in one's personal universe. The Path of Peh describes those periods when the aspirant becomes aware of being assailed by personal conflicts and inner complexes which have contaminated the spiritual progress. Having these "complexes" abruptly moved from the hidden depths of the subconscious (where they could be forgotten) to the exposing light of the conscious mind can be quite an uncomfortable ordeal. These are literally tests of inner strength, where the candidate must summon the courage to examine these undesirable parts of the psyche and deal with them properly. This may include the need to eliminate some excess psychic "garbage." As strenuous as these experiences are, they are also one of the hallmarks of a successful initiation. This represents the first half of the alchemical phrase "*solve et coagula.*"

As in Alchemy, the process of analysis and dissolution must always precede assimilation. The Philosopher's gold is always obtained from the gross matter, through a chemical process which the Alchemical texts often describe as noxious and disagreeable. Yet in every case, the Alchemists also hold that this unpleasant condition always precedes the most exalted results. The task of the Philosophus is to balance the combined energies of Fire and Water, emotion and intellect. This foreshadows the second half of the Alchemical phrase, the *coagula* process, which comes into full power in the Portal grade, where the previous chaos is sublimated and infused with Spirit, making possible a higher level of spiritual attainment.

The name bestowed upon an initiate of this grade, *Philosophus,* is based on a Greek word which means, "lover of Wisdom."✿

The Biblical Passages

Many of the speeches recited in the Philosophus ceremony during the candidate's passage through the 27th Path are taken from various passages in the Old Testament which deal specifically with the fall of the Kings of Edom. A few of the versicles are taken from the Books of Genesis and Exodus, but the bulk of them are from the books of Judges, Psalms, and Habakkuk. A reoccurring theme in most of these passages is the sudden and warlike (Martial) fury in which the old kingdom of Chaos represented by the Edomites was destroyed. The "reign of Edom" was the reign of the unbalanced and chaotic forces of the primordial worlds. Ushered in after the reign of Edom was the period of balance and order called the "reign of

Israel." There are also many passages in the ritual which refer to the majesty and might of the Creator of the universe.

The Babylonian Influence

The Biblical passages that occur in the Philosophus grade can be traced directly to the more ancient beliefs of the Babylonians, the inheritors of the geographic remnants of Eden. As stated in the previous chapter, the words *Eden* and *Adam* are far older than the Sumerian civilization in which they came to be used. Also, the concept of *Yahweh* being "a man of war," and "lord of armies," sounds remarkably like the descriptions of *Marduk* and *Baal*, principle gods of war in the Babylonian pantheon. The authors of the Old Testament were no doubt very familiar with this pantheon, and were writing for an audience who also knew of the power that these gods were said to possess. The Biblical writers knew that in order to impress their audience with the might of Yahweh (יהוה), the deity must have the same warrior attributes, and be able to vanquish the same ancient enemies that Marduk and Baal had vanquished. For both Marduk and Baal were involved in Creation Myths wherein the forces of Light and Order overcome the Forces of Darkness and Chaos.

In the Babylonian text known as the *Enuma elish* ("when on high"), the story of Creation unfolds as follows: In the beginning, nothing existed but a watery Chaos made up of the *Apsu*, the sweet waters, *Tiamat*, the sea, and *Mummu*, the clouds and mist. From this combination of different waters came the birth of two gods named *Lahmu* and *Lahamu*, deities of fertility and expanse, who in turn sired the gods *Anshar* and *Kishar*, both aspects of the horizon. This pair gave birth to *Anu*, the great sky god, and other generations of deities followed.

Eventually, as the story goes, a generational gap formed between the older gods and the younger, active gods. A conflict occurred wherein the most ancient god Apsu regretted having sired such noisy children and vowed to obliterate them. When the wise *Ea* (Enki) learned of this, he cast a magic spell over Apsu which caused him to fall asleep. Ea then killed the ancient one and established a portion of the world as it now is: the waters of Apsu sank down, and over them Ea established the earth. (This was the first great victory over chaos.)

Over time Tiamat convinced her allies to avenge the death of her husband, Apsu, and negotiations between the two factions fell through. Because of the impending crisis the gods decided to elect a warrior to lead them in the fight against Tiamat and her army of monster serpents and fierce dragons. They chose Marduk, son of Ea, who armed himself with thunder and lightning (the weapons of a storm god), bow and arrow, a mace, a net, four winds, seven storms and an Evil, disease-carrying wind.

At the sight of the great Marduk in his chariot, Tiamat's army fled—only Tiamat herself stood her ground. Marduk forced her to swallow the Evil Wind and then killed her with an arrow. He split her body into two halves, one of which he used to create the starry heavens. He posted guards over her and bade them "to allow not her waters to escape." After banishing the waters of Chaos and establishing Order, Marduk was enthroned as the Sovereign of Babylon and of the universe with the proclamation *Marduk sarru*, "Marduk is King."

In ancient Canaan, Baal was the god of storm and of war. This god, along with his warrior sister *Anath*, did battle with a mighty opponent called *Yamm*, the sea (also known as *Naher*, "the River"). The legend says that the god *El*, head of the gods, instructed that a palace be built for Prince Yamm, thus giving Yamm authority over the other gods. Baal cursed Yamm, who then demanded that Baal be handed over to him as a slave. Eventually Baal breaks the back of Yamm, and is made King.

In ancient Mesopotamia, the waters of the flooded rivers would have been a threat to life, and their orderly control signified a victory over Chaos (Marduk over Tiamat). And in Canaan the battle between Baal and Yamm seems to have taken place in the late fall when the sea was too rough for safe sailing. The sea pounding against the shore and threatening to flood (*Rabbim*) the lower regions, was understood to be a chaotic force waging war against Order. In both legends Tiamat/Yamm is seen as the sum of all Water that is destructive to human life, whereas Marduk/Baal, gods of the storm, bring rains which help maintain the growth of vegetation and human survival.

In another story, Baal is said to have conquered a rival named *Lotan*, the serpent. Lotan is also referred to as *Shalyat*, the seven-headed. It is possible that Yamm (the destructive sea) and Rabbim, (the flood) are names of the same Chaos god who is also referred to as Lotan/Shalyat, the serpent or Dragon.[115]

When the writers of the Old Testament inherited the mythos of ancient Babylonia, they used it to express that the idea that Yahweh, god of the Hebrews, was King of the universe, as was previously said of Marduk. Yahweh, like Marduk and Baal before him must also vanquish the powers of Chaos and Darkness. And as in the previous legends, these chaotic powers take the form of the Deep or *Tehom* (תהום—reminiscent of Tiamat), Yamm (ים), the sea, and the seven-headed dragon called *Leviathan* (לויתן) [Lotan]. The Biblical passages that were employed in the Philosophus Ritual emphasize these Hebraized Babylonian legends of the battle between the Forces of Order (Light) and the Forces of Chaos (Darkness) at the time when the universe was created.

Examples of the Hebrew god of war doing battle with the monsters of Chaos can be found in other passages as well:

> *Awake! Awake! Arm of Yahweh, put on strength!*
> *Awake, as in the days of old, everlasting generations!*
> *Was it not you cutting in pieces Rahab*
> *and piercing the sea monster?*
> *Was it not you drying up the sea (yam) and the waters*
> *of the great deep (tehom),*
> *who made the depths of the sea (yam) a way for the*
> *redeemed to pass? (Isaiah 51:9—10)*

---

[115] In ancient Egypt the Chaos deity is called *Apophis*, the dragon or serpent of Darkness, who attempted to swallow *Re*, the Sun god.

> *For Elohim is my king of old,*
> *who works salvation in the midst of the land.*
> *You broke the sea (yam) by your strength.*
> *You broke the heads of sea-monsters in the waters.*
> *You broke the head of Leviathan in pieces.*
> *You made made him food for the people*
> *of the wilderness. (Psalm 74:12—14)*

One of the passages given in the Philosophus Ritual (Psalm 18),[116] is a song of praise to Yahweh by one who was rescued from the pits of hell. This passage could have easily been used to describe the storm god, Marduk/Baal doing battle with the forces of Tiamat/Yamm:

> *He also bowed the Heavens, and came down*
> *and Darkness was under his feet. (v. 9)*
> *Out of the brightness before Him,*
> *his dark clouds passed through,*
> *Hailstones and and coals of fire. (v.12)*
> *Yahweh also thundered in the heavens;*
> *and the Highest uttered his voice—*
> *Hailstones and coals of fire. (v. 13)*
> *Yea, he sent out his arrows and scattered them,*
> *and he shot out lightnings and confounded them. (v.14)*
> *Then the stream beds of the waters were seen,*
> *and the foundations of the world were bared,*
> *at your rebuke, O Yahweh, at the blast*
> *of the breath of your nostrils. (v. 18)*

A large section of the Biblical passages in this ritual come from the third chapter of the Book of Habakkuk, which portrays Yahweh marching as a divine warrior from Teman and Mount Paran ready for battle, causing the land of Midian to tremble. It describes Yahweh's furious anger at the sea and the rivers. The river (Naher) was cut in two and the Deep (Tehom) groaned under the wrath of the god. The enemy was smashed and pierced with arrows, as the warrior god trampled the sea—the "many waters." This imagery is almost completely lifted from the Canaanite story of Baal conquering Yamm.[117] It is another example of the ancient story of Chaos being vanquished by Order.✡

A few of the words and references made in these Biblical verses deserve further exploration and thought:

---

[116] This passage is virtually identical to that given in 2 Samuel 22.

[117] After the discovery of certain Ugaritic texts, scholars have concluded that Psalm 29 also is a Hebraisized Hymn to Baal.

KISHON: meaning "curved, laborious, hard, inflexible, difficult" and also "torture." An important river in Palestine. Those who were swept away by the river represent external impulses that sway the Soul away from spiritual matters. To cut off these external things that have given one pleasure is indeed difficult.

MOAB: meaning "the seed of the Father" or "flowing from the Father." The name for the land now called Jordan. The word can be said to represent the Lower or limited Self, the external conditions of Life.

SEIR: named after Mt. Seir. The land of the Edomites. This symbolize physical or external consciousness.

MEROZ: meaning "shrinking, contracting, becoming compact." A place in Palestine belonging to the Israelites. Curses were pronounced against Meroz because its inhabitants did not join in the fight against the Canaanites.[118] Ideas related to the word include a retreat, secret place, or place of refuge. This might allude to a place in the consciousness that receives Wisdom but does not give out Wisdom. It indicates that if Wisdom is gained, it is to be used, but if this Wisdom is not used, it may be lost.

LEBANON: meaning "white, clean, pure." A place in Palestine. It symbolizes the pure portions of the psyche.

KADESH:[119] meaning "pure, holy, sacred." This can be said to represent an inherently pure state that exists within the depths of the individual psyche. As various aspects of the psyche come into the Divine Light of this sacred place, they are measured according to sacred ideals. A judgment or adjustment then takes place. What portions fall short are revealed and a further process of psychic cleansing takes place.

TEMAN: meaning "South, on the right side." A place in Edom known for abundance. It can be said to refer to a rich storehouse of Truth and Wisdom hidden in the subconscious mind that is under the influence of material and external thoughts.

PARAN: A region full of caverns between Sinai and Canaan, where much of the wanderings of the Israelites took place. It symbolizes to a place of confusion and disorder, but also a place or period of much passionate searching after truth. The beginning of redemption or enlightenment.

KARNAIM: meaning "two horns" and also "radiated." This word may also mean two rays or beams of Light issuing.

CUSHAN: meaning "blackness, falsehood." It refers to a king of Mesopotamia. It symbolizes the erroneous belief that the external and secular Life is all-important, and that humanity has no need for spiritual truths.

---

[118] As the story goes, *Jabin*, the King of *Canaan* (symbolizing intellect ruled by ego) reigned in the city of *Hazor* ("castle" or "fortification"). The king sent the captain of his armies, *Sisera*, ("Enraged," "battle array") to make war on Israel. An Israelite captain named *Barak* ("lightning flash," "thunderbolt") managed to defeat the hosts of Jabin with the aid of the Prophetess *Deborah* ("bee" or "wasp"). Sisera is killed by a woman who drives a tent pin (*vav*) through his temples.

[119] Or Qadesh.

MIDIAN: meaning "rule, government, judgment, strife." It refers to a sense of domination ruled by strife and contention. Discordant or contentious thoughts.✿

The Godforms

Two different godform triads reveal themselves to the aspirant in the Philosophus ceremony. The first triad is composed of *Osiris, Horus* and *Isis,* who in this ritual represent the various forms of Water and aspects of time. A triangle is the strongest architectural figure known, as well as the only polygon that all other such polygons can be reduced to. The triad symbolizes two opposing forces and one which "anchors" and stabilizes them. This is why the idea of the divine triad is so universal to many traditions. The speeches in this ceremony taken from the Chaldean Oracles concerning the Monad, the Duad and Triad, reiterate this fact.

In the 4 = 7 grade Osiris represents the Divine Light which is so brilliant that it is every bit as blinding as absolute darkness, concealing and reflecting all. At this stage, he symbolizes the Past, the brilliance and stillness that was Eden before the Fall. Osiris alludes to the beginning act of creation—the Ruach Elohim who moved upon the face of the Waters.

The second godform in this triad is Horus. In the Philosophus grade he is the destroyer, the Martial arm of YHVH Elohim wielding the Sword of Justice and Severity. He symbolizes a raging storm, the harsh instrument of purification that is employed to banish the Kings of Chaos and put an end to disorder. Horus also suggests the future, which is changed forever due to the fall of the Edomite kings.

Isis is the reconciler between Osiris and Horus—between stillness and storm, past and future. She is Water flowing in steady movement toward the sea. She is also the Present which mediates between the purity of Eden past, and the stormy future of the post-Edomite realm. It is she who acts on humanity's behalf to gently guide us back to Eden.

The second triad of godforms in the Philosophus ritual represent the Celestial Waters of Life. These Stellar Waters of Creation are the Waters of the subconscious mind, which flow back through the layers of time to the rivers of Paradise. This is the flow of Light and Wisdom from its eternal Source to the psyche of the initiate. The triad involved consists of the three goddesses, *Isis, Nephthys* and *Hathor.* These feminine godforms illustrate the idea of the Fountain of Wisdom—a receptive and sacred vessel which distills Knowledge to all lower vessels.

In this triad, Isis symbolizes the direct influence of the Divine upon the mind of the initiate. She interacts on behalf of the Supernal Light directly through sudden illumination and realization.

Nephthys personifies the subtle influence of the Divine upon the aspirant. She is responsible for clandestine knowledge and cryptic messages which are planted gradually through the deepest parts of the subconscious mind and through dreams.

Hathor delineates the intermediary type of divine influence which depends upon both direct illumination and subtle communication. She alludes to the conscious mind actively petitioning the subconscious mind for knowledge obtained through meditation and contemplation.✿

After taking the 4 = 7 initiation, the task of the Philosophus is to thoroughly digest all knowledge associated with the Element of Fire and the Planet Venus. Most of the necessary information is contained in the Fifth Knowledge Lecture, which also contains additional information on the Shem ha-Mephoresh, the Qlippoth and the restoration of the Tree of Life. Ritual work and meditations suitable to the grade, are also covered.

The Philosophus initiate undergoing some of the rough-and-tumble aspects of this grade should bear in mind that the harmony between Fire and Water is the key to a new Renaissance in the Garden of Eden. *"And the Ruach Elohim moved upon the Face of the Waters."*✿

THE INITIATION CEREMONY

Temple setup: The aspirant will need to set up the Hall beforehand in accordance with the temple diagram. The black cubical altar is placed in the center of the room. Upon it should be placed the Tarot card of *The Moon.* Two large candle holders complete with candles flank the Northern and Southern side of the altar. The pillars are placed in the Southeast part of the Hall before the Dais. The Hebrew letter Qoph is shown on a large plaque in the Northeast. Directly East is the letter Tau, while in the Southeast is Shin. The Banners of the East and West are located near their respective officers. The Enochian Tablet of Fire is placed in the South, and the Tablets of Earth, Air and Water are also shown. Place the lamens and implements in accordance with the temple diagram, in the positions of the officer-forms. The station of Hierophant is located in the Northeast, while the station of Hegemon is in the Southeast. The Hiereus is stationed in the West. In addition, you will need three cups of Water to be placed by each officer's station.

As in the previous ritual, all of the Elemental candles should be placed around the circumference of the room, with a white candle in the East. The red Fire candle is to be placed before the Enochian Tablet of the South, along with a censer of incense. The lights on the pillars should be unshaded.

(Note: For later segments of the ritual, the aspirant will need the following items close at hand: plaques of the Hebrew letters Resh, Samekh, Tzaddi, Peh, Mem, Ayin, Kaph and Nun, as well as the Qamea, seal and sigils of Venus (see Chapter Four), the Tarot cards of *The Star* and *The Tower,* and the diagram of the Garden of Eden after the Fall (see Plate 4). You will need four Admission Badges for this ceremony: the Calvary Cross of Twelve Squares, the Solid Pyramid of the Elements, the Calvary Cross of Ten Squares, and the Cross of the Hegemon's Badge.)

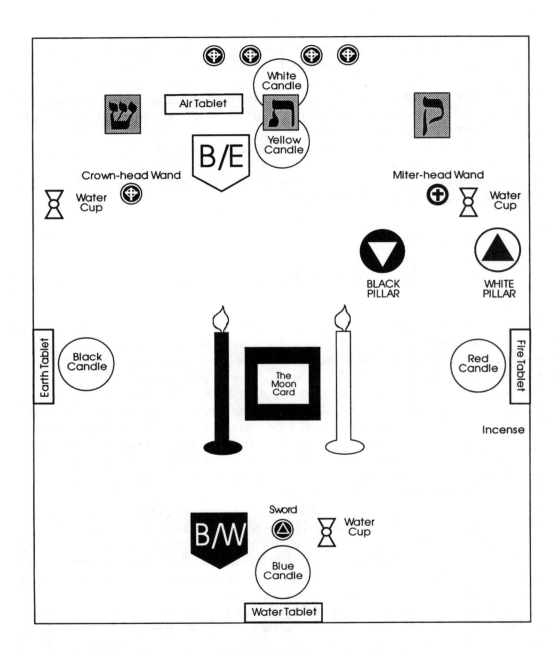

The Philosophus Temple for Self-Initiation: First Setup

Ritual preparations: The aspirant should fast for a period of twelve hours prior to the ritual. A ritual bath is required after which the aspirant may put on the black Tau robe, and red slippers. The sash will need to be decorated with the Philosophus emblems, but it is not to be worn by the candidate at this time. Place the sash inside the altar.

The aspirant must meditate for a certain length of time on a drawing of the symbol of Fire—a Fire triangle (apex upwards) in red. Next s/he must spend a period of time (20—30 minutes) in a darkened room or antechamber to the temple seated in quiet meditation while wearing a hoodwink or blindfold. The Admission Badge for the 29th Path, the Calvary Cross of Twelve Squares, should be held in the right hand throughout this period. A small red candle is to be the only source of light in the room. During this time, darkness and silence are to be maintained. The aspirant should imagine him/her self under the watchful eye of Anubis of the West. After this period of time, the hoodwink may be removed. The aspirant may then enter the temple and begin the ritual.

Upon entering the temple, imagine that you are leaving your physical body outside as a sentinel to guard the temple, so that your spiritual self has the freedom to accept initiation.

PART 0: The Opening

Enter the temple with the Admission Badge of the Calvary Cross of Twelve Squares. Salute the Banner of the East with the Neophyte Signs. Leave the cross in the Western part of the temple. Once inside walk deosil to the East. With the Hiereus' Sword perform the LBRP.

Give one knock with the pommel of the sword against the floor or side of the chair and say: "HEKAS, HEKAS, ESTE BEBELOI!"

Put the sword aside and go to the West of the temple, facing East. Kneel down and invoke the godform of Thmê as in the previous initiation. Vibrate strongly:

> *THMÊ! THMÊ! THMÊ! Thou daughter and eye of RA! Lady of Heaven, Queen of Earth and mistress of the Underworld! Great Lady of all the gods and goddesses. Thou whose name is MAAT! Lady of Truth! Goddess of Justice and Order! Mediator between Darkness and Light, Chaos and Order! THMÊ! THMÊ! THMÊ! Thou who assesseth the heart of every man and woman in the Hall of Judgment before Ousiri and the assembly of the gods. Thou who art the eye and heart of balance! THMÊ! THMÊ! THMÊ! I invoke thee!*

Visualize the familiar image of the goddess Thmê before you, with human head and yellow-gold skin. She wears a black and white nemyss and a white linen gown. She carries the miter-headed scepter of the Hegemon. Above her head is the white glowing outline of the cross and triangle, symbolic of the outer magical current of the Golden Dawn.

Slowly and with feeling, perform the Qabalistic Cross, drawing the Light down from the Kether of the universe into the Kether at the crown of your head as you continue the QC. Strongly visualize the cross of Light you have formed in the center of your body. Trace within your heart the Hebrew letters of the name THMÊ in glowing white. Project a white ray of thought from your heart toward the image of Thmê you have created before you. See the figure breathe in life as your thought-ray animates it. Address the form:

> THMÊ! Beautiful One of the Feather of Truth! I beseech thee to act upon my behalf in this my quest for the Light Divine! Guide me, O thou who art none other but my own Higher Self. Aid me and escort me in this Venusian Realm which is the emotional power of the manifest universe. I am a true and willing Seeker of Light and Knowledge. Act as my overseer and reconciler on the paths and in the temple of Netzach. Speak for me amidst the assembly of the gods and the guardians of this sacred Hall. My intentions are honest. I am ready to undergo test and trial. I am willing to be examined by the Triad of Time Eternal! I wish to be purified and consecrated to the Light. Grant that my heart is made MAAT! Grant that my Will is made MAAT! Merciful THMÊ! Let me be judged aright! Grant that this humble aspirant before you be not turned away from that resplendent Light which resides in the East. Permit me to tread the watery paths that lead to the fiery temple of Netzach. Award me a vision of the mysteries of the Fallen Garden of Paradise! Grant that I may safely digress from the middle path, and grant me the ability to return to that stable pillar! Permit me to enter the victorious sphere! Let me penetrate the Threshold in the path of the Enterer!

Thmê speaks to you in your own mind.

> And the Ruach Elohim moved upon the Face of the Waters. The voice of Adonai is powerful. He that dwelleth in the secret place of the most High shall abide under the shadow of the Almighty. Thou shalt not be afraid for the terror by night, nor for the arrow that flieth by day. I am the representative of your Higher and Holy Self. It is only through my arbitration that thou canst even approach the sphere of Victory. In this Hall I am thy tongue, thy heart and thy mind. Fear not, for I shall guide thee through the deluge of the Waters, and I shall keep thee safe. Fear not, for I shall lead thee through the fiery temple of Netzach. I shall direct thee in the pathways before the mighty Triad of Reconciliation! I shall speak for thee in this assembly of the gods before the powers of Elohim and the current of the Light.

Visualize the goddess Thmê communicating in silence with the energies in the East. She speaks on your behalf to the divine guardians of the Hall. Once again you hear her voice as she calls out the names of other godforms in the East of the temple: ESE, NEBETHO, THOOUTH and another, HOOR OUER. Again, you have a vague perception of four figures in the East, seated before a veil. Thmê proceeds to address the figures, and the scene becomes hazy. The goddess stands once more before the gigantic form of Djehoti, god of Wisdom. Thmê carries on a silent conversation with Thoth. After a few moments Thmê turns toward you, salutes with the Signs toward the West and says silently:

Thou mayest proceed, O aspirant; thou art MAAT.

Thmê descends from the East and walks to her own station of Hegemon in the Southeast where she traces the figures of a cross and triangle with her scepter. She then goes to the West and traces the figures at the station of the Hiereus. As she does so, vibrate the name *"HOOR"* (Hoor or Hoh-or) The figure of Horus begins to formulate rapidly. She returns to the Northeast and traces the figures at the station of Hierophant. As she does this, intone the name *"OUSIRI"* (Oo-seer-ee) The mummy-wrapped form of Osiris starts to take shape.

Thmê takes you by the hand, and leads you to the East of the altar. Say:

> *The 4 = 7 grade of Philosophus is attributed to the Planet Venus and the 29th, 28th, and 27th Paths. The 29th Path of QOPH refers to the reflection of the sphere of PISCES. The 28th Path of TZADDI alludes to the reflection of the sphere of AQUARIUS. The 27th Path of PEH alludes to the reflection of the sphere of MARS. Let the Element of this grade be named that it may be awakened within my sphere, in the spheres of those beings who are present, and in the sphere of this magical current. The Element is FIRE.*

Visualize the symbol of the red Fire triangle that you meditated on before entering the Hall. Imagine its presence in your sphere of sensation at your Kether[120] center, above the crown of your head. (Note: You should become aware of a feeling of harmonic resonance between the Fire triangle and your Geburah sphere—the right shoulder. Then visualize the triangle in green reflected into your Netzach center—the left hip.) Imagine that these same images are activated in all of the various astral officer-forms of the Hall.

Thmê leads you to the figure of Osiris in the Northeast. The god traces in the air before you the figure of a cross and circle. He then hands you his crown-headed scepter. Picking up the Wand of Power, you take on the office of Hierophant that Osiris has bestowed upon you. Give the Sign of the Spiraling Light toward the East, and then say, *"Let the white brilliance of the Divine Spirit descend!"* Feel a flood of Divine Light flow through your body from the Kether of the universe. Equili-

---

[120] The *Yod-Fire* area of the Four Qabalistic Worlds.

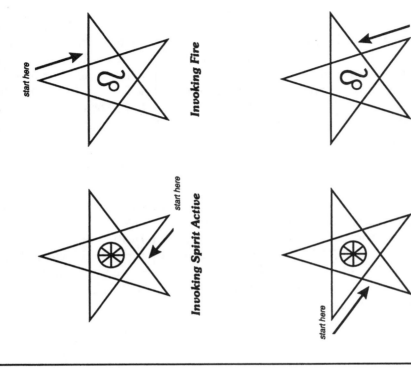

Invoking Spirit Active

Invoking Fire

Banishing Spirit Active

Banishing Fire

The Pentagrams of Fire

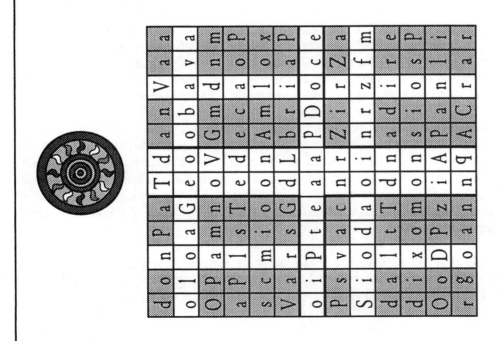

The Enochian Tablet of Fire

brate this Light through your body by performing the Qabalistic Cross, vibrating the Hebrew names.

Give a knock and say: *"Let us adore the Lord and King of Fire!"* Turn to the East and continue: *"YHVH TZABAOTH. Blessed be Thou—Leader of Armies is Thy Name, Amen."* Salute with the Sign of Philosophus.

The Philosophus Sign

Go clockwise to the South and stand before the Fire Tablet. Visualize the other officer-forms facing South also.

Through the authority of the office of Hierophant bestowed upon you by Osiris, invoke the powers of the Fire Tablet. Give a knock, then trace with the wand a large circle in front of the Tablet. Then draw the invoking pentagram of Spirit Active. As you do so vibrate *"BITOM"* (Bay-ee-toh-em). Trace the sigil of Spirit in the center and intone *"EHEIEH"* (Eh-heh-yay). Give the Sign of the Spiraling Light. Then trace the invoking pentagram of Fire. As you do so vibrate the name *"OIP TEAA PEDOCE"* (Oh-ee-pay Tay-ah-ah Pay-doe-kay). Draw the sigil of Leo in the center and intone *"ELOHIM."* (El-oh-heem) Give the Sign of Philosophus. Say:

> *And the Elohim said, "Let us make ADAM in our Image, after our own likeness and let them have dominion. In the Name of ELOHIM, Mighty and Ruling, and in the name of YHVH TZABAOTH, Spirits of Fire adore your Creator!*

Take up the incense and trace with it the Sign of Leo in the air before the Tablet. Say:

> *In the Name of MICHAEL, the Great Archangel of Fire, and in the Sign of the Lion, Spirits of Fire, adore your Creator!*

Trace a cross with the incense. Say:

> *In the Name and Letters of the great Southern Quadrangle revealed unto Enoch by the Great Angel Ave, Spirits of Fire adore your Creator!*

Hold the incense high and say:

> *In the Three Great Secret Names of God, born upon the Banners of the South, OIP TEAA PEDOCE, Spirits of Fire adore your Creator! In the Name of EDELPERNA, Great King of the South, Spirits of Fire adore your Creator!*

Replace the incense and return to the station of the Hierophant to face West. Visualize the other officers at their stations. Say:

In the Name of YHVH TZABAOTH, I declare this temple opened in the
4 = 7 grade of Philosophus.

Give the following knocks with the pommel of the scepter: ווו ווו ו (3—3—1). Visualize the officer/godform of the Hiereus repeating the Battery of knocks: 3—3—1. Visualize the officer/godform of the Hegemon repeating the Battery of knocks: 3—3—1.

Step out of the office of Hierophant and return it to the dominion of Osiris. The goddess Thmê then leads you to the West of the temple.

PART 1: Advancement in the 29th Path of Qoph

Visualize all of the astral officer/godforms at their respective stations. At this point, the temple has been opened under the guidance of the Guardians of the Hall, with your very active participation. You have already done a great deal to activate the Element of Fire within your sphere of sensation. As in your past initiations you must now take a few moments to re-establish yourself as a *candidate* who seeks for entrance into this Hall. Perform the Qabalistic Cross to maintain a psychic balance of all the Elements within your aura. Recall the experience in the antechamber, where you were blindfolded in the darkness. Restore the persona of the aspiring candidate within you.

Take up the Calvary Cross of Twelve Squares in your right hand. Give the Battery of knocks: 3—3—1. Stand in the Western part of the Hall facing East and say:

> *This candidate seeks for entrance. I vow it to be true that I (magical motto) have made such progress in the paths of occult science to have enabled me to pass certain examinations in the requisite knowledge. Having accomplished this, I am now eligible for advancement to the grade of Philosophus.*

The goddess Thmê replies:

> And the Ruach Elohim moved upon the face of the Waters.

She leads you to the South before the Tablet of Fire. As you face the East, she demands the 3 = 8 Signs and words from you:

> Give me the Sign of the grade of Practicus. (You give it.)

> Give me the Grip or Token.

You exchange the Outer Order Grip with the goddess.

Give me the Grand Word of the 3 = 8 grade.

You give it: *"Elohim Tzabaoth."*

Give me the Mystic Number of the 3 = 8 grade.

You give it: *"36."*

What is the Password formed from the Mystic Number?—She asks.

You answer: *"Aleph Lamed Heh."*

What is the Mystic Title of the 3 = 8 grade?

You give it: *"Monocris de Astris."*

What symbol did you receive in that grade?

You give it: *"Maim."*

From the Northeast, you hear the voice of Osiris:

Monocris de Astris, are you ready to take this oath of the 4 = 7 grade?

You answer: *"I am ready to take this oath."*

Face the Fire Tablet and say:

> I (state magical motto) *solemnly pledge to maintain and uphold the mysteries of the 29th, 28th, and 27th Paths, and of the 4 = 7 grade of Philosophus, just as I am pledged to maintain those of the preceding grades.*

Stretch forth your arms above your head to their full limit and say: *"I swear by the Torrent of Fire."* Take up the incense that is before the Tablet of the South. Wave it thrice in front of the Tablet and say, *"Let the powers of Fire witness my pledge."* Replace the incense.

Thmê as Hegemon leads you between the pillars in the Northeast. She remains at the outer side of the black pillar. Give a knock and say:

> Before me are the Portals of the 31st, 32nd, and 29th Paths as in the grade of Zelator. The two former I have already traversed, and the portal of the 29th Path leading to the grade of Philosophus is now open to me.

Osiris speaks:

> Take in your right hand the Calvary Cross of Twelve Squares, and
> follow your guide through the path of the Waters.

The Hegemon turns to the right. You pass between the pillars and follow her as she
leads you slowly around the Hall. Take time however to visualize the following:

> At this point, briefly imagine in your mind's eye that you are pass-
> ing through a gate marked with the Hebrew letter Qoph—leaving
> the sphere of Malkuth behind and following your guide through a
> red-violet tunnel or passageway. You are leaving the material
> world behind as you begin to traverse the watery path of the sub-
> conscious mind that connects the Active World with the Realm of
> the Emotions and Instincts. The energy of the path is feral and
> untamed, as if you have stepped out of a time machine and into a
> primeval marshland that exists at the edge of a vast ocean. Sounds
> of insects and creatures that live near the wetlands are all around
> you. Your senses seem unusually sharp on this path, as if you had
> somehow regained some of the instincts of humanity's primitive
> ancestors. The air has the humid, muddy smell of a swamp teem-
> ing with life and death. Your guide leads onward.

After one circumambulation around the Hall, the Hegemon leads you to the
Hierophant's throne. The officer-form of the Hierophant rises, and you perceive
the features of dark Osiris, very familiar to you now. Holding a cup of Water, the
figure approaches you and begins to speak:

> The priest with the mask of OSIRIS spake and said: "I am Water stag-
> nant and silent and still, reflecting all, concealing all. I am the Past—I
> am the Inundation. He who riseth from the Great Waters is my Name.
> Hail unto ye, Dwellers of the Land of Night! For the rending of Dark-
> ness is near."

After hearing the god's speech, a hush comes over the Path of Qoph, as if the creatures of the marsh had suddenly detected a new presence. The Water at your feet is
like the glass of a black mirror—offering both reflections and enigmas. The Hegemon leads you round to the station of the Hiereus, who rises at your approach with
Water cup in hand. The hawkish eyes of Horus flash with a greenish glare as the
figure speaks to you:

> The Priest with the Mask of HORUS spake and said: "I am Water,
> turbid and troubled. I am the Banisher of Peace in the vast abode of
> the Waters. None is so strong that can withstand the Great
> Waters—the vastness of their Terror—the magnitude of their
> Fear—the Roar of their Thundering Voice. I am the Future, mist-
> clad and shrouded in gloom. I am the Recession of the Torrent. The

storm veiled in Terror is my Name. Hail unto the Mighty Powers of Nature and the Chiefs of the Whirling Storm!"

Visualize the following:

> The feel of the path has changed from a still and quiet swamp to a tropical wetland in the beginnings of a typhoon. The wind lashes at the trees surrounding the marsh. Foam-crested waves begin to inundate the still waters of the swamp, pounding the marshland reeds with relentless force. The creatures of the wetlands have either burrowed deeper into the mud or escaped to higher ground.
>
> The eerie howling of the wind reminds you of the baying of wild dogs. In the shifting Moonlit shadows of the storm, you see monstrous bestial shapes slinking along the outskirts of the swamp, just beyond your peripheral vision—always moving ahead of your ability to see them clearly. They resemble shapes from long-ago memories and stories which frightened you as a child. They also resemble phobias that you may still cling to—unreasoning fears. Although the shapes are alarming, you resist the human urge to run away in fear. You are determined to stay the course.
>
> The appearance of the phantom shapes, together with the ferocity of the storm gives you a rush of adrenaline and excitement. You feel very much alive on this ominous path.

The officer-form of the Hegemon leads you round to her own station where she takes up the cup of Water. The face of Thmê is gone—in its place is the countenance of the great goddess Isis, calm and reflective. She speaks to you:

> The Priestess with the mask of ISIS spake and said: "The traveler through the Gates of Anubis is my Name. I am Water, pure and limpid, ever flowing on toward the sea. I am the Ever-passing Present that stands in the place of the Past. I am the fertilized land. Hail unto thee Dwellers of the Wings of the Morning!"

Visualize the following:

> The "feel" of the path has changed again now that the storm has passed. Gone are the phantom shapes of the night, banished with the night itself as the rays of morning embrace the sky. It is as though the stagnant Water of the swamp has been cleansed by the overflow of Water from the sea, mingling with the fresh Water from the marsh. Shells, seaweed and dead sea creatures have also been tossed into the marshland, providing an unexpected bounty for the wetland's own creatures. A crayfish pulls itself up onto the muddy land to scavenge. Meanwhile the rain supplied by the storm causes

an increase in the current of fresh Water which flows downstream towards the sea.

Return to the West of the altar facing East. Osiris as Hierophant speaks to you:

I arise in the place of the Gathering of the Waters, through the rolled back Cloud of Night. From the Father of Waters went forth the Spirit, rending asunder the veils of Darkness. And there was but a Vastness of Silence and of Depth in the place of the Gathering Waters. Terrible was the Silence of that Uncreated world—Immeasurable the depth of that Abyss. And the Countenances of Darkness half-formed arose— they abode not—they hasted away—and in the Darkness of Vacancy, the Spirit moved and the Lightbearers existed for a space.

I have said Darkness of Darkness—are not the Countenances of Darkness fallen with Kings? Do the Sons of the Night of Time last for ever? And have they not yet passed away?

You continue the speech:

Before all things are the Waters and the Darkness and the Gates of the Land of Night. And the CHAOS cried aloud for Unity of Form—and the Face of the ETERNAL arose. Before the Glory of that Countenance the Night rolled back and the Darkness hasted away. In the Waters beneath was that Face reflected, in the Formless Abyss of the Void. From those Eyes darted rays of terrible splendor which crossed with the currents reflected. That Brow and those Eyes formed the triangle of the Measureless Heavens—and their reflections formed the triangle of the Measureless Waters. And thus was formulated the eternal Hexad—the number of the Dawning Creation.

Hold the Admission Badge for the Path of Qoph high and say:

The Calvary Cross of Twelve Squares fitly represents the ZODIAC which embraces the Waters of Nu as the ancient Egyptians called the Heavens, the Waters which be above the Firmament. It also alludes to the eternal River of Eden, divided into four Heads which find their correlations in the four triplicities of the Zodiac.

Put the cross aside and focus your attention on the plaque of the letter Qoph. Say:

The Twenty-ninth path of the Sepher Yetzirah which answereth unto the letter QOPH is called the Corporeal Intelligence, and it is so-called because it forms the very body which is so formed beneath the whole Order of the Worlds and the increment of them. It is therefore the reflection of the watery Sign of Pisces and the path connecting Malkuth with the Pillar of

Mercy and the side of Chesed, through the Sephirah NETZACH, and through it do the Waters of Chesed flow down.

Focus your attention on the Tarot Key of The Moon and say:

The Eighteenth Key of the Tarot symbolically resumes these ideas. It represents the MOON with four Hebrew Yods like drops of dew falling, two dogs, two Towers, a winding path leading to the Horizon, and in the foreground, Water with a Crayfish crawling through it to the land.

The Moon is in its increase on the side of Mercy, Gedulah, and from it proceed sixteen principle and sixteen secondary rays, which make 32, the number of the paths of Yetzirah. She is the Moon at the feet of the Woman of Revelations, ruling equally over the cold and moist natures and the passive Elements of Earth and Water. It is to be noted that the symbol of the Sign is formed of two Lunar crescents bound together. It thus shows the Lunar nature of the Sign. The Dogs are the Jackals of the Egyptian ANUBIS, guarding the Gates of the East and of the West, shown by the two Towers between which lies the path of all the heavenly bodies ever rising in the East and setting in the West. The Crayfish is the Sign Cancer and was anciently the Scarabeus or Khepera, the emblem of the Sun below the Horizon as he ever is when the Moon is increasing above. Also, when the Sun is in the Sign Pisces the Moon will be well in her increase in Cancer as shown by the Crayfish emblem.

Visualize the following:

Imagine that you are at the end of the red-violet Path of Qoph. In your mind's eye imagine that you now stand before the green gate that is the entrance leading to the Fire temple of Netzach. You realize that your journey through the 29th Path has been a primary step into the evolution of your own sub-conscious mind. Once again you have traversed a path which has veered off the safety of the Middle Pillar. You have encountered the Waters of the Unconscious on this path, in all its darkness, fury and timeless depth. You have learned not to fear the dark phantoms of the lower astral and of your own subconscious mind. Instead you have ridden out the storm in anticipation of the Light. Progression into spiritual Truth only takes place when all fears are confronted and dealt with.

Osiris speaks to you:

I hereby confer on you the Title of Lord (Lady) of the Twenty-ninth Path.

(Say:) *"I claim the Title of Lord (Lady) of the 29th Path."*

Thmê speaks to you:

> You have passed the gate of the Path of Qoph in the footsteps of an initiate. Prepare this Hall to reflect the 28th Path of Tzaddi. Prepare thyself for passage into the path of the Star.

The goddess leads you out into the antechamber where you spend a few moments rehearsing the Fourfold Breath and meditating on the Moon Card. Perform the Qabalistic Cross to once again equilibrate the Elemental energies within your aura. When ready, set the temple in accordance with Part Two of the ritual.

Changes in the temple setup for the Second Part of the ritual—the 28th Path: Replace the plaque of the letter Qoph in the Southeast with the letter Tzaddi. Replace Tau with Samekh. Replace Shin with Resh. Also replace the Tarot card of The Moon with that of The Star. All other temple furnishings remain as they are.

PART 2: Advancement in the 28th Path of Tzaddi

Spend a few moments in the antechamber in a state of relaxed meditation. Perform the Qabalistic Cross. Take up the Admission Badge of the Solid Pyramid of the Elements. Visualize all of the astral officer/godforms at their respective stations. Take a few moments to re-establish yourself as a candidate who seeks for entrance into this Hall.

With the Pyramid in your right hand, stand in the Western part of the Hall facing East.

The goddess Thmê comes to your side and says,

> *And ever forth from their Celestial Source, the Rivers of Eden flow.*

Thmê as Hegemon leads you between the pillars in the Southeast. She remains at the outer side of the black pillar. Give a knock and say:

> *The path now open to me is the 28th leading from the 2 = 9 grade of Theoricus to the 4 = 7 grade of Philosophus.*

Osiris speaks:

> Take in your right hand the Solid Pyramid of the Elements, and follow the guide of the path.

The Hegemon turns to the right. You pass between the pillars and follow her as she leads you slowly around the Hall. During this time visualize the following:

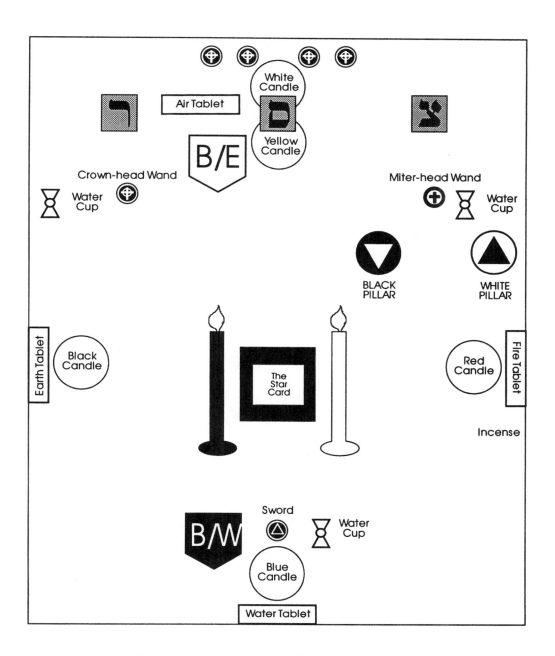

The Philosophus Temple for Self-Initiation: Second Setup

At this point, briefly imagine in your mind's eye that you are passing through a gate marked with the Hebrew letter Tzaddi—leaving the sphere of Yesod behind and following your guide through a violet tunnel or passageway. You are leaving the astral sphere behind as you begin to traverse the celestial path of the human imagination that connects the sphere of Foundation with the Realm of the Emotions. The energy of the path is comforting and dreamy, as if you have suddenly entered a place of great serenity and beauty— a place where you could look out unto the vastness of Nature and be awestruck by the marvel of its grand design. It opens you to a state of meditation and contemplation which lends itself to a stream of consciousness that is very receptive to inner spiritual knowledge.

After one circumambulation around the Hall, the Hegemon leads you to the Hierophant's throne. The officer-form of the Hierophant rises, but this time it is the face of the goddess Isis that you behold. Holding a Water cup, the figure approaches you and begins to speak:

> The Priestess with the Mask of ISIS spake and said: "I am the Rain of Heaven descending upon Earth, bearing with it the fructifying and germinating power. I am the plenteous Yielder of Harvest. I am the Cherisher of Life."

Visualize the following:

> After hearing the speech of the goddess, your journey on the path of Tzaddi is accompanied by a warm and steady rainfall. The rumbling of distant thunder reminds you of the contented purr of some gigantic celestial cat. The gentle patter of the Water falling on the leaves of trees and ground vegetation is hypnotic. You don't mind the feel of the warm rain upon your head; you feel strangely delighted and emotionally satisfied. You realize that the calm meditative stillness of your mind is being fertilized by the bountiful waters of the goddess. Even now the seeds of Wisdom are taking root in the fertile soil of your subconscious mind.

The Hegemon leads you round to the station of the Hiereus, who rises at your approach with Water cup in hand. However in the place of Horus, you perceive the dark countenance of the goddess Nephthys. She speaks:

> The Priestess with the mask of NEPHTHYS spake and said: "I am the Dew descending viewless and silent, gemming the Earth with countless diamonds of Dew, bearing down the influence from above in the solemn darkness of Night."

Visualize the following:

> The rain has ended and the path leads on into the darkness of night. Stars glitter like jewels on the body of some celestial goddess. Beads of condensation form upon the leaves around you as you continue silently on the nocturnal path. You feel as though many of the greatest mysteries of the 28th Path are being transmitted to you subconsciously, in a way that you cannot yet comprehend. Like diamonds of dew, they form silently and will gradually reveal themselves to the light of day, when conscious meditation draws them out.

The officer-form of the Hegemon leads you round to her station, where she takes up the Water cup. But instead of Thmê, you see before you the face of the goddess Hathor. The figure speaks:

> The Priestess with the Mask of HATHOR spake and said: "I am the Ruler of Mist and Cloud wrapping the Earth, as it were, in a Garment, floating and hovering between Earth and Heaven. I am the Giver of the Mist-veil of Autumn, the successor of the Dew-clad Night."

Visualize the following:

> The "feel" of the path has changed slightly, as the beams of the morning sun meet the dew-drenched foliage and begin to turn Water into vapor. It is a transmutation; a changing of one form of energy into another form—from Water to Air. You experience a conscious realization of some unconscious spiritual Truth which had previously eluded you.

Return to the West of the altar facing East. Visualize all of the astral officer/god-forms shedding their outer appearance as the three goddesses and assuming their regular demeanor. Osiris as Hierophant speaks to you:

> Where the Paternal Monad is, the Monad is enlarged and genereth two, and beside Him is seated the Duad and glittereth with Intellectual Sections. Also to govern all things and order everything not ordered. For in the whole universe shineth the Triad over which the Monad ruleth. This Order is the beginning of all sections.

You continue the speech:

> *For the Mind of the Father said that all things should be cut into Three. Whose will assented and then all things were divided. For the mind of the eternal Father said, into Three, governing all things by Mind. And there*

appeared in it the Triad: Virtue, Wisdom and Multicient Truth. Thus being Pre-existent, not the first Essence, but that whereby all things are measured.

The Hierophant continues the speech:

For thou must know that all things bow before the Three Supernals. The first Course is Sacred—but in the midst thereof, the third aerial, which cherisheth Earth in Fire, and the Fountain of Fountains and of all Fountains—the Matrix containing All. Thence springeth forth abundantly the generation of multifarious Matter.

Hold the Admission Badge for the Path of Tzaddi high and say,

This Pyramid is attributed to the four Elements. On the four triangles are their Hebrew Names: Asch—Fire, Maim—Water, Ruach—Air, Aretz—Earth. On the Apex is the word ETH composed of the first and last letters of the alphabet and implying Essence. The square base represents the material universe and on it is the word OLAM meaning World.

Put the Badge aside and focus your attention on the plaque of the letter Tzaddi. Say:

The 28th Path of the Sepher Yetzirah which answereth to the letter Tzaddi is called the Natural Intelligence—and it is so called because through it is consummated and perfected the Nature of every existing being under the Orb of the Sun. It is therefore the reflection of the Airy Sign Aquarius, the Water-bearer, unto which is attributed the Countenance of Man, the ADAM who restored the world.

Focus your attention on the Tarot Key of The Star and say:

The 17th Key of the Tarot symbolically resumes these ideas. The large STAR in the center of the Heavens has seven principal and fourteen secondary rays and this represents the Heptad multiplied by the Triad. This yields 21—the Number of the Divine Name EHEIEH which, as you already know, is attached to Kether.

In the Egyptian sense, it is SIRIUS, the Dog-Star, the Star of Isis-Sothis. Around it are the Stars of the Seven Planets each with its sevenfold counterchanged operation.

The nude female figure with the Star of the Heptagram on her brow is the synthesis of Isis, of Nephthys, and of Hathor. She also represents the Planet VENUS through whose sphere the influence of Chesed descends. She is Aima, Binah, Tebunah, the Great Supernal Mother—Aima Elohim, pouring upon the Earth the Waters of Creation which unite and form a River at her feet, the River going forth from the Supernal Eden which floweth and faileth not. In this Key she is completely unveiled while in the 21st Key she is only partially so.

The two Urns contain the influences from Chokmah and Binah. On the right springs the Tree of Life, and on the left the Tree of the Knowledge of Good and Evil whereon the Bird of Hermes alights, and therefore does this Key represent the restored World, after the formless and the Void and the Darkness, the New ADAM, the Countenance of the Man which falls in the Sign AQUARIUS. And therefore doth the astronomical ripple of this Sign represent, as it were, Waves of Water—the ripples of that River going forth out of Eden—but, therefore also, is it justly attributed to Air and not unto Water because it is the Firmament dividing and containing the Waters.

Visualize the following:

Imagine that you are at the end of the violet Path of Tzaddi. In your mind's eye imagine that you now stand before the green gate that is the entrance leading to the Fire temple of Netzach. You realize that your journey through the 28th Path has been a personal one of meditation, imagination and spiritual contemplation. You have consciously delved into the realm of pure subconsciousness to retrieve knowledge and transmute it into a form that your Intellect can understand. Imagination and meditation are the tools that you need to do this. The Water that you encountered through the goddesses Isis and Nephthys (Light and Dark) symbolized the Waters of the universal unconscious, the Eternal spring which feeds the Soul of humanity. The goddess Hathor represented a transmutation of one form of energy to another—from Water to Air (from the unconscious to the conscious intellect). This foreshadows the act of drawing out hidden spiritual truths from the unconscious into the conscious mind through the act of meditation.

Osiris speaks to you:

I hereby confer on you the Title of Lord (Lady) of the 28th Path.

(Say:) *I claim the Title of Lord (Lady) of the 28th Path.*

Thmê speaks to you:

You have passed the gate of the Path of Tzaddi in the descending rays of the Star. Prepare this Hall to reflect the 27th Path of Peh. Prepare thyself for passage into the Path of Mars.

The goddess leads you out into the antechamber where you spend a few moments rehearsing the Fourfold Breath and meditating on The Star Card. Perform the Qabalistic Cross to once again equilibrate the Elemental energies within your aura. When ready, set the temple in accordance with the next part of the ritual.

Changes in the temple setup for the Third Part of the ritual—the 27th Path: Place the pillars in front of the Fire Tablet as shown in the diagram. Upon the altar should be the Tarot Card of *The Tower*. The stations of all three officers are now situated in the East: Hiereus in the Northeast, Hierophant in due East, and Hegemon in the Southeast. Beside each officer's station should be a red lamp. The Banners of East and West are located near the Hierophant and Hiereus respectively. The plaques of the Hebrew letters are needed as follows: East—Mem, Southeast—Ayin, South—Peh, Southwest—Resh, Northwest—Shin.

PART 3: Advancement in the 27th Path of Peh

After setting up the Hall, spend a few additional moments in relaxed meditation in the antechamber. Visualize the Fire triangle once more and then perform the Qabalistic Cross. Take up the Admission Badge to the 27th Path—the Calvary Cross of Ten Squares. When finished, stand just outside the temple door and give the Battery of knocks: 3—3—1. Briefly visualize all of the astral officer/godforms at their respective stations. Then imagine Thmê at the entrance facing you. The goddess motions for you to enter and says:

> The River Kishon swept them away, that Ancient River, the River Kishon. O my Soul, thou hast trodden down strength.

She leads you to the South and places you between the pillars, facing the Tablet. Give a knock and say:

> *The path now open to me is the 27th, which leads from the 3 = 8 grade of Practicus to the 4 = 7 grade of Philosophus.*

Osiris speaks:

> Take in your right hand the Calvary Cross of Ten Squares, and follow your guide through the Path of Mars.

Visualize the following:

> At this point, briefly imagine in your mind's eye that you are passing through a gate marked with the Hebrew letter Peh, leaving the sphere of Hod behind and following your guide through a red tun-

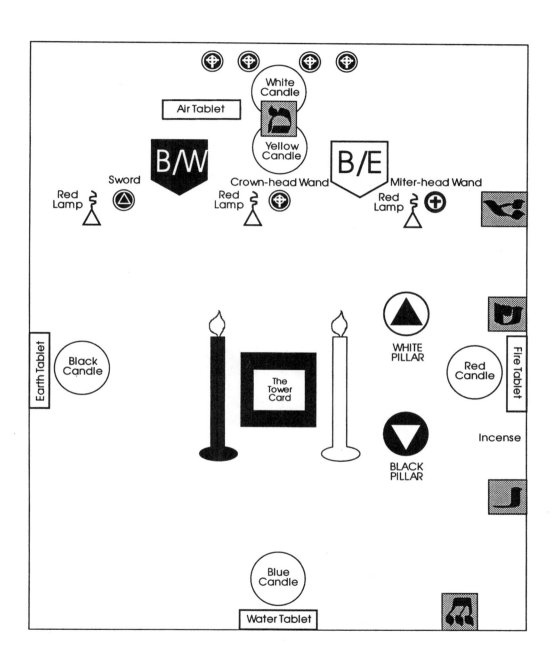

The Philosophus Temple for Self-Initiation: Third Setup

nel or passageway. You are leaving the Mercurial sphere behind as you begin to traverse the Martial path of psychic restructuring that connects the sphere of Intellect with the Realm of the Emotions. The energy of the path is uncomfortable and unnerving. Your senses are on edge, as if you were expecting something unpleasant to happen.

Thmê leads you between the pillars and round to the Hierophant. The god-form of Osiris rises with red lamp in hand. He speaks:

Ere the Eternal instituted the Formation, Beginning and End existed not. Therefore, before Him, He expanded a certain Veil, and therein He instituted the Primal Kings. And these are the Kings who reigned in Edom before there reigned a King over Israel.

You take up the red lamp at the station of Hierophant and continue the speech:

But they subsisted not. When the Earth was formless and void—behold this is the reign of EDOM. And when the Creation was established, lo, this is the reign of Israel. And the Wars of titanic forces in the Chaos of Creation, Lo, these are the Wars between them.

From a Light-bearer of unsupportable brightness, proceeded a radiating flame, hurling forth, like a vast and mighty Hammer, those sparks which were the Primal worlds. And these Sparks flamed and scintillated awhile, but being unbalanced, they were extinguished. Since lo, the Kings assembled, they passed away together, they themselves beheld, and so they were astonished. They feared. They hasted away.

Osiris finishes the speech:

And these be the Kings of Edom who reigned before there reigned a King over Israel.

Visualize the following:

The heat of the path has increased. You are aware of chaotic shapes and images along the border of the path, but they are not the ghostly images and phantoms that you encountered on the 29th Path. These are the chaotic embodiments of your own thoughts. They are not only your own personal thoughts, there are many thoughts that have been implanted into your mind long ago by others—parents, teachers, clergy, peer groups, friends, and rivals. In many instances you discover that your thoughts are not truly our own—your beliefs about self-worth, the worthiness of others, religion, race, and the things that are truly meaningful and important in life—many of your ideas on these matters have come from sources outside of yourself. It is difficult to tell which beliefs come exclusively from your own psyche, and this makes you uncomfortable. You do not wish to merely react to a given situation because a psychological button, implanted long ago by someone else, is pushed. You are not a robot. You have the right to examine your own beliefs.

Replace the red lamp. Thmê leads you around to the station of Hiereus. The godform of Horus rises with red lamp in hand and speaks:

> **The Dukes of Edom were amazed, trembling they took hold of the Mighty MOAB. Lord, when Thou wentest out of SEIR, when Thou marchest out of the Field of Edom, the Earth trembled and the Heavens dropped—the Clouds also dropped Water.**

You take up the red lamp at the station of Hiereus and continue the speech:

> *Curse ye MEROZ, said the Angel of the Lord—curse ye bitterly, the inhabitants thereof, because they came not to the help of the Lord—to the help of the Lord against the Mighty.*
>
> *The River Kishon swept them away—that ancient River, the River Kishon. O my Soul, thou hast trodden down Strength!*
>
> *He bowed the Heavens, also, and came down and the Darkness was under His Feet. At the brightness that was before Him, the thick clouds passed— Hailstones and flashings of Fire. The Lord thundered through the Heavens and the highest gave forth His Voice—Hailstones and flashings of Fire. He sent out His Arrows and scattered them: He hurled forth His Lightnings and destroyed them.*

Horus finishes the speech:

> **Then the channels of the Waters were seen and the Foundations of the World were discovered. At Thy rebuke, O Lord—at the blast of the Breath of Thy Nostrils, the Voice of Thy Thunder was in the Heavens and Thy Lightnings lighteneth the World. The Earth trembled and shook. Thy way is in the Sea and Thy path in the Great Waters and Thy Footsteps are not known.**

Visualize the following:

> The electricity of the path is now very pronounced. The chaotic shapes that inhabit the path are agitated. You have discovered the

Truth that they are in fact foreign archetypes implanted into your psyche long ago by others. Some are even beliefs that you yourself have created, but which you have now outgrown. To invoke order out of this chaos, you call upon your own inner spiritual self. There is an instant flash of Divine Light. Some of the chaotic shapes are immediately incinerated. Others are blown apart. By the very act of self-realization, you have destroyed these outmoded archetypes. They have lost their hold upon you.

Replace the red lamp. Thmê leads you back around to her own station and takes up the red lamp. She speaks:

O Lord, I have heard Thy Speech and was afraid.

You take up the red lamp and continue the speech:

The Voice of the Lord is upon the Waters. The God of Glory thundereth. The Lord is upon many Waters. The Voice of the Lord is powerful. The Voice of the Lord is full of Majesty. The Voice of the Lord breaketh the Cedars of Lebanon. The Voice of the Lord divideth the Flames of Fire.

Thmê finishes the speech:

The Voice of the Lord shaketh the wilderness of Kadesh.

Visualize the following:

There is an eerie calm upon the path, and the air smells of ozone. Around you are the devastated remains of the chaotic archetypes, lying about like so many charred bricks. As you walk along the path, you spot portions of the archetypes that you can still use—a healthy belief concerning your own self-worth that your parents instilled within you—a positive belief about the welfare of others that was given to you by a clergyman. There are also beliefs that you no longer care to keep—a belief that one religion has the right to dictate to other religions—a belief that you cannot succeed at something that you are striving for. Now that the old archetypes lay in pieces upon the ground, you can closely examine each one. As you walk along the Path of Peh, you retain those beliefs that you wish to retain, and discard those that you wish to discard.

Return to the West of the altar facing East. Osiris as Hierophant speaks to you:

ELOAH came from Teman of EDOM and the Holy One from Mount Paran. His Glory covered the Heavens and the Earth was full of His praise. His brightness was as the Light. He had **KARNAIM** in His Hands and there was the hiding of his Power.

You continue the speech of the Hierophant:

> *Before the Lord went the pestilence and Flaming Fire went forth at His Feet. He stood and measured The Earth. He beheld and drove asunder the Nations. And the Everlasting Mountains were scattered—the Perpetual Hills did bow. His ways are everlasting. I saw the tents of Cushan in affliction and the curtain of the Land of Midian did tremble.*

> *Was the Lord displeased against the Rivers? Was Thy Wrath against the Sea that Thou didst ride upon Thy horses and Chariots of Salvation? Thou didst cleave asunder the Earth with the Rivers. The Mountains saw Thee and they trembled. The deluge of Waters rolled by. The Deep uttered His voice and lifted up His hands on high. The SUN and the MOON stood still in their habitations. At the Light of Thine arrows they went— at the shining of Thy Glittering Spear.*

The Hierophant finishes the speech:

> Thou didst march through the Land in indignation. Thou didst thrash the Heathen in Thine Anger. Thou didst march through the Sea with Thy Horses—through the depth of the Mighty Waters.

Hold the Admission Badge for the Path of Peh high and say:

> *The Calvary Cross of Ten Squares refers to the Ten Sephiroth in balanced disposition, before which the Formless and the Void rolled back. It is also the opened out form of the Double Cube and of the Altar of Incense.*

Put the cross aside and focus your attention on the plaque of the letter Peh. Say:

> *The Twenty-seventh Path of the Sepher Yetzirah which answereth unto the letter PEH is called the EXCITING Intelligence, and it is so-called because by it is created the Intellect of all created Beings under the Highest Heaven, and the Excitement or Motion of them.*

> *It is therefore the reflection of the sphere of Mars, and the reciprocal path connecting Netzach with Hod, Victory with Splendor. It is the lowermost of the three reciprocal paths.*

Focus your attention on the Tarot Key of The Tower and say:

> *The 16th Key of the Tarot symbolically resumes these ideas. It represents a Tower struck by a Lightning Flash proceeding from a rayed circle and ter-*

minating in a triangle. It is the Tower of Babel struck by the Fire from Heaven. The triangle at the end of the flash, issuing from the circle, forms exactly the astronomical symbol of Mars.

It is the Power of the Triad rushing down and destroying the columns of Darkness. Three holes are rent in the walls, symbolizing the establishment of the Triad therein and the crown at the summit of the Tower is falling, as the crowns of the Kings of Edom fell, who are also symbolized by the men falling headlong. On the right hand side of the Tower is LIGHT and the representation of the Tree of LIFE by ten circles thus disposed.

On the left hand side is DARKNESS and eleven circles symbolizing the QLIPPOTH.

Visualize the following:

Imagine that you are at the end of the reddish path of Peh. In your mind's eye imagine that you now stand before the green gate that is the entrance leading to the Fire temple of Netzach. You realize that your journey through the 27th Path has been a personal psychic restructuring. This has meant a necessary and sudden destruction of the old and the unbalanced in order to completely overhaul and rebuild a new orderly psychic reality. The Kings of Edom represented chaotic thoughts, some of which are your own, and some of which have been implanted in your mind by others. Only by taking the tower of your personal beliefs apart and examining the merits of each belief can you achieve spiritual growth. This also entails a balancing of the Intellect with the Emotions. Some beliefs are based purely on irrational emotional responses, devoid of reason. Other beliefs are cold intellectual abstractions with no basis in real life. A healthy balance must be struck between these two extremes in order to build order out of chaos.

Osiris speaks to you:

I hereby confer on you the Title of Lord (Lady) of the Twenty-seventh Path.

(Say:) *I claim the Title of Lord (Lady) of the 27th Path.*

Thmê speaks to you:

You have passed the Gate of the Path of Peh in the Lightning Flash of Mars. Prepare this Hall to reflect the Fire temple of Netzach. Prepare thyself for advancement into the 4 = 7 grade of Philosophus.

The goddess leads you out into the antechamber where you spend a few moments rehearsing the Fourfold Breath and mediating on The Tower Card. Perform the Qabalistic Cross to once again equilibrate the Elemental energies within your aura. When ready, set the temple in accordance with the final part of the ritual.

Changes in the temple set for the remainder of the ritual—the temple of Netzach: Place the pillars slightly West of the altar. Just East of the altar should be a diagram stand with the drawing of The Garden of Eden after the Fall placed thereon. Upon the altar the cross should be placed below the triangle. The triangle is pointed apex upwards, and its three points are surrounded by the three red lamps which had accompanied the officers in the previous part of the ritual.

The station of Hiereus is situated North of the altar, while the station of Hegemon is located South of the altar. The station of the Hierophant remains in the East. The plaques of the Hebrew letters are needed as follows: East—Kaph, Northeast— Nun, North—Peh, Northwest—Tzaddi, Northwest—Qoph. In the East should be the Qamea of Venus, along with the Planetary sigils and the symbol of Venus on the Tree of Life.

PART 4: Entry into Netzach

After setting up the Hall, spend a few additional moments in relaxed meditation in the antechamber. Visualize the Fire triangle once more and then perform the Qabalistic Cross. Take up the Admission Badge to the temple of Netzach—the Cross of the Hegemon's Lamen. When finished, stand just outside the temple door and give the Battery of knocks: 3—3—1. Briefly visualize all of the astral officer/godforms at their respective stations. Then imagine Thmê at the entrance facing you. The goddess motions for you to enter and then gestures toward the Portals in the Northwest. Say:

> *In the Northwest are the Portals of the 29th and 28th Paths by which I have symbolically entered this grade from the 1 = 10 and 2 = 9 grades respectively, while in the North is the Portal of the 27th Path by which I have just passed from the grade of Practicus.*

She leads you forward to the figure of the Hiereus. Horus inquires:

By what symbol dost thou enter herein?

(You answer:) *I enter by the peculiar emblem of the Hegemon, which is the Calvary Cross of Six Squares. This cross embraces Tiphareth, Netzach, Hod and Yesod, and rests upon Malkuth. Also, the Calvary Cross of Six Squares forms the Cube, and is thus referred to the Six Sephiroth*

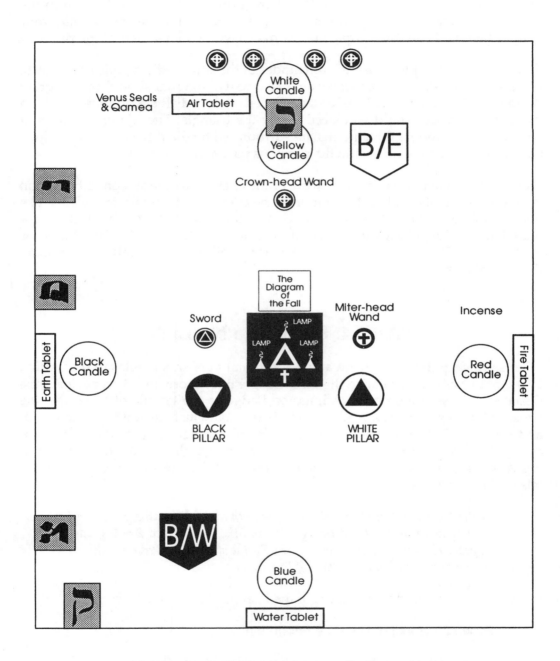

The Philosophus Temple for Self-Initiation: Fourth Setup

508

of Microprosopus which are Chesed, Geburah, Tiphareth, Netzach, Hod and Yesod.

Thmê leads you to just West of the altar. All three officer/godforms turn inward to face the altar.

Visualize the following:

In your mind's eye see yourself standing at the end of the red Path of Peh, facing the Gate to the astral temple of Netzach. A large green door is in front of you. Carved into this door is the letter Nun painted in red. Osiris, Horus and Isis stand before you, holding up their red lamps and blocking your final passage into Hod with the Banner of the West. You hold up the Hegemon's Lamen and proclaim that you have received the Title of Lord/Lady of the 29th, 28th and 27th Paths. The Banner of the West is withdrawn and the guardians permit you final entrance into the Fire temple of Netzach. Astrally, you give the Neophyte Signs followed by the Sign of a Philosophus and then step through the door into Netzach.

The temple is a seven-sided chamber draped in curtains of green silk. The floor and ceiling are constructed of pure emerald, while the ceiling itself is ornamented with the ruby figure of a heptagram. The scent of rose is in the Air. Seven columns surround the red central altar, upon which are a temple flame, a sistrum and seven roses.

The winged Archangel Haniel is also here, a fair-haired feminine being in robes of green chiffon. She leads you to a curtain at the far end of the temple. Giving the Sign of the Spiraling Light, you step through the curtain.

Again you find yourself in the familiar Courtyard of the Tabernacle. Quickly you walk past the brazen altar and the laver, entering the outer chamber of the Holy Place before the golden altar. As always, you offer up coals and incense and perform the Qabalistic Cross. Then crossing the chamber, the veil before you separates and you behold once again the sacred Ark.

You stare into the Divine Light that is perched atop the golden Mercy Seat between the two winged Kerubim. A further vision of the Garden of Eden presents itself to you:

You see again before you the Tree of Life, connected by the rivers of Paradise that you first encountered in the Practicus grade. But the vision before you has lost all of its former tranquillity. In Malkuth the mighty crowned goddess Eve, had supported the entire Tree of Life by single-handedly holding up the two great opposing pillars of Fire and Cloud, Light and Darkness. Yet just as in the story of Prometheus who stole the divine Fire from Heaven assisted by Pallas Athene, the goddess of Wisdom, Eve reached down to partake of the fruits of knowledge. She performed what could be considered the first act of Free Will, by which primitive humanity took a step forward in the physical evolution which separated humankind from the rest of Nature. In doing so she changed the destiny of the human race forever, because a sentient animal had no place in the Garden of Paradise.

As Eve reached down to grasp knowledge and secure it for humanity, she left the two mighty pillars unsupported. As a result, the Sephirotic Tree was shattered. Once knowledge was attained, the great red dragon of seven heads and ten horns, which had been asleep below Malkuth, was awakened and set loose.

Loosing her steady footing, Eve fell and so did the great Adam. They could no longer remain like the other creatures in the forest, motivated by instinct alone. They now possessed the ability to think, to be self-aware, to make tools, and to use knowledge— whether for good or ill—only their Free Will could decide which. Together they fell from the garden.

The coils of the dragon enveloped Malkuth, and its heads rose up into the seven lower Sephiroth, even up to Daath at the feet of the Great goddess *Aima Elohim*. The Dragon grew an eighth head, and from this hissing mouth of Leviathan, the Infernal Waters began to flow into Daath, threatening even the Supernals themselves.

For a moment you have a glimpse of the Supernal Realm: The goddess *Aima Elohim* has turned her face away from the Garden in sorrow. The great god *Yah* looks on with compassion. Above them both is the crown of Kether.

Then *YHVH Elohim* placed the four letters of the Unutterable Name, the Mighty Kerubim, and the Flaming Sword between the devastated Garden and the Supernal Eden, protecting it from the Dragon of Chaos. The Mighty Kerubim fought back the serpent and a great chasm known as the Abyss was formed to mark the battlefield, cutting off the Supernal Eden from the lower branches of the Tree. Thick dark clouds rolled in to obscure the Garden and hide it from humanity's sight.

Gradually, this vision of the Garden of Eden fades once more into the brilliant Light above the mercy Seat of the Ark. The curtain before you closes and obscures the Ark and its guardians. You are again in the astral temple of Netzach.

Bring the focus of your conscious mind back to the Philosophus Hall. Perform the Adoration to the Lord of the Universe. The officer-form of the Hierophant comes to your side and directs your attention to the diagram of The Fall, East of the altar. When you are ready, continue and say:

Before me is represented the symbolism of the Garden of Eden after the Fall. For, the great goddess, Eve, who in the 3 = 8 grade was supporting the Columns of the Sephiroth, in the Sign of the 2 = 9 grade, being tempted by the Tree of Knowledge (whose branches indeed tend upward into the Seven lower Sephiroth, but also tend downward unto the Kingdom of Shells) reached downward unto the Qlippoth, and immediately the Columns were unsupported and the Sephirotic system was shattered, and with it fell ADAM, the MICROPROSOPUS.

Then arose the Great Dragon with Seven Heads and Ten Horns, and the Garden was made desolate, and MALKUTH was cut off from the Sephiroth by his intersecting folds, and linked unto the Kingdom of Shells. And the Seven lower Sephiroth were cut off from the Three Supernals in DAATH, at the feet of AIMA ELOHIM.

And on the Heads of the Dragon are the names and crowns of the Edomite Kings. And because in DAATH was the greatest rise of the Great Serpent of Evil, therefore is there, as it were, another Sephirah, making for the Infernal or Averse Sephiroth, Eleven instead of Ten.

And hence were the Rivers of Eden desecrated, and from the Mouth of the Dragon rushed the Infernal Waters in DAATH. And this is LEVIATHAN, the Crooked Serpent.

But between the Devastated Garden and the Supernal Eden, YHVH ELOHIM placed the letters of the NAME and the FLASHING SWORD that the uppermost part of the Tree of Life might not be involved in the Fall of Adam. And thence it was necessary that the SECOND ADAM should come to restore all things and that, as the First Adam had been extended on the cross of the Celestial Rivers, so the SON should be crucified on the cross of the Infernal Rivers of DAATH. Yet, to do this, he must descend unto the lowest first, even unto Malkuth and be born of her.

The officer-form of the Hierophant captures your attention to give you the secrets of the grade. You hear the voice of Osiris:

The 4 = 7 grade of Philosophus is referred to the Sephirah Netzach and the 29th, 28th and 27th Paths are bound thereto.

Osiris then prompts you to give the Sign of Philosophus and explains:

This Sign is given by raising the hands to the forehead, and with the thumbs and index finger forming a triangle, apex upward. This represents the Element of Fire, to which this grade is allotted, and also the Spirit which moved upon the Waters of Creation.

The figure continues:

> The Grip or Token is the general Grip of the First Order. The Grand Word is a Name of nine letters, YHVH TZABAOTH, which means Lord of Armies. The Mystic Number is 28, and from it is formed the Password of this grade, KAPH CHETH, which should be lettered separately when given. It means POWER.

You repeat the words:

> *The Grand Word is YHVH TZABAOTH. The Mystic Number is 28. The Password of the grade is KAPH CHETH.*
>
> (You continue:) *Unto this grade and unto the Sephirah Netzach, the Seventh Path of the Sepher Yetzirah is referred. It is called the Recondite Intelligence, and it is so called because it is the Refulgent Splendor of all the Intellectual Virtues which are perceived by the Eye of the Mind and by the Contemplation of Faith.*

Osiris continues:

> The Distinguishing Badge of this grade, which you are now entitled to wear is the sash of a Practicus with the addition of a green cross above the orange cross and the number 4 in a circle and 7 in a square on either side of its summit, and below the 31, the numbers 27, 28 and 29 in green, between narrow bars of the same color.

Open the altar and remove the Philosophus sash. As you put it on, visualize the god Osiris investing you with the sash. The god then points out the Enochian Tablet of the South. As you inspect the Tablet say:

> *This grade is especially referred to the Element of Fire and therefore the Great Watchtower or Terrestrial Tablet of the South forms one of its principal emblems. It is known as the Fourth or Great Southern Quadrangle and it is one of the Four Great Tablets delivered unto Enoch by the Great Angel Ave. From it are drawn the Three Holy Secret Names of God—OIP TEAA PEDOCE—which are borne upon the Banners of the South, and numberless Divine and Angelic Names which appertain unto the Element of Fire.*

The officer-form of the Hierophant indicates the cross and triangle upon the altar. Say:

> *The triangle surmounting the cross upon the altar represents the Fire of the Spirit surmounting the Cross of Life and of the Waters of Edom. It forms the Alchemical Emblem of Sulfur. The red lamps at the angles of the triangle are the threefold form of Fire.*

The officer-form of the Hierophant returns to his throne in the East. Osiris speaks, pointing to the Hebrew letter plaques:

> The Portals in the East and North East conduct to higher grades. The others are those of paths you have already traversed.

Osiris then directs your attention to the Qamea of Venus. You continue:

> *The grade of Philosophus is especially related to the Planet VENUS, Ruler in Netzach. Its symbol, when inscribed on the Tree of Life is shown in the East. It embraces the whole of the Sephiroth, and is therefore a fitting emblem of the Isis of Nature, hence also, its circle is represented larger than that of Mercury.*

Hear the voice of Osiris speaking to you:

> I now congratulate you on having passed through the ceremony of the 4 = 7 grade of Practicus, and in recognition thereof, I confer upon you the Mystic Title of PHAROS ILLUMINANS, which means "Illuminating Tower of Light"; and I give you the symbol of ASCH which is the Hebrew name for Fire. I also give you the further symbol of PHRATH or Euphrates, the Fourth River.

Go to the East and face the godform of Osiris. The god traces the sigil of the cross and circle before you. Take up the crown-headed scepter and turn to face the East. Taking on the officer-form of the Hierophant, give a knock and say:

> *In the Name of YHVH TZABAOTH, hear ye all, that I (state magical motto) proclaim that I have been duly advanced to the grade of 4 = 7 of Philosophus, as a Lord (Lady) of the 27th, 28th and 29th Paths, and that I have received the Mystic Title of PHAROS ILLUMINANS and the symbols of ASCH and PHRATH.*
>
> *I further vow to study thoroughly the Mysteries which have been unfolded to my view in my progress from the humble position of Neophyte, so that mine may not be the merely superficial knowledge which marks the conceited and ignorant person, but that I may really and thoroughly understand what I profess to know.*

PART 5: The Closing

Give a knock and say: *"Let us adore the Lord and King of Fire!"* Knock again. Face the East and visualize the Fire triangle. Say, *"YHVH TZABAOTH Mighty and Terrible! Commander of the Ethereal Armies art Thou! Amen!"*

Go to the South of the temple facing the Enochian Tablet of Fire. Visualize the other officer/godforms standing behind you in balanced formation. Give a knock with the scepter and recite the Prayer of the Salamanders or Fire Spirits:

> *Immortal, eternal, ineffable and uncreated Father of all, borne upon the Chariot of Worlds which ever roll in ceaseless motion. Ruler over the ethereal vastness where the throne of Thy Power is raised, from the summit of which Thine Eyes behold all and Thy Pure and Holy Ears hear all—help us, Thy children, whom Thou hast loved since the birth of the Ages of Time! Thy Majesty, Golden, Vast and eternal, shineth above the Heaven of Stars. Above them art Thou exalted.*

> *O Thou Flashing Fire, there Thou illuminatest all things with Thine Insupportable Glory, whence flow the Ceaseless Streams of Splendor which nourisheth Thine Infinite Spirit. This Infinite Spirit nourisheth all and maketh that inexhaustible Treasure of Generation which ever encompasseth Thee—replete with the numberless forms wherewith Thou hast filled it from the Beginning.*

> *From this Spirit arise those most holy kings who are around Thy throne and who compose Thy Court.*

> *O Universal Father, One and Alone! Father alike of Immortals and Mortals. Thou hast specially created Powers similar unto Thy Thought Eternal and unto Thy Venerable Essence. Thou hast established them above the Angels who announce Thy Will to the world.*

> *Lastly, Thou hast created us as a third Order in our Elemental Empire.*

> *There our continual exercise is to praise and to adore Thy Desires: there we ceaselessly burn with eternal Aspirations unto Thee, O Father! O Mother of Mothers! O Archetype Eternal of Maternity and Love! O Son, the Flower of all Sons! Form of all Forms! Soul, Spirit, Harmony and Numeral of all things! Amen!"*

Through the authority of the office of Hierophant bestowed upon you by Osiris, banish the powers of the Fire Tablet. Trace with the wand a large circle in front of the Tablet. Then draw the banishing pentagram of Spirit Active. As you do so vibrate *"BITOM"* (Bay-ee-toh-em). Trace the sigil of Spirit in the center and intone

"*EHEIEH*" (Eh-heh-yay). Give the Reversal Sign of the Spiraling Light. Then trace the banishing pentagram of Fire. As you do so vibrate the Name "*OIP TEAA PEDOCE*" (Oh-ee-pay Tay-ah-ah Pay-doe-kay). Draw the sigil of Leo in the center and intone "*ELOHIM*" (El-oh-heem). Give the Sign of Philosophus.

Give the License to Depart by saying:

> *Depart ye in peace unto your habitations. May the blessing of YHVH TZABAOTH be upon you. Be there peace between us and you, and be ready to come when ye are called!* (Give a knock.)

Return the office of Hierophant to the dominion of Osiris in the Eastern part of the Hall.

The goddess Thmê comes to your side. She leads you to the station of the Hiereus where she traces the figure of the cross and triangle in the Air. The godform of Horus salutes with the Projection Sign—Thmê answers with the Sign of Silence. Horus slowly fades from view. In this manner, Thmê releases the other godforms in the Hall, Osiris and the godforms on the Dais. All the astral entities in the Hall begin to fade from view.

Thmê herself is the last godform to dissolve. You thank the goddess for guiding you in the Philosophus Hall. You trace the figures of the cross and triangle before her. She salutes you with the Projection Sign. You answer with the Sign of Silence. Withdraw the white ray which had activated the godform back into your heart center. Perform the Qabalistic Cross one last time to equilibrate all energies within your sphere of sensation.

Take up the sword and perform the Lesser Banishing Ritual of the Pentagram. Then go to the East and say:

> *In the Name of YHVH TZABAOTH, I declare this temple closed in the 4 = 7 grade of Philosophus.*

Give the Battery of knocks: 3—3—1. Go to the station of the of Hiereus and repeat the Battery: 3—3—1. Go to the station of Hegemon and repeat the Battery: 3—3—1.

Give the Philosophus Sign before exiting the temple.✿

The Fifth Knowledge Lecture

SECTION 1: Qabalah—The "Body" of the Divine

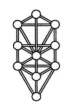 **AZOTH** is a word often used in magic and in alchemy. It is formed from the initial and final letters of the Greek, Latin, and Hebrew alphabets thus: A and Z, Aleph and Tau (את), Alpha and Omega (AΩ). It is used with various meanings by different writers, but for the most part it symbolizes the beginning and the end, or rather the *Essence. Azoth* is considered the Universal Medicine of Alchemy, or the universal remedy said to contain within itself all other medicines. The term is oftentimes used for Alchemic Mercury, and some consider Azoth to be a living essence or Spirit, containing a Soul.

In addition to the Sephiroth on the Tree of Life, many other concepts and names occur in Qabalistic writings. These include what are known as the *Three Veils of Negative Existence*. They are:

AIN (אין): which means "Negativity," "Nothing," or "Not." Ain is the outermost Veil.

AIN SOPH (אין סוף): or "Limitless." Ain Soph is the middle Veil. Ain Soph is the vessel that contains the Ain.

AIN SOPH AUR (אין סוף אור): or "the Limitless Light." The Innermost Veil from which the Sephirah of Kether was formed. Ain Soph Aur is the restricted Light which is the result of the junction of Ain and Ain Soph.

The idea of the *Three Negative Veils* is a concept that defies human attempts to describe the Veils as *something*. They are planes of existence which lie outside of all human realms of experience. Humankind naturally thinks in terms of "some-things" rather than "nothings." We simply cannot understand these Veils in terms of anything we can compare them to. The student is reminded of yet another polarity of the Qabalah—just as the Light cannot exist with Darkness, "some-thing" cannot exist without "nothing." Ain is truly the only constant in the universe, it has always been, and will always be. "Somethings" always need a point of beginning, even the highest sphere of Kether. The Limitless Nothing, on the other hand, has always existed. All of creation springs from and returns to it. It is the calm silence—the Limitless Light of being—infinity. These unmanifested Veils of negativity contain within themselves the seeds of positive existence and the manifest universe as we know it. This negativity can be symbolized by the Greek letters Alpha and Omega, the beginning and the end.

That being stated at the outset, we will attempt the impossible—to describe the Veils in terms that the reader can relate to. The main characteristic of the Veil of Ain is to give or bestow of its own essence. Thus the Veil of Ain is said to be a masculine/positive aspect of God which seeks to stimulate or impart of its own essential Light.

The attribute of Ain Soph, the feminine/negative aspect of God is to take in the Light. Ain Soph is said to be the perfect vessel which seeks to receive and contain the Light in order to bestow it. The Ain Soph suppressed her desire to receive the Light in order to transmit the Light. Thus the Ain Soph formed into an empty circle which was surrounded by a circle of Light. A shaft of the Light penetrated the empty circle to its center, resulting in a succession of concentric circles which marked the divisions of creation. The primary point of Light formed at the center of Ain Soph is Ain Soph Aur, the Limitless Light from which the universe was created. In Lurianic Qabalah,[121] the creation of Kether is said to have come from a process of *zimzum* or "contraction" of the Ain Soph from the surrounding Light—not unlike an empty set of lungs inhaling to gather in and contain (and therefore limit) the surrounding air.

ADAM KADMON (אדם קדמון): From the Light point of Ain Soph Aur the "Body" of the Divine was formed—the primordial man that preceded all other primordials. This is *Adam Kadmon*, the "archetypal man" or prototype of humanity which is circumscribed on the Tree of Life. Kether, the crown is above his head, and Malkuth is at his feet. This *divine human* contains the essence of YHVH, for Yod of the Four-Lettered Name is symbolized by the head of Adam Kadmon, the letter Heh alludes to the arms and shoulders, the letter Vav refers to the torso, and Heh Sophith is attributed to the legs and feet.

Conceived prior to the world of Atziluth, Adam Kadmon was the first of four reflections of the Eternal which become manifest as existence evolved from the Divine to the Material. He is an intervening link between the Ain Soph and the order of Qabalistic Worlds yet to come into manifestation. Adam Kadmon is the consciousness of the Divine, containing within himself everything that is needed to create the manifest universe as a reflection of the divine universe. He contains within his being Will (Atziluth), Intellect (Briah), Emotion (Yetzirah) and Assiah (the capacity for action). Adam Kadmon is the mirror of reflection that is used by the Divine to *experience itself* through the Four Worlds of the Qabalah, for only a descent into all four Worlds will enable the Divine to apperceive all aspects of divinity. However, once Adam Kadmon descends into the Active World of Manifestation, he must be reflected back to the original Atziluthic Source. The body of Adam Kadmon on the Sephiroth of the Tree of Life is a larger reflection of the human body superimposed on the spheres of the Tree. (Therefore the Pillar of Mercy is located at Adam Kadmon's right-hand side and the Pillar of Severity at his left-hand side. When applying the Tree of Life to your own body, a *reflection* of the Godhead is achieved. The Pillar of Mercy is on your left side while the Pillar of Severity is on your right.)

The Qabalistic restriction of the Divine Light into spheres which made up the body of Adam Kadmon was for the purpose of the creation of humanity. But the Light was still too potent to fulfill that purpose. Thus the Light was divided into Four Worlds, each world successively veiled from the one which preceded it. (Review Chapter Two for information on the Four Worlds of the Qabalah.)

---

[121] Named after Rabbi Isaac Luria.

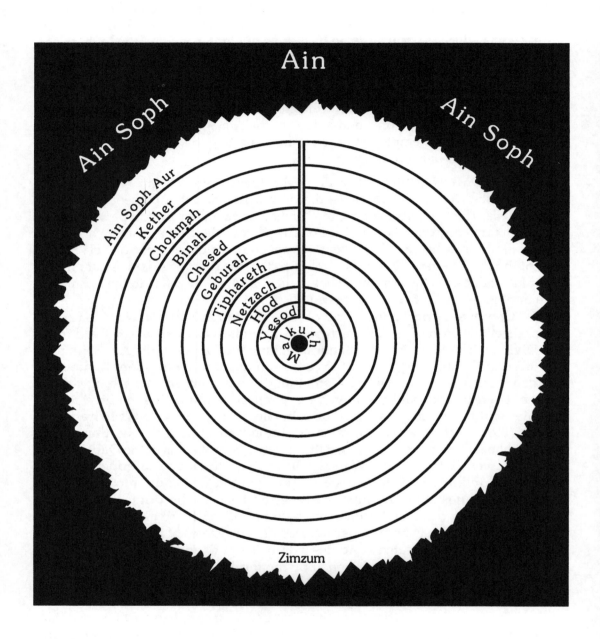

Concentric Sephiroth

THE BREAKING OF THE VESSELS: The Breaking of the Vessels is another version of the Fall of the Garden of Eden (as espoused by Lurianic Qabalah). This event corresponds to the destruction of the initial, failed worlds of the previous Qabalah—the universe of Chaos or *Tohu*. According to the tradition, there are two aspects of the emanation of the Divine Light. One is linear, in the form of the body of Adam Kadmon, (or the glyph of the Tree of Life as we know it). The second is circular, wherein the Sephiroth took form within Adam Kadmon in a series of concentric circles. The outermost circle was Kether, which abided in close proximity to the encompassing circle of Ain Soph Aur. At this early stage the Sephiroth were not yet separate, but bound together as a series of Lights or Points. These Sephirotic Lights were then given "vessels" or fields of containment, in which to organize their substance and operations.

What occurred next was what is called the "Breaking of the Vessels" or "the death of the Kings." The vessels of containment belonging to the three Supernal Sephiroth were sturdy enough to receive the Divine Light issuing into them, but the force of the Light was unstable and lacked direction. When the Light struck the next six spheres from Chesed to Yesod, it did so with such potency that the vessels shattered one by one, sending fragments falling. The vessel of Malkuth also cracked but did not shatter.

Some of the Light returned to its source, but the remainder of it was propelled down along with the broken vessels. The shattered pieces of the vessels became the Qlippoth and the origins of gross matter. The Light which was trapped by the Qlippoth, supplied the lifeforce and substance for the Qlippotic realm, which affected all but the Supernal realms after the breaking of the Vessels.

One of the most serious consequences of the devastating pressure of the Light shattering the Vessels was that every level of World below the Supernals dropped downward from its normal location. (The death of the Edomite kings in Genesis is said to refer to the breaking of the Vessels and their consequent fall to a lower level.) Nothing was to remain in its proper position. The World of Assiah, the Active World has plunged into and intermingled with the lowest abodes of the Qlippoth. The universal process became at odds with its former order.

One of the explanations as to why the Vessels shattered is that in this stage of *Tohu*, the primitive Sephiroth could receive the Light of the Divine as Vessels, but being simple points of emanation, they could neither give back Light nor interact with each other. In this way, they could not resemble the Divine and consequently were incomplete. Thus they were unable to hold the Light of the Divine, were overwhelmed by the Light, and shattered. The reason that these unstable Vessels were created in the first place (according to Lurianic tradition) was so that Evil should come into being. This would supply humanity with the freedom to choose; something which is prerequisite for the restoration of the Vessels. In addition, because Evil emanated from the first and highest of the Vessels, it can be reconstructed and restored to this level.

PARTZUFIM (פרצופים): There is a teaching in the *Zohar* (or Qabalistic *Book of Splendor*) that divides the Sephiroth into five archetypal countenances. The word *partzufim*

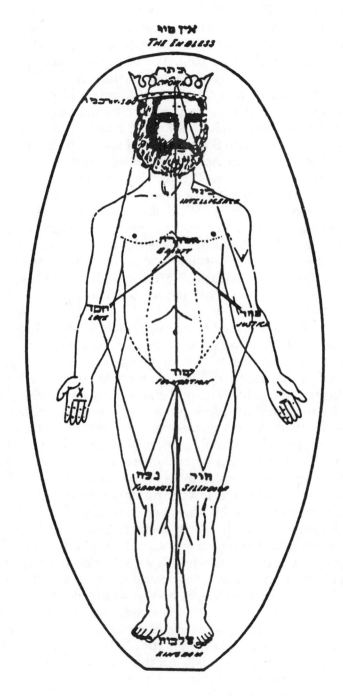

Adam Kadmon, The Body of God

means "faces" (singular—*partzuf*). It refers to five forces or archetypal personas which take the place of the Sephiroth as the primary manifestations of Adam Kadmon after the "Breaking of the Vessels." After the "Breaking," the Vessels were then reconstructed and rebuilt into the "Faces." This constituted the *Universe of Rectification* which replaced the *Universe of Chaos*. The Partzufim include Arik Anpin, Abba, Aima, Zauir Anpin and Nukba de-Zauir (also known as Malkah).[122] These five points are centers of force through which the creative energy of the Divine is able to operate and manifest. These five also establish the final form of Adam Kadmon after the Breaking of the Vessels—a form that is very different from the figure of the "archetypal man" that existed prior to the Fall. The partzufim constitute the World of Atziluth, which is reflected into the three lower Worlds. Most importantly, the partzufim were strong enough to contain the Light which had shattered the previous Vessels. They were able to both give and to receive Light. These "faces" resembled humanity and were able to interact with each other in an anthropomorphic fashion.

ARIK ANPIN (אריך אנפין): meaning the "Vast Countenance" or the "Greater Countenance" (literally "long faced"). Also known as *Macroprosopus*. One of the titles of Kether. Other titles of Kether include *Aatik Yomin* (עתיך יומין), the "Ancient of Days," and *Aatik Qadosh* (עתיך קדוש), "the Holy Ancient One."

ABBA (אבבא): Kether or the Vast Countenance emanates first as *Abba* the Supernal Father, and *Aima*, the Supernal Mother. Abba the Supernal Father is referred to the Hebrew letter Yod of Tetragrammaton. Abba is associated with the Sephirah Chokmah.

AIMA (אימא): The Supernal Mother, *Aima*, is referred to the letter Heh. Aima is attributed to the Sephirah of Binah. Abba and Aima function as a dual potential. They perform as models of differentiation which divide all emanations into either active or passive, stimulating or receiving, masculine or feminine. *Elohim* is a name given to these two beings united.

ZAUIR ANPIN (זעיר אנפין): Literally "short faced." Also called *Microprosopus* or the Lesser Countenance. Zauir Anpin is the son of the Elohim, Abba and Aima. The son represents a "birth" into the lower worlds of manifestation below the Supernals. Zauir Anpin corresponds to the six Sephiroth of Chesed, Geburah, Tiphareth, Netzach, Hod, and Yesod; and of these especially to Tiphareth. It is also associated with the letter Vav of Tetragrammaton. This partzuf is central to the process of restoring the Tree of Life to its original state before the Fall.

NUKBA DE-ZAUIR (נקבה דזעיר): Literally the "Female of Zauir." This partzuf symbolized the female counterpart of Zauir Anpin. Additional titles of this "face" include Malkah and Kalah: **MALKAH** (מלכה)"the Queen" and **KALAH** (כלה) "the Bride." These are titles of the Sephirah Malkuth, which is considered the spouse of the Microprosopus. It is also referred to Heh Sophith of Tetragrammaton.

---

[122] Some sources refer to a total of seven Partzufim, including two which are referred to the upper level of Kether, *Aatik Qadosh* and *Aatik Yomin*; while *Arik Anpin* is sometimes considered the lower part of Kether.

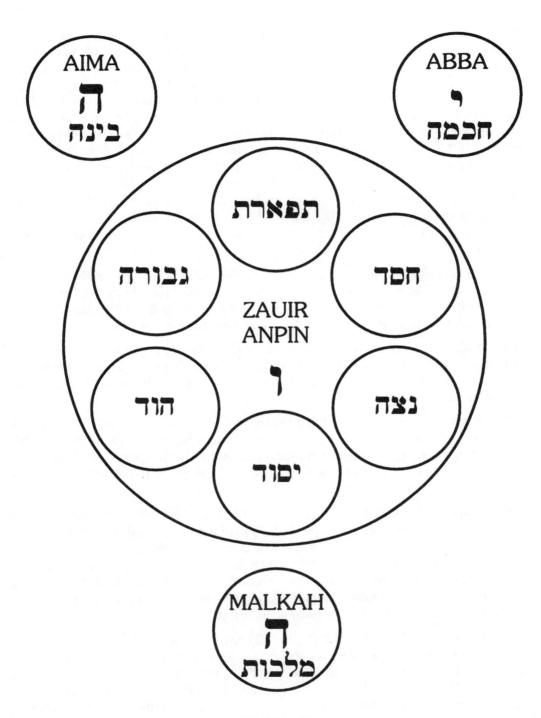

The Partzufim

TIKKUN (תקון): which means "redemption" is the restoration of the universe to its primal purity and design—it is the correction of the confusion and chaos that was the outcome of the breaking of the Vessels. The creation of the partzufim (faces) which introduced a new pattern of dynamics to the Tree of Life, is a part of the process of tikkun, a process of cleansing and reconstruction of the Tree. The Divine Light from Atziluth (the world of the partzufim) is passed down into the other worlds and altered or filtered as it descends. The full potency of the Light is modified on its descent. Thus the process of tikkun is commenced, but it can only be completed by humanity. The human task is to restore the system of the Tree of Life by restoring the World of Assiah, the physical world, to its original state of spirituality—to remove it from the realm of the Qlippoth and permit a state of ultimate unity to exist between every being and the Divine, uninterrupted by the Qlippoth. This task is an inner spiritual cleansing which every human being must strive for.

Qabalistic Correspondences

The *Secret Names* of the Four Qabalistic Worlds were given in Chapter Two. These names are based upon numerical correspondences: Atziluth—*Ab* (עב)—72, Briah—*Seg* (סג)—63, Yetzirah—*Mah* (מה)—45, Assiah—*Ben* (בן)—52. These four realms are ones that eventually manifest in the four letters of the Name, in the four lower "faces" of Atziluth in the body of Adam Kadmon, and finally, in the Four Worlds themselves.

The Letter Tau: In each of the Four Worlds are the Ten Sephiroth of that World, and each Sephirah has its own ten Sephiroth, making 400 Sephiroth in all—the number of the Hebrew letter Tau, the cross, the universe, the completion of all things. (This helps to explain why the Zelator grade is referred to Malkuth of Malkuth, and Theoricus to Yesod of Malkuth, etc.)

The Seven Palaces: The ten Sephiroth are combined into what are known as the Seven Palaces (*Sheva Hekhaloth*) of Briah. The First Palace contains the Three Supernal Sephiroth. The Second Palace consists of Chesed, the Third—Geburah, the Fourth—Tiphareth, the Fifth—Netzach, the Sixth—Hod, and the Seventh contains Yesod and Malkuth. By assigning the ten Sephiroth to Seven Palaces, the energies of the Sephiroth may be differentiated along the lines of Planetary energies, since the Seven Palaces correspond to the Seven Planets of the ancients.

This can be likened to the Macrocosmic Hexagram whose uppermost point is assigned to Saturn (or the Supernals of the First Palace which are generally grouped together and symbolized by the sphere of Binah reflected through Daath). The lowest point of the Hexagram is attributed to Luna (or the Seventh Palace containing Yesod and Malkuth).

The Seven Palaces also correspond to the Tree of the Knowledge of Good and of Evil, for upper seven branches relate to the Seven Heavens in Assiah, and the lower seven branches refer to the Seven Qlippotic Palaces.

The Trinity on the Tree: The Trinity operates through the Sephiroth and is reflected downward in the four triangles of the Elements. Air is reflected from Kether through Tiphareth to Yesod. Water is reflected from Binah through Chesed to

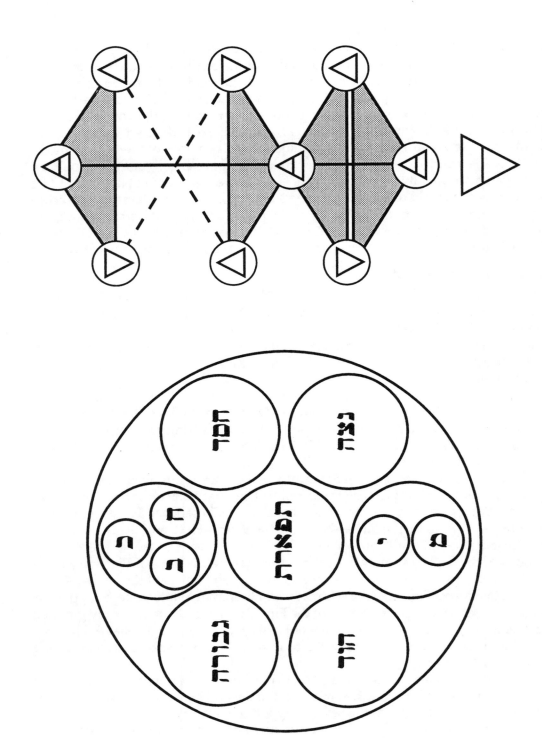

The Trinity operating through the Sephiroth

The Seven Palaces attributed to the Sephiroth

The Serpent of Brass

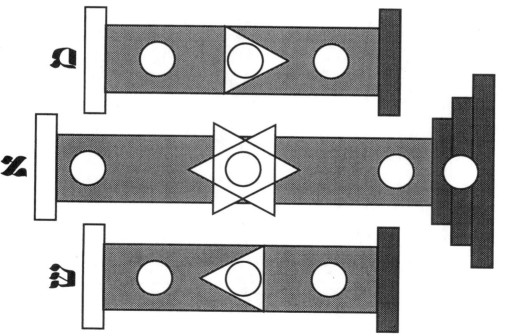

The Tablet of Three Columns

The Image of Nebuchadnezzar

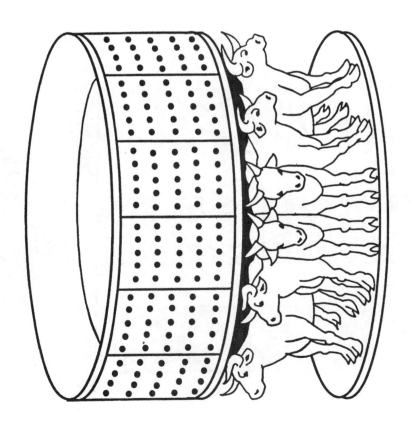

The Brazen Sea

Hod. Fire is reflected from Chokmah through Geburah to Netzach, while Earth is Malkuth, the receptacle of the other Three.

The Serpent of Brass: The Serpent *Nehushtan*, which Moses made when the Children of Israel were bitten by Serpents of Fire in the Wilderness, is the Serpent of the paths of the Tree. And he set it on a pole—that is, twined it round the Middle Pillar of the Sephiroth. And the word used in the passage in *Numbers 21* for "Fiery Serpents" is the same as the Name of the Angels of Geburah, the same spelling, the same pointing, *Seraphim.* Round the Middle Pillar of the Sephiroth, because that is the Reconciler between the Fires of Geburah or Severity, and the Waters of Chesed or Mercy—and hence it is said in the New

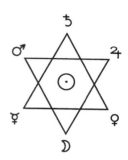

The Macrocosmic Hexagram

Testament that it is a type of Christ, the Reconciler. And the Serpent is of Brass, the Metal of Venus, whose sphere is called *Nogah,* or External Splendor, as shown further by the Alchemical Symbol of Venus, wherein the Circle of the Sun is exalted above the Cross of Corrosion. And therefore it is said in the *Zohar* that "Alone of the Shells is the Serpent Nogah found in Holiness" and he is called the Balance of Justice. Why, then, is he called the External or False Splendor? Because he indeed uniteth the Paths, but comprehendeth not the Sephiroth. Nevertheless, he is also the Celestial Serpent of Wisdom. But the Serpent of the Temptation is the Serpent of the Tree of Knowledge of Good and of Evil, and not that of the Tree of Life. The Celestial Serpent is green and gold, colors which indicate growth and vegetation. Its antithesis is the stooping dragon or serpent of the Qlippoth which is red, the color of destruction.

The Hexagram of Tiphareth: The formation of the *Macrocosmic Hexagram* is from the pillars on each side of the Tree of Life. (See the Diagram of the Tablet of Three Columns.) The Water triangle is from the side of Chesed, while the Fire triangle is from the side of Geburah. In Tiphareth, these two triangles are combined and reconciled in the figure of the Hexagram. Just as the Hebrew letter Aleph is the reconciling force between Mem (Water) and Shin (Fire), the central pillar of the Tree stands, unites and mediates between the pillars of Fire and Cloud (the pillars of Jachin and Boaz of King Solomon's temple).

The Brazen Sea: The Brazen Sea which stood in the courtyard of Solomon's temple was a total of ten cubits in diameter, alluding to the ten Sephiroth, and 5 cubits in height, a reference to the Hebrew letter Heh. Its curcumference was 30 cubits—the number of the Sephiroth multiplied by the Triad. Beneath the rim of the vessel were 300 knobs or rounded protrusions, referring to the number of the letter Shin (spirit) and the name of *Ruach Elohim,* the Spirit of God. It stood upon 12 oxen, representing the 12 Signs of the Zodiac, and the 12 stars upon the crown of Aima Elohim, the Great Mother. The whole of it is a synthesis of Binah, containing the Waters of Creation.

The Image of Nebuchadnezzar: Representing the prophetic dream of the Babylonian king, Nebuchadnezzar. The head of the figure is gold, the breast and arms are silver, the thighs and belly are brass, the legs are iron, and the feet are partially iron and partially clay. The hands hold the symbols of the hot and the moist Natures respectively.✿

SECTION 2: The Shem Ha-Mephoresh:

The *Shem Ha-Mephoresh* (שם המפרש) or "Divided Name" refers to the seventy-two fold Name of God, or to be exact, the seventy-two Names of the Expounded Name of the Tetragrammaton, YHVH. It is a divine name of 216 letters derived from the Book of Exodus 14:19-21. Each of these three verses from Exodus contains seventy-two letters which are then organized (by boustrophedon) to generate the seventy-two syllables of the Name. In due time the Shem Ha-Mephoresh was condensed into the letters of the Tetragrammaton.

The verses involved read as follows:

> **19th Verse:** *And the Angel of the Elohim, that went before the camp of Israel, removed and went behind them; and the pillar of cloud removed from before them and stood behind them.*

> **20th Verse:** *And it came between the camp of the Egyptians and the camp of Israel; and it was a cloud and darkness (to the first) but it gave light by night (to these); and the one came not near unto the other all the night.*

> **21st Verse:** *And Moses stretched out his hand over the sea, and the Lord drove back the sea with a strong east wind all that night and made the sea dry land, and the waters divided.*

The names are obtained by writing these three verses in Hebrew with alternating lines in opposing directions. In other words, the verses are to be written out one above the other, the first verse from right to left, the second verse from left to right, and the third from right to left.[123] The result is seventy-two columns of three letters apiece. The seventy-two names are thought of as expansions of YHVH; they are separated under four groupings of eighteen letters. Each group (read from top to bottom) corresponds to one of the letters of Tetragrammaton:

In assigning the decanates of the Zodiac to the names of the Shem Ha-Mephoresh (as well as the Tarot) the Golden Dawn system assigns the first decanate to the Sign of Leo. Thus in the list that follows, the first column of names derived from the three verses of Exodus is to be found in the grouping of HEH (Water) under the Sign of Leo. The reason for this is explained in a paper by Mathers entitled "The Tree of Life as Projected in a Solid Sphere."[124]

---

[123] It is also possible to construct 72 such Names out of the three required verses by writing them all in the same direction, or by using any of the methods described by Temurah. However, the meanings of the Names as derived from the Psalms remain the same.

[124] "Another very important difference is that, throughout the true Tarot, the teaching assigns the commencing Point of the Zodiac to the bright Star "Regulus" which is in Leo. And it measures Right Ascension and Longitude from that point, and not from a suppositious point divided by the Equinox and called the 0° of Aries (though in reality now far removed from the constellation of that name), which has been adopted by modern or Western Astronomy and Astrology. By this now usual way of reckoning, and the Procession of the Equinoxes, it has gradually come to pass that the signs (or divisions, each of 30°, of the Zodiac) no longer coincide with the constellations of the same name, and

The Shem Ha-Mephoresh is also sometimes referred to as the "seventy-two leaves of the Tree of Life," the "healing leaves," or the "divided name of Zauir Anpin," the Microprosopus.

From the seventy-two names of the deity, seventy-two Angels bearing these divine names are formed by adding the suffix *Yod Heh* (יה—*iah*) or the suffix *Aleph Lamed* (אל—*al*) to the end of the Name. *Iah* signifies mercy and beneficence, whereas *al* embodies severity and judgment. Each deity Name contains three letters,[125] while each Angelic Name formed therefrom has five letters.

Each of these Angels also rules over one of the seventy-two quinances (or sets of 5⁰ divisions) of the Zodiac. Two quinances are contained in each decanate (or sets of 10⁰ divisions) of a Zodiacal Sign,

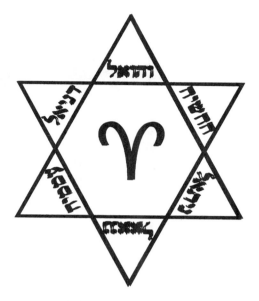

*Aries Hexagram Talisman
with Angelic Names*

therefore each of the Signs has six of these Angelic names associated with it. The number seventy-two is also equal to the total number of Zodiacal Signs (twelve) multiplied by the number six, the number of Angels assigned to each Sign. Thus each sign and its corresponding Angelic names can be symbolized in the form of a hexagram. (Each angle of the hexagram represents one of the Angelic names, while the sigil of the Sign itself is to be placed in the center.)

The wheel of the Zodiac is equal to 360⁰. This number divided by five yields 72⁰ which is the angle of degrees that exist between each point of a pentagram.

These seventy-two Angels are divided into groups of nine sets of eight, each associated with one of the nine choirs of Angels of the Sephiroth.[126] These Angels are also grouped under the four Elemental divisions of the Tetragrammaton. The first three Signs beginning with Kerubic Fire (Leo, Virgo, Libra) are referred to *Yod*—Fire. The second triad of Signs (Scorpio, Sagittarius, Capricorn) falls under the Presidency of *Heh*—Water. The third division (Aquarius, Pisces, Aries) is allotted to *Vav*—Air. The final three Signs (Taurus, Gemini, Cancer) are referred to *Heh*

---

each decade of years shows them slowly but surely receding. But the Tarot method of reckoning from the star named Regulus has, it will be seen, the effect of making the Signs and the Constellations coincide.

Regulus is also named *Cor Leonis*—'The Heart of the Lion.' *Regulus* means 'Star of the Prince.' *Regulus* coincides with the position of the *heart* in the figure of Leo upon the Star Maps."— from a paper by MacGregor Mathers published in *The Golden Dawn* by Israel Regardie. This shows that much of the esoteric Astrology taught in the Golden Dawn is based on a fixed Sidereal rather than Tropical Astrology. There is evidence to support the view that in parts of ancient Egypt, this Astrological method (beginning with 0⁰ Leo) was employed.

[125] It should be noted that Gimel (3) is the only letter not used in the Shem Ha-Mephoresh.

[126] Minus the Choir of Angels associated with Kether.

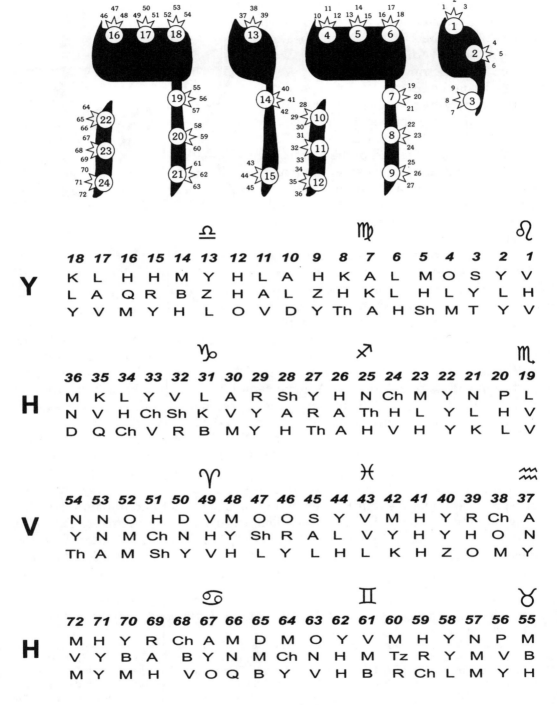

♎   ♍   ♌

	18	17	16	15	14	13	12	11	10	9	8	7	6	5	4	3	2	1
Y	K	L	H	H	M	Y	H	L	A	H	K	A	L	M	O	S	Y	V
	L	A	Q	R	B	Z	H	A	L	Z	H	K	L	H	L	Y	L	H
	Y	V	M	Y	H	L	O	V	D	Y	Th	A	H	Sh	M	T	Y	V

♑   ♐   ♏

	36	35	34	33	32	31	30	29	28	27	26	25	24	23	22	21	20	19
H	M	K	L	Y	V	L	A	R	Sh	Y	H	N	Ch	M	Y	N	P	L
	N	V	H	Ch	Sh	K	V	Y	A	R	A	Th	H	L	Y	L	H	V
	D	Q	Ch	V	R	B	M	Y	H	Th	A	H	V	H	Y	K	L	V

♈   ♓   ♒

	54	53	52	51	50	49	48	47	46	45	44	43	42	41	40	39	38	37
V	N	N	O	H	D	V	M	O	O	S	Y	V	M	H	Y	R	Ch	A
	Y	N	M	Ch	N	H	Y	Sh	R	A	L	V	Y	H	Y	H	O	N
	Th	A	M	Sh	Y	V	H	L	Y	L	H	L	K	H	Z	O	M	Y

♋   ♊   ♉

	72	71	70	69	68	67	66	65	64	63	62	61	60	59	58	57	56	55
H	M	H	Y	R	Ch	A	M	D	M	O	Y	V	M	H	Y	N	P	M
	V	Y	B	A	B	Y	N	M	Ch	N	H	M	Tz	R	Y	M	V	B
	M	Y	M	H	V	O	Q	B	Y	V	H	B	R	Ch	L	M	Y	H

The Seventy-two Names of the Shem ha-Mephoresh

Sophith—Earth. However the most potent rule of the letter *Yod* is over the Zodiacal Triplicity of Fire, the rule of *Heh* is most powerful over the Triplicity of Water, *Vav* governs the Air Triplicity, while *Heh Sophith* rules over the Triplicity of Earth.

A special relationship exists between the Tetragrammaton and the Shem Ha-Mephoresh, which is truly an expanded form of YHVH. In the previous chapter, the Name IAHDVNHY (a combination of YHVH with ADNI) was described. The number of letters in this name totals eight. This number multiplied by three, the number of the Supernals yields twenty-four, a significant number:

> *And round about the throne were four and twenty seats: and upon the seats I saw four and twenty elders sitting, clothed in white rainment; and they had on their heads crowns of gold. (Rev. 4:4)*

The Elders of Apocalypse were twenty-four in number, and each was equipped with a golden three-pointed crown. Each point of the crown signified a name or ruling principle of the Tetragrammaton. The three crown-points multiplied by the number of Elders yields seventy-two, the hidden and expanded name of YHVH. The meanings of the divine and Angelic names of the Shem Ha-Mephoresh are derived from those Biblical verses of the Psalms in which the name of the Tetragrammaton appears.[127]

The 72 Names of The Shem Ha-Mephoresh

Divine 3 Letters	Angel	Meaning	Sign	Decan	YHVH Letter	Tarot Card
1. VHV	*Vahaviah*	God the Exalter	♌	Saturn	Y	5 Wands
2. YLY	*Yelayel*	Strength	♌	Saturn	Y	
3. SYT	*Sitael*	Refuge, fortress	♌	Jupiter	Y	6 Wands
4. OLM	*Almiah*	Concealed, strong	♌	Jupiter	Y	
5. MHSh	*Mahashiah*	Seeking safety	♌	Mars	Y	7 Wands
6. LLH	*Lelahel*	Praiseworthy, declaring his works	♌	Mars	Y	
7. AKA	*Akayah*	Long suffering	♍	Sol	Y	8 Pent.
8. KHTh	*Kehethel*	Adorable	♍	Sol	Y	
9. HZY	*Haziel*	Merciful	♍	Venus	Y	9 Pent.
10. ALD	*Eldayah*	Profitable	♍	Venus	Y	
11. LAV	*Laviah*	To be exalted	♍	Mercury	Y	10 Pent.
12. HHO	*Hihaayah*	Refuge	♍	Mercury	Y	
13. YZL	*Yezalel*	Rejoicing over	♎	Luna	Y	2 Swords
14. MBH	*Mebahel*	Guardian, preserver	♎	Luna	Y	
15. HRY	*Hariel*	Aid	♎	Saturn	Y	3 Swords

---

[127] With the exception of the 70th Name.

16.	HQM	*Haqamiah*	Raise up, praying day and night	♎	Saturn	Y	
17.	LAW	*Levayah*	Wonderful	♎	Jupiter	Y	4 Swords
18.	KLY	*Keliel*	Worthy to be invoked	♎	Jupiter	Y	
19.	LVV	*Luvayah*	Hastening to hear	♏	Mars	H	5 Cups
20.	PHL	*Phaheliah*	Redeemer, liberator	♏	Mars	H	
21.	NLK	*Nelakhel*	Thou alone	♏	Sol	H	6 Cups
22.	YYY	*Yeyayel*	Thy right hand	♏	Sol	H	
23.	MLH	*Melohel*	Turning away evil	♏	Venus	H	7 Cups
24.	ChHV	*Chahaviah*	Goodness in himself	♏	Venus	H	
25.	NThH	*Nethahiah*	Wide in extent, the enlarger, wonderful	♐	Mercury	H	8 Wands
26.	HAA	*Haayah*	Heaven in Secret	♐	Mercury	H	
27.	YRTh	*Yerathel*	Deliverer	♐	Luna	H	9 Wands
28.	ShAH	*Saahiah*	Taker away of evils	♐	Luna	H	
29.	RYY	*Reyayel*	Expectation	♐	Saturn	H	10 Wands
30.	AVM	*Umael*	Patient	♐	Saturn	H	
31.	LKB	*Lekhabel*	Teacher, instructor	♑	Jupiter	H	2 Pent.
32.	VShR	*Veshiriah*	Upright	♑	Jupiter	H	
33.	YChV	*Yechaviah*	Knower of all things	♑	Mars	H	3 Pent.
34.	LHCh	*Lehachiah*	Clement, merciful	♑	Mars	H	
35.	KVQ	*Kuqiah*	To be rejoiced in	♑	Sol	H	4 Pent.
36.	MND	*Menadel*	Honorable	♑	Sol	H	
37.	ANY	*Eniel*	Lord of Virtues	♒	Venus	V	5 Swords
38.	ChOM	*Chaamiah*	The hope of all the ends of the earth	♒	Venus	V	
39.	RHO	*Rehael*	Swift to condone	♒	Mercury	V	6 Swords
40.	YYZ	*Yeyezel*	Making joyful	♒	Mercury	V	
41.	HHH	*Hehahel*	Triune	♒	Luna	V	7 Swords
42.	MYK	*Mayakhel*	Who is like unto him	♒	Luna	V	
43.	VVL	*Vuliah*	King and ruler	♓	Saturn	V	8 Cups
44.	YLH	*Yelahiah*	Abiding forever	♓	Saturn	V	
45.	SAL	*Saaliah*	Mover of all things	♓	Jupiter	V	9 Cups
46.	ORY	*Eriel*	Revealer	♓	Jupiter	V	
47.	OShL	*Esheliah*	Just judge	♓	Mars	V	10 Cups
48.	MYH	*Mayahel*	Sending forth as a father	♓	Mars	V	
49.	VHV	*Vehuel*	Great and Lofty	♈	Mars	V	2 Wands
50.	DNY	*Deniel*	Merciful	♈	Mars	V	
51.	HChSh	*Hechashiah*	Secret and impenetrable	♈	Sol	V	3 Wands
52.	OMM	*Amemiah*	Covered in darkness	♈	Sol	V	
53.	NNA	*Nanael*	Caster down of the proud	♈	Venus	V	4 Wands

54.	NYTh	*Nithael*	Celestial King	♈	Venus	V	
55.	MBH	*Mibahayah*	Eternal	♉	Mercury	Hs	5 Pent.
56.	PVY	*Puyael*	Supporting all things	♉	Mercury	Hs	
57.	NMM	*Nemamiah*	Lovable	♉	Luna	Hs	6 Pent.
58.	YYL	*Yeyelel*	Hearer of cries	♉	Luna	Hs	
59.	HRCh	*Herachel*	Permeating all things	♉	Saturn	Hs	7 Pent.
60.	MTzR	*Mitzrael*	Raising up the oppressed	♉	Saturn	Hs	
61.	VMB	*Vembael*	The name which is over all	♊	Jupiter	Hs	8 Swords
62.	YHH	*Yahohel*	The supreme ends, or essence	♊	Jupiter	Hs	
63.	ONV	*Anuel*	Rejoicing	♊	Mars	Hs	9 Swords
64.	MChY	*Machiel*	Vivifying	♊	Mars	Hs	
65.	DMB	*Dambayah*	Fountain of wisdom	♊	Sol	Hs	10 Swords
66.	MNQ	*Meneqel*	Nourishing all	♊	Sol	Hs	
67.	AYO	*Ayael*	Delights of the sons of men	♋	Venus	Hs	2 Cups
68.	ChBW	*Chavuyah*	Most liberal giver	♋	Venus	Hs	
69.	RAH	*Raahel*	Beholding all	♋	Mercury	Hs	3 Cups
70.	YBM	*Yebemiah*	Producing by his word	♋	Mercury	Hs	
71.	HYY	*Hayayel*	Lord of the universe	♋	Luna	Hs	4 Cups
72.	MVM	*Mumiah*	End of the universe	♋	Luna	Hs	

PART 3: Correspondences of Netzach

The Philosophus grade is attributed to the sphere of Netzach on the Qabalistic Tree of Life. Netzach is the seventh Sephirah on the Tree and the third sphere encountered by the aspirant. It is the sphere of emotion, passions, the Element of Fire, god-images, the creative arts, and the group mind. (Review all information on Netzach given in Chapter One.)

Name in English: Victory
Divine (Atziluthic) Name: YHVH Tzabaoth
Archangel (Briatic) Name: Haniel
Angelic (Yetziratic) Choir: Elohim
Planet or House of Assiah: Nogah (Venus)
Spiritual experience: Vision of Beauty Triumphant
Qabalistic Number: Seven
Color (Briatic): Green
Element: Fire

Part of Anatomy: Left hip
Tarot cards: The four Sevens
Magical Image: A beautiful naked woman
Incense: Benzoin, rose, red sandal
Gemstone: Emerald
Symbols: Lamp, girdle, rose
Lineal Figure: Heptagram
Virtue: Unselfishness
Vice: Lust

SECTION 4: Correspondences of Fire

Fire symbolizes the active and stimulating part of the human psyche. It is the Element of passion, purification and transcendence. Fire is masculine, regenerating, exciting and transforming. The color given for Fire is red, and the cardinal point is South. (Review all information on the Element of Fire given in Chapter One.) Candles colored in the various Planetary, Sephirotic and Zodiacal pigments are often used in ritual to attract those forces with the aid of the potent and invigorating energy of Fire.

Hebrew and Other Names Connected with Fire

Element Name: Asch (אש)
Outer Divine Name: YHVH Tzabaoth (יהוה צבאות)
Cardinal Point: Darom (South) (דרום)
Archangel: Michael (מיכאל)
Angel: Ariel (אריאל)
Ruler: Seraph (שרף)
Elementals: Salamanders
King of Salamanders: Djin

MICHAEL (Specifically *Michael Ashel*): is the great winged Archangel of Elemental Fire, whose name means "Perfect One of God." Stationed in the South, Michael is visualized as a masculine Archangel dressed in robes or armor of red and green. He stands in the attitude of a warrior amid flames. Bearing either a sword or a spear as both a weapon and a symbol of masculine Fire energy, Michael is the vanquisher of evil and protector of humanity.

ARYEH: The name of the Kerub of Fire symbolized by the Zodiacal Sign of Leo. Aryeh is visualized as a powerful winged sphinx-like figure with a human body and a lion's head. His colors are primarily red and green.

Beings and Deities of Fire:

NUSKU: An Assyro-Babylonian Fire god. Nusku's symbol was a lamp shaped like a wooden clog. He represented the sacred Fire which consumed offerings made to the gods and made possible the burning of the sacred incense. Invoked during sacrifices, Nusku was also known as "Bel's sublime messenger." **GIBIL** was another Fire god who together with Nusku sometimes dispensed justice upon the wicked in the form of a purging Fire. Gibil was often invoked by sorcerers who wished to destroy their enemies. A variation of this god is **BILKAN**, who might have some connection with the Biblical *Tubal Cain* and the Roman god *Vulcan*. He was a potent Fire deity who was invoked often in spells.

Bast

SEKHET (or **SEKHMET**): An Egyptian goddess of war and battle. Her name means "the powerful." She is represented as a woman with the head of a lioness and she was known as "the beloved of Ptah." Sekhet personified the burning, Fiery and destructive heat of the sun in late summer. Sekhet and the goddess *Bast* worked together to destroy the enemies of the Sun god *Re*. Her lust for battle was so extreme that Re had to restrain her from killing off the human race.

BAST: An Egyptian Fire goddess who symbolized the mild heat of early summer which encouraged the growth of vegetation and the germination of seeds. She was originally depicted as a woman with the greenish head of a lioness, but later she was portrayed as cat-headed. The goddess holds in her right-hand a sistrum and in her left hand a basket. Although she was associated with Sekhet as a fiery defender of Re, the sun god, she later became associated with the Moon and with the ideas of pleasure, music and dance. Joyous festivals were held in her honor.

HERU-BEHUTET: One of the most important forms of Horus (many of which are associated with Fire and heat.) Heru-Behutet personified the most powerful heat of the sun at midday. Usually depicted as a man with the head of a hawk and carrying a club or spear, this god has sometimes been portrayed as a lion or lion-headed. He was the warrior god who battled the evil god *Set* or *Typhon*, slayer of Osiris. Called "smiter of the rebel," Heru-Behutet symbolizes the power which dispels evil and darkness and fills the world with brilliant Light.

Ptah

MONT (or **MENTHU**): A Solar war god of Egypt who symbolized the destructive heat of the Sun. Mont is generally represented as man with a hawk's (or a bull's) head surmounted by the Solar disk and two tall plumes. His attributes are the *khepesh* or curved sword used to vanquish the enemies of the Pharaoh. Mont was the supreme Solar god until he was "demoted" to second in rank by the god Amon.

PTAH: One of the oldest known of the Egyptian deities. His name means "sculptor, engraver" and he is associated with metal-

Bennu

smithing, casting, and sculpting. (The Greeks identified this god with *Hephaestus* and the Romans equated him with *Vulcan*.) Ptah is the great architect of the universe—designer of heaven and Earth. He is usually portrayed as a bearded balding man who wears a tight headband, and is clothed in a close-fitting garment or mummy-wrappings. From an opening in his garment his two hands project to grasp a phoenix scepter, an ankh and a *Djed* wand.

The **BENNU** bird was the Egyptian version of the phoenix, which was sacred to Osiris. The Bennu was said to have created itself out of the Fire that burned on the summit of the sacred Persea Tree of Heliopolis. Once every five hundred years the Bennu made its appearance bearing the body of his father in an egg of myrrh to the temple of the Sun to be buried. Resembling a heron, the Bennu's plumage was colored gold and red.

HEPHAESTUS (Equivalent to the Roman *Vulcan*): The Greek god of terrestrial Fire. The son of Hera and Zeus, his name is derived from a Greek word meaning

Hephaestus

"hearth" or "Kindle." The Element that this god represents is not the destroying Fire, but the beneficial Fire that permits humans to smelt metal and advance civilization. Like the Egyptian Ptah, Hephaestus is the divine blacksmith, the artisan who taught humans the mechanical arts and built the divine palaces of Olympus. The god appears as a powerful bearded smith who is lame in both legs. He is depicted wearing a short sleeveless chiton and holding a hammer and thongs, often working by flaming furnaces and pounding out metal on an enormous anvil. The metal-working companions of Hephaestus were a variety of subterranean Fire genii, which included the Cyclopes and Dactyls.

PROMETHEUS: The Greek Titan who stole sacred Fire from the forges of Hephaestus to give to the human race. (An angry Zeus had ordered Fire withheld from humankind.) For this crime Zeus had the Titan chained to a mountain crest where every day a vulture would feast upon his liver, which grew back every night. After many years of defiant suffering he was rescued by the hero Hercules. Prometheus was regarded by the Athenians as the father of the arts and sciences.

HESTIA (Equivalent to the Roman *Vesta*): The Greek goddess of the hearth-fire of the household—Fire which is benevolent and helpful to humankind. Considered the oldest of the Olympian gods, Hestia was venerated in all of Greece, and the Fire of the *hestia* or public hearth was used in sacrifices.✿

Hestia

SECTION 5: Correspondences of Venus

The Planet attributed to the Philosophus grade is Venus. Venus rules attractions, social interactions, partners, marriages, unions, aesthetics, cultural pursuits, the emotions associated with natural love, beauty, sensuality, the creative arts, and adornments. Venus governs the nonrational emotive part of the human mind as well as that part of us that wishes to socialize with others and express our creativity and affections. It is the "right-brain" portion that seeks to sing, dance, act, paint and express things that words cannot express. The energy of Venus is mild and harmonious.

The Planet Venus takes 224.5 days to complete one orbit of the Sun, and it is never located more than 46° from the Sun. Venus is the Morning and Evening Star It is considered feminine and a "fruitful" or benefic Planet. In an Astrological sense, Venus is said to be "warm." The ancients described Venus as the ruler of the period of life dominated by *emotion* from the ages 15 to 22.

In human anatomy, this Planet rules the throat, the kidneys, internal reproductive organs, the venous blood circulation, and the skin. Physical ailments associated with Venus include blood impurities, pustural and contagious diseases such as measles and small pox, poisonings, and venereal diseases.

Objects attributed to Venus include jewelry and ornaments, women's apparel, and bed linens. Flowing and veined substances.

In magic, the days and hours of Venus are used for forming friendships, for pleasant undertakings, for kindness and love, and for traveling. In the days of the week, Venus rules Friday.

The symbol of Venus on the Tree of Life embraces the whole ten Sephiroth. It is a fitting emblem of the Isis of Nature. As it contains all the Sephiroth, its circle is always represented larger than that of Mercury.

Hebrew Name: Nogah
Sephiroth: Netzach
Archangel: Anael
Day: Friday
Planetary Intelligence: Hagiel
Planetary Spirit: Qedemel
Olympic Planetary Spirit: Hagith
Metal: Copper, brass
Gemstones: Emerald, turquoise, jade, malachite
Incenses: Sandalwood, myrtle
Trees: Elder, fruit trees
Herbs/plants: Rose, myrtle, geranium, hyacinth, thyme, licorice
Animals: Dove, dolphin, bee, tortoise

Venusian Deities *(Gods and Goddesses of Love and the Arts)*

Ishtar

ISHTAR (The Sumerian *Inanna*): The Assyro-Babylonian goddess who personified the Planet Venus. A complex goddess of many functions, Ishtar was the supreme goddess of the Heavens. Self-proclaimed "goddess of the morn and goddess of the Evening," Ishtar was both a divinity of love and of war. (Worshiped as the daughter of the Moon god, *Sin*, Ishtar was perceived as a goddess of war, but seen as the daughter of *Anu*, the sky, she fulfilled her role as the goddess of love.) The warrior goddess Ishtar, as venerated especially by the Assyrians was the "Lady of Battles, valiant among goddesses." In this form she is depicted standing in a chariot pulled by seven lions, and holding a bow or a lion-headed club. Her sister is *Ereshkigal*, dark queen of the Underworld.

Ishtar as the goddess of love controlled the power to arouse desire and the ability to procreate in all creatures. She was "courtesan to the gods" and sacred prostitution formed an important part of her cult. Although she often displayed her kindness, she was also regularly cruel to her many lovers, and her affections were sometimes fatal. Her love for the harvest god Tammuz, caused his death. In her grief, she journeyed into the Underworld to find Tammuz, only to become Ereshkigal's prisoner. Eventually she was freed with a powerful magic spell by the god Ea.

Ishtar is usually portrayed wearing a triple-horned crown and clothed in flowing golden robes. Her necklace and bracelets are made of lapis lazuli.

HATHOR: A sky goddess who became associated with the morning and evening star because the Sun god resided within her breast, enclosed every night within the body of Hathor, to be born anew each morning. She was revered as the goddess of love, joy, and merriment, and was the mistress of dance and music. Her temple was the home of intoxication and a place of enjoyment. Hathor was sometimes represented as the great celestial cow, whose milk nourished the young Horus. More often she is depicted as a cow-headed woman, or a woman with cow's ears, sometimes crowned with horns and the Solar disk. The sistrum, a musical instrument used to drive away evil Spirits, is Hathor's special implement—and is usually engraved with her image.

BES: Egyptian god of marriage, merriment and the adornment of women. Of Semetic or African origin, Bes is represented as a robust dwarf with a large head, hairy cheeks and protruding tongue. He wears a headdress of ostrich feathers, and around his body the skin of a leopard. Bes is known as the god of music, dance, pleasure and amusement. He delights in playing the harp and entertaining the gods with his jovial antics and contortions.

QETESH: A Semtic/Egyptian goddess of love and beauty, who is another form of Hathor. Qetesh is usually represented as a nude woman standing upon a lion, holding lotus flowers.

APHRODITE (Equivalent to the Roman *Venus*): The Greek goddess of love in all its aspects: *Aphrodite Urania*, or the heavenly Aphrodite, was the goddess of pure and ideal love. *Aphrodite Genetrix* was the goddess of marriage. *Aphrodite Pandemos* was the goddess of lust and mistress of prostitutes.

In legend, Aphrodite was born out of the sea, from the foam of the severed genitalia of Uranus. All of the gods were struck by her beauty and grace, for the goddess emitted an aura of seduction and charm. She owned a magic girdle which was endowed with the power of enslaving the hearts of mortals and immortals alike. Aphrodite often delighted in arousing the amorous passions of the gods and sending them chasing after mortals. Protectress of legitimate unions between men and women, the normally benign goddess could punish her enemies by driving them mad with passion. Companions of the goddess included the child god Eros (Cupid) and the three Graces whose presence gladdened the hearts of humanity. Although she was the wife of the deformed god Hephaestus, her lovers were many, including the god of war, Ares. Aphrodite is usually portrayed as a voluptuous woman partially draped with a robe or nude.

DIONYSUS: A complex Greek god who became known as the god of wine, pleasure and the forces of life. Called "the deliverer of men from their cares," Dionysus is depicted as a youth crowned with vine leaves and grapes and robed in the skin of a panther. In one hand he bears a cup of wine and in the other a thyrsus staff surmounted by a pine cone. The god is often accompanied in his travels by a band of satyrs, centaurs, maenids, nymphs and sileni. The festivals of Dionysus were marked by frenzied activity, orgies, dancing, music and pleasure. Later the god acquired the more mystical aspects of death and resurrection, thus becoming a symbol of the forces of life.

FREYA (or **FRIGG**): Teutonic goddess of love and fertility. Her name means "lady" or "mistress." She is usually depicted as a beautiful woman in a cloak, and riding a boar or driving a chariot pulled by cats. Freya is sometimes shown weeping.

Hathor

Bes

Aphrodite

Complementary Planet: MARS

In conjunction with the study material given on the Planet Venus, the student should review information supplied in Chapter One on Mars, the Planet which complements Venus on the Macrocosmic Hexagram.

Mars is the Planet of initiative, aggression, action, strife, competition and death. It is also the Planet which governs sexual desires, animal nature, wounds, weapons and warfare. The energy of Mars is sudden and disruptive.

In an astrological sense, Mars is said to be "hot" and "dry," and it is associated with Fire. It is sometimes thought of as a "malefic" and "barren" Planet. The ancients defined Mars as the ruler of the period life dominated by *ambition* from the ages 43 to 57 symbolized by "the soldier."

In human anatomy, this Planet rules the muscles, the head, external sex organs, red blood cells and the motor nerves. Physical ailments associated with Mars include infectious diseases, fevers, inflammations, burns, high blood pressure and delirium associated with fever.

In magic, the days and hours of Mars are used for war, military honor, to acquire courage, strength, and self-assertion, to overthrow enemies and to cause discord and ruin. In the days of the week, Mars rules Tuesday.

Deities associated with the Planet Mars (war gods) include: **NINURTA**, **NINIP**, and **NERGAL** (Assyro-Babylonian gods of hunting and of warfare) **SEKHET** (Egyptian) **MONT** (Egyptian), **HORUS** (Egyptian) **ARES** (Greek), **THOR** (Teutonic) and **TIW** (Teutonic).

The following is a list of Martial associations:

Hebrew Name: Madim
Sephirah: Geburah
Archangel: Zamael
Day: Tuesday
Planetary Intelligence: Graphiel
Planetary Spirit: Bartzabel
Olympic Planetary Spirit: Phaleg
Metal: Iron
Gemstones: ruby, garnet, bloodstone
Incenses: Pepper, dragon's blood
Trees: Pine
Herbs/plants: Sage, nutmeg, hyssop
Animals: Unicorn, eagle, swan, whale

SECTION 6: Qabalah—The Qlippoth

 The Qlippoth came into existence at the catastrophic event known as the Breaking of the Vessels when the instability of the Tree of life could not support the pressure of the Divine Light. Thus from an excess of energy the Qlippoth came into being. The Broken Vessels were still open to the process of reconstruction, but their "shells" which are the equivalent of waste by-products, were not affected. It was in this manner that the Qlippoth in their most strict definition as the forces of corruption and evil began—(as god's garbage heap).

The Qlippoth are a group of ten chaotic and imbalanced Sephiroth, which are the direct opposites of the harmonious spheres of the Tree of Life, and thus they form a second Tree which is called evil. They are simply the destructive and unequilibrated aspects of the Sephiroth. (Just as every Sephirah is said to have a "virtue" there is a corresponding "vice.") The Qlippotic Tree is usually represented as a mirror image of the Tree of Life, reflected from the base of Malkuth. The tenth Sephirah is said to be "fallen" because after the Fall when the Vessels were broken, Malkuth descended and came to rest upon the Kingdom of Shells (the Qlippoth), which is why their influence is so potent in the world of humanity. And just as they were formed from an excess of unstable energy, their power is connected with all forms of overindulgence and excess—imbalance in general. Whereas as the Sephiroth symbolize progressive evolution and spiritual reunion with the Divine, the Qlippoth represent de-evolution and spiritual disintegration.

In the same manner as the figure of the upright pentagram (with the Spirit point on top) is utilized to symbolize the balanced forces of the Sephiroth and the Elements, the inverted pentagram is used to indicate the unbalanced or Qlippotic forces (Spirit inverted).

The ten averse and evil Sephiroth of the Qlippoth are also collected into the Seven Evil Palaces (the great red dragon, Leviathan of the Qlippoth with seven heads and ten horns). The Infernal Order of the Qlippoth corresponds somewhat to the various Angelic Orders. Samael is said to surround the whole of the Evil Sephiroth, thus making eleven instead of ten. (This is why eleven is seen as a number which especially refers to the Qlippoth.) The names of the Qlippotic forces attributed to the Three Negative Veils are:

000.	Ain	*Qemetiel*	—	The Crowd of gods
00.	Ain Soph	*Belial*	—	Without God
0.	Ain Soph Aur	*Athiel*	—	Uncertainty

The ten Qlippotic forces assigned to the Sephiroth and the Seven Averse Palaces are:

1.	Kether	*Thaumiel*	—	Twins of God
		(also *Kerethial*	—	Cut off from God)
2.	Chokmah	*Ogiel*	—	The Hinderers
3.	Binah	*Satariel*	—	The Concealers
4.	Chesed	*Gasheklah*	—	The Smiters, The Breakers
5.	Geburah	*Golachab*	—	The Burners
6.	Tiphareth	*Tageriron*	—	The Hagglers, The Disputers
7.	Netzach	*Oreb Zaraq*	—	The Ravens of Dispersion
8.	Hod	*Samael*	—	The Liar or Poison of God
9.	Yesod	*Gamaliel*	—	The Obscene Ones
		(also *Nachashiel*	—	Evil Serpents)
10.	Malkuth	*Lilith*	—	Queen of Night and Demons

The Qlippoth of the Planets are the same as those of the corresponding Sephiroth. There are also twelve Princes and tribes of Qlippotic forces that are attributed to the Zodiacal Signs and the Months of the year. These include:

11.	♈	Aries	*Bairiron*	—	The Herd
12.	♉	Taurus	*Adimiron*	—	The Bloody Ones
13.	♊	Gemini	*Tzelilimiron*	—	The Clangers
14.	♋	Cancer	*Shichiriron*	—	The Black Ones
15.	♌	Leo	*Shalhebiron*	—	The Flaming Ones
16.	♍	Virgo	*Tzaphiriron*	—	The Bloody Ones
17.	♎	Libra	*Abiriron*	—	The Clayish Ones
18.	♏	Scorpio	*Necheshthiron*	—	The Brazen Ones
19.	♐	Sagittarius	*Nachashiron*	—	The Snaky Ones
20.	♑	Capricorn	*Dagdagiron*	—	The Fishy Ones
21.	♒	Aquarius	*Bahimiron*	—	The Bestial Ones
22.	♓	Pisces	*Nashimiron*	—	Malignant Women

000. **QEMETIEL:** Takes the image of a vast black man-headed dragon-serpent who unites under him the force of the Qlippotic Kether.

00. **BELIAL:** He who denies God, takes the shape of a black bloated Man-dragon who unites under him the force of the Qlippotic Chokmah.

0. **ATHIEL:** Appears as a black bloated Man-insect who unites under him the force of the Qlippotic Binah.

1. **THAUMIEL:** The Two Contending Forces. The Thaumiel appear as dual, giant heads without bodies but having bat-like wings. They continually seek to combine with the bodies

of other entities or forces. (Also **KERETHIAL:** Cut off from God. The Kerethial take the form of evil black giants.)

2. **OGIEL:** The Ogiel take the form of black giants covered in twining serpents. (The so-called Dukes of Esau are also attributed the Qlippotic Chokmah.)

3. **SATARIEL:** The Satariel appear as gigantic horned and veiled heads whose eyes are seen through the veil. They are followed by malignant hairy centaurs known as the Seriel of Esau.

4. **GASHEKLAH:** The Breakers in Pieces, Disturbers of all things. They take the form of black cat-headed giants.

5. **GOLACHAB:** The symbolic forms of the Golachab are large black heads which erupt like volcanoes.

6. **TAGERIRON:** The forms of the Disputers are those of great black giants constantly working one against the other.

7. **OREB ZARAQ:** The Dispersing Ravens. They take on the appearance of demonic ravens flying out of a volcano.

8. **SAMAEL:** The Deceivers. Their symbolic shapes are those of demon-headed dog-like monsters.

9. **GAMALIEL:** The Obscene Ones whose heads are like corrupting bull-men joined together. The Blind Dragon force is also attributed to Qlippotic Yesod.

10. **LILITH:** The appearance of Lilith is that of a beautiful woman who changes into a black monkey-like demon.

11. **BAIRIRON:** The Herd, evolved from Samael. Their symbolic form is that of Dragon-Lion in the colors of black and dull red.

12. **ADIMIRON:** The Bloody Ones, who resemble Lion-Lizards in the colors of dull yellow, gray and blood mixed with water.

13. **TZELILIMIRON:** The Clangers, who take the forms of feral triangular-headed dogs. Their colors are blood-red and bronze.

14. **SHICHIRIRON:** The Black Ones, whose forms are a combination of crayfish, reptile and insect with a demonic face.

15. **SHALHEBIRON:** The Flaming Ones, who resemble fierce wolves and jackals in the colors of flaming red and yellow.

16. **TZAPHIRIRON:** The Bloody Ones, who resemble putrefying yet living corpses in the colors of Earth.

17. **ABIRIRON:** The Clayish Ones, who take on the forms of gray bloated and cloud-colored goblins.

18. **NECHESHTHIRON:** The Brazen Ones, who appear like copper-colored human-headed insects.

19. **NACHASHIRON:** The Snaky Ones, who resemble dog-headed snakes.

20. **DAGDAGIRON:** The Fishy Ones, shaped like large ravenous flat-headed fishes in gleaming reddish tones.

21. **BAHIMIRON:** The Bestial Ones, who are fantastic-looking creatures like elephants or hippos, but crushed flat. They crawl yet have great strength. Their colors are brown and black, and their skins are pulled taught as if over the body of a large beetle.

22. **NASHIMIRON:** Malignant Women who resemble skeletons joined to the bodies of fish and snakes. Their colors are watery.

BEHEMOTH is an averse creature that represents the synthesis of all the Qlippoth of the Zodiacal Signs. He resembles the creature described under the Qlippoth Behimiron.

LEVIATHON is a creature formed from many dragons joined together. Each of his red scales represents a separate evil serpent. He is the synthesis of the Sephirotic Qlippoth.

GEHENNA—THE INFERNAL ABODES: Anciently, this referred to Ge-Hinnom, or the Valley of Hinnom, the garbage dump and crematorium for criminals and the poor. It came to symbolize Hell. In Qabalah, there are seven Hells, just as there are seven Heavens or Palaces. Each Hell has associated with it one of the Seven Earths:

1. The Supernals. **SHEOL**—"Abyss." Type of Earth: *Aretz*—dry crumbling Earth.

2. Chesed. **ABADDON**—"Destruction." Type of Earth: *Adamah*—reddish mould.

3. Geburah. **BAR SHACHATH**—"Pit of Ruin." Type of Earth: *Gia*—undulating ground, like the slopes of a valley.

4. Tiphareth. **TIT HA-YAWEN**—"Mire of Mud." Type of Earth: *Neshiah*—meadow, pasture.

5. Netzach. **SHAARE-MAWETH**—"Gates of Death." Type of Earth: *Areqa*—Earth.

6. Hod. **TZAL-MAWETH**—"Shadow of Death." Type of Earth: *Tziah*—sandy desert soil.

7. Yesod and Malkuth. **GE-HINNOM** — "Valley of Hinnom." Type of Earth: *Thebal* or *Cheled*—Earth and Water mixed.

These Seven Infernal Palaces are surrounded by the Four Seas: (1) the Waters of Tears, (2) the Waters of Creation, (3) the Waters of Ocean and (4) the False Sea.

We have omitted Hebrew spellings for all the Qlippotic names. One of our initiates has suggested that when writing the names of the Qlippoth for study, the student write a corresponding divine name next to it, in order to balance out the negative energies with positive ones. For example, for Binah: *YHVH Elohim*—next to *Satariel*. By doing this the student will not become overly fixated upon the degenerative forces of the Qlippoth when studying. When writing the names of the Qlippoth of the Zodiacal Signs, the Archangels of the Signs could be employed for balance. Review Chapter Two for the Zodiacal Archangels.

The objective of teaching students about the Qlippoth in the Philosophus grade is not to supply the aspirant with a list of demonic names to work with. We certainly do *not* recommend that students experiment with or meditate upon any of the entities listed in this section. The point of all this is to teach the student not to be fearful of such beings, but rather to understand their place within the Qabalistic

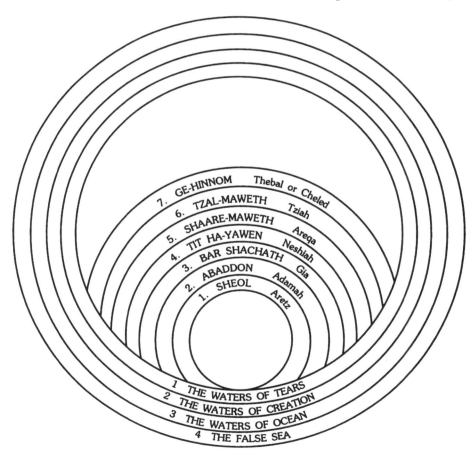

Gehenna, or the Seven Infernal Mansions and the Four Seas

scheme of the universe. When a person fears something so completely that s/he shuns even the thought of such beings, the result is often that the Qlippothic portions of the psyche are given force, thus increasing their degenerative powers. Often the individual who thinks that s/he has vanquished these entities by rejecting any reference to them at all, may find that their imbalancing tendencies leak out of the psyche in various unforeseen ways, causing obsessive behavior patterns (gluttony, self-abuse, drug-addiction, etc.). In studying this section, the student would do well to remember the speach of Hiereus in the Neophyte Ritual, *"Fear is failure, so be thou without fear—for he who trembles at the Flame and at the Flood and at the Shadows of the Air, hath no part in God."*✿

SECTION 7: Alchemy—The Tools of Practical Alchemy

 One great difference between chemical and Alchemical processes is that Alchemy only employs a gradual heat which is continually but carefully increased.[128] Chemistry on the other hand commences with a violent, rapid heat. Qabalistically, the entire process of Alchemy can be explained as the cleansing and purifying of Malkuth in order to purge it from the influence of the shells and return it to its rightful spiritual origins. The practicing Alchemist uses a variety of implements to aid in his work. These include the following items:

ALUDEL (or **SUBLIMINATORY**): A gourd-shaped clay pot which was constructed so that a series of such vessels could be built up, one on top of the other, to a height of five or six feet. Used for sublimation, the bottom pot was placed on a stove. The vapors that rose during the heating process, condensed on the inside of the upper vessels, and were removed later by scraping.

ALEMBIC: A container which was used for distillation. Its shape was said to resemble a dancing bear. In early days the alembic was made of two pieces with a removable head. Later alembics of glass were sometimes made in one piece. The receiver, a globular glass vessel, was fitted over the open end of the alembic's tube in order to catch the distillate.

ATHANOR: A forge or oven known as the *Philosophical Furnace* which is used to produce a graduated heat. Approximately five feet in height, the oven was constructed so that it could be divided into various parts, of which the bottom portion contained a small fireplace for providing a uniform heat. Used for digestion and evaporation of certain liquids. The Athanor contains the glass vessel (egg-shaped) which lies in a sand bath or ash-pit just above the fire. A symbol of the human being. (In sexual symbolism, a penis or active masculine force.)

---

[128] In the early days of the Order, some Alchemical references taken from a text known as the *Aesh Metzareph* ("Purifying Fire") were included in the Knowledge Lectures of the Outer Order. The *Aesh Metzareph* was originally written in Hebrew, translated into Latin sometime later, and included in the book *Cabala Denudata* by Knorr von Rosenroth. (The original is thought to be lost.) The *Aesh Metzareph* is significant only in that it is the source of the most awful and pointless of the Alchemical correspondences in the Outer Order Knowledge Lectures. It is obvious that the author of the work knew very little about Alchemy. Therefore we will not include it here.

BALLOON: a spherical-shaped glass vessel with two or three short spouts. It was used to collect the distillate.

BALNEUM MARIAE: or "The bath of Mary," named after Mary the Jewess, who was the sister of Moses and an ancient Alchemist. The modern water bath—a vessel of hot water in which was placed the vessel to be heated. It consisted of a double vessel set over another kettle. A warm water bath kept at a temperature which is bearable to humans. A method of controlled heat.

BALNEUM VAPORIS: The steam bath.

CLOCHE: an early form of bell jar used for subliming.

CRUCIBLE (THALAMUS or CURCUBITE): A gourd-shaped glass boiler attached to the lower part of the Alembic. It consists of a tube, a head, and a receiver added thereto for purposes of distillation. The melting pot, employed in the dry method by which the First Matter is exposed to direct Fire. (In sexual symbolism it represents the womb, or female principle used in conjunction with the Athanor or male principle.) A place of trial and test prior to rebirth into an exalted state. Also called the Bridal Chamber or Glass House.

CRUCIFIX: Comprised of three curcubites around a central glass vessel, used for subliming.

EVAPORATING DISH: A shallow circlular-shaped bowl which was placed over the Balneum Mariae.

IGNIS CINERUM: An ash heat wherein the vessel of the work is buried. It is not a violent Fire unless it is agitated.

LUTE: A mixture of substances which was used to seal the various flasks and vessels. Some common lutes included glass-sand and loam, or flour and water.

MATRASS: A long-necked flask that was employed for various purposes in Alchemy. Said to resemble an ostrich.

PELICAN: A glass container with two necks for continuous distillation. Named after the seabird.

PHILOSOPHIC EGG: An oval glass vessel in which is placed the water or liquid to be acted upon, and which could be hermetically sealed. Composed of a round bulb and a short neck by which it could be attached to another container. Used as a symbol of creation, it was said to contain the four Elements.

RETORT: A long-necked vessel used for gentle distillation and cohobation. It was said to resemble a long-necked goose.

SERPENT: A metal spiral or zigzag tube used in distillation by acting as a condenser connected to the curcubit. Cooled by air.

Other instruments used include bell jars, beakers, flasks, funnels, condensers and glass tubes.

Athanor

Matrass

Retort

Pelican

Alembic

Alchemic Principles on the Tree

SULFUR: The Alchemical symbol of sulfur on the Tree of Life does not touch any of the four lower Sephiroth. The cross terminates in Tiphareth, whereby as it were, the Supernal triangle is to be grasped. Tiphareth is the purified human being.

MERCURY: The Alchemical symbol of mercury on the Tree of Life. As is the symbol of the Planet Mercury, it embraces all but Kether. The horns spring from Daath, a conjunction of Chokmah and Binah. The triple foliation at the bottom of the cross alludes to Fire (Shin) represented by the addition of the Sign of Aries. It also symbolizes the three principles of sulfur, mercury and salt.

SALT: The Alchemical symbol of salt on the Tree of Life embraces all of the Sephiroth but Malkuth, and is as it were, the *Reconciler* between the sulfur and mercury. The horizontal dividing line implies the precept of Hermes, "As above, so Below." (Note: review information given in Chapter Two concerning the Three Alchemic Principles.)

The Astrological and Alchemical Symbols of the Planets[129]

These are derived from the three primary forms of the Cross, the Crescent and the Circle, either singly or in combination. The Circle denotes Sun and Gold; the Crescent the Moon and Silver, respectively analogous to the Red and White Alchemical natures.

The Cross is the symbol of corrosion. The corrosion of metals is usually of the complementary color to that to which they naturally approximate. Thus Copper, which is reddish, becomes green in its corrosion of verdigris, etc.

Mercury is the only Planet which unites these three primary forms in one symbol. Saturn is composed of the cross and the crescent showing that Lead is corrosive internally and Luna externally. Jupiter is the reverse. Mars is Solar externally but corrosive externally.

Venus is opposite. Copper is externally of the nature of Gold, but internally corrosive. Hence the name of the sphere of Venus is Nogah—denoting External Splendor but internal corruption.✿

SECTION 8: Admission Badges and Diagrams

The Calvary Cross of Twelve Squres is the Admission Badge to the Path of Qoph. It is formed of twelve squares which fitly represent the Zodiac which embraces the Waters of Nu as the ancient Egyptians called the Heavens (the Waters which are above the Firmament). It also alludes to the eternal river of Eden, divided into four heads which find their correlations in the four triplicities of the Zodiac.

---

[129] From Regardie's *The Golden Dawn*.

The Symbol of Sulfur on the Tree

The Symbol of Salt on the Tree

The Symbol of Mercury on the Tree

550

The great river is called *Naher*, which flows out of Eden, namely from the Supernal Triad. At Daath, it is divided into four heads. The first river is called *Pison*, the river of Fire, which flows into Geburah. Second is the river *Gihon*, the river of the Waters which flows into Chesed. The third is *Hiddikel*, the river of Air, flowing into Tiphareth, and the fourth, which receives the virtues of the other three, is *Phrath* (Euphrates), which flows down upon the Earth.

Cancer, the Cardinal Sign of Water is placed at the junction of the cross (and of the four rivers). All the Cardinal and Mutable Signs are placed in alternating positions on the central shaft of the cross, beginning with Aries and ending with Pisces. The cross bar is composed of the Kerubic Signs.

The Pyramid of the Four Elements is the Admission Badge for the 28th Path of Tzaddi. On the four triangles which comprise the sides of this Badge are the Hebrew names of the four Elements: *Asch*—Fire, *Maim*—Water, *Ruach*—Air, and *Aretz*—Earth. On the apex of the Badge is the word *Eth*, composed of the first and last letter of the Hebrew alphabet and implying essence or Spirit. The square base represents the material universe and on it is the word *Olam* meaning "World."

The word "pyramid" is derived from a root word which means "Fire," signifying that it is the symbolic representation of the one divine Flame. A pyramid can easily be likened to the "Mountain of God," which was believed to stand in the center of the Earth. The four sides of the pyramid are triangular to represent the threefold aspect of the Divine enthroned within every aspect of the fourfold universe. The square base is a reminder that the structure is firmly based on the immutable laws of nature. The truncated pyramid shows the essence of the Divine firmly planted at the top of the design. It, too, is a square to indicate that the fourfold model of the cosmos begins with the Tetragrammaton.

The Calvary Cross of Ten Squares is the Admission Badge to the 27th Path of Peh. It is formed of ten squares which fitly represent the ten Sephiroth in balanced disposition, before which the Formless and the Void rolled back. It is also the opened out form of the Double Cube and of the Altar of Incense. (The Altar of Incense before the Veil of the Holy of Holies, was overlaid with gold to represent the highest purity.) This alludes to the path of Peh as a vehicle of purification, where the Microcosm of man (represented by the ten Sephiroth) learns to separate the pure from the impure in order to become a perfect mirror of the greater Tree, the Macrocosm of the universe.

The Cross of the Hegemon's Badge grants the candidate entry into the temple of Netzach. The Calvary Cross of Six Squares embraces Tiphareth, Netzach, Hod and Yesod, and rests upon Malkuth. Also, the Calvary Cross of Six Squares is the opened-out form of the cube, and is thus referred to the Six Sephiroth of Microprosopus which are Chesed, Geburah, Tiphareth, Netzach, Hod, and Yesod.

This Badge is given to the Philosophus to emphasize the balance that must be attained in the 4 = 7 grade between the energies of Water and Fire, emotions and intellect. The Calvary Cross of Six Squares underscores the reconciling sphere of Tiphareth tempering and equilibrating between the opposing energies which meet head-to-head in this grade.

Side View

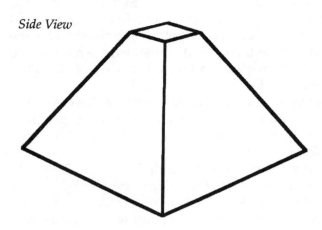

Top View

Hebrew on Base

The Pyramid of the Four Elements

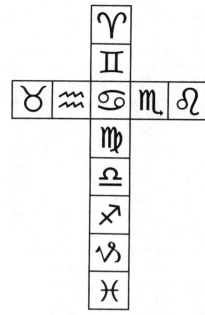

The Calvary Cross of 12 Squares

	1. כתר			
3. בינה	5. גבורה	6. תפארת	4. חסד	2. חכמה
		7. נצח		
		8. הוד		
		9. יסוד		
		10. מלכות		

The Calvary Cross of 10 Squares

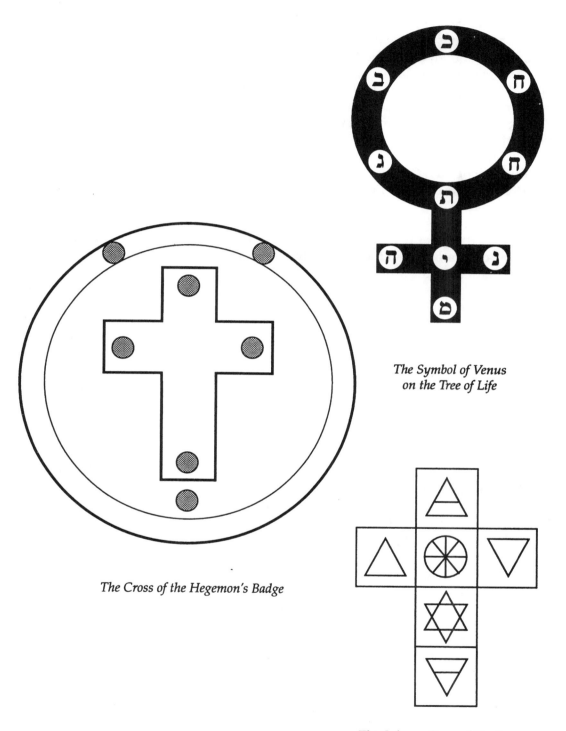

The Symbol of Venus
on the Tree of Life

The Cross of the Hegemon's Badge

The Calvary Cross of Six Squares

The Symbol of Venus on the Tree of Life: The Venus symbol embraces the whole Ten Sephiroth. It is a fitting emblem of the Isis of Nature. As it contains all the Sephiroth, its circle should be made larger than that of Mercury.

The Garden of Eden after the Fall: (See Plate 4.) This diagram is described in the Philosophus Ritual. It shows in a glyph the teaching proper to a Philosophus on entering the Sephirah Netzach which s/he has reached by the Three Paths of Qoph, Tzaddi, and Peh from the Sephiroth—Malkuth, Yesod and Hod respectively.

The great goddess *Eve*, being tempted by the fruits of the *Tree of Knowledge* whose branches tend upwards to the seven lower Sephiroth, but also downward to the Kingdom of Shells, reached down to them and the two pillars were left unsupported.

Then the Sephirotic Tree was shattered. She fell and with her fell the great *Adam*. And the great red Dragon arose with his seven heads and ten horns, and *Eden* was desolated—and the folds of the Dragon enclosed Malkuth and linked it to the Kingdom of the Shells.

And the heads of the Dragon rose into the seven lower Sephiroth, even up to *Daath* at the feet of Aima Elohim.

Thus were the four Rivers of Eden desecrated and the Dragon's mouth gave forth the Infernal Waters in Daath—and this is *Leviathan*, The Piercing and Crooked Serpent.

But *Tetragrammaton Elohim* placed the four letters YHVH of the *Name* and the Flaming Sword of the Ten Sephiroth between the devastated Garden and the Supernal Eden, that this should not be involved in the Fall of Adam.

And it became necessary that a Second Adam should arise to restore the System, and thus, as Adam had been spread on the Cross of the Four Rivers, so the Second Adam should be crucified on the Infernal Rivers of the four armed Cross of Death—yet to do this he must descend into the lowest, even Malkuth, the Earth, and be born of her. (Psalm 74. "Thou breakest the Heads of Leviathan in pieces.")

And on the Dragon Heads were the names of the eight Kings of *Edom* and on his horns the names of the Eleven Dukes of Edom, for Daath having developed in the Dragon a new Head, the Seven Headed Dragon with Ten Horns became Eight Headed and Eleven Horned. (Genesis, 36 31 to 43. Chronicles 1.43 to 54.)

NOTE: The Edomites were the descendants of Esau who sold his birthright. Their Kings came to symbolize unlawful and chaotic forces.

This diagram is somewhat similar to the one encountered in the preceding grade. The previous drawing portrayed the tranquillity of the Garden as in the grade of Water, while this one depicts the calamity within Eden caused by the power of imbalance. The red dragon has awakened and its heads ascend the Tree to Daath.

The Lower Self (symbolized by Eve) was lured downwards by the Tree of Knowledge to grasp the fruits of Knowledge. The cause of the problem, however, was an undeveloped understanding of creative power. Thus the Lower Self became entranced by the power of the awakening psyche, and momentarily suspended its support of the Higher Self (symbolized by Adam).[130] She has in a sense stooped down into that "darkly splendid world" which was forewarned against in the previous grade.

Yet the Fall is only a disaster from a single point of view. The knowledge derived from the waking dragon gave humanity consciousness and the awareness of power, which is the ability to evolve spiritually. Leviathan is in fact an emblem of a great obstacle which must be overcome. As all such impediments are designed to strengthen us, the dragon also represents the ultimate success of surmounting these difficulties at the end of the equilibration process.

The Garden of Eden after the Fall is equivalent to a state of consciousness often called "the Dark Night of the Soul." This is usually followed by a sense of despair wherein the powers of the Soul seem numbed and the mind wants to shut itself off against the discipline and practice of the Great Work. Numerous temptations to cease the Work will present themselves, attempting to entice the initiate away from his/her spiritual goal. At times the aspirant may feel as if the mind is becoming unbalanced, and that it would be best to cease all magical work. (The Alchemists symbolized this state of mind with a venomous dragon.) However, if the initiate persists and bears up through this unpleasant condition, it will eventually fade and be replaced by a higher state of spiritual awareness.

The ascent of Leviathan into Daath (knowledge) signifies an overflowing of subconscious archetypes into the individual psyche, which can be highly unsettling until they are absorbed and balanced out within the consciousness of the aspirant. Daath is the passageway between the Supernals (the Divine Self) and the lower parts of the Tree (the lower parts of the Self) through which Wisdom and Understanding are transmuted into *knowledge through experience.* Thus the Fall of Paradise, when the heads of the dragon reached up into Daath, refers to a procurement of self-knowledge. Daath is a connecting link between the tranquillity of the Divine Self and the human self confined to the realm of matter and delusion.

In the Macrocosmic view, the Fall from Eden represents an event in humanity's distant past when the collective psyche of our primitive race was stimulated and the beginnings of intelligence and self-awareness developed. In the Microcosmic view this process is repeated through the stimulation of the psychic Elements within the mind of the initiate. The routine activities of daily living, amplified by a spiritual focus (along with the arousal of the sphere of Daath) bring calamity at the outset because the revitalized psyche is usually misunderstood and misused for private gain. However, it is only through this state of calamity, where the initiate is forced to face these obstacles rather than pushing them to the back of the mind, that s/he can actually perceive and overcome the hidden causes of the distress. This is in fact the beginnings of real spiritual growth and awareness. So long as the necessary equilibrium is avoided, and the self-consciousness conferred upon the aspirant is abused for personal ends alone, then the serpent

---

[130] This continues to be a problem for magicians today who get sidetracked from the goal of the Great Work into an obsessed fascination with their own magical abilities. When this occurs however, the Higher Powers usually respond with a swift kick in the pants as an "attitude adjustment" against ego inflation.

Leviathan shall be relentless in its attack upon the self. Conquering this obstacle does not require suppressing or denying its existence—rather it entails acceptance of the dragon and forcing it back to its appropriate abode. The various levels of the initiate's personal Tree, separated from its Supernal origins are to be reintegrated and the colossal forces of the Dark side of one's psyche are to be trained like the lion in the Tarot card of Strength; a mighty beast which has been tamed and kept always under the firm control of the Higher Will.✿

SECTION 9: The Greek Alphabet

Ω The Greek alphabet is another magical set of building blocks that is very important to the mystical tradition of the West. Greek became a wide-spread language of the known (Western) world at a time when the culture of Egypt was becoming "Hellenized." This ancient tongue was the language of all the archaic mystery cults, including those of Samothrace, Eleusis, Orpheus, and the Hellenized rites of Isis and Serapis. Many mystical texts including the Magical Papyri, the New Testament, the Gnostic books and the writings of Hermes Trismegistus were written in Greek. And in the Golden Dawn, the names of the grades and the officiating officers themselves are Greek, in keeping with those earlier mystic rites at Delphi, Athens and Alexandria. It is therefore quite appropriate to include the study of the Greek alphabet in the Outer Order.

Like Hebrew, the letters of the Greek alphabet were assigned to different numeral values. This "Greek Gematria" is called *Isopsephos* which means "equal stones." Isopsephos is similar to Gematria in that words that added up to the same numeral value were considered to be related. (Some of the obscure numerical passages in the New Testament, including those in the Book of Revelations, were undoubtedly a result of Isopsephos. The most widely used system of assigning numbers to the Greek letters originated around 400 B.C. and is based on the Hebrew system. Both the upper and lower case forms of these letters are shown on the following page.

Letter	Name	Value	English Equivalent
A α	Alpha	1	A (*father*)
B β	Beta	2	B
Γ γ	Gamma	3	G
Δ δ	Delta	4	D
E ε	Epsilon	5	short e (*better*)
Z ζ.	Zeta	7	Zd (wis*d*om)
H η	Eta	8	long e (p*ai*r)
Θθ	Theta	9	Th (ca*th*ouse)
Iι	Iota	10	I (either *fee*t or *fi*t)
Kκ	Kappa	20	K
Λλ	Lambda	30	L
Mμ	Mu	40	M
Nν	Nu	50	N
Ξξ	Xi	60	X
Oο	Omicron	70	short o (h*o*t)
Ππ	Pi	80	P
Pρ	Rho	100	R, Rh (*always trilled*)
Σσ	Sigma	200	S (z if before B, Γ, Δ, or M)
Tτ	Tau	300	T
Yυ	Upsilon	400	U (long or short)
Φφ	Phi	500	Ph (mo*ph*ead)
Xχ	Chi	600	Kh (bac*kh*oe)
Ψψ	Psi	700	Ps
Ωω	Omega	800	aw (s*aw*)

The following letters were only used for their numeral values:

F or ς Digamma (w) or Stau (st) — 6

ϙ Qoppa (q) — 90

ϡ Sampi (s) — 900

Greek diphthongs can be somewhat complex. The following list of *classical* Greek pronunciations is based upon suggestions given in David Godwin's book, *Light in Extension:*

αι	(ai)	as in K*ai*ser
ευ	(au)	as in S*au*erkraut
ει	(ei)	as in V*ei*l
ευ	(eu)	"ay-oo"
οι	(oi)	as in *Oi*l
ου	(ou)	as in Gr*ou*p
υι	(ui)	"ü-ya"

Pronunciation of ancient Greek is different from that of modern Greek. The ancient form of pronunciation would be more beneficial to the magician, who seeks to approximate the tongue of the ancient mystery rites. Any reader who desires more information on this language is advised to pursue other books on ancient Greek.✿

SECTION 10: Tarot Divination

In the previous grade the initiate committed to memory the various meanings of the Tarot cards. Once these principles are understood, the student may begin using the cards for the practice of divination. The Zelator first encounters the art of divining through Geomancy. Divination with Tarot, however, is a more comprehensive and tactile method which fully engages all of the practitioner's Qabalistic and Astrological knowledge, together with his/her psychic abilities and creative powers.

Our book, *The New Golden Dawn Ritual Tarot* will provide the student with much information on the subtle relationships that exist between two or more cards in a divination.[131] However, a proper Tarot reading requires much more than book knowledge alone. Familiarizing oneself with the symbolism of the cards is merely the first step. This symbolism must be constantly built up in the mind of the reader. This information is progressively absorbed and regularly contemplated until there is a gradual alignment between the operation of the higher consciousness and that of the normal consciousness. The powers of psychic perception and awareness begin to develop greater accuracy and precision.

The second step in performing accurate divinations is to *practice constantly*. This is the only tried and true method for success in this area. The student should regularly examine the relationships that can occur between certain cards in an actual reading. Keep in mind, however, that it is pointless to coerce a reading. All of the symbolism in the universe will not avail one who is under strain or simply too tired to properly activate the psyche. If a reading is forced, it will probably be more untruth than truth.

Finally, one specific card reading method or Tarot spread should be chosen for regular and consistent use in divination. Three different Tarot spreads are presented here: The first is the *Celtic Cross Spread*, a ten card layout that was made

---

[131] A ritual for consecrating a deck of Tarot cards is given on page 166 of that book.

popular by A.E. Waite. This was the layout recommended to Outer Order initiates in Mather's day, because it was simple and direct.[132]

The method that we prefer to teach our students is the *Ten Card* or *Cicero Spread* which we have found to be quite reliable. Its advantage over the Celtic Cross Spread is that it eliminates the need for reversed or inverted cards, relying instead upon neighboring cards for interpretation.

At the start of any reading, it is appropriate to relax, meditate and to invoke the Divine. This not only aligns the reader with the Higher Forces, but it also sets the stage for reliable psychic interpretations. The initiate may decide to put on ritual garb and insignia as additional aids which focus the mind on the divine nature of the operation. The lesser invoking pentagram may be traced over the cards with a wand or index finger.[133] Visualize a brilliant ball of Light just over one's head and say the following invocation:

> *In the divine name IAO, I invoke thee, thou Great Angel HRU (Her-oo) who art set over the operations of this Secret Wisdom. Lay thine hand invisibly on these consecrated cards of art, that thereby I may obtain true knowledge of hidden things, to the glory of the ineffable Name. Amen.*

The Tarot cards may be shuffled thoroughly, while the diviner maintains a clear still mind and an attitude of psychic receptivity. The cards may then be spread out using one of the following methods.

The Celtic Cross Spread

The diviner must first select a card to represent the Querent or the question itself. This first card is known as the Significator. In many cases a Court card which corresponds to the personal or physical description of the Querent is chosen as the Significator. At times a Trump or small card may be selected as the Significator if the card's meaning conforms to the matter at hand.

Once the Significator is selected, the diviner should place it on the table, face upwards. The rest of the deck should be shuffled and cut three times, always keeping the cards face down.

CARD 1: Turn up the top or first card of the deck and place it over the Significator. *This covers him.* The first card portrays the general influence that is effecting the Querent or the matter of the question.

CARD 2: Turn up the second card and lay it across the first. *This crosses him.* The second card shows the character of the obstacles in the matter. If the card is favorable, this may indicate that the obstacles can be overcome. It may also indicate that something which is normally considered good will not be good in this particular situation.

---

[132] The more complex method, known as the *Opening of the Key*, was taught in the Second Order.

[133] The Philosophus may use the Outer Wand of Double Power or the Tarot Wand. Both of these implements are described in our book *Secrets of a Golden Dawn Temple.*

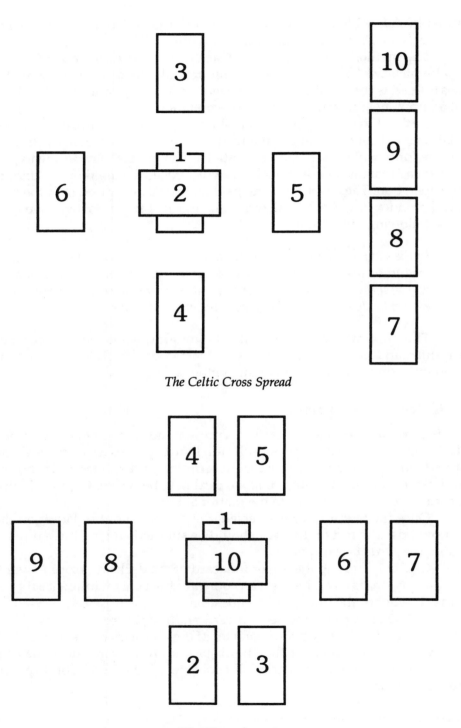

The Celtic Cross Spread

The Cicero Spread

560

CARD 3: Turn up the third card and place it above the Significator. *This crowns him.* The Third card can represent either the Querent's goal in the matter or the best that can be attained under the circumstances (but has not yet come to pass).

CARD 4: Turn up the fourth card and place it below the Significator. *This is beneath him.* The fourth card portrays the foundation of the matter—that which as already occurred and which the Significator has made his own.

CARD 5: Turn up the fifth card and place it either to the right or left of the Significator, away from the direction the Significator is facing. *This is behind him.* (Note: if the card does not "face" any particular direction, the diviner must decide ahead of time which direction will be viewed as "facing." Often the card on the right side of the Significator will be viewed as the one "behind." This card portrays the influence on the matter that has just passed, or is in the process of passing.

CARD 6: Turn up the sixth card and place it on the side that the Significator is facing (opposite Card 5). *This is before him.* The sixth card shows the influence on the matter that is just beginning to occur and which will be operating in the immediate future.

The cards are now arranged in the form of a cross, with the Significator in the center, underneath Card 1. The next four cards are placed consecutively one card above the other in an ascending line to the right of the cross.

CARD 7: This card represents the Significator or Querent *himself.* It portrays the position or attitude of the Significator in the unfolding circumstances.

CARD 8: This card indicates *his house*—the Querent's environment and the inclinations involved that have an effect on the matter. (For example: responsibilities, career, position in life, influence of family or friends, etc.)

CARD 9: This card represents the Querent's *hopes or fears* in the matter.

CARD 10: This card portrays the *end result or final outcome* which is brought about by the influences of all the previous cards in the reading. The tenth card should be regarded as especially significant to the entire reading.

The Ten Card Spread (The Cicero Spread)

After a preliminary meditation the cards should be shuffled thoroughly. The diviner should take the first ten cards from the deck and spread them out in accordance with the diagram.

CARD 1: This represents the *person asking the question* as well as the primary influences surrounding him or her. A Court card here might refer to the Querent or to some dominant person in his/her life.

CARDS 2 and 3: These cards represent the *subconscious mind* of the person asking the question. They give information on the hidden influences which effect, but are not detected by the Querent. These cards may have a strong yet concealed influence that can effect the entire reading.

CARDS 4 and 5: These cards represent the *conscious mind* of the Querent. They give information on the current thoughts and immediate feelings of the Querent toward the nature of the question.

CARDS 6 and 7: These cards shed light on the Querent's *past*. They indicate past events or influences which relate to the current question or problem.

CARDS 8 and 9: These cards represent the *final outcome*, or *potential future events or influences*.

CARD 10: This is the *cross-over card from the past to the future*. It reveals the psychological implications upon the Querent, as well as the actions he/she will take in making whatever decision may be necessary. It may also indicate forces operating beyond the control of the Querent, to which s/he must adapt.

The Fifteen Card Spread

After a preliminary meditation the cards should be shuffled thoroughly. The diviner should take the first fifteen cards from the deck and spread them out in accordance with the diagram.

CARD 1: This card represents the Querent, the *nature of the question or problem*, and the main influences which surround him/her.

CARDS 2 and 3: Along with Card 1, these are the primary cards of the spread. They describe the *nature of the circumstances and the personality* of the Querent.

CARDS 4, 8, and 12: These cards show *potential future events and influences*. They show what direction the Querent's life will naturally take, unless alternate steps are employed to change the course of events.

CARDS 5, 9, and 13: These cards represent an *alternative course of action* that the Querent may choose to take.

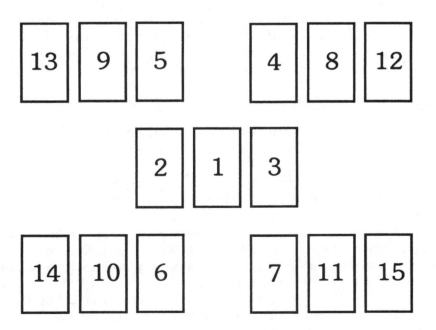

The Fifteen Card Spread

CARDS 6, 10, and 14: These cards indicate the *psychological basis and implications of the situation*. They assist the Querent in making whatever decision is needed.

CARDS 7, 11, and 15: These cards show forces at work that are beyond the Querent's control (*destiny or karma*). The Querent must be able to adapt and learn from them.✿

ADDITIONAL READING
The Tattwas of the Eastern School[134]

(Note: This paper was officially issued to all members of the Philosophus grade since the earliest days of the Order, although it was withdrawn from some branches of the Order later on. Regardie noted that these teachings from the Eastern School did not particularly blend well with the rest of the G∴D∴ system: "As to whether it accords with the general content of the rest of the Order system must be left to the discrimination of the individual student. That it has several points of value will be doubted by none, though few will care to subscribe to the paper in its entirety. Personally, I feel it to be definitely an alien system, which touches the Order teaching in but very few places. The mode of skrying in the Spirit-vision using the Tattwas symbols is sound enough, and has been described elsewhere. But other aspects suggest that the two systems are not likely to mix particularly well."[135]

It is our feeling as well that the Tattwas are a completely foreign addition to the Order teachings—introduced early on as a result of the popularity of Tattwas in the London Theosophical groups which were frequented by several Adepts of the G∴D∴ at the time. Today, study of the Tattwas within our Order is considered as an elective rather than required grade work. Our students are encouraged to employ the Western Elemental and Sub-Elemental symbols of the Spirit Wheel and the Elemental triangles or the Kerubic sigils rather than the Tattwas. Using the Western forms will provide the student with symbols which are completely integrated with every other aspect of the G∴D∴ teachings, from Neophyte studies to advanced Enochian work. These Western symbols also correspond to the Golden Dawn's attribution of color to the Elements, whereas the Eastern Tattwas do not.

We have included this paper for those students who choose to study the Tattwa system.—CC & STC)✿

---

[134] From Regardie's *The Golden Dawn*.

[135] Ibid. page 514.

General Observation. There are five Tattwas or Principles:

1. *Akasa*—Ether.
2. *Vayu*—the Aerial principle.
3. *Tejas*—the Principle of Light and Heat.
4. *Apas*—Watery Principle.
5. *Prithivi*—the Earthly Principle.

But the first Cause of these is the Great Controller of all things, the One Light, the Formless. From Him first came into appearance Ether; thence the Air, the motion producing Ether waves which causes Light and Heat, and so on in the above order.

The Yogi comes to know the principle of these five Tattwas, their Sukshma Sharira, but how? Further on you will see how. The Astrologer who has no knowledge of the Swara is as worthless as a man without a wife. It is the Soul itself; it is the Swara, the Great Controller of all, who creates, preserves, and destroys, and causes whatsoever is in this World. Experience and Tradition both say no knowledge is more precious than this knowledge of the Swara. None else lays bare the workings of the machinery of this world, or the secret workings of this world.

By the power of Swara may be destroyed an enemy. Power, wealth, and pleasure, all these can be commanded by Swara. The beginner in our Science must be pure and calm in mind and in thought, virtuous in actions, and having unmixed faith in his spiritual teacher. He must be strong in his determination, and grateful.

Swara in the Body. Ten manifestations of this Swara are in the body. But before the Neophyte is told this, he must gain a thorough knowledge of the nervous system. This is very important, and according to his knowledge of this science, the Neophyte gains success. To give a rough outline of the parts we have chiefly to deal with in our endeavor to explain the elementary treatise: There are ten principal nerves, this includes the tubes, etc. It is in the ten manifestations of Swara that the ten so-called Vayus move. We mean by this ten forces which perform ten different functions. The three most important nerves are the following, as the beginner has only to deal with these:

1. *Ida*—the left bronchus.
2. *Pingala*—the right bronchus.
3. *Sushumna*—in the middle.

The ten Vayus are:

1. *Prana*, in the breast.
2. *Apana*, about the excretory organs.
3. *Samana*, in the navel.
4. *Undana*, middle of the throat.
5. *Vyana*, pervading the whole body.
6. *Kurmana*, the eyes, helping them open.
7. *Kirkala*, in the stomach, producing hunger.
8. *Nag*, whence comes vomiting.
9. *Devadatta*, causes yawning.
10. *Dhananjaya*, that which doth not leave the body after death.

These ten vayus, or forces, have their play in the ten principal nerves, not one in each. They are the regulators of the body of man. If they go on working properly, a man remains perfectly healthy; if not, different kinds of diseases spring up.

A Yogi keeps them always working, and consequently diseases never come to him. The key to all these nerves lies in the working of the Prana Vayu, or vital principle drawing the Air through the Ida, the Pingala, and the Sushumna. When the Air is drawn through the Ida it is felt coming out or going in through the left nostril. When through the Pingala, in the right nostril. When through the Sushumna it is felt through both nostrils simultaneously. The Air is drawn or felt through either or both of the nostrils at certain appointed times. Whenever in any given time, the Breath goes in and comes out of the wrong nostril it is a sure sign some sort of disease is coming on.

The Ida is sometimes called the Chandra Nadi, or the Moon Nerve. The Pingala, the Surya Nadi or Sun nerve. These are called, the former, the Chandra Swara and the latter the Surya Swara.

The reason is that when the breath is in the Ida it gives coolness to the body, and that when in the Pingala it gives heat to the body. The ancient Magi used to say the place of the Moon in the human body was in Ida, and the Sun in Pingala.

The Course of the Breath. The Lunar month, it is well known, is divided into two parts, the fortnight of the Waxing and the fortnight of the Waning. On the first fortnight, or the Bright Fortnight, just at Sunrise of the first day the Breath must come into the left nostril and must be so for three days successively. At the beginning of the 4th day the Breath must come through the right nostril and must do so for the three succeeding days, when again the 7th day must begin with the Moon breath, and so on in the same order. Thus we have said that such and such days begin with such and such a breath.

But how long is our breath to remain in one nostril? For five Gharis, or 2 hours. Thus when the first day of the Bright fortnight begins with the Moon Breath, after five Gharis, the Sun Breath must set in, and this again must change into the Moon Breath after the same interval of time. So on for every day.

Again, the first day of the dark fortnight must begin with the Sun Breath, and proceed in the same way, changing after five Gharis and the three succeeding days. It will be seen that all the days of the month have been divided into the Ida and the Pingala. In the Sushumna, the Swara flows only when it changes, either in its natural course or in certain other conditions to be afterwards mentioned. This is the course of Nature. But a Yogi commands Nature. He turns everything into his own way. Rules for this will be given in the proper place.

Course of the Tattwas

For five Gharis, as we have above said, the breath flows through our nostrils. In these 5 Gharis, or two hour periods, the Tattwas have their course. In the first we have Akasa, in the second Vayu, in the third Tejas, in the fourth Apas, in the fifth Prithivi. Thus in one night and day, or 60 Gharis, we have twelve courses of these 5 Tattwas each remaining one Ghari and returning again in two hours. There are again further five subdivisions of each Tattwa in a Ghari. Thus, Akasa is subdivided into Akas-Akasa; Akas-Vayu; Akas-Tejas; Akas-Apas; Akas-Prithivi—and similarly with the other four.

How to know which of the Tattwas is at a certain time in course, not merely by a mathematical calculation but with the certainty of an eye witness, is of the greatest importance in the practical part of this science. We shall come to it further on.

The Ida. When the Breath is in Ida, that is in the left Nostril, then only is it well to perform the following actions. Stable works such as erecting a building, or the construction of a well or tank, going on a distant journey, entering a new house, collection of things, giving gifts, marriage, making jewels or clothes, taking medicines and tonics, seeing a superior or master for any purpose of trade, amassing of wealth, sowing of seed in a field, negotiations, commencement of trade, seeing of friends, works of charity and faith, going home, buying of animals, doing work for the benefit of others, placing money on security, singing, dancing, taking up abode in any village or city, drinking or making water at the time of sorrow, pain, fever, etc. All these acts should be done when the Swara is in Ida. It must however be kept in mind that the Tattwas Vayu and Tejas are to be excluded from these actions, likewise Akasa.

During the Tattwas Prithivi and Apas only, are these actions to be done. In a fever, the Yogi keeps his Chandra Swara going, and brings the Apas or Water Tattwa in course, so the fever is all over in a very short time. How mastery is gained over the Tattwas will come further on.

The Pingala. In the Surya Swara only, are the following actions to be done. Reading and teaching hard and difficult subjects of knowledge, sexual intercourse, shipping, hunting, mounting a hill or fort, riding a donkey, camel or horse, swimming over a powerful stream or river, writing, painting, buying and selling, fighting with swords or hands, seeing a king, bathing, eating, shaving, bleeding, sleeping—and such like. All these secure success and health, as the case may be, if done in the Surya Swara.

The Sushumna. When the Breath comes not out of both nostrils at the same time, it is flowing in the Sushumna. Nothing ought to be done under these conditions, for everything turns out badly. The same is the case when the Breath is now in one and now in the other nostril. When this is the case, sit down and meditate upon or over the Sacred Hansa. This joining of the Breath is the only time for Sandha, meditation.

NOTE: Zanoni[136] secured success in gaming for Cetosa and overcame the effects of the poisoned wine of the Prince di D——— as follows. In the first place, he changed his breath to the right nostril, and threw an envelope of the Akasa Tattwa over his antagonist, who consequently became all empty, the money in gaming flowing towards the Surya Swara. In the latter case he brought the Water, Apas, Tattwa into course, directed it with the full force of his trained will towards the poisoned wine, and consequently the burning heat of the poison was counteracted for a very long time, and before it could recover strength enough to act on the system, it was there no longer.—S.R.M.D.)

The Tattwas

To each of the five Tattwas a special color has been assigned. Akasa— Black; dark or no color really. Vayu—Green (blue by some). Tejas—Red. Apas, White or really all colors. Prithivi—Yellow. It is by these colors that a practical man finds on the spur of the moment which Tattwa is at the time in course. Besides, these Tattwas have different shapes and tastes. These figures are seen by taking a bright mirror and letting the breath fall upon it, as it comes out of the Nose. The divided part takes one of the following forms according to the Tattwa then in course. Prithivi— a figure having four Angles. Apas, a half moon, or crescent. Tejas, triangular. Vayu, spherical. Akasa, oval like a human ear. To sum up their qualities:

Prithivi—moves always in the middle of the paths of Air and Water. Apas— downwards, straight through the nose. Tejas—upwards. Vayu— obliquely towards the right or left arm, as the case may be. Akasa—transversely always.

Tattwa	Color	Form	Taste	Distance of Breath below Nose	Natural Principle
Prithivi	Yellow	Having Angles	4 Sweet	12 fingers	Bulky
Apas	White or all colors	Half Moon	Astringent	16 fingers	Cold
Vayu	Green or Blue	Sphere	Acid	8 fingers	Always in motion
Tejas	Red	Triangle	Hot tastes such as pepper, etc.	4 fingers	Hot
Akasa	Black, Dark, or no color	Human ear, oval, egg	Bitter	Upwards	Universally pervading

---

[136] A main character in a novel by Edward Bulwer Lytton.

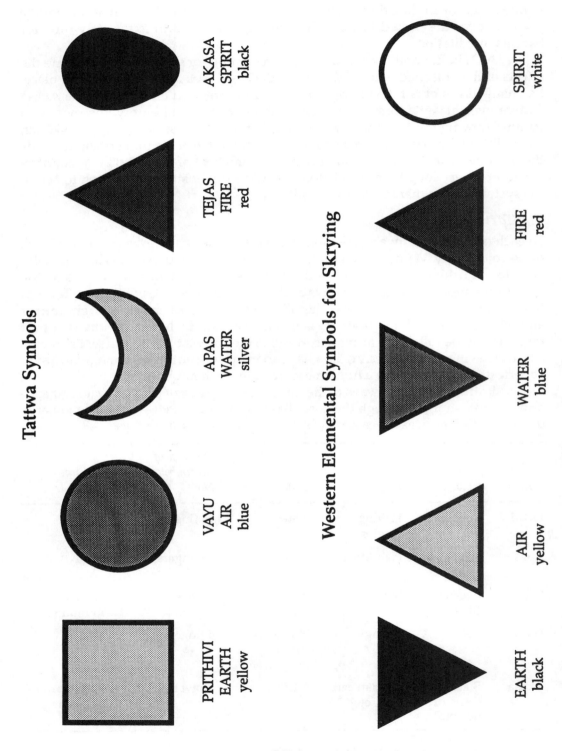

568

Tests of the Tattwas. For practice, let a man take five little bullets or counters colored: red, yellow, green or blue, white or silver, and black. And place or carry them in his pocket. Now let him close his eyes and take one of them out of his pocket. The color of the bullet will be that of the Tattwa then in course. Whilst still keeping the eyes closed, let him see if the color of the bullet floats before them.

He must not suppose he will be correct all at once. By and by the confusion will disappear, and colors well-defined, staying for the proper length of time, will begin to come before him, and the color of the bullet will be the same as that seen before his eyes. And then he will have gained the power of knowing which of the Tattwas is in course, and can at pleasure find them.

There is a particular method of concentrating the mind and practicing the eyes for this purpose, which will come with practice.

Let him ask any of his friends to imagine one of the five colors, say a flower. He will only have to shut his eyes to find the Tattwa then in course, and he can astonish his friends by naming the color. Again, if a man sitting amongst his friends finds the Vayu Tattwa set in, let him be sure that those of his friends who are in perfect health and in a normal state both of body and mind, wish to go away. Let him ask them to say frankly, and they will answer "yes."

In what way other Tattwas affect both the body and mind of man will be stated in another place. Some higher secrets are purposely reserved for those who safely and honestly pass the elementary stage. When the man has reached the stage of finding at will any of the Tattwas, let him not imagine he has become perfect.

If he goes on practicing, his inward sight becomes keener, and he will recognize the five subdivisions of the Tattwas. On and on let him go with his meditation, and innumerable shades of color will be recognized according to the different proportions of the Tattwas. Whilst during these intervals he is trying to distinguish from all external things; and sitting in an easy chair, let him fix his eyes on any particular part of the blue sky, and go on looking at it without allowing them to twinkle. At first he will see the waves of the water, this is the watery vapor in the atmosphere which surrounds the whole world. Some days later, as the eyes become practiced, he will see different sorts of buildings and so on in the Air, and many other wonderful things as well. When the Neophyte reaches this stage of practice, he is sure of gaining success.

After this he will see different sorts of mixed colors of Tattwas in the sky, which will after a constant and resolute practice show themselves in their proper and respective colors.

To test the truth of this, the Neophyte during the practice should occasionally close his eyes and compare the color floating in the sky with that which he sees inwardly. When both are the same the operation is right. Other tests we have given before, and other wonders resulting from this will of themselves present themselves to the Yogi. This practice is to be done in the daytime.

For the night, let the student rise about two o'clock in the morning, when everything is calm, when there is no noise, and when the cold light of the stars breathe holiness, and a calm rapture enters into the Soul of man. Let him wash his hands, feet, the crown of his head, and the nape of his neck with cold water. Let him put his shin bones on the ground, and let the back of his thighs touch his calves, and let him put his hands upon his knees, the fingers pointing towards the body. Let him now fix his eyes on the tip of his nose. To avoid this tediousness, he must always, especially during the meditation, meditate upon his breath, coming in and going out.

Besides the above, this has many other advantages given elsewhere. It may here be said that by constant practice of this meditation over his breath, the man is to develop two distinct syllables in his thought. It is evident that when a man draws his breath in, a sound is produced which is imitated in Han. When out, the sound Sa. By constant practice, the going in and coming out of the breath is so much connected with these sounds that without any effort the mind understands Han-sa with the production of these sounds. Thus we see that one full breath makes Han-Sa, this is the Name of the Ruler of the Universe, together with his powers. They are exerted in the working out of natural phenomena. At this stage of perfection, the Yogi should commence as follows:

Getting up at two or three in the morning, and washing himself in the aforementioned manner, let him know and fix his mind upon the Tattwa then in course. If the Tattwa in course be then Prithivi, let him think of it as something having 4 angles, a good yellow color, sweet smelling, small in body, and taking away all diseases. Let him at the same time repeat the word LAM. It is very easy to imagine such a thing.

If it be the Apas Tattwa, let him imagine something of the shape and brightness of the half moon, putting down heat and thirst, and that he is immersed in the ocean of Water. Let him at that time repeat the word VAM.

If the Tattwa be Tejas, let him imagine it as something triangular in shape, shedding a red glare, consuming food and drink, burning away everything, and thus making itself unbearable. At the same time let him repeat RAM.

If the Tattwa be Vayu, let him imagine it as something of a spherical shape, of a color Green, or Blue, like the green leaves of a tree after rain, and carrying him with a mighty power away from the ground and flying in space like the birds. And let him repeat the syllable PAM.

If the Tattwa be Akasa, let him imagine it as having no shape but giving forth a brilliant light, and let him repeat the syllable HAM.

By diligent practice, these syllables uttered by the tongue of a Yogi become inseparable from the Tattwas. When he repeats any of these, the special Tattwa appears with as much force as he may will, and thus it is that a Yogi can cause whatever he likes; lightning, rain, wind, and so forth.

Cure of Diseases

Every disease causes the breath to flow out of the wrong nostril, and the wrong Tattwa to come into course. When the breath therefore is restored to the proper nostril, and the proper Tattwa has been brought into course, let not anyone expect that all that is necessary has been done. If the disease be obstinate and the attack a very violent one, the man will have to persevere in battle a very long time before he conquers.

If a beginner cannot succeed very soon, let him aid the power of his breath by a suitable medicine, and Swara will be restored very soon.

It may be noticed that the Chandra Swara is generally the best for all diseases. Its flow is an indication of the soundness of Health. In cold, cough, and other diseases, this breath ought to flow.

Of the Tattwas as well as of the Swaras, no one causes pain if it goes on properly. In this state it ought not generally to be meddled with. But when anyone gains an undue predominance and causes diseases, it ought to be at once changed. Experience shows that the Apas and the Prithivi Tattwas are the only ones generally good for health, and indeed, the fact that during the course of the Apas Tattwa the breath is felt 16 fingers breadth below the nose, and during the Prithivi 12 fingers, argues at those times a more sound and powerful working of the functions of the body, than when it is felt only 8, or 4, or no finger-breadth below the nose.

Akasa therefore is the worst for health, and in a state of ill-health, a man will generally find in course, either Akasa, Vayu, or Tejas.

Let him therefore, when need be, proceed in the following manner. After having changed his Breath, from the wrong nostril to the proper one, generally the Left, and pressing the opposite side by a cushion so that it may not change again, let the man sit in an easy chair and bind his left thigh a little above the knee joint with his handkerchief. In a short time, whose length, varies inversely as the deficiency of practice, and directly as the violence of the disease, he will perceive that the Tattwa changes to the one immediately below it and so on; and then the next, and so forth. If he be an acute observer of the conditions of his body, he will perceive that slowly his mind is becoming more and more easy. Let him tighten his bandage still more if need be. When at last he reaches the Prithivi Tattwa, he will find in the state of his health a great change for the better. Let him preserve in this state, or, still better, the Apas Tattwa for some time, and return to it occasionally for some days, even after the attacks of the disease have ceased. He will no doubt be cured.

Forecast of Futurity

Although a Yogi obtains the power of knowing everything that is, has been, or is to be, beyond the reach of the senses, yet generally he becomes indifferent to such knowledge, forgetting himself, as he does, in his eternal presence before the Light which breathes beauty into all we see in the world. We shall therefore represent him here revealing if not all his knowledge of futurity, only on questions being put to him by others. But our Neophytes may as well put the questions themselves, and then answer them according to the laws here laid down.

When a man comes and says to the Yogi that he has a question to ask, let him:

(a) see which of the Tattwas is in course. If the Tattwa be Prithivi, the question is about some root, something belonging to the vegetable kingdom, or something in which the Earthy nature is predominant.

(b) If it be Apas, it is about some Life, birth, death, etc.

(c) If Tejas, the question is of metals, gain, or loss, etc.

(d) If Akasa, he means to ask nothing.

(e) If Vayu, about some journey.

These are but elementary things. The practical Yogi who can distinguish between the mixture of the Tattwas can name the particular things.

Now let him see through which of his nostrils the Breath is flowing, which is the fortnight then in course of passing, which the days, and what direction of himself, the enquirer.

If the breath comes through the Left nostril, to secure complete success in the work which makes the subject of the question, and which will be of the sort specified under Ida, he must have the following coincidences. The fortnight must be bright, that is of the Waxing Moon. The day must be even; 2, 4, 6, and so on; the direction must be East or North. If these things coincide the man will get what he wants.

Again, if the Surya and Swara coincide with the dark fortnight, the day odd, the direction South and West, the same result may be predicted but not so thoroughly. The action will be of the sort prescribed under Pingala.

According as any of these do not coincide, will the success be more or less imperfect. It must be remembered that the breath at the time must not be flowing through the wrong nostril. This has many bad consequences; we only just touch the subject.

Of the Wrong Swara. If at the commencement of the day the wrong Swara arises, the Luna for the Solar, and vice versa, a man may expect something wrong. If it happens the first day, there is sure to be some sort of mental uneasiness. If the second, some loss of wealth. If the third, a journey will come. If the fourth, some dear object will be destroyed. If the fifth, loss of kingdom. If the sixth, loss of everything. If the seventh illness and pain sure to come. If the eighth, death.

If the Sun breath flows in the morning and at noon and the Moon in the evening, a sad discomforture will be the result, the reverse being a sign of Victory.

If a man, going to travel, raises his foot which coincides in direction with the empty nostril at the time being, he will not get what he desires from his travels.✿

Ritual Work for the Philosophus

Continue the Fourfold breath technique as taught in the Neophyte grade. Add to this the following visualizations:

Inhale	—	YHVH
Full Hold	—	ADONAI
Exhale	—	EHEIEH
Empty Hold	—	AGLA

The Philosophus should construct all of the following talismanic emblems to aid in meditation and ritual. These emblems should be painted green on red.

- The sigil of Elemental Fire
- The sigil of Venus
- The sigil of Aries
- The sigil of Leo
- The sigil of Sagittarius

The following symbols should be painted black on white:

- The number seven
- The letter Qoph
- The letter Tzaddi
- The letter Peh
- The name YHVH Tzabaoth in Hebrew
- The heptagram and heptangle

MEDITATION
for the 3 = 8 grade of Practicus[137]

Let the Philosophus meditate upon the symbol of the Fire Triangle in all its aspects.

Let him contemplate the symbol of the Planet VENUS until he realizes the Universal Love which would express itself in perfect service to all mankind and which embraces Nature both visible and invisible.

Let him identify himself with the powers of FIRE, consecrating himself wholly until the Burnt Sacrifice is consummated and the Christ is conceived by the Spirit.

Let him meditate upon the Triplicity of Fire—its attributes and correspondences.✿

DEVOTION

It is a fact that a powerful emotion will cause very intense mental concentration and focus. For example, a person in the beginning stages of emotional love often becomes completely obsessed with the object of his/her desire—sometimes

---

[137] From Regardie's *The Golden Dawn.*

neglecting all other responsibilities in the process. Fear, another potent emotion, often evokes the same response in those persons who seem wholly consumed and preoccupied by their phobias. All strongly felt emotions (whether love, hate, envy, etc.) can induce a high degree of concentration.

Emotion is therefore a tool that the initiate can use to deliberately focus the mind solely upon one idea. Desire and deep conviction are the necessary creative catalysts in this process. The aspirant must discover something that will arouse within him/her a deeply inspiring emotional reaction. This could include a poem, a work of art, a Biblical or literary passage, a place, a memory, or even a relationship.

No matter what the inspiring image is, the initiate should think upon it and examine it carefully. The image can be summed up within a single glyph or symbol that will serve as an emblem of that which awakens the emotion; the *Symbol of Devotion*. This symbol of Devotion can easily be expanded to contain or even become the ultimate goal of the Great Work undertaken by the aspirant. The Symbol of Devotion which summarizes one's spiritual goal can be either drawn or painted as a sacred object, or it can be preserved abstractly within the canvas of the mind.

Whatever Symbol of Devotion is used, the initiate should bestow great attention to it until it becomes such a potent force that simply gazing at it or thinking about it is all that is necessary to inspire a profound feeling of devotional passion. When this occurs, the symbol becomes an integral part of the aspirant's psyche, growing stronger each time it is recalled.

It is a good practice to employ the Symbol of Devotion to consecrate the most routine activities of daily life to the service of the Divine. Thus even the most ordinary act is accomplished for the sake of the completion of the Great Work. This eventually results in the dedication of one's life to the Divine and to make every act a sacred act. The totality of the initiate's being becomes highly focused in one persistent act of devotion to the Divine Light.

If the aspirant so desires, the Symbol of Devotion can be mentally linked to the deity of his/her choice. (This deity can be derived from any pantheon or tradition.) In this way the image of the deity is firmly connected to the spiritual emotion, making the essence of the deity come to spiritual fruition in the mind of the initiate. Thus any conscious act which invokes the deity becomes an invocation to complete the Great Work.✿

SACRED GROUND

Initiation is a twofold process which entails both the elevation of the Lower Self to the Higher and the invocation of the Higher Self into the Lower vehicle. This exercise involves the consecration of the initiate's Malkuth in order to sublimate it to the Higher awareness of Kether—to render the kingdom sacred for the descent of Spirit.

To begin this exercise, first remove your shoes so that your feet are bare. Remain seated and begin the method of rhythmic breathing. Once this breathing pattern has been established, visualize flames covering the floor beneath your feet. (Note: you may choose to heighten this visualization by first applying a small amount of analgesic cream used for arthritis to the soles or ankles of your feet, so long as you are not allergic to these substances. (Regardie often employed an oriental medication called *Tiger Balm* for such purposes.)

Visualize the red flames both around and through your feet.

Invoke the divine names of Malkuth (for Earth) and Netzach (for Fire) while maintaining the image of sacred ground. For Malkuth, intone: "*ADONAI HA-ARETZ. SANDALPHON. ASHIM.*" For Netzach vibrate "*YHVH TZABAOTH. HANIEL. ELOHIM.*" Continue the exercise for approximately fifteen minutes once or twice daily while in the grade of Philosophus.✡

The 29th Path of Qoph

The *Sepher Yetzirah* calls the 29th Path (from Malkuth to Netzach) the Corporeal Intelligence, because it forms the very body which is so formed beneath the whole Order of the Worlds and the increment of them. It is therefore a path of organization and formation. Case describes the "Corporeal Intelligence" as "body consciousness" representing that stage of incarnation in which the physical body is organized into a form that the Soul may inhabit. This path is ultimately concerned with the acts of reproduction and physical evolution. It is a sexual path, full of passions, reflexes and instincts. The process of journeying upon the paths of the Tree can have a definite effect on the physical body as well as the psychic body. The physical temple of the body is gradually refined as the Divine Light enters into it, and as the Lower Self becomes steadily aware of the Higher.

The occult meaning of the letter Qoph is "sleep," referring to the subconscious state. This is also indicated by the literal meaning of the letter Qoph, which is "the back of the head." In addition, this is also a path of the lower astral, where the student must face and overcome the phantoms and illusions reflected back from the material plane. This is a harsh, probationary path of Water, where the student must confront and conquer the "creations of the created," meaning the phantasms which dwell in the darkest parts of his/her own mind, as well as the ghosts of humanity's collective subconscious. The 29th Path can in fact be a frightening one to traverse, but to the initiate who successfully crosses it, great insight into the inner workings of the astral realm is gained. The Dark is not to be feared, but accepted as the counterpart of the Light.

The 18th Key of the Tarot *The Moon*, is attributed to this path. The Magical Title of this card is "The Ruler of Flux and Reflux, the Child of the Sons of the Mighty." The path of The Moon is known as "The Victory of the Material." Venus acting through Pisces upon the Cosmic Elements. It refers to the deceptive effect of the apparent power of Material Forces, due to the proximity of the Material plane. In other words this path exposes the individual to the allure and pleasure (Venus) that the physical world holds over the psyche (Cosmic elements) using watery Pisces energy. It is up to the initiate to confront and understand this seduction in order to master it and not be mastered by it.

Symbols included within the Tarot card of The Moon are: The orb of the Moon waxing on the side of Chesed (Mercy), four Hebrew Yods falling from Luna like drops of rain, two wild dogs cavorting by moonlight, two towers marking the Path of Qoph in the background, a crayfish in the foreground pulling itself out of the Water onto the path to dry land. The crayfish climbing onto land represents the initiate, starting up the path of evolution from a low-level consciousness to a high-level consciousness (from mundane to spiritual). It seeks the path of growth, which leads out of darkness and into the Light. In its progression, the crayfish must pass by the fierce dogs who are the representatives of the Anubian guards of the path. The crayfish, like the initiate, must overcome all fear and confront what ever phantoms await, for eventually the sun will rise.✿

A JOURNEY ON THE 29TH PATH OF QOPH[138]

For this ritual the Philosophus will need the robe, nemyss, red sandals, the Calvary Cross of Twelve Squares, and the Outer Wand of Double Power. The temple is to be arranged as in the Opening of the 4 = 7 grade. Upon the altar should be the Tarot Trump of THE MOON. A comfortable place to sit and meditate should be arranged West of the pillars.

After a period of relaxation has passed, go to the Northeast and say: *"HEKAS, HEKAS, ESTE BEBELOI! Far from this sacred place be the profane!"*

Go to the East. With the black end of the wand, perform the Lesser Banishing Ritual of the pentagram.

Go to the West of the altar. With the Wand of Double Power, trace a large letter Qoph over the tarot card with the white end of the wand. Visualize it in Red-violet. Intone the name of the letter thrice. Give the Neophyte Signs toward the card. Put the wand aside, and take the Calvary Cross in your right hand.

With all your powers of concentration, look upon the card and comprehend it, consider all its meaning and symbolism. Give the Sign of the Philosophus. At this point you may sit comfortably if you wish, but maintain a disassociation from the

---

[138] From our book *Secret of a Golden Dawn Temple.*

surrounding room. Behind the darkness of your closed eyelids, you begin to formulate the astral temple of the Sephirah Malkuth, as the journey begins:

Astrally, you give the Sign of the Zelator. The now familiar temple of Malkuth formulates around you. The central flame burns brightly with a renewed passion upon the central altar.

As before, you intone the names which call forth the inhabitants of this temple, *Adonai ha-Aretz, Sandalphon, Ashim,* and finally, *Malkuth.* Sandalphon appears as in your previous journeys and you exchange the usual Signs. She asks "Why have you come to the bridal chamber of Kalah in the realm of the Active World?" This time you hold up the Calvary Cross of 12 Squares for the Archangel to see. She leads you to a curtain in the Southeast of the temple upon which is painted the Tarot card of The Moon. She traces the symbol of Pisces and the veil fades into mist. In its place is a door carved from Mother of Pearl upon which is the Hebrew letter Qoph in red-violet. Giving the Sign of the Philosophus, you hold out the Cross and trace the letter Qoph before the door, which dissolves.

A great sea stretches before you blanketed by a thick fog. You are uncertain how to cross this expanse of Water until you notice a white shape rising from the deep. A large scallop shell breaks the surface of the Water at your feet. You step down into it and sit down. Sandalphon is not coming with you, but she gives you a talisman carved from cuttlebone. On one side of it is the symbol of two fish joined by a rope—the sigil of Pisces. On the other side is the representation of a crayfish. Biding the Archangel farewell, you set out upon your journey, drifting across the Waters. The temple of Malkuth is soon lost from sight in the mist.

The Water gently rocks the shell as you glide along. Not being able to see in any direction, you look down and are amazed at the variety of life just under the surface of the Waters. Your sight seems greatly intensified; you see unicellular life forms such as protozoans or single-celled animals, feeding on microscopic food particles and reproducing by cell division. They are eaten by larger multi-celled creatures which are in turn devoured by small jellyfish and crustaceans. Fish hungrily snap up these tasty invertebrates. It is all quite fascinating to you. Nearby the fin of a dolphin cuts through the surface. The animal seems to be following you, or perhaps it is leading your unusual vessel.

Ahead of you the mist parts and you see land. As you glide toward the shore, you see two great stone towers. The portal unto dry land is guarded by the twin Anubian Guards whom you have seen before on the 32nd Path. You stand and face them as your craft pulls into shore. Just as before, they cross their weapons and bar your approach with a snarl. "In what signs and symbols ye come?" they demand.

Standing in the Sign of the Philosophus you state, "In the divine name of *YHVH Tzabaoth,* in the word *Kaph Cheth,* and in the symbol of the Calvary Cross of 12 Squares." The figures step back and allow you to pass. You give the Sign of the Enterer followed by the Sign of Silence and enter the realm of Qoph.

The path leads though a thick, humid jungle of scale-covered trees, giant cycads, huge ferns, and dense thickets of horsetails or scouring rushes. Strange animal sounds can be heard intermittently through the forest. A small yet colorful feathered animal with claws and teeth glides through the treetops, catching a huge dragonfly in mid-flight. In a clearing ahead, you see two large animals locked in mortal combat. A large carnosaur kicks at the belly of a smaller crested plant-eater with deadly clawed feet. The wounded animal bellows in pain as the final blows are inflicted. The victor hungrily tears meat from the not-quite-dead victim, and turns its bloodied head to inspect you with a cold, dull eye. Hunger brings its attention back to the meal at hand. Relieved, you continue though the forest.

Farther up the trail you nearly stumble into a pit of tar. A giant lumbering haired beast has already expired in the black pool. Its body is torn at by a pack of wolves who snap at one another over the possession of choice bits of flesh. Some of the animals have themselves become mired in the tar. The fearful cries of the unfortunates who lay exhausted in the pool are ignored by the rest of the hungry pack.

The jungle opens out into a swamp which makes travel difficult and precarious. It is dark and eerie in this place. Vapors from rotting vegetation rise to the surface of the fetid Waters and cause strange phosphorescent lights and movements. It is easy to see why bogs of this type were thought to be haunted by the Spirits of the dead. The swamp gases play about you, forming phantom shapes and faces against the dark canopy of the trees. In the middle of the marsh stands a large black stone carved into the shape of some terrifying ancient deity. From the scattered bones around the stone, you deduce that humans were once sacrificed here to avoid the wrath of an angry god who might withhold food-animals and plants from hungry tribes. The ghosts of the sacrificed seem to linger here in the iridescent gasses. Without fear, but nonetheless anxious to leave this dreadful place, you press on.

Eventually, the swamp feeds into a river, and the ground on either side of it becomes more firm. The path leads along the river bank amid tall rushes and cattails.

Feeling that you are being watched, you turn toward the river and see the unnerving form of a large crocodile eyeing you curiously. This is the Water god, Sebek, whom the Egyptians worshiped and feared. On the shore near him is an altar upon which a goat has been sacrificed and offered—to persuade the god not to wander about the canals of Egypt searching for hapless victims. For the moment, he is appeased. You are thankful when the road finally leads away from the river.

Beyond the marshlands, the trail takes you up a hill at the top of which is a lion with two heads, one at either end of its body. The menacing beast sits squarely in your path. "Thou canst not enter the realm of Nature and witness the act of Creation unless thou canst tell us our names." The heads warn.

"Thou art the god SEF and the god TUAU. Thou art the twin gods of Yesterday and Tomorrow."

"In what signs and symbols do ye come?" they ask.

You answer with the Sign of the Philosophus and say, "In the divine name *YHVH Tzabaoth*, in the word *Kaph Cheth*, and in this symbol of the Four Rivers." You hold out the Calvary Cross. The creature steps out of your way and you continue up the hill.

At the summit, you look out over a barren landscape. This was the world that existed before the present one. This was the Aeon of time when god begot god, before the stars were positioned. This was the time when Tem, the god of the setting sun produced from his own body by masturbation, his two children—Shu, the god of Air and Tefnut, the goddess of the rains. From the mating of these two gods came the births of Nut and Geb.

The form of Nut fills the sky above you. Her skin is dark and bespangled with stars. Her arms are projected over her head. Her legs are straight with feet together. She is the goddess of the starry heavens, mistress and mother of the gods, and coverer of the sky. Upon her head is a vase of Water, for she is the Water of the firmament, and the starry ocean above.

Her consort Geb, the green god of Earth lays upon the dry and barren ground, propped up on one elbow. With one arm he reaches toward his heavenly lover, who comes to him. The goddess bends her great body into a semicircle which covers the reclining form of the Earth god. Sky and Earth become locked in an intimate and passionate embrace which seems to last indefinitely.

Ra, the mighty Sun god is angered by this great coupling. How will the Solar boat be carried across the sky if the Heavens are eternally mating with the Earth? He orders their father, Shu, to separate the amorous pair. The Air god does so, stepping between the lovers and lifting Nut off of Geb. Her body then forms the arch of the heavens, her arms and legs become the four pillars of the sky and the cardinal points. The raising up of Nut from the embrace of Geb is the first act of creation—the Earth is now separate from the Waters above it. The sun is now set between the Earth and the sky by the reconciling element of Air. The sky, now pregnant, is able to give birth to Osiris, Isis, and other gods and goddesses. Overhead, you witness the process of birth, as the Constellations and Planets are produced from the belly of Nut. The fertile Geb is enabled to cover the Earth with trees, plants, animals and humans. The landscape before you, barren before the great mating, springs to new life with herbs, grains and wildflowers. Before your very eyes, the vegetation thrives and produces fruit.

The path leads on toward a temple surrounded by a colonnade of lotus-topped pillars. The temple itself is built from bricks of pure emerald overgrown with vines. The surrounding courtyard is lush with all manner of plants and wild-flowers. A large disc-shaped brazier in front of the building contains a roaring Fire.

A tap on your shoulder causes you to turn around. A short and stout being with a huge bearded face, large ears and shaggy hair sticks his tongue out and throws an armful of flowers at you. The god, Bes, dressed in animal skins and wearing a tiara of feathers, lets out a huge belly laugh at his jest. He is the god of joy, pleasure and amusement. He welcomes you to the courtyard with a comic dance which is deliberately clumsy and you cannot help but laugh at his antics. In the dance, he humorously mimics your journey through the prehistoric jungle and the fetid swamp—snapping at your backside like Sebek the crocodile. At the end of his dance, the god takes a seat and begins to play a soft melody on a harp, for the goddess of Nature is about to make her appearance.

The beauty of Hathor, the Lady of love, music and dance captivates you as she descends the steps of the temple. The dark skin of her breasts and arms is soft and all-inviting. Her full lips and high cheek bones are accentuated by the slender curve of her neck. She wears a green half-tunic and the crown of cow's horns surmounted by the Solar disc. She is known as the great power of Nature which is perpetually conceiving and creating, rearing and nurturing all things great and small. She is the mother of her father and the daughter of her son. A train of attendant gods follow her every move, for she is known as the mother of every god and goddess. Plants bear seeds in every patch of Earth where her foot has touched. Antelope drop their young at her passing.

Within an instant, the goddess transforms into a great cow. The child Horus comes forth to suckle from her. When he has had his fill, Hathor changes again, into her previous form, but with the head of a cow. Horus falls asleep in the lap of his nursemaid. She gestures at a small shrine in one corner of the garden, indicating that you should investigate.

Upon closer inspection, you notice two nude figures before the door of the grotto. On one side is Min, the god of the Moon and the bestower of fertility in men. His strong body testifies to his sexual powers. The other figure is Qetesh, a moon goddess whose voluptuousness and powers of love relate her to Hathor. A dish of lettuce, considered to be an aphrodisiac by the Egyptians, is placed in offering before each of the figures. You approach and present the signs of a Philosophus and the symbol of the Cross, but in order to enter the shrine, you must honor one of the Lunar deities with a kiss.

Past the entrance into the building it is dark. Before you is a still pool of Water. Beyond that is hill with two forbidding towers. Two black dogs snap and bay at the ghostly face of the Moon, hanging low in the darkening sky. The Lunar energies have stirred the wild animal passions within them. A lowly crayfish starts up the path of evolution which leads between the two higher animal forms. The creature must thread its way carefully through the terrors of the night, that it may live to see the glory of the morning sun. You realize that this is also the path of the initiate, who must face the demons in the back of his/her mind—illusions created in the race consciousness as well as personal illusions and phobias. Like the crayfish, the initiate must be prepared to move up the path of evolution. Although the journey is fraught with unpleasantness, the end result is growth and beauty.

You leave the shrine of the Moon and walk down into the garden of Hathor. She is again as you saw her in the beginning with human features. Beside her is Sandalphon, ready to accompany you on the journey back. You bid farewell to the company of gods and return down the path to the river. Swiftly you pass the fetid swamp and the ancient jungle. The twin Anubis guards watch motionlessly from the shore as you and the Archangel sail away on the white scallop across the expanse of the sea. The temple of Malkuth soon appears in the ocean mist. You enter and take a few moments to warm yourself by the hearth as Sandalphon seals the portal of Qoph. After standing awhile at the altar to take in its spiritual Fire, you salute the Archangel with the Neophyte Sign. She in turn gives the Sign of Silence.

At this point bring your astral body back to the physical temple around you. Do not hurry.

Perform the LBRP with the black end of the wand. Declare the temple duly closed.✿

The 28th Path of Tzaddi

The Sepher Yetzirah calls the 28th Path (from Yesod to Netzach) the Natural Intelligence, because through it is consummated and perfected the Nature of every existing thing beneath the Sun. This points to the coarse powers of Nature attributed to Netzach. This path is a reflection of the Airy Sign Aquarius, the Water-bearer, unto which is attributed to the Countenance of Man, the ADAM who restored the world. For the initiate, the path that runs between Yesod and Netzach represents the hope of rebuilding the Garden of Eden by the deliberate changing of consciousness through the act of meditation.

Meditation is a combination of knowledge and imagination, and it is through the awakening of the centers of consciousness in the body (with meditation) that the initiate "perfects his/her own nature." Case describes meditation as "an unbroken flow of knowledge in a particular object." The "fish-hook" of Tzaddi is cast into the ocean stream of the subconscious mind to catch a bit of divine truth. It is a period of inner quest and searching. The process of meditation is both the procedure and the goal of spiritual attainment, for the act itself results in a change of energy from one form to another. The initiate on this upper astral path is exploring the very basic mysteries behind creation, life and death. However, the aspirant on the 28th Path must take care not to become "bewitched" by the glamours and illusions which commence in the sphere of Yesod. This path contains the hopes, dreams and visions of humankind infused with the fertile lifeforce of Netzach. The only way back to a restored Eden is to function in accordance with the universal Will.

The 17th Key of the Tarot *The Star*, is attributed to this path. The Magical Title of this card is "The Daughter of the Firmament; the Dweller between the Waters." The path of The Star is known as "The Victory of Fundamental Strength." Venus acting through Aquarius upon Luna. This is a path of hope that shows the initiate that imagination combined with emotive force (Venus) has great power in the astral realm (Luna) through the Airy energies of Aquarius.

Symbols included within the Tarot card of The Star are: a great feminine figure pouring two vases of Water which form a river at her feet, a large star overhead with seven principle rays and fourteen secondary rays, seven smaller stars, the Tree of Life, the Tree of the Knowledge of Good and Evil, and the ibis of Thoth. The Water that the goddess pours out is pure fluid consciousness—the Waters of Life which receive an everlasting supply of creative energy from Venus. This fluid consciousness is the universal consciousness or wellspring of the imagination which feeds the meditative faculties of humanity, and provides the initiate with an endless stream of spiritual wealth.✿

A JOURNEY ON THE 28TH PATH OF TZADDI[139]

For this ritual the Philosophus will need the robe, nemyss, red sandals, the Pyramid of the Elements, and the Outer Wand of Double Power. The temple is to be arranged as in the second part of the 4 = 7 grade. Upon the altar should be the Tarot Trump of THE STAR. A comfortable place to sit and meditate should be arranged West of the pillars.

After a period of relaxation has passed, go to the Northeast and say:*"HEKAS, HEKAS, ESTE BEBELOI! Far from this sacred place be the profane!"*

Go to the East. With the black end of the wand, perform the Lesser Banishing Ritual of the pentagram.

Go the West of the altar. With the white end of the Wand of Double Power, trace a large letter Tzaddi over the Tarot card. Visualize it in violet. Intone the name of the letter thrice. Give the Neophyte Signs toward the card. Put the wand aside, and take the Pyramid in your right hand.

With all your powers of concentration, look upon the card and comprehend it, consider all its meaning and symbolism. Give the Sign of the Philosophus. At this point you may sit comfortably if you wish, but maintain a disassociation from the surrounding room. Behind the darkness of your closed eyelids, you begin to formulate the astral temple of the Sephirah Malkuth as the journey begins:

Astrally, you give the Sign of the Zelator. The now familiar temple of Malkuth formulates around you. The altar flame lends its comforting warmth to the chamber.

As before, you intone the names which call forth the inhabitants of this temple, *Adonai ha-Aretz, Sandalphon, Ashim,* and finally, *Malkuth.* Sandalphon appears as she has in all your previous journeys and you exchange the usual Signs. You hold up the Truncated Pyramid for her to see, and she takes you quickly through the Eastern portal of Tau. Soon you are at the entrance to the temple of Yesod. You enter without the Archangel, giving the Neophyte Signs.

The nine violet walls of the chamber along with the enneangle carved into the floor is a sight which never fails to heighten your sense of awareness. The thick scent of jasmine hangs in the Air, bringing with it the tingling sensation of the Kundalini along the nerves of your spine. The phases of the moon carved in quartz and ebony seem to float eerily in the ceiling above the incense. The four kerubic statues around the silver altar and its central flame again bring an etheric feeling of awe and timelessness.

---

[139] From our book *Secret of a Golden Dawn Temple.*

As before, you vibrate the divine name of *Shaddai El Chai*, the Archangel *Gabriel*, the order of the *Kerubim*, and finally, the name of the temple itself, *Yesod*.

The beautiful Gabriel takes shape in the clouds of incense. The same dark hair, green eyes and fine-boned features are there, but this time the robes of violet and yellow cover a female form—the Archangel has chosen to emphasize her feminine aspects. She speaks:

"Behold around you, the realm of Foundation—the sphere of the art of magic. You have entered the current of the astral Light. By what Sign hast thou entered into the temple of Flux and Reflux?

You answer by giving the Sign of the Theoricus.

"Why have you come to the chamber of change and alteration?" she asks. You hold up the Pyramid of the Four Elements.

The Archangel anoints you with perfume as you again step into the sandals of a Firm Foundation which provide you a better footing in the astral plane. Gabriel then takes you to a curtain in the Southeast upon which is depicted the Tarot card of The Star. She traces the sigil of Aquarius and the veil evaporates, disclosing a door of glass, upon which is a panel of violet stained glass shaped in the form of the letter Tzaddi. Before it, you hold up the Pyramid and trace the letter of the fishhook. The door opens and the journey on the 28th Path of The Star begins.

The scenery along this trail is the most lush and beautiful of any you have yet encountered. Not only is the sight of it beautiful, but the whole atmosphere of the landscape is one of overwhelming peace and promise. It is ideal—the perfect Garden of Eden. Gabriel walks swiftly, but you are in no hurry and pause frequently to admire some singularly lovely flower or butterfly, or listen to a songbird. The guide stops often to let you catch up to her.

The path ahead leads between two olive trees where a single figure stands guard with no weapon at all. He is not nearly as menacing as the portal guardians of other paths have been. Nevertheless, he blocks your entrance.

"Thou canst not enter the Garden of Perfected Nature, unless thou canst tell me my name." he states.

"SAA, god of feeling and intelligence is Thy name. Thou art the god that causes men and women to perceive, to feel, to understand and to become wise through experience," you reply.

"In what signs and symbols do ye come?"

Giving the Sign of Philosophus you answer, "In the divine name *YHVH Tzabaoth*, in the word *Kaph Cheth* and in this symbol of the Pyramid of the Four Elements."

The god traces the sigil of Aquarius in the Air before you and lets you pass, but not without a word of warning. "Respect the garden for its beauty, but also for its thorns which are felt but rarely seen." With that enigmatic word of caution, you continue up the path. Gabriel indicates that this is as far as she will take you.

In the main part of this paradise, there is a cool spring of pure running Water which trickles through a grove of lilacs. Unhurried, you sit down on a large rock which overhangs the stream. A long blade of grass provides you with something to hold between your teeth. You lazily chew the stem, tasting the strong green fluid. The Water beside the stone reflects your face back at you. After a short while you notice three large yellow butterflies carrying a lily between them. They hover close enough for you to smell the sweet odor of the flower. "Come closer," they whisper, "Come and drink the nectar of the Garden of Paradise. Live here with us in eternal happiness!" The smell of the honey-liquid within the flower is intoxicating and inviting. You can imagine how sweet it would taste. But something holds you back. You are suddenly aware of the sandals of Yesod on your feet. The thought of the Firm Foundation suddenly thrusts itself into your mind. If you drink the fluid, you could become immortal and live in the Garden of Eden forever. But at what price? This way to immortality seems too easy. What good is it to become immortal if you have not yet learned the lessons of this incarnation? It is very tempting, but in the end, you refuse to drink.

Turning away, you glance down into the stream beneath your feet. To your surprise, the face that is reflected back at you is not your own. The triangular head of Sebek the crocodile, complete with a toothy grin, has stealthily glided into position below you. Instinctively, you give the Attacking Sign at him, followed by the Sign of Silence. The scaly head disappears under the Water.

The sound of laughter makes you look up. The butterflies have become sylphs who are amused that you almost fell for their illusion. The flower that they hold is a carnivorous pitcher plant. In a cloud of fairy dust, they vanish.

The glamour gone, you stand up and realize that you almost did not complete this journey. Much time as passed, and it is late evening. Luckily, the Moon is high and full, with no clouds to obscure the light it provides. Looking around for the trail, you spot it and continue up the 28th path, this time with more respect and fewer misconceptions.

The road winds through thick vegetation and eventually into a grassy meadow. There stands a great and beautiful goddess with long golden hair and milky skin. She is nude save for the symbol of the seven-pointed star at her brow. In each hand she grasps a vase, one gray and one black. Water from both vases pour out upon the ground at her feet, forming the headwaters of a great river. She is Isis, the mighty goddess. But she is also Hathor and Nephthys, the dark-skinned beauty. In fact she is all goddesses, but perhaps she is best described by the title *Aima Elohim*, the great Supernal Mother. The vases contain the essences of Chokmah and Binah, respectively, pouring out upon the Earth to restore the decimated garden of Eden. A large heptagonal star surrounded by fourteen secondary rays sits in the sky above her head. This is the dog star, Sirius, as well as *Sept* or *Sothis*, the Star of Hathor, which is known as the second sun in heaven. The seven Planets of the ancients appear as smaller stars which encircle the Sept star like a halo.

To the right (Geburah) side of the figure is the Tree of the knowledge of Good and Evil, which symbolizes the mixed state of the human condition after the expulsion from the Garden of eternal happiness, pleasure and pain, love and anger, harmony and disorder. An Ibis, the bird of Thoth perches itself on the forbidding tree as if to emphasize that only through the willpower of the magician can the garden be restored—through the proper use of knowledge in accordance with the universal will.

To the left (Chesed) side of the figure is the Tree of Life, the map which humankind may follow to reconstruct the Garden of Eden within the Personality of each individual through meditation and spiritual intuition.

You give the Sign and Words of a Philosophus, hold out the truncated pyramid and ask for guidance and inspiration from the great goddess. She says nothing and scarcely seems to notice you, but continues to pour Water into the river. For a brief moment you are perplexed, but decide to take a different approach. Seating yourself in the grass at the edge of the river, you begin to focus on the large star in the sky. You concentrate on the number of rays, seven primary plus fourteen secondary—a total of twenty-one. Closing your eyes, you begin to mentally intone the divine name of Kether, *Eheieh*, meditating only upon the quiet vibration of the name, and shutting out all else.

After vibrating the name for a period of time, the voice of goddess enters your mind. You listen as she speaks:

"Dost thou imagine that thou hast come to this place of thine own accord searching for Wisdom? Nothing is farther from the Truth. I have sought *Thee* out. I have brought thee here as a fish on the hook of Tzaddi cast into the shadowy ocean—to bring thee into the Light. I seek thee as a bride seeks the groom. I seek thee as a reflection of mine own face in a mirror.

"I am the gate which looks out upon the world and back in at myself. I lead humanity from falsity into Truth—from the separateness of the outer into the wholeness and holiness of the Inner. This I work through *Inner* vision and hearing. The eyes and ears of the body are concerned only with the veneer of reality. The senses of the Soul perceive far more that is Truth. The seeds of Truth and Wisdom are sown in silence and grow in silence and mystery. Not in confusion and noise is the work of Nature perfected, but in the calm meditation that seeks out thine own true self. Here shalt thou find me reflected. Herein lies the return to the Garden. Herein also is the universe resolved into its ultimate elements under the presidency of the divine ETH."

When the goddess is done speaking, you open your eyes. She stands there as before, pouring out the essence of the Supernals into the river. As the Water from the vases mix with that of the river, quartz crystals are formed, as though energy is transforming from a fluid into a solid form. This metamorphosis of energy reminds you of your own transformation—from a secular individual into an initiate of the Hermetic mysteries.

The vision of the star re-enters your thoughts. You are reminded of the story of Lucifer, not the devil of the Dark Ages, but the beautiful Angel whose name means "Light Bearer" identified with the Planet Venus—the Morning and Evening Star. Venus, the physical chakra of the Sephirah, Netzach, hangs in the sky with the other stars.

You sit on the river bank a long time, basking in the rays of starlight, filled with inspiration and creativity. The stars multiply into a galaxy. Each constellation presents itself to you, one after another. Soon the fingers of morning begin to grasp the Eastern edge of the sky, pushing the stars ever higher above the horizon. As dawn breaks over the Garden, you know it is time to leave.

Backtracking the way you came, you soon arrive at the twin olive trees guarded by the god Saa. Gabriel is there waiting for you. Together you return to the temple of Yesod where you return the violet sandals to their place at the foot of the altar. She then guides you back to the temple of Malkuth. Sandalphon seems particularly pleased to see you after this journey and welcomes you with an embrace worthy of an Archangel. She then closes the portal of Tzaddi. As always you take a few moments of silent communion over the altar flame with Sandalphon. After this journey, such moments of silence seem pregnant with conversation. Finally, bidding her farewell, you salute with the Projection Sign. She in turn gives the Sign of Silence.

At this point bring your astral body back to the physical temple around you. Do not hurry.

Perform the LBRP with the black end of the wand. Declare the temple duly closed.✪

The 27th Path of Peh

The *Sepher Yetzirah* calls the 27th Path the Exciting Intelligence, because by it is created the Intellect of all created Beings under the Highest Heaven. It is therefore a reflection of the sphere of Mars and the path connecting Netzach with Hod. The "Exciting Intelligence" refers to the power of this path to arouse sudden change. The Hebrew letter Peh means mouth, which alludes to the power of speech and vibration. This is the first of the reciprocal paths (straddling all three pillars) that the initiate encounters while scaling the paths of the Tree.

This most difficult path involves the abrupt and complete destruction (purification) of old "realities." It signifies sudden illumination or realization. The Higher Forces are brought in through this harsh path in order to exhaust the Lower Personality and literally force spiritual growth to take place.

The 16th Key of the Tarot *The Tower*, is attributed to this path. The Magical Title of this card is "The Lord of the Hosts of the Mighty." The path of The Tower is known as "The Victory over Splendor." Venus acting through Mars upon Mercury. This gives some indication of the conflict between heart and mind that occurs on this path. Emotion and Desire (Venus) struggle to strike a balance with Intellect (Mercury) using fiery Martial force. This balance must be accomplished before any real spiritual progress can take place.

Symbols included within the Tarot card of The Tower are: a stone tower struck by a lightening bolt in the shape of the Mars sigil, two figures falling headlong from the blasted crown of the tower, the Tree of Life and the Tree of the Qlippoth. The Tower symbolizes the "I" consciousness or Personality awareness. It represents those beliefs which each person has built up through life since childhood—those beliefs that were programmed into the child by parents, teachers, institutions and peers. The Tower is built in this fashion, one brick, one belief at a time, and is fortified in adulthood like a tower under siege. This tower is protected by the Lower Personality from attack by other belief systems which are in disagreement with it. Thus it becomes a closed armory, firmly shut against free flow of expression from the outside as well as from the inside.

The Tower struck by lightning represents the Ego awareness collapsing under an inflow of force which exposes something of the essence of the Higher Self. Thus the old "realities" so cherished by the Lower Personality are changed forever—destroyed for all intents and purposes. Once the Tower has been shattered, it must be re-examined. Some remnants of the old Tower may then be re-integrated, while others are discarded. It is up to the initiate to decide.✿

A JOURNEY ON THE 27TH PATH OF PEH[140]

For this ritual the Philosophus will need the robe, nemyss, red sandals and the Outer Wand of Double Power. The temple is to be arranged as in the Third part of the 4 = 7 grade. Upon the altar should be the Tarot Trump of THE TOWER. A comfortable place to sit and meditate should be arranged West of the pillars.

After a period of relaxation has passed, go to the Northeast and say, "*HEKAS, HEKAS, ESTE BEBELOI! Far from this sacred place be the profane!*"

Go to the East. With the black end of the wand, perform the Lesser Banishing Ritual of the pentagram.

Go the West of the altar. With the white end of the Wand of Double Power, trace a large letter Peh over the Tarot card. Visualize it in Red. Intone the name of the letter twice. Give the Neophyte Signs toward the card. Put the wand aside, and take the Calvary Cross in your right hand.

With all your powers of concentration, look upon the card and comprehend it, consider all its meaning and symbolism. Give the Sign of the Philosophus. At this point you may sit comfortably if you wish, but maintain a disassociation from the surrounding room. Behind the darkness of your closed eyelids, you begin to formulate the astral temple of the Sephirah Malkuth, as the journey begins:

Astrally, you give the Sign of the Zelator. The ten-sided chamber of Malkuth appears around you. As on previous journeys, you intone the names which call forth the inhabitants of this temple, *Adonai ha-Aretz, Sandalphon, Ashim,* and finally, *Malkuth.* Sandalphon comes forth and you exchange the usual Signs. When she asks why you have come this time, you hold up the Calvary Cross of 10

---

[140] From our book *Secret of a Golden Dawn Temple.*

Squares for her to see. Swiftly, the Archangel leads you through the portal of Shin in the Northeast of the temple and up the 31st Path to the temple of Hod. Leaving Sandalphon, you enter the Water temple giving the Neophyte Signs.

A great eight-sided room surrounds you. The walls are draped in curtains of orange silk and the floor is covered with glittering Fire opals. The scent of storax is heavy in the Air. In each corner of the room is a statue of the god of Knowledge, given various names and appearances throughout history: Tahuti-Thoth, Enki, Hermes, Mercury, Nabu, Turms, Odin and Cilans. A statue of an hermaphrodite, Hapi, god of the Nile occupies a small shrine in one part of the temple. The ceiling above you is dominated by a large blue sigil of Mercury. Within the circle of the sigil is the image of a cup. Your attention is drawn to the center of the room where eight alternating columns of Water and Fire enclose a small inner sanctuary. There is a blue altar in the middle of this sacred chamber, covered by an apron, upon which is a disc of opal containing the temple flame. In addition, there is a chalice of Water and the Book of Knowledge with the figure of an octagram gracing its cover.

To announce your presence in the temple and call forth its inhabitants, you vibrate the divine name *Elohim Tzabaoth* and the name of the Archangel, *Michael.* You then call upon the order of Angels known as the *Beni Elohim.* Finally, you intone the name of the temple itself, Hod.

Almost immediately, the great flaming being of Michael appears, just as you remember him from the Path of Shin, clothed in a Fireball of red and orange flames with fingers of flame running the entire length of his body. His vaporous wings form a halo of pure heat around his head, and he carries a large sword, for he is the Prince of Light and the Leader of the Heavenly Hosts. He speaks:

"Behold the Vision of Splendour and the reflection of Mercy! By what sign does thou enter herein?"

You answer by giving the Sign of the Practicus.

"Why hast thou come to this temple of the Perfect and Absolute Intelligence?"

You hold up the Calvary Cross of Ten Squares for the Archangel to see. Satisfied, he changes into a form that is easier for you to approach. The halo of flames vanishes and in its place is a suit of armour, Roman in design, which makes Michael look more like a winged human warrior than a being of living flame. His sword has become a long spear.

The Archangel takes you to the right side of the chamber and draws back a portion of the orange drapery to reveal another curtain with the image of The Tower painted upon it. He traces the symbol of Mars and the veil fades into mist. In its place is a door carved from ruby, upon which is the Hebrew letter Peh. Giving the Sign of the Philosophus, you hold out the Cross and trace the form of the letter Peh before the door, which dissolves. Together, you and your guide start down the path.

It is sunrise, and the Solar disc is just beginning to mark its ascent to your left. You pass low rolling hills dotted with grazing sheep. The grazing is sparse, however, because the land is similar to a high plains desert with meager amounts of rainfall. Joshua trees, cactus and desert scrub seem to be the norm here, and the arid odor of pepper is in the Air.

Eventually, the landscape begins to change, becoming more rocky and mountainous. Even the hardy desert scrub seems unable to get a foothold between the impartial granite slabs of this harsh place. Devoid of even the most durable of Nature's flora, the region looks as though it might just as well be a martian land-scape. The trail seems treacherous, full of potholes and sharp, loose stones that cause you to misstep often. Michael says not a word as he walks effortlessly in front of you, but his protective presence is reassuring.

Just ahead of you, behind a craggy hillside, a wondrous image presents itself to your eyes—a great crown which sparkles with many jewels. As you get closer, you see before you an enormously high stone tower with a shining crown at its summit. The mighty fortress looks impenetrable and there are no windows. The path you are traveling leads straight to the entrance of the structure, where two well-worn battering rams have ended their days of combat only to be implanted in the ground as columns—their carved horns and ram-faces chipped and broken in many places. Before these crude pillars two figures hold watch over the entrance. Michael sends you on ahead. From here on you must face whatever awaits you alone, and act upon your own decisions. As you near the tower, you begin to make out the features of the two guardians.

The form on the right has a muscular form covered by a red tunic. The piercing eyes of a hawk glare at you from under a nemyss surmounted by the double crown of Egypt. In one hand the swarthy being holds a club, and in the other an iron-tipped spear.

The left-hand figure is feminine, also dark in limb, who holds a lotus staff and ankh. She too, wears a tunic of red linen.

At your approach, the figures cross their implements, spear to staff, and block your advance. "Thou canst not enter the Tower of the Vibration of the Word unless thou canst tell us our names," they command.

You turn to the hawk-headed figure and say, "Thou art *Horus*, god of bat-tles, Slayer of Set and the enemies of Ra. *Heru* the Piecer, Son of the Sun." To the left-hand figure you answer, "Thou art *Nephthys*, sister of Isis, lady of the invisible, dark goddess of death and life."

"In what signs and symbols do ye come?" They question.

Your answer is given in the Sign of the Philosophus. "In the divine name *Elohim Tzabaoth*. In the word *Kaph Cheth*. And in this symbol of the Sephirotic Cross."

The figures step back and allow you to pass. A solid oak door stands in your way. You project at it with the Attacking Sign and it opens inward. Giving the Sign of Silence, you enter.

Once inside the damp, musky building, you feel a bit closed-in. The tower has been badly neglected and is in need of repair. Cobwebs and dust are every-where. The floorboards are rotten and crumble under your weight. Before you is a stone staircase that looks as though it leads to the crown of the tower. Perhaps there is something of value in this dingy old tower that you need to explore. With renewed confidence you begin the ascent to the top. The stairs are slippery with mold, so you must watch your step. As you climb, you pass armaments of all kinds: cannons, gunpowder, shields, lances, broadswords and more. Apparently, the tower has been under siege for some time, but it is well-fortified and armed to the teeth.

Nearing the top of the fortress, you hear sounds of music, dancing and laughter. Who, you wonder, could call such a place as this home? Your Will and curiosity drive you forward. Thrusting open a crumbling door at the top of the stairs, you gaze out onto a richly dressed group of nobles in silken robes and jeweled headpieces. They sit atop the crown of the tower under the shade a raised cloth. They are bloated and immobile from sheer gluttony. A few undernourished servants in rags do their best to minister to the needs and amusements of the group—playing flutes, dancing and bringing food. The only reward of these attendants is disregard at best. The more unfortunate servants receive a kick or fist. The wealthy barons and dukes argue with one another over luxurious trinkets which fall unnoticed to the fall when some new bauble grabs their attention. In front of this opulent group are enormous quantities of food and drink, so much food in fact that some of it appears to be spoiling. Yet tethered to a stone away from the food is a small monkey weak from hunger, with nothing to eat. The pitiful animal, kept only for amusement has obviously been forgotten like the other court toys. This makes you angry. How dare these people be so neglectful and selfish?

Your presence has startled them. They stare at you with absolute astonishment. It is as if they have never seen anyone besides themselves in their domain. They seem to consider you an intruder. Frightened, they sound an alarm. From the door behind you and another opening behind the nobles, armored guards come running with raised swords. What you wouldn't give to have Michael by your side now!

Before any hands are able to grasp you, there is another sudden commotion. The aristocrats are now frantic because the sun has abruptly disappeared behind a great black cloud. Without warning there is a huge explosion of light and stone. A great bolt of lightning has struck the tower! At the same moment, you hear a roaring vibration of sound as if all the Angelic choirs above the Firmament suddenly opened their mouths and uttered the true name of Tetragrammaton. Within an instant there are no longer bricks beneath your feet and you are sailing through the Air. For a moment you are certain that this must be the end of your journey. As you fall, you yell out, "ADONAI! I am free from the bonds of Darkness!"

Hands are suddenly there to grasp you. Michael, hearing your cry of willing sacrifice, has taken wing to keep you from falling into the void and sharing the fate of the Dukes of Edom. For the Lords of Chaos there is no rescue. From the Archangel's strong arms you watch as the nobles and the tower's crown are swept away in the darkness—into the waiting mouth of Moloch—and the nothingness from whence they came. Fascinated, you can do nothing but watch. A voice enters your mind, and you listen quietly as you learned to do on the Path of Tzaddi:

"I am the Logos and the mouth that utter it. I beget life and I consume life. I am the Alpha and the Omega. All things which I create return unto me. Do not be mislead by this apparent demolition, for I destroy only to rebuild into a greater design. The Soul of the humankind evolves from this destruction, always growing and fading, changing yet living. Through this destruction is the Soul preserved, that it may at length become One with the Source. Let those who would be free from the bonds of darkness learn to separate the spiritual from the material. Temper the Water of the Intellect with the Fire of Emotion. The Fire of Spirit moves and descends into the Fire of Form. Those who feel this divine Fire within their Souls shall ascend to live eternally within the new tower which I alone shall build. The Logos shall be my building stone and the vibration of the Word shall be my mortar."

You are lying on the ground, but you did not feel the landing. Michael is standing above you smiling. The Archangel offers you his hand and pulls you to your feet. Remembering everything that has happened, you stare at the tower in amazement.

The mighty crown which surmounted the structure has been utterly destroyed. Not one of its bricks remain. The entire upper portion of masonry has been knocked away. Three gaping holes have been blown into the wall revealing that the Fire inside the fortress rages on. The openings resemble three blazing roses.

Squeezing your shoulder in a gesture of affection, Michael informs you that you have done well on this difficult test. What you rebuild out of the ashes of the Tower struck by Lightning will be far greater than anything you can now imagine. It is up to you to create a better, more balanced structure—discarding pieces of the old tower which are obsolete, while keeping those pieces which are usable. The new tower of the Personality must be built in the image of the Higher Design, using knowledge and compassion, never the one without the other. But for the moment you must return to the temple of Hod.

The landscape becomes less rugged and the road widens as you leave the desolate region of the old tower. The desert vegetation returns to view. You feel revitalized by having survived the ordeal of the Tower. Michael walks beside you now, as if he is more confident of your abilities.

A noise off to the right brings your attention to an apple tree beside the path that you had not noticed earlier. The monkey from the tower sits amid the branches, happily munching on a piece of fruit. It is as if the ape of Thoth has been nourished by the blasting of the old fortress.

Once again you find yourself back at the Water temple. You are reluctant to leave this place of learning, but you know that what you have accomplished today will take time to fully comprehend. Michael takes you down the path of Shin to the temple of Malkuth. As you say goodbye to the Archangel, he transforms back into his true flaming appearance—the Light of God in the center of the ball of flame.

Sandalphon quickly seals the portal of the 31st Path behind you. She fetches a chalice to give you a long cool drink from the fountain. The Ashim are quite noticeable in the temple after your journey on the Path of Peh. They resemble Yods of flame dancing above the altar. You enjoy their company awhile before leaving. Finally, you bid goodbye to the inhabitants of the temple and salute with the Projection Sign. Sandalphon gives the Sign of Silence.

At this point bring your astral body back to the physical temple around you. Do not hurry.

Perform the LBRP with the black end of the wand. Declare the temple duly closed.✿

AN INVOCATION OF THE ELEMENT OF FIRE

For the grade of Philosophus

For this ritual the Philosophus will need a black Outer Order robe, black and white striped nemyss, and the Outer Wand of Double Power. A red candle and one or more of the talismanic emblems mentioned on page 573 should be placed on the altar. The temple is to be arranged in accordance with the Philosophus Hall (as in the final part of the initiation ceremony).

Relax for a few moments and perform the Fourfold Breath.

Go to the Northeast and say, *"HEKAS, HEKAS, ESTE BEBELOI!"*

With the black end of the wand, perform the Lesser Banishing Ritual of the Pentagram.

> (Say the following invocation:) *And when after all the phantoms are banished, thou shalt see that holy and formless Fire, that Fire which darts and flashes through the hidden depths of the universe. Hear thou, the Voice of Fire!*

Go clockwise to the East. With the white end of the wand, trace the lesser invoking pentagram. Thrust the wand through the center of the figure and vibrate, *"ADONAI!"* Draw the same figure and intone the same name in all four quarters going from East to South, West and North. Return to the South. Say:

> *In the divine name YHVH TZABAOTH, I open this temple in the Element of Fire. May the Archangel MICHAEL look with favor upon this ceremony! May the Angel ARIEL and the ruler SERAPH be also in attendance! I have gained admission to this temple through the Cross of the Hegemon's Badge. Hear me! I am one who has received the Mystic Title of Pharos Illuminans and the symbols of ASCH and PHRATH. As an Illuminating Tower of Light, I invoke the powers of Fire to bear witness to my spiritual endeavor. Grant me the knowledge of the Element of Fire and the divine realm, so that I may obtain greater understanding of hidden things and thereby advance in the Great Work.*

Circumambulate the temple three times, saluting with the Neophyte Signs when passing the East.

Go to the West and face East. Give the Adoration to the Lord of the Universe:

> *Holy art Thou, Lord of the Universe!*
> *Holy art Thou, Whom Nature hath not formed!*
> *Holy art Thou, the Vast and the Mighty One!*
> *Lord of the Light, and of the Darkness!*

Go to the South and give the Philosophus Sign. Recite the Prayer of the Salamanders:

> *Immortal, Eternal, Ineffable and Uncreated Father of all, borne upon the Chariot of Worlds which ever roll in ceaseless motion. Ruler over the Ethereal Vastness where the Throne of Thy Power is raised, from the summit of which Thine Eyes behold all and Thy Pure and Holy Ears hear all— help us, Thy children, whom Thou hast loved since the birth of the Ages of Time! Thy Majesty, Golden, Vast and Eternal, shineth above the Heaven of Stars. Above them art Thou exalted.*
>
> *O Thou Flashing Fire, there Thou illuminatest all things with Thine Insupportable Glory, whence flow the Ceaseless Streams of Splendour which nourisheth Thine Infinite Spirit. This Infinite Spirit nourisheth all and maketh that inexhaustible Treasure of Generation which ever encompasseth Thee—replete with the numberless forms wherewith Thou hast filled it from the Beginning.*
>
> *From this Spirit arise those most holy kings who are around Thy Throne and who compose Thy Court.*
>
> *O Universal Father, One and Alone! Father alike of Immortals and Mortals. Thou hast specially created Powers similar unto Thy Thought Eternal and unto Thy Venerable Essence. Thou hast established them above the Angels who announce Thy Will to the world.*
>
> *Lastly, Thou hast created us as a third Order in our Elemental Empire.*
>
> *There our continual exercise is to praise and to adore Thy Desires: there we ceaselessly burn with Eternal Aspirations unto Thee, O Father! O Mother of Mothers! O Archetype Eternal of Maternity and Love! O Son, the Flower of all Sons! Form of all Forms! Soul, Spirit, Harmony and Numeral of all things! Amen!*

Give the Philosophus Sign. Go to the West of the altar. With the white end of the wand, trace the lesser invoking pentagram over the red candle. Place the wand aside.

Take a few moments to feel the heat of the candle flame. As you partake of the Element, meditate on the talismanic emblem you have chosen. Take as much time as you need for the meditation.

Perform the Reverse Circumambulation. Go to the East and say:

> *I now release any Spirits that may have been imprisoned by this ceremony. Depart in peace to your abodes and habitations. Go with the blessings of YHVH TZABAOTH!*

Perform the LBRP with the black end of the wand. Then say: *"I now declare this temple duly closed."*✿

Suggested Reading

Egyptian Religion by E.A. Wallis Budge
> (Write a report on the book. Examine the parallels between the religion of the ancient Egyptians and Judaeo-Christian beliefs.)

Egyptian Magic by Florence Farr

Awakening Osiris by Normandi Ellis

Meditation and Kabbalah by Aryeh Kaplan
> (An excellent book which explores the meditative techniques, mantras and mandalas of the ancient Qabalists. Write a report on the book. Explore and put into practice some of the techniques given.)

Sefer Yetzirah, The Book of Creation by Aryeh Kaplan

Psychology & Kabbalah by Z'en ben Shimon Halevi
> (Write a report on the book.)

The Book of Tokens by Paul Foster Case
> (A potent little book of Tarot Meditations. Perform one meditation daily in conjunction with the Qabalistic Cross and the Adoration to the Lord of the Universe, or with the daily meditations given in Chapter One.)

The Equilibration of Jehovah by M. Isidora Forrest
> (Published in *The Golden Dawn Journal, Book 2: Qabalah*. If possible, perform this ritual with a group of competent magicians, priests and priestesses. Record your impressions and take note of how the fiery energy of Jehovah is transformed during the ceremony.)

The Restoration and Alchemy by Steven Marshall.
> (Published in *The Golden Dawn Journal, Book 2: Qabalah*)

The Gnostics and Their Remains by C. W. King

The Gnostic Gospels by Elaine Pagels

The Varieties of Religious Experience by William James

Religions, Values, and Peak Experiences by Abraham H. Maslow

Up from Eden: A Transpersonal View of Human Evolution by Ken Wilber

Some Final Suggestions

- Obtain a black-and-white 8.5 x 11 copy of the Tarot card *The Moon* and paint it, or draw your own version of the card.

- Obtain a black-and-white 8.5 x 11 copy of the Tarot card *The Star* and paint it, or draw your own version of the card.

- Make colored drawings of Osiris, Horus and Isis. Devise your own meditation for incorporating these figures.

- Make colored drawings of Isis, Nephthys and Hathor. Devise your own meditation for incorporating these figures.

- Draw your personal impression of a Salamander.

- Practice divination by Pyromancy. (See the introduction of *The Golden Dawn Journal, Book 1: Divination.*)

- Take periodic observations of the Planet Venus (at both dawn and dusk) Also take note what Zodiacal Sign the Planet is in.

- Take note of where Venus falls in your own Zodiacal chart. Write a brief report on how you think you are affected by the Planet's position in your natal chart.

- Take note of any Planets that are located in Fire Signs in your own Zodiacal chart. Write a brief report on how you think you are affected by them.

- Prepare your own mixture of perfumed oils, herbal baths, magic inks or herbal teas for the Sephirah of Venus, using your ingenuity and the source book *The Complete Book of Incense, Oils and Brews* by Scott Cunningham.

- Perform Tarot divinations twice daily while in the grade of Philosophus.

- Take a trip to a foundry or metal smith. Meditate on the importance of the Fire Element to human invention and interaction.

- Gaze into a camp fire or lighted hearth. Meditate on the importance of the Fire Element to all aspects of Life on this Planet.

- Find out how you can become personally involved in Fire prevention and responsible management of this potent Element.

Examinations

(Answers for all exams are given in the back of this book.)

QUIZ 0 *(The Ritual)*

1. What is the Grand Word of the grade of Philosophus?
2. What is the Mystic Number of the Philosophus grade?
3. What is the password of the Philosophus grade derived from the Mystic Number?
4. What is the Battery of knocks attributed to the Philosophus grade?
5. What is the Grip of the Philosophus grade?
6. What is the Sign of the Philosophus grade?
7. What is the Elemental symbol given to the Philosophus?
8. List the name of the Element attributed to this grade (in English and in Hebrew.)
9. Which direction is associated with this Element?
10. What is the Mystic Title conferred upon a Philosophus?
11. What does the Mystic Title mean?
12. Which Sephirah is associated with this grade?
13. List the Divine (Atziluthic) Name of this Sephirah.
14. Name the Great Archangel of the Element of this grade.
15. Name the Kerubic Sign of this Element.
16. What are the Three Great Secret Names of God borne upon the Enochian Banners of the Quarter?
17. Name the Great Enochian King of the Quarter.
18. How are the Cross and triangle arranged on the altar?
19. What does the arrangement of the Cross and triangle symbolize?
20. What does "4 = 7" signify?
21. What is the Admission Badge to the 29th Path?
22. What is the Admission Badge to the 28th Path?
23. What is the Admission Badge to the 27th Path?
24. What is the Admission Badge to the temple of the 7th Sephirah of Netzach?
25. The Admission Badge is identical to the lamen of which officer?
26. The distinct sections of a ritual are called "points." Each grade ritual has at least three points: an opening, a closing, and at least one middle point between the opening and the closing. How many middle points are there in the Philosophus Ritual?
27. Briefly describe what happens in each of the middle points of this ritual.
28. During the Philosophus oath, what gesture does the candidate make in swearing his/her oath the Powers of the Element?
29. List the names of the gods encountered by the candidate on the 29th Path.
30. On the 29th Path, what type of Water is associated with the godform in the Northeast? What aspect of time is associated with this figure?

31. What type of Water is associated with the godform in the Southeast? What aspect of time is associated with this figure?
32. What type of Water is associated with the godform in the West? What aspect of time is associated with this figure?
33. Describe the 18th Key of the Tarot.
34. Describe the 17th Key of the Tarot.
35. Describe the 16th Key of the Tarot.
36. In addition to the Tarot Keys and the Admission Badges, what diagrams are displayed in this grade?
37. What additional symbol is given to the Philosophus?

QUIZ—SECTIONS 1, 2, and 3 (*Qabalah,*
Shem ha-Mephoresh, The Correspondences of Netzach)

1. How is the word "Azoth" formed?
2. What is Azoth?
3. List the 3 Negative Veils. Give both English and Hebrew spellings.
4. Which Veil indicates the "Limitless?"
5. Which Veil indicates the "Limitless Light?"
6. Which Veil is sometimes referred as the feminine/negative aspect of God that takes in Light?
7. Which Veil can be described as an empty circle surrounded by a circle of Light?
8. What is the Hebrew word for "contraction?"
9. What is the Hebrew name of the "archetypal man?"
10. Which Veil indicates "Nothing?"
11. On the archetypal man, which side is the Pillar of Mercy located on?
12. What is Tohu?
13. What Lurianic phrase is used to signify the Fall of Eden or the Death of the Kings?
14. What Hebrew word means "faces?"
15. List the five "faces." Give both English and Hebrew spellings.
16. What "face" is known as "short-faced?"
17. What "face" is known as "long-faced?"
18. What "face" is attributed to the second letter Heh of YHVH?
19. What "face" is attributed to Chokmah?
20. What "face" is attributed to Heh Final? What are two additional names given to this face?
21. What Hebrew phrase means "Ancient of Days?" Give both English and Hebrew spellings.
22. What Sephirah is associated with the "Ancient of Days?"
23. What Hebrew phrase means "the Holy Ancient One?"
24. What Sephirah is associated with "the Holy Ancient One?"
25. What name means "the Lesser Countenance?" What Sephirah/Sephiroth does it correspond to?

26. What name means "the Greater Countenance?" What Sephirah/Sephiroth does it correspond to?
27. What is the name given to the Supernal Father and Mother united?
28. What Hebrew word means "Redemption?"
29. List the Secret names of the Four Qabalistic Worlds. Give both English and Hebrew spellings.
30. Why is the letter Tau important with regard to the Four Qabalistic Worlds?
31. What is the Hebrew name for the Seven Palaces?
32. What Sephiroth are assigned to the 1st Palace?
33. What Sephiroth are assigned to the 7th Palace?
34. What is so important about the Seven Palaces?
35. Air is reflected from _____ through _____ to _____.
36. Water is reflected from _____ through _____ to _____.
37. The formation of the Macrocosmic Hexagram is from the _____ on each side of the _____ __ _____.
38. What is the name of the Serpent of Brass?
39. What does the name Shem ha-Mephoresh mean? What does it refer to?
40. Where does the Shem ha-Mephoresh originate from (How was it formed)?
41. In assigning the decanates of the Zodiac to the names of the Shem ha-Mephoresh, the Golden Dawn system assigns the first Decan to which Zodiacal Sign?
42. What additional titles are sometimes used to describe the Shem ha-Mephoresh?
43. How many letters appear in each divine name of the Shem ha-Mephoresh?
44. How are Angelic names formed from the Shem ha-Mephoresh?
45. What do the Angels of the Shem ha-Mephoresh rule over?
46. Which suffix to the divine names indicates Mercy and beneficence?
47. Which suffix to the divine names indicates Severity and judgment?
48. Which is the only Hebrew letter not used in the Shem ha-Mephoresh?
49. What is the literal meaning of Netzach?
50. What is the Divine (Atziluthic) Name of Netzach?
51. What is the Archangelic (Briatic) Name of Netzach?
52. What is the Angelic Choir of Netzach?
53. What House of Assiah is associated with Netzach?
54. What is the Spiritual Experience of Netzach?
55. What is the Briatic Color of Netzach?
56. What Tarot cards are attributed to Netzach?
57. What is the Magical Image of Netzach?
58. List some incenses that are associated with Netzach.
59. What are the symbols of Netzach?
60. What is the Lineal figure of Netzach?
61. What is the Virtue associated with Netzach?
62. What is the Vice associated with Netzach?
63. What part of the human anatomy is attributed to Netzach?

QUIZ—PARTS 4, 5, and 6

(Correspondences of Fire, Venus and The Qlippoth)

1. Describe the energy of Fire.
2. What is the Hebrew name for Fire? Give both English and Hebrew spellings?
3. What is the Outer Divine Name of Fire? Give both English and Hebrew spellings.
4. What is the Hebrew name for the Cardinal Point of the South? Give both English and Hebrew spellings.
5. What is the name of the Archangel of Fire? Give both English and Hebrew spellings.
6. What is the name of the Angel of Fire? Give both English and Hebrew spellings.
7. What is the name of the Ruler of Fire? Give both English and Hebrew spellings.
8. What is the name of the King of Fire?
9. What is the name of Order of Elementals associated with Fire?
10. What is the name of the Kerub of Fire?
11. What is the name of the Egyptian goddess of war and the destructive heat of late summer?
12. What is the name of the Assyro-Babylonian Fire god who was invoked during sacrifices?
13. What is the name of the Egyptian god associated with Fire and Heat who is also a form of Horus?
14. What is the name of the Egyptian Fire goddess with the head of a cat?
15. What is the name of the Assyro-Babylonian Fire god who invoked by sorcerers to destroy their enemies?
16. What is the name of the Egyptian god who was known as the "smiter of the rebel?"
17. What is the name of the Egyptian phoenix?
18. What is the name of the Egyptian war god who is often portrayed with the head of a bull?
19. What is the name of the Egyptian god of metalsmithing?
20. What is the name of the Greek Titan who stole Fire from the gods?
21. What is the name of the Greek god of terrestrial Fire?
22. What is the name of the Greek goddess of the Hearth Fire?
23. List some of the things that are ruled by the Planet Venus.
24. List some of the things that the days and hours of Venus are used for in magic.
25. What is the Hebrew name for Venus?
26. The ancients described Venus as the ruler of the period of life dominated by _____ from the ages ____ to ____.
27. Describe the symbol of Venus on the Tree of Life.
28. What is the name of the Archangel of Venus?

29. What day is associated with Venus?
30. What is the name of the Planetary Intelligence of Venus?
31. What is the name of the Planetary Spirit of Venus?
32. What is the name of the Olympic Planetary Spirit of Venus?
33. What is the metal of Venus?
34. Name some of the gemstones associated with Venus.
35. Name some of the trees associated with Venus.
36. Name some of the herbs/plants associated with Venus.
37. Name some of the animals associated with Venus.
38. What is the name of the Egyptian god of marriage and merriment?
39. What is the name of the Assyro-Babylonian goddess of love and war?
40. What is the name of the Egyptian goddess of love, dance and music?
41. What is the name of the Assyro-Babylonian goddess who was the courtesan to the gods?
42. What is the name of the Egyptian goddess whose special instrument was the sistrum?
43. What is the name of the Egyptian goddess of love who is often portrayed as a nude woman standing on a lion?
44. What is the name of the Greek goddess of love?
45. What is the name of the Greek goddess of marriage?
46. What is the name of the Greek goddess of lust and prostitutes?
47. What is the name of the Teutonic goddess of love?
48. What Greek god is known as "the deliverer of men from their cares?"
49. What Planet complements Venus on the Macrocosmic Hexagram? List some characteristics that the two Planets share.
50. What event resulted in the creation of the Qlippoth?
51. What are the Qlippoth?
52. Why is Malkuth said to be "fallen?"
53. What number is especially referred to the Qlippoth?
54. What are the names of the Negative Qlippotic Veils?
55. What are the names of the Qlippoth of the Sephiroth?
56. What are the names of the Qlippoth of the Zodiacal Signs?
57. What creature represents the synthesis of all the Zodiacal Qlippoth?
58. What creature represents the synthesis of all the Sephirotic Qlippoth?

QUIZ—SECTIONS 7, 8, 9 and 10 (*Alchemy, Admission Badges and Diagrams, The Greek Alphabet, Tarot Divination*)

1. What is one great difference between chemical and Alchemical processes?
2. How can the entire process of Alchemy be explained Qabalistically?
3. What Alchemical implement is used for continuous distillation?
4. What Alchemical implement resembles a dancing bear?
5. What Alchemical implement may be hermetically sealed?
6. What Alchemical implement is known as the Philosophical Furnace?
7. What Alchemical implement resembles a long-necked goose?

8. What is the Alchemical name for a steam bath?
9. What is the Alchemical name for a modern water bath?
10. Describe the Alchemical symbol of sulfur on the Tree.
11. Describe the Alchemical symbol of salt on the Tree.
12. Describe the Alchemical symbol of mercury on the Tree.
13. What three symbols are the emblems of the Planets derived from?
14. The _____ is a symbol of corrosion.
15. The Planet _____ is the only one which unites these 3 forms in one symbol.
16. True or False. The corrosion of metals is usually of the complementary color to that which they naturally approximate.
17. Describe the Admission Badge to the Path of Qoph.
18. Describe the Admission Badge to the Path of Tzaddi.
19. Describe the Admission Badge to the Path of Peh.
20. Describe the Admission Badge to the temple of Netzach.
21. Briefly describe the diagram of the Fall of Eden.
22. In terms of the various parts of the Self (i.e., Higher Self, Lower Self, etc.) what does the diagram of the Fall represent?
23. What does the diagram of the Fall represent from a Macrocosmic viewpoint?
24. What does the diagram of the Fall represent from a Microcosmic viewpoint?
25. What was the Tarot card spread that was originally recommended to First Order students in the early days of the Golden Dawn?
26. What is the name of the Great Angel who is set over the operations of the Tarot?
27. List the letters of the Greek alphabet along with their names (in English), their numerical values and their English letter equivalents.

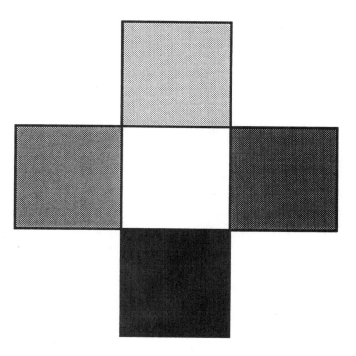

CHAPTER SIX

The Portal

he Portal grade does not bring the initiate to any one Sephirah as in the previous grade initiations, although it may be considered as an outer court of Tiphareth. Moreover, this grade is especially referred to the Veil of Paroketh which falls in the Path of Samekh between Yesod and Tiphareth. This time the initiate is brought back squarely to the Middle Pillar and the Way of Balance. The Portal is very much a compendium of the earlier grades as well as a completion of them. This is also the final grade in this course of *self-initiation*. The Portal grade in particular is concerned with the process of inner alchemy—of separating and examining the parts of one's own psychological and spiritual working—in order to balance and merge them again into a more unified whole which makes true spiritual attainment possible.

The previous grade entailed the Alchemical processes of *analysis* and *dissolution* wherein the candidate was forced to examine his/her own chaotic inner workings. This included a kind of Alchemic "exorcism" if you will, of inner conflicts and the purging of any excess psychic "baggage." If the aspirant has honestly and diligently pursued the work of introspection and psychic balance that is the *core work* of the Golden Dawn at this level, then it is assumed that the candidate who has successfully completed the Philosophus grade is ready to begin the Alchemical process of *assimilation* wherein the purified portions of the aspirant's Elemental self are exalted by an infusion of the Light-giving Spirit and recombined into a balanced "whole" which is greater than the sum of its parts. This is the second half of the *solve et coagula* formula, where the sublimated Elements begin to coagulate into a more balanced psyche which is consecrated to the work of the Divine Will. This not only makes a higher level of spiritual growth possible, it is in fact the goal of the Alchemists—the procurement of the Philosopher's Stone.

The Element encountered in this grade is the fifth and final Element of Spirit. It is the guiding spiritual essence within the aspirant's psyche which transcends all of the Qabalistic Worlds. Spirit is the crowning Element which forms the uppermost point of the pentagram, ruling above the Elements of Fire, Water, Air and Earth, and announcing the dominion of the Divine Light over (and permeating throughout) the manifest Kingdom. It is the cornerstone of the magical tradition. Until the initiate receives an influx of this highest Element and makes an initial contact with the Higher and Divine Self (sometimes referred to as the Holy Guardian Angel or HGA), all magical workings undertaken will be undermined to a lesser or greater extent due to the fact that they will be under the governance of the ego rather than the guidance of the Angel or spiritual Self.

The Portal grade equilibrates all the various portions of the Elemental Self which are symbolically sacrificed upon the altar and submitted to the service of the Higher and Divine Genius. In addition, this grade not only emphasizes the *Quintessence* or Philosophic Mercury, it takes the Alchemical process one step further by focusing on specific Alchemic symbolism to drive the point home. Thus the Portal grade clearly represents a definite stage in the Spagyric Art. The Second and Third Adepts in this ritual bear wands which are surmounted by the Alchemical symbols of sulfur and salt respectively. The Chief Adept (who replaces the Hierophant in this ritual) bears a wand surmounted by a pentagram, to represent collectively the three Alchemic Principles of sulfur, salt and mercury. This points out that the Spirit or Quintessence is more than the union of the four Elements, it is that which contains the three hidden Alchemical Principles. After taking this initiation, it is the duty of the aspirant to expand upon these Three Principles, to separate them from their base, and to engage and comprehend them fully within the consciousness.

There are a number of unique aspects to the ceremony of the Portal. Whereas all of the Outer Order grades represent what in the strictest interpretation of the Golden Dawn calls the "First Degree," the Portal is referred to the "Second Degree." This is also the first time throughout all of the initiations that the candidate is formally presented with the white pillar. Up until this point the initiate has been working with the black pillar which represents the Outer Order. A primary theme in the Portal Ceremony is the candidate's coming out of Darkness into the Light. Only after the Darkness of the black pillar (i.e., the initiate's lower personality symbolized in the Elemental grades) has been explored and synthesized can the white pillar be safely approached.

There is also a curious mixture of both Outer Order and Inner Order officers present in this grade. This is because in the traditional scheme of the Golden Dawn, the Portal grade occupies a position "between the worlds," so to speak, between the Golden Dawn and the R.R. et A.C. It partakes of both, and yet is a part of neither. As already stated, the Hierophant has been replaced by the Chief Adept in this ceremony. (In the earlier grades the Inner Order was represented by the Dais officers, and the Hierophant acted as an intermediate between the Inner and the Outer. Here there is no need for an intermediate officer—the Inner Order officers are full participants in this rite.) The Hiereus and the Hegemon are all that remain of the Outer Order initiatory team. These officers are in charge of the secondary Elements of Air and Earth while the 2nd and 3rd Adepts are in charge of the primary Elements of Fire and Water. (These four officers also correspond to the four pillars which were established within the aspirant's sphere of sensation in the Neophyte Ceremony.) The Chief Adept is in charge of the crowning Element of Spirit. (This officer corresponds to the white triangle of Supernal Light that was established in the Neophyte's aura.) Whereas the Neophyte grade was the *Alpha* stage of the initiatory process, the Portal is the *Omega* stage, crowning and completing the operation.

The four previous grades referred to the Sub-Elements of Malkuth in Assiah. The Portal grade emphasizes Yesod of Yesod in Assiah.

The Portal Sash

The plain white sash is a symbol of the initiate's attainment to the Second Degree. It fits over the candidate's right shoulder (crossing the black sash). While the black sash symbolized the watery current of the black pillar, the white sash alludes to the Fiery current of the white pillar.

The Portal Implements

The Portal grade employs wands and lamens that are unique to this grade. The wand and sword of the Hegemon and the Hiereus are the same as in all of the previous grades, however the wands of the remaining officers and all of the Lamens needed are different. These are described in detail later in this chapter.[141]

The Portal ceremony can be summarized as follows: After the standard (self-initiatory) rite of opening, the temple is in darkness, reminiscent of the darkness of Edom. Light is then brought into the temple from behind the Veil. By the word *Paroketh*, the Veil is opened and the four Elements are invoked into the four quarters of the temple (and into the cross of the Elements). The fifth Element of Spirit is invoked last to complete the other four. After an Adoration to the Lord of the Universe, the Veil is then closed.

The next part of the ceremony is called the *Ritual of the Cross and the Four Elements*. The candidate swears further oaths and must prove that s/he has grasped the secrets (signs and words) of *all* the preceding Elemental grades. The aspirant then circumambulates the hall with each respective Element (of the four lesser Elements) while vibrating the appropriate Elemental names and making the appropriate signs and figures. (Thus the candidate re-establishes the four Elements of the cross within his/her sphere of sensation and equilibrates them.) The symbolism of certain diagrams is also explained, including: The Cross of Four Triangles, the Circle and Point, the symbol of Malkuth, the Great Hermetic Arcanum, the Vision of Nebuchadnezzar, V.I.T.R.I.O.L., and the Seraphim in the Vision of Isaiah.

The next part of the ritual is known as the *Rite of the Pentagram and the Five Paths*. Here the candidate attempts to traverse five paths which lead to higher levels of the Tree of Life (the 21st, 24th, 25th, 26th, and 23rd Paths).

The aspirant attempts the Path of Kaph but is barred from undertaking it. The Path of Nun is then partially traversed and the Tarot card of the Death and a diagram of Typhon are revealed.

The aspirant then attempts the Path of Mem but is barred from venturing upon it. The Path of Ayin is then partially traversed and the Tarot card of the Devil and a diagram of Pan are unveiled.

The candidate, wearing the Cross of the Four Elements, advances to the Veil by the balanced Path of Samekh. In the word *Paroketh*, the initiate rends the Veil and offers up the Elemental portions of him/her self upon the white altar by burning a small portion of the Elemental symbols in a small cauldron. This signals the aspirant's willingness to consecrate his/her life to the service of the Divine.

---

[141] The construction of these implements is described in our book *Secrets of a Golden Dawn Temple*.

Also burned is the candidate's magical motto. (A new motto will be employed after this grade.)

The aspirant is then formally presented with the white pillar and the sash of the grade. The Secrets of the Portal grade are revealed, along with the crowning Element of Spirit and the Enochian Tablet of Union. Two forms of the Temperance Card from the Tarot (the 25th Path) are shown. The importance of striking a balance between opposing forces is stressed. Certain symbols are explained further, including the Hierophant's Lamen, the Banner of the East, and the Chief Adept's Lamen. Finally the powers of the Elements are released.

Five officers are stationed in the Portal Hall in the form of a cross with the altar just below the "crossbar" (the station of the Hegemon). The Outer Order officers who represent Earth and Air (Hiereus and Hegemon) form the "shaft" of the cross in the West and center of the Hall respectively. The Chief Adept's station is at the top of this shaft in the East (Tiphareth), indicating that within the candidate's psyche, Spirit must be firmly grounded in Earth, while the reconciling Element of Air is ever at the point of balance. The 2nd Adept, who represents the Element of Fire and the white pillar is stationed in the South (Netzach), while the 3rd Adept who symbolizes the powers of Water and the black pillar is stationed in the North (Hod). (These officers too, are balanced by the Hegemon and the Element of Air in Yesod.) It is important to keep in mind however, that some of these officers are *not* stationed by their respective Element. The Hiereus is stationed in the West (Malkuth), but must move to the North when necessary to work with the Element of Earth. Likewise the 3rd Adept is stationed in the North (Hod), but must move to the West whenever a working of the Element of Water is called for. During key parts of the ritual the Elemental officers move to form a cross around the altar— each officer on the side of the altar that corresponds to the appropriate Element. When the Chief Adept (Spirit) joins the other four, s/he takes up a position just West of the altar—stepping between the altar and the 3rd Adept. Thus standing, they form the Greek Cross of Five Squares (or the Cross of the Elements).✿

The Godforms of the Portal Grade

As mentioned in Chapter Two, the various "traditional" godforms that exist in the grades beyond that of Neophyte are not set and carved in stone. Therefore the godforms that we have chosen to represent the various Elements in the Portal grade are *not* the only possible ones that may be used. The godforms listed below, however, correspond with the Elemental Deities first hinted at in the Theoricus Ceremony given in Chapter Three.

SERAPIS: The godform of the Hiereus and the deity associated with Elemental Earth. Serapis has a man's body and the head of a bull. The skin of the god is black and he wears the Solar disk and a uraeus between his crescent horns. His tunic is white bordered with black and his pectoral collar is banded red, yellow and blue. His nemyss is striped black and white and his wristbands are banded black and white. He bears either the Crook of Mercy and the Scourge of Severity or the sword of the Hiereus. Serapis is seated upon a throne of black ornamented with white, and stands upon a pavement of black and white squares.

NUET: The godform of the Hegemon and the deity associated with Elemental Air. Nuet has the head and body of a golden-skinned woman. Upon her head she wears the crescent horns and solar disk surmounted by a vase of Water. In one hand she bears an ankh, and in the other either a yellow Lotus Wand or the miter-headed wand of the Hegemon. The goddess wears a tunic of violet ornamented with yellow stars. Her pectoral collar is banded black, red, and blue. Her nemyss is striped yellow and violet and her wristbands are banded yellow and violet. Nuet is seated on a throne of yellow ornamented with violet, and stands upon a pavement of black and white squares.

TEFNUT: The godform of the 3rd Adept and the deity associated with Elemental Water. Tefnut has the body of a woman and the head of a lioness. Upon her head she wears the Solar disk encircled by a serpent. Her skin is blue and she wears an orange tunic. Her pectoral collar is banded yellow, black and red. The Goddess wears a nemyss striped blue and orange and her wristbands are banded blue and orange. In one hand she bears an ankh, and in the other either a blue Lotus Wand or the salt-headed wand of the 3rd Adept. Tefnut is seated on a throne of blue ornamented in orange, and stands upon a pavement of black and white squares.

MAU: The godform of the 2nd Adept and the deity associated with Elemental Fire. Mau has the body of a man and the head of a male cat. Upon his head he wears the Solar disk encircled by a serpent. His skin is red and his tunic is green. His pectoral collar is banded blue, yellow and black. The god wears a nemyss striped red and green, and his wristbands are banded red and green. In one hand he bears an ankh, and in the other either a red Lotus Wand or the Sulphur-headed wand of the 2nd Adept. Mau is seated on a throne of red ornamented with green, and stands upon a pavement of black and white squares.

OSIRIS: The godform of the Chief Adept and the deity associated with Elemental Spirit. Osiris has a human head, and wears a nemyss striped white and yellow, surmounted by the white *Stenu* crown of the Upper Regions. He is mummy-wrapped in white except for his head and hands. His pectoral collar is banded white, red, blue, yellow, black. His wristbands are banded yellow and white. Osiris bears a white Djed Wand or a white pentagram-headed scepter of the Chief Adept. The god sits upon a Throne of white ornamented in yellow, which stands upon a white pavement.✿

THE PORTAL CEREMONY

Temple setup: The aspirant will need to set up the Hall beforehand in accordance with the temple diagram. The black cubical altar is placed in the center of the room. Upon it should be placed rose petals, several incense sticks (preferably sticks that are solid incense, so that they can be easily broken up), a cup of Water and a platter of salt (in the East, South, West and North respectively) around the symbol of a five-squared Greek Cross. A hook suspended from the ceiling by a string, should be positioned over the center of the black altar.

In the Eastern part of the Hall is the Veil of Paroketh[142] behind which is a white altar and the two pillars. On the white altar should be placed the Tablet of Union, the Lamen of the Hierophant, a brazier or small cauldron containing charcoal, matches, a small pentacle, a plain white votive candle, a container of powdered incense, and a piece of paper whereon is written the aspirant's motto. All four Elemental Tablets are placed in their respective quarters.

The Hebrew letter Samekh is shown on a large plaque in the East, hanging above the center of Paroketh. Also in the East, but occupying a lower position to the left and right of Samekh are the letters Mem, Ayin, Nun and Kaph. Tau is in the West. The Banner of the East is before the Veil, while the Banner of the West is located near the station of the Hiereus.

Place the lamens and implements in accordance with the temple diagram, in the positions of the officer-forms. The station of the Chief Adept is behind the Veil, while the stations of Second and Third Adept are in front of Paroketh, to the right and left respectively. The Hegemon is just East of the altar and the Hiereus is stationed in the West.

As in the previous rituals, all of the Elemental candles should be placed around the circumference of the room, with a white candle in the East. (Note: At the beginning of this ritual all candles except for the white Spirit candle are to be unlit.)

Have the following diagrams close at hand. In the West: The Maltese Cross, the Circle and the Point, and the symbol of Malkuth. In the East near the throne of Hegemon: The Great Hermetic Arcanum, the two forms of the Temperance card. In the North: The Tarot card of the Devil, Pan, the Vision of Nebuchadnezzar, and the diagram of Vitriol. In the South: the Death card, Typhon, and the Seraphim and Kerubim.

(Note: For a later segment of the ritual, the aspirant will need the Hiereus Lamen Admission Badge and a white sash which fits over the right shoulder. Leave the white sash in the Eastern part of the Hall.)

Ritual preparations: The aspirant should fast for a period of twelve hours prior to the ritual. A ritual bath is required after which the aspirant may put on the black Tau robe, back sash, and red slippers.

The aspirant must meditate for a certain length of time on the symbol of the Spirit wheel in white. Next s/he must spend a period of time (20—30 minutes)

---

[142] See *Secrets of a Golden Dawn Temple.*

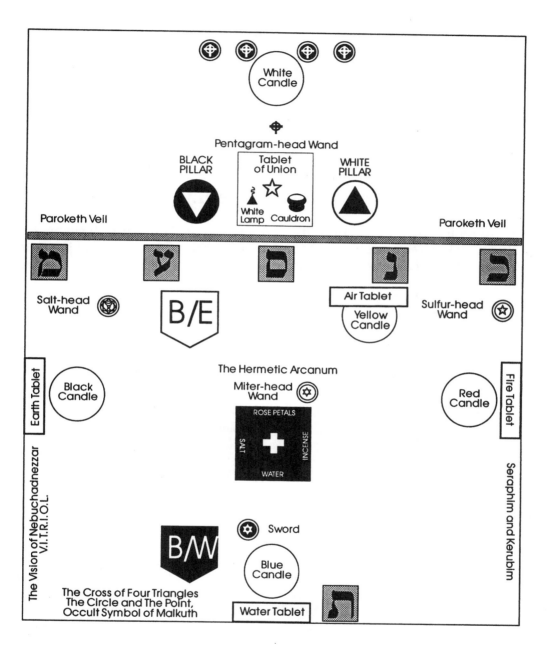

The Portal Temple for Self-Initiation: First Setup

in a darkened room or antechamber to the temple seated in quiet meditation. No hoodwink is required. The Admission Badge for the 29th Path, the Greek Cross of Five Squares, should be worn around the neck. A small white candle is to be the only source of light in the room. During this time, darkness and silence are to be maintained. After this period of time has passed, the aspirant may then enter the temple and begin the ritual.

     Upon entering the temple, imagine that you are leaving your physical body outside as a sentinel to guard the temple, so that your spiritual self has the freedom to accept initiation.

PART 0: The Opening

Enter the Temple with the Admission Badge about your neck. Salute the Banner of the East with the Neophyte Signs. Take off the cross and place it on top of the altar. Walk deosil to the East. With the Hiereus' sword perform the LBRP.

Give one knock with the pommel of the sword against the floor or side of the chair and say *"HEKAS, HEKAS, ESTE BEBELOI!"*

Put the sword aside and go to the West of the temple, facing East. Kneel down and invoke the godform of Thmê as in the previous initiation. Vibrate strongly:

> *THMÊ! THMÊ! THMÊ! Thou daughter and eye of RA! Lady of Heaven, Queen of Earth and mistress of the Underworld! Great Lady of all the gods and goddesses. Thou whose name is MAAT! Lady of Truth! Goddess of Justice and Order! Mediator between Darkness and Light, Chaos and Order! THMÊ! THMÊ! THMÊ! Thou who assesseth the heart of every man and woman in the Hall of Judgment before Ousiri and the assembly of the gods. Thou who art the eye and heart of balance! THMÊ! THMÊ! THMÊ! I invoke thee!*

Visualize the familiar image of the goddess Thmê before you, with human head and yellow-gold skin. However this time, you see the goddess in different attire. For the first time, she now appears to you in her advanced form, wearing a yellow and violet striped nemyss and a yellow linen gown. About her nemyss is bound a violet headband from which a white Shu feather stands. Her pectoral collar is banded red, yellow and blue. Her left wristband is banded yellow and red, while her right wristband is yellow and blue. She carries a yellow Phoenix Wand. Above her head is the white glowing outline of the cross and triangle, symbolic of the outer magical current of the Golden Dawn.

Slowly and with feeling, perform the Qabalistic Cross, drawing the Light down from the Kether of the universe into the Kether at the crown of your head as you continue the QC. Strongly visualize the cross of Light you have formed in the center of your body. Trace within your heart the Hebrew letters of the name THMÊ in glowing white. Project a white ray of thought from your heart toward the image of Thmê you have created before you. See the figure breathe in life as your thought-ray animates it. Address the form:

> *THMÊ! Beautiful One of the Feather of Truth! I beseech thee to act upon my behalf in this my quest for the Light Divine! Guide me, O thou who art none other but my own Higher Self. Aid me and escort me in the Portal before the Veil of Paroketh! I am a true and willing Seeker of Light and Knowledge. Act as my overseer and reconciler as the Elements of this Hall are equilibrated within me. Guide me through the rites of the Pentagram and the Five Paths. Speak for me amidst the assembly of the gods and the guardians of this sacred Hall. My intentions are honest. I am ready to undergo test and trial. I am willing to be examined by the Elemental gods! I wish to be purified and consecrated to the Light. Grant that my heart is made MAAT! Grant that my Will is made MAAT! Merciful THMÊ! Let me be judged aright! Grant that this humble aspirant before you be not turned away from that resplendent Light which resides in the East. Permit me to tread the paths that lead to the edge of the Veil —and beyond! Award me a vision of the mysteries which lie past the curtain of Paroketh! Permit me safe return to that Middle Column from which I have digressed in exploration. Grant me the harmony and guidance of the Fifth Element; the crowning jewel of Life! Let me penetrate the Threshold in the path of the Enterer!*

Thmê speaks to you in your own mind.

> The Light shineth in Darkness, yet the Darkness comprehendeth it not. Waiting, I awaited upon YHVH, and he bent down unto me and heard my cry. And he brought me up out of the tumultuous pit, out of the mire of clay, and he set my feet upon a rock, he directed my steps. I am the representative of your Higher and Holy Self. It is only through my arbitration that thou canst even approach the Curtain of the Sanctuary. In this Hall I am thy tongue, thy heart and thy mind. Fear not, for I shall guide thee through the abode of the Elements, and the paths of tribulation, and I shall keep thee safe. Fear not, for I shall lead thee through the Veil of Paroketh. I shall speak for thee in this assembly of the gods before the powers of Eth and the current of the Light.

Visualize the goddess Thmê as she parts the Veil of Paroketh to communicate in silence with the energies in the East. The Veil closes behind her. She speaks on your behalf to the divine guardians of the Hall, though this time you can neither see nor hear them. After a few moments Thmê returns and salutes with the Signs toward the West and says silently:

Thou mayest proceed, O aspirant; thou art MAAT.

Thmê goes clockwise to the West, where she traces the figure of the cross and triangle with the Phoenix Wand. As she does so, you vibrate the Coptic name of "*OSIR-HAPI*" (Sarapis) (Au-oo-sar-hap-hee). The dark form of the god takes shape before you. He holds the Crook and Scourge. Visualize the figure strongly.

Thmê goes to the station of the Hegemon (East of the altar) and traces the figures of the cross and triangle. As she does so vibrate the Coptic name of "*NUET*" (Nau-oo-eh). The figure of the Sky goddess begins to formulate. She holds a yellow Phoenix Wand.

Thmê goes to the station of the 3rd Adept in the Northeast and traces the figure of a circled cross (like the lamen of the Hierophant). As she does so vibrate the Coptic name of "*TEFNUT*" (Tef-nau-oo-eh). The figure of the lioness-headed goddess dressed in blue and orange begins to formulate. She holds a blue Lotus Wand.

Thmê goes to the station of the 2nd Adept in the Southeast and traces the figure of a circled cross. As she does so, vibrate the Coptic name of "*MAU*" (Mau-oo). The figure of the cat-headed god dressed in red and green begins to formulate. He holds a red Phoenix Wand.

Thmê goes behind the Veil to the station of the Chief Adept and traces the figure of the circled cross. As she does so vibrate the Coptic name of "*OSIRIS*" (Ou-see-ree). The mighty figure of Osiris forms in the East. Thmê returns to stand West of the altar.

Still in the West, give the Projection Sign of a Neophyte and remain in the position of the Sign. Visualize a small but brilliant white Light coming from behind the Veil. It lingers for a few moments in front of the Curtain and is then withdrawn. As the Light vanishes behind the Veil, give the Sign of Silence. Say:

> *The Light shineth in Darkness, but the Darkness comprehendeth it not. The Dukes of Edom ruled in Chaos, Lords of unbalanced force. Yet upon the altar is the symbol of equated forces of the four Elements. Banished be the Power of the Dukes of Edom and let the Power of the Cross be established.*

The white Light again appears in the East. Slowly and deliberately, it traces the figure of a cross.

In the West Thmê leads you to the station of Hiereus. The godform of Sarapis traces in the air before you the symbol of Malkuth and hands you his implement. Picking up the Hiereus' sword, you take on the office of Hiereus that the godform has bestowed upon you, and advance to the East.

With the sword, perform the LBRP. (During the final recital of the Qabalistic Cross, imagine all the astral godforms in the Hall repeating the words with you.)

Return to the West and face East. Make the Zelator Sign and give one knock with the hilt of the sword. Step out of the office of Hiereus and return the officer-form to the dominion of Sarapis. Thmê then leads you to the station of Hegemon. The godform of Nuet traces in the air before you the figure of a hexagram within a circle and hands you her scepter. Picking up the Hegemon's Wand, you take on the office of Hegemon that the goddess has bestowed upon you. Make the Sign of the Theoricus and give a knock. Step out of the office of Hegemon and return the officer-form to the dominion of Nuet.

Thmê brings you to the station of the 3rd Adept. The godform of Tefnut traces in the air before you the figure of a cup within an octagram and hands you her scepter. Picking up the 3rd Adept's Wand, you take on the office that the goddess has bestowed upon you. Make the Sign of the Practicus and give a knock. Step out of the office of the 3rd Adept and return the officer-form to the dominion of Tefnut.

Thmê brings you to the station of the 2nd Adept. The godform of Mau traces in the air before you the figure of a triangle within a pentagram and hands you his scepter. Picking up the 2nd Adept's Wand, you take on the office that the god has bestowed upon you. Make the Sign of the Philosophus and give a knock. Step out of the office of 2nd Adept and return the officer-form to the dominion of Mau. Return to West of the altar and say:

> *The cross upon the altar is also a cross of corrosion, corruption, disintegration and death. Therefore, doth it fall in the paths of Death and the Devil, unless in Hod, the Glory triumpheth over matter and the corruptible putteth on incorruption, thus attaining unto the beauty of Tiphareth, unless in Netzach, Death is swallowed up in Victory and the Transformer becometh into pure Alchemic Gold. "Except ye be born of Water and the Spirit, ye cannot enter the Kingdom of God."*

> *The additional mystic symbol I received in the Philosophus grade was PHRATH, the fourth river of Eden. TAU. RESH. PEH. To this may be added—*

> *Kaph* (knock)
> *Tau* (knock)
> *Resh* (knock)
> *Peh* (knock)

> *The whole Word is Paroketh, which is the Veil of the Tabernacle.* (Make the Sign of the Rending or Opening of the Veil.)

From behind the Veil, you hear a knock followed by the deep voice of the god, Osiris, who declares:

Invoking Spirit Active

start here

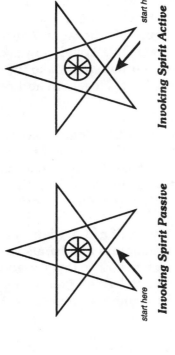

Invoking Spirit Passive

start here

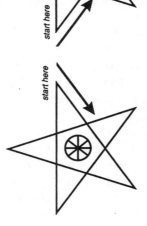

Banishing Spirit Active

start here

Banishing Spirit Passive

start here

The Pentagrams of Spirit

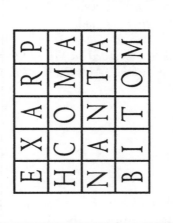

E	X	A	R	P
H	C	O	M	A
N	A	N	T	A
B	I	T	O	M

The Tablet of Union

In and by that Word, I permit the Portal of the Vault of the Adepti to be opened.

Draw aside the curtains and strongly visualize the godform of Osiris. The god rises and traces in the Air before you the symbol of the circled cross and hands you his scepter. Pick up the Chief Adept's Wand, the white candle and the pentacle, as you take on the office that the godform has bestowed upon you. Turn to face West and visualize all the astral godforms in their respective positions. Say:

Let us establish the dominion of the mystic ETH over the four Elements.

Take the rose Petals and place them before the Tablet of the East. Imagine the officer/godform of Hegemon standing behind you in the Sign of Theoricus. Give a knock, then trace with the wand a large circle in front of the Tablet. Draw the invoking pentagram of Spirit Active. As you do so vibrate *"EXARP"* (Ex-ar-pay). Trace the sigil of Spirit in the center and intone *"EHEIEH"* (Eh-heh-yay). Give the Sign of Rending of the Veil. Then trace the invoking pentagram of Air. As you do so vibrate the name *"ORO IBAH AOZPI"* (Or-oh Ee-bah-hay Ah-oh-zohd-pee). Draw the sigil of Aquarius in the center and intone *"YHVH."* Give the Sign of Theoricus. Light the yellow candle from the flame of the white candle. Take the rose petals back to the black altar and place them on the yellow arm of the Greek Cross. The officer/godform of Hegemon remains East of the altar facing West.

Take the incense sticks and place them before the Tablet of the South. Imagine the astral officer/godform of the 2nd Adept standing behind you in the Sign of Philosophus. Give a knock, then trace with the wand a large circle in front of the Tablet. Then draw the invoking pentagram of Spirit Active. As you do so vibrate *"BITOM"* (Bay-ee-toh-em). Trace the sigil of Spirit in the center and intone *"EHEIEH"* (Eh-heh-yay). Give the Sign of Rending of the Veil. Then trace the invoking pentagram of Fire. As you do so vibrate the name *"OIP TEAA PEDOCE"* (Oh-ee-pay Teh-ah-ah Pay-doh-kay). Draw the sigil of Leo in the center and intone *"ELOHIM."* Give the Sign of Philosophus. Light the red candle from the flame of the white candle. Take the incense sticks back to the black altar and place them on the red arm of the Greek Cross. The officer/godform of the 2nd Adept remains South of the altar facing North.

Take the Cup of Water and place it before the Tablet of the West. Imagine the officer/godform of the 3rd Adept standing behind you in the Sign of Practicus. Give a knock, then trace with the wand a large circle in front of the Tablet. Then draw the invoking pentagram of Spirit Passive. As you do so vibrate *"HCOMA"* (Hay-coh-mah). Trace the sigil of Spirit in the center and intone *"AGLA"* (Ah-gah-lah). Give the Sign of Rending of the Veil. Then trace the invoking pentagram of Water. As you do so vibrate the name *"EMP ARSEL GAIOL"* (Em-pay Ar-sell Gah-ee-ohl). Draw the sigil of the Eagle in the center and intone *"Aleph Lamed, AL."* Give the Sign of Practicus. Light the blue candle from the flame of the white candle. Take the

Cup back to the black altar and place it on the blue arm of the Greek Cross. The officer/godform of the 3rd Adept remains far West of the altar facing East.

Take the salt and place it before the Tablet of the North. Imagine the officer/godform of the Hiereus standing behind you in the Sign of Zelator. Give a knock, then trace with the wand a large circle in front of the Tablet. Then draw the invoking pentagram of Spirit Passive. As you do so vibrate *"NANTA"* (Eh-nah-en-tah). Trace the sigil of Spirit in the center and intone *"AGLA"* (Ah-gah-lah). Give the Sign of Rending of the Veil. Then trace the invoking pentagram of Earth. As you do so vibrate the name *"EMOR DIAL HECTEGA"* (Ee-mor Dee-ahl Heck-tay-gah). Draw the sigil of Taurus in the center and intone *"ADONAI."* Give the Sign of Zelator. Light the black candle from the flame of the white candle. Take the salt back to the black altar and place it on the black arm of the Greek Cross. The officer/godform of the Hiereus remains North of the altar facing South.

Complete the circle by returning to the East, then go to the West of the altar facing East. Say *"In the Great Name YOD HEH VAV HEH!"*

Give the Neophyte Signs toward the altar. Then give the Signs of Zelator, Theoricus, Practicus and Philosophus. Trace a circle over the Greek Cross followed by the invoking pentagram of Spirit Active. Vibrate, *"EXARP"* and *"EHEIEH."* Next trace the invoking pentagram of Spirit Passive and vibrate *"HCOMA"* and *"AGLA."* Trace again the figure of the invoking pentagram of Spirit Passive and vibrate *"NANTA"* and *"AGLA."* Finally draw the invoking pentagram of Spirit Active and intone, *"BITOM"* and *"EHEIEH."* Give the Sign of the Rending of the Veil.

Perform the Qabalistic Cross. Then go to the East of the altar facing West. Lay the pentacle upon the central white portion of the cross. Hold the wand and white candle high and say:

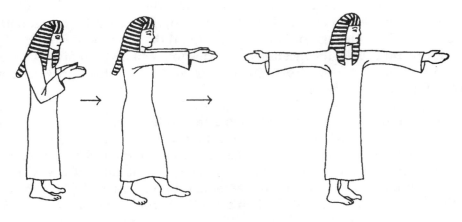

The Rending of the Veil

May the Cross of the four Elements become truly purified and planted in Incorruption. Wherefore in the name of YHVH and in the concealed name of Yeheshuah, do I add the power of the pentagram constituting the glorified Body of Osiris, the Sign of the Microcosmos.

After a brief pause, pick up the pentacle and hang it on the hook above the cross. Return to the West of the altar and raise the white candle and the scepter high and intone the following Enochian invocation:

OL SONUF VAORSAGI GOHO IAD BALATA. ELEXARPEH. COMANANU. TABITOM. ZODAKARA, EKE ZODAKARE OD ZODAMERANU. ODO KIKLE QAA PIAPE PIAMOEL OD VEOAN."[143] *(Oh-ell son-oof vay-oh-ar-sah-gee go-ho ee-ah-dah bahl-tah. El-ex-ar-pay-hay. Coh-mah-nah-noo. Tah-bee-toh-em. Zohd-ah-kah-rah eh-kah zohd-ah-kah-ray oh-dah zohd-ah-mehr-ah-noo. Oh-doh kee-klay kah-ah pee-ah-pay pee-ah-moh-el oh-dah vay-oh-ah-noo.)*

Return to the station of the Chief Adept. Visualize the 2nd and 3rd Adepts standing by the pillars. Also imagine the Hiereus and the Hegemon at the North and South of the black altar, facing East. Say: *"Let us adore the Lord and King of Hosts."* Perform the Adoration to the Lord of the Universe.

Holy art Thou, Lord of the Universe. (Projection Sign)
Holy art Thou, Whom Nature hath not formed. (Projection Sign)
Holy art Thou, the Vast and the mighty One. (Projection Sign)
Lord of the Light and of the Darkness. (Sign of Silence)

(Say:) By the Word Paroketh and in the Sign of the Rending of the Veil, I declare that the Portal of the Vault of the Adepti has been opened.

Give the Battery of knocks with the scepter. וחוו (4—1). Visualize the officer/godform of the 2nd Adept repeating the Battery of knocks: 4—1. Visualize the officer/godform of the 3rd Adept repeating the Battery of knocks: 4—1. Visualize the officer/godform of the Hiereus repeating the Battery of knocks: 4—1. Visualize the officer/godform of the Hegemon repeating the Battery of knocks: 4—1.

Circumambulate the temple once, then step out of the office of Chief Adept and return control of the officer-form to Osiris. Replace the scepter and the white candle. Draw the curtains closed, concealing Osiris once more behind the Veil. Shade all the Elemental candles with the glass covers and replace the Elements by their respective astral officer/godforms. The goddess Thmê then leads you to the West of the Temple where she will remain for much of the ritual. Take the Greek Cross with you.

---

[143] This translates as "I reign over you, says the God of Justice. (Three Angelic Names.) Move, therefore, move and appear. Open the mysteries of creation: balance, righteousness and truth."

PART 1: The Ritual of the Cross and Four Elements

Visualize all of the astral officer/godforms at their respective stations. At this point, the temple has been opened under the guidance of the Guardians of the Hall, with your very active participation. You have already done much to equilibrate the Elements within your sphere of sensation under the guidance of Spirit. At this point you must now take a few moments to re-establish yourself as a candidate who seeks for entrance into this Hall. Perform the Qabalistic Cross to maintain a psychic balance of all the Elements within your aura. Restore the persona of the aspirant within you.

Place the Greek Cross around your neck. Give the Battery of knocks: 4—1. Stand in the Western part of the Hall facing East. The officer/godforms of Hiereus and Hegemon bar your advance. Say:

> *This candidate seeks for entrance. I vow it to be true that I (state magical motto) have been a member of the 4 = 7 grade of Philosophus for the space of seven months, and have passed the fivefold examination prescribed for study. Having accomplished this, I am now eligible to approach the Portal of the Vault of Adepti.*

The goddess Nuet speaks to you:

> The realm of Chaos and of ancient Night, ere ever the Aeons were, when there was neither Heaven or Earth, nor was there any Sea, when naught was, save the Shape unluminous, formless and void.

The god Sarapis speaks to you:

> To and fro in the Deeps, swayed the coils of the Dragon with eight Heads and eleven Horns. Eleven were the curses of Mount Ebal, eleven the Rulers of the Qlippoth, and at their head were the Dual Contending Forces.

The two officer/godforms lower their weapons and step back. Go clockwise to the East of the altar and say:

> *Then breathed forth THO-OTH out of the Unutterable Abyss the Word! Then stood forth THO-OTH in the Sign of the Enterer, on the Threshold of the Hall of Time as Time was born of the Eternal. (Give the Projection Sign and stay in that position.) So stood THO-OTH in the Power of the Word, giving forth Light, while the Aeons that were unbegotten unfolded before him. (Pause and then say:) And ELOHIM said "Let there be Light."*

Imagine a bright Light coming from behind the Veil. Then reach through the curtain and take up the white candle. Give the Sign of Silence. Visualize the officer/godform of the 3rd Adept leading you clockwise to the West. Take up the Banner of the West. Say:

> *I stand within this sacred hall as one who has received the title of Honoured Frater (Soror) Pharos Illuminans. I stand amid this company of gods assembled here to open the Portal of the Vault of the Adepti which admits me to the Second Degree and brings me to the Inner Threshold.*
>
> *But because of the increased influence that such advancement necessarily confers, and because of the increased power for good or for evil that will follow if, with steadfast will and aspiration, I take this step in essence as well as in form, it is necessary that I make further pledges which, as in the Previous Degree, contain nothing contrary to my civil, moral or religious duties.*

You hear the voice of the god Mau:

Are you willing to take these pledges?

(You answer:) *I am willing to take these pledges.*

Holding both the white candle and the Banner of the West in your right hand, imagine your left hand placed in that of the officer/godform of the 3rd Adept, who is the symbol of the black pillar which rules the grades of the Outer Order. Visualizing your hand thus, touch the corresponding emblem of the black sash of restriction upon your breast. Raise the banner and candle on high and say:

> *I Frater (Soror) _____ pledge never to flaunt or parade the secrets of this ceremony to those who are not true seekers of the Light. I shall not abase my mystical knowledge in such a mundane manner.*
>
> *Secondly, I solemnly promise to use whatever practical knowledge I may now or at any future time possess, for a good end alone.*
>
> *Thirdly, I promise to regard all the knowledge imparted to me as a trust, given into my hands, not for my selfish advantage, but for the service of all mankind, that the ancient tradition of initiation be kept pure and undefiled, and the Light be not lost for those that seek it in this path.*
>
> *Lastly, I solemnly promise to exercise brotherly love, charity and forbearance toward all true Seekers of the Divine Light.*

Then realizing the cross about your neck, lift the banner and candle in your right hand on high and say:

May the Powers of the Elements bear witness to my pledges.

Replace the banner, but keep the white candle. Visualize the officer/godform of the 3rd Adept returning to her station. Say:

> *The symbol of the first grade of Neophyte is 0 = 0. To the first 0 is attached a circle—to the second, a square. The union of the circle and the square hath many meanings, one of which I must accomplish in my own being, ere I can advance further. For if in the mystic sphere of Truth, the way of initiation may be trodden alone, yet in another sphere, it hath a threefold aspect. Part that can be given to humanity from without—part that can be attained by humanity ourselves—and part that can only come from the Divine. Thus far in my studies I have been given intellectual teaching, and I won my grades in tests of what was taught. Here I must prove that I have truly attained thus far of my own strength, and after, I may progress by the Higher Soul within me.*

Again you hear the voice of Mau as he speaks to you.

> Round your neck, you wear the symbol of the Cross of Four Elements, equilibrated and equated. Establish it firmly in the sphere of your own being and advance with courage.

The officer/godforms of the Hiereus and Hegemon bar your advance as in the Zelator grade. Sarapis demands the 1 = 10 signs and words from you:

> Give me the Sign of the grade of Zelator. (You give it.)

> Give me the Grip or Token.

You exchange the Outer Order Grip with the bull-headed god.

> Give me the Grand Word of the 1 = 10 grade.

You give it: *"Adonai Ha Aretz."*

> Give me the Mystic Number of the 1 = 10 grade.

You give it: *"55."*

> What is the Password formed from the Mystic Number?

You answer: *"Nun-Heh."*

> What is the Mystic Title of the 1 = 10 grade?

You give it: *"Periclinus de Faustus."*

> What symbol did you receive in that grade?

You give it: *"Aretz."*

The astral officer/godforms step back and allow you to advance. Sarapis traces the symbol of Malkuth in the air before you. Taking on the office of Hiereus that Sarapis has bestowed upon you, take up the sword of the Hiereus and go (with the white candle) to the Earth Tablet. The godform of Sarapis stands in the North in the Sign of the Zelator. Trace with the sword the figure of a cross over the platter of salt. Leave the sword in the North and circumambulate the Hall one time slowly with the candle and the salt while vibrating the divine names of Earth:

> *Adonai ha-Aretz. Emor Dial Hectega. Uriel. Ic Zod Heh Hal.*

Upon returning to the North, trace with the sword the invoking Earth pentagram over the salt. Remove the glass cover from the Elemental (Earth) lamp to reveal its light. Place the platter of salt on the Northern side of the black altar. Step out of the office of Hiereus and return the officer-form to the dominion of Sarapis.

The officer/godform of Sarapis takes you clockwise to the West and gestures at the diagrams there. Observe the diagram of the Maltese Cross and say:

> *The Cross of Four Triangles called the Maltese Cross, is a symbol of the four Elements in balanced disposition. It is here given in the colors of the King's scale, and is also assigned to the four Sephiroth ruling the grades of the Outer—Earth to Malkuth, Air to Yesod, Water to Hod and Fire to Netzach.*
>
> *It is again, the cross which heads the Praemonstrator's Wand, who represents the Sephirah Chesed, the fourth Sephirah. Four is also the number of Jupiter, whose path unites Chesed to Netzach. The cross is therefore a fit emblem for a Philosophus of the grade of 4 = 7.*

Turn your attention to the diagram of the Circle and Point. Say:

> *In this diagram are represented the circle, the point, the line, the cross, the square and the cube. For the circle is the Abyss, the nothingness, the AIN. The point is Kether. Now, the point has no dimension, but in moving, it traces the line. This gives the first number—unity—yet therein, lies duality unmanifest, for two points mark its ends. The movement of the line maketh the plane or square. The motion of the point at angles to its first direction and intersecting it maketh the cross. So therefore, are the square and the cross but one symbol, deriving from the circle and the point.*

Direct your attention to the diagram of Malkuth. Say:

> *In this diagram is shown the occult symbol of Malkuth, the tenth Sephirah. It is in four parts, corresponding to the Maltese Cross. They are Fire of Earth, Water of Earth, Air of Earth, Earth of Earth, as is indicated by the symbol. They correspond to the four grades of the First Order, which in one sense, quitteth not Malkuth, being the grades of the four lowest Sephiroth of Malkuth in Assiah. Upon them is surcharged a white hexagram in a circle. The six and the four make ten, the number of Malkuth on the Tree. The hexagram is also the sign of the Macrocosm—of Tiphareth, and of the six upper Sephiroth, wherefore here it is white—Spirit ruling over matter. Six is a perfect number, for its whole equals the sum of its parts.*
>
> *Six are the middle points of the planes bounding a cube, which derives from the square, and from the cross, if the center point moves outwards.*
>
> *In these numbers and figures are hid many revelations. The whole number of Malkuth is 496—which is again a perfect number. Malkuth must then be equated and perfected by the six ruling the four—and the link between six and four is the number of the pentagram.*

The officer/godform of Hiereus goes to the East. The god Mau speaks to you:

> Having achieved entry into Malkuth, it is needful that you should pass through the Path of Tau, the dark path of the astral plane. Go therefore, to the Tablet of the East.

Go sunwise to the East where the astral officer/godforms of Hiereus and Hegemon again bar your approach. The goddess Nuet demands the 2 = 9 signs and words from you:

> Give me the Sign of the grade of Theoricus. (You give it.)
>
> Give me the Grip or Token.

You exchange the Outer Order Grip with the sky goddess.

> Give me the Grand Word of the 2 = 9 grade.

You give it: *"Shaddai El Chai."*

> Give me the Mystic Number of the 2 = 9 grade.

You give it: *"45."*

> What is the Password formed from the Mystic Number?

You answer: *"Mem-Heh."*

What is the Mystic Title of the 2 = 9 grade?

You give it: *"Poraios de Rejectis."*

What symbol did you receive in that grade?

You give it: *"Ruach."*

The officer/godforms step back and allow you to advance. Nuet traces the symbol of the hexagram within a circle in the air before you. Taking on the office of Hegemon that Nuet has bestowed upon you, take up the Hegemon's Wand and go (with the white candle) to the Air Tablet. The godform of Nuet stands in the East in the Sign of the Theoricus. Trace with the wand the figure of a cross over the rose petals. Leave the wand in the East and circumambulate the Hall one time slowly with the candle and the rose petals while vibrating the divine names of Air:

Shaddai El Chai. Raphael. Oro Ibah Aozpi. Bataivah.

Upon returning to the East, trace with the wand the invoking Air pentagram over the rose petals. Remove the glass cover from the Elemental (Air) lamp to reveal its light. Place the rose petals on the Eastern side of the black altar. Step out of the office of Hegemon and return the officer-form to the dominion of Nuet.

The godform of Nuet takes you to her station East of the altar (in Yesod) where she directs your attention to the diagram of the Great Hermetic Arcanum. Observe the diagram and say:

> *This symbol represents the Great Hermetic Arcanum. The feet of the figure rest upon the Earth and the Sea. In the Hands are represented the hot and moist natures, symbolized by the torch and the horn of Water. These are further strengthened by the Solar and fiery emblems of the king and the Lion, and the Lunar and the watery emblems of the Queen and Dolphin. Above the whole figure rise the wings of the aerial nature, the Reconciler between the Fire and the Water. This symbol can be compared with the Angel described in the 10th Chapter of the Apocalypse of St. John:—"And I saw another mighty Angel come down from Heaven clothed with a cloud; and a rainbow was upon his head, and his feet were as pillars of Fire, and he set his right foot upon the sea and his left foot upon the Earth, and he cried with a loud voice as when a lion roareth,[144] and when he cried, seven thunders uttered their voices.[145] The Dragon issuing from the cave represents volcanic Fires."*

---

[144] In the Order symbolism, this refers to Teth; the Green Lion and the Path of Leo above Tiphareth.

[145] The Seven Aeons represented under the regimen of the Planets.

The sky goddess leads you sunwise to Sarapis in the North. The godform of Nuet then returns to the South. The Earth god directs your attention to the diagram of Nebuchadnezzar's Vision in the Northern part of the Hall. Observing the diagram you say:

> This is the Image of the Vision of Nebuchadnezzar, described in the second chapter of the Book of Daniel: "Thou, O King, sawest and beheld a great image. This Great Image, whose brightness was excellent, stood before thee, and the form thereof was terrible. This Image's head was pure gold, his breast and his arms were silver, his belly and his thighs were brass, his legs of iron and his feet part of iron and part of clay. Thou sawest till that a stone was cut without hands, which smote the Image upon its feet, which were part of iron and part of clay, and brake them to pieces. Then was the iron, the clay, the brass, the silver and the gold broken to pieces together and became like the chaff of the summer threshing floors; and the wind carried them away and no place was found for them; and the stone that smote the Image became a great mountain and filled the whole Earth." Thou, O King, art a King of Kings, for the God in heaven hath given—(Perform the Qabalistic Cross) Unto Thee, the Kingdom, the Power and the Glory!

The God Sarapis speaks to you:

> Thou art this head of Gold! Thou art this head of Gold! Thy head represents in thee the dominion of the Divine ruling over the rest of the body.

You continue:

> The silver is the world of the heart, the brass is the material passion, the iron is the firm purpose, and the feet, part of iron and part of clay, are the mingled strength and infirmity of the natural man. And the Stone made without hands is the eternal Stone of the Wise, which will become the Mountain of Initiation, whereby the whole Earth shall be filled with knowledge of God.

Turn your attention to the diagram of the V.I.T.R.I.O.L. Say:

> This tablet shows the symbolic manner in which certain names have been used by our ancient brethren. The initials of this sentence make the Latin word, VITRIOLUM or Sulfuric acid. Furthermore, the words VITRIOL, SULFUR and MERCURY each consist of seven letters answering to the Alchemic powers of the seven Planets. The initials of the following sentence in Latin make the word S.A.L.T.— salt, and further, the four words of the sentence answers to the four Elements, SUBTILIS—Air, AQUA—

> Water, LUX—Fire, and TERRA—Earth. And the four words yield twenty letters, that is, the product of four, the number of the Elements, multiplied by five, the number of the pentagram.
>
> The words FIAT LUX, meaning "Let there be Light," consist of seven letters. The letters of FIAT form the initials of: FLATIS—Air, AQUA—Water, IGNUS—Fire, and TERRA—Earth. Which four names again yield twenty letters as in the previous case. And the word LUX is formed from the angles of the cross, L.V.X.

Sarapis leads you sunwise to the officer/godform of the Hegemon in the South. The goddess Nuet directs your attention to the diagram of the Seraphim and the Kerubim. Observe the diagram and say:

> The Seraphim in the Vision of Isaiah[146] are described as having six wings:—"With twain He covered his face, and with twain he covered his feet, and with twain did he fly." That is, his synthesis is to be found in the hexagram and in the idea of the Seven, more especially dominating the Planetary region.
>
> But the Kerubim of Ezekiel have each four faces—those of the Lion, the Bull, the Man and the Eagle counterchanged with each other by revolution, whence the symbolic forms of the wheels beside them, wherein was the Spirit; and with two of the wings they covered their bodies and two were stretched upwards one to another. So the synthesis of the Kerubim is found in the revolving cross, in the pentagram, and in the idea of one Spirit dominating four Elements.
>
> But the Kerubim of St. John's vision in the Apocalypse are uncompounded, having single heads, but they have six wings and thus unite the powers of the seven with the four. And their cry is similar to that of the Seraphim of Isaiah:—"Holy, Holy, Holy."

The astral officer/godforms of Hiereus and Hegemon return to their stations. The figures of the 2nd and 3rd Adepts bar your advance in the Southwest. The goddess Tefnut demands the 3 = 8 Signs and words from you:

> Give me the Sign of the grade of Practicus. (You give it.)
>
> Give me the Grip or Token.

You exchange the Outer Order Grip with the Water goddess.

> Give me the Grand Word of the 3 = 8 grade.

---

[146] Isaiah 6:2.

You give it: *"Elohim Tzabaoth."*

> Give me the Mystic Number of the 3 = 8 grade.

You give it: *"36."*

> What is the Password formed from the Mystic Number? Tefnut asks.

You answer: *"Eloah."*

> What is the Mystic Title of the 3 = 8 grade?

You give it: *"Monocris de Astris."*

> What symbol did you receive in that grade?

You give it: *"Maim."*

The officer/godforms step back and allow you to advance. Tefnut traces the symbol of a Cup within an octagon in the air before you. Taking on the office of 3rd Adept that Tefnut has bestowed upon you, take up the 3rd Adept's Wand and go (with the white candle) to the Water Tablet. The godform of Tefnut stands in the West in the Sign of the Practicus. Trace with the wand the figure of a cross over the Cup of Water. Leave the wand in the West and circumambulate the Hall one time slowly with the candle and the Cup while vibrating the divine names of Water:

> *Elohim Tzabaoth. Gabriel. Emp Arsel Gaiol. Raagiosel.*

Upon returning to the West, trace with the wand the invoking Water pentagram over the Cup. Remove the glass cover from the Elemental (Water) lamp to reveal its light. Place the Cup on the Western side of the black altar. Step out of the office of 3rd Adept and return the officer-form to the dominion of Tefnut.

The figures of the 2nd and 3rd Adepts bar your advance in the Northwest. The god Mau demands the 4 = 7 Signs and words from you:

> Give me the Sign of the grade of Philosophus. (You give it.)

> Give me the Grip or Token.

You exchange the Outer Order Grip with the Fire god.

> Give me the Grand Word of the 4 = 7 grade.

You give it: *"YHVH Tzabaoth."*

Give me the Mystic Number of the 4 = 7 grade.

You give it: *"28."*

What is the Password formed from the Mystic Number? —Mau asks.

You answer: *"Kaph Cheth."*

What is the Mystic Title of the 4 = 7 grade?

You give it: *"Pharos Illuminans."*

What symbols did you receive in that grade?

You give it: *"Asch and Phrath."*

The officer/godforms step back and allow you to advance. Mau traces the symbol of a triangle within a pentagram in the air before you. Taking on the office of 2nd Adept that Mau has bestowed upon you, take up the 2nd Adept's Wand and go (with the white candle) to the Fire Tablet. The godform of Mau stands in the South in the Sign of the Philosophus. Trace with the wand the figure of a cross over the incense sticks. Leave the wand in the South and circumambulate the Hall one time slowly with the candle and the incense sticks while vibrating the divine names of Fire:

> *YHVH Tzabaoth. Michael. Oip Teaa Pedoce. Edelperna.*

Upon returning to the South, trace with the wand the invoking Fire pentagram over the incense sticks. Remove the glass cover from the Elemental (Fire) lamp to reveal its light. Place the incense sticks on the Southern side of the black altar. Step out of the office of 2nd Adept and return the officer-form to the dominion of Mau. Go to the West of the altar, facing East.

Visualize the four astral officer/godforms surrounding the altar on all sides—facing it: Sarapis in the North as Hiereus stands in the Sign of Zelator, Nuet in the East as Hegemon stands in the Sign of Theoricus, behind you in the West, Tefnut as 3rd Adept stands in the Sign of Practicus, Mau in the South as 2nd Adept stands in the Sign of Philosophus.

Take the cross from around your neck and place it in the center of the Elements upon the altar. Place the white candle on the center of the cross, beneath the pentacle. Surrounded by the officer/godforms standing in the grade Signs, you give the Sign of the Enterer and remain in the position during the following speech:

> *From the center outwards, so moveth the point as it traceth the line and the cross. Equated and equilibrated lie here the four Elements of the body of Osiris slain.*

> *May the corrosive cross return upon itself, from without inward, from the*
> *four quarters to the center, and become by sacrifice and transmutation, an*
> *offering acceptable, a body glorified.* (Give a knock.)

The goddess Thmê appears at your side and speaks to you:

> You have passed the hour of cloud and of night. You have disassem-
> bled, examined and reassembled the four Elements of your Inner Self.
> You must now animate these pieces of the body of Osiris with the
> vitalizing power of Spirit. Prepare this Hall for the Rite of the Penta-
> gram and prepare thyself for advancement through the Veil and the
> indwelling guidance of ETH.

Take the four Elements from the black altar and place them on the white altar, passing them one by one through the Veil. The goddess Thmê leads you out into the
antechamber where you spend a few moments rehearsing the Fourfold Breath and
meditating on the equilibrated Elements of the Greek Cross. Perform the Qabalistic
Cross to once again equilibrate the Elemental energies within your aura.

PART 2: The Rite of the Pentagram and the Five Paths

Spend a few additional moments in relaxed meditation in the antechamber. Take
up the Hiereus Lamen Admission Badge. When finished, stand just outside the
temple door and give four knocks, one for each Element. Briefly visualize all of the
astral officer/godforms at their respective stations. Again visualize a small bright
Light coming through the Veil. The Light lingers for a moment in front of
Paroketh, then traces the figure of a pentagram and is withdrawn.

Imagine Thmê at the entrance facing you. The goddess motions for you to enter.
You give the Battery of knocks (4—1) and then perform the Qabalistic Cross. The
goddess Thmê performs it with you. For much of the ceremony she will remain
near the entrance.

The officer/godform of Hiereus leads you to the West and directs your attention
to the diagram of Malkuth. You hear the voice of Sarapis as you contemplate the
diagram:

> Herein has been established the Equated Cross, which is the ruler
> over the Kingdom of Matter. This symbol may be found even upon
> the crowns of the Kings of this Earth.

The god gestures at the Tau Portal. You pick it up and say:

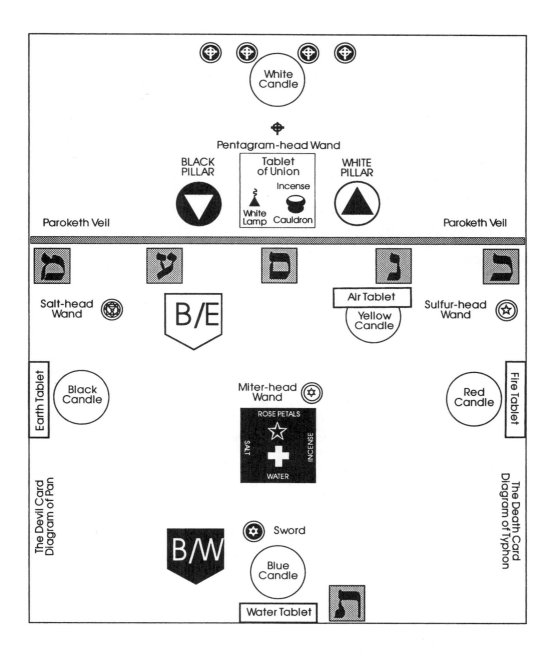

The Portal Temple for Self-Initiation: Second Setup

The letter Tau leads from the airy quarter of Malkuth into Yesod. Air is uppermost in the symbol as in the Planet Earth where the atmosphere is furthest from the core. Moreover, the letter Tau signifieth the cross, the impact of Spirit upon matter.

The Lamen of the Hiereus is my Badge of Admission, for he is the ruler in Malkuth, and the guardian against the Underworld. The Hiereus is also Lord of the Path of Tau, the link between the First and Second Degrees, and also between the Outer and the Inner.

This Path of Tau, dark and full of mystery, under the presidency of Saturn and the Tarot Key of The Universe leads, as I learned in the 2 = 9 grade, through the astral plane. Therefore, in the ritual of the 32nd Path I passed by the four Kerubic stations, as a fore-shadowing of the Rites of the Cross, the full completion of the Elemental grades which I have now accomplished.

Sarapis speaks:

Having traversed the Path of Tau, the darkness of the astral plane and of the black pillar, stand firm in Yesod, that the black pillar may become the white.

Replace the Portal of Tau in the West. The officer/godform of Hiereus leads you to the station of the Hegemon. Nuet directs your attention to the Portals in the East. Say:

Before me in the East, are the Five Portals of the 21st, 24th, 25th, 26th and 23rd Paths. Five will divide the number of the letter of each of them, as it will divide without remainder that of every path from Yod, the 20th, to Tau, the 32nd.

The Five paths here visible are assigned to MEM—Water; AYIN—Capricornus, an Earthy Sign; SAMEKH—Sagittarius, a Fiery Sign; NUN—Scorpio, a Watery Sign, but in its highest aspect also a Ruler of Fire; and Kaph —Jupiter, which Planet is akin to Spirit, and rules especially Aspiration. Thus both in number and in significance these Planets jointly set forth the eternal symbol of the pentagram.

Nuet speaks:

This symbol of the pentagram must now be established—wherefore advancing by the Kerubic Path of Aquarius approach the highest in Netzach.

Advance to the station of the 2nd Adept, before the Portals of Kaph and Nun. The god Mau questions you:

Wherefore do you stand at the base of the white pillar, being but the Lord (Lady) of the First Degree?

You answer: *"I seek the Path of Kaph, the Path of Aspiration."*

The officer/godform of Hiereus gives a knock. Sarapis speaks:

> Beware! Temerity is not courage, Lord(Lady) of the First Degree. Remember the warning of the Tower struck by Lightning that was revealed in the highest path you have yet adventured. As a house built upon the sand cannot endure, so without the strength of Geburah, the height of Chesed cannot be scaled. Stay, therefore, ere your limbs be broken upon the wheel.

Mau speaks:

> The Portal of Kaph is barred, yet it is well to aspire, though it may be folly to attempt. This path is governed by the Wheel of Life and Death, and hard it is to be freed from that Wheel.

You reply, *"Let me seek then the Path of Nun."*

Mau answers:

> It is open to you unto the limit of your strength.

He leads you to the West where the officer/godform of the Hiereus bars your advance.

Sarapis gives a knock and says:

> In the Power of Typhon the Destroyer, and the Death the Transformer, stand!

Mau speaks:

> Thus far and no farther is it permitted to penetrate into the Path of Nun. The mysteries may now be partially revealed.

He leads you to the Tarot Key of Death in the South. Observe the diagram and say:

> *The 13th Key of Tarot represents the figure of a Skeleton, upon which some portions of flesh still remain. In a field he is reaping off with the Scythe of Death the fresh vegetation which springs from corrupting bodies buried therein—fragments of which—such as hands, heads and feet appear above the soil. Bones also are strewn upon the surface. One of the heads wears a*

kingly crown; another is apparently that of a person of little note, showing that Death is the equalizer of all conditions. The five extremities, the head, hands and feet, allude to the powers of the number five, the letter Heh, the pentagram—the concealed Spirit of Life and the four Elements—the originator of all living form. The Sign of Scorpio especially alludes to stagnant and foetid Water—that property of the moist nature which initiates putrefaction and decay. The eternal change from life into death through death into life, is symbolized by the grass which springs from and is nourished by putrefying and corrupting carcasses; the herbage, in its turn affords food to animals and man, which again when dead, nourisheth vegetable life and bring to growth and perfection the living herbage. This is further shown by the figure itself putrefying and decaying as it reaps the grass of the field. "As for man, his days are as grass, as a flower of the field, so he flourisheth." The top of the scythe forms the Tau Cross of Life, showing that what destroys also renews.

The whole is a representation of the eternal transmutation of the life of nature, which reforms all things into fresh images and similitudes. This symbol represents the corrosive and destructive action of the infernal Fire as opposed to the Celestial—the Dragon of the Waters, the Typhon of the Egyptians, the Slayer of Osiris—which later yet rises again in Horus. The Scorpion, Serpent of Evil, delineated before the figure of Death in the more ancient form of the Key, refers to the mixed and transforming, therefore deceptive, nature of this emblem. Behind him, is the symbol of the Nameless One, representing the Seed and its germ, not yet differentiated into Life, therefore incapable of definition. The Scorpion is the emblem of ruthless destruction; the Snake is the mixed and deceptive nature, serving alike for good and evil; the Eagle is the Higher and Divine Nature, yet to be found herein, the Alchemical Eagle of distillation, the Renewer of life. As it is said:—"Thy youth shall be renewed like the Eagles." Great indeed, and many are the mysteries of this terrible Key."

The figures of the 2nd Adept and the Hiereus direct your attention to the **diagram of Typhon**. Observing the diagram you say:

This drawing represents the symbolic figure of Typhon, the Destroyer. The eleven circles represent the eleven Averse Sephiroth. He stands upon Earth and Ocean, his head lost in the clouds, a colossal image of evil and destruction. The brow denotes the confusion of opposing Elemental Forces in the higher regions of the Air, and confusion of mind and madness in man. The eyes are the devouring flames of lust and violence—the breath is storm, devastation and rage, alike in the universe which is the greater world, and in man who is the lesser. The arms and the hands are the swift executors of evil works, the bringers of pestilence and disease. The heart is malice and envy in man, the nourisher of evil in the atmosphere, which later are again symbolized by the numerous and twining serpents.

The 24th Path of the Sepher Yetzirah to which the Tarot Key of Death is referred is the Imaginative Intelligence, and it is so called because it giveth form to all similitudes which are created in like manner similar to its harmonious elegances. For the outward form always follows the hidden law, thus from chaos is produced harmony, just as a beautiful flower is produced from decaying matter.

Mau speaks:

> Return now to Yesod, for here no more may be spoken.

Go clockwise to the station of Hegemon where the godform of Nuet confronts you and says:

> Approach now the station of Hod by the Path of Resh, the Sun.

Advance to the station of the 3rd Adept, before the Portals of Mem and Ayin. The goddess Tefnut speaks to you:

> Already the sash of the black pillar is upon you—already you have passed the dark Path of Tau. What more do you seek of me, Lord(Lady) of the 1st Degree?

You answer, *"I seek the Path of Mem, the Path of Sacrifice."*

The officer/godform of Hiereus gives a knock. Sarapis speaks:

> Be warned, O, vainglorious one. Samson broke down the two pillars and perished. Having but one pillar, can you bear up the might of Geburah, can you attain strength without the Life of Tiphareth?

Tefnut speaks:

> The Portal of Mem is barred. Yet it is well to be willing for the Sacrifice itself, if as yet, not fully prepared. For in the Path of Mem rules the Hanged man, the power of the Great Waters. Can your tears prevail against the Tide of the Sea, your might against the waves of the storm, your love against the sorrows of all the world?

You reply, *"Let me seek then the Path of Ayin."*

Tefnut answers:

It is open to you unto the limit of your strength.

She leads you sunwise to the North where the officer/godform of the Hiereus bars your advance. Sarapis gives a knock and says:

By the Power of Pan and the Goat of Mendes, stand!

Tefnut speaks:

Thus far and no farther are you permitted to penetrate the Path of Ayin. The mysteries may now be partially revealed.

She leads you to the Tarot Key of the Devil in the North. Observe the diagram and say:

The 15th Key of the Tarot represents a goat-headed, satyr-like Demon whose legs are hairy—his feet and claws, standing upon a cubical altar. He has heavy bat-like wings. In his left hand, which points downwards, he holds a lighted torch, and in his right, which is elevated, a horn of Water. The left hand points downwards to show that it is the infernal and burning, not the celestial and lifegiving flame which is kindled in his torch— just as when the Sun is in Capricornus, to which cold and earthy Sign this Key corresponds, Solar light is at its weakest and the natures of cold and moisture triumph over heat and dryness. The cubical altar represents the universe—right and left of it, bound thereto by a cord attached to a circle which typifies the center of the Earth, are two smaller demons, one male and one female. They hold a cord in their hands. The whole figure shows the gross generative powers of nature on the material plane, and is analogous to the Pan of the Greeks and Egyptian Goat of Mendes (the symbol of Khem). In certain aspects, this Key represents the brutal forces of nature, which to the unbelieving man only obscure and do not reflect the luminous Countenance of God. It also alludes to the sexual powers of natural generation. Thus therefore the Key fitly balances the symbol of Death on the other side of the Tree of Life. Of the smaller demons, one points downwards and one upwards, answering to the positions of the hands of the central figures. Beneath his feet are pentagrams on which he tramples (whence comes their title of Wizard's foot) and his head is covered with the evil and reversed pentagram. As his hands bear the torch and horn—the symbols of Fire and Water, so does his form unite the Earth in his hairy and bestial aspect, and the Air in his bat-like wings. Thus he represents the gross and materialized Elemental Forces of nature; and the whole would be an evil symbol, were it not for the pentagram of Light above his head which regulates and guides his movements. He is the eternal renewer of all the changing forms of Creation in conformity with the Law of the All-Powerful One (Blessed be He) which controlling law is typified by the con-

trolling pentagram of Light surmounting the whole. This Key is an emblem of tremendous force; many and universal are its mysteries.

The god Sarapis directs your attention to the diagram of Pan. Observe the diagram and say:

This drawing represents the symbolic figure of Pan, the Greek god of Nature. He stands upon the cube of the universe, holding in his right hand the pastoral staff of rural authority, and in his left the seven-reeded pipe symbolical of the harmony of the Planetary spheres. The nine circles represent the Sephiroth with the exception of Kether, exactly those which are included in the symbol on the Tree of Life. The ruddy face is the heat of the Earth—the horns are the rays—the body contains the Elements and the cube is the firm basis. Observe that the higher part of the figure is human, growing more bestial as it nears the Earth.

The 26th Path of the Sepher Yetzirah, to which the Tarot Key of the Devil is referred, is called the Renovating Intelligence, because, by it, God the Holy One reneweth all the changing forms which are renewed by the creation of the world.

Tefnut speaks:

Return again to Yesod, for here no more may be spoken.

Go to the West of the altar facing East. Visualize the officer/godforms of 2nd and 3rd Adepts back at their stations, right and left of the Veil. The officer/godform of Hegemon is at your right side, while the Hiereus is on your left.

Sarapis speaks to you:

In guardianship and not in enmity, have I barred your venturing, O Philosophus. Now may it be revealed how in the Lamen of the Hiereus is hidden the Key which you seek.

Observe the Admission Badge and say:

The triangle in the circle is the high symbol of the Holy Trinity, and the first three Sephiroth, and of Binah wherein is the sphere of Saturn, Ruler of the Path Tau. Therefore it is worn by the Hiereus, and when I entered the Hall of the Neophytes in the 0 = 0 grade, I beheld the sword that barred and the symbol which overcometh the barrier.

The lamen in its more special attribution to the Hiereus, has the following meanings. In the circle are the four Sephiroth of Tiphareth, Netzach, Hod and Yesod. The first three mark the angles of the triangle inscribed within, while the sides are the Paths of Nun, Ayin and Peh, respectively. In the center is marked the letter Samekh indicating the 25th Path.

While the wheel revolves, the hub is still. Ever shall I seek the center, looking from without to within. This is the Key of my path.

Nuet directs your attention to the Portals in the East and says:

Five paths are before you—four have you attempted and each was guarded by a symbol sinister and dread.

(Say:) *In the 1 = 10 grade it was revealed that above Malkuth were the Paths Qoph, Shin, Tau,—Qesheth, the Bow of promise. From the many colored Bow, is loosed in Yesod, the Arrow of Sagittarius—Samekh, soaring upward to cleave open the Veil unto the Sun in Tiphareth. Thus it is a fit symbol for hope and aspiration, for in the Sign Sagittarius, Jupiter, Ruler of Kaph is Lord. Thus, by this straight and narrow way only, is advance between the dangers that have threatened me possible.*

Tefnut speaks:

But Sagittarius, the Archer, is a bi-corporate Sign—the Centaur, the Man and the Horse combined. Recall what was said in the 3 = 8 grade of Practicus.

You continue:

"Also there is the vision of the Fire flashing Courser of Light, or also a child borne aloft upon the shoulders of the Celestial Steed, fiery or clothed with gold, or naked and shooting from the bow, shafts of Light, and standing on the shoulders of a horse. But, if thy meditation prolongeth itself thou shalt unite all these symbols in the form of a lion."

For thus will I cleave upward by the Path of Sagittarius, through the Sixth Sephirah into the Path of Teth, answering to Leo, the Lion—the reconciling path between Mercy and Severity, Chesed and Geburah, beneath whose center hangs the glorious Sun of Tiphareth. Therefore, by the straight and narrow Path of Sagittarius, I shall advance, like the arrow from the center of Qesheth, the Bow. And as this Sign of Sagittarius lieth between the Sign of Scorpio—Death and Capricornus the devil, so had Jesus to pass through the Wilderness, tempted by Satan.

Pause and then observe the symbols upon the altar and say:

Before me upon the altar, lie the four Elements of my purified body, and over them is the symbol of the pentagram, while beneath in the midst is the Spirit within them. I am willing in service and in sacrifice to offer the purified Elements of my body.

Bind the Greek Cross once more around your neck, and take the white candle in your right hand. Stretch forth the light over the four Elements and pause for a moment of meditation, prayer or personal dedication.

Go to the East of the altar. Visualize all of the astral officer/godforms doing likewise. (Mau as 2nd Adept is to your right, Tefnut as 3rd is on your left. Nuet as Hegemon is behind Mau. Sarapis as Hiereus is behind Tefnut.)

Mau speaks:

Honoured Philosophus, what was the additional symbol given you in the 4 = 7?

(You reply:) *"Phrath. O Hidden Warden of the Portal of the Vault, here is one who cometh in the Word Phrath."*

Osiris speaks to you from behind the Veil:

If you would rend the Veil, then complete the Word.

Say: *"I will complete the Word."*

Osiris asks:

What know you of the Word?

You answer:

TAU—the letter of Saturn, ruling the path of Malkuth to Yesod, linked to Earth. RESH—the letter of Sol, of the path joining Yesod to Hod, and it is also the letter linked with rule over Air as the Sun ruleth the Air in Tiphareth. PEH—the letter of Mars, of the path joining Hod to Netzach, which is also a letter linked to Water, as Mars ruleth Water, and to Fire, as Mars ruleth Fire in Geburah.

Mars in Peh, linketh the base of the black pillar to the base of the white pillar, and the converse of Mars is Jupiter—for Jupiter is Lord of Fire, but in Chesed he ruleth Water, balancing Mars in Geburah. The letter of Jupiter is Kaph, linking Netzach with Chesed; and Kaph continueth the Path Peh to Chesed, and is the highest path now visible unto me. It is the path of aspiration and its Planet Jupiter rules also in Sagittarius.

Mau speaks:

> Take the Light of the Highest for Guide and complete the word.

Say the following words and perform the appropriate gestures:

> *"Peh"* (Knock and give the Sign of Water.)
> *"Resh"* (Knock and give the Sign of Air.)
> *"Kaph"* (Knock and give the Sign of Fire.)
> *"Tau"* (Knock and give the Sign of Earth.)
> *"Paroketh"* (Perform the Qabalistic Cross, vibrating the words.)

> (Say:) *In the Word Paroketh, in the Power of the cross and the pentagram, I claim to behold the Portal of the Vault of the Adepti. It is the Word of the Veil, the Veil of the Tabernacle, of the temple, before the Holy of Holies, the Veil which was rent asunder. It is the Veil of the four Elements of the Body of Man, which was offered upon the cross for the service of Man.*

Osiris speaks:

> In the Word Phrath, in the Spirit of service and sacrifice draw nigh.

Mau speaks:

> Give the Sign of the Rending of the Veil, and thus standing, you form the Tau Cross.

You give the Sign, physically Opening the Veil as you do so. Revealed before you the god Osiris also stands in the Sign of Tau with scepter and white lamp. Pause in this position for a few moments of meditation. Then light the charcoal in the cauldron. When ready say:

> *Freely and of full purpose and with understanding I offer myself upon the altar of the Spirit.*

> *In the letter TAU.*

Sprinkle some salt into the cauldron and give the Sign of Earth.

> *In the letter HEH.*

Sprinkle some powered incense into the cauldron and trace over it the invoking pentagram of Earth.

> *In the letter RESH.*

Sprinkle some rose petals into the cauldron and give the Sign of Air.

> *In the letter VAV.*

Sprinkle some powered incense into the cauldron and trace over it the invoking pentagram of Air.

> *In the letter PEH.*

Sprinkle some Water into the cauldron and give the Sign of Water.

> *In the letter HEH.*

Sprinkle some powered incense into the cauldron and trace over it the invoking pentagram of Water.

> *In the letter KAPH.*

Break off some pieces of the incense sticks and place them into the cauldron. Give the Sign of Fire.

> *In the letter YOD.*

Sprinkle some powered incense into the cauldron and trace over it the invoking pentagram of Fire.

> *In the letter SHIN.*

Place the paper (upon which is written your motto) into the cauldron.

Imagine the god Osiris tracing before you the symbol of the circled cross. Take up the Chief Adept's Wand and trace the invoking pentagrams of Spirit Active and Passive over the cauldron. Visualize Osiris doing likewise. Touch the head of the wand to your breast and say:

> *May this offering be as the offering of Abel, which ascended unto God.*

Return the office of Chief Adept back to the godform of Osiris and put the pentagram-headed wand aside.

Osiris speaks to you:

> Stretch out your hand to touch the black pillar, *(done)* the pillar of the
> FIRST DEGREE, wherein all was as yet in the darkness of the Path
> Tau. This was a period of restriction and of groping, as was shown by
> the black sash, the Sign of the First Degree. Among its symbols were

the cross, upon which meditate, that the mysteries of growth and change may become revealed.

Stetch out now your hand to touch the white pillar, *(done)* the pillar of the SECOND DEGREE, wherein is the Fire of the Path Samekh. Its token is the white sash. Standing thus you are in the point of equilibrium, master of both, Lord(Lady) of the Second Degree, Lord(Lady) of the Paths of the Portal of the Vault of the Adepti— wherefore, in recognition of your achievement, I confer upon you the white sash of probation.

At this, put on the white sash, and say:

Standing thus in the Path of Samekh, I am in the point of equilibrium, Master of both pillars, Lord(Lady) of the Second Degree, Lord(Lady) of the Paths of the Portal of the Vault of the Adepti.

Osiris continues:

The grip of this Degree is the Grip of the First Order, but given with the left hand, and represents the Sephirah Chesed, and the white pillar.

Visualize yourself exchanging the grip with the godform. The godform gives the Sign of the Rending of the Veil and says:

The Sign of the Opening or Rending of the Veil symbolizes the rending asunder of a curtain. The answering Sign, the Closing of the Veil, is a complete reversal of the first.

He demonstrates the Sign. You also give the Sign. Osiris continues:

The Password is PAROKETH, which is the Veil of the Tabernacle, and it is exchanged by letters.

You repeat this:

The Password is PAROKETH, which is Veil of the Tabernacle, and it is exchanged by letters: PEH. RESH. KAPH. TAU.

The godform continues:

Further, I give you the Word ETH which crowns the Pyramid of the Four Elements in the 4 = 7 grade, and is one symbol of the Spirit which converts the cross into the pentagram. Wherefore upon the white altar is this Tablet which is called the Tablet of Union, and binds together the four Tablets into one under the presidency of Spirit.

(Say:) *From this day forward I shall strive ever to be worthy of the eternal ETH, the crown of the pyramid and the transmuter of the cross into the pentagram. The Element of Spirit shall be within me a securing force, like that of the Tablet of Union, binding the four Elements into One under the governance of Spirit.*

Thus far by work of the intellect, and aid of the sacred rites have I come. I must now labor to establish the pentagram within myself. That it be the pentagram of Good, upright and balanced, not the evil and reversed pentagram of the Goat of Mendes. I shall strive to make myself truly a Microcosm reflecting the Macrocosm whose symbolic hexagram of Tiphareth presides above me.

Osiris speaks:

This Degree is in one sense attributed to YESOD, base of the path of probation, Sagittarius.

(Say:) *In YESOD is the sphere of Luna, who in her fullness reflects the Sun of Tiphareth. The number given to the Moon in the 2 = 9 grade is nine, but in a more esoteric sense the number of Luna is Five, the number of the pentagram and the Microcosm.*

If need be, pause for reflection or meditation. Then take the Elements and place them before their respective Tablets. Place the white candle and the Tablet of Union on the black altar. Also place the two forms of the Temperance Key upon the altar. Then go to the West of the altar facing East. Visualize the four Elemental officer/godforms surrounding the black altar forming a cross as before.

When ready, observe the Tarot Keys before you and say:

This drawing represents the more ancient form of the 14th Key of Tarot, for which the later and more usual form was soon substituted, as better representing the natural symbolism of the Path Sagittarius. The earlier figure was considered not so much a representation of this path alone, as the synthesis of that and the others conjoined. The later figure, therefore, is better adapted to the more restricted meaning.

The more ancient form shows a female figure crowned with the crown of five rays, symbolizing the five Principles of Nature, the concealed Spirit and the four Elements of Earth, Air, Water and Fire. About her head is a halo of Light. On her breast is the Sun of Tiphareth. The five-rayed crown further alludes to the Five Sephiroth Kether, Chokmah, Binah, Chesed and Geburah. Chained to her waist are a Lion and an Eagle, between which is a large cauldron whence arise steam and smoke. The Lion represents the

Fire in Netzach—the Blood of the Lion; and the Eagle represents the Water in Hod, the Gluten of the Eagle—whose reconcilement is made by the Air in Yesod, uniting with the volatilized Water arising from the cauldron through the influence of the Fire beneath it. The chains which link the Lion and the Eagle to her waist, are symbolic of the Paths of Scorpio and Capricornus as shown by the Scorpion and the Goat in the background. In her right hand, she bears the Torch of Solar Fire elevating and volatilizing the Water in Hod by the Fiery influence of Geburah, while with her left hand, she pours from a vase the Waters of Chesed to temperate and calm the Fires of Netzach.

This later form is the usual figure of Temperance, symbolizing in a more restricted form than the preceding, the peculiar properties of this path. It represents an Angel with the Solar emblem of Tiphareth on her brow, and wings of the aerial and volatilizing nature, pouring together the fluidic Fire and the Fiery Water—thus combining, harmonizing and tempering those opposing Elements. One foot rests on dry and volcanic land, in the background of which is a volcano whence issues an irruption. The other foot is in the Water by whose border springs fresh vegetation, contrasting strongly with the arid and dry nature of the distant land. On her breast is a square, the emblem of rectitude.

The whole figure is a representation of that straight and narrow way of which it is said "few there be that find it" which alone leads to the higher and glorified life. For to pursue that steady and tranquil mean between two opposing force, is indeed difficult, and many are the temptations to turn aside either to the right or to the left—wherein are but to be found the menacing symbols of Death and the Devil.

The 25th Path of the Sepher Yetzirah to which the Tarot Key of Temperance is referred, is called the Intelligence of Probation, and it is so called because it is the primary temptation by which the Creator tries all righteous persons. That is, that in it, there is ever present the temptation to turn aside to the one hand or to the other.

Take up the cup from the West and the red lamp from the South. Return to the altar and stand in the Sign of the Tau Cross, holding the cup in the left hand and the lamp in the right. Say:

Only in and by the reconciliation of opposing forces is the pathway made to true occult knowledge and practical power. Good alone is mighty and Truth alone shall prevail. Evil is but weakness and the power of evil magic exists but in the contest of unbalanced forces, which in the end, will destroy and ruin him who hath subjugated himself thereto. As it is said, "Stoop not down, for a precipice lieth beneath the Earth—a descent of seven steps; and therein, is established the throne of an evil and fatal force.

Stoop not down unto that dark and lurid world. Defile not thy brilliant flame with the earthly dross of matter. Stoop not down, for its splendor is but seeming, it is but the habitation of the Sons of the Unhappy."

Replace the cup and the lamp and restore them to their Tablets. Visualize all the astral officer/godforms returning to their stations. Go to the East of the Hall facing the Veil. Say:

As a Lord (Lady) of the Paths of the Portal of the Vault of the Adepti, and a initiate of the Second Degree, it is fitting that I should have the knowledge of certain emblems to complete my understanding of the Powers of the officers of the First Order. Both refer in natural succession of numbers to the six following the five. Thus all progress is by steps, gradual and secure. The inner revelation may come suddenly to some, even in the twinkling of an eye or it may be after long waiting, yet ever the liquid must be prepared to the point of saturation.

Observe the Hierophant's lamen and say:

The Hierophant's lamen is a synthesis of Tiphareth, to which the Calvary Cross of Six Squares, forming the cube opened out, is fitly referred. The two colors, red and green, the most active and the most passive, whose conjunction points out the practical application of the knowledge of equilibrium, are symbolic of the reconciliation of the celestial essences of Fire and Water, for the reconciling yellow unites with blue in green, which is the complementary color to red, and with red in orange which is the complementary color to blue. The small inner circle placed upon the cross alludes to the rose that is conjoined therewith in the symbolism of the rose and cross.

Observe the Banner of the East and say:

The field of the Banner of the East is white, the color of Light and purity. As in the previous case, the Calvary Cross of Six Squares is the number six of Tiphareth, the yellow cross of the Solar gold, and the cubical stone bearing in its center the sacred Tau of Life, and having bound together upon it the form of the Macrocosmic hexagram, the red triangle of Fire and the blue triangle of Water—the Ruach Elohim and the Waters of Creation. The six angles of the hexagram described upon the Tree of Life will yield the Planets referred to it: DAATH—Saturn, CHESED—Jupiter, GEBURAH—Mars, NETZACH—Venus, HOD—Mercury, YESOD— Luna, while in the center is the Sun of Tiphareth.

Return to face the officer/godform of the Chief Adept. Observe the lamen of the officer and say:

The Chief Adept's lamen is no symbol of the Golden Dawn, nor of the Second Degree. It is the symbol of red rose and the cross of gold, uniting the powers of the four and the five and of the six within itself, but to learn its full meaning, it is needful that I discover further hidden truths to which the teachings of the Golden Dawn are but one of the Veils.

Additional wisdom can be earned no more by excellence in intellectual learning alone, although that is also required. All true knowledge cometh of grace, not of right. It is granted not upon demand, but at the discretion of the Higher Powers.

PART 3: The Closing

Spend as much time as you need to meditate on any of the knowledge given to you during the course of this ritual. Then visualize all the astral officer/godforms at their stations. When ready, give the following consecutive grade Signs: Neophyte. Zelator. Theoricus. Practicus. Philosophus. The Rending of the Veil. The Closing of the Veil.

Imagine the figure of Osiris tracing the symbol of the circled cross in the Air before you, bestowing upon you the office of Chief Adept. Stepping into the office, take up the pentagram-headed scepter. Say:

PEH. RESH. KAPH. TAU. The whole Word is PAROKETH, which is the Veil of the Tabernacle. In and by that Word, I declare the Portal of the Vault of the Adepti duly closed.

Draw the curtain closed. Go West of the altar facing East. Say:

In the Power of the name YOD HEH VAV HEH, and in the might of the concealed name YEHESHUAH, in the symbol of the Tablet of Union and by the word ETH, Spirits of the five Elements, adore your Creator.

With scepter in hand, go to the Tablet of the North and make the banishing pentagrams of Earth while saying the appropriate names and giving the correct Signs. *(Nanta—Agla, Emor Dial Hectega—Adonai.)*

Go to the Tablet of the East and make the banishing pentagrams of Air. *(Exarp—Eheieh, Oro Ibah Aozpi—YHVH.)*

Go to the Tablet of the West and make the banishing pentagrams of Water. *(Hcoma—Agla, Emp Arsel Gaiol—Al.)*

Go to the Tablet of the South and make the banishing pentagrams of Fire. *(Bitom— Eheieh, Oip Teaa Pedoce—Elohim.)*

Return to the West of the black altar and say:

> *Depart in peace unto your habitations. May there be peace between us, and be ye ready to come when you are called.*

Make the banishing pentagrams of Spirit over the Tablet of Union, saying the appropriate names. *(Exarp—Eheieh, Hcoma—Agla, Nanta—Agla, Bitom—Eheieh.)*

Give the Sign of the Closing of the Veil. Still facing East perform the Qabalistic Cross in English: *"Unto Thee Tetragrammaton, be ascribed Malkuth, Geburah, Gedulah, unto the Ages, AMEN."* Give a knock.

Return the office of Chief Adept to the dominion of Osiris in the Eastern part of the Hall.

The goddess Thmê comes to your side. She leads you to the station of the Hiereus where she traces the figure of the cross and triangle in the Air. The godform of Sarapis salutes with the Projection Sign—Thmê answers with the Sign of Silence. Sarapis slowly fades from view. In this manner, Thmê releases the other godforms in the Hall: Nuet, Tefnut, Mau, and Osiris. All the astral entities in the Hall begin to fade from view.

Thmê herself is the last godform to dissolve. You thank the goddess for guiding you in the Portal of the Vault of the Adepti. Trace the figures of the cross and triangle before her. She salutes you with the Projection Sign. You answer with the Sign of Silence. Withdraw the white ray which had activated the goddess back into your heart center. Perform the Qabalistic Cross one last time to equilibrate all energies within your sphere of sensation.

Take up the sword and perform the Lesser Banishing Ritual of the Pentagram. Then go to the East and say:

> *In the names of YEHESHUAH and YEHOVASHAH, I now declare this temple closed.*

Give the Battery of knocks: 4—1. Give the Sign of the Closing of the Veil before exiting the Temple.✿

The Sixth Knowledge Lecture

SECTION 1: On the Work to be Undertaken in the Portal

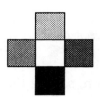 Traditionally speaking, there was no Sixth Knowledge Lecture for Order members of the Portal grade. Initiates were given a manuscript entitled "On the Work to be Undertaken between Portal and 5 = 6"[147] which outlined what gradework was expected of them. An adaptation of this manuscript is incorporated here. The Portal work described in the paper includes: a thesis on the ritual, a meditation on the crosses, a complete diagram of the Tree of Life, the practice of control of the aura, the Tree of Life in the aura, Tattwas, Astrology and divination. In addition there was no written examination for the Portal grade, since after taking the Philosophus examination, the aspirant has "passed the fivefold examination prescribed for admission to the Second Order." Some of our temples require an additional sixth examination for Portal initiates, while others only require them if the student has not fully absorbed the material of the Outer Order.✿

The Thesis

Initiates in the Portal grade are required to review all of the initiation ceremonies and experiences gathered in the preceding grades and reflect upon them. A Thesis of at least twenty (single-spaced) pages which summarizes these experiences is required. The information given below describes how to go about writing the thesis:

The Thesis. Read the initiation rituals. Build them up in the imagination. Compare the Opening and Closing in the various grades. Note the general underlying scheme for each Elemental grade—and note where the differences occur. Follow the careers of the various Officers. Note at what grade an officer disappears.

Make a precis of ritual, so that the general scheme becomes apparent. Draw up a separate outline for each officer.

Note the positions of the various officers—what mathematical shapes they make among themselves from time to time as they take up their places in the Temple. It may be a triangle, a cross, a pentagram, etc.

Read the speeches carefully, and read them often aloud. Note that some speeches are designed to create atmosphere by their archaic form and should be read rhythmically and sonorously, while others are informative and should be read in such a way as to make their points clear.

Examples of archaic passages are challenges of the gods: "Thou canst not pass the Gate of the Western Heaven unless thou canst tell me my name." And the speeches of the Kabiri in the grades of Practicus and Philosophus. Information is given in speeches about Tarot Keys and diagrams.

---

[147] Regardie's *The Golden Dawn*, pages 87-94. In the sixth edition of that book, this paper is mistakenly grouped together with the Fifth Knowledge Lecture. Please note that in Regardie's book the meditation for the Portal Grade on page 94 is followed by a section entitled "Concerning the Tree of Life." This separate paper is part of the gradework of an Adeptus Minor and it, too, is not a part of the Fifth Knowledge Lecture (or of the Portal work.)

Note the technique for traversing the various paths—the words, and the badges with which the path is entered, the length of the circumambulation and the special symbolism described therein.

Let all these things soak into your mind, make notes as ideas occur to you. Finally, and most importantly, take into consideration your own personal feelings, experiences and perceptions of what took place in each of your initiations and during the months spent in each particular grade.✿

The Crosses

Make a list and drawings of the crosses which you have used as Admission Badges throughout the grades, from the Swastika of the Zelator to the Five-Squared Cross worn about the neck in the Portal grade. In addition, read all information about them in the rituals and the Knowledge Lectures and write a brief paper on them.✿

A Drawing of the Tree of Life

This should be done fairly large in order that the writing and symbols should be clear. It is essential to show the deity names, names of Archangels and Angels in Hebrew in the Sephiroth, and to number the paths and give their attributions. Apart from this, the Tree should be your personal synthesis of the Golden Dawn symbolism as it applies to the Tree of Life. The drawing may be colored.✿

Control of the Aura

If the initiate is not already familiar with the parts of the human body such as the nervous system, respiratory system, and digestive system, obtain a simple text book such as *Gray's Anatomy*, so that before starting to work on the subtle body, the student may know something about the physical body.

The physical body is interpenetrated by a subtle body or aura which also surrounds the physical body like an egg of Light. You should now begin to practice controlling this aura or *sphere of sensation*. This includes attempting to keep all emotional reactions under conscious control. Instead of automatically liking this and disliking that, the student should strive to understand the mechanism which underlies these feelings. For assistance in this, the study of human psychology is recommended. (See the list of books recommended at the end of this chapter.)

Having built up some idea of the mechanism of the mental processes, try to make yourself negative or positive at will towards people or ideas. If you are likely to meet someone who always makes you argumentative and irritable, decide that your aura is closed to their power of irritating you and that your mind will not be disturbed by what they say. Being able to listen without comment to someone whose views you disagree with is good practice which helps to control your emotions. In this way, you can also come to understand just how much of your dislike is due to prejudice or personal factors, and how much is due to your regard for abstract truth.

Practice opening your aura to other people or ideas in an endeavor to see things from another point of view.

The practice of deep breathing (like the practices recommended in Chapter Three) is also of help in establishing balance and controlling nervousness. One such practice is to expand the chest to its fullest extent and then expand the diaphragm below the ribs as well and finally let the breath out slowly and steadily on a vowel sound such as "ah" or "oh."

If you are nervous, you will find that your breathing is shallow and that your muscles are tense. You tend to clench your hands and tighten up the abdominal muscles. To cure this, take a deep breath to full capacity, hold it while tensing and relaxing alternately the abdominal muscles. Practice the tensing and relaxing of the muscles three times and then relax completely into a chair. Allow your muscles to go limp and let your breath out to the last gasp. Do the whole process three times, if necessary. It is designed to stimulate the solar plexus which is the heart of the nervous system (which governs emotion).

Another good exercise is to say the deity names aloud. Take a deep breath and say them softly, smoothly and slowly, imagining all the while that your voice travels out to the confines of the Universe. This can be done in conjunction with the Pentagram Ritual.✿

The Tree of Life in the Aura

In the aura which interpenetrates and surrounds the physical body, the magician regularly builds up a replica of the Tree of Life. The Pillar of Severity is on the magician's right side, the Pillar of Mercy is on the left, and the Pillar of Mildness is in the center of the body. The astral construction of the Middle Pillar within the initiate's body should be practiced regularly as part of a lifelong spiritual routine.

THE EXERCISE OF THE MIDDLE PILLAR

(This exercise can be performed either standing, siting, or lying down.) After a few minutes of relaxation, imagine a sphere of white Light just above your head. Vibrate the name *"EHEIEH"* (I am). Keep vibrating this word until it is the only thought in your conscious mind. Then imagine a shaft of light descending from your Kether center to your Daath center at the nape of the neck.

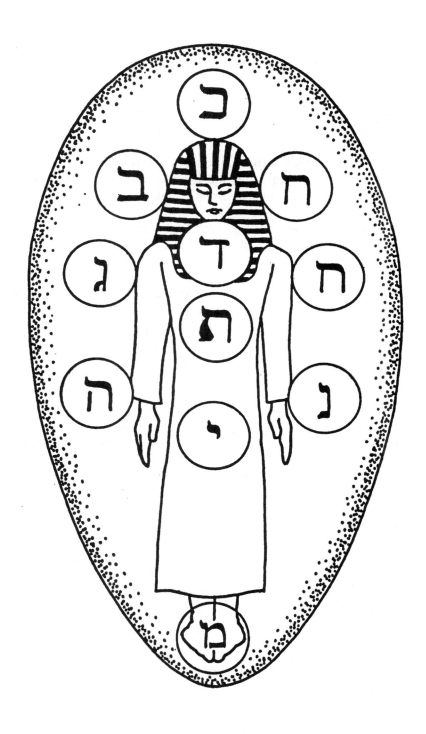

The Tree of Life in the Aura

651

Form a sphere of Light at the Daath center. Vibrate the name *"YHVH ELOHIM"* (the Lord God). Intone the name until it is the only thing in your conscious mind.

Bring a shaft of Light down from the Daath center to the Tiphareth center around your heart. Form a sphere of Light there. Vibrate the name *"YHVH ELOAH VE-DAATH"* (Lord God of Knowledge) several times until it fills your consciousness.

See the shaft of Light descending from Tiphareth into the Yesod center in the genital region. Imagine a sphere of Light formed there. Intone the name *"SHADDAI EL CHAI"* (Almighty Living God) several times as before.

Visualize the shaft of Light descending from Yesod into your Malkuth center at the feet and ankles. Vibrate the name *"ADONAI HA ARETZ"* (Lord of Earth) a number of times as before.

Imagine the Middle Pillar complete. Then circulate the Light you have brought down through the Middle Pillar around the outside of your body to strengthen your aura. Using the cycles of breathing, bring the Light up the right side of the body and down the left, from Malkuth to Kether and back again. After performing this for a short period of time, imagine the ribbon of Light descending down the front of your body and rising up your back.

Still employing rhythmic breathing, visualize the shaft of Light rising up the Middle Pillar in the center of your body. When it reaches Kether, imagine a shower of Light surrounding the outside of your body as it descends to Malkuth again. Circulate the Light in this manner for some time. Then see the Light rise again in a ribbon that spirals round the outside of your body.

Finally focus some of the energy back into your Tiphareth center, the seat of equilibrium and balance.

You may decide to end the exercise with the Qabalistic Cross to indicate that you have called down the Light of your Kether and balanced it in your aura. Then let your imagination dwell on the aura and see it oval and clear, pulsating with the glow from Tiphareth. (Note: this simple exercise of Middle Pillar is the basis for many complex formulas of magic.)

If you are called to see anyone who is ill, depressed, or who has a depressing effect on you, you should perform this exercise beforehand. You may also imagine that your aura is hardened at the edge, so that the person is unable to penetrate it and deplete you of vitality.

It is better at first to keep your aura to yourself, rather than try to flow out towards other. Unless you are particularly vital and well-balanced, you will only waste energy. Modes of healing should be tabled for the time being. Such methods have a technique of their own and require trained and balanced minds and bodies to carry them out. The initiate is advised to "get right" with him/her self before interfering in any way with others.

When you have practiced the exercise of the Middle Pillar for some time and can visualize easily, you can establish the other Sephiroth within your aura by vibrating the deity names.

The exercise of the Middle Pillar can be done as an alternative to the Pentagram Ritual as a preparation for meditation.✿

Tattwas and Triangles

 As already stated in Chapter Five, we feel that the Tattwas are a foreign addition to the Order teachings, which have little in common with the rest of the Golden Dawn system. Study of the Tattwas within our Order today is considered as an elective. Rather than using the Tattwas, we encourage our students to employ the symbols of the Spirit Wheel and the Elemental triangles. These forms will provide the student with completely integrated Golden Dawn symbols for skrying and meditative work. Students are examined on their ability to skry with the Western Elemental symbols, just as in Mather's day when Inner Order members were examined in their proficiency to produce Tattwa visions. (Thus most skrying work takes place in the Adept grades.) In the Portal grade, however, the student is free to choose between which emblems to skry with— the Elemental symbols of the West (the triangles) or of those of the East— the Tattwas. (Both forms are shown in Chapter Five.) Here we will provide only the most basic techniques for skrying with the emblems.

This technique can be described as a form of auto-hypnosis which employs symbols as doorways into controlled astral visions. They are lucid, significant and conscious visions wherein the practitioner maintains all powers of Will, choice and judgment. Creating visions in this fashion also enables the aspirant to tap into the deepest levels of the universal consciousness.

These symbols are designed to assist you in your researches into the Soul of Nature. They should never be allowed to become uncontrolled day-dreams. The method taught should be strictly adhered to—a definite time, preferably in the morning, should be set aside for this practice, once a week. The exercise should not be attempted when one is tired or preoccupied. Notes of the pictures and symbols seen should be kept together in a book.

The student should construct all of the Elemental symbols and have a set of them for working. The Elemental symbol should be made about 2.5 or 3 inches in height and painted in the appropriate colors on 3 x 5 note cards. (Compound Elements, which indicate the Sub-Element *such as Air of Water*, are depicted by painting a smaller emblem, symbolic of the Sub-Element in the center of the larger, primary Element. There are five primary Elements and twenty-five Sub-Elements.)

The method for using the symbols is as follows: Have one of the symbol cards and a white sheet of paper handy. Perform the LBRP. Then be seated in a relaxed and calm attitude. Take one of the symbol cards in your hand and gaze at it intently, until the mind is completely focused on the symbol and nothing else. If the symbol is Watery, feel the fluid around you. If it is Fiery, feel the heat against your skin.

Quickly transfer your attention from the symbol to the white sheet of paper. An optical effect will produce an exact image of the symbol on the paper, but in the complementary or flashing color to the original. When this happens close your eyes and visualize the symbol as a large door. Mentally project yourself through this symbol-door with the Sign of the Enterer. (You may wish to rise and give the Sign physically as well, before sitting down to continue the vision.) Then visualize the door behind you.

Maintaining your abstraction from your physical surroundings and, still concentrating on the symbol and its related ideas, seek out a perception of a scene or view on the Element's plane. There should be landscapes, objects, entities, and a strong sense of being *within* the Element.

At this point, vibrate the highest divine names associated with the Element several times. The vision should become more dynamic and clear. Keep close to the doorway until an Elemental "guide" appears or is felt to be near. This being should be tested with every means at the aspirant's disposal to insure that it is indeed a true guide. Give the grade sign of the Element and see if the being can return it. You may trace the appropriate pentagram before the figure. Also ask the being clearly if it comes to act as your guide in the name of the appropriate divine name. If the guide is found to be true, you may let it lead you anywhere through the vision and ask questions of it.

For the *Sub-Elements* the same methods should be applied. After the primary Elemental names, the divine names of the secondary Element should be vibrated and its grade sign given. You may find yourself being escorted from one guide to another.

Always treat these beings with courtesy. Pay respect to the superior Orders, the Archangels, Angels and Rulers. To those of lower rank, bear yourself as an equal, and those lower still such as Elementals, should be treated politely but firmly. Always imagine yourself taller than the being confronting you.

At the end of the vision, thank your guide and bid him/her farewell. Retrace your steps to the door and pass through it with the Sign of the Enterer. Return to your physical consciousness and stand up, firmly giving the Sign of Silence.

It is wise not to practice this procedure too often. Once every few days is plenty. Also avoid skrying if you are tired or ill. If at any time during the visions you encounter something inappropriate or inconsistent with the vision, repeat the appropriate names, signs and symbols. Always strive to avoid deluding yourself—test everything in the vision and take nothing for granted.

(For more information on skrying techniques, the advanced student may refer to manuscripts printed in Regardie's *The Golden Dawn*. These include:

"Clairvoyance" pg. 456-466, and "Of Skrying and Traveling in the Spirit Vision" pg. 467-476.)✡

Astrology

 From the Order Lectures, the student should be able to set up a true birth horoscope for any place and any time. The student should continue to draw up horoscopes for several people (both known and unknown to the initiate). Focus on the accurate interpretation of a horoscope is of utmost importance to this practice.

Horary Astrology

The Order requires only that the initiate be able to set up an accurate horoscope and know how to work out the aspects. Also required is the knowledge of how to make a simple assessment of the favorable and unfavorable factors in a horary figure.

Whereas Natal Astrology focuses on the birth time of a person, Horary Astrology deals with *the birth time of a question.* This clearly marks Horary Astrology (the Astrology of the Hours) as a form of divination. The methods of Horary Astrology are quite archaic, having been developed much earlier than Natal Astrology. Through the ages, this type of Astrology has cultivated a strict set of rules designed to aid in objective divination by *providing an answer to a specific question.* The Astrologer becomes the diviner and medium between a sharply focused question and the answer embodied in the Zodiacal chart that is drawn up at that moment of intense focus. Very briefly, the ancient rules of Horary Astrology can be summarized as follows:

The *birth time* of a particular question is essential to the reading. By this is meant the actual time when the question reaches the awareness of the Astrologer. This is when the focus of the question is brought by the Querent to the diviner for an answer. Communication must be personal and direct. Frivolous questions are not suitable for this type of Astrology, and the question must be specific. The question must also be presented in its own time. (If the Querent impulsively telephones the diviner with a focused inquiry, then the question will have been "born" naturally, not within the context of a predetermined appointment.) To reiterate, *the birth time occurs when the diviner completely comprehends the question.*

Once the birth time of the question has been determined, several rules are traditionally applied to ascertain whether or not the chart is valid for further interpretation:

1. *Void-of-Course Moon.* (A Planet is said to be void-of-course if it forms no complete aspect before leaving the Sign in which it is positioned at birth. Such a Planet is said to be without a purpose or objective.) Luna is very important in Horary Astrology. If Luna will not make an aspect with any other Planet in the horoscope before leaving its Sign, the horary chart is null and void. Such a chart would basically indicate that nothing good or bad will come of the matter. If the Void-of-Course Moon makes a favorable aspect to the Part of Fortune (a synthesis

of Sol, Luna and Ascendant positions) it would indicate success and benefit. If it forms an unfavorable aspect to the Part of Fortune it would indicate loss.

2. *Position of the Ascendant.* If the Ascendant lies between twenty-seven degrees of one Sign and three degrees of another, then the chart is invalid. In such cases, the question is considered either to close to the final outcome or premature. (Some Astrologers make an exception if the normally "void" Horary Ascendant forms an exact conjunction with a planet in the Natal chart.)

3. *Via Combusta (the Fiery Way).* Ancient Astrologers called the area between fifteen degrees Libra and fifteen degrees Scorpio "the Fiery Way." If Luna lies within this section of the chart, the horoscope is invalidated.[148]

4. *Saturn in the Seventh House.* In horary Astrology, the Ascendant represents the Querent, while the seventh house symbolizes the diviner. The placement of Saturn in the seventh house indicates that the diviner is: not objective, in error, has misunderstood the question, or is unable to come up with an answer. It sheds doubt on the validity or productivity of the Reading.[149]

If none of the above rules apply, the analysis of the chart may continue. *The house of the question must then be determined.* (The meanings of the houses are basically the same as in Natal Astrology, as are the Planets and Signs. Remember however, that Horary Astrology is more specific—less generalized.)

The ruler of the house in question is considered a vitally important part of the chart. The Horary answer is based upon the aspect relationships formed between that particular house ruler and the rest of the Planets. In addition to this, Luna and its aspects (until it leaves its Sign) portrays the development of the matter and its ultimate resolution.

Another rule to keep in mind is that any Planet or angle degree which shares the same number of degrees as Luna's nodal axis (regardless of which Sign the Planet or nodal axis is in) will promote a "fateful" influence on the matter in question. Whether this influence is favorable or unfavorable depends upon the Planet in question.

In any of the divinatory arts, the question of *time* is an important factor. In horary Astrology, the time of a *recent past event* is made by determining the number of degrees between the Planet last passed (the Moon's last conjunction) and Luna's actual location (in degrees) in the chart. The number of degrees, not the Sign, is what is important here. The subtracted difference between these two degree numbers is relevant. Then using the placement of Luna in conjunction with the chart below, the diviner is able to ascertain the time frame involved:

---

[148] We feel that this particular rule seems rather like the one in Geomancy where the Diviner is told to destroy the chart if Rubeus or Cauda Draconis show up in the First House. Apply it if you wish to be traditional.

[149] In many cases the Querent and the Diviner may be one and the same. Follow the same advice as in the previous footnote.

	CARDINAL SIGN	KERUBIC SIGN	MUTABLE SIGN
ANGULAR	days	months	weeks
SUCCEDENT	weeks	years	months
CADENT	months	many years or unknown	years

Example: If the difference between Luna and its most recent "passed" Planet is four degrees and Luna was positioned in a Kerubic Sign in an Angular house, the timing in question was four months earlier.

The same table may be used to estimate the timing of future events. Example: Let's say that Luna is in eight degrees of Libra in the eleventh house. If another planet such as Jupiter is in fourteen degrees of Cancer, then we can see that a square aspect between Luna and Jupiter will occur six degrees "into the future" (14-8=6). Since Luna is in a Cardinal Sign and a Succedent house, this means that the square will occur in six weeks.

Electional Astrology

This type of Astrology concerns the planning of the "birth time" of a *desired event* before it occurs. It is a form of "planning ahead" which utilizes Astrological knowledge to determine beforehand the most favorable time to begin an idea or event, in order to obtain a desired outcome. This type of Astrology is very important to the ceremonial magician, who often uses it to plan the most favorable time to perform a specific ritual or magical working.

In Electional Astrology, like Horary Astrology, the Moon is of crucial importance. Its position must be strengthened in an Election chart for any pre-planned event. The void-of-course Moon should always be avoided in planning any event.

Synastry

(From the Greek "syn" meaning "with, together, along with.") This is the technique and practice of chart comparison in Astrology. Its focus is the relationship that exists between two natal charts when they are compared. It is used to evaluate the interaction between two people. Many kinds of human relationships can be explored through synastry, including marriages, business relationships and friendships.

Imagine synastry as two natal charts placed one top of the other and held up to the light, so that both can be seen at the same time and compared. The Planets of one chart will form aspects with the Planets of the other. The charts interact, create stresses and bring added comforts.

Begin by comparing the positions of Sol and Luna in the two charts: trines created between the charts will indicate support, while squares and oppositions mean strained relations. Conjunctions will imply a unity of focus but perhaps not enough tension to allow for combined growth. However, even if there are numerous unfavorable aspects between two charts, a trine of the Suns will make compatibility possible if not probable. The Sol/Luna combination of both horoscopes must be examined together with emphasis placed upon the support or stress points formed by the cross-aspects between the charts.

Synastry allows for wide orbs and places particular emphasis on Elemental qualities. In addition, the closer the aspect, the more prominent will be the relationship factors obtained by interpretation.

If the Suns or Moons do not form aspects with each other, the Astrologer must turn his/her attention to the individual Sol/Luna blends and Elemental harmonies. Then examine the house positions of one individual's Sun and Moon in the other person's chart. Next, the positions of the remaining planets are compared by Sign, aspect and house. The relationship of the Mercuries will portray where the minds of the two individuals meet. The relationship of the Venuses points to emotional compatibility. The Mars' relationship will depict energy or sex. The Jupiters will portray hopes and enthusiasm. The Saturns will show alignment of ambitions. The Uranus' factors will point to where one individual will cooperate in the other's self-concept and self-awareness. The Neptunes will portray fantasies and possible deceptions. The Plutos will indicate major points of blended perspective. (If a Planet of one horoscope falls on the South Node of the other, the first person will tend to dominate and exploit the latter.)

The last step in synastry is to compare the aspects made between the Planets from one chart to the other. These aspect relationships become active networks of one individual's needs and tensions interacting with those of the other person. In ideal relationships, tension must be present to sustain growth and attraction, while ease must exist to affirm comfort and fulfillment.

Composite

Two charts may also be compared by the construction of a composite chart. To make such a *relationship horoscope*, the Planetary positions, Midheaven and Ascendant points in both charts are converted to degree positions. Then the positions of each of the pairs (two Ascendants, two Midheavens, etc.) are added together and divided by two. The resulting composite points arrived at are the *synthesis* of the two charts. (The composite House alignment is determined by the composite Midheaven and the table of houses for the latitude marking the locale of the relationship.) In a composite chart, the Zodiacal Signs are not significant, whereas the aspects and house positions are of utmost importance.

Astrology in all its forms is a complex and fascinating subject. The student is well advised to seek out a couple of good books on the subject to flesh out the "bare bones" of the system provided here. The various forms of Astrology presented here should *all* be practiced at least once a week while in the Portal grade.✿

Divination

The Portal initiate should strive as much as possible to develop the faculty of intuition through the use of Horary and Natal Astrology, Geomancy and Tarot. It is best to attempt only questions in which you are not emotionally involved, because methods of divination can be a fruitful source of self-deception to those who are psychic but not self-aware. It is only natural to advertise your successful intuitions and disregard your unsuccessful ones. If you are given to having intuitions, you must learn to assess them honestly. Failure, too, is a part of the learning process. Have the courage to say, "I was right about this, but wrong about that."✿

Self-Exploration

The time spent in the Portal should be given to the study of the whole makeup of the initiate. All of these methods are designed to assist the student in his/her progression along the road to self-knowledge. You are to realize the different layers of your being—some of which you have been symbolically led through in the Outer grades—"Which in one sense quitteth not Malkuth"—the Kingdom of *yourself*.

This line of thought, coupled with the study of the rituals, may lead you to realize what it was you gathered together in the first point of the Portal Ritual, and what it is you are trying to perfect on the altar of the Spirit.

The traditional period of time spent in the Portal grade is nine months, for this grade has a correspondence to the nine months of gestation before birth. As the unborn child, stage by stage, grows through the ancestral history of the race, so the initiate in the Portal, by a single circumambulation for each, recalls the past grades. And at the end of the first point of the ritual the initiate regards the Elemental grade symbols upon the altar as parts of the aspirant's body and mind, and contemplates them as coming together—the unity of his/her spiritual self.

In the second point, the initiate sacrifices his/her name—the symbol of the old idea of "self"—in order that the idea of a new self and a new consciousness may be attained.

This has a correspondence in the birth of a child. It emerges from the membranes and placenta which hitherto have been its body and source and finds itself not "dead" after the dread change, but translated to a larger consciousness. Thus the Portal foreshadows the kind of change and development necessary for understanding the higher teachings. The symbolism of birth gives us the courage to believe that even now, our personal growth is evolving to a stage where our physical bodies will share the same fate as the placenta, which "dies" at our spiritual birth.

But tradition, as embodied in the Golden Dawn and shown somewhat less directly in the organized religions, teaches that this development can be assisted by conscious effort—in fact, there comes a time when this effort must be made through the present body and mind. And realizing that we are indeed in a path of Darkness groping for Light, we must feel our way to an understanding of the meaning of Life—and the reason for death.

To those who feel the call to make this effort, comes the teachings of the Golden Dawn with a series of pictures, symbolic of the growth of the Soul to new life. The meditations given with each grade are designed to lead the mind towards ideas which will assist in self-knowledge—universal impersonal ideas which each must find in his/her own way—*"the secrets which cannot be told save to those who know them already."*

The aspirant is led to look backwards. First the initiate must acknowledge the debt to evolution through which has been perfected the instrument of the mind. Then, through meditation, the aspirant is led to see him/her self as not only self-conscious; as one who receives impressions—as one who criticizes and watches—one whose will is interfered with—one who is misunderstood—one to whom others are "persons" or masks (from the Latin *persona*, a mask)—but, standing outside himself, the initiate now becomes one who endeavors to sense how his/her mask appears to others; as one who impresses, one who is criticized and watched, one who interferes with the will of others, one who misunderstands.

The aspirant may recall earlier periods in life when his/her convictions were sure, judgments were harsh and unjust, and actions were shameful. The initiate may view this past life in that picture as dispassionately as an entity operating in the give and take of life—something growing out and as outside the category of blame as is the bitterness of unripe fruit.

As the knowledge of the aspirant's place and relative importance in the Universe matures, s/he will attain strength to be self-honest—ashamed of nothing that is found within the mind—one watching the antics of the lower personality with tolerant amusement—yet always learning.

The aspirant will reflect on words, and the power of words. The initiate will catch him/her self weaving them—twisting their meaning—deceiving self and others with them. S/he will at time come under obsession to them—s/he will see how they fix and make possible the recall of events and emotions, and with this knowledge s/he will become aware of how words affect other people.

As the aspirant begins to realize the tremendous miracle of words, the magic, both good and evil, of human communication by words, s/he will begin to grasp why the Order reiterates the importance of silence. The true magician must understand all the tools of magic, and in periods of silence, s/he must contemplate words as one of them.

As the initiate thus traverses the long road to dispassionate self-knowledge, and no longer has to waste energy in doing battle for and indulging wounded feelings in defense of a totally false idea of self, s/he is led to meditate on the varied symbols of the cross, and from this to contemplate the Crucified One, known variously in the Western Esoteric Traditions as Osiris or Jesus Christ.

The Life and sayings of Christ given in the Portal Meditation should be studied and pictured in the mind.

The mind must be taught to die to useless churnings over past times and vain apprehensions about future things. This is difficult, for human fantasies die hard, but once the effort is made, however transient the result, it becomes easier with time to replace wasteful thoughts with those that cluster around a powerful symbol of eternal truth.

Definite times should be set aside for Meditation wherein ideas may be formulated as far as possible. Before going to sleep, the aspirant should do the Pentagram Ritual and impress on the mind that s/he must recall on waking any teaching that has been obtained in dream or vision. This may be assisted, if on waking, s/he calls to mind the Sun rising, thinly veiled in clouds.

The previous ceremonies and gradework shall be as true initiations for the aspirant only in so far as s/he has prepared the self to receive them. Like words, these ceremonies are as symbols, the communication of whose essence depends on the understanding and experience of the recipient.✿

REGRESSION EXERCISE

Perform the LBRP. Sit in a comfortable position or lie down, eyes closed. Spend a few minutes inducing relaxation and rhythmic breathing. Visualize yourself within your present surroundings.

As you continue the Fourfold breath, see yourself going backwards in time. As you inhale to the count of four, think of last spring. Hold the breath for four counts and think of last Winter. Exhale to the count of four and imagine last Fall. On the empty hold to the count of four, think of last summer. Continue the exercise in this fashion going backwards into time, from Spring to Winter, Fall and Summer. Ever backwards, keeping pace with the Fourfold breath.

You may decide to go back in time in five year intervals: five years, ten years, fifteen years, twenty years, etc. At any one of these intervals, stop and visualize yourself at that particular point in time. Observe how you looked, how your surroundings looked, the people around you at that time, how you felt about yourself, your view of the world. Examine significant events that occurred which shaped your view of the world and of yourself.

When ready to end the exercise, use the Fourfold breath to visualize time moving forward again. (Inhale—Spring, full hold—Summer, exhale—Fall, Empty hold—winter.) Move time forward again until you arrive at the present. End the exercise with the LBRP. Always record your observations.

You should practice this exercise several times, deciding beforehand what time in the past you wish to examine further. If you become quite proficient in this technique, you can go back one year at a time, all the way back to birth.✿

SECTION 2: Correspondences of Spirit

Spirit is the Fifth Element which crowns and completes the other four. The word "Spirit" comes from the Latin word *spiritus* meaning "breath." Spirit symbolizes the eternal and divine part of the psyche and the Infinite mind. It is the Element of ultimate transcendence and divine essence. Spirit is androgynous and ever-present. The color given for Spirit is white. The "direction" assigned to Spirit is in the center (although it permeates through everything).

Hebrew names especially connected with the Element of Spirit are *Eth* (essence), *Yeheshuah* (the Pentagramaton), *Ruach* (breath) and *Eheieh* (I am). Greek words for the Divine Soul is *Nous*, and *Pneuma* (Spirit). Godforms associated with the Element of Spirit include Inanna, Osiris, Dionysus, Mithras, Christ and all of the dying and resurrected gods and goddesses. Great Mother goddess such as Isis, who is the synthesis of all types of universal conciousness, can also be applied to the Element of Spirit. The Hebrew letter Shin in white is also attributed, as are the images of the sphinx, the circle, the cross and the Christian Holy Ghost.

In the Enochian system the Tablet of Union is attributed to the Element of Spirit. This Tablet binds together the four other Elemental Tablets under the presidency of Spirit and the divine names *Exarp* (Air), *Hcoma* (Water), *Nanta* (Earth) and *Bitom* (Fire).

NETER: The Egyptian word which means roughly "God" or "Lord." The Hieroglyph for this word was an axe-head fastened to a long handle by thongs of leather or string. There is no exact translation of the word, although it was often used by the Egyptians to indicate something which is "divine." The word Neter includes ideas of "renewal" and "perpetual." It can be described as an active principle which creates things in regular recurrence, to renew its own perpetual self-existence, with the power to renew life indefinitely.

OSIRIS: Originally an Egyptian vegetation god, the son of Geb and Nuet who died with the harvest only to be reborn in the Spring, Osiris later became the god of the Dead and of Resurrection. In early legend he was also a Water god who represented the fertility brought by the Nile. In certain texts he is simply referred to as "God,"something which was not done with other deities. And no other Egyptian god was equal to the exalted position of Osiris, or thought to possess his specific characteristics.

Legend has it that Osiris instituted the cult of the gods, built the first towns and temples and laid down the law governing religious worship. He was given the title "Onnophris" or "un-nefer" (Greek and Egyptian respectively), which some claim means "the good one." As the story goes, the evil brother of Osiris, Set, who represented everything which opposed Osiris, eventually plotted to kill him. Set entombed the body of Osiris within a chest and flung it into the waters. The chest later ended up on a shore where a tree trunk grew around it. The tree was later cut down and used as a column of a king's house. The chest containing the body of Osiris was eventually recovered by his wife, Isis, but Set found it and dismembered the body into fourteen pieces, which he scattered. Isis patiently searched for the remnants and reconstitued the body, accept for the phallus. Isis, aided by Thoth, Anubis and Horus, was able to restore the dead god to life.

From early times Osiris represented to the Egyptians a being that was both a man and a god; someone who by virtue of his suffering and death, humans could identify with—more so than the other gods. But he also offered the hope of resurection after death—that humans, too, could triumph over death and attain everlasting life. Thus Osiris became the god of the Underworld, with the power to bestow eternal life upon the dead, who after passing the ordeal of the judgment (the Weighing of the Soul) were allowed to live in the Underworld. Osiris became known as *Osiris Khenti Amenti* or "Lord of the Westerners," that is, the dead who dwell in the direction where sun sets.

Eventually Osiris was thought to be even more powerful than Ra, the Sun god—taking on the powers of a cosmic Being and the creator of all. He is represented standing or sitting on a throne, dressed in mummy wrappings. He wears the *Atef* crown which is a high white miter or cone flanked by two ostrich feathers. His hands which are folded across his breast, hold the crook and scourge. Another symbol which is associated with Osiris is the *Djed*, which was said to symbolize the god's spinal column.✡

Djed

SECTION 3: Wands, Lamens and Admission Badges

The Wands

The implements of the Hiereus and the Hegemon remain the same as they were in the Outer grades.

The Third Adept's Wand: The blue salt-headed wand is the scepter of the Third Adept in the Portal Temple of the Order. The Third Adept in this particular ceremony always represents the feminine qualities of moisture and receptivity. (There is valid speculation within the Order as to the correctness of the symbolism concerning this particular wand—whether or not the symbol of mercury should actually replace the salt symbol as the wand-head. However we shall not enter into this discussion here. What we have provided is a description of the Third Adept's Wand as portrayed in the original Order documents.)

Of these three Alchemic essentials, salt is the physical vehicle of manifestation for the other two. (The phrase "salt of the Earth" takes on new meaning in this regard.) Sulfur characterizes each thing in a particular way—mercury gives animation—but salt provides the matrix. Salt is the receptive Body—the material substance. Salt is in a continual state of evolution, taking on a new Body as the old Body is steadily cast away. This is a process of purification which arises out of separation. To cleanse is purification, but the work of purification is more than a degree of cleansing. That which is pure is freed from that which is impure. The purification of the salt in its triune parts: the *Body, Soul* and *Spirit*, is an important step in the initiate's spiritual evolution.

The Second Adept's Wand: The red sulfur-headed wand is the scepter of the Second Adept in the Portal Temple. The Second Adept in this ceremony represents

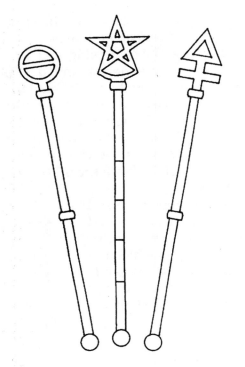

The Chief Adept's Lamen

The Portal Wands

The Third Adept's Lamen

The Second Adept's Lamen

The Hiereus' Lamen

The Hegemon's Lamen

the qualities of heat and the active male principle. That is why the most Fiery of the three Alchemic principles is attributed to this particular officer.

Sulfur is that which gathers together and fashions all that is of the Earth. The nature of Sulfur is both tangible and intangible. Within its tangible aspect sulfur is an oil which is to be found in all substances. Its intangible aspect is that of consciousness—to be found in all substances in varying degrees. Sulfur corresponds to the superconsciousness or the cosmic consciousness. It is the desire for positive action and vital heat.

The Chief Adept's Wand: The pentagram-headed wand is the scepter of the Chief Adept in the Portal Temple of the Order. The pentagram represents the four Elements of nature crowned by the fifth—Spirit. As far back as the days of the Egyptians, the five-pointed star has signified "rising upward towards the point of origin." In the Portal ceremony it is wielded by the Chief Adept to instill these ideas deeply within the psyche of the candidate, who in this ritual symbolically receives the fifth and final Element. This wand also represents the Three Alchemic Principles combined.

The shaft of the scepter is painted in the five Elemental colors of the pentagram: Spirit—white (the longest section on the wand), Fire—red, Air —yellow, Water—blue, and Earth—black.

The Lamens

The Second and Third Adepts wear lamens that symbolize their specific Elemental affiliation. The Hiereus and the Hegemon wears lamens that are adorned with hexagrams—references to the Macrocosm and to the Perfected Human Being.

The Hegemon's Lamen in the Portal Hall reveals her important duties as the keeper of the balance within the temple. The lamen depicts the opposing red and blue triangles of Fire and Water conjoined and in perfect equilibrium—the Macrocosmic Hexagram. This lamen is not unlike a simplified Banner of the East (minus the crosses), showing the Hegemon's importance in bringing the candidate throughout all the grades to the Antechamber of the Light of L.V.X. In the Portal Ritual, she is also the officer who performs all of the workings of Elemental Air. She therefore indicates that Air is the Reconciler between the Forces of Fire and Water, and that only through perfect balance of these two extremes is the Portal to the Light traversed.

The Hiereus' Lamen in the Portal is identical to one of the diagrams shown in this grade: "Below, is shown the Occult Symbol of Malkuth, the tenth Sephirah. It is in four parts, corresponding to the Maltese Cross. They are Fire of Earth, Water of Earth, Air of Earth, Earth of Earth, as indicated by the symbol. They correspond to the four grades of the First Order, which in one sense, quitteth not Malkuth, being the grades of the four lowest Sephiroth of Malkuth in Assiah. Upon them, is surcharged a white hexagram in a circle. The six and the four make ten, the number of Malkuth on the Tree. The hexagram is also the Sign of the Macrocosm—of Tiphareth, and of the six upper Sephiroth, wherefore it is white—Spirit ruling over matter. Six is a perfect number, for its whole equals the sum of its parts....Remember that the whole number of Malkuth is 496—which again is a perfect number.

Malkuth must then be equated and perfected by the six ruling the four: and the link between six and four is the number of the pentagram."

The Hiereus is the officer who sits in the lowest point of Malkuth in the Hall at the border of the Qlippotic Realm, enthroned upon matter and robed in Darkness. In the Portal, he is the Officer in charge of the workings of Elemental Earth. His lamen in this grade primarily shows that Spirit must always govern matter (represented by the four Sub-Elemental colors of Malkuth). If Spirit does not crown matter, the result is chaos and evil, symbolized by the Qlippoth.

The Third Adept's Lamen portrays the forces of Water, and she thus oversees all the workings of Water in the Portal grade. Her lamen is painted in the flashing colors of Elemental Water, blue and orange. She represents the powers of the black (feminine) pillar in this grade. The lamen shows a octagram in the center of which is a Water cup drawn in the style of the Stolistes Badge. The octagram is formed from two squares superimposed one over the other at an angle. It thus refers not only to the sphere of Hod, but also to that of Chesed (i.e., the two watery Sephiroth).

The Second Adept's Lamen depicts the Powers of Fire, and he is in charge therefore of all the workings of Fire in the Portal grade. He represents the powers of the white (masculine) pillar in the Portal Ceremony. His lamen is painted in the flashing colors of Elemental Fire, red and green. Upon it are shown an upright Fire triangle within a pentagram. The pentagram refers to the sphere of Geburah, the fiery Sephirah.

The Chief Adept's Lamen differs from the others in that it is in the shape of a Rose Cross, which more properly belongs to, and foreshadows the Rosicrucian symbolism of the Second Order.

This outer form of the Rose Cross Lamen is a symbol which unites the numbers four, five, and six. (The four arms of the cross, the number of Tiphareth (six), to which the Rose Cross is attributed, and the five Elements represented by the four arms of the cross plus the circle of Spirit.)

The cross is a complex symbol whose main meanings include that of "conjunction" of opposing forces. The cross represents the mystic center of the cosmos—the place of junction for the forces of the universe. Consequently, the cross affirms the primary relationship between the two worlds of the celestial and the Earth-bound (Spirit and Matter). It represents the Spirit or Divine Light, brought into the physical world of manifestation—Life (the human body) symbolized by the four Elements which are the components of Life.

The rose is primarily a symbol of completion, total achievement and perfection. It also alludes to the mystic center, and the heart. The rose is a yonic symbol associated with regeneration, productivity and purity. Because the flower unfolds when it blossoms, it is a worthy symbol of spiritual growth. To the Greeks it was a symbol of sunrise. The rose is the sacred flower of Venus, goddess of love, attributed to the seventh Sephirah. (Seven is described as the most blessed of all the numbers, and it is also the number assigned to the act of initiation into the mysteries.)

The golden cross and red rose together refer to the synthesis of all these ideas. The red rose also alludes to the compassion and sacrifice of the Slain and

Resurrected One. The golden cross alludes to the spiritual gold concealed within human nature.✿

The Admission Badges

The Greek Cross of Five Squares is the Admission Badge to the Ritual of the Cross and the four Elements in the Portal grade. It symbolizes the equated forces of the four Elements ruled by the fifth Element of ETH or Spirit. In addition, the number five alludes to the powers of the pentagram—this cross could well be described as a pentagram in the shape of a cross.

It is also described in the Portal Ceremony as: "a cross of corrosion, corruption, disintegration and death. Therefore doth it fall in the paths of Death and the Devil, unless in Hod, the Glory triumpheth over matter and the Corruptible putteth on Incorruption, thus attaining unto the beauty of Tiphareth; unless in Netzach, Death is swallowed up in Victory and the Transformer becometh the Transmuter into Pure Alchemic Gold. 'Except ye be born of Water and the Spirit, ye cannot enter the Kingdom of God.'"

This refers to some very basic Alchemic principles. In the science of Alchemy, purification arises out of separation, out of the various processes that transpire during the work with separation. Dissolution, also known as separation, is a form of decomposition—a breaking up. This is a crucial part of Alchemic purification. That which is not essential is separated from that which is. That which is pure is freed from the impure. There is a natural and hidden Fire within humanity that brings forth a cleansing process through heat, putrefaction and distillation—until the Pure Essence is revealed. Only that which has endured the Trial by Fire has been purified. Only that which complies with the Trial of devotion and love, is pure.

This cross is given to the candidate as a symbol of his/her various component "parts." The candidate symbolically examines and scrutinizes these separate parts, an act which represents the process of decomposition. The different Elements must be carefully equilibrated—any imbalance must be sacrificed. (Although we are discussing symbolic ritual acts, these processes must also occur in the psyche of the individual.) Until the initiate has prepared the psyche through separation and purification, he/she cannot receive the *Eth*, the philosophical Mercury, (Spirit) whereby through knowledge and understanding the lesser is transmuted into the greater. Only then can the true and indissolvable Stone of the Wise, be found within as a source of strength and inspiration.

The Badge of the Hiereus' Lamen: This Badge is described earlier in this chapter thus: "The triangle in the circle is the high symbol of the Holy Trinity, and the first three Sephiroth, and of Binah wherein is the sphere of Saturn, Ruler of the Path Tau. Therefore it is worn by the Hiereus, and when I entered the Hall of the Neophytes in the 0 = 0 grade, I beheld the sword that barred and the symbol which overcometh the barrier.

The lamen in its more special attribution to the Hiereus, has the following meanings. In the circle are the four Sephiroth of Tiphareth, Netzach, Hod and Yesod. The first three mark the angles of the triangle inscribed within, while the sides are

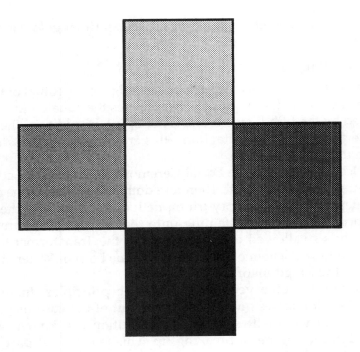

The Greek Cross of Five Squares

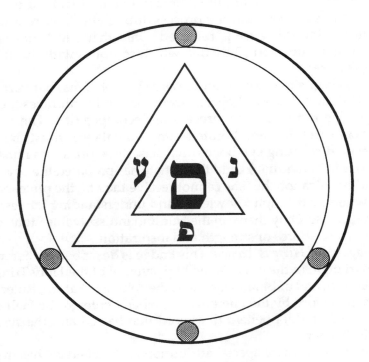

The Badge of the Hiereus' Lamen

668

the Paths of Nun, Ayin and Peh, respectively. In the center is marked the letter Samekh indicating the 25th Path. While the Wheel revolves, the hub is still. Ever shall I seek the center, looking from without to within. *This is the Key of my path."* ✿

SECTION 4: Ritual Diagrams

The Portal Ceremony includes the explanations of several diagrams. Some of these are described quite adequately within the text of the ritual itself (including: the Cross of Four Triangles, the Circle and Point, the Occult symbol of Malkuth, the Diagram of V.I.T.R.I.O.L. and the Tablet of Union[150]). The other diagrams require a bit more explanation.

The Great Hermetic Arcanum: This diagram is from the *Musaeum Hermeticum*, a 17th century alchemical book. Briefly described in the Portal ceremony, this diagram not only contains symbolism of the three alchemical principles, but also the seven mystical numbers as well. The central point (the face) in the diagram refers to the synthesis of the whole inherent within the monad. The duad is symbolized by the Queen of Luna and the King of Sol (the two gender archetypes as well as the two great contending forces of the Universe.) The triad is portrayed in the triangle of Spiritus, Anima and Corpus (Spirit, Soul and Body) as well as in the smaller triad of the Three Alchemical Principles. The number four is depicted by the four Elements (two of which are shown by their Kerubic animals) in the corners of the drawing. The number five is represented by the five parts of the initiate (hands, feet and head) which are each associated with one of the five Elements in the diagram. The number six is symbolized by the two triangles in the drawing. The heptad is shown by the heptagram of the Planets.[151]

The face of the figure is contained with a triangle formed from sulfur, mercury and salt. At the base is salt, which is identified with the planet Saturn of the heptagram, pointing downward at a cube, the emblem of the body (corpus). Sulfur is placed on the Mars angle, pointing toward a torch-bearing hand on the side of the Soul (anima). Alchemical Mercury is located on the angle of the Planet Mercury, which points to a hand holding a sack or matrix on the side of Spirit (spiritus). The greater triangle of Body, Soul and Spirit, represent the Macrocosm, whereas the lesser triangle containing the face is the Microcosm.

The image of the sun is situated on the side of anima-Soul, because it is sometimes considered as male, active and fiery. The salamander above affirms this. The female principle, Spirit, is shown alongside the image of Luna, above which is the eagle of Scorpio (the Water Element). On the side of Sol and Jupiter is a King. On the side of Luna and Venus is a goddess riding a dolphin.

Sol and Luna (or Anima and Spiritus) are the male and female principles, which are separated in nature. Through the Spagyric Art the two are united and the resulting offspring is the Philosopher's Stone—the hermaphrodite—male and

---

[150] For more information about all the Enochian Tablets, refer to our book, *Secrets of a Golden Dawn Temple*.

[151] Refer to Adam McLean's book, *The Alchemical Mandala*.

The Great Hermetic Arcanum
(from the Musaeum Hermeticum)

670

The Vision of Nebuchadnezzar

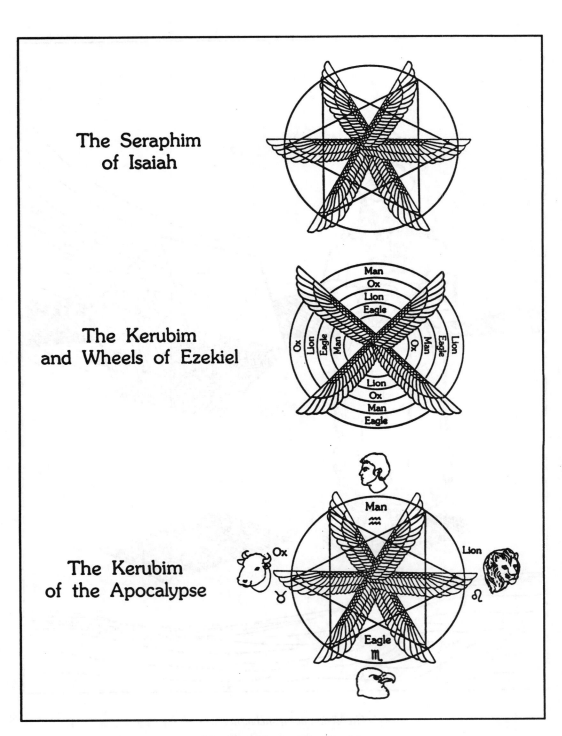

The Seraphim
of Isaiah

The Kerubim
and Wheels of Ezekiel

The Kerubim
of the Apocalypse

The Seraphim and the Kerubim

Pan
(from Athanasius Kircher's Œdipus Ægyptiacus)

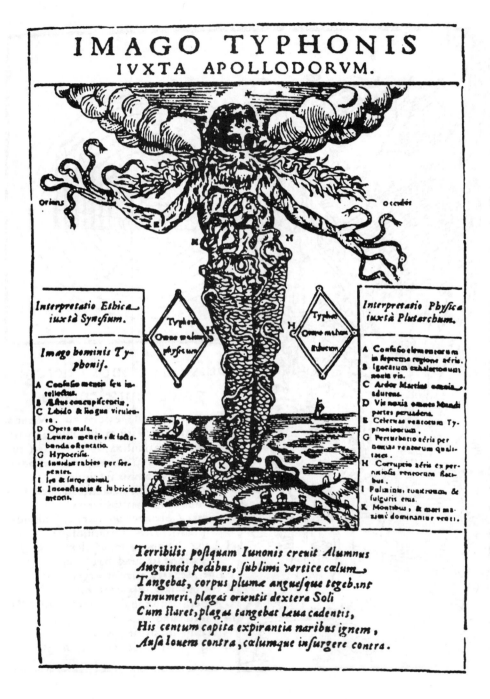

Typhon
(from Athanasius Kircher's Œdipus Ægyptiacus)

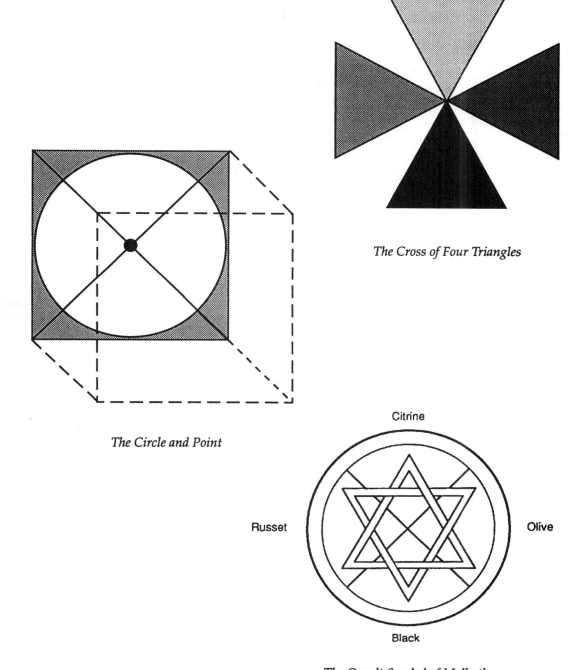

The Cross of Four Triangles

The Circle and Point

Citrine

Russet

Olive

Black

The Occult Symbol of Malkuth

Visita Interiora Terrae Rectificando
Invenies Occultam Lapidem Veram Medicinam
V.I.T.R.I.O.L.U.M.

1. 2. 3. 4. 5. 6. 7.

V. 1. T. R. I. O. L.

S. U. L. P. H. U. R.

M. E. R. C. U. R. Y.

△ ▽ △ ▽

Subtilis Aqua Lux Terra
S.A.L.T.

Flatus Ignis Aqua Terra

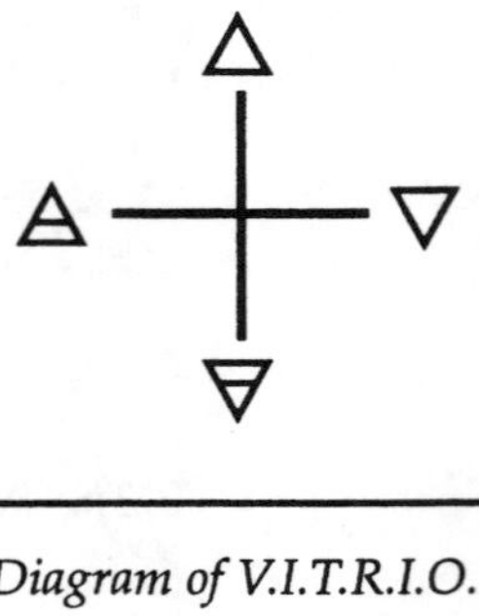

Diagram of V.I.T.R.I.O.L.

676

female, Soul and Spirit merged into one. This is indicated by the feet of the figure, one in the Water and one on dry land.

In the circle which surrounds the figure, a Latin sentence of seven words is shown: *Visita Interiora Terrae Rectifando Invenies Occultum Lapidem,* "visit the interior of the Earth, in rectifying you will discover the hidden stone." Each word of the sentence relates to an Alchemical process. The first letters of all of these words form the word *Vitriol.* Within seven smaller circles are depicted various allegorical scenes of the Alchemical process from putrefaction to resurrection.

To obtain this type of perfection, the Alchemist attempts to "fix that which is volatile." (The fixed volatile is represented at the top of the diagram by the two wings tied together.) In practical Alchemy, the "volatile" is the evaporating Mercury, while the "fixed" is the Mercury remaining at the bottom of the container. During condensation, the volatile will drip from the top of the vessel to the bottom. The goal of this process of sublimation is to separate the (fixed) male and the (volatile) female portions of the Mercury. Then the two portions are each purified before they are joined in ultimate union.

The Vision of Nebuchadnezzar: In the early days of the Order a variation of this diagram was briefly described in the Philosophus grade. The Portal diagram is based upon a description given in the Book of Daniel (2:31-38). Nebuchadnezzar was a king of Babylon whose name meant "Nebo chief protector." Nebo was the Babylonian king of Wisdom (the Lord of Brightness). As a king, Nebuchadnezzar symbolizes the human will backed up by intellect, which brings about human judgment. The human will supported by intellect is very powerful up to a point (the metal body), until it realizes it's own weaknesses and limitations (the feet, part of iron and part of clay). These represent the limitations of the unpurified base material before the alchemical process is begun.

The kings' vision portrays a great figure composed of different substances which are the planetary metals used in Alchemy. These metals describe the different psychic aspects of the initiate. These are the base materials that the aspirant must analyze, separate and sublimate (*solve et coagula*) unto the highest state of purity. The Stone cut without hands is the goal of the process—Philosophers Stone—unto which all else is like the chaff of grain blown by the wind.

The Seraphim and Kerubim: This diagram portrays various descriptions of Angelic beings from three different Biblical passages. The first passage is from Isaiah Chapter 6:1-3 where the prophet describes a vision:

> *In the year that king Uzziah died I saw also the Lord sitting upon a throne, high and lifted up, and his train filled the temple. Above it stood the Seraphim: each one had six wings; with twain he covered his face, and with twain he covered his feet, and with twain did he fly. And one cried unto another, and said, Holy, Holy, Holy, is the Lord of hosts: the whole Earth is full of his glory.*

The six wings refer to the hexagram and the idea of the number seven (the synthesis of the six ancient Planets plus the luminary of the Sun) which dominates the heavens.

The next passage concerns the Kerubim in the vision of the Prophet Ezekiel (Ezekiel, Chapter 1).

> *Also out of the midst thereof came the likeness of four living creatures. And this was their appearance; they had the likeness of a man. And every one had four faces and every one had four wings....Their wings were joined one to another; they turned not when they went, they went every one straight forward. As for the likeness of their faces, they four had the face of a man, and the face of a lion, on the right side; and they four had the face of an ox on the right side; they four also had the face of an eagle. Thus were their faces: and their wings were stretched upward; two wings of every one were joined to another, and two covered their bodies....Now as I beheld the living creatures, behold one wheel upon the Earth by the living creatures....And when the living creatures went, the wheel went by them: and when the living creatures were lifted up from the Earth, the wheels were lifted up. Whithersoever the Spirit was to go, they went, thither was their Spirit to go; and the wheels were lifted up over against them: for the Spirit of the living creatures was in the wheels....And under the firmament were their wings straight, the one toward the other: every one had two which covered on this side, and two which covered that side on their bodies."*

Here the Kerubim are seen to be the powers of the four Elements under the name Tetragrammaton and the form of the cross (joined one to another) The wheel of the Spirit adds the fifth and final Element (ETH) which is the guiding principle of the whole, thus completing the pentagram.

The final description of the Kerubim is from John's vision (Revelations 4:7-8).

> *And the first beast was like a lion, and the second beast like a calf, and the third beast had a face as a man, and the fourth beast was like a flying eagle. And the four beasts had each of them six wings about him; and they were full of eyes within: and they rest not day and night, saying Holy, Holy, Holy, Lord God Almighty, which was, is, and is to come.*

Here the Kerubim are seen as single-headed, but having six wings. They thus unite the powers of the number seven (the planets) with the number four (the Elements).

Typhon: The diagram is taken from Athanasius Kircher's *Œdipus Ægyptiacus.* Typhon is also called Set. He is the Evil One, the unclean one, the enemy and murderer of Osiris. Typhon later became known as the dragon of ignorance, destruction and perversion.

The harsh sand storms and dry desert winds of Egypt were said to have been created by Apophis-Typhon, the maker of the blistering heat, drought and the sting of the scorpion. Typhon was reputed to rule when the Sun entered the Sign of Scorpio. Typhon was also believed to cause blindness by means of the wind-swept dessert sands.

To initiates, Typhon represents the devourer of Souls and the lower world which "swallows" the spiritual side of the individual, whose essence is divine, but must be born (reborn) into the manifest Universe (a descent into a lower imperfect world). Defeating Typhon means freedom from the cycle of rebirth into the physical world (continuous devouring by Typhon) and ultimate union with the godhead.

Pan: The drawing of Pan employed in this grade is from a diagram called "The Hieroglyphical Representation of Jupiter or Pan" from Athanasius Kircher's *Œdipus Ægyptiacus.* The Greek god of nature was considered the leader of the sacred dances which he was said to have created to represent the circular orbits of the Planets. The god Pan is a composite of man and goat, an archetype of natural energy. He is also associated with the Planet Saturn (ruler of Capricorn) and his pipes represent the harmony of the Planetary bodies. Later, the Graeco-Egyptians considered Pan a form of Jupiter. The god was also regarded as the power of the Sun and the ruler of the lower worlds. (Review information on Pan given in Chapter Three.)✿

Ritual Work for the Portal Grade

Continue the Fourfold breath technique as taught in the Neophyte grade. Add to this the following visualizations:

Inhale	—	Yod
Full Hold	—	Heh
Exhale	—	Vav
Empty Hold	—	Heh

The Portal initiate should construct all of the following talismanic emblems to aid in meditation and ritual. These emblems should be painted black on white:

- The sigil of the Spirit wheel
- A pentagram
- The number five
- The letter Shin
- The letter Samekh
- The name ETH in Hebrew
- The name PAROKETH in Hebrew
- The name YEHESHUAH in Hebrew
- A drawing containing all forms of the cross as depicted in the Admission Badges of the Elemental grades.

MEDITATION

for the Portal grade[152]

Let the Aspirant meditate upon the cross in its various forms and aspects as shown in the Admission Badges throughout the grades.

Let him consider the necessity and prevalence of sacrifice throughout nature and religion.

Let him realize the saying of the Master, 'Whosoever shall save his life shall lose it, and whosoever shall lose his life shall save it.'

'Except a corn of wheat fall into the ground and die, it abideth alone, but if it die, it bringeth forth much fruit.'

Let him endeavor to realize his own place and relative importance in the Universe, striving to stand outside himself and allowing only such claims as he would allow to another.

Let him carefully abstain from talking of himself, his feelings or experiences that he may gain continence of speech, and learn to control the wasteful activities of his mind.

Let him contemplate the Sun as thinly veiled in clouds.✿

---

[152] From Regardie's *The Golden Dawn*.

Development of the Will

The development of the Will is one of the most important tasks faced by a magician. It is a principal factor in the attainment of spiritual progress.

A practical and most effective method for training the Will is to consciously set up specific goals for a predetermined period of time, and if diverted from keeping these goals, to withhold something that gives enjoyment. This method is based on a type of behavior modification therapy. Keep in mind that there is nothing moralistic in this procedure. The student who undertakes this practice is not "avoiding (bad) vices in favor of (good) virtues."

The point is to strengthen the Will, which in and of itself is neither good nor bad. This exercise is a disciplinary vow that a certain habitual action will be denied by the aspirant. In order to perform this technique properly, the student should deliberately set a goal which is not in any way connected with a "bad" habit, such as smoking, swearing or drinking. An impersonal and guilt-free attitude of detachment should be maintained. The aspirant should select a personal idiosyncrasy such as tapping the foot to music, saying a certain word, or crossing the legs when sitting. This will help insure that the student does not make a senseless virtue out of the discipline exercise.

One of the most effective ways to reinforce the Will is to dispense a mild electric shock. (One can usually find a small device which will deliver a slight shock in any store that sells supplies for stage magic.) The shock is very light, but can be quite surprising. If this device is employed immediately following the broken vow, a mental connection is made which will become a fixed and potent reminder which sets up a continual alertness on the part of the Will. It is important to carry the device with you at all times so that the disciplinary action can be delivered immediately after the transgression. By doing this the student will reinforce the connection between the unwanted action and the electric shock. It is through this discipline that the Will obtains its training and effectiveness. All violations of the oath should be rapidly "punished" in order to make an enduring impression on the student's mind. This can be done either by administering a light shock as described above, or by denying oneself something that is pleasurable.

This technique accomplishes two things. Firstly, a constant vigilance is established which generates a potent Will-power. Second, the mind itself is placed gradually under the control of the aspirant's Will. This in turn helps the student's faculty of concentration immensely.✡

THE PRACTICE OF THE DIVINE ESSENCE

For this exercise the student should review and practice all of the relaxation and body-awareness exercises prescribed earlier.

To perform this exercise, lie down in a comfortable position. Once relaxed, reflect on the fact that the entire surface of your body is covered by millions of tiny pores. In truth, every muscle and organ in the body is composed of cells which have minute areas of space between them.

Imagine the pores on the skin of your face (nose, cheeks and brow) are stretched wide open. (This should only take a matter of seconds if you have performed the previous exercises regularly.) Then proceed to visualize the skin on the scalp and back of the head in the same fashion. Continue on to the skin of the neck, shoulders, arms, chest, abdomen, hips, thighs, legs and feet. Imagine the surrounding membrane of every part of the body, including the internal organs permeated by a series of pores loosely weaved together by a net-like substance.

Once you have obtained a feeling of the opening of all the pores in your body, return to reflect upon your head. Imagine the brain, also has become full of open pores—somewhat sponge-like. Apply this visualization to every part in the body—the bones, muscles and soft organs—all becoming like sponges.

When this visualization is complete, imagine that the surrounding atmosphere is able to easily penetrate through your body, as if the air itself flowed right through the pores and holes of your body. The air saturates you, entering into every pore. Imagine that when you inhale, the air enters your body through the bottom of your feet; when you exhale, the air leaves your porous body from the top of your head. Experiment with similar visualizations, pushing the inhalations and exhalations of air through your body in various directions.

A relationship exists between the Elements of Air and Spirit. Therefore imagine that the air cascading through your body is the air of the Divine Spirit—the Ruach Elohim. It is the Divine which exists everywhere, surrounding you on all sides—omnipotent and infinite. This Spirit is without limitation or opposition. It is eternal Truth, Wisdom and Love. It is Light and Life. This is what you should imagine flowing freely through every pore of your body and mind.

This exercise is designed to bring the student to a high level of divine-consciousness. Every aspect of mystical experience and knowledge may be brought fully into play during this meditation. Although it is an extension of the aspirant's earlier work, this meditation is designed to bring about a true realization concerning the infinity of the eternal Spirit and the complete fulfillment of the Divine within.✿

A GUIDED VISUALIZATION FOR THE PORTAL[153]

After taking a ritual bath and performing a rite of relaxation, put on the regalia of the First Order and the crossed black and white sashes. Two candles, one black and the other white should be placed upon the altar, North and South respectively.

Close your eyes and continue breathing in the exercise of the Fourfold Breath. See yourself leaving your personal temple behind. The room slowly fades from your view.

Imagine yourself standing in a great arched stone doorway. Before you is a magnificent temple with marble pillars, an immense stone altar, black-and-white tiled floor, an assembly of Egyptian gods and goddesses and Kerubic guardians. Anubis. Horus. Thme. Osiris. This is a place you are very familiar and comfortable with. It is the Hall of the goddess, Thme, the Hall of Two Truths. This is where your admission into the mysteries first took place, and your journey on the path of initiation began. For many months you have worked in this temple, learning its secrets and studying its foundation. Now it is time to journey beyond the confines of this temple and explore what lies ahead. Near the doorway in which you are standing there is one enormous black pillar. Figures and hieroglyphs are carved into its smooth obsidian surface. A red stained glass pyramid burns brightly upon its summit. You reach out your hand to touch this pillar, the symbol of the temple you are leaving behind. You know that once you leave this temple, the touch of the black pillar will never feel the same as it does now. The assembly of gods seem curiously elated at your parting, as if they understand more about your impending journey than you do. Saluting them with the Signs of a Neophyte, you turn and step out of the archway into a mist-covered landscape.

This is the strangest terrain you have ever encountered. It is neither day nor night. There are no trees nor plants of any kind. No rocks or hills. There is little of anything except a gray haze and fog-enshrouded ground. This is a complete detachment from anything you have yet experienced.

You look around for a guide, for caution tells you not to proceed until one appears. You withdraw for a while into a quiet meditation, imagining yourself as the child-god, Harpocrates, seated upon a Lotus flower. At length you are aroused from this meditation by an unimpressive figure in a simple brown robe. You test the authenticity of the guide by vibrating the divine name of *Eheieh*. You then exchange the Neophyte Signs. Your guide then leads you into the mist.

You continue walking for some time, uncertain of your direction, or if a path even exists under your feet. If only there were something, some marker or symbol to give you a clue as to where you are going. But again there is nothing. You might be walking in a circle for all you know. It is as though you and your guide exist in a state of limbo.

You ask the guide where you are going. He indicates that at this point in your spiritual development, it is up to you to decide where your path truly lies.

---

[153] From our book *Secrets of a Golden Dawn Temple.*

You must find a way out of the fog. Taking the advice of your guide, you reach into yourself to find the knowledge you accumulated as an initiate. This knowledge will aid you now. But knowledge is not enough, you must begin to put that knowledge to wise and practical use. You are not even certain of the direction you are facing, therefore you close your eyes and ask for the guidance of the Divine Light. Behind the darkness of your closed eyelids, you see an Angelic hand appear, a flaming Yod held in its palm. Turning your body until the hand is directly in front of you, then you open your eyes. You now know what direction is East.

You invoke the four Elements, saying the proper words and saluting each quarter with the Sign of the Rending of the Veil. As you salute the North, mountains, hills and lush forests appear around you. As you salute the East, a cool gust of wind rushes over you and clouds begin to form. As you open the Veil toward the West, vast oceans and pristine rivers are created. As you make the Sign toward the South, a bolt of lightning strikes a tree starting a small brush Fire that clears away dead vegetation.

A rich landscape has been formed around you where once there was nothing. You pause a moment to perform the Qabalistic Cross. Your guide gives a nod of approval. The two of you continue on in the direction of the Eastern wind. A wheel appears off in the sky ahead, but you are too far away to see it clearly.

It is not long before a dreadful sight appears on the right-hand side of the path you are traveling. In a field is a skeleton swinging a scythe back and forth, cutting the long stems of wild grass. Beneath its bony feet are human body parts protruding from the Earth, which are nourishing the fresh vegetation. The skeleton stops swinging his implement and gives you a long eyeless stare. A deadly scorpion picks over the bones for food, and a poisonous serpent curls around the scrawny legs of the reaper. Off in the distance beyond the figure is the colossal form of Typhon, spewing smoke and ash from his mouth like some infernal volcano.

This is the image of transformation, which most people fear intensely. It is a frightening image because many individuals fear change of any kind. Change is however, a natural occurrence in the cycle of the universe. Change of consciousness is necessary for spiritual evolution. You notice a white eagle soaring above the head of the skeleton, a symbol of purity and transmutation. You give the Sign of the Enterer at the figure. It answers with the Sign of Silence. You and your guide proceed on the Eastern path.

The landscape continues as before, unchanged in its richness. Far ahead of you, there appears to be a large tree in the shape of the letter Tau. A figure is hanging from it, but you are too far away to see any details.

To the left of the path another strange sight is evident. A hairy creature with a goat's head, huge bat-like wings and clawed feet stands on top of a cubical black stone. To the rock are chained two smaller horned creatures who dance and mimic the larger being. The great demon spits and laughs at you as it flaps its leathery wings and rocks back and forth upon the altar, trampling protective pentagrams underfoot. The figure hurdles a stream of obscenities at you and tells you to return from whence you came.

However you are aware of the humor of this situation. The figure of the devil is truly a comedy of errors, a conglomerate of various animal parts put together as an illusion to mislead you. The Devil is a boogieman, a creation built up from humanity's own fears and corruption and projected outwards into the form of a demon—a scapegoat for all evil acts committed by human beings. This illusion, like all illusions placed as obstacles to your spiritual growth, must be dealt with, exposed, and seen for what it truly is, or else you will remain like the two smaller creatures, held in bondage by their own misconceptions. You must see beyond the limited vision of your two physical eyes. The greater sight of the inner vision is called for. The figure of the devil does not alarm you, in fact it provokes you into laughter.

The apparition of the Devil vanishes without a trace. Off in the forest beyond, you see the figure of gentle Pan, Greek god of nature, much maligned by Christianity, which turned the peace-loving god into a monster. Pan is grateful that you have shattered the false illusionary form of the devil. With a flick of his goat's tail, he smiles and slips quietly into the woods. Soon after, you hear the sweet sound of music from his hollow-reed pipes.

Continuing on in the direction of the East, you and your guide eventually find yourselves in the middle of a great valley where a clear river divides the land. A mighty volcano spews ash into the distant sky, but even that impressive sight cannot draw your eyes away from the gigantic form of an Angel who straddles the river, one foot resting on dry land, and the other foot in the Water. The eyes of the Angel are closed, and you get the impression that she does not need eyes to see you with. Soft reddish hair frames her face and falls in long locks against her blue robe. Her wings are like two prismatic crescents which rise vapor-like into the air beyond. A single golden square adorns her azure garment, and the brilliant orb of the sun graces her brow. In her slender hands she holds two vases, one containing Water, and the other containing Fire. She mixes the two primal Elements together, creating steam and liquid gold.

The Angel then releases the two vases which remain floating in the air, completely unsupported. The mixing of the Elements continues as before, the Fire and Water now form an infinity sign as they flow from one vessel into the other. Her hands free, the Angel makes the Sign of the Philosophus. Without warning, a fierce lion appears from behind a bush, ready to spring at you. Somehow you realize that what is about to occur is necessary, and you resist the urge to banish. The great cat lunges at you and knocks you off your feet. The beast delivers a painful bite to your left hip then simply walks away and begins licking its paw. The sting of the wound is intense. The sight of blood on your hand causes you to enter a trance-like state:

Flames are all around you, engulfing your entire body. The pain of the wound increases as you feel the purging Fire burning away the impurities of your personality—all the untruths, jealousies, cruelties and injustices you have ever committed against others and against your own Higher Self. All these evils are brought to the surface like a boil. They arise out of your skin to surround your body like the foul smoke of a rubbish-fire. The stench of your own naked evils is enough to gag you, and you suddenly feel exposed and ashamed.

The Angel then makes the Sign of the Practicus, forming a cup over her heart with her hands. As she does so, you become aware of a pure white eagle flying low, skimming across the surface of the river. As you lay exhausted on the ground, the great bird circles above you and finally lands, sinking its sharp talons into your right hip.

The pain is almost a relief. A sudden rainstorm appears. Heavy drops of Water wash over your face and into your mouth. The foul black cloud is washed away without a trace by the redeeming rain. The bird of prey is not at all bothered by the downpour. It regards you with stern eyes, but it seems to be saying, "mercy, forgiveness, peace."

The rain stops as suddenly as it began and the bird takes to flight. The sun appears from behind a cloud and its rays form the most perfect rainbow you have ever seen in the East. A wondrous feeling of freedom overtakes you. You feel healed and rejuvenated. Standing up to face the Angel, you reach down to touch with both hands, the wounds left by the kerubic creatures. Holding out your hands toward the Angel, you notice that your hands are not bloodied. In the palm of one hand is a small tongue of flame and in the other is a handful of Water.

The Angel makes the sign of the equated cross over you. Bringing both hands together over your heart, you absorb the equilibrated Elements into your Tiphareth center, and a rush of white brilliance reverberates throughout all the spheres and paths of your inner Middle Pillar.

The Angel begins to fade from view, transforming into glistening drops of mist which hang in the air and catch the suns rays to form flowing prismatic shapes. The shimmering forms gather together into a thin wisp of a veil which extends before you in the East. Your guide, whom you had all but forgotten, takes you by the arm and places you in front of this etheric curtain. Giving the Sign of the Rending of the Veil, you part the curtain.

An immense white pillar, counterpart to the black pillar that you saw earlier looms before you, stretching very nearly to the sky. Its white marble surface is fully etched with sacred scenes and symbols. Its red pyramid capital is almost lost to view in the clouds. You touch this pillar just as you embraced its black twin. An inner part of you rejoices at this union. For a long time you remain in communion with the energies of the pillar of Light.

At length it is time to end this journey. Your guide takes you back along the path, past Pan's forest and the figure of Death swinging his scythe. Finally, you come to the door of the familiar temple in the West. You exchange the Signs of the Opening and the Closing of the Veil with your companion and bid him farewell. Then, giving the Neophyte Signs, you enter the Hall of Dual Manifestation.

The assembly of gods and goddesses seems elated to see you. The temple is the same, but you feel different—changed somehow. It is as though you have reached a different level or plateau in your spiritual development, and your perspective is no longer the same as it was. You spend a brief period of time at the altar flame before deciding to end the meditation.

Finally, you see your own physical temple room and see yourself seated within it. Bring your consciousness slowly back into your physical body, sensing the room around you. After adjusting yourself to your surroundings, you may bring the visualization to its completion.

At the end of the meditation, you may write down any impressions or experiences in a magical diary before closing with the LBRP.✿

Additional Work for the Portal Grade

In our book *Secrets of a Golden Dawn Temple*, Volume Two, there are several rituals written specifically for the Portal grade. They include: the Rite of Self-Purification, the Rite of Self-Consecration, the Rite of Self-Consecration through Sulfur, the Rite of Self-Purification through Salt, a Simple Meditation on the Portal Lamens, and the Purifications of the Elements Within. The student may also begin regular performance of the Supreme Invoking Ritual of the Pentagram (SIRP) and the Supreme Banishing Ritual of the Pentagram (SBRP). Although these last two rituals are traditionally Adept-level, we believe that the Portal initiate may begin to practice them by virtue of the fact that s/he has now been introduced to all five Elements.

The LVX Signs vs. the Portal Signs.

In some of the rituals suggested in this chapter, (the SIRP, the SBRP, the BRH, and Regardie's Opening by Watchtower) call for the initiate to give the LVX Signs after tracing the Spirit pentagrams. This is because traditionally, advanced rituals of this type were performed only by initiates in the grade of Adeptus Minor (or higher). The LVX Signs are the *grade signs* of an Adeptus Minor, not necessarily the grade sign of the Element of Spirit. The Fifth Element is conferred on an initiate in the Portal grade, and therefore the grade signs of Spirit are the Opening and Closing of the Veil, just as the grade sign for Air is that of the Theoricus. It is therefore appropriate for the Portal initiate to freely substitute the Portal Signs for the LVX Signs. We realize, however, that many students have already been performing these rituals with the traditional LVX Signs, and may be reluctant to switch to the Portal Signs. Therefore we have presented the rituals in this course with the traditional LVX Signs, and leave the option open for the individual to choose.✿

Suggested Reading

The Art of True Healing by Israel Regardie
> (Deals with the aura and the Middle Pillar from a therapeutic view point. Perform the exercises suggested in the book.)

The Middle Pillar by Israel Regardie
> (This book also deals with the Middle Pillar technique. It attempts to link the results of magical training with the terminology of Analytical Psychology.)

The Alchemical Mandala by Adam Mclean
> (Describes various Western symbols for contemplation and meditation. Write a report on the book and perform the meditations it describes.)

Three Books of Occult Philosophy by Henry Cornelius Agrippa, edited and annotated by Donald Tyson. (A book which was the source of many of the Order's teachings.)

The Rosicrucians by Christopher McIntosh
> (An excellent book on Rosicrucianism.)

The Sacred Magician by William Bloom
> (A <u>must-read</u> book that is a dairy of a magician who performed the six month long ceremony known as the *Sacred Magic of Abra-Melin the Mage*. A no-nonsense look at the difficulty involved in attaining true knowledge and conversation with one's Holy Guardian Angel.)

Books on Psychology

The Spectrum of Consciousness by Ken Wilber

Memories, Dreams, Reflections. by C.G. Jung

Psyche and Symbol by C.G. Jung

A Primer of Jungian Psychology by Calvin S. Hall and Vernon J. Nordby

Selected Writings; An Introduction to Orgonomy by William Reich

Wilhelm Reich: The Evolution of his Work by David Boadella

The Possible Human by Jean Houston

Books on Astrology

The Principles and Practice of Astrology (series) by Noel Tyl

Horary Astrology: The History and Practice of Astro-Divination by Anthony Louis

Work for the Advanced Magician

Traditionally, an initiate remains in the Portal grade for a minimum of nine months. Since the process of spiritual gestation is no less important for the Self-initiated student, we suggest adhering to this time frame. After completing this course, the student should be well prepared to move on to more advanced studies and rituals. Much of this work is to be found in Israel Regardie's *The Golden Dawn*, including several rituals written by Regardie for Adept-level working. Regardie's Introduction to the First Edition gives an overview of the some of the traditionally required gradework for an Adept.[154] The student may at this time begin to explore the more advanced studies of skrying, Enochian, the Tarot divination known as the "Opening of the Key," and many other techniques described in that book.[155]

In *Secrets of a Golden Dawn Temple*, Volume Two, there are a number of rituals designed for the Adept-level magician. These include: a Meditation on the Throne of Stolistes, the Consecration of a Tipharetic Talisman, Ritual for Spiritual Development, an Invocation of Hermes-Thoth, Assumption of God-forms, a Guided Meditation, The Rite of Assumption to the Godform of Thme, the Supreme Convocation of the Watchtowers, A Guided Alchemical Journey for the Adept, The Supreme Invocation of Eth, Consecration of a Lunar Talisman, The Opening of the Spheres by Key, the Rite of Assumption to the Godform of Osiris, A Meditation on the Cross of Victory, Charging the Guardians of the Temple, A Meditation on the Miniature Vault Wall, An Invocation of Aries, A Rite of Healing, Invocations of the Powers of the Elements, and an Invocation of Binah.

Chapter Five of *Secrets of a Golden Dawn Temple* (Volume Two), also provides some traditional Adept gradework: the construction and consecration of the four Elemental Weapons, the Lotus Wand, the Magic Sword, and the Rose Cross Lamen. ✡

THE LESSER BANISHING RITUAL OF THE HEXAGRAM (BRH)

(This ritual uses the four lesser forms of the hexagram assigned to the quarters in accordance with the Cardinal Signs on the Zodiacal wheel. Thus Aries-Fire is in the East, Cancer-Water is in the North, etc.)

Face East and perform the Qabalistic Cross.

With right index finger or implement, trace the banishing hexagram of Fire toward the East. Thrust through the center of the figure and vibrate the word *"ARARITA."*

---

[154] The Grade work listed in the introduction is for the subgrades of Neophyte Adeptus Minor and Zelator Adeptus Minor.

[155] A book describing the Inner Order rituals and advanced workings of the Golden Dawn in more detail will be published sometime in the near future by Adam Forrest.

EAST
Banishing Hexagram
of Fire

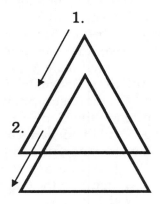

SOUTH
Banishing Hexagram
of Earth

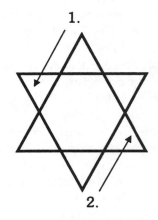

WEST
Banishing Hexagram
of Air

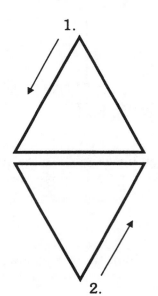

NORTH
Banishing Hexagram
of Water

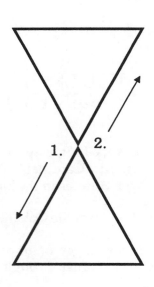

The Hexgrams for the BRH

Move to the South and trace the banishing hexagram of Earth. Charge the center of the figure as before and vibrate *"ARARITA."*

Move to the West and draw the banishing hexagram of Air. Energize it by thrusting through the center of the figure and vibrate as before, *"ARARITA."*

Go to the North and draw the banishing hexagram of Water. Thrust and intone as before, *"ARARITA."*

Return to the East and perform the Analysis of the Keyword: Extend your arms out in the shape of the Tau Cross. Say with feeling, *"I.N.R.I."* (Pronounce each letter) *"YOD NUN RESH YOD"*(Yode-noon-raysh-yode). As the names of the Hebrew letters are pronounced, trace them in the air before you, from right to left. Then say:

> *Virgo, Isis, mighty Mother,*
> *Scorpio, Apophis, Destroyer,*
> *Sol, Osiris, Slain and Risen,*
> *Isis, Apophis, Osiris.*

Through the previous oration, gradually raise the arms and lift the head upwards. Vibrate strongly, *"IAO."*

Return to the stance of the Tau Cross saying, *"The Sign of Osiris Slain."*

Put your right arm straight up in the air from the shoulder. The left arm should be straight out from the left shoulder so that the position of the two arms together resemble the letter L. Hands are to be open flat with palms forward. Turn your head so that you are looking over your left arm. Say, *"L, the Sign of the Mourning of Isis."*

Raise the arms overhead to an angle of sixty degrees so that they form the letter V. Keep the arms straight and the palms facing forward. Throw the head back and say, *"V, the Sign of Typhon and Apophis."*

Cross the arms on the chest to form the letter X. Bow your head and say, *"X, the Sign of Osiris Risen."*

Say slowly and powerfully, *"L.V.X."* (Spell out each letter separately and give the sign of each as you do so.) Say, *"LUX"* (lukes).

Remain in the Sign of Osiris Slain and say, *"The Light..."* (hold arms out in the Tau Cross position for a moment then recross them again on the chest) *"...of the Cross."*

(Note: This is the end of the Analysis of the Keyword as performed in the Banishing Ritual of the Hexagram [BRH]. However the Analysis of the Keyword is performed slightly different from this in the Rose Cross Ritual.)✿

THE L.V.X. SIGNS

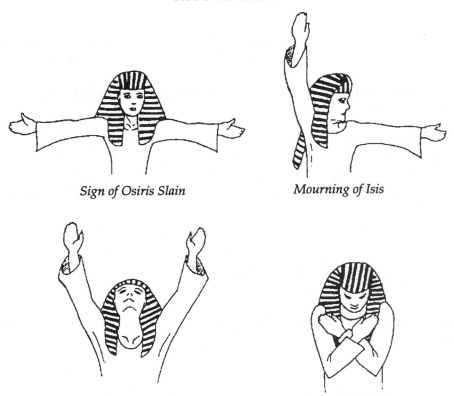

Sign of Osiris Slain   *Mourning of Isis*

Apophis and Typhon   *Sign of Osiris Risen*

THE OPENING BY WATCHTOWER

(Note: This is a ritual written by Israel Regardie that is based upon the Golden Dawn's SIRP and the Consecration of the Vault of the Adepti.)[156]

Preparation of the Hall: The temple is to be arranged in accordance with the Neophyte Hall. The Elemental tablets should be placed in the appropriate quarters. On the center of the altar should be the Tablet of Union with the Elemental weapons around it. (Air Dagger—East, Fire Wand—South, Water Cup—West, Earth Pentacle—North.) The magician should be relaxed and robed in full ceremonial regalia. A black-handled dagger, sword, or Outer Wand of Double Power may be employed for the LBRP and BRH.

---

[156] Regardie and I discussed the subject of self-initiation several times. We both agreed that at this level of attainment, the magician should perform the Opening by Watchtower daily in order to activate the astral (Yetziratic World) and become a magician who truly walks between the worlds.—CC.

Commence the ritual with five knocks. Go to the Northeast and say in a loud voice, *"HEKAS, HEKAS ESTE BEBELOI!"*

Go to the East and perform the LBRP. Perform the BRH.

Go to the South side of the altar and take up the Fire Wand. Turn to the Elemental Tablet of Fire in the South and wave the implement three times in front of the Tablet's sigil. Then, holding the wand high, slowly circumambulate the room in a clockwise (deosil) direction saying:

> *And when, after all the phantoms are banished, thou shalt see that Holy and Formless Fire, that Fire which darts and flashes through the hidden depths of the Universe, hear thou the Voice of Fire.*

Upon reaching South, face the Elemental Tablet and wave the wand in front of it again, three times. With the wand, trace a large circle in the air in front of the Tablet and imagine it in brilliant white light. Within this circle draw a large flaming white invoking Spirit Active pentagram and vibrate *"BITOM."* In the center of the figure, draw the Spirit sigil in bright white light and vibrate *"EHEIEH."* Give the LVX Signs. Draw another circle. Trace the invoking pentagram of Fire over the one just drawn while vibrating, *"OIP TEAA PEDOCE."* In the center draw the sigil of Leo and visualize it in red, while intoning *"ELOHIM."*

Place the wand before the Tablet and give the Sign of Philosophus. Remain in this position and say:

> *In the Names and Letters of the Great Southern Quadrangle, I invoke ye, ye Angels of the Watchtower of the South!*

Leave the Fire Wand in front of the Tablet. Take up the Water Cup and turn to the West. Wave the cup thrice before the Water Tablet. Hold the cup high while circumambulating slowly doesil around the room and say:

> *So therefore first the Priest who governeth the works of Fire must sprinkle with the Lustral Water of the Loud Resounding Sea.*

On reaching the West, wave the cup three times again and trace the circle in white light before the Tablet. Draw the invoking Spirit Passive pentagram in white with the cup while vibrating *"HCOMA."* In the center trace the Spirit sigil in white light and vibrate *"AGLA."* Give the LVX Signs. Trace another circle. Draw the invoking pentagram of Water over the Spirit pentagram while intoning *"EMPEH ARSEL GAIOL."* Draw the blue sigil of the Eagle in the center and vibrate, *"Aleph Lamed, AL."*

Place the cup in front of the Tablet and give the Sign of Practicus. While in this position say:

In the Names and Letters of the Great Western Quadrangle, I invoke ye,
ye Angels of the Watchtower of the West.

Leave the Water Cup in front of the Tablet. Go clockwise to the East of the altar and take up the Air Dagger. Turn to the East and wave the implement three times in front of the Air tablet. Begin the slow circumambulation while saying,

Such a Fire existeth, extending through the rushings of Air—or even a
Fire formless whence cometh the Image of a Voice, or even a flashing
Light, abounding, revolving, whirling forth, crying aloud.

Stop again in the East and wave the implement thrice in front of the Tablet. Trace the circle and the invoking Spirit Active pentagram in white while vibrating *"EXARP."* Draw the sigil of Spirit in the center and vibrate, *"EHEIEH."* Give the LVX Signs. Draw another circle. Trace the invoking pentagram of Air while intoning *"ORO IBAH AOZPI."* Draw in the center the yellow sigil of Aquarius and vibrate *"YHVH."*

Place the Dagger in front of the Tablet and give the Sign of Theoricus. Say:

In the Names and Letters of the Great Eastern Quadrangle, I invoke ye, ye
Angels of the Watchtower of the East.

Leave the Air Dagger in front of the Tablet. Go clockwise to the North of the altar and take up the Earth Pentacle. Turn to the North and wave the implement thrice in front of the Earth Tablet. Begin the slow circumambulation while saying:

Stoop not down into that darkly splendid world wherein continually lieth
a faithless depth, and Hades wrapped in gloom, delighting in unintelligi-
ble images, precipitous, winding, a black, ever-rolling Abyss, ever espous-
ing a body, unluminous, formless and void.

Stop upon reaching the North and wave the implement thrice again in front of the tablet. With the Pentacle trace the circle and the invoking Spirit Passive pentagram in white. Vibrate *"NANTA."* Trace the white Spirit sigil in the center while intoning *"AGLA."* Give the LVX Signs. Trace another circle. Draw the invoking pentagram of Earth over the previous figure while vibrating *"EMOR DIAL HECTEGA."* Draw the black sigil of Taurus in the center and intone *"ADONAI."* Place the Pentacle in front of the Tablet and give the Sign of Zelator. In this position, say:

In the Names and Letters of the Great Northern Quadrangle, I invoke ye,
ye Angels of the Watchtowers of the North.

Leave the Pentacle in front of the Tablet. Move clockwise to the West of the altar and face East. Trace a circle over the Tablet of Union. Then draw each of the Spirit pentagrams in white and vibrate the appropriate words:

EXARP EHEIEH. HCOMA AGLA. NANTA AGLA. BITOM EHEIEH.

Then say:

> *In the Names and Letters of the mystical Tablet of Union, I invoke ye, ye Divine Forces of the Spirit of Life.*

Make the Sign of the Rending of the Veil. Visualize the Veil opening as you step through it.

Remain West of the altar and say the following Enochian oration:

> *OL SONUF VAORSAGI GOHO IAD BALATA. ELEXARPEH. CO-MANANU. TABITOM. ZODAKARA, EKA ZODAKARE OD ZODAMERANU. ODO KIKLE QAA PIAPE PIAMOEL OD VAOAN.*
> *(Oh-ell son-oof vay-oh-air-sah-jee go-ho ee-ah-dah bahl-tah. El-ex-ar-pay-hay. Co-mah-nah-noo. Tah-bee-toh-em. Zohd-ah-kah-rah eh-kah zohd-ah-kah-ray oh-dah zohd-ah-mehr-ah-noo. Oh-doh kee-klay kah-ah pee-ah-pay pee-ah-moh-el oh-dah vay-oh-ah-noo.)*

> *(Say:) I invoke ye, ye Angels of the celestial spheres, whose dwelling is in the invisible. Ye are the guardians of the gates of the Universe, be ye also the guardians of this mystic sphere. Keep far removed the evil and the unbalanced. Strengthen and inspire me so that I may preserve unsullied this abode of the mysteries of the eternal gods. Let my sphere be pure and holy so that I may enter in and become a partaker of the secrets of the Light Divine.*

Go deosil to the Northeast and say:

> *The visible Sun is the dispenser of Light to the Earth. Let me therefore form a vortex in this chamber that the Invisible Sun of the Spirit may shine therein from above.*

Circumambulate the temple three times and give the Projection Sign and the Sign of Silence each time you pass the East. After the third pass, go to the West of the altar and face East. Utter the following adoration:

> *Holy art Thou, Lord of the Universe. (Projection Sign.)*
> *Holy art Thou, whom Nature hath not formed. (Projection Sign.)*
> *Holy art thou, the Vast and the Mighty One. (Projection Sign.)*
> *Lord of the Light and of the Darkness. (Sign of Silence.)*

(This marks the completion of the Opening by Watchtower and the beginning of the actual ritual or meditation at hand. At this point the magician should clearly state his/her intent for performing the ritual. Then the main ritual working [consecration of a talisman, invocation, rite of healing, etc.] can be proceeded with. When the actual working is completed, the magician may perform the Closing by Watchtower.)

Closing by Watchtower

Circumambulate the temple three times counterclockwise, giving the Sign of the Enterer and the Sign of Silence each time you pass the East. Feel the energy that you have carefully built up throughout the ceremony begin to dissipate.

Banish all the Tablets with the proper pentagrams and using the appropriate Elemental weapons. Then replace the four Elemental implements upon the altar.

Perform the LBRP. Perform the BRH.

> (Say:) *I now release any spirits that may have been imprisoned by this ceremony. Depart in peace to your abodes and habitations. Go with the blessings of YEHESHUAH YEHOVASHAH.*

Knock five times as in the beginning. Say:

> *I now declare this temple duly closed.*✿

THE RITUAL OF THE ROSE CROSS

The room should be clear of any obstructions (the altar should be moved aside). The only implement needed will be a stick of incense or the Rose Cross Wand.[157]

Go to the Southeast (SE) corner of the room and face outward. Trace a large cross and circle there with the incense or wand. As you draw the cross, visualize it in a golden light. The circle should be imagined as flaming red. While tracing this symbol, vibrate the name, *"YEHESHUAH."* On the last syllable, thrust through the center of the circled cross, charging it.

Keep the tip of the implement at the level of the center of the cross and walk to the Southwest (SW) corner of the room. Draw the cross and circle (rose) as before and thrust the implement through the center of the figure intoning, *"YEHESHUAH."*

Move to the Northwest (NW) and repeat this process.

---

[157] See *Secrets of a Golden Dawn Temple* for instructions on how to construct this wand.

Move to the Northeast (NE) and repeat.

Return to the SE to complete the circle. Touch the head of the implement to the cross already drawn there, but do not retrace or intone the name.

Now move diagonally across the room toward the NW, but stop in the center of the temple and make the Rose Cross above your head. Intone the name as before. With the implement held straight up in the air, walk to the NW corner of the room. Touch the tip of the implement to the center of the cross already formulated there. Do not retrace the cross or say the name.

Move diagonally across the room again toward the SE but stop in the center of the temple. Trace the Rose Cross below you and vibrate the name. Keep the tip of the implement held down and continue to walk to the SE corner. Touch the tip of the implement to the center of the Rose Cross already traced there. Do not retrace or intone.

Move deosil to the SW and touch the head of the implement to the cross already traced there. Vibrate the name *"YEHESHUAH."*

Walk diagonally toward the NE but stop in the middle of the room to touch the center of the cross above your head. Intone the name. Continue on to the NE and touch the implement to the center of the cross formulated there.

Move diagonally across the room toward the SW but stop in the middle of the temple to touch the cross below you. Intone the name. Continue on to the SW corner and touch the center of the cross already there.

Move clockwise and link up with all the crosses by touching their centers with the wand (NW, NE and SE). No need to intone as you do so.

Upon returning to the SE, the site of the first cross, touch the center and pause. Then retrace the golden cross over the original, only much larger. Vibrate, *"YEHESHUAH."* Trace a larger red circle over the original and intone, *"YEHOVASHAH."*

Walk deosil to the center of the room. Observe all six Rose Crosses surrounding you, all connected by ribbons of light. Return to the East and perform the Analysis of the Keyword:

Extend your arms out in the shape of the Tau Cross. Say with feeling, *"I.N.R.I."* (Pronounce each letter) *"YOD NUN RESH YOD"* (Yode-noon-raysh-yode). As the names of the Hebrew letters are pronounced, trace them in the air before you, from right to left.

Return to the stance of the Tau Cross saying, *"The Sign of Osiris Slain."*

Put your right arm straight up in the air from the shoulder. The left arm should be straight out from the left shoulder so that the position of the two arms together resemble the letter L. Hands are to be open flat with palms forward. Turn your head so that you are looking over your left arm. Say, *"L, the Sign of the Mourning of Isis."*

Raise the arms overhead to an angle of 60 degrees so that they form the letter V. Keep the arms straight and the palms facing forward. Throw the head back and say, *"V, the Sign of Typhon and Apophis."*

Cross the arms on the chest to form the letter X. Bow your head and say, *"X, the Sign of Osiris Risen."*

Say slowly and powerfully, *"L.V.X."* (Spell out each letter separately and give the sign of each as you do so.) Say, *"LUX"* (lukes).

Remain in the Sign of Osiris Slain and say, *"The Light..."* (hold arms out in the Tau Cross position for a moment then recross them again on the chest) *"..of the Cross."*

Then say:

> *Virgo, Isis, mighty Mother. Scorpio, Apophis, Destroyer.*
> *Sol, Osiris, Slain and Risen. Isis, Apophis, Osiris.*

Through the previous oration, gradually raise the arms and lift the head upwards. Vibrate strongly, *"IAO."*

End the Analysis by vibrating the four Tablet of Union names to equilibrate the Light: *"EXARP. HCOMA. NANTA. BITOM."*[158] Then aspire to the Light and draw it down over your head to your feet. Say, *"Let the Divine Light Descend!"*✡

Invoke Often

The Chaldean Oracles reveal that the magician is to "Invoke often" and "Inflame himself with prayer." This is the best possible advice that we or anyone else could give to the student who has reached the end of this book. The aspirant who has persevered through many months of studying these pages and the rituals described herein will have come to a realization that every aspect of the manifest universe is connected to and directed by the Divine. Every action, no matter how seemingly trivial is endowed by the Divine. Even the aspirant's own ego, which is a steady source of consternation throughout these studies, is determined by the Divine. No part of a divine universe is without meaning or importance.

---

[158] These names would not be vibrated if the magician were to perform the ritual in the Vault of the Adepti.

For all ceremonial workings, the magician must remember to always invoke the Highest first. It is equally important to invoke one's Higher Self or Holy Guardian Angel when performing the higher workings. This is because the magician's Angel is his/her own *personal link* with the universal Divine. A magician who has not made an initial connecting link to the Angel will never be able to accomplish the complex rituals of high magic. For the purposes of this course, we have clothed the Higher Self in the garb of the goddess Thmê. At this point, however, the aspirant should make an attempt to connect with the Angel without such scripting—discovering the personal nuances of the Angel on one's own. Anyone who attempts such workings under the governance of the Lower personality rather than the Higher Self is almost certain to fail, if not corrupt the magic.

Communication with one's Holy Guardian Angel is not to be found through good deeds or virtues, nor through one's beliefs in religious or occult dogma. No grade certificate or business card given by an occult organization can bestow it. It is only found through patience, perseverance, self-discipline and aspiration. The effort must be made and followed up with self-honesty and sincerity. But above all else *invoke often and inflame thyself with prayer!* There are many prayers and invocations that the magician can look to for inspiration, including the Egyptian Book of the Dead, the Greek Magical Papyri and certain Biblical writings such as the Psalms. Regular meditation—time spent alone in communion with the Godhead is a way to focus the divine presence within the Soul and the psyche.

Daily discipline is required. The magician must also trust the Holy Guardian Angel for guidance in all areas of life, even the most seemingly mundane. Through aspiration, prayer and invocation, the magician will certainly come to an understanding of what it means to find the True Stone of the Wise and to rest *"under the shadow of Thy wings, YHVH."* ✿

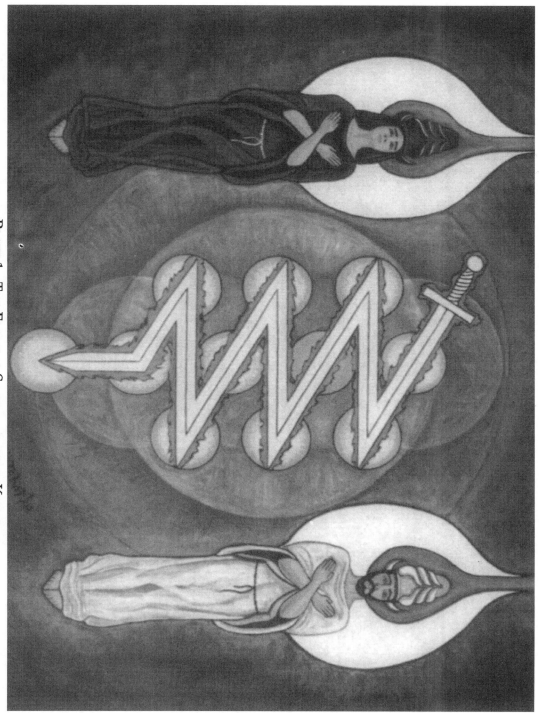

PLATE 1: THE FLAMING SWORD AND THE KERUBIM

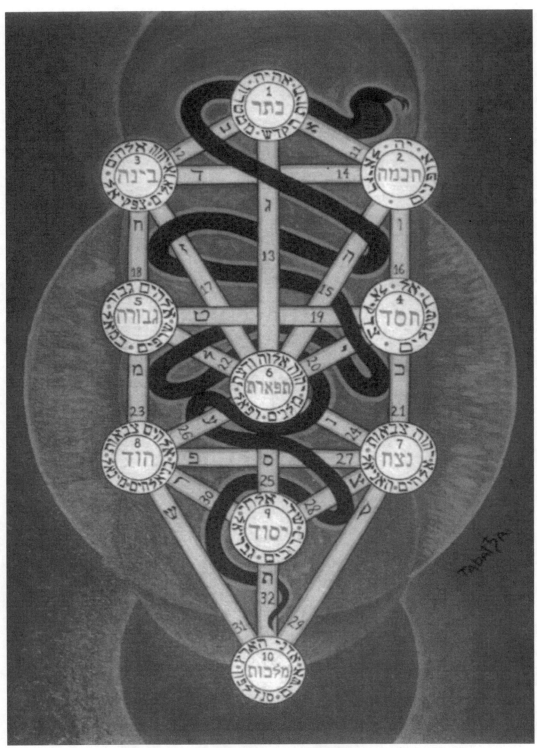

PLATE 2: THE SERPENT OF WISDOM ON THE TREE OF LIFE

PLATE 3: THE GARDEN OF EDEN BEFORE THE FALL

PLATE 4: THE GARDEN OF EDEN AFTER THE FALL

Afterword

by Mitch Henson

n this New Age of neo-pagan revivalism the term "initiation" gets bandied about much too frequently. If one attends the numerous neo-pagan gatherings, one hears a great deal about initiation (hence questionable qualifications). Let us not kid ourselves. Initiation means beginning and perhaps, something more. This is no less true within the Golden Dawn, the O.T.O. or the three degree system of Wicca. A beginning qualifies no one—a beginning is where the work starts. Usually an initiation is seen as a ceremony pulling in specific energies to introduce the candidate to the path he/she has chosen. Sometimes this is done in the form of a dedication, as in Wicca, or by the actual manipulation of the LVX in the Golden Dawn by the Hierophant (the chief initiating Officer).

In Wicca the candidate pledges to dedicate him/herself to the Goddess and the God. This is usually followed by three primary degrees and a great deal of training. In the O.T.O. the candidate participates in a dramatic ritual designed to open the chakras. In the Golden Dawn the candidate is imbued with the divine energy needed to begin the Great Work. Realistically it makes no difference which path one follows. Each system has advantages and disadvantages.

Israel Regardie wrote that by revising the Golden Dawn group initiation rituals for self-initiation, one could become initiated within the structure of the Golden Dawn.

At least one disenfranchised member of the Golden Dawn did just that. When Aleister Crowley left the Order after the revolt of 1900, he formed his own Ordo A∴ A∴. It was his opinion that the Golden Dawn failed to provide a structure which took the all too fallible human ego into consideration. He felt that the interaction of personalities distracted the student from accomplishing the Great Work. He also recognized a need for a membership that could exist on a one on one exclusivity relationship between master and student. Since he conceived his Order to be an initiatory body, he rewrote the Golden Dawn Neophyte Ritual for self-initiation. The result was *Liber Pyramidos*. Unfortunately *Pyramidos* was written within the framework of Crowley's religion, Thelema, and is consistent with those who fully believe in the validity of the Aeon of Horus.

For far too long the initiatory rituals of fraternal/magical organizations have been shrouded in a cloak of secrecy. Having been involved with, at least one such Order, I can attest that whether one is aware of the ritual prior to one's advancement or not, it simply makes not a shred of difference as to the validity of the initiatory process. I believe that Crowley even came to this conclusion, because with *Liber Pyramidos* he required the candidate to memorize the full text. This had to be done because it was, and is a ritual of self-initiation which the aspirant had to complete while hoodwinked.

Having stepped up the ladder of O.T.O. degrees to the Fifth Degree, with each ritual more protected than the last, and having moved through the grade rituals of today's *Hermetic Order of the Golden Dawn* without that dark cloak laying over the process, I , for one, would be willing to conclude that the Golden Dawn is far superior within their initiation process. Secrecy is not the motivating factor for advancement within the structure of any group. I'm sorry, but I believe that the road to self-illumination resides in the acquisition of knowledge. The only way one acquires that knowledge is to study the rituals of the organization that one affiliates oneself with. The Neophyte Ritual provides the entire body of magical teaching as adumbrated by the Order. Since it is the intent of the Golden Dawn to teach the processes of magic, it is absolutely necessary that the candidate have full access to the rituals through which he or she receives their initiation.

The book you have just read is based on the original Neophyte and grade rituals of the Hermetic Order of the Golden Dawn. There is no underlaying cloud *Under the Rose*, ostensibly to protect the integrity of the Golden Dawn. The text of this book maintains the integrity of the original group rituals by not insisting on a specific creed, for it is the knowledge and practice of *magic* that the Golden Dawn disseminates.

The reader will note that the knowledge lectures have been fully expanded, updated and organized so as to promote the best possible method one has at one's disposal for learning the material. At the end of each section are fully realized examinations which, if the student is honest with him or herself, will prepare one fully for Adepthood. Though one should never mistake the realization of Adepthood as one's principle goal. The goal is not to become an Adept, for that is just a single bridge that one will cross on the road to self-realization.

With the advent of this volume there should be a great deal less confusion, on the part of the student, about what material is pertinent to the gradework. When Israel Regardie originally issued the Aries Press edition of his seminal work, his intent was to insure the availability of the Golden Dawn technique of initiation and the methods of ceremonial magic as taught by the Order. Organization of the material was not his intent—preservation was. Almost fifty years have elapsed and, to my knowledge, this material has been fully reorganized and expanded here for the first time.

Though Chic and Tabatha Cicero have geared the text of this book as an instruction of self-initiation, it should become very apparent to the reader that this volume can be used with a clear intent to promote group work. It should also become apparent that any single individual or group of individuals have a clear choice in preparing the background for any path they wish to take inside or outside the Golden Dawn, based on the Western Tradition of ceremonial magic. Virtually the entire range of occult teaching available today has been influenced by the teachings of the Golden Dawn in one capacity or another since Regardie originally published this material. This will undoubtedly be truer with the book you are now holding, which is seminal in its own right. It is certainly true that this book is one of the most complete and unique books on the initiation work of the Western Esoteric Tradition. Similar texts seem to be content with somewhat meaningless descriptions of an initiatory process. This one is unique in that it fully presents the work necessary to the student in a complete format within a single volume.

It is unique in that Chic and Tabatha recognize the need for an initiator and provide a means for the aspirant to access the current that will be responsible for a valid initiation. For the first time the student has the means to fully initiate oneself into the 120 current of the Golden Dawn.

It is unique in that it places the initiation rituals in a traditional format as initially conceived by Mathers, Westcott and Woodman, the founders of the original Order. You certainly will not find muddied embellishments and bovine scatology. Clear, concise and no nonsense.

It is unique in that the text, rituals and knowledge lectures are consistent with Israel Regardie's *The Golden Dawn*, the cards produced by Chic and Sandra Tabatha Cicero, the *New Golden Dawn Ritual Tarot* book and *Secrets of a Golden Dawn Temple*.

It is unique in that they make no pretentious claims regarding their range of experience, which is considerable, or nonsense about secret teachings that Israel Regardie was not aware of. The material they present is traditional though flexible.

For the student who plans to continue the Great Work after the material in this volume has been assimilated, Israel Regardie's *The Golden Dawn* will provide the work of the Second Order. The present volume will provide the studies necessary to fully realize a competent level for the student to pursue the more advanced work of the R.R. et A.C. While utilizing the material in both this book and Regardie's, the reader will benefit greatly by supplementing these works with additional material provided in *The Golden Dawn Journal*, an ongoing series of volumes, edited by Chic and Sandra Tabatha Cicero, featuring multiple perspectives on the Golden Dawn by a variety of prominent occult writers.

The book you hold in your hands is unique in that you will not find material rewritten, reevaluated and changed simply to satisfy the ego-oriented urge that seems to be so important to some occult-oriented writers these days.

Now that you have read the text, take the time to go back and work through the material. Begin the greatest adventure of your life—the Knowledge and Conversation of your Holy Guardian Angel. *Scire, Velle, Audere, Tacere.*✿

Examination Answers

Chapter One: Neophyte

Quiz 0 (The Ritual)

1. The Hiereus
2. The Censer of Incense
3. The Hierophant
4. Four
5. The Hidden Knowledge
6. Light in Extension

7. The Cross and Triangle, a rose, cup of wine, red lamp, bread and salt.
8. The darkness, ignorance and mortality which has blinded humanity.
9. The threefold bondage of mortality; material inclination which has bound humanity.
10. The altar is an emblem of visible Nature which reflects the Hermetic axiom "As above, so below."

11. The rise of Light
12. The Hegemon
13. The Stolistes

14. The candidate's condition in a state of Darkness, groping for Light.
15. The two great opposing forces of Light and Dark.

16. Wisdom
17. Names; Images

18. The Egyptian god of Silence.
19. The directing power of the Hidden Knowledge.
20. Seeking guidance in Darkness.
21. The Keryx
22. The Hiereus
23. The Hierophant

Quiz—Sections 1, 2, and 3 (Elements, Zodiac, Planets)

1. Fire △
   Water ▽
   Air △
   Earth ▽
2. Air
3. Earth
4. Fire
5. Water
6. Fire
7. Air
8. Air
9. Water

10. Aries ♈
    Taurus ♉
    Gemini ♊
    Cancer ♋
    Leo ♌
    Virgo ♍
    Libra ♎
    Scorpio ♏
    Sagittarius ♐
    Capricorn ♑
    Aquarius ♒
    Pisces ♓

11. Virgo

12. Zodical Signs which are grouped by Element.

13. Quality

14. Libra, Aquarius, Gemini

15. Capricorn, Taurus, Virgo

16. Cardinal Signs

17. Leo, Scorpio, Aquarius, Taurus

18. The Mutable Signs

19. The Kerubic Signs

20. Virgo

21. Gemini

22. Aries

23. Libra

24. Sagittarius

25. Leo

26. Cancer

27. Scorpio

28. Pisces

29. Capricorn

30. Sagittarius

31. Saturn ♄
    Jupiter ♃
    Mars ♂
    Sol ☉
    Venus ♀
    Mercury ☿
    Luna ☽

32. Venus

33. Jupiter

34. Mars

35. Jupiter

36. Sol

37. Saturn

38. a. Pisces
    b. Capricorn
    c. Aries, Scorpio
    d. Aries
    e. Capricorn
    f. Capricorn, Aquarius
    g. Sagittarius, Pisces
    h. Taurus
    i. Taurus, Libra
    j. Leo
    k. Pisces
    l. Taurus

39. Saturn

40. Uranus ♅
    Neptune ♆
    Pluto ♇

41. Caput Draconis—the North Lunar Node.

42. Pluto

43. Uranus

44. Neptune

45. Sol

46. Mars

47. Cauda Draconis—the South Lunar Node.

48. Luna

49. Sol

50. Water

51. Fire

52. Water

53. Earth

54. Earth

55. Air

56. Aquarius

57. Cancer, Scorpio, Pisces

58. Adaptable, versatile, changeable, subtle, intuitive, understanding.

59. Stable, determined, persevering, acumulative, able to concentrate.

60. Active, fervent, independent, enthusiastic, ambitious, initiating.

61. Mercury.

62. Venus.

63. Venus.

64. Venus.

65. Mars.

66. Venus.

67. Mercury.

68. Mars.

Quiz—Sections 4, 5, and 6 (Qabalah, Sephiroth, Hebrew Alphabet)

1. Tradition
2. Dogmatic, Practical, Literal, Unwritten

3.

Kether	the Crown	כתר
Chokmah	Wisdom	חכמה
Binah	Understanding	בינה
Chesed	Mercy	חסד
Geburah	Severity	גבורה
Tiphareth	Beauty	תפארת
Netzach	Victory	נצח
Hod	Splendor	הוד
Yesod	Foundation	יסוד
Malkuth	the Kingdom	מלכות

4. Chokmah	5. Chesed	6. Tiphareth	7. Hod
8. Chokmah	9. Kether	10. Hod	11. Netzach
12. Geburah	13. Yesod	14. Tiphareth	15. Malkuth
16. Tiphareth	17. Geburah	18. Yesod	19. Kether

20. Binah
21. Binah, Geburah, Hod
22. Kether, Tiphareth, Yesod, Malkuth
23. Chokmah, Chesed, Netzach
24. The Pentateuch
25. Teth, Tau

26. Samekh, Shin   27. Cheth   28. Qoph   29. Beth

30.

Letter	Power	Value	Final	Name	Meaning
א	A	1		Aleph	ox
ב	B	2		Beth	house
ג	G, Gh	3		Gimel	camel
ד	D, Dh	4		Daleth	door
ה	H	5		Heh	window
ו	O, U, V	6		Vav	pin, hook
ז	Z	7		Zayin	sword, armor
ח	Ch	8		Cheth	fence, enclosure
ט	T	9		Teth	serpent
י	I, Y	10		Yod	hand
כ	K, Kh	20—500	ך	Kaph	fist, palm of hand
ל	L	30		Lamed	ox goad
מ	M	40—600	ם	Mem	Water
נ	N	50—700	ן	Nun	fish
ס	S	60		Samekh	prop

				Name	Meaning
ע	Aa	70		Ayin	eye
פ	P, Ph	80—800	ף	Peh	mouth
צ	Tz	90—900	ץ	Tzaddi	fish hook
ק	Q	100		Qoph	back of the head
ר	R	200		Resh	head
ש	S, Sh	300		Shin	tooth
ת	T, Th	400		Tau	cross

Chapter Two: Zelator

Quiz 0 (The Ritual)

1. Adonai ha-Aretz
2. 55
3. Nun Heh
4. 4-3-3
5. The 6 x 6 step
6. The raising of the right arm to an angle of 45 degrees.
7. Aretz
8. Aretz—Earth
9. North
10. Periclinus de Faustis
11. Wanderer in the Wilderness
12. The Egyptian Zaruator, signifying searcher of Athor, Goddess of Nature.
13. Malkuth
14. Adonai ha-Aretz, Adonai Melekh
15. Uriel
16. Taurus
17. Emor Dial Hectega
18. Ic Zod Heh Hal
19. The Cross is placed within the Triangle.
20. The triangle represents the three Paths which lead to further Grades, while the Cross is the Hidden Knowledge—together they represent Life and Light.
21. The Banner of the West.
22. The first Elemental Grade (the first step onto the Tree of Life), and the tenth Sephirah of Malkuth.
23. The Fylfot Cross, also called the Hermetic Cross, Swastika, and Hammer of Thor.
24. The Dadouchos
25. Two.
26. First part—the candidate encounters the Kerubim from the Garden of Eden. Second part—the candidate is symbolically shown the mysteries of the ancient Hebraic Tabernacle in the Wilderness.
27. With the left hand, salt is cast to the North.
28. Shin, Tau, Qoph
29. The three Paths which join Malkuth to the other Sephiroth—these letters also make the word Qesheth—a bow or reflection of the rainbow of promise.

30. Samael   31. Metatron   32. Sandalphon   33. Metatron
34. Samael   35. Sandalphon   36. Metatron

37. a. The Altar of Burnt Offering—which represents the Qlippoth.
    b. The Laver of Brass—which represents the Waters of Creation.
    c. The Altar of Incense—which represents the highest degree of purity.

38. The Table of Shewbread—which represents the Mystery of the Rose of Creation—the twelve Signs of the Zodiac and the twelve simple letters of the Hebrew alphabet.

39. The Seven-branched Candlestick—which represents the seven Planets and the seven Double Letters of the Hebrew Alphabet.

Quiz—Section 1 (The Zodiacal Houses)

1. A 30 degree arc which is one-twelfth of the Zodiacal Wheel.

2. Planets; Zodiacal Signs   3. The Ascendant or Rising Sign
4. Medium Coeli   5. Imum Coeli
6. The Fourth House Cusp   7. The Seventh House Cusp
8. True   9. Second, Sixth, and Tenth
10. Fourth, Eighth, and Twelfth

11. False   12. False   13. False   14. True
15. True   16. First   17. Tenth   18. Eleventh
19. Third   20. Fourth   21. Ninth   22. Twelfth
23. Eighth   24. Seventh   25. Fifth   26. Second
27. Fourth   28. Third & Sixth   29. Ninth   30. Second & Seventh
31. Fifth   32. Twelfth   33. Eleventh   34. True
35. True   36. False   37. True   38. False
39. Eighth   40. Seventh   41. Fourth

42. Two lines (each known as an axis) which are drawn on a Zodiacal chart to help interpret the horoscope.

43. The Horizon   44. The Meridian

45. A free and strong Will—the embodiment of a sowing incarnation.
46. Flexibility and involvement with the future of others—indicates a harvesting incarnation.

47. A Cusp   48. A Decanate

Quiz—Section 2 (Alchemy)

1. The article "al" and the Coptic name of Egypt, "Khem."

2. Hermes Trismegistus   3. Metalsmiths
4. To cure illness   5. A philosophy
6. Chemistry   7. Nature

8. Sulphur, Mercury, Salt
9. Separation, Purification, Cohobation
10. The Quintessence or Philosophic Mercury
11. To bring all things, including humanity to a preordained state of perfection.

12. Spiritual purity　　　　　13. Sulphur
14. Salt　　　　　　　　　　15. Mercury

16. Lead　　　　♄　Saturn
　　Tin　　　　　♃　Jupiter
　　Iron　　　　♂　Mars
　　Gold　　　　☉　Sol
　　Copper/Brass　♀　Venus
　　Quicksilver　☿　Mercury
　　Silver　　　　☽　Luna

17. Luna Philosophorum　　　18. Sol Philosophorum
19. Red Lion　　　　　　　　20. Death, putrefaction, decay
21. The King　　　　　　　　22. The Queen
23. The King　　　　　　　　24. The Green Lion
25. Prima Materia　　　　　　26. Magnum Opus
27. Sophic Fire; Our Mercury　28. Philosopher's Stone
29. The Philosopher's Stone

30. The idea that the First Matter contains within itself all that is needed for transformation and purification.
31. Rebis
32. The fact that transformation is occuring.

33. The Phoenix　　　　　　　34. Black
35. Antimony　　　　　　　　36. Aes Hermetis
37. Antimony　　　　　　　　38. Amalgam
39. Aqua Permanens　　　　　40. Azoth
41. Aquila Philosophorum　　　42. Earth
43. The Raven　　　　　　　　44. Ignis Leonis
45. Primum Ens　　　　　　　46. Electrum
47. Mysterium　　　　　　　　48. Mater Metallorum
49. Menstruum　　　　　　　　50. Iron or sulphur
51. Mysterium Magnum

52. The root of metals which harmonizes with them and is the medium which combines the tintures.
53. Philosophic Mercury; Fiery Water; Philosophic Vinegar.
54. The Philosopher's Stone.
55. "The separative Art," a term for Alchemy.
56. The part of a substance which is extracted by a solvent.
57. The Three Alchemic Principles of Sulphur, Mercury and Salt.

58. Ultima Materia
59. "Dissolve and coagulate." To reduce the solids into a liquid, and then
       back into a solid.
60. Vitriol
61. The "soul" of matter being released.
62. The combining of opposites required for the production of the
       Philosopher's Stone.

63. Sandarace	64. Lapis Lucidum Angularis
65. Initiation; immortality	66. The male principle
67. The Dog and Wolf	68. Caput Mortem
69. The tail of the peacock	70. Aurum Album
71. Spiritus Mundi	72. Tapis
73. The female principle	

Quiz—Sections 3, 4, and 5 (Elementals, Tetragrammaton, Hebrew Letters, Four Worlds, Divine Names)

1. A non-physical entity having a nature that is composed entirely of one of the
       four magical Elements.

2.
Gnomes	Earth spirits
Sylphs	Air spirits
Undines	Water spirits
Salamanders	Fire spirits

3. Gnomes.	4. Paralda.	5. Ghob.
6. Salamanders.	7. Sylphs.	8. Nichsa.

9. Four-lettered Name
10. The unknown and unpronounceable name of God symbolized by
       the Hebrew letters Yod Heh Vav Heh.

11.
Yod	Fire
Heh	Water
Vav	Air
Heh (final)	Earth

12. Yod; Vav
13. Heh; Heh (final)
14. The Strong Ones
15. The Fixed or Kerubic Signs

16.
Aryeh	Fire
Adam	Air
Nesher	Water
Shor	Earth

20. Aleph, Mem, Shin
21. Beth, Gimel, Daleth, Kaph, Peh, Resh, Tau

22.   Heh, Vav, Zayin, Cheth, Teth, Yod, Lamed, Nun, Samekh, Ayin,
        Tzaddi, Qoph.
23.   The Double letters each have two sounds and a duel set of qualities
        associated with them.
24.   Seven Planets
25.   The ancient Elements of Fire, Air and Water.

26.   Atziluth   אצילות
        Briah   בריאה
        Yetzirah   יצירה
        Assiah   עשיה

27.   Briah.   28. Atziluth.   29. Atziluth.   30. Yetzirah.
31.   Assiah.   32. Assiah.   33. Assiah.   34. Yetzirah.
35.   Atziluth.

36.   1st—Rashith ha-Gilgalim ראשית הגלגלים the First Whirlings
        2nd—Mazloth מזלות the Zodiac
        3rd— Shabbathai שבתאי Saturn
        4th—Tzedek צדק Jupiter
        5th—Madim מדים Mars
        6th—Shemesh שמש Sol
        7th—Nogah נוגה Venus
        8th—Kokab כוכב Mercury
        9th—Levannah לבנה Luna
        10th—Olam Yesodoth עולם יסודות the sphere of the Elements.

37.   Kether—Eheieh אהיה
        Chokmah—Yah יה
        Binah—YHVH Elohim יהוה אלהים
        Chesed—El אל
        Geburah—Elohim Gibor אלהים גבור
        Tiphareth—YHVH Eloah ve-Daath יהוה אלוה ודעת
        Netzach—YHVH Tzabaoth יהוה צבאות
        Hod—Elohim Tzabaoth אלהים צבאות
        Yesod—Shaddai El Chai שדי אלהי
        Malkuth—Adonai ha-Aretz אדני הארץ

38.   Kether—Metatron מטטרון
        Chokmah—Raziel רזיאל
        Binah—Tzaphqiel צפקיאל
        Chesed—Tzadqiel צדקיאל
        Geburah—Kamael כמאל
        Tiphareth—Raphael רפאל
        Netzach—Haniel האניאל
        Hod—Michael מיכאל
        Yesod—Gabriel גבריאל
        Malkuth—Sandalphon סנדלפון

39. Kether—Chayoth ha-Qadesh חיות הקדש
Chokmah—Auphanim אופנים
Binah—Aralim אראלים
Chesed—Chashmalim חשמלים
Geburah—Seraphim שרפים
Tiphareth—Melekim מלכים
Netzach—Elohim אלהים
Hod—Beni Elohim בני אלהים
Yesod—Kerubim כרובים
Malkuth—Ashim אשים

40. Elohim Gibor   41. Eheieh   42. YHVH Eloah ve-Daath
43. Elohim Tzabaoth   44. Shaddai El-Chai   45. Metatron
46. Kamael   47. Raziel   48. Raphael
49. Gabriel   50. Auphanim   51. Chashmalim
52. Beni Elohim   53. Ashim   54. Melekim

55. Saturn—Cassiel כסיאל
Jupiter—Sachiel סחיאל
Mars—Zamael זמאל
Sol—Michael מיכאל
Venus—Anael אנאל
Mercury—Raphael רפאל
Luna—Gabriel גבריאל

56. Saturn—Agiel אגיאל
Jupiter—Iophiel יהפיאל
Mars—Graphiel גראפיאל
Sol—Nakhiel נכיאל
Venus—Hagiel הגיאל
Mercury—Tiriel תיריאל
Luna—Malkah be Tarshism ve-ad Ruachoth Schechalim
מלכא בתרשישים ועד רוחות שחלים

57. Saturn—Zazel זאזל
Jupiter—Hismael הסמאל
Mars—Bartzabel ברצבאל
Sol—Sorath סורת
Venus—Qedemel קדמאל
Mercury—Taphthartharath תפתרתרת
Luna—Chasmodai חשמודאי
or—Schad Barshemoth ha-Shartathan שד ברשמעת השרתתן

58. Cassiel.   59. Sachiel.
60. Iophiel.   61. Graphiel.
62. Shelachel שלחאל

63. Aries—Malkhidael מלכידאל
    Taurus—Asmodel אסמודאל
    Gemini—Ambriel אמבריאל
    Cancer—Muriel מוריאל
    Leo—Verkhiel ורכיאל
    Virgo—Hamaliel המליאל
    Libra—Zuriel זוריאל
    Scorpio—Barkhiel ברכיאל
    Sagittarius—Adnakhiel אדנכיאל
    Capricorn—Hanael הנאל
    Aquarius—Kambriel כמבריאל
    Pisces—Amnitziel אמניציאל

64. Muriel.   65. Barkhiel.   66. Amnitziel.   67. Verkhiel.
68. Zuriel.   69. Malkhidiel.   70. Adnakhiel.

Quiz—Sections 6, and 7 (Earth Correspondenses and Geomancy)

1. Kether—Diamond
   Chokmah—Star Ruby, Turquoise
   Binah—Star Sapphire, Pearl
   Chesed—Amethyst, Sapphire
   Geburah—Ruby
   Tiphareth—Topaz, Yellow Diamond
   Netzach—Emerald
   Hod—Opal, especially Fire Opal
   Yesod—Quartz
   Malkuth—Rock Crystal, Salt

2. Aries—Diamond, Red Jasper, Garnet
   Taurus—Emerald, Red Coral, Lapis Lazuli
   Gemini—Pearl, Agate, Alexandrite
   Cancer—Ruby, Amber, Moonstone
   Leo—Sardonyx, Cat's Eye, Chrysolite
   Virgo—Sapphire, Peridot
   Libra—Opal, Malachite, Emerald
   Scorpio—Topaz, Obsidian, Bloodstone
   Sagittarius—Turquise, Blue Zircon
   Capricorn—Garnet, Jet, Onyx
   Aquarius—Amethyst, Aquamarine
   Pisces—Bloodstone, Pearl.

3. Saturn—Onyx, Jet, Anthracite
   Jupiter—Amethyst, Sapphire, Lapis Lazuli
   Mars—Ruby, Garnet, Bloodstone
   Sol—Topaz, Chrysolite, Helidor, Zircon
   Venus—Emerald, Turquoise, Jade, Serpentine

Mercury—Opal, Fire Opal, Agate, Serpentine
Luna—Moonstone, Pearl, Quartz, Flourspar

4. Fire—Ruby, Fire Opal
   Water—Aquamarine, Coral, Moonstone
   Air—Topaz, Opal
   Earth—Moss Agate, Rock Salt, Onyx, Galena

5. Aretz ארץ Ophir עפיר
6. Adonai ha-Aretz אדני הארץ
7. Tzaphon (North) צפון
8. Uriel אוריאל
9. Phorlakh פורלאך
10. Kerub כרוב

11. Ghob	12. Gnomes	13. Geb	14. Tammuz
15. Cybele	16. Gaea	17. Persephone	18. Demeter

19.

Figure	Sign	Figure	Sign
Acquisitio	*Sagittarius*	Amissio	*Taurus*
Albus	*Gemini*	Rubeus	*Scorpio*
Puella	*Libra*	Puer	*Aries*
Laetitia	*Pisces*	Tristitia	*Aquarius*
Caput Draconis	*North Node*	Cauda Draconis	*South Node*
Populus	*Cancer*	Via	*Cancer*
Conjunctio	*Virgo*	Carcer	*Capricorn*
Fortuna Major	*Leo*	Fortuna Minor	*Leo*

20. The Mothers	21. The Daughters
22. The Nephews	23. Tetragram

24. By Adding together the two Witnesses.

25. By adding together the final two Nephews.
26. Part of Fortune

27. False   28. False   29. True   30. False

31. The Significator

32. True   33. True   34. False   35. Dexter

36. Sinister   37. The Fourth House
38. The Reconcilor   39. Squilling
40. The Nephews   41. A Ruler or Genius
42. Planetary Spirits

43. The strength of a Planet when it is in a particular Sign.
44. The strength of a Planet when it is in a particular House.
45. ————

Quiz—Section 8 (Ritual Images and Diagrams)

1. The Altar of Incense
2. The Laver of Brass
3. Evil Demons of Matter and the Shells of the Dead.
4. The Altar of Burnt Offering
5. The Flaming Sword
6. The Ten Sephiroth together with the Twenty-two Paths.
7. Black, passive, negative, feminine, form
8. White, active, positive, masculine, force
9. The Fylfot Cross
10. 17
11. 25
12. The Sun
13. The Elements and the Twelve Signs of the Zodiac.
14. Hermetic Cross, Hammer of Thor, Swastica and Gammadion.
15. The center of the Universe giving rise to the Celestial Signs and the Elements.
16. The Table of Shewbread depicts the twelve Simple Letters of the Hebrew alphabet connected by a dodekagram which surrounds a pentagram. The twelve circles are the twelve Signs of the Zodiac while the central lamp is an image of the sun. The four Triangles represent the Elements, while five (the pentragram) indicates the great feminine Letter Heh, Malkah, the Bride, ruling in her kingdom Malkuth, crowned with a crown of Twelve Stars. Also shown are the Elemental Archangels and the Kerubim.
17. The Seven-branched Candlestick depicts the Seven Double Letters of the Hebrew Alphabet connected by a heptagram. It is an image of the mystery of the Elohim, the seven Creative ideas. The seven circles are the seven Planets, and they also allude to the seven days of the week and the seven localities.

18. | | |
|---|---|
| Aries | Gad |
| Taurus | Ephraim |
| Gemini | Manasseh |
| Cancer | Issachar |
| Leo | Judah |
| Virgo | Naphthali |
| Libra | Asshur |
| Scorpio | Dan |
| Sagittarius | Benjamin |
| Capricorn | Zebulun |
| Aquarius | Rueben |
| Pisces | Simeon |

19. Ephraim   20. Rueben   21. Judah   22. Dan

Chapter Three: Theoricus

Quiz 0 (The Ritual)

1. Shaddai El Chai   2. 45
3. Mem Heh   4. 3—3—3

5. The General Grip of the First Order.
6. The Sign emulates a figure supporting a great weight.

7. Ruach   8. Air; Ruach   9. East

10. Poraios de Rejectis
11. Brought from Among the Rejected

12. Yesod   13. Shaddai El Chai   14. Raphael
15. Aquarius   16. Oro Ibah Aozpi   17. Bataivah

18. The Cross is within the Triangle, which is apex downward.
19. The cross refers to the four Rivers of paradise, while the Triangle refers to the Three Sephiroth of Netzach, Hod and Yesod.
20. The Second of the Elemental Grades and the Ninth Sephirah of Yesod.
21. The Solid Greek Cubical Cross
22. The Caduceus Admission Badge
23. The Keryx
24. 2
25. The first medial point of the Ritual focuses on the Journey on the Path of Tau where the candidate encounters the Four Kerubim. The second medial point emphasizes the entry into Yesod where the secrets of this grade are revealed.
26. The Candidate holds the Cubical Cross in the right hand in the position of the Zelator Sign.
27. Shin, Tau, Qoph

28. Paths which lead from the Zelator to three other Grades which are beyond.
29. Human-headed; lion-headed; Eagle-headed; Bull-headed.

30. Adam; Nuet; Harmachis
31. Aryeh; Mau; Re
32. Nesher; Tefnut; Tum
33. Shor; Serapis; Osiris

34. The Universe Card—Within an oval formed of 72 circles is a female form crowned with the lunar cresent and holding two wands. A scarf floats around her, and above her is a heptagram. The four Kerubim surround the whole. The card is attributed to Saturn.
35. A fan, lamp, cup and salt
36. The Garden of Eden
37. Gehenna, the Abode of Shells
38. The Flaming Sword and the Kerubim; the Serpent on the Tree of Life; The Qamea, Seal and sigils of Luna, Luna on the Tree of Life.
39. The Cross within the Triangle, apex downward. It refers to the Four Rivers of Paradise, while the angles of the Triangle refer to the Three Sephiroth of Netzach, Hod and Yesod.

Quiz—Section 1 (Astrology)

1. Orb
2. 180°
3. 60°
4. Inconjunct

5. When three Planets are in trine with one another, all in the same triplicity or Element.

6. Four
7. Three
8. Opposition
9. Platic
10. Partile
11. 0°
12. Opposition
13. Two

14. A Conjuction of three or more Planets.

15. False
16. True
17. Conjunction
18. Six
19. False
20. 90°
21. False

22. When three Planets are involved, two of which are in Opposition.

23. Quincunx
24. Five
25. 120°
26. False
27. True
28. True
29. True

30. When four Planets are involved, with two pairs in Opposition.

31. Opposition
32. False
33. True
34. 30°
35. 360°
36. 30°

37. A theoretical circle which surrounds the middle of the globe from North to South and is used to measure distance East or West of the Prime Meridian, the 0° mark at Greenwich, England.

38. Parallels.
39. Meridians of Longitude.
40. Greenwich Mean Time.
41. Sidereal Time.

42. Acceleration on the Interval. It is found by adding or subtracting ten seconds for every hour and one second for every six minutes of interval time.
43. By multiplying the birthplace longitude by four, naming the resulting numbers as hours, minutes and seconds.
44. The Ascendant and the Midheaven.
45. By consulting an Ephemeris to determine the degrees and minutes of the Planets for the date of birth. Within the inner circle of the chart, draw a series of marks opposite the marked positions of the Planets. If two Planets are in aspect to each other, having the correct angle within the accepted orb, join the appropriate markings.

46. Forming or Applying   47. Separating or Waning

Quiz—Section 2 (Alchemy)

1. Iosis	2. Xanthosis	3. Leukosis	4. Melanosis
5. Albedo	6. Rubedo	7. Nigredo	8. Citrinitas
9. Leukosis	10. Xanthosis.	11. Iosis	12. Melanosis
13. Conjunction	14. Fermentation	15. Cibation	16. Congealation
17. Sublimation	18. Projection	19. Putrefaction	20. Calcination
21. Multiplication	22. Exaltation	23. Ligation	24. Rotation

25. BLACK: Saturn (lead)
BLUE: Jupiter (tin)
PEACOCK'S TAIL: (multi-colored) Mercury (quicksilver)
WHITE: Luna (silver)
YELLOW: Venus (copper)
RED: Mars (iron)
VIOLET: Sol (gold)

26. Desponsation   27. Distillation   28. Solution

Quiz—Sections 3, 4 and 5 (Spiritual Entities, Qabalah, Yesod)

1. The Foundation
2. A beautiful, strong naked man
3. The Vision of the machinery of the Universe

4. Enneagram	5. Perfumes and sandals
6. Gabriel	7. Shaddai El Chai
8. Kerubim	9. Violet
10. Reproductive organs	11. Levannah
12. The four Nines	13. Independence

14. Idleness	15. Yetzirah	16. True	17. True
18. False	19. False	20. False	

21. Nous. Also Daimon and Pneuma.

22. Psyche   23. False

24. Neshamah נשמה, Ruach רוח, Nephesh נפש
25. Yechidah יחידה, Chiah חיה, Neshamah נשמה

26. Chiah   27. Neshamah   28. Yechidah   29. Nephesh
30. Ruach   31. Nephesh   32. Nephesh   33. Neshamah
34. Neshamah   35. Ruach   36. G'uph

Quiz—Section 6 (Correspondences of Air)

1. KETHER   Ambergris
    CHOKMAH   Musk
    BINAH   Myrrh, Civet
    CHESED   Cedar
    GEBURAH   Tobacco
    TIPHARETH   Olibanum
    NETZACH   Benzoin, Rose, Red Sandal
    HOD   Storax
    YESOD   Jasmine, Ginseng
    MALKUTH   Dittany of Crete

2. ARIES   Dragon's Blood
    TAURUS   Storax
    GEMINI   Wormwood
    CANCER   Onycha
    LEO   Olibanum
    VIRGO   Narcissus
    LIBRA   Galbanum
    SCORPIO   Siamese Benzoin, Opoponax
    SAGITTARIUS   Lign-Aloes (Wood-Aloe)
    CAPRICORN   Musk, Civet
    AQUARIUS   Galbanum
    PISCES   Ambergris

3. SATURN   Assafoetida, Scammony, Sulphur
    JUPITER   Saffron
    MARS   Pepper, Dragon's Blood
    SOL   Olibanum, Cinnamon
    VENUS   Sandalwood, Myrtle
    MERCURY   Mastic, White Sandal, Mace, Storax
    LUNA   Camphor, Aloes

4. FIRE   Olibanum
    WATER   Onycha, Myrrh
    AIR   Galbanum
    EARTH   Storax

5. Ruach, רוח
6. Shaddai El Chai, שדי אל חי
7. Mizrach, מזרח
8. Raphael, רפאל
9. Chassan, חשן
10. Aral, אראל

11. Paralda	12. Sylphs	13. Anu	14. Enlil; Adad
15. Nuet; Hathor	16. Shu	17. Zeus	18. Hera

19. Boreas—the North Wind
    Zephyrus—the West Wind
    Eurus—the East Wind
    Notus—the South Wind

20. Aeolus   21. Thor

Quiz—Section 7 (Correspondences of Luna)

1. The subconcious mind, cycles and patterns, plant and animal life, tides, and all instinctive process in nature.
2. Voyages, femininity, alternation, change, receptivity, sleep, prophetic dreams, visions, messages, navigation, love, fertility, envoys, and aquisition of merchandise by water.
3. 28-29 days
4. The Second Quarter; the Fourth Quarter.

5. The Third Quarter	6. The First Quarter
7. The Fourth Quarter	8. The Second Quarter
9. The Third Quarter	10. The First Quarter

11. In its increase, it embraces the side of Mercy; in its decrease the side of Severity, and at full, it reflects the Sun of Tiphareth.

12. Levannah   13. Gabriel   14. Monday

15. Malkah be Tarshism ve-ad Ruachoth Schechalim. Shelachiel.
16. Schad Barshemoth ha-Shartathan. Chasmodai.

17. Phul   18. Silver

19. Moonstone, Pearl, Quartz, Fluorspar, Beryl
20. Willow, Bay, Hazel, Papaya, Coconut Palm, Almond
21. Lotus, Opium, Mushroom, Poppy, Gourds, Moonwort
22. Cat, Hare, Dog, Owl

23. Sin	24. Khonsu	25. Hecate	26. Aah-Djehuti
27. Selene	28. Artemis	29. Hecate	

30. Saturn. Both are attributed in a similar sense to the concept of the Great Mother and the passage or cycles of time. Isis, Cronos, Hera, Ptah, Rhea, Saturnus, Ea, Ishtar.

Quiz—Sections 8 and 9 (Plants, Admission Badges and Diagrams)

1. Photosynthesis
2. Assimilation
3. Air
4. They die
5. The Creative Mystery of Life, and spiritual enlightment.
6. The Tree
7. Some herbs are poisonous
8. Color, scent, form, habitat
9. SATURN—Ivy, Yew, Hemlock, Nightshade, Amaranth, Hemp, Aconite
   JUPITER—Hyssop, Fig, Sage, Star Anise, Nutmeg, Sassafras
   MARS—Pine, Wormwood, Ginger, Nettle, Basil, Radish, Holly
   SOL—Sunflower, Acacia, Bay, Marigold, Saffron, Rowan, Peony
   VENUS—Rose, Myrtle, Elder, Geranium, Hyacinth, Thyme, Licorice
   MERCURY—Marjoram, Fennel, Mandrake, Caraway, Dill, Pomegranate
   LUNA—Willow, Moonwort, Lotus, Lemon, Gardenia, Mushroom, Poppy
10. FIRE—Ash, Mustard, Cactus, Pepper, Garlic, Onion, Thistle
    WATER—Most Fruit Trees, Water plants, Lotus, Melon, Orchid
    AIR—Palm, Mistletoe, Dandelion, Mint, Lavender, Goldenrod
    EARTH—Oak, Cypress, Grains, Potato, Turnip, Cotton, Patchouli
11. Nymphs
12. Naiads
13. Dryads
14. Dryads
15. Oreads
16. Napaea, Auloniads, Hylaeorae, Alsaeids
17. Hamadryads
18. Sileni
19. Satyrs
20. The Solid Greek Cubical Cross
21. The equilibrated and balanced powers of the Elements through the forces represented by the Hebrew Letters.
22. The Four Elements and the Sun; Aleph, Shin, Mem, Tau, and Resh.
23. Resh—Sol
24. The remaining Planets; Beth, Peh, Gimel, Daleth, and Kaph.
25. Resh and Tau. These letters are on the front side.
26. Cheth, Nun, Qoph; the Water Triplicity.
27. Ayin, Vav, Yod; the Earth Triplicity.
28. Lamed, Tzaddi, Zayin; the Air Triplicity.
29. Heh, Teth, Samekh; the Fire Triplicity.
30. The Caduceus of Hermes.

31. The upper point of the Wand rests upon Kether, and the wings stretch out to Chokmah and Binah. The lower seven Sephiroth are touched by the serpents whose heads rest upon Chesed and Geburah. The wings and top of the wand form the letter Shin. The upper parts of the serpent form the letter Aleph, while the tails enclose Mem.
32. The balanced forces of the Eternal Light working invisibly in the darkness.
33. Nekhebet is the serpent on the left, while Uatchet is the serpent on the right. They are the twin serpents of Egypt and the currents of the Astral Light.

Chapter Four: Practicus

Quiz 0 (The Ritual)

1. Elohim Tzabaoth

2. 36   3. Eloah   4. 1—3—1—3

5. The general Grip of the Outer Order.
6. Holding the hands together while raising the arms till the elbows are level with the shoulders. With thumbs and fore-finger, make a triangle (apex downward over the breast).

7. Maim   8. Water, Maim
9. West   10. Monocris de Astris
11. Unicorn from the Stars   12. Hod
13. Elohim Tzabaoth   14. Gabriel
15. Scorpio   16. EMPEH ARSEL GAIOL
17. Raagiosel

18. The Cross above the Triangle (apex downward).
19. It represents the Spirit of Life rising above the triangle of the Waters and reflecting the Triune therein, as further marked by the Lamps at the angles. The Cup of Water at the junction of the Cross and Triangle represents the maternal letter Mem.
20. The third Elemental Grade and the eighth Sephirah of Hod.
21. The Solid Triangular Pyramid.
22. The Greek Cross of Thirteen Squares.
23. The Cup of Stolistes Lamen.

24. Stolistes   25. Three

26. The First medial point concerns the journey on the Path of Shin where the candidate encounters the Samothracian Kabiri and the various aspects of Fire. The second medial point focuses on the journey on the Path of Resh, where the candidate is again confronted by the Kabiri and shown the various types of Solar energy. In the third medial point the candidate enters the Water Temple of Hod where the mysteries of the Grade are revealed.

27. The Saluting Sign of a Neophyte; sprinkling water toward the Tablet of the West.
28. Axieros—the 1st Kabir. Axiokersos—the 2nd Kabi. Axiokersa—the 3rd Kabir.
29. Axiokersa—the 3rd Kabir; Astral Fire; the sun at Equinox.
30. Axieros—the 1st Kabir; Solar; the Summer sun.
31. Axiokersos—the 2nd Kabir; Terrestial Fire; the Winter sun.
32. The Judgment Card depicts a mighty angel blowing a trumpet and figures rising from earth, water, and a tomb. It is a glyph of the various forms of Fire, to which Element this card is attributed.
33. The Sun Card portrays two children playing in a garden under the rays of a large sun. The sun embraces the whole of Creation in its rays. The card is attributed to Sol.
34. The Garden of Eden before the Fall; the Qamea and Seals of Mercury.

Quiz—Sections 1, 2, and 3: (Admission Badges, Lineal Figures, Magical Squares, Literal Qabalah)

1. The Solid Triangle or Tetrahedron, whose sides represent various types of Fire.
2. The Greek Cross of 13 Squares has depicted upon it the twelve signs of the Zodiac with the symbol of the Sun in the center.

3. Aud   4. Aur   5. Aub   6. Asch

7. The Cup of Stolistes Lamen partakes to some extent of the symbolism of the Laver of Moses and the Sea of Solomon. On the Tree of Life, it embraces nine of the Sephiroth exclusive of Kether. It further represents the Three Elements of Water, Air, and Fire. The Crescent is the Water which is above the Firmament, the Circle is the Firmament, and the triangle is the consuming Fire below.
8. It embraces all of the Sephiroth except Kether. The horns spring from Daath.
9. Aima Elohim.
10. Naher; the "perennial stream."

11. Hiddikel; Tiphareth.   12. Pison; Geburah.
13. Phrath; Malkuth.   14. Gihon; Chesed.
15. Eve; the Nephesh.

16. Adam; Geburah; Gedulah; The Ruach.
17. The Three basic principles in humanity—the three Qabalistic parts of the Soul.

18. A Rhombus   19. A Vesica   20. A Triangle

21.
Saturn	Triangle
Jupiter	Square
Mars	Pentagram
Sol	Hexagram
Venus	Heptagram
Mercury	Octogram
Luna	Enneagram

22. Chokmah   23. Kether   24. Chesed
25. The Triangle 26. The Endekangle 27. The Square
28. The Pentagram 29. The Pentagram 30. The Pentagram
31. The Hexagram 32. False   33. False
34. The Heptagram 35. The Octagram

36. The names YHVH and Adonai bound together, representing the binding together of the concentrated Positive and Negative Forces of the Elements.

37. The Enneangle   38. The Dekangle   39. The Dodekangle

40. A Hebrew root word meaning talisman or amulet.

41. Sigillum; sign or signature   42. The Qameoth
43. Spirit   44. Intelligence
45. The Planetary Seal   46. The Magic Constant
47. The Grand Total   48. The Planetary Seal

49. $\dfrac{N^3 + N}{2}$

50. A hidden number which controls how the numbers are placed on a Qamea.

51. $\dfrac{N^2 + 1}{2}$

52. $N^2 + 1$ 53. Gematria   54. Aiq Beker

55. The Pythagorean Table

56. Notariqon   57. Temurah   58. Notariqon
59. Avgad   60. Thashrag   61. Tziruph

Quiz—Sections 4, 5, 6, and 7 (Hod, Water, Mercury, Olympic Planetary Spirits)

1. Splendor   2. Hermaphrodite
3. The Vision of Splendour   4. An Octogram
5. Names, versicles, apron   6. Michael
7. Elohim Tzabaoth   8. Beni Elohim
9. Orange   10. The right hip
11. Kokab   12. The four Eights
13. Truthfulness   14. Dishonesty

15. Maim; מים

16. Elohim Tzaboath; אלהים צבאות

17. Maarab; מערב

18. Gabriel; גבריאל

19. Taliahad; טליהד

20. Tharsis; תרשים

21. Nichsa
22. Undines
23. Apsu
24. Tiamat
25. Nammu
26. Ea; Enki
27. Nanshe
28. Nanshe
29. Nun
30. Tefnut
31. Khnemu
32. Hapi
33. Poseidon
34. Amphitrite
35. Pontus
36. Oceanus
37. Nereus
38. Triton
39. Achelous
40. Prophesy
41. Manannan
42. Mimir
43. Ran
44. Nixies

45. Education; 5; 14
46. Rational thinking
47. Active, dexterous, quick, inpredictable and volatile.
48. It embraces all of the Sephiroth except for Kether. The horns spring out from Daath.
49. Science, divination, eloquence, intelligence, skill in business, wonders, apparitions, writings, deceit, theft, and merchandise.

50. Kokab
51. Raphael
52. Wednesday
53. Tiriel
54. Taphthartharath
55. Ophiel

56. Quicksilver
57. Opal, fire opal, agate, serpentine
58. Birch, aspen, mulberry
59. Marjoram, fennel, mandrake, lavendar, carraway, dill
60. Jackel, ibis, ape, swallow, twin serpents
61. Jupiter; the aspects of Water and wisdom; Amon-Ra, Maat, Zeus, Poseidon, Athene, Marduk, Adad.

62. Enki
63. Nabu
64. Djehoti
65. Tashmetum
66. Seshat
67. Hermes
68. Iris
69. Athene
70. Athene
71. Athene
72. Iris
73. Asclepius
74. Lug
75. Odin
76. Odin
77. Khnemu
78. Phorcys
79. Mimir
80. Ea
81. Seshat
82. Hermes
83. Hygieia

84. Saturn   Aratron
    Jupiter   Bethor
    Mars   Phalegh
    Sol   Och
    Venus   Hagith
    Mercury   Ophiel
    Phul   Luna

Quiz—Section 8 (The Tarot)

1. 78
2. 22
3. 56

4. Wands   Clubs
   Cups   Hearts
   Swords   Spades
   Pentacles Diamonds

5. Wands   Yod
   Cups   Heh
   Swords   Vav
   Pentacles Heh

6. Wands   Atziluth
   Cups   Briah
   Swords   Yetzirah
   Pentacles Assiah

7. Objective centers of energy
8. Subjective conduits or energy channels
9. To represent the twenty-two Paths on the tree and the Hebrew letters.
10. Elemental, Zodiacal, Planetary
11. The ten Sephiroth and the Twenty-two Paths

12. *Elemental—The 3 Mother Letters*

    The Fool (AIR—Aleph)
    The Hanged Man (WATER—Mem)
    Judgment (FIRE—Shin)

    Planetary—The 7 Double Letters

    The Magician (MERCURY—Beth)
    The High Priestess (LUNA—Gimel)
    The Empress (Venus—Daleth)
    The Wheel of Fortune (JUPITER—Kaph)
    The Tower (MARS—Peh)
    The Sun (SOL—Resh)
    The Universe (SATURN—Tau)

    Zodiacal—The 12 Simple Letters

    The Emperor (ARIES—Heh)
    The Hierophant (Taurus—Vav)
    The Lovers (GEMINI—Zayin)
    The Chariot (CANCER—Cheth)
    Strength (LEO—Teth)
    The Hermit (VIRGO—Yod)

Justice (LIBRA—Lamed)
Death (SCORPIO—Nun)
Temperance (SAGITTARIUS—Samekh)
The Devil (CAPRICORN—Ayin)
The Star (AQUARIUS—Tzaddi)
The Moon (PISCES—Qoph)

13. Air, Aries, Virgo, Aries. ♈ ♍ ♈ △
14. Air, Libra, Aries, Virgo, Water. ▽ ♍ ♈ ♎ △

15. The Emperor	16. The Fool
17. The Hierophant	18. The High Priestess
19. The Magician	20. The Empress
21. The Universe	22. The Lovers
23. Judgment	24. The Chariot
25. The Sun	26. Stength
27. The Star	28. The Hermit
29. The Tower	30. The Wheel of Fortune
31. Justice	32. The Devil
33. The Hanged man	34. Death
35. Temperance	36. Justice
37. The Star	38. The Emperor
39. The Hierophant	40. The Sun
41. The Empress	42. Death
43. The Lovers	44. The Hanged Man
45. Temperance	46. Jupiter; Virgo; Sol
47. Zodiac; Taurus; Jupiter	48. Venus; Aquarius; Luna

49. Mercury; Fire; the Cosmic Elements
50. Saturn; Cancer; Mars
51. Sephiroth; Four Worlds
52. Great energy and dynamic power. Masculine power.
53. Suggests material or worldly affairs, business or money.
54. Form-building capacity. Feminine Power.
55. Intellect, communication, mental faculties and sometimes trouble.

56. A Decanate	57. The Two of Wands
58. The Four of Wands	59. The Three of Wands
60. The Eight of Wands	61. The Six of Wands
62. The Two of Cups	63. The Three of Cups
64. The Five of Cups	65. The Seven of Cups
66. The Two of Swords	67. The Three of Swords
68. The Six of Swords	69. The Nine of Swords
70. The Ten of Swords	71. The Two of Pentacles
72. The Seven of Pentacles	73. The Six of Pentacles
74. The Eight of Pentacles	75. The Ten of Swords
76. The Ten of Cups	77. The Seven of Wands

78. The King of Wands
79. The Queen of Swords
80. The Prince of Cups
81. The Princess of Wands
82. The Princess of Pentacles
83. The King of Cups
84. The Princess of Wands
85. The Prince of Swords
86. The Queen of Pentacles
87. The Queen of Swords

Chapter Five: Philosophus

Quiz 0 (The Ritual)

1. YHVH Tzabaoth
2. 28
3. Kaph Cheth
4. 3—3—1
5. The General Grip of the Outer Order.
6. Raising the hands to the fore-head, palms outward, with the thumbs and index fingers forming a triangle.

7. Asch
8. Fire, Asch
9. South
10. Pharos Illuminans
11. Illuminating Tower of Light
12. Netzach
13. YHVH Tzabaoth
14. Michael
15. Leo
16. OIP TEAA PEDOCE
17. Edelperna
18. The Triangle above the Cross

19. The Triangle surmounting the Cross upon the Altar represents the Fire of the Spirit surmounting the Cross of Life and of the Waters of Edom.
20. The Fourth Elemental Grade and the Seventh Sephirah.
21. The Calvary Cross of Twelve Squares
22. The Solid Pyramid of the Elements
23. The Calvary Cross of Ten Squares
24. The Cross of the Hegemon's Lamen
25. The Hegemon
26. Four
27. In the first medial point, the candidate undertakes a Journey on the Path of Qoph where the various forms of Elemental Water and different aspects of Time are revealed. In the second medial point, a journey on the Path of Tzaddi is undertaken and the different types of celestial water are exposed. In the third medial point the candidate traverses the Path of Peh where the story of the Fall of the Edomite kings (the Fall of Eden) is explained. In the fourth medial point the Candidate enters the Fire Temple of Netzach where the mysteries of the Philosophus Grade are revealed.
28. The Candidate raises both arms above the head
29. Osiris, Horus, Isis
30. Water that is stagnant, silent and still; the Past
31. Water that is pure, limid and flowing; the Present
32. Water that is turbid and troubled; the Future

33. The Moon Card shows two dogs frolicking near two towers under the Moon-light. A crayfish crawls up from the water unto the Path which leads to the Horizon. The card is attributed to the Sign of Pisces.

34. The Star Card shows a nude female figure crowned with a heptagram who pours water from two vases, forming a river at her feet. She is the Great Mother pouring forth the Waters of Creation. The card is attributed to Aquarius.

35. The Tower Card shows a stone tower being blown apart by a lighting bolt. The figures falling from the tower are the Edomite Kings. The card is attributed to Mars.

36. The Diagram of Eden after the Fall, and the Qamea and seals of Venus.

37. Phrath

Quiz—Sections 1, 2, and 3 (Qabalah, Shem ha-Mephoresh, Netzach)

1. From the first and last letters of the Greek, Latin and Hebrew alphabets thus: A and Z, Aleph and Tau, Alpha and Omega.

2. The beginning and the end—the living essence.

3. Ain אין, Ain Soph אין סוף, Ain Soph Aur אין סוף אור

4. Ain Soph   5. Ain Soph Aur   6. Ain Soph

7. Ain Soph   8. Zimzum   9. Adam Kadmon

10. Ain   11. The right-hand side

12. Chaos

13. The Breaking of the Vessels

14. Partzufim

15. Arik Anpin אריך אנפין
Abba אבבא
Aima אימא
Zauir Anpin זעיר אנפין
Nukba de-Zauir נקבה דזעיר

16. Zauir Anpin   17. Arik Anpin

18. Aima   19. Abba

20. Nukba de-Zauir; Malkah; Kalah

21. Aatik Yomin עתיך יומין

22. Kether   23. Aatik Qadesh   24. Kether

25. Microprosopus; Chesed, Geburah, Tiphareth, Netzach, Hod, Yesod.

26. Macroprosopus; Kether.

27. Elohim.   28. Tikkun.

29. Atziluth—Ab עב. Briah—Seg סג. Yetzirah—Mah מה. Assiah—Ben בן.

30. In each of the Four Worlds are the Ten Sephiroth of that world, and each Sephirah has its own ten Sephiroth, a total of 400—the number of Tau.

31. Sheva Kekhaloth
32. The three Supernal Sephiroth
33. Yesod and Malkuth
34. By assigning the ten Sephiroth to seven palaces, the energies of the Sephiroth may be differentiated along the lines of planetary energies.
35. Kether, Tiphareth, Yesod
36. Binah, Chesed, Hod
37. Pillars, Tree of Life
38. Nehushtan
39. The Divided Name; the seventy-two fold Name of God.
40. It is derived from the Book of Exodus 14:19-21. Each of these three verses contains 72 letters which are then organized to generate the 72 syllables of the Name.
41. Leo
42. The Seventy-two Leaves of the Tree of Life; the Healing Leaves; the Divided Name of Zauir Anpin.
43. Three
44. By adding the suffix "iah" or the suffix "al."
45. The 72 Quinances of the Zodiac

46. "Iah"	47. "al"	48. Gimel
49. Victory	50. YHVH Tzabaoth	51. Haniel
52. Elohim	53. Nogah	

54. The Vision of Beauty Triumphant.

55. Green	56. The four Sevens
57. A beautiful naked woman	58. Benzoin, rose, red sandal
59. Lamp, gridle, rose	60. The Heptagram
61. Unselfishness	62. Lust
63. The left hip	

Quiz—Sections 4, 5, and 6 (Fire, Venus, The Qlippoth)

1. Masculine, regenerating, exciting, transforming
2. Asch, אש
3. YHVH Tzabaoth, יהוה צבאות

4. Darom, דרום	5. Michael, מיכאל	6. Ariel, אריאל
7. Seraph, שרף	8. Djin	9. Salamanders
10. Aryeh	11. Sekhet	12. Nusku
13. Heru-Behutet	14. Bast	15. Gibil
16. Heru-Behetet	17. Bennu	18. Mont
19. Ptah	20. Prometheus	21. Hephaestus
22. Hestia		

23. Attractions, social interactions, partners, marriages, unions, aesthetics, cultural pursuits, emotions beauty, sensuality, creative arts, adornments.

24. Forming friendships, pleasant undertakings, kindness and love, traveling.
25. Nogah
26. Emotion, 15, 22
27. It embraces all ten Sephiroth, and is a fitting symbol for the Isis of Nature.

28. Anael   29. Friday   30. Hagiel
31. Qedemel   32. Hagith   33. Copper, Brass

34. Emerald, turquise, jade, malachite
35. Elder, fruit trees
36. Rose, myrtle, geranium, hyacinth, thyme, licorice
37. Dove, dolphin, bee, tortoise

38. Bes   39. Ishtar   40. Hathor
41. Ishtar   42. Hathor   43. Qetesh

44. Aphrodite   45. Aphrodite Genetrix
46. Aphrodite Pandemos   47. Freya
48. Dionysus

49. Mars; both planets are associated with Fire and passion.
50. The Breaking of the Vessels.
51. A group of choatic, destructive and imbalanced forces.
52. After the fall, Malkuth descended and came to rest upon the Kingdom
      of Shells.
53. Eleven
54. Ain—Qemetiel, Ain Soph—Belial, Ain Soph Aur—Athiel.

55. Kether   Thaumiel—Twins of God
    Chokmah   Ogiel—The Hinderers
    Binah   Satariel—The Concealers
    Chesed   Gasheklah—The Smiters, The Breakers
    Geburah   Golachab—The Burners
    Tiphareth   Tageriron—The Hagglers, The Disputers
    Netzach   Oreb Zaraq—The Ravens of Dispersion
    Hod   Samael—The Liar or Poison of God
    Yesod   Gamaliel—The Obscene Ones
    Malkuth   Lilith—Queen of Night and of Demons

56. Aries   Bairiron—The Herd
    Taurus   Adimiron—The Bloody Ones
    Gemini   Tzelilimiron—The Clangers
    Cancer   Shichiriron—The Black Ones
    Leo   Shalhebiron—The Flaming Ones
    Virgo   Tzaphiriron—The Bloody Ones
    Libra   Abiriron—The Clayish Ones
    Scorpio   Necheshthiron—The Brazen Ones
    Sagittarius   Nachashiron—The Snaky Ones

Capricorn   Dagdagiron—The Fishy Ones
Aquarius   Bahimiron—The Bestial Ones
Pisces   Nashimiron—Malignant Women

57. Behemoth   58. Leviathon

Quiz—Sections 7, 8, 9, and 10 (Alchemy, Admission Badges and Diagrams, Greek Alphabet, Tarot)

1. Alchemy only employs a gradual heat which is continually but carefully increased whereas chemistry commences with a violent, rapid heat.
2. As the cleansing and purifying of Malkuth in order to purge it from the influence of the shells and return it to its rightful spiritual origins.

3. The pelican   4. The Alembic   5. The Philosophic Egg
6. The Athanor   7. The Retort   8. Balneum Vaporis
9. Balneum Mariae

10. The symbol of Sulphur does not touch any of the four lower Sephiroth. The Cross terminates in Tiphareth, where the Supernal Triangle is to be grasped.
11. The symbol of Salt embraces all of the Sephiroth but Malkuth.
12. The Symbol of Mercury embraces all of the Sephiroth but Kether. The horns spring from Daath.
13. The Cross, the Crescent and the Circle.

14. Cross   15. Mercury   16. True

17. The Calvary Cross of Twelve Squares is formed of twelve squares which fitly represent the Zodiac. It also alludes to the Eternal River of Eden divided into four heads which correspond to the four triplicities of the Zodiac.
18. The Pyramid of the Four Elements is a truncated pyramid. On the four triangles which comprise the sides are the Hebrew names of the Four Elements, Asch—Fire, Maim—Water, Ruach—Air, and Aretz—Earth. On the apex is the word Eth (Spirit) and the square base contains the word Olam (world) implying the material universe.
19. The Calvary Cross of Ten Squares is formed of 10 squares which fitly represent the ten Sephiroth in balanced disposition. It is also the opened out form of the Double Cube and the Altar of Incense.
20. The Cross of the Hegemon's Badge embraces Tiphareth, Netzach, Hod and Yesod, and rests upon Malkuth. Also the Calvary Cross of Six Squares is the opened-out form of the Cube, and is thus referred to the six Sephiroth of Microprosopus.
21. The Great Goddess Eve tempted by the fruits of Knowledge, reaches down and thus the Pillars are left unsupported. The Tree was shattered, and Adam and Eve fell from the garden. The dragon Leviathan arose with seven heads and ten horns, and Eden was desolated. The folds of the Dragon

enclosed Malkuth and linked it to the kingdom of shells. Leviathan reached as high as Daath on the Tree, but YHVH Elohim placed the Four Letters of the Name and the Flaming Sword between the devastated garden and the Supernal Eden, that it should not be involved in the Fall of Adam.

22. The Fall of Eden represents the Lower Self symbolized by Eve, becoming entranced the power of the awakening psyche, and momentarily suspending its support of the Higher Self, symbolized by Adam.

23. An event in humanity's distant past when the collective unconscious of our primitive race was stimulated and the beginnings of intelligence and self-awareness developed.

24. The stimulation of the psychic Elements within the Mind of the initiate.

25. The Celtic Cross spread

26. Hru

27.

Letter	Name	Value	English equivalent
A α	Alpha	1	A (father)
B β	Beta	2	B
Γ γ	Gamma	3	G
Δ δ	Delta	4	D
E ε	Epsilon	5	short e (better)
Z ζ	Zeta	7	Zd (wisdom)
H η	Eta	8	long e (pair)
Θ θ	Theta	9	Th (cathouse)
Ι ι	Iota	10	I (either feet or fit)
Κ κ	Kappa	20	K
Λ λ	Lambda	30	L
Μ μ	Mu	40	M
Ν ν	Nu	50	N
Ξ ξ	Xi	60	X
O o	Omicron	70	short o (hot)
Π π	Pi	80	P
Ρ ρ	Rho	100	R, Rh (trilled)
Σ σ	Sigma	200	S (sometimes z)
Τ τ	Tau	300	T
Υ υ	Upsilon	400	U (long or short)
Φ φ	Phi	500	Ph (mophead)
Χ χ	Chi	600	Kh (backhoe)
Ψ ψ	Psi	700	Ps
Ω ω	Omega	800	aw (saw)

The Table of Combinations of Tziruph
(Transliterated into English Letters)

ALBTh	K	Y	T	Ch	Z	V	H	D	G	B	A
	M	N	S	O	P	Tz	Q	R	Sh	Th	L
ABGTh	L	K	Y	T	Ch	Z	V	H	D	G	A
	M	N	S	O	P	Tz	Q	R	Sh	Th	B
AGDTh	M	L	K	Y	T	Ch	Z	V	H	D	A
	S	O	P	Tz	O	R	Sh	B	N	Th	G
ADBG	N	M	L	K	Y	T	Ch	Z	V	B	A
	O	P	Tz	Q	R	Sh	Th	H	S	G	D
AHBD	S	N	M	L	K	Y	T	Ch	Z	B	A
	P	Tz	Q	R	Sh	Th	V	O	G	D	H
AVBH	O	S	N	M	L	K	Y	T	Ch	B	A
	Tz	Q	R	Sh	Th	Z	P	G	D	H	V
AZBV	P	O	S	N	M	L	K	Y	T	B	A
	Q	R	Sh	Th	Ch	Tz	G	D	H	V	Z
AChBZ	Tz	P	O	S	N	M	L	K	Y	B	A
	R	Sh	Th	T	Q	G	D	H	V	Z	Ch
ATBCh	Q	Tz	P	O	S	N	M	L	K	B	A
	Sh	Th	Y	R	G	D	H	V	Z	Ch	T
AYBT	R	Q	Tz	P	O	S	N	M	L	B	A
	Th	K	Sh	G	D	H	V	Z	Ch	T	Y
AHBY	Sh	R	Q	Tz	P	O	S	N	M	B	A
	L	Th	G	D	H	V	Z	Ch	T	Y	K
ALBK	Th	Sh	R	Q	Tz	P	O	S	N	B	A
	M	G	D	H	V	Z	Ch	T	Y	K	L
AMBL	N	Th	Sh	R	Q	Tz	P	O	S	B	A
	G	D	H	V	Z	Ch	T	Y	K	L	M
ANBM	S	G	Th	Sh	R	O	Tz	P	O	B	A
	D	H	V	Z	Ch	T	Y	K	L	M	N
ASBN	O	D	G	Th	Sh	R	O	Tz	P	B	A
	H	V	Z	Ch	T	Y	K	L	M	N	S
AOBS	P	H	D	G	Th	Sh	R	O	Tz	B	A
	V	Z	Ch	T	Y	K	L	M	N	S	O

APBO	Tz	V	H	D	G	Th	Sh	R	O	B	A
	Z	Ch	T	Y	K	L	M	N	S	O	P
ATzBP	Q	Z	V	H	D	G	Th	Sh	R	O	B	A
	Ch	T	Y	K	L	M	N	S	O	P	Tz
AQBTz	R	Ch	Z	V	H	D	G	Th	Sh	B	A
	T	Y	K	L	M	N	S	O	P	Tz	Q
ARBQ	Sh	T	Ch	Z	V	H	D	G	Th	B	A
	Y	K	L	M	N	S	O	P	Tz	Q	R
AShBR	Th	Y	T	Ch	Z	V	H	D	H	B	A
	K	L	M	N	S	O	P	Tz	Q	R	Sh
AThBSh	K	Y	T	Ch	Z	V	H	D	G	B	A
	L	M	N	S	O	P	Tz	Q	R	Sh	Th
ABGD	Th	L	K	Y	T	Ch	Z	V	H	G	A
	M	N	S	O	P	Tz	Q	R	Sh	D	B
ALBM	K	Y	T	Ch	Z	V	H	D	G	B	A
	N	S	O	P	Tz	Q	R	Sh	Th	M	L

The Right Table of Commutations

Th	Sh	R	Q	Tz	P	O	S	N	M	L	K	Y	T	Ch	Z	V	H	D	G	B	A
A	Th	Sh	R	Q	Tz	P	O	S	N	M	L	K	Y	T	Ch	Z	V	H	D	G	B
B	A	Th	Sh	R	Q	Tz	P	O	S	N	M	L	K	Y	T	Ch	Z	V	H	D	G
G	B	A	Th	Sh	R	Q	Tz	P	O	S	N	M	L	K	Y	T	Ch	Z	V	H	D
D	G	B	A	Th	Sh	R	Q	Tz	P	O	S	N	M	L	K	Y	T	Ch	Z	V	H
H	D	G	B	A	Th	Sh	R	Q	Tz	P	O	S	N	M	L	K	Y	T	Ch	Z	V
V	H	D	G	B	A	Th	Sh	R	Q	Tz	P	O	S	N	M	L	K	Y	T	Ch	Z
Z	V	H	D	G	B	A	Th	Sh	R	Q	Tz	P	O	S	N	M	L	K	Y	T	Ch
Ch	Z	V	H	D	G	B	A	Th	Sh	R	Q	Tz	P	O	S	N	M	L	K	Y	T
T	Ch	Z	V	H	D	G	B	A	Th	Sh	R	Q	Tz	P	O	S	N	M	L	K	Y
Y	T	Ch	Z	V	H	D	G	B	A	Th	Sh	R	Q	Tz	P	O	S	N	M	L	K
K	Y	T	Ch	Z	V	H	D	G	B	A	Th	Sh	R	Q	Tz	P	O	S	N	M	L
L	K	Y	T	Ch	Z	V	H	D	G	B	A	Th	Sh	R	Q	Tz	P	O	S	N	M
M	L	K	Y	T	Ch	Z	V	H	D	G	B	A	Th	Sh	R	Q	Tz	P	O	S	N
N	M	L	K	Y	T	Ch	Z	V	H	D	G	B	A	Th	Sh	R	Q	Tz	P	O	S
S	N	M	L	K	Y	T	Ch	Z	V	H	D	G	B	A	Th	Sh	R	Q	Tz	P	O
O	S	N	M	L	K	Y	T	Ch	Z	V	H	D	G	B	A	Th	Sh	R	Q	Tz	P
P	O	S	N	M	L	K	Y	T	Ch	Z	V	H	D	G	B	A	Th	Sh	R	Q	Tz
Tz	P	O	S	N	M	L	K	Y	T	Ch	Z	V	H	D	G	B	A	Th	Sh	R	Q
Q	Tz	P	O	S	N	M	L	K	Y	T	Ch	Z	V	H	D	G	B	A	Th	Sh	R
R	Q	Tz	P	O	S	N	M	L	K	Y	T	Ch	Z	V	H	D	G	B	A	Th	Sh
Sh	R	Q	Tz	P	O	S	N	M	L	K	Y	T	Ch	Z	V	H	D	G	B	A	Th

The Averse Table of Commutations

A	B	G	D	H	V	Z	Ch	T	Y	K	L	M	N	S	O	P	Tz	Q	R	Sh	Th
Th	A	B	G	D	H	V	Z	Ch	T	Y	K	L	M	N	S	O	P	Tz	Q	R	Sh
Sh	Th	A	B	G	D	H	V	Z	Ch	T	Y	K	L	M	N	S	O	P	Tz	Q	R
R	Sh	Th	A	B	G	D	H	V	Z	Ch	T	Y	K	L	M	N	S	O	P	Tz	Q
Q	R	Sh	Th	A	B	G	D	H	V	Z	Ch	T	Y	K	L	M	N	S	O	P	Tz
Tz	Q	R	Sh	Th	A	B	G	D	H	V	Z	Ch	T	Y	K	L	M	N	S	O	P
P	Tz	Q	R	Sh	Th	A	B	G	D	H	V	Z	Ch	T	Y	K	L	M	N	S	O
O	P	Tz	Q	R	Sh	Th	A	B	G	D	H	V	Z	Ch	T	Y	K	L	M	N	S
S	O	P	Tz	Q	R	Sh	Th	A	B	G	D	H	V	Z	Ch	T	Y	K	L	M	N
N	S	O	P	Tz	Q	R	Sh	Th	A	B	G	D	H	V	Z	Ch	T	Y	K	L	M
M	N	S	O	P	Tz	Q	R	Sh	Th	A	B	G	D	H	V	Z	Ch	T	Y	K	L
L	M	N	S	O	P	Tz	Q	R	Sh	Th	A	B	G	D	H	V	Z	Ch	T	Y	K
K	L	M	N	S	O	P	Tz	Q	R	Sh	Th	A	B	G	D	H	V	Z	Ch	T	Y
Y	K	L	M	N	S	O	P	Tz	Q	R	Sh	Th	A	B	G	D	H	V	Z	Ch	T
T	Y	K	L	M	N	S	O	P	Tz	Q	R	Sh	Th	A	B	G	D	H	V	Z	Ch
Ch	T	Y	K	L	M	N	S	O	P	Tz	Q	R	Sh	Th	A	B	G	D	H	V	Z
Z	Ch	T	Y	K	L	M	N	S	O	P	Tz	Q	R	Sh	Th	A	B	G	D	H	V
V	Z	Ch	T	Y	K	L	M	N	S	O	P	Tz	Q	R	Sh	Th	A	B	G	D	H
H	V	Z	Ch	T	Y	K	L	M	N	S	O	P	Tz	Q	R	Sh	Th	A	B	G	D
D	H	V	Z	Ch	T	Y	K	L	M	N	S	O	P	Tz	Q	R	Sh	Th	A	B	G
G	D	H	V	Z	Ch	T	Y	K	L	M	N	S	O	P	Tz	Q	R	Sh	Th	A	B
B	G	D	H	V	Z	Ch	T	Y	K	L	M	N	S	O	P	Tz	Q	R	Sh	Th	A

The Rational Table of Commutations

ABGCh	L	K	Y	T	Ch	Z	V	H	D	G	A
	M	N	S	O	P	Tz	Q	R	Sh	Ch	B
AGDB	M	L	K	Y	T	Ch	Z	V	H	D	A
	N	S	O	P	Tz	Q	R	Sh	Th	B	G
ADHG	N	M	L	K	Y	T	Ch	Z	V	H	A
	S	O	P	Tz	Q	R	Sh	Th	B	G	D
AHVD	S	N	M	L	K	Y	T	Ch	Z	V	A
	O	P	Tz	Q	R	Sh	Th	B	G	D	H
AVZH	O	S	N	M	L	K	Y	T	Ch	Z	A
	P	Tz	Q	R	Sh	Th	B	G	D	H	V
AZChV	P	O	S	N	M	L	K	Y	T	Ch	A
	Tz	Q	R	Sh	Th	S	G	D	H	V	Z
AChTZ	Tz	P	O	S	N	M	L	K	Y	T	A
	Q	R	Sh	Th	B	G	D	H	V	Z	Ch
ATYCh	Q	Tz	P	O	S	N	M	L	K	Y	A
	R	Sh	Th	B	G	D	H	V	Z	Ch	T
AYKT	R	Q	Tz	P	O	S	N	M	L	K	A
	Sh	Th	B	G	D	H	V	Z	Ch	T	Y
AKLY	Sh	R	Q	Tz	P	O	S	N	M	L	A
	Th	B	G	D	H	V	Z	Ch	T	Y	K
ALMK	Th	Sh	R	Q	Tz	P	O	S	N	M	A
	B	G	D	H	V	Z	Ch	T	Y	K	L
AMNL	B	Th	Sh	R	Q	Tz	P	O	S	N	A
	G	D	H	V	Z	Ch	T	Y	K	L	M
ANSM	G	B	Th	Sh	R	Q	Tz	P	O	S	A
	D	H	V	Z	Ch	T	Y	K	L	M	N
ASON	D	G	B	Th	Sh	R	Q	Tz	P	O	A
	H	V	Z	Ch	T	Y	K	L	M	N	S
AOPS	H	D	G	B	Th	Sh	R	Q	Tz	P	A
	V	Z	Ch	T	Y	K	L	M	N	S	O
APTzO	V	H	D	G	B	Th	Sh	R	Q	Tz	A
	Z	Ch	T	Y	K	L	M	N	S	O	P
ATzOP	Z	V	H	D	G	B	Th	Sh	R	O	A
	Ch	T	Y	K	L	M	N	S	O	P	Tz
AQRTz	Ch	Z	V	H	D	G	B	Th	Sh	R	A
	T	Y	K	L	M	N	S	O	P	Tz	Q
ARShQ	T	Ch	Z	V	H	D	G	B	Th	Sh	A
	Y	K	L	M	N	S	O	P	Tz	Q	R
AShThR	Y	T	Ch	Z	V	H	D	G	B	Th	A
	K	L	M	N	S	O	P	Tz	Q	R	Sh
AThBSh	K	Y	T	Ch	Z	V	H	D	G	B	A
	L	M	N	S	O	P	Tz	Q	R	Sh	Th
ABGD	Th	O	P	S	M	K	T	Z	H	G	A
	Sh	R	Tz	Q	M	L	Y	Ch	V	D	B

Bibliography

Agrippa, Henry Cornelius. *Three Books of Occult Philosophy*. St. Paul, MN: Llewellyn Publications, 1993.

Albertus Spagyricus, F.R.C. *The Alchemist's Handbook*. Salt Lake City, Utah: The Paracelsus Research Society, 1960.

Budge, E.A. Wallis. *An Egyptian Hieroglyphic Dictionary*, Vol. 1 & 2. New York, NY: Dover Publications, Inc., 1969.

Budge, E.A. Wallis. *Egyptian Religion*. New York, NY: Citadel Press, 1987.

Budge, E.A. Wallis. *The Book of the Dead*. London: Routledge & Kegan Paul Ltd., 1949.

Budge, E.A. Wallis. *The Gods of the Egyptians*, Vol. 1 & 2. New York, NY: Dover Publications, Inc., 1969.

Burckhardt, Titus. *Alchemy*. Longmead, Shaftesbury, Dorset: Element Books, Ltd., 1986.

Cicero, Chic and Cicero, Sandra Tabatha. *The New Golden Dawn Ritual Tarot*. St. Paul, MN: Llewellyn Publications, 1991.

Cicero, Chic and Cicero, Sandra Tabatha. *Secrets of a Golden Dawn Temple*. St. Paul, MN: Llewellyn Publications, 1992.

Cirlot, J.E. *A Dictionary of Symbols*. 2nd ed. New York, NY: Philosophical Library, 1983.

Crowley, Aleister. *777*. York Beach, Maine: Samuel Weiser, Inc., 1973.

Cunningham, Scott. *The Complete Book of Incense, Oils and Brews*. St. Paul, MN: Llewellyn Publications, 1992.

Cunningham, Scott. *Crystal Gem & Metal Magic*. St. Paul, MN: Llewellyn Publications, 1992.

Cunningham, Scott. *Cunningham's Encyclopedia of Magical Herbs*. St. Paul, MN: Llewellyn Publications, 1990.

Davidson, Gustav. *A Dictionary of Angels.* New York, NY: The Free Press,
    A Division of Macmillan, Inc., 1992.

Denning & Phillips. *Planetary Magick.* St. Paul, MN: Llewellyn Publications, 1989.

D'Olivet, Fabre. *The Hebraic Tongue Restored.* New York, NY: Samuel Weiser, Inc.,
    1981.

De Vore, Nicholas. *Encylopedia of Astrology.* New York, NY: Philosophical
    Library, 1947.

Essentia, Journal of Evolutionary Thought in Action. Summer 1981, Vol. 2.

Essentia, Journal of Evolutionary Thought in Action. Winter 1983 - Spring 1984, Vol. 5.

Fortune, Dion. *The Mystical Qabalah.* New York, NY: Ibis Books, 1981.

Gilbert, R.A. *The Golden Dawn Companion.* Wellingborough, Northamptonshire:
    The Aquarian Press, 1986.

Gilbert, R.A. *The Sorcerer and His Apprentice.* Wellingborough, Northamptonshire:
    The Aquarian Press, 1983.

Godwin, David. *Godwin's Cabalistic Encyclopedia.* 2nd ed. St. Paul, MN: Llewellyn
    Publications, 1989.

Godwin, David. *Light in Extension.* St. Paul, MN: LlewellynPublications, 1992.

Godwin, Malcolm. *Angels, an Endangered Species.* New York, NY: Simon and
    Schuster, 1990.

Gonzalez-Wippler, Migene. *A Kabbalah for the Modern World.* St. Paul, MN:
    Llewellyn Publications, 1990.

Gray, William G. *The Ladder of Lights.* York Beach, Maine: Samuel Weiser, Inc.,
    1981.

Hall, Manly P. *The Philosophy of Astrology.* Los Angeles, CA: The Philosophical
    Research Society, Inc., 1947.

Hall, Manly P. *The Secret Teachings of All Ages.* Los Angeles, CA: The
    Philosophical Research Society, Inc., 1977.

Holmyard, E.J. *Alchemy.* New York, NY: Dover Publications, Inc,. 1990.

Kaplan, Aryeh. *Sefer Yetzirah.* York Beach, Maine: Samuel Weiser, Inc., 1990.

Knight, Gareth. *A Practical Guide to Qabalistic Symbolism.* New York, NY:
    Samuel Weiser, Inc., 1983.

Kraig, Donald Michael. *Modern Magick.* St. Paul, MN: Llewellyn Publications,
    1988.

Lapidus. *In Pursuit of Gold.* New York, NY: Samuel Weiser, Inc., 1976.

Larouse Encyclopedia of Mythology. New York, NY: Prometheus Press, 1959.

Lewis, Naphtali. *Samothrace*. New York, NY: Bolligen Series LX-1, Pantheon Books, 1958.

March, Marion D. and McEvers, Joan. *The Only Way to Learn Astrology*. Vol. 1, 2 & 3. San Diego, CA: Astro-Analytic Publications, Inc., 1976.

Mathers, S.L. MacGregor. *The Kabbalah Unveiled*. York Beach, Maine: Samuel Weiser, Inc., 1989.

McCurley, Foster R. *Ancient Myths and Biblical Faith*. Philadelphia, PA: Fortress Press, 1983.

McLean, Adam. *The Alchemical Mandala*. Grand Rapids, MI: Phanes Press, 1989.

McLean, Adam. *A Treatise on Angel Magic*. Grand Rapids, MI: Phanes Press, 1990.

Regardie, Israel. *The Golden Dawn*. 4th ed. St. Paul: Llewellyn Publications, 1982.

Regardie, Israel. *Foundations of Practical Magic*. 2nd ed. Wellingborough, Northamptonshire: The Aquarian Press, 1983.

Regardie, Israel. *The Complete Golden Dawn System of Magic*. Phoenix, Arizona: Falcon Press, 1984.

Regardie, Israel. *A Garden of Pomegranates*. 2nd ed. St. Paul, MN: Llewellyn Publications, 1988.

Regardie, Israel. *The Philosopher's Stone*. St. Paul, MN: Llewellyn Publications, 1978.

Regardie, Israel. *The Tree of Life*. York Beach, Maine: Samuel Weiser, Inc., 1972.

Regardie, Israel. *The One Year Manual*. York Beach, Maine: Samuel Weiser, Inc., 1981.

Sauneron, Serge. *The Priests of Ancient Egypt*. New York, NY: Grove Press, Inc., 1960.

Schlcicher, Joan L. "The Chaldean Oracles." *Ancient Wisdom for Modern Living*. January/February/March 1993, Vol. 53, No. 1, pp. 20-22.

Silberer, Herbert. *Hidden Symbolism of Alchemy and the Occult Arts*. New York, NY: Dover Publications, Inc., 1971

Smith, George. *The Chaldean Account of Genesis*. London, UK: Sampson, Low & Co. 1876.

Spretnak, Charlene. *Lost Goddesses of Early Greece*. Boston, Mass: Beacon Press, 1978.

Stanley, Thomas. *The Chaldaean Oracles*. Gillette, New Jersey: Heptangle Books, 1989.

Stebbing, Lionel. *A Dictionary of the Occult Sciences*. London: Emerson Press, Date Unknown.

Thompson, C.J.S. *The Lure and Romance of Alchemy.* New York, NY: Bell Publishing Company, 1990

Torrens, R.G. *The Secret Rituals of the Golden Dawn.* New York, NY: Samuel Weiser, Inc., 1973.

Tyl, Noel. *Horoscope Construction: Volume 1: The Principles and Practice of Astrology.* St. Paul, MN: Llewellyn Publications, 1973.

Waite, Arthur Edward. *The Hermetic Museum.* York Beach, Maine: Samuel Weiser, Inc., 1991.

Whitcomb, Bill. *The Magician's Companion.* St. Paul, MN: Llewellyn Publications, 1993.

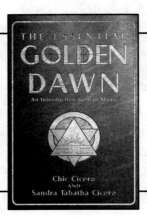

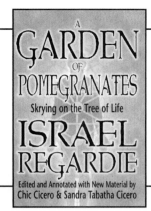

A Garden of Pomegranates
Skrying on the Tree of Life
ISRAEL REGARDIE
EDITED AND ANNOTATED WITH NEW MATERIAL BY CHIC CICERO AND SANDRA TABATHA CICERO

When Israel Regardie wrote *A Garden of Pomegranates* in 1932, he designed it to be a simple yet comprehensive guidebook outlining the complex system of the Qabalah and providing a key to its symbolism. Since then it has achieved the status of a classic among texts on the Hermetic Qabalah. It stands as the best single introductory guide for magicians on this complex system, with an emphasis on direct experience through meditation on the twenty-two paths.

Now, Chic Cicero and Sandra Tabatha Cicero—Golden Dawn adepts and personal friends of the late Regardie—have made the book even more useful for today's occult students with full annotations, critical commentary, and explanatory notes. They've added practical material in the form of path-workings, suggested exercises, and daily affirmations—one for each Sephirah and each path. Brief rituals, meditations, and Qabalistic mantras complement Regardie's section on gematria and other forms of numerical Qabalah.

1-56718-141-4
336 pp., 6 x 9 $14.95

The Middle Pillar
The Balance Between Mind & Magic
Israel Regardie
Edited and annotated with new material by Chic Cicero & Sandra Tabatha Cicero

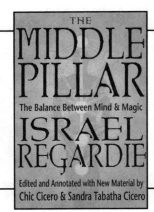

Break the barrier between the conscious and unconscious mind through the Middle Pillar exercise, a technique that serves as a bridge into magic, chakra work, and psychology. This classic work introduces a psychological perspective on magic and occultism while giving clear directions on how to perform the Qabalistic Cross, The Lesser Banishing Ritual of the Pentagram, the Middle Pillar exercise, along with its accompanying methods of circulating the light, the Vibratory Formula, and the building up of the Tree of Life in the aura.

The Ciceros, who knew Regardie personally, have made his book much more accessible by adding an extensive and useful set of notes, along with chapters that explain Regardie's work in depth. They expand upon it by carrying it into a realm of new techniques that are directly related to Regardie's core material. Especially valuable is the chapter on psychology, which provides a solid frame of reference for Regardie's' numerous remarks on this subject.

1-56718-140-6
312 pp., 6 x 9, illus.　　　　　　　　　　　　　　　　　　　**$14.95**

To order, call 1-877-NEW-WRLD
Prices subject to change without notice

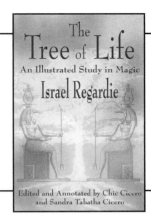

The Tree of Life
An Illustrated Study in Magic
ISRAEL REGARDIE
EDITED AND ANNOTATED BY CHIC CICERO AND SANDRA TABATHA CICERO

In 1932, when magic was a "forbidden subject," Israel Regardie wrote The Tree of Life at the age of 24. He believed that magic was a precise scientific discipline as well as a highly spiritual way of life, and he took on the enormous task of making it accessible to a wide audience of eager spiritual seekers. The result was The Tree of Life, which adroitly presents a massive amount of diverse material in a remarkably unified whole.

From the day it was first published, this book has remained in high demand by ceremonial magicians for its skillful combination of ancient wisdom and modern magical experience. It was Regardie's primary desire to point out the principles of magic that cut across all boundaries of time, religion, and culture—those fundamental principles common to all magic, regardless of any specific tradition or spiritual path.

1-56718-132-5
552 pp., 6 x 9, 177 illus., full-color, 4-pp. insert $19.95

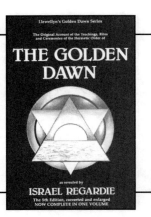